KU-316-231

Contents

Birmingham
Metropolitan
College LRC

Accession

292942

Class

Date Catalogued

How to use this book

Welcome to your BTEC National Business course!

A BTEC National in Business course is one of the most popular BTEC courses. There are many reasons why this course is in such demand, and you will experience some of these at first hand during the next year or so.

Your qualification will help you succeed in your future career, not matter what you choose to go on to do. The principles of business that you will learn on your course underpin every shop, office and organisation in the UK economy – from presenting positive marketing messages and developing effective customer service skills to operating within a legal framework and managing finances. The skills you will develop on your course will be valued by employers in every sector.

Your BTEC National in Business is a vocational or work-related qualification. This does not mean that you will be given all the skills you need to do a job, but that you will have the opportunity to gain specific knowledge, understanding and skills that are relevant to your chosen subject or area of work.

How your BTEC is structured

Your BTEC National is divided into **mandatory units** (M, the ones you must do) and **optional units** (O, the ones you can choose to do). The number of units you need to do, and the units you cover, will depend on the type of BTEC National qualification you are doing.

▶ BTEC Level 3 National Certificate in Business (180 GLH): two units, both mandatory, of which one is external
▶ BTEC Level National Extended Certificate in Business (360 GLH): four units of which three are mandatory and two are external
▶ BTEC Level 3 National Foundation Diploma in Business (510 GLH): six units of which four are mandatory and two are external
▶ BTEC Level 3 National Diploma in Business (720 GLH): eight units of which six are mandatory and three are external
▶ BTEC Level 3 National Extended Diploma in Business (1080 GLH): thirteen units of which seven are mandatory and four are external

The table below shows how the units covered by the books in this series cover the different types of BTEC qualifications.

Unit number	GLH	Unit name	Cert	Ext Cert	Foundation Dip	Dip	Ext Dip
1	90	Exploring Business	M	M	M	M	M
2	90	Developing a Marketing Campaign	M	M	M	M	M
3	120	Personal and Business Finance		M	M	M	M
4	90	Managing an Event			M	M	M
5	90	International Business				M	M
6	120	Principles of Management				M	M
7	120	Business Decision Making					M
8	60	Recruitment and Selection Process		O	O	O	O
14	60	Investigating Customer Service		O	O	O	O
16	60	Visual Merchandising			O	O	O

BIRMINGHAM METROPOLITAN COLLEGE

292942

endorsed for
BTEC

Pearson
BTEC National
Business

Student Book 1

PEARSON

Published by Pearson Education Limited, 80 Strand, London, WC2R 0RL.

www.pearsonschoolsandfecolleges.co.uk

Copies of official specifications for all Edexcel qualifications may be found on the website: www.edexcel.com

Text © Pearson
Edited by Cally Harris
Page design by Andy Magee
Typeset by Tech-Set Ltd, Gateshead
Original illustrations © Pearson Education Ltd
Illustrated by Tech-Set Ltd, Gateshead
Cover design by Vince Haig
Cover photo/illustration © leungchopan, Ufuk ZIVANA / Shutterstock.com

Picture research by Rebecca Sodergren

The rights of Helen Coupland-Smith, Jenny Phillips, Catherine Richards, Ann Summerscales and Julie Smith to be identified as authors of this work have been asserted by them in accordance with the Copyright, Designs and Patents Act 1988.

First published 2016

19 18 17

10 9 8 7 6 5 4 3

British Library Cataloguing in Publication Data
A catalogue record for this book is available from the British Library

ISBN 978 1 292 12624 1

Copyright notice
All rights reserved. No part of this publication may be reproduced in any form or by any means (including photocopying or storing it in any medium by electronic means and whether or not transiently or incidentally to some other use of this publication) without the written permission of the copyright owner, except in accordance with the provisions of the Copyright, Designs and Patents Act 1988 or under the terms of a licence issued by the Copyright Licensing Agency, Barnards Inn

86 Fetter Lane, London EC4A 1EN (**www.cla.co.uk**). Applications for the copyright owner's written permission should be addressed to the publisher.

Printed in Italy by LEGO S.p.A.

Acknowledgements
The publisher would like to thank the following for their kind permission to reproduce their photographs:

(Key: b-bottom; c-centre; l-left; r-right; t-top)

123RF.com: 8tr, 145, 179, 296, 360, 426, Frank Merfort 369, Karel Miragaya 77, Hongqi Zhang 291; **Alamy Images:** Blend Images 345, Kevin Britland 81, David Colbran 94, Ian Dagnall 91, 133, Ian Dagnall 91, 133, Mim Friday 296t, Matthew Horwood 29, D. Hurst 172, Yanice Idir 377, incamerastock 337b, itdarbs 161, Juice Images 8br, 150, Wavebreak Media ltd 97, Phanie 36, Alex Segre 1, 165, Tony Tallec 39, Jane Tregelles 343, Westend61 GmbH 247, 341, Westend61 GmbH 247, 341; **Bokeh Photographic – Aldeburgh 2015:** 211; **Charter Selection:** 299; **Crikey Bikey :** 12; **Digital Vision:** 55; **Flipside Festival:** 227; **Fotolia.com:** blvdone 58, Diego Cervo 154, Dangubic 351, DragonImages 373, DW labs Incorporated 361b, Elenathewise 68, highwaystarz 14, 410, idea_studio 189, JackF 75, Janni 310, JJAVA 173, joegast 306, lichaoshu 125, Dario Lo Presti 76, Nina Malyna 304, Monkey Business 157, nandyphotos 71, Yakobchuk Olena 300, Pakhnyushchyy 337c, Rawpixel.com 204, robinmhl 185, Gina Smith 159, StockPhotoPro 106, Syda Productions 118, Uber Images 138, vadymvdrobot 430, WavebreakMediaMicro 389; **Getty Images:** Heather Berisford 331, Bloomberg 121, 142, 391, Vladimir Khmelnytsky 313, Glyn Kirk 26, Peter Macdiarmid 135, B Marshall 298, Ben A. Prunchnie 335, Oli Scarff 339, Karwai Tang 130; **Good Bubble:** 31; **Her Honour Judge Hilary Manley:** 429; **Paul Wilkinson Photography:** 18; **Pearson Education Ltd:** Peter Evans 403, Lord and Leverett 7; **Jenny Phillips:** 57; **PhotoDisc:** John A Rizzo 21; **Shutterstock.com:** AlexanderJE 215, Anthony Shaw Photography 254, Arena Creative 203, Anna Baburkina 337t, baranq 275, Ryan Rodrick Beiler 395, Peter Bernik 349, bikeriderlondon 115, Chaoss 152, Roberto Chicano 336b, Eric Crama 16, Phil Date 290, Zhu Difeng 347, Elena Elisseeva 245, Felix Mizioznikov 289, Marie C Fields. 86, Drima Film 350, Goodluz 206, Dmitry Kalinovsky 8bl, Kletr 8tl, Robert Kneschke 265, Leungchopan 246, Vaclav Mach 336t, Arek Malang 330, Minerva Studio 329, Monkey Business Images 59, 168, 250, 407, Pres Panayotov 316, pkchai 122, Pressmaster 113, Rawpixel.com 147, Rido 390, Tommaso79 287, Vladimir Tronin 90, Wavebreak Media 194, Wckiw 319
Cover images: *Front:* **Shutterstock.com:** Ufuk ZIVANA

All other images © Pearson Education

The authors and publisher would like to thank the following individuals and organisations for their approval and permission to reproduce their materials:

p.7–8: adapted from Care and Share Associates (CASA) - social care with a difference, http://www.uk.coop/about/case-studies/social-care-co-ops-casa, with permission from Co-operatives UK; **p.8:** Guy Turnbull, Care and Share Associates (CASA) - social care with a difference, http://www.uk.coop/about/case-studies/social-care-co-ops-casa, with permission from Co-operatives UK; **p.10:** BIM57601 - Measuring the profits (particular trades): Franchising: general, http://www.hmrc.gov.uk/manuals/bimmanual/bim57601.htm, Contains public sector information licensed under the Open Government Licence (OGL) v3.0.http://www.nationalarchives.gov.uk/doc/open-government-licence.; **p.21–22:** adapted from Press release West Midlands businesses boost profits with a little help from the virtual world from Department for Communities and Local Government and Baroness Hanham CBE, 18 October 2012, https://www.gov.uk/government/news/west-midlands-businesses-boost-profits-with-a-little-help-from-the-virtual-world, Contains public sector information licensed under the Open Government Licence (OGL) v3.0.http://www.nationalarchives.gov.uk/doc/open-government-licence.;**p.30:** Villages Housing Association; **p.53:** 'Never knowingly undersold', with permission from John Lewis; **p.53:** from BMW slogan, with permission from BMW Group; **p.57:** with permission from Andrew Churchill; **p.81, Fig 2.4:** *Evaluation of Research and Development Tax Credit, March, HMRC Working Paper 17* (Fowkes, R.K., Sousa, J., Duncan, N. 2015), Contains public sector information licensed under the Open Government Licence (OGL) v3.0.http://www.nationalarchives.gov.uk/doc/open-government-licence; **p.83:** slogan from Red Bull, reproduced with permission from Red Bull GmbH, this project has not been supported by Red Bull GmbH and there has not been any cooperation with Red Bull GmbH regarding this book; **p.86, Tab 2.6:** adapted from Pocket databank: economic indicators, https://www.gov.uk/government/statistics/weekly-economic-indicators, Contains public sector information licensed under the Open Government Licence (OGL) v3.0.http://www.nationalarchives.gov.uk/doc/open-government-licence; **p.99:** Ronseal slogan, with permission from Ronseal, Sherwin-Williams Diversified Brands Ltd; **p.192:** adapted from Norfolk Network, http://www.norfolknetwork.com/about, used with kind permission from Norfolk Network; **p.299:** adapted from http://www.charterselection.com/; **p.271:** from www.birmingham.gov.uk, Contains public sector information licensed under the Open Government Licence v2.0; **p.359:** with thanks to Lauren Massey; **p.429:** reproduced with kind permission from Her Honour Judge Hilary Manley.

Every effort has been made to trace the copyright holders and we apologise for any omissions. We would be pleased to insert the appropriate acknowledgment in any subsequent editions.

Pearson Education Limited is not responsible for the content of any external internet sites. It is essential for tutors to preview each website before using it in class so as to ensure that the URL is still accurate, relevant and appropriate. We suggest that tutors bookmark useful websites and consider enabling students to access them through the school/college intranet.

A note from the publisher
In order to ensure that this resource offers high-quality support for the associated Pearson qualification, it has been through a review process by the awarding body. This process confirms that this resource fully covers the teaching and learning content of the specification or part of a specification at which it is aimed. It also confirms that it demonstrates an appropriate balance between the development of subject skills, knowledge and understanding, in addition to preparation for assessment.

Endorsement does not cover any guidance on assessment activities or processes (e.g. practice questions or advice on how to answer assessment questions), included in the resource nor does it prescribe any particular approach to the teaching or delivery of a related course.

While the publishers have made every attempt to ensure that advice on the qualification and its assessment is accurate, the official specification and associated assessment guidance materials are the only authoritative source of information and should always be referred to for definitive guidance.

Pearson examiners have not contributed to any sections in this resource relevant to examination papers for which they have responsibility.

Examiners will not use endorsed resources as a source of material for any assessment set by Pearson.

Endorsement of a resource does not mean that the resource is required to achieve this Pearson qualification, nor does it mean that it is the only suitable material available to support the qualification, and any resource lists produced by the awarding body shall include this and other appropriate resources.

19	60	Pitching for a New Business			O	O	O
21	60	Training and Development				O	O
22	60	Market Research		O	O	O	O
23	60	The English Legal System		O	O	O	O

Units in grey are covered in this book. Units in white are covered in BTEC Nationals Business Student Book 2 (ISBN: 9781292126258).

Your learning experience

You may not realise it but you are always learning. Your educational and life experiences are constantly shaping you, your ideas, your thinking, and how you view and engage with the world around you.

You are the person most responsible for your own learning experience so it is really important you understand what you are learning, why you are learning it and why it is important both to your course and your personal development.

Your learning can be seen as a journey which moves through four phases.

Phase 1	Phase 2	Phase 3	Phase 4
You are introduced to a topic or concept; you start to develop an awareness of what learning is required.	You explore the topic or concept through different methods (e.g. research, questioning, analysis, deep thinking, critical evaluation) and form your own understanding.	You apply your knowledge and skills to a task designed to test your understanding.	You reflect on your learning, evaluate your efforts, identify gaps in your knowledge and look for ways to improve.

During each phase, you will use different learning strategies. As you go through your course, these strategies will combine to help you secure the core knowledge and skills you need.

This student book has been written using similar learning principles, strategies and tools. It has been designed to support your learning journey, to give you control over your own learning and to equip you with the knowledge, understanding and tools to be successful in your future studies or career.

Features of this book

In this student book there are lots of different features. They are there to help you learn about the topics in your course in different ways and understand it from multiple perspectives. Together these features:
▶ explain what your learning is about
▶ help you to build your knowledge
▶ help you understand how to succeed in your assessment
▶ help you to reflect on and evaluate your learning
▶ help you to link your learning to the workplace.

In addition, each individual feature has a specific purpose, designed to support important learning strategies. For example, some features will:
▶ get you to question assumptions around what you are learning
▶ make you think beyond what you are reading about
▶ help you make connections across your learning and across units
▶ draw comparisons between your own learning and real-world workplace environments
▶ help you to develop some of the important skills you will need for the workplace, including team work, effective communication and problem solving.

Features that explain what your learning is about

Getting to know your unit

This section introduces the unit and explains how you will be assessed. It gives an overview of what will be covered and will help you to understand *why* you are doing the things you are asked to do in this unit.

Getting started

This appears at the start of every unit and is designed to get you thinking about the unit and what it involves. This feature will also help you to identify what you may already know about some of the topics in the unit and acts as a starting point for understanding the skills and knowledge you will need to develop to complete the unit.

Features that help you to build your knowledge

Research

This asks you to research a topic in greater depth. These features will help to expand your understanding of a topic and develop your research and investigation skills. All of this will be invaluable for your future progression, both professionally and academically.

Worked example

Our worked examples show the process you need to follow to solve a problem, such as a maths or science equation or the process for writing a letter or memo. This will also help you to develop your understanding and your numeracy and literacy skills.

Theory into practice

In this feature you are asked to consider the workplace or industry implications of a topic or concept from the unit. This will help you to understand the close links between what you are learning in the classroom and the affects it will have on a future career in your chosen sector.

Discussion

Discussion features encourage you to talk to other students about a topic in greater detail, working together to increase your understanding of the topic and to understand other people's perspectives on an issue. This will also help to build your teamworking skills, which will be invaluable in your future professional and academic career.

Key terms

Concise and simple definitions are provided for key words, phrases and concepts, allowing you to have, at a glance, a clear understanding of the key ideas in each unit.

Link

This shows any links between units or within the same unit, helping you to identify where the knowledge you have learned elsewhere will help you to achieve the requirements of the unit. Remember, although your BTEC National is made up of several units, there are common themes that are explored from different perspectives across the whole of your course.

Step by step:

This practical feature gives step-by-step descriptions of particular processes or tasks in the unit, including a photo or artwork for each step. This will help you to understand the key stages in the process and help you to carry out the process yourself.

Further reading and resources

This feature lists other resources – such as books, journals, articles or websites – you can use to expand your knowledge of the unit content. This is a good opportunity for you to take responsibility for your own learning and prepare for research tasks you may need to complete academically or professionally.

Features connected to your assessment

Your course is made up of a series of mandatory and optional units. There are two different types of mandatory unit:
▶ externally assessed
▶ internally assessed.

The features that support you in preparing for assessment are below. But first, what is the difference between these two different types of units?

Externally assessed units

These units give you the opportunity to present what you have learned in the unit in a different way. They can be challenging, but will really give you the opportunity to demonstrate your knowledge and understanding, or your skills in a direct way. For these units you will complete an assessment, set directly by Pearson, in controlled conditions. This could take the form of an exam or it could be a type of task. You may have the opportunity in advance to research and prepare notes around a topic, which can be used when completing the assessment.

Internally assessed units

Most of your units will be internally assessed. This involves you completing a series of assignments, set and marked by your teacher. The assignments you complete could allow you to demonstrate your learning in a number of different ways, from a written report to a presentation to a video recording and observation statements of you completing a practical task. Whatever the method, you will need to make sure you have clear evidence of what you have achieved and how you did it.

Assessment practice

These features give you the opportunity to practise some of the skills you will need when you are assessed on your unit. They do not fully reflect the actual assessment tasks, but will help you get ready for doing them.

Plan – Do – Review

You'll also find handy advice on how to plan, complete and evaluate your work after you have completed it. This is designed to get you thinking about the best way to complete your work and to build your skills and experience before doing the actual assessment. These prompt questions are designed to get you started with thinking about how the way you work, as well as understand why you do things.

Getting ready for assessment

For internally assessed units, this is a case study from a BTEC National student, talking about how they planned and carried out their assignment work and what they would do differently if they were to do it again. It will give you advice on preparing for the kind of work you will need to for your internal assessments, including Think about it points for you to consider for your own development.

Getting ready for assessment

This section will help you to prepare for external assessment. It gives practical advice on preparing for and sitting exams or a set task. It provides a series of sample answers for the types of questions you will need to answer in your external assessments, including guidance on the good points of these answers and how these answers could be improved.

Features to help you reflect on and evaluate your learning

II **PAUSE POINT** Pause points appear after a section of each unit and give you the opportunity to review and reflect upon your own learning. The ability to reflect on your own performance is a key skill you'll need to develop and use throughout your life, and will be essential whatever your future plans are.

Hint
Extend

These sections give you suggestions to help cement your knowledge and indicate other areas you can look at to expand it.

Reflect

This allows you to reflect on how the knowledge you have gained in this unit may impact your behaviour in a workplace situation. This will help not only to place the topic in a professional context, but also help you to review your own conduct and develop your employability skills.

Features which link your learning with the workplace

Case study

Case studies throughout the book will allow you to apply the learning and knowledge from the unit to a scenario from the workplace or industry. Case studies include questions to help you consider the wider context of a topic. They show how the course content is reflected in the real world and help you to build familiarity with issues you may find in a real-world workplace.

THINK ▶FUTURE

This is a special case study where someone working in the industry talks about the job role they do and the skills they need. This comes with a *Focusing your skills* section, which gives suggestions for how you can begin to develop the employability skills and experiences that are needed to be successful in a career in your chosen sector. This is an excellent opportunity to help you identify what you could do, inside and outside of your BTEC National studies, to build up your employability skills.

Exploring Business 1

Getting to know your unit

Assessment
You will be assessed by a series of assignments set by your tutor.

Whatever your aspirations are for the future, you will need to understand about business. In this introductory unit, you will study purposes of different businesses, their structure, the effect of the external environment, and how a business must be dynamic and innovative to survive.

A business is any activity that provides goods or services, whether to make a profit or not. The main aim in business, that owners and employees strive for, is satisfied customers. Nowadays, customers are more informed and have more options in terms of what they buy and who they buy from, so a successful business is one that balances satisfying their customers and selling products or providing services.

This unit will help you gain an overview of key ingredients for business success, how businesses are organised, how they communicate, the characteristics of the environment in which they operate, and how this shapes them and their activities. You will also look at the importance of innovation and enterprise to the success and survival of businesses, with the associated risks and benefits.

This unit will help prepare you for progressing into employment, vocational training and apprenticeships or higher education, and underpins all the other units in this qualification.

How you will be assessed

This unit will be assessed by a maximum of three internally assessed tasks set by your tutor. Throughout this unit, you will find assessment practices to help you work towards your assignment. Completing them will mean that you have undertaken useful research and preparation, which will be relevant when it comes to your final assignment.

To achieve the tasks in your assignment, check that you have met all the Pass grading criteria. These criteria require clear explanations in your own words, for example describing how contrasting businesses operate. Check against the criteria as you work your way through your assignment. To gain a Merit or Distinction, you should make sure that you present the information in your assignment in the style required by the relevant assessment criterion. For example, Merit criteria require you to analyse and discuss relationships, effects of business environments and changes to businesses in response to market forces. Distinction criteria require you to assess, evaluate and justify your conclusions and make convincing assumptions about future business changes which may be required.

The assignments set by your tutor will consist of tasks designed to meet the criteria in the table. They may include a written assignment and also include activities such as:
▶ creating diagrams or models of different organisational structures and how they operate
▶ reviewing, comparing and analysing several business case studies
▶ producing a report using your own research which examines different types and sizes of businesses
▶ presenting your investigations and findings of innovative and enterprising successful businesses.

Assessment criteria

This table shows you what you must do in order to achieve a **Pass**, **Merit** or **Distinction** grade, and where you can find activities to help you.

Pass	**Merit**	**Distinction**
Learning aim **A** Explore the features of different businesses and what makes them successful		
A.P1 Explain the features of two contrasting businesses. **Assessment practice 1.1 and Assessment practice 1.2**	**A.M1** Assess the relationship and communication with stakeholders of two contrasting businesses using independent research. **Assessment practice 1.1**	**AB.D1** Evaluate the reasons for the success of two contrasting businesses, reflecting on evidence gathered. **Assessment practice 1.1 and Assessment practice 1.2**
A.P2 Explain how two contrasting businesses are influenced by stakeholders. **Assessment practice 1.1**		
Learning aim **B** Investigate how businesses are organised		
B.P3 Explore the organisation structures, aims and objectives of two contrasting businesses. **Assessment practice 1.1**	**B.M2** Analyse how the structures of two contrasting businesses allow each to achieve its aims and objectives. **Assessment practice 1.1**	
Learning aim **C** Examine the environment in which businesses operate		
C.P4 Discuss the internal, external and competitive environment of a given business. **Assessment practice 1.2**	**C.M3** Assess the effects of the business environment on a given business. **Assessment practice 1.2**	**C.D2** Evaluate the extent to which the business environment affects a given business, using a variety of situational analysis techniques. **Assessment practice 1.2**
C.P5 Select a variety of techniques to undertake a situational analysis of a given business. **Assessment practice 1.2**		
Learning aim **D** Examine business markets		
D.P6 Explore how the market structure and influences on supply and demand affect the pricing and output decisions for a given business. **Assessment practice 1.3**	**D.M4** Assess how a given business has responded to changes in the market. **Assessment practice 1.3**	**D.D3** Evaluate how changes in the market have impacted on a given business and how this business may react to future changes. **Assessment practice 1.3**
Learning aim **E** Investigate the role and contribution of innovation and enterprise to business success		
E.P7 Explore how innovation and enterprise contribute to the success of business. **Assessment practice 1.3**	**E.M5** Analyse how successful the use of innovation and enterprise has been for a given business. **Assessment practice 1.3**	**E.D4** Justify the use of innovation and enterprise for a business in relation to its changing market and environment. **Assessment practice 1.3**

Getting started

Consumers rely on businesses every day. Make a list of of businesses, starting with any you have used this week. How many sell products? Which provide services? Compare your list with a peer. How many have you identified? Expand this list as you work through your course and use it during research.

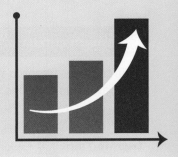

A Explore the features of different businesses and analyse what makes them successful

Most businesses rely on making a profit. The bigger the profit, the more successful the business. Although, remember that not every business measures its success by the amount of profit it makes. You will explore why that is a little later. However, the way a business is organised to deliver its aims and meet the needs of its customers is critical to its success. In this unit you start to explore types of businesses and what influences success and failure.

Features of businesses

Another word for 'feature' is 'characteristic' or 'attribute'; therefore business features comprise the characteristics that make up every organisation. For example, if you refer to the list you created earlier, you may have identified some businesses as one-man-bands, known as a sole traders, such as a plumber or mobile hairdresser offering a service to customers who live locally. Other businesses might be very big and sell their products or services around the world, such as the BBC, Virgin Atlantic and GlaxoSmithKline.

Your list should include businesses of different sizes, purposes and possibly the types of customers who use their services or buy their products. You, your peers, friends and family will favour some of the same and different businesses and no doubt share different experiences. You will now explore the range of features as separate characteristics.

Ownership and liability

Businesses are owned in one of three ways: private, public and not-for-profit.

Private

Research

Identify businesses for every category in Table 1.1. Seek information about businesses in your local area and those you listed earlier.

Private businesses are those owned by citizens and therefore they are liable for all aspects of the business. Owners of private businesses are likely to take many risks as they are in business to make a profit. Privately owned businesses can be of any size and owned by many partners. Some of the largest include:

▶ Virgin
▶ Toys "R" Us
▶ Mars
▶ Tesco.

Public

Public businesses which are identified as belonging to the public sector are owned by the government. These types of businesses may have been set up by the government or subsequently bought by the government from the private sector for investment or to save them from financial ruin, such as Northern Rock and the Royal Bank of Scotland.

As the government is then liable for the success or failure of the business, they are less likely to take risks than businesses in the private sector because they aim to benefit the public.

Not-for-profit

Businesses which do not aim to make a profit are often charitable organisations, such as the international Médecins Sans Frontières which provides doctors and nurses across the globe to in-need areas. Businesses like this often share many of the same features as private and public businesses, such as running on normal business lines, and have many paid workers but only seek to make enough money to cover running costs.

Voluntary organisations are also not-for-profit businesses. They are set up, organised and staffed by people working on a purely voluntary basis. Examples include the Royal Voluntary Service (RVS) and Voluntary Service Overseas (VSO).

Table 1.1 suggests a few examples of businesses under each of the three categories which you could investigate further or use to help identify your own businesses to research. There are variables, however, within each category. For example, limited companies do not need to have large numbers of employees and some, such as specialist consultancy services, may be sole traders.

> **Key term**
>
> **Partnership** – comprising two or more people who set up in business together and share all profits and losses.

▶ **Table 1.1:** Suggested examples of business ownership

Private, for example:		Public, for example:		Not-for-profit, for example:	
Sole trader	• Decorator • Gardener • Photographer • Pilates instructor • Childminder • Taxi driver	Government department	• Departrment for Education • Department for Business, Innovation and Skills (BIS) • Ofsted • NS&I • Ministry of Defence	Charitable trust	• Buttle UK • Hospice UK • WWF
Partnership	• Accountants • Solicitors • Dental practice			Voluntary	• Rotary Club • Round Table • MAIN – Taking Autism Seriously • Voluntary Service Overseas • MacMillan Cancer Support
Private limited company	• Estate agents • John Lewis Partnership (JLP) • McLaren Technology Group • River Island				
Public limited company	• Aer Lingus Group • Rolls-Royce Holdings plc • Tesco plc • Manchester United plc				
Cooperative	• The Co-operative Bank • FC United of Manchester • Brighton Energy Co-operative				

Tip

For more details on limited companies, visit the UK government website at www.gov.uk/business-legal-structures/limited-company.

Key term

Economy – the state of a country, such as its wealth, production and consumption of goods and services.

Tip

Useful places include Companies House for information about limited companies (Ltd) and the London Stock Exchange for public limited companies (plc).

Key term

Liability – an obligation of a company, or amounts owed to lenders and suppliers.

Research

Select one business from each type of ownership from your list. Identify at least three insurance companies offering business insurance and compare the extent of protection against liability each of them offers.

Privately owned businesses can decide to become limited companies at any time. A decision to do so might be made to ensure that business profits and liabilities are properly shared based on the percentage of ownership by each of its directors. Business finances are kept separate from personal finances, therefore, if the business fails, owners' personal assets, such as homes, cars, etc, cannot be used to pay off any debt.

Owners of limited companies have to pay corporation tax and can draw dividends from their businesses. Depending on personal tax liabilities, it may be beneficial to change the business structure to a limited company.

Some owners find they can increase their business opportunities by becoming a limited company as it may give the impression that they are larger or more established than they are. Some large organisations will only contract with limited companies.

Partnerships, such as the John Lewis Partnership (JLP), may have many employees. Keep an open mind when exploring types of business and their features – not all estate agencies are private limited companies, just as not all accountants, dentists or solicitors are partnerships.

JLP is particularly interesting because it operates as a cooperative, although not in the formal sense like the examples listed in Table 1.1. Cooperatives contribute significant annual revenue (£37 billion) to the UK's **economy** and are owned by nearly 15 million people. The word cooperative suggests working together, sharing aims and objectives, which can be implemented in different ways and reward those who cooperate in the business differently.

Liability

To protect the business against the risk of being sued or held legally responsible, anyone owning or running a business should insure against such **liability**.

There are multiple insurance companies offering such cover and, as with any insurance (for example, car or house insurance), they offer it at different rates and with different terms and conditions. Insurance for liability includes Public Liability Insurance and Directors' and Officers' Insurance (D & O).

Depending on the ownership, size and type of business, the cover will also vary. You will explore this further throughout this unit.

Unlimited liability

Some businesses (as suggested in Table 1.1) are owned by sole traders or partnerships. If the owners share the business responsibilities equally, they are responsible not just for the profits but also the losses, such as debts and claims against the business. This means that all owners are responsible for any shortfall of money if the business has insufficient funds. This could mean all savings and possessions including car, house, etc are at risk.

Limited liability

Where liability is limited, this means there is a limit (or cap) placed upon the amount that can be claimed. This type of liability might seem to be the obvious choice, but setting up in business is relatively easy and the risks attached can be overlooked, especially without the benefit of knowledge gained through studying.

Just as some insurance companies specialise in house, car or travel insurance, others specialise in business insurance and insurance for different types of businesses.

Ⅱ **PAUSE POINT**   After comparing with a peer, add an extra column or comments to your research from the Getting started activity.

    Hint   Highlight gaps and conflicting results.

    Extend   What worked well? What would you change and why?

Purposes

Most businesses supply products or services, or occasionally both. For example some businesses, such as dentists, provide a service and also sell a small range of products such as toothpaste, floss, toothbrushes, etc. Halfords provide products such as car and bicycle parts and they also provide a service whereby they fit windscreen wipers or bicycle tyres.

You could argue that all businesses are providing a service when selling or making their products.

Difference between for profit and not-for-profit businesses

As mentioned earlier, not all businesses measure success by profit. Dr Turnbull, MD of Care and Share Associates (CASA) said: 'Profit is not wrong – but it is our belief that a reasonable and sustainable profit is best generated by delivering a quality service, not by cutting costs, corners and ultimately, quality.' This does not suggest that profit seeking businesses are more likely to cut corners and compromise quality, although you could possibly identify some examples where you believe that is true.

Some examples of large profitable businesses include utility companies such as British Gas and major retailers such as JLP, Next and Marks and Spencer. Profits can and do fluctuate year on year. Some of the UK's most profitable companies include Burberry and the telecommunications giant Vodafone.

Information on the performance of the top 100 businesses measured by shares on the stock market are listed in the **FTSE 100**. You will explore shareholding a little later in this unit.

Examples of smaller businesses making a profit in 2014–15 are PeopleTree: ethical clothing; Levi Root's: Reggae, Reggae Sauce; Mad Marc's Sublime Science: making science fun.

> **Discussion**
>
> Compare your growing lists of businesses to identify which provide products, which provide services and which provide both. Discuss what proportion of each (products and services) they are likely to offer.

> **Key term**
>
> **FTSE** – the Financial Times Stock Exchange.

> **Link**
>
> In *Unit 6: Principles of Management* you will explore in detail what is meant by quality and in *Unit 14: Investigating Customer Service* you will explore how to find out whether or not you are providing a quality service. How you calculate business profit will be explained in *Unit 3: Personal and Business Finance*.

Case study

Care in crisis

With people living longer, changes in the way they live, the recession and reduced public funding and strains on the NHS, social care provision is experiencing a

negative impact alongside claims that elderly people are being put at risk. A group of caring individuals formed a cooperative to help redress this problem, starting on a small scale locally and expanding over the last 10 years. They called the business CASA, an acronym for Care and Share Associates and grew to employ more than 850 staff by 2014. Shares in CASA are held by an Employee Ownership Trust, an Employee Benefit Trust, and individual employees.

CASA is an employee-owned social enterprise with a clear purpose. Their primary concern is providing care for older people, the disabled (including children) and those with learning difficulties. CASA's Managing Director explains their successful business is due to:

'Engaged employee owners provide the highest quality care and we also have low staff turnover, making the business more successful. Profits are then reinvested in staff and growth ... and shared amongst the workforce.'

Because the business does not have any external shareholders, the business can focus on delivering its aims for social care. One employee testimonial states:

'Because we are the owners it's easier to see that we can have a brilliant future if we manage it correctly and really get involved.'

Check your knowledge

1 Which sector and type of ownership is this business?

2 What do you think are the aims and objectives of this business?

3 What is CASA's innovative approach to this business?

4 What are the most important assets of this business?

5 List the priorities for the Managing Director (MD). Can you put them in order of importance?

 PAUSE POINT Why is profit not the most important goal for this business?

Hint Without referring to the case study, list all the reasons that profit is not the main aim.

Extend What non-financial rewards do employees receive from their involvement with this business?

Tip

There are also case studies featured in the 10,000 small business brochure from Goldman Sachs. Finance information about limited companies can be explored through Companies House, the Stock Exchange and the Financial Times while private sector small business quarterly economic data is collated by the British Chamber of Commerce.

Sectors

Businesses operate in different sectors according to the nature of their business and the product or service they provide. These sectors are known as primary, secondary, tertiary and quaternary and are the four stages of the journey from sourcing a material to being ready for the customer.

Primary

Secondary

Tertiary

Quaternary

▶ Business sectors from primary to quaternary

These terms also relate to the positioning of the business in relation to the customers' requirements. Every sector and every type of business services customers.

Primary

Let's take an example of a customer such as a builder who requires the roof trusses for a house – the builder relies on the primary sector to source the raw materials and on the secondary sector to prepare those materials from their raw state so that they can form the frame for a roof.

Secondary

The secondary sector processes the raw materials produced by the primary sector so that they can be sold on. For example, farmed vegetables, mined diamonds or coal, felled wood and caught fish, all need to be prepared or manufactured in some way by the secondary sector so that they are fit for sale.

Tertiary

This sector provides the supporting services which store and distribute the goods which have been manufactured. It also provides insurances against, for example, damage or possibly late delivery. Businesses often rely on advertising to promote their products – another service provided by the tertiary sector.

The tertiary sector also sells skills support such as training for staff, for example for people who clean and pack vegetables to sell in shops and supermarkets. Types of tertiary businesses include services such as travel and tourism, entertainment, education and training, and transport.

Quaternary

Together with the tertiary sector, employees working in the quaternary sector currently account for approximately 75 per cent of the UK workforce. This sector also provides support services and can appear to overlap the tertiary sector. Examples include the communications infrastructure for day to day operations, such as telephoning and emailing.

The quaternary sector could be seen as the beginning and the future of every business as this sector includes the research and development stage. Therefore this fourth (quaternary) sector relies on information from the other sectors to test existing products and methods, and to develop new ways of sourcing and producing new products or approaches.

Scope of business activities

Local

The scope of a business means the range covered by that business. Earlier you looked at the features of businesses and suggested that some business types are more likely to offer their services locally, for example mobile hairdressers, plumbers and gardeners. A local business is usually one which is owned locally and serves just the local area, such as an independent village shop or perhaps a pub which is owned by local residents. There are, of course, exceptions and you could probably identify some. Some local businesses, such as your local council office, are part of a much bigger organisation although they provide a service to the local area.

National

You probably use businesses which operate nationally fairly frequently and possibly have not considered this before. Some could appear to be a local business (especially if you are served by the same staff) but the business might be a **franchise**.

> **Link**
>
> *Unit 14: Investigating Customer Service.*

> **Discussion**
>
> As a group, name as many businesses as you can in each sector. Use the list you created at the beginning.

You may know some franchised businesses in your area, for example Dunkin' Donuts, Harvey's Furniture Store, Kwik Fit and possibly one of the most well known, McDonald's.

The government defines a franchise as 'the owner of an established business format (the franchiser) grants to another person (the franchisee) the right to distribute products or perform services using that system' and a fee is paid to the franchiser according to the terms of their agreement.

International

International businesses do business transactions that take place across national borders. Since the birth of the internet, international business has been provided with worldwide opportunities to sell products and services. Since the first email was sent in the early 1970s and the internet became widely available from 1990, the world appears to have become smaller and certainly more accessible.

Measuring the size of a business

So far, this unit has referred to businesses of different sizes as small or large. To accurately quantify the size of a business, strict definitions exist and these are outlined in Table 1.2.

▶ **Table 1.2:** Defining a business by size

Size type	Number of employees/staff
Micro	Up to 9
Small	10–49
Medium	50–249
The above are all known as SMEs (Small and Medium Enterprises)	
Large	More than 250

Link

The contribution these businesses make to the economy is calculated in turnover, which you will learn about in *Unit 3: Personal and Business Finance*.

The UK parliament publishes reports on the contribution businesses have made to the economy. According to the data supplied by BIS in its Business Population Estimates (2014) there were 4.9 million businesses in 2013, which increased to 5.2 million in 2014. More than 99 per cent were SMEs and employed almost 14.5 million people, contributing to almost half of the UK economy. The number of micro businesses also rose slightly to 5 million.

Reasons for success

Earlier, the concept that not every business measures success by the amount of profit made was introduced. There are different reasons for success depending on the type of business (profit or non-profit) and its aims and objectives, which you will explore shortly.

Profit seeking business

Businesses seeking to make a profit are motivated by various reasons. For example, to pay the bills for everyday living, have money for extras and realise some aspirations such as owning your own home, buying a nice car, having holidays, etc.

Link

You will learn more about profit in *Unit 3: Personal and Business Finance*.

As businesses get larger they generate more responsibility. For example, a growing business might employ additional staff, pay for premises and develop products or services to expand on its market share so the business can continue to grow. Managing the profits becomes more complex and specialised.

Just because a business grows it does not automatically follow that it becomes more profitable. This is because its costs might increase and the interest rates paid on loans or investments could fluctuate. Sometimes businesses call on the services of other sectors, for example for specialist financial advice from a consultancy service (perhaps on running the business more efficiently to make more profit and reduce costs).

Discussion

Discuss with another learner, or as a small group, what sector these types of service come under. Explore which businesses made a profit last year and which are declining and compare with your peers. You can probably name several businesses which have gone bankrupt over recent years during the recession and explore some reasons.

Non-profit seeking business

Discussion

Why run a non-profit (or not-for-profit) business? Before you read on, think why you might and share your ideas with a peer, colleague, friend or member of your family. Refer back to your list based on Table 1.1 – it should be growing as you work through this unit.

The primary goal of these businesses is not to make substantial profits but enough to continue the business. Therefore they also need to keep a very close eye on their finances to ensure that what they spend does not exceed the income they receive, known as **revenue**.

Revenue is not necessarily gained from selling a product or service but could come from successful bids for funding or grants, donations from members of the public or perhaps lottery funding. Examples include:

▸ donations for The Royal National Lifeboat Institution (The RNLI)

▸ lottery funding for causes such as sports and the arts

▸ cultural heritage groups, such as those celebrating the 70th anniversary of the end of the Second World War.

Aims and objectives

Every business needs aims and objectives – just as every lesson you attend has aims defining the purpose and outcome of the lesson and objectives which identify how to achieve the aim. You will look at some examples later. Although these aims and objectives might be less formal in a micro business, every business must have a purpose and outcome. You will have your own aims and objectives and a plan of some sort identifying how you are going to get there.

Clarity of vision

Just as your plan will change and a tutor's plan can change, so will the aims and objectives of a business. These changes are influenced by **market forces**, for example customers' needs. Market forces help a business to focus on its direction and how it can continue to operate. In other words, they are designed to provide clarity of vision – without this it is unlikely that the business will succeed.

Think about an experience you have had with a business where you have been confused about its purpose or got the impression that the business had no direction. For example, think about whether it would make business sense to set up a market stall selling sportswear and other unrelated products, for example toiletries.

Key term

Revenue – the income received by a business for selling its products and services.

Research

Businesses including community groups can apply for lottery funding grants for a variety of causes. Research the application process and think about what type of business would be likely to apply.

Tip

Create a plan for successfully completing this unit. Identify your aims and objectives and timeframes.

Key term

Market forces – factors created by the economy for the demand and availability of products and services which influence costs.

Innovative products or processes

Innovative products, or creative ways to go about a process, can lead to business success. Examples include Mad Marc's idea to enthuse children in science, child innovators of the Crikey Bikey harness and Rob Law's Trunki.

Having a great idea for an innovative product or idea is a good start. But your perception of a great product or idea may not be someone else's. What makes good business sense is to be creative – employers are always looking for employees who can think for themselves and propose more efficient ways to manage a process or identify innovative products or services.

▶ How do you think the innovative idea of the Crikey Bikey helped it become a success?

Stakeholders and their influence

Every business has stakeholders. You may have heard the term used before but you will now learn what it actually means and look at who the various stakeholders in a business are.

Stakeholders

There are two types of stakeholders, internal and external. In other words, those within the business, such as its employees, and those outside the business, including customers and anyone else with an interest in the business. They all have a stake in the business.

Internal

The internal stakeholders include:
▶ managers (decision makers and bosses)
▶ employees (reporting to managers)
▶ owners (overall responsibility for the business).

Therefore every sector has internal stakeholders although, for example, a sole trader will not have managers and employees.

External

Businesses also have external stakeholders. Without them they wouldn't have a business. These stakeholders are described below.

Suppliers

Suppliers supply raw materials (considered earlier in this unit). Examples include bricks supplied to builders, electricity to light our homes and streets, fabric to manufacture our clothes, etc.

Lenders

These are stakeholders who lend money or possibly services to the business, such as start up business loans. These loans are available through banks and other sources such as government loans. Other loans might include a mortgage for the business premises for those owners who don't want to rent premises.

Competitors

Anyone who is in competition with a business is also referred to as a stakeholder. In order to operate a successful business, you will need to know who your competitors are and what they are offering. This enables a business owner to be better informed about the choices they can make and whether a change of direction is required, or if an opportunity is arising due to a gap in the market. One such example is the supermarket chain Lidl UK. They identified a need for competitively priced food that does not compromise on taste, as claimed by their adverts.

Debtors

Every business has debtors, although this does not mean all businesses run without making a profit. A debtor is any person or organisation which owes money to the business. The financial crisis in Greece may well have made you familiar with the term debtor in relation to a country which owes money. If you have been given a period of time to pay for a product or service you have received, you are a debtor of that business.

Creditors

Just as every business has its debtors, it will also have creditors. Creditors are those to whom money is owed, and this may be an individual or another business. If you take the example of raw materials supplied to a business, the supplier becomes a creditor of the business until they have paid for the materials.

Customers

Businesses have both internal and external customers. Everyone can relate to being an external customer whether enquiring about or purchasing a product or service such as an item of clothing, a train ticket or a haircut. You are also a customer when you receive a service for which no money changes hands, such as hospital treatment or careers advice. The last point is especially interesting because, while an external customer might not be required to pay for a service, payment for that service will still come from somewhere, such as government funding. Basically, an external customer is someone who brings revenue into the business.

Internal customers include anyone directly related to the business. They include employees of a business whether they are physically present in that business or are representatives of the organisation. For example, historically, the majority of sales personnel travelled around promoting and selling their company's wares for the majority of their time. This type of customer has changed significantly over the last few years due to developments in technology that reduce the need for travel, for example email and the internet.

Internal customers also include employees working in different departments and those working at different sites. They also include suppliers who are crucial to the operation of the business. A successful business relies on everyone working together harmoniously, therefore it is important you recognise that we are all customers of each other. In other words, we become a team, relying on each other's knowledge, strengths and expertise. Having this philosophy leads to greater job satisfaction as everyone has a stake in the business.

> **Link**
>
> Debtors and creditors will be covered in more detail in *Unit 3: Personal and Business Finance*, along with financial terms such as deficit.

'Bring me back'

Walkers Crisps Ltd, owned by PepsiCo, is one of Britain's biggest brands and strives to retain its popularity in a highly competitive market.

Having an innovative idea does not mean that existing ideas or products are obsolete. For example, the UK consumption of crisps, snacks and nuts has risen significantly and generates revenue of almost £129 million. Therefore it appears that there is still room for expansion into the snack industry.

Walkers' innovation lies not just in how it expands its product range, such as its 'Do us a flavour' campaign in the mid-2000s, but, more recently, by asking the public to vote for their favourite flavours previously removed from its range. Walkers' process of deciding how to expand its range is also innovative and it does this very well by seeking **stakeholder feedback**. For example, in an earlier campaign, Walkers received more than a million votes from stakeholders for flavour ideas. The campaign got people talking about Walkers, both online and in daily conversations, subsequently raising their profile. The company promised a large monetary reward and a percentage of all future sales, with the winning announcement exposed to media coverage.

To ensure success, Walkers produced a focussed campaign. It is likely that some of their aims were:

- to remain a popular snack brand with the public
- to find out the nation's favourite flavours
- to increase sales through daily public interest
- to resurrect a previously tried and tested recipe.

The benefits to stakeholders of this campaign included:

- extended flavours to the product range
- a significant financial reward for the stakeholder selected as winner and their moment of fame in the media
- a sense of belonging and involvement with Walkers.

Walkers Crisps has also been investing heavily in research and development and, during the mid-2000s, it reduced the salt content of its products following trends towards healthier living. Further extensions to their range include the Market Deli range, in 2014, to stay ahead in a highly competitive market. Despite being owned by an American company, PepsiCo, crisps are considered a traditionally British snack food; sales have increased due to the recession as people stay at home more rather than socialising in public places.

Check your knowledge

1 What are the business features of Walkers Crisps?

2 Who are Walkers Crisps' stakeholders?

3 How would you describe the relationship Walkers Crisps has with its stakeholders?

4 What innovative approaches are Walkers Crisps using?

5 What factors influenced Walkers Crisps to try such innovative ideas?

Key term

Stakeholder feedback – surveying stakeholders for ideas, compliments, suggestions and complaints.

PAUSE POINT

Which aspects of this case study did you find most interesting and why? What new information have you learned?

Hint

Identify a different type of business and explore how they involve stakeholders to develop their product range.

Extend

Consider other reasons for the success of these businesses based on factual information.

Theory into practice

Reflect on your experiences, either at work (paid or voluntary) or perhaps in your place of study or at home. Identify a single process you want to change, perhaps to make it simpler, quicker or more interesting. Examples could be getting up in the morning, or commuting. Write down the existing process and the changes you propose, thinking about the reasons why, just as Walkers Crisps justified their reasons for change. Explain your ideas to a peer and ask for feedback. Review your idea in light of their comments. Make further changes and try again. Compare the previous way and the new process to identify which works best and why.

Tip

You will need to justify your findings just as you will in your assignment. Personal opinion or hearsay is not enough!

Government agencies and departments

Other external stakeholders include government agencies and departments, which may be local, national or international. Some examples of government departments have been mentioned already in this unit, such as the Department for Business, Innovation and Skills. Other examples of agencies and departments are outlined in Table 1.3.

▶ **Table 1.3:** Examples of government agencies and departments

Local	National	International
County Councils	Department for Education	Foreign and Commonwealth Office
City/Borough/District Councils	Department for Work and Pensions	URENCO
Parish Councils	Department for Transport	
	Ministry of Justice	

Local government includes your local council. In some areas there are two councils, for example in Leicestershire, where they have a county council and a city council. Each of these councils are responsible for services which affect the whole county, such as education, roads, planning, fire and safety, etc.

London boroughs each have a council and the metropolitan area has another. District councils are responsible for the detail of how, for example, rubbish collections are organised and how the council tax is structured. You may have a parish or community council which deals with very local matters such as allotments and street lighting. Each has a stake in the business and the community, for example to ensure houses are not built on farmland unless permission is granted.

Each government department works with a number of agencies. If you take the example of the Department for Education, a national department working with nine agencies (including Ofsted), they have a stake in your education and provide the funding for your schooling and possibly your education still.

An example of international government is the Foreign and Commonwealth Office. It is responsible for: promoting the UK; working with other countries to seek ways to increase our economy; reporting on global developments and travel; informing policy.

Government has a stake in businesses and also informs and legislates how businesses must operate. Government rules and regulations are constantly changing and businesses can find it difficult to keep up to date.

Link

You will learn more about business legislation throughout your course and particularly in *Unit 23: The English Legal System.*

Communities

Just as government operates locally, nationally and internationally, so do our communities. You may know of examples where a community has influenced a new or existing business. For example, members of a community may become involved in the operation of a business such as a training centre or a post office, working in partnership with communities.

Pressure groups

Communities can take on small and large projects and put considerable pressure on whether a business proposition will succeed or fail. For example, a farmer who proposed to sell some of his land to a developer for a crematorium but met with opposition.

▶ Community demonstrators expressing their views about crematorium proposals

Another example is where communities nationally have placed pressure upon the government to reconsider their plans for the high speed railway (HS2). Longstanding pressure groups exist on a larger and longer-standing scale, such as:

▶ animal rights activists
▶ Amnesty International
▶ Greenpeace
▶ Christian Aid.

Interest groups

These groups include members with an interest in a business or specific businesses who strive for a common cause. They look to influence the business or factors such as policy or **regulators**. These include:

▶ trade unions
▶ chambers of commerce
▶ professional associations such as those representing:
  - accountants
  - doctors
  - lawyers
  - architects.

Key term

Regulator – external body acting as supervisor to ensure businesses comply with relevant legislation.

The influence of stakeholders on business success

Stakeholders can influence business success. The London Stock Exchange is where public limited companies (plcs) offer shares in the company. This raises funding for the business by selling off parts of it as shares. Shareholders are looking for value for money; in business terms this is called **shareholder value**.

As you probably know, the value of these shares can go down as well as up and therefore shareholders are keen to ensure their investment is worthwhile. This can create a tension between those who run the business and those who simply have an interest in it. Shareholders vote on proposals for the way the business is run, which depends on majority votes.

Customers are also stakeholders and should be considered as long-term assets. Customers who feel valued and receive a good service are more likely to remain loyal. Strong customer service, such as that provided by M&S, Waitrose and JLP, enables **customer retention**.

Surprisingly, some businesses are constantly chasing new business and overlook the power of using their existing customer base by retaining their customers. Some businesses make assumptions that if a customer has just purchased a product or service they may not purchase again for a while, if at all. You can probably give examples of businesses who promote special offers to 'brand new customers only'.

> **Key term**
>
> **Shareholder value** – the benefits received by shareholders relative to the number of shares they hold in a business.

> **Discussion**
>
> Discuss with another learner, or in a small group, the percentage of your business you would need to retain to ensure overall control. Discuss how a shareholder might bring value to the business.

> **Key term**
>
> **Customer retention** – customers who remain loyal to specific brands and businesses.

> **Discussion**
>
> In a small group, discuss how often you have relied on 'word of mouth' as justification for using a business. Explore the impact of the message existing customers receive when they can't get the best offers. Find examples of businesses which encourage retention of existing customers and those which don't, and what stops these customers from taking their custom elsewhere.

Employee involvement

As employees are stakeholders of the business they contribute to the success of the business, whether it is as a direct or indirect result of their actions.

Some businesses have employee contribution schemes, such as JLP, Waitrose, Brompton Bikes and Dyson. In a similar way, your place of study will seek feedback from its employees as well as its students. Suggestions and recommendations can indirectly impact on the success of a business by initiating ideas.

In the early 20th century, a shop assistant in a major department store in New York suggested to a customer that they visit their main competitor when they could not supply the item sought. Despite opposition from the management, the sales in this store increased as a direct result and, subsequently, other stores followed the example.

> **Reflect**
>
> Some businesses also offer incentives for making suggestions, sometimes through a short survey. Can you think about a time when you have seen this in practice?

Corporate social responsibility

Often shortened to CSR, corporate social responsibility means the contribution that a business has committed to make to society and the environment. To deliver such a commitment, employees are encouraged to volunteer in a community project and work with community groups. The business might allocate the equivalent of one day a year to such an activity. Several major businesses are known for this strategy.

Tip

Read about the Marine Management Organisation's (MMO) strategy for undertaking their commitment. You can find this at https://www.gov.uk/government/publications/corporate-social-responsibility-strategy. What other volunteering examples can you find?

As consumers, we are probably made more aware of our responsibilities to society and environment than ever before. There are businesses which alert public interest, such as the nuclear industry, and others which may be of particular interest to you, such as endangered species. It is probably unlikely that you can avoid daily media interest about local or global examples of poverty or waste or damage to the environment. British-owned, international business URENCO (Uranium Enrichment Company) has a CSR strategy which includes its policy for engaging with stakeholders.

Interest groups influence and support CSR strategies. One such example is the Banyan Tree Resorts which endeavours to protect the environment by investing in research projects and educating visitors to their resorts. They have invested in a team of specialists led by a Group Director of Conservation to deliver their aim.

Research

Look up URENCO's CSR strategy on their website. Then find some other examples from other international businesses. What are the differences and similarities? Why do you think this is?

Case study

Little Italy

Little Italy started as a business in a small Vespa van with an old 1960s 'pull lever' espresso machine at a village railway station in 2004. It provided hot drinks and freshly baked breakfast snacks to commuters. Norwegian born Cathrine stood outside the station daily in snow, sleet, wind and rain.

After a year of being exposed to the elements, Little Italy Espresso Bar moved inside the newly refurbished station and, from humble beginnings, they now have four branches on the Chiltern line and a permanent coffee shop in the heart of the village where it all began.

Their culture is simple: fun, fast and friendly with a belief that you can't be successful by just making good coffee – it's all about the people. The Norwegian-born couple like to lead from the front and also involve customers in publishing their free magazine, created in house by staff. Local businesses and customers feature throughout.

Check your knowledge

1 What are the features of this business that make it so successful?

2 In which sector does this business belong?

3 What do you think are the aims and objectives of Little Italy?

4 How important are their stakeholders to the success of the business?

5 List all of Little Italy's stakeholders.

PAUSE POINT   Which aspects of this case study were difficult? Which were the easiest?

Hint   Identify another similar case study, for example another local business. Ask yourself the same questions.

Extend   Compare your responses to those you gave to the questions about Little Italy. Are there any similarities? Differences?

Effective business communications

Without effective business communications, a business is unlikely to succeed. So far in this unit, you have learned about a variety of businesses from different sectors and of different sizes. Since the latter part of the 20th century, people have relied on the introduction and development of digital communications and, as you will explore shortly, these require a different approach towards how to communicate with the diverse audiences with which businesses need to engage.

While English is widely spoken around the globe, it is too easy to assume that everyone understands exactly what we mean. For example, a simple message shown in the first column in Table 1.4 might be clear, but the same message written in slang (second column) could be difficult for a UK resident to interpret, let alone an overseas customer. The interpretation shown in the third column might be clear, but is it appropriate in a business context?

The example in Table 1.4 shows possible differences in dialect in just a small part of the UK. Consider how many other differences there are in the way people speak because of geographical diversity alone.

▶ **Table 1.4:** Examples of how a message could be misinterpreted

Intended message	Slang version	A more friendly tone
Good afternoon Could you supply us with 2000 barrels of oil for next Tuesday to arrive at Tilbury by 5pm? Please confirm the cost per barrel in dollars. Regards	Awright geeezzaa! Hiya We wan' ter buy 2000 barrels ov oil an' need i' next Tuesday at Tilbury docks by 5. Can yew tell us da cost in dollars? Ta. Sorted mate.	Hiya We want to buy 2000 barrels of oil and need it next Tuesday at Tilbury docks by 5. Can you tell us the cost in dollars? Ta

Although the message might be understood, the way in which it is conveyed might be not be received so well. It is important to use the right language for the right audience to get the right result. Everyone uses different ways of speaking depending on who they are communicating with and the method they are using to convey the message.

Reflect

What information would you rely on to undertake this task and what should you have been given automatically?

What should the business have in place to avoid unnecessary panic, mistakes or delays?

Theory into practice

Your supervisor asks you to order more stock as it is running low unexpectedly soon. Several customers have gone elsewhere and your supervisor is concerned about the impact on sales targets. Before you place the order, do you know who to order from and what you need to order? Consider the following.

1 What do you need to know to ensure you order the right amount of stock?

2 What communication method will you choose to ensure the order gets through?

3 How will you know if the order:
   • has arrived
   • can be serviced
   • will be delivered on time
   • is the price expected?

4 What else do you need to know about?

Tip

Businesses should have clear procedures which guide employees on how to do their job. These procedures can help the way in which colleagues communicate with customers because, where confusion arises, stress levels are also likely to increase. Poor communication may also affect the business leading to under or over ordering, possibly losing potential revenue and damaging their reputation.

Appropriate presentation and delivery of information to a given audience

You may have been asked to give a presentation to your tutors and classmates in school or college. If you have a part-time job, consider how often you have been required to give a presentation to colleagues or managers. In this situation, it is possible you would be told what format is required.

However, if you have been asked by a family member to explain something to them or describe an idea, the way you present it to them is likely to be very different. In a business context, you may be required to produce a written report, presentation of slides or use a flip chart and pens to explain a concept. It is highly unlikely that any of these methods will be needed with family or close friends where you are communicating on a more **informal** basis. Yet people tend to associate a presentation with an electronic output.

Written presentations

In business, presentations take place almost continually. Reports can be **formal**, for example those which deal with business matters relating to finance or policy, such as government reports. A finance department (which may comprise just one or two people in a SME) will routinely produce a set of written monthly accounts as a formal report.

While electronic software is probably used to produce the financial accounts and the report, an explanation of what the figures actually mean will be more appropriate than providing lots of graphs or colourful slides. This means that the accounts need to be explained in a different format so that others can understand them clearly. This could be informal, for example by using a flip chart, or talking others through the information. Informal reports can also describe progress on a project or idea. In this case, the language will reflect a less formal and less business-like approach.

With all written presentations it is important that the information provided is accurate and presented in an appropriate format.

Table 1.5 gives some examples of ways to communicate in business.

> **Table 1.5:** Examples of ways to communicate in business

<table>
<tr><th colspan="9">Method</th></tr>
<tr><th rowspan="12">Reason</th><th></th><th>Video-conference call</th><th>Fax</th><th>Letter</th><th>Telephone call</th><th>Text message</th><th>Email</th><th>Slide presentation</th><th>Written report</th></tr>
<tr><td>Chase order</td><td></td><td>✓</td><td></td><td>✓</td><td></td><td>✓</td><td></td><td></td></tr>
<tr><td>Apologise to customer</td><td>✓</td><td></td><td>✓</td><td>✓</td><td></td><td></td><td></td><td></td></tr>
<tr><td>Negotiate price</td><td></td><td>✓</td><td></td><td>✓</td><td></td><td>✓</td><td></td><td></td></tr>
<tr><td>Make a complaint</td><td></td><td>✓</td><td>✓</td><td>✓</td><td></td><td>✓</td><td></td><td></td></tr>
<tr><td>Chase payment</td><td></td><td>✓</td><td></td><td>✓</td><td></td><td>✓</td><td></td><td></td></tr>
<tr><td>Arrange meeting</td><td></td><td></td><td></td><td>✓</td><td></td><td>✓</td><td></td><td></td></tr>
<tr><td>Book accommodation</td><td></td><td>✓</td><td></td><td>✓</td><td></td><td>✓</td><td></td><td></td></tr>
<tr><td>Check a delivery</td><td></td><td>✓</td><td></td><td>✓</td><td>✓</td><td>✓</td><td></td><td></td></tr>
<tr><td>Meeting notes</td><td></td><td></td><td></td><td></td><td></td><td></td><td></td><td>✓</td></tr>
<tr><td>Sales performance</td><td></td><td></td><td></td><td></td><td></td><td></td><td>✓</td><td>✓</td></tr>
<tr><td>Customer quotation</td><td></td><td></td><td>✓</td><td></td><td></td><td>✓</td><td></td><td></td></tr>
</table>

Key terms

Informal – less business-like, friendlier and could also mean ad hoc. Informal can refer to information given verbally.

Formal – business-like, factual, technical and professional, providing a record. It can refer to writing, such as formal written feedback.

Video conferencing may be used to present some reports, especially where employees are unable to attend one site or always work cross-site. Faxes are used infrequently these days but do still exist, especially overseas or in remote locations where internet connection is less reliable.

Oral presentations

Presentations are often accompanied by a speaker, where professional presenting software is used. This is because each slide should only provide a headline account, with the detail explained by the presenter. Presentations are especially useful when communicating to larger audiences or when giving a series of presentations. They may be accompanied by speaker notes.

It is important to consider the purpose of communicating and whether the language used needs to be adapted to different audiences. For example, technical language is understood by a specialist, such as a mechanical engineer or IT technician, but it needs to be adapted if you are proposing changes to a network system to non-expert users of that system.

Importance of communication to aid business success

Social media can be a great way of promoting a small business and getting it known across a wider community (like Little Italy promoting its services to customers through its website and newsletter). Regardless of business size, social media is being used more widely each year and those dominating business communications include LinkedIn, Instagram, Facebook and Twitter. Government offices also rely on social media. Although there are reservations about using social media, it can reap rewards if it is used responsibly.

Social networks which develop through the use of social media become virtual communities, spanning diverse geographical locations and ignoring political boundaries. Less obvious examples of virtual communities include those initiated by inventor James Dyson and Brompton Bikes.

These virtual communities can thrive on common interests and develop fresh ideas, extend knowledge and be useful for business owners who are considering ways to expand or even start up a business. Virtual communities can make or break a business and word can travel fast. Sites such as TripAdvisor use virtual communities for gathering reviews from customers on their experiences.

Some businesses, such as Microsoft, use discussion boards to generate ongoing interaction whether to promote a product or service, or to report or solve problems. Sites such as Educator Network evolved to bring tutors together across the globe to share their teaching and training ideas and challenges. They have helped to provide innovative ways to teach 'hard to learn' topics and better understand cultural diversity.

Case study

Manufacturing in the West Midlands

West Midlands businesses have boosted profits with a little help from the virtual world.

Manufacturing businesses in the West Midlands now have the chance to try out and test new product prototypes and ideas through virtual simulation technology.

Use of the innovative technology on offer at the University of Birmingham and the Manufacturing Technology Centre in Coventry will help businesses save time and money with costly repeat experiments which normally go hand in hand with testing new ideas.

'In order for businesses to survive and thrive new ways of working that save time and money but still gain the results is key. This project offers businesses an exciting opportunity to try out and explore the innovative technology by putting their new products and ideas to the test in a cost effective, reliable and safe environment. I am pleased that we are able to provide support to a project that will be really beneficial to the future development of businesses in the West Midlands,' said Communities Minister Baroness Hanham CBE.

The project called CASiM2 is supported by £2.6 million from the European Regional Development Fund, which is managed by the Department for Communities and Local Government and matched through funding and staff skills by the University of Birmingham, the Manufacturing Technology Centre, Airbus and Rolls-Royce. 'We will engage SMEs in the West Midlands through demonstrating the commercial benefits of using innovative technologies to deliver step changes in their business offering.'

Check your knowledge

1 What types of communication is this project using?

2 In what ways is this project benefiting from communication?

3 Who are the stakeholders and how have they influenced the project?

4 Which sector does this business belong in and who are its owners?

5 What would you describe as related to its success so far?

❚❚ PAUSE POINT Has your approach to exploring a case study changed since you started this unit? If so, why and how?

Hint What examples can you find where social media has driven the success of a business either from micro to SME or larger, or in initiating a new business idea?

Tip

If you don't have a job, approach local businesses and ask if they would be willing to let you use them as a case study.

Research

If you have a job, what would happen if you were asked to propose a new way for the business to promote products or services? Talk to your employer or supervisor. Would they mentor you on this task or even through your qualification?

1 What else could you do to improve your communication skills?

2 Are there forms of communication where you would benefit from extra training (such as video conferencing)?

B Investigate how businesses are organised

Structure and organisation

Organisational structure

Organisations need a structure to enable the business to operate effectively. As a business grows, the structure will evolve but needs to be considered carefully so that:

▶ all jobs that need doing are identified and allocated
▶ lines of communication are established
▶ levels of responsibility are identified and allocated
▶ levels of authority are attributed.

Although you probably think a sole trader will not have an organisational structure, the jobs still have to get done. Examples include keeping the accounts, ordering supplies, promoting the business, etc. Therefore some jobs are likely to be outsourced, meaning that someone else with the right expertise will be paid to do that aspect of the work. In a way, this 'expert' could be viewed as part of the organisational structure, as the sole trader will depend on them for the smooth operation of the business.

There are different types of organisational structure and these are explored below.

Hierarchical

As the name suggests, this structure shows a hierarchy of responsibility and authority showing who is responsible for what and who has authority to make decisions regarding business operations. This type of structure is fairly easy to understand and, as Figure 1.1 shows, there is one person with overall responsibility and authority for the business and everyone else has a clear position in the organisation.

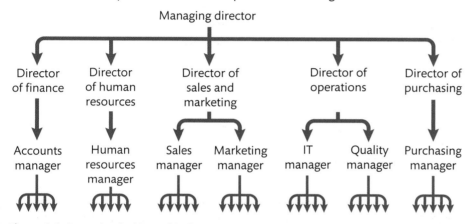

▶ **Figure 1.1:** Example of a hierarchical structure

As shown in Figure 1.1, it is clear who is responsible for their subordinates and that some employees have the same level of responsibility or authority as each other. Each manager leads a team of employees and in large organisations these teams might also have team leaders. This type of structure might apply to SMEs, although not exclusively. Some local authorities operate similar organisational structures.

Another example of a hierarchical structure is shown in Figure 1.2. This is a dental practice. In this example, one dentist owns the practice and associate self-employed dentists are contracted by the owner.

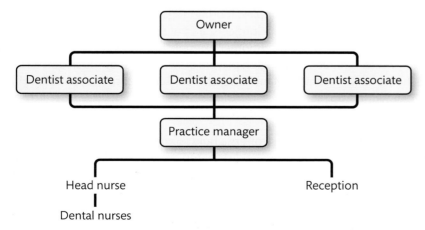

▶ **Figure 1.2:** An alternative example of a hierarchical structure

Discussion

Do you know of anyone who works for a business with a similar structure in a different sector?

Other examples of hierarchical structures include pubs with restaurants where the bar and restaurant are likely to be managed separately, for example by the bar manager and head chef, with staff reporting directly to the boss of their section. The owner has overall authority and responsibility and this can impact on the time it takes for decisions to be made.

Flat structure

A flat structure is a simple example of what might be a micro business. Larger businesses may also have this type of structure. Each structure has advantages and disadvantages, which you will explore later.

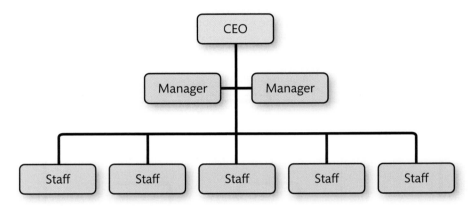

▶ **Figure 1.3:** Example of a flat structure

As Figure 1.3 shows, the lines of responsibility are very clear and the routes to those in authority are also clearly defined. However, as a business grows the number of subordinates (people who the managers are responsible for) can become unwieldy. Examples include:
▶ the amount of time it takes managers to deal with a large number of teams
▶ the impact on their workload.

Key term

Bureaucracy – detailed procedures which have to be followed (sometimes known as 'red tape').

Flat structures may operate with less **bureaucracy** and therefore decision making can be quicker. However, with one overall leader, they are likely to be more protective of their business and can be reluctant to change. There are also likely to be fewer opportunities for promotion or progression than in other structures. The structure and organisation of the business may need to be changed as it grows.

Matrix

The matrix type of structure is complex. It brings together teams of people depending on their abilities to work on specific projects. BT put together teams of employees to work on projects, as do Microsoft. Another example is a national football team such as England which is made up of English players drawn from individual football clubs around the world (for example Manchester United, Real Madrid, Bayern Munich) for the football World Cup.

Research

If you have a business mentor, ask them about their experience of being in charge of others.

Holocratic

A holocratic organisation structure offers a holistic approach to running a business where responsibility and authority are distributed amongst the workforce. One disadvantage of other structures is the level of bureaucracy that can appear to get in the way of getting on with the job. Holocracy claims to remove this problem by devolving responsibility and relying on very clear roles, aims and objectives, which, in turn, rely on very clear communication and trust. Figure 1.5 shows how this structure can be associated with departments.

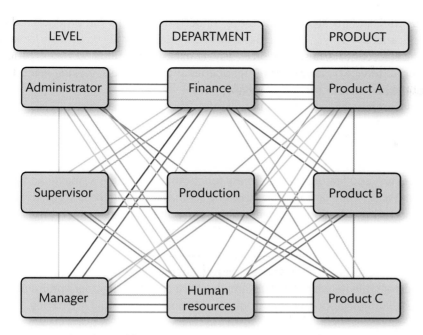

Each coloured line represents a team made up of members from one or more of the levels, departments and products

▶ **Figure 1.4:** An example of a matrix structure

▶ **Figure 1.5:** Concept of a holocratic structure

The advantage of this type of structure is the equal distribution of responsibility and authority. In other words, no single individual takes on the role of boss and everyone can operate autonomously. As you may imagine, this requires considerable trust due to the lack of bureaucracy. Employees need to understand their role without the constraints of job descriptions. This type of structure can help a business to adapt rapidly to change and could be viewed as generating greater job satisfaction and feeling part of the business. An example of a business using this type of structure could be Microsoft, whereby teams are put together to work on specialist projects.

Research

Explore how these organisations structure their businesses and list the similarities and differences between their organisational structures:
- Eddie Stobart
- Mercedes Benz
- Fitness First
- Whitbread.

Compare your findings with another learner.

Functional/operational areas

Businesses have several functions in order to operate efficiently.

Functions

A brief definition of each function is:
▶ human resources (HR) (responsible for managing the people in the organisation to include their welfare, job roles, progression opportunities)
▶ research and development (R&D) (of new products or concepts)
▶ sales (selling products or services)
▶ marketing (promotion of business)
▶ purchasing (supplies, products, stationery)

- production and quality (manufacturing, undertaking checks that products meet specifications)
- finance (accounting, raising invoices, paying bills, wages)
- customer service (resolving customer queries and complaints, seeking feedback to improve products or service, or develop ideas)
- IT (telecommunications and computer infrastructure such as website)
- administration (the ongoing support for the business to function, such as following processes, dealing with correspondence, organising meetings and any travel).

While this list may apply to large organisations such as BT, Microsoft and BMW, smaller businesses will also feature many of these functions although on a smaller and possibly less formal scale. For example, a hairdressing salon will still purchase stock, deal with finance and administration, and need HR for personnel matters, but it is less likely to undertake research and development functions in the way large businesses do.

Smaller businesses may contribute to R&D by giving feedback to suppliers or listen to customer feedback to pick up ways to improve their service or what they offer. The case study of Little Italy is a typical example where employees gather comments from customers, learning about what customers and commuters would like to buy.

While larger organisations such as Waitrose, Ryanair, Staysure and Wiltshire Farm Foods may have entire departments to manage customer service matters, smaller businesses rely on every member of staff to know how to resolve customer service issues, and employees are more likely to be in close contact with customers on a frequent basis.

Operations

If the functional areas of a business are not suitably structured, then efficient operations will be affected. For example, when some businesses set up customer service departments or help desks outside the UK, customers might complain about communication difficulties if they are unable to understand the support assistant.

Due to the recession, many businesses have had to streamline their functions. Some have reduced their workforce, leading to job cuts in marketing teams, administrative staff or sales assistants. You may be able to identify where staff shortages appear to be impacting on service.

Reducing the workforce does not automatically lead to a reduction in service quality. By taking advantage of technological advancements, businesses such as banks and manufacturing industries might feel the investment in expensive equipment has led to a reduction in staff but no reduction in the service offered to customers.

Link

You will explore customer service in more detail in *Unit 14: Investigating Customer Service.*

Research

If you have a part-time job, find out about the business's organisational structure. Compare the structure with those you have explored already and consider why that structure was chosen for this business. If you don't have a part-time job or volunteer, perhaps ask family and friends about the businesses they work for.

Aims and objectives

Earlier in this unit, you reviewed your aims and objectives and were asked to put together a plan for achieving this qualification. The purpose for doing this is to focus on the main goal and break down what appears to be a large task into smaller bite-sized chunks. You may have created a Gantt chart or you may have preferred to use another method.

▶ Robotic 'barstaff' on new cruise ships

Aims of businesses in different sectors

The same applies to businesses needing to plan out their aims and objectives to strive for success. These are built around three key areas:

▶ mission (a promise of commitment to the business cause)

▶ vision (the direction the business aims to travel in the future, short or longer term)

▶ values (the philosophy and ethos of a business which underpin the vision).

Mission

You may have heard or seen the mission statement of the place where you are studying. Mission statements are often found at the front of any marketing materials and websites. While a mission statement is intended to represent the overall aim of the business, it should be informed by the vision and values of the business. Here are three examples from different business types.

Salon: Body Beautiful

Our team aims to provide excellent customer care in a friendly and professional environment. We pledge to deliver this care via a first class service.

We are sure of success when clients are delighted with the products and treatments we have supplied. We will continue to seek to improve the services we offer by continual staff training and by embracing all new technology.

Our aim for our clients is to achieve the salon's motto of 'Embrace your body beautiful!'.

Carefree Coaches

Safety, security and comfort form the foundation of everything we aim to give our customers.

Our future success will build on these by focusing on both business and leisure markets and by ensuring the customer always comes first.

Ingleham Community Project

1. To represent all the residents and businesses of Ingleham, Benton and Clapdale.

2. To hear and respond to the needs of all residents and businesses.

3. To work in partnership with all stakeholders and interest groups within the area and their representatives.

Each of these statements varies in length and complexity. Ultimately, these should be supported by the business objectives representing how the business intends to deliver these promises. Analyse these three statements. These questions will help you.

▶ What are the main messages?

▶ Do they represent the company image to you as a customer?

▶ Are they understandable for a variety of audiences?

▶ What expectations do they give you?

▶ Do they communicate their vision and values to the customer?

▶ What changes would you recommend?

▶ How well do you think each mission statement reflects the overall business aim?

Business aims are not solely the intentions of owners as these will depend on the stakeholders of the business and which sector it belongs to.

Vision

A vision statement is easily confused with a mission statement. Its aim is to clearly communicate the future plans for the business, particularly to its employees. They can become involved in the plans for the business and their jobs and organisation structure will need to support this vision.

Values

Organisational values will vary across businesses depending on their overall aim. Businesses such as Sainsbury plc promote their eagerness for growth, while Coca-Cola are keen to promote their commitment to a sustainable environment. British Gas also promote their commitment to the environment.

Research

Look at the websites for Sainsbury plc, Coca Cola and British Gas. How prominent do they make their values on their website? Can you identify the key values for each business? How do you think each company chose their values?

Private

The aims of businesses are likely to vary depending on whether or not the overall aim is:

▶ making profits – most multi-national businesses aim to make a profit

▶ profit maximisation, where efficiency and cost of supplies, service or production are streamlined to ensure a greater margin between those costs and the revenue received, therefore maximising profits; examples include some budget airlines which charge extra for in-flight meals, drinks and baggage

▶ breakeven – the critical measure identifying at what point a business will make a profit or become non-viable; the breakeven point is the basis of business plans and especially a new business, where a calculation identifies how many products or services are needed to generate sufficient income to cover all outgoing costs, such as buying supplies, premises, wages, paying taxes etc

▶ survival – such as the struggles reported over recent times being faced by Mulberry and Ladbrokes; other businesses such as Clinton Cards and Jessops have struggled to stay afloat – the former has sold off many of its stores and Jessops has closed almost 100 stores and reduced staff numbers by at least 550 in 2013; Clinton Cards may have overlooked the growth in sending ecards

▶ growth – for example pound shops and pawn brokers which always do well in times of austerity (the number of UK pawn brokers was reported to have increased substantially during the recession)

▶ market leadership – Sainsbury plc is an example where the company's mission is to gain market leadership, while British Gas strives to retain its leadership in the utilities sector and BT to regain the lead across all its services.

The private sector also needs to take into account the expectations of stakeholders and that includes government. Business and personal taxes must be paid and businesses must comply with legislation and regulations.

Public

In the public sector, especially those companies which are not-for-profit, business aims are accountable to the government which may be a major stakeholder providing government funding from public taxes and other means. Therefore the organisation's mission, vision and values are influenced by government expectations as well as other stakeholders.

Service provision to government agencies is often contracted from profit making private sector businesses such as refuse collectors, building contractors, cleaners, etc. Each of these suppliers will undergo significant checks and be expected to comply with agency contracts, usually known as service level agreements.

Cost control is fundamental to the survival of any business. A public sector business is accountable to the public for how it spends money and controls costs. For example, households are informed about how their contributions from council taxes to local government will be spent and how well they performed to provide the service expected.

Value for money – the public and private sector is no different in wanting to provide value for money. Therefore when seeking a supplier, such as sourcing a contractor to repair roads, bids will be requested from several contractors and the following will be judged:

▶ cost (cheapest is not necessarily best or worst; fixed price or estimated; what is not included?)

▶ quality (workmanship, resources, customer satisfaction)

▶ timeframe (overall timeframe, impact on other services).

Link

You will be introduced to business legislation in learning aim C later in this unit and taxes in *Unit 3: Personal and Business Finance.*

Each aspect is important and it is often difficult to compare like for like. You may be able to identify other factors which would influence you when making a choice.

Service quality

Everyone prefers quality service. For example, deliveries which turn up on time and shelf stackers who stand aside to let you reach a product, just as a bus driver appreciates a thank you from a departing passenger and the public values the bus driver who avoids splashing waiting passengers or passers-by.

One example of a business committed to quality is London-based Brompton Bikes. They manufacture bespoke bicycles to order and every part is traceable to the employee responsible for its manufacture. Their aim is for every customer to be confident of service quality because every employee takes responsibility.

Meeting government standards

Think back to the dental practice structure shown in Figure 1.2. That type of business aims to make a profit from private patients while also servicing patients through the NHS. However, not all dental practices provide government-funded dental treatment and you might be aware of examples in your local area.

Service provision

Regardless of who is paying for the treatment, the patient should receive the same level of care and service. However, the type of treatment may vary because not all treatments are funded (or may only be partially funded) by the NHS, such as teeth whitening, white fillings and veneers.

Cost control

All businesses need to keep control of their outgoing costs and generate income, otherwise the business might close. Several businesses closed during the recession, some of which seemed to be part of the British heritage, such as Woolworths and MFI, along with Blockbusters, Comet and JJB Sports. This is not to suggest that these businesses lost control of their costs, but when demand drops (for whatever reason) profits fall to the point where they cannot continue to pay their way and businesses close.

Woolworths suffered from a lack of vision. It was hard to pinpoint what it offered that was unique. Low-cost products, especially those no longer sought by consumers, do not pay expensive rents in prime locations and customers' needs were being met by out-of-centre supermarkets which expanded their ranges.

▶ Woolworths was one of several large and well-known businesses to close down during the last recession

Key term

Austerity – the difficult economic conditions resulting from the government putting measures in place to reduce public spending.

Value for money

Customers expect value for money, especially during times of **austerity** such as a recession. These customers include stakeholders such as the contractor purchasing bricks who will want to get the best deal on the bricks and other building supplies without compromising quality.

Service quality

Service quality is judged by the customer in relation to their expectations. This can be difficult as our expectations are very subjective and so they differ. Take, for example, a simple transaction in a shop. What factors shape your assessment of the experience? Can you find what you are looking for? How long do you wait to be served? Is the assistant courteous or over-friendly? Are you charged the correct amount? Are you given the right change, etc.? All these factors are influential regardless of cost.

Strangely, customers can get very agitated over very minor transactions while a major purchase or service might be overlooked, for example buying a holiday or a new home. People are becoming more critical about service quality and reports feature frequently about the NHS or how BT has fought to repair a failing reputation for its support services. It is now the norm to check review websites, such as TripAdvisor or Amazon reviews, before visiting a business or making a purchase. However, there is a danger that people are more likely to leave a review after a negative experience, rather than a positive one.

Meeting government standards

Research

Explore the government's website for the responsibilities laid out by government departments and agencies. Think about how a local business or your school or college can meet these responsibilities.

All businesses have to comply with rules laid out by the government. For example, all businesses must comply with legislation such as health and safety, which you will explore a little later in this unit and throughout this book. However, depending on the nature of the business, there are specific standards to meet such as:

▶ care standards for those working in the care sector

▶ food standards for any business providing food and drink to the public

▶ Ofsted regulating education and training, including schools, nurseries, child minders

▶ organic certification for those growing organic produce

▶ disease notification regulations for farmers.

Not-for-profit

While providers of education share the same overall goal, their objectives will vary depending on the type of education they supply and, especially, who they are educating.

Key term

Multi-collaborative – collaborating with multiple partners.

The National Science Learning Centre is an education provider and therefore a not-for-profit organisation offering tutor education in the UK and Northern Ireland. As a **multi-collaborative** charity registered organisation, it operates as a joint venture between the Department for Education and the Wellcome Trust. It has multiple funding sources so has many stakeholders to satisfy.

Housing associations, such as the Villages Housing Association situated in the north-west of England, also publish their mission statement: 'To Be More Than Just A Landlord. Working In Partnership To Create An Environment For Communities To Flourish'. Their aim is clear and succinct and their website describes how and why they work in partnership and lists their values in support of their vision.

Charitable organisations aimed at alleviating poverty at home and overseas, such as Oxfam, UNICEF and NSPCC, have clear mission statements, although their aims and objectives will also change according to a perceived area for need. One recent example of need is the Nepalese earthquake early in 2015, while others are longstanding, such as UNICEF's aim to improve sanitation in places such as Angola.

Shops to raise funds for charities such as these have appeared in many shopping centres and high streets during the recession, taking advantage of the opportunity of prime location premises paying lower rents. You may have seen some local authorities making temporary use of empty stores to promote community projects, such as mobility services or careers advice, occupying government owned empty space which might otherwise become derelict.

> **Research**
>
> Locate the mission statement of your place of study or work. Explore how their aims and objectives relate to the mission statement.

Case study

'Good Bubble'

In the summer of 2015, Amy Wordsworth presented her company, Ella Banks Ltd, to the Channel 4 programme *Dragons' Den*. Her company produces 'natural superfruit' children's toiletries labelled 'Good Bubble' and she was seeking extra investment. Amy's business aim and values are evident in that, while striving to make a profit and grow the business, the intention is that the business stays true to its values.

Good Bubble aims to stay true to its values by being kind to skin and using 98 per cent natural ingredients in their products. Superfruit ingredients provide extra nourishment for hair and skin without the use of chemicals or irritants.

The business values also promote a commitment to reducing their carbon footprint by using and promoting recyclable packaging. Good Bubble also recognise hard economic times and aim to keep prices down, selling their products online with stockists based around the UK and Ireland.

Check your knowledge

1 Which sector is the Good Bubble business in?
2 What are Amy's business values?
3 What type of organisational structure is Good Bubble likely to be?
4 Why do you think Amy was seeking additional investment?
5 Who are her likely stakeholders?
6 If you were Amy, is there anything you would do differently?

Objectives: SMART

Putting together a plan, whether it is for a business or your personal use, requires frequent reviewing and updating. This process can be extremely rewarding when you can 'tick off' your achievements without getting downhearted if some of the targets set have not been achieved. It is possible that they were overly ambitious and more complex or time consuming than originally expected.

Managers of businesses will have similar experiences and will need to justify to others, such as their stakeholders, why some business objectives were not achieved. The key to a successful plan is to carefully consider each objective and ensure that it is SMART and that, ultimately, taken together, all the aims meet the overall aim.

A 'SMART' objective should be:
▶ Specific
▶ Measurable
▶ Achievable
▶ Relevant
▶ Time constrained.

Reflect

You'll recall that, earlier in the unit, you were encouraged to create a plan to help you to achieve the aims and objectives of this unit, and to think about your timeframe. Now that you have explored more about business aims and objectives, review your plan and adjust it where relevant. You might need to break down some of the objectives into smaller chunks with varying dates for completion. Ask yourself these questions about your objectives.

- Are my objectives specific and clear? Will I know what I mean next time I review my plan?
- How will I measure my progress and achievements?
- Are my objectives achievable, for example do I have the resources?
- Are my expectations realistic?

Am I confident I can achieve in the allocated time? What are the time constraints? Have I been unrealistic? Have I considered other factors and built in some flexibility (buffer time)?

Assessment practice 1.1

A.P1   A.P2   B.P3   B.M2   A.M1   AB.D1

You and a friend decide to set up a small business to help support your community. You want the business to be a non-profit, but your friend would like it to be profit-making.

To compare ideas and ensure that you are fully prepared for conversations with likely investors, you write a report exploring two contrasting businesses, one for-profit and one not-for-profit. You also want this report to help you decide how best to organise the business.

In your report you should:
- identify the features, organisation structure, aims and objectives of each business
- identify the stakeholders of each business.

Think about how the organisation's structure enables your chosen businesses to achieve their aims and objectives and how this contributes to the business' success.

Discuss how the businesses manage the relationship and communication with their stakeholders, and how they influence the business.

The report should include a detailed analysis of the reasons behind the success of each business, using the evidence you have gathered.

Plan
- How do I pick my chosen businesses? How do I find enough information out about each?
- What aspects of this task will I struggle with? How can I combat this?
- Is it clear what I need to do? Do I need any clarification?

Do
- Am I sticking to the timeframe and order of my plan – unless it doesn't work?
- Am I keeping details of my sources, together with dates I accessed each one?
- Am I using a variety of sources and not relying just on the internet, and making notes around which sources look trustworthy and which are dubious?
- As I work through the activity, am I ticking or highlighting the learning aims covered?

Review
- I can read through my work thoroughly, checking for mistakes and poor presentation.
- I can reflect on my work and my contribution. How did it go? Could I have done better?
- I can swap with my peers and critique each other's work. I can give considered feedback, which is constructive, developmental and most of all, honest.

Examine the environment in which businesses operate

The term 'environment' has multiple features. During this unit, you will have recognised how the economic environment has influenced businesses, for example **retail** outlets and businesses closing down due to the recession. Some shops such as high-end brand retailers, pound shops, technology, gambling sites and pawn brokers have thrived, while others have had to close down due to lack of sales.

External environment

The external environment impacts on businesses and is comprised of many factors. These factors are often used by businesses to analyse how and why they will be successful or unsuccessful – this analysis is known as '**PESTLE**' which stands for:

Political
Economic
Social
Technological
Legal
Environment.

Political

Government support, such as monetary grants or promotion, can inject considerable enthusiasm into new business ideas such as wind farms and solar panels. Although grants are time constrained, you have probably noticed both of these examples springing up around the country. Of course, there is a motive for government support according to government policy and promises.

The government website regularly updates with announcements. You may also recall the example of government bail-out when Northern Rock and the Royal Bank of Scotland (RBS) were in financial trouble. However, there are plenty of business owners who claim government do little to support their sectors.

Membership of trading communities

Businesses can benefit from being members of trading communities. These are often sector related, such as retail, health, publishing, tourism, catering, etc. and provide networking opportunities, advice, news and opportunities to buy or sell equipment, services, training, etc.

The European Union

The European Union (EU) is another form of trade association. The EU promotes itself as 'the best way to realise our global future'. Being a member of any trade association gives credibility in the eyes of the customer, just as you would expect a gas fitter or service engineer to be Gas Safe registered. It can be seen to open doors to opportunities that are closely guarded or seen as exclusive.

Economic

Economic factors greatly influence the success or demise of businesses. As you know, the recession has been blamed for the closure of thousands of high street stores. These businesses may have failed to take into account economic needs, competition and technological advancements. You have also learned about the success of new or diversified businesses, informed by government initiatives such as solar panels and air source heating.

> **Key term**
>
> **Retail** – the sale of goods, usually on a small scale, directly to the public for consumption rather than resale.

> **Key term**
>
> **PESTLE** – political, economic, social, technological, legal, environmental.

> **Link**
>
> *Unit 19: Pitching for a New Business* Learning aim B, also considers PESTLE analysis.

> **Research**
>
> Research examples of businesses that complain of too little government intervention. Can you explain why this might be?

Key term

Fiscal – relates to government revenue, for example from taxes.

Fiscal

Fiscal policy affects every type of business. It is government controlled and dictates levels of taxation based on the cost of borrowing. This is how the government generates its income and decides its budget. Every business owner and its decision makers cannot ignore changes to fiscal policy.

Research

Can you find any examples of the effect of fiscal policy on small businesses? In groups, see if you can find any examples of the effect of fiscal policy on large businesses.

Monetary and other government policies

Monetary policy affects everybody as it relates to the value of our currency and interest rates. This policy is determined by the government and decisions about how to meet expectations are controlled by the Bank of England and the Monetary Policy Committee (MPC). All businesses are affected by decisions made by the MPC.

Supply side policy

These policies aim to improve productivity and produce economic growth. Ways to achieve this include reducing taxes, such as income tax in 2014, and reducing corporation tax (the tax paid by private and public limited companies) in 2015.

Economic growth

The government is striving to grow the economy so that the UK does not return to a recession. If you imagine that the government is you, look at your own financial circumstances. Calculate how much money you have coming in and how much you expect to spend. What is left? Everyone needs money to survive, so you have to ensure that you do not spend more than you can afford or else you have to find ways of generating more income.

The country is no different and the government has to find ways to grow our economy at international, national, regional and local levels according to opportunity and need, for example, building projects, the Help to Buy scheme, and increasing job and training opportunities.

Exchange rates

Key term

Inflation – a general increase in prices and fall in the purchasing value of money.

Another factor influencing the success or failure of businesses and our economy is exchange rates. These can fluctuate greatly and how our UK currency, pounds sterling, compares with the US dollar, euros and the Japanese yen is analysed daily. Each of these currencies is influential in the UK's purchasing and selling power globally, although not exclusively, depending on the countries trading. Exchange rates are influenced by many factors such as unemployment, **inflation** and other complex factors such as the activity on the stock exchange and speculation. In other words, how much our currency is worth when trading with other countries. You may well have experienced fluctuations if you have ever bought foreign currency to go on holiday.

Imagine how fluctuating exchange rates impact on the travel industry. Airlines, rail and logistics companies are just a few of the businesses which must try to forecast their income while anticipating the costs of running the business, for example vehicle maintenance, fuel costs and the predicted number of passengers, etc.

Exchange rates are partly responsible for fluctuating oil prices. For example, in the summer of 2015 the price of petrol was 30p per litre less than two years previously. Consider what other factors might have influenced this reduction.

Social

Attitudes to saving

Banks and the government rely on people to save money. The money saved is used to boost the economy as it is borrowed by businesses and householders for mortgages, etc. However, with less money in people's pockets (disposable income) and interest rates remaining at a low rate previously unheard of, banks and government are finding it difficult to encourage saving. This is why the government has introduced initiatives such as increasing the amount that can be invested in **ISAs** and premium bonds.

Key term

ISA – individual savings account (a good way to save money without having to pay tax on it).

Spending and debt

Changes to spending habits influence the types of business that can start up and expand. For example, recent times have seen an increase in pawn brokers, gambling sites, pound and charity shops, payday lenders and businesses like Bright House which offer weekly payment schemes. (Charity shops do not have to pay business rates.) By contrast, pubs, building contractors, clothing, furniture and photography stores, etc are struggling to survive.

Social responsibility requirements

A sense of social responsibility also influences spending habits. For example, with the increase of charity shops people can make their money go further while also helping a good cause. Consumers are being encouraged to consider ethical matters and the consequences of their actions much more. According to the Office of National Statistics (ONS), sales of tobacco and alcohol have dropped while the biggest growth area is recreation and culture, although this includes mostly electronic goods.

Change

Changes, for example to the **demographic trends**, can have a significant influence on business. For example, in Slough, Berkshire, there is a wide diversity of ethnicity which has led to new businesses catering for specialist foods, local government services and training opportunities. In Kent, there are large Nepalese settlements while, in other areas of the UK, immigrants from Somalia are building communities. These are just a few of the factors influencing our businesses.

Key term

Demographic trends – the characteristics of a country's population.

Consumers' tastes/preferences

Changes to consumers' tastes or preferences also influence the nature of businesses. For example, the food industry is now strongly influenced by foreign foods and recipes, while fast food remains very popular. There have been increases in restaurants such as burger chains and 'simple' food restaurants: for example, one London restaurant is dedicated to grilled cheese sandwiches and one to just cereal.

However, tastes can also remain unchanged – reports from the Foreign and Commonwealth Office (FCO) reveal that our favourite takeaway food is still traditional fish and chips.

Research

How many different nations are represented by fast food outlets and restaurants in your local area?

Discussion

Discuss your research findings with your peers. How do your findings compare and how do you think these businesses reflect the local population? Now look at your nearest city. Are your findings different? Or do they reflect the same as your local area?

Technological change

Technological advancements and changes influence businesses and create opportunities for new businesses. During the mid 1980s, businesses started to introduce fax machines, and electronic typewriters and word processors became more commonplace. Early adopters used computers although few employees were skilled in their use. By the mid 1990s, this led to a change in the training courses and qualifications being offered to meet demand and public interest; by the early 21st century internet usage was almost a necessity for businesses to function.

Automation

Automation has been in existence for a long time, with robots building cars, but, if traced back, it could be claimed that automation appeared as early as the 8th century. The first programmable robot was developed in 1954 and robots were first introduced into the motor industry in 1962.

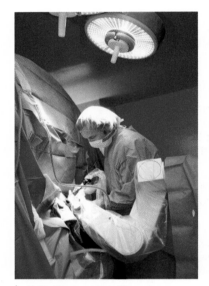

▶ Robotic surgery taking place

Of course robots are not the only form of automation. Today we take it for granted that we spend much of our everyday lives interacting with some form of automation. This includes buying tickets, setting alarm clocks, timers for heating, water, cooking, programming washing machines, etc. Even certain surgical procedures or treatments are carried out to some extent by automation.

Improved communications

Technologically, improved communications have changed the way businesses operate and especially how they are structured, for example more people can now work from home or remotely. This had led to WiFi connections being provided on trains, in stations, on ships, in aeroplanes, in restaurants, coffee shops, shopping centres and open spaces. All this encourages us to take work on holiday or maximise travel time into business time.

New businesses are increasing rapidly and some innovative ideas may even operate from a 'back bedroom' – these are sometimes based on a new craze, such as the aluminium scooter in the mid 1990s. However, unless business owners know how to sustain their business idea, and can cope with changes in demand, they can be short lived. One recent 'back bedroom' innovation is that of Marc, 'inventor' of Sublime Science children's parties.

Legal

Certain legislation must be complied with in business otherwise heavy fines are imposed and even imprisonment. Some of the laws affecting businesses are outlined in Table 1.6.

▶ **Table 1.6:** A sample of laws which affect business

Laws and regulations	Business type affected	What it means
Partnership Act 1890 (undergoing changes late 2015)	Partnerships	All partnerships are governed by this Act regardless of whether the partnership has been registered as a legal partnership or limited company. A partnership can only be dissolved if one partner wishes to retire or unfortunately dies. A partner cannot be sacked or made redundant. Regardless of the time as a partner or contribution to the business, partners must have equal share of all profits and losses, unless other legal contracts are in place stating otherwise.
Companies Act 2006 (undergoing updates late 2015)	Limited, unlimited, private and public companies	This Act sets a code of conduct for businesses to operate to protect the business and its operations (both internally and externally), its employees and shareholders. This Act informs company policies and their operations including financial, rules for forming and dissolving a business.
Charities Act 2011	Registered charities, non-profit	The aim of this Act is to protect the charity and its fundraising activities in line with business expectations. All fundraising activities exceeding £10,000 per year must register as a charity. Charities have to set up trustees to ensure the charity operates within the law. They are not being responsible for debts but can face greater public liability.
Competition Act 1998 (undergoing amendments late 2015)	Any business	This Act came into force to prevent domination by any one business by addressing: • anti-competitive agreements which prevent, restrict or distort competition in the UK • abuse of dominant market positions which prohibits limiting production, markets or technical development to the detriment of the consumer.
UK Corporate Governance Code	Public sector including schools, colleges	This Code comprises the rules and regulations which all governing bodies need to comply with and legal requirements for operating, including: • formal financial accounts • record keeping of decision-making such as minutes of all meetings • rules by which governing bodies conduct themselves including requirements for holding meetings (frequency, attendance) • who can and cannot be a governor.
Financial services regulation	Financial organisations	These are rules which act to protect consumers and provide monitoring of financial activities by third parties, for example auditors. The Stock Exchange is regulated by these guidelines, just as banks and other financial services are supervised.
Industry regulators	Sector specific	These regulators act as supervisors to ensure conformity and compliance across business sectors. For example, Gas Safe regulate gas appliances, fitting, servicing and manufacture. The Care Quality Commission is a health regulator. The Health and Safety Executive (HSE) regulates all aspects of business (and personal) operations. All businesses have their regulators, including registered charities (Charity Commission of England and Wales). Your qualifications are regulated by Ofqual to ensure they are relevant, appropriate and of sufficient quality.
Government departments	All businesses and the public	The government has many departments aimed at ensuring everyone operates in a responsible and trustworthy manner and for the benefit of public good.

Research

Check for anticipated changes to existing legislation and the introduction of new rules and regulations.

Key terms

Environmental factors – those factors outside of the business over which you mostly have no control.

Ethical trends – trends determined by moral principles.

Businesses are responsible for keeping up to date with developments and changes to legislation and regulations. Ignorance cannot be used as an excuse for non-compliance.

All rules and regulations, including laws, can be difficult to understand and are easily misinterpreted. Always seek professional advice if in doubt. This is why large organisations often employ their own legal department, just as the place of your study may have a specialist in their governing body.

Environmental factors and ethical trends

More than ever, businesses and individuals are concerned about **environmental factors** and **ethical trends**. We all share a sense of social responsibility for our survival and that of the planet. Factors are outlined below.

▸ Carbon emissions.
  • This means an impact on business costs such as increased taxes imposed on fuel.
▸ Waste.
  • Household rubbish must now be segregated between different bins which the council collect and dispose of in controlled ways. Landfill sites are also heavily regulated, as is how water and sewage are disposed of.
  • In order to reduce the waste from bags given out by supermarkets and larger stores, the government imposed a charge on plastic bags from October 2015.
▸ Recycling.
  • Businesses must comply with the government's green policies which ultimately impact on all our lives. The government's 'lets recycle' policy is under review in their quest for zero waste.
  • Examples of businesses built on recycling include The Recycling Factory, which sells ink cartridges, and Traid, which remakes donated clothes for resale.
▸ Pollution.
  • The amount of pollution produced impacts on our health, buildings and surroundings. Demand for reduced pollution is forcing businesses to close, such as Didcot Power Station, demolished almost 43 years after it opened in 1970.

Businesses can benefit from being seen to support environmental issues, for example those affecting the planet, the food we eat and people's welfare, such as Fairtrade food production, recyclable products, free range eggs, etc.

Organisations can also be forced out of business if they don't consider environmental factors and ethical trends. One of the biggest law suits ever in the USA was won in 1996 when Pacific Gas and Electric were forced to pay damages due to chromium water contamination which impacted on hundreds of people's lives.

Some businesses choose to adapt their business operations, for example Pret A Manger have made changes to their plastic packaging to make it more environmentally friendly.

Internal environment

Corporate culture

Business (corporate) culture is a hot topic. You might have heard people talk about a blame culture – how an organisation is structured can have a great impact on whether or not there is a blame culture and, more importantly, whether employees and managers share the same view of this. Corporate cultures vary hugely from business to business. For example, large banks in the city are known for their long hours and cut-throat attitudes whereas technology start-ups, such as those found in Silicon Valley and Old Street, are known for their relaxed, casual atmosphere. What impact do you think different cultures have on businesses?

Corporate Social Responsibility (CSR)

You will have learned a little about CSR earlier in this unit. Three such examples given were URENCO, Banyan Tree Resorts and MMO.

CSR can greatly influence the operations of a business. For example, in the nuclear industry many people jump to conclusions about the dangers of enriching uranium: they readily conjure up stories which frighten others or embellish stories from historic events such as Chernobyl in 1986. These examples are usually driven by fear of the unknown and incorrect assumptions, but they can impact greatly on the success of a business. A more recent example in the nuclear industry was the Tsunami disaster at Fukushima in March 2011. This led to reductions in demand and lack of confidence in investing in planned nuclear power stations.

Ethics

Businesses are also shaped by ethical considerations. One such example is the range of services offered by the NHS. In 1978, the birth of Louise Brown, the world's first ever test tube baby, led to some disapproval and claims that such intervention was unethical.

The health service is probably the most obvious example of the importance of ethics – IVF being almost commonplace and R&D appearing to make rapid progress, committees and government are challenged constantly about the ethics, for example, of body transplants. Very recently the announcement of human hand transplants and the proposal for 3D printing of body parts are undergoing an ethical debate.

Such matters impact on the way businesses are organised and operate, and on their funding and company values. For example, new businesses have emerged to meet the demand and supply of automated prostheses, pacemakers and computer software to stimulate brain function.

Businesses need policies and procedures in place to ensure their employees behave ethically. One example of where government stepped in to stop unethical practice was the decision to cap exorbitant interest rates charged by unscrupulous payday lenders.

CSR is an ethical consideration and you may also have been introduced to policies during your induction at your place of study or work. Other examples of ethical policies are **whistle-blowing** and those associated with equality such as homophobic bullying.

Competitive environment

Just as some people are more competitive than others, businesses vary in how they regard competition. Those businesses which view competition as destructive may have overlooked competition as an opportunity.

Competition can be at different levels:
- local
- national
- international.

Having competitors does not mean that a business will automatically succeed or fail – rather, it relies on careful business planning and a consideration of all factors. For example, if Little Italy decided to open a coffee bar at a small rural railway station

▶ Can you think of the type of business that would have an office as shown in the photo?

Key term

Whistle-blowing – informing on someone who is doing something wrong or illegal.

which already had one, it could be viewed as a bad business decision. However, if their reputation preceded them by offering a superior product, better customer satisfaction or improved value for money, then their business might well wipe out their competitor. Decisions like this cannot be taken lightly. You can probably name several examples where competitors appear to work alongside each other in harmony such as opticians, dental practices, estate agents, chemists, department stores, supermarkets, fast food chains, electrical retailers, etc.

Factors influencing competitive advantage

In order to keep a competitive advantage, it is vital that a business keeps its eye on what its competitors are doing and tries to anticipate what they are planning to do. Factors which influence are outlined below.

▶ Differentiation: for example developing new products, branching out into new products or services, especially something unique from your competitors, such as the Dyson Ball cylinder vacuums.

▶ Pricing policies: how a business determines prices for **wholesale** and retail products or services to achieve its planned profits.

▶ Market leadership: defines a business which has the largest or larger share of the market in relation to its competitors, for example Coca Cola and British Airways.

▶ Reputation: something a business cannot buy and which has to be earned. Businesses such as Waitrose, Virgin Atlantic, M&S and Walt Disney thrive on their reputation which has been developed and maintained over many years. Customers also highly rate Amazon, Microsoft, Apple and Plusnet. A bad reputation can rapidly ruin a business no matter how large or small. BT has been working hard to improve its reputation. Security company Blackwater even changed its name to X, and then to Academi, in an attempt to improve its reputation, without success, after a terrible incident in Iraq in 2007 that resulted in lost lives.

▶ Market share: the percentage of a given market that a business holds. Holding a market share does not mean that the business is the market leader, however. For example, in 2014 Samsung was reported to hold 26 per cent of the global market share in Smart televisions whereas in 2009 it was market leader with its range of LCD TVs.

▶ Cost control: managing and controlling costs for a business to remain viable. For example, Phones 4U acted as an interface or broker between mobile phone companies but the businesses it provided its services to decided to sell its services directly. Unfortunately, these other business declined to pay Phones 4U, leading to its bankruptcy.

▶ Technology relationships with customers: different means of technology are relied upon heavily for communicating with customers such as:
  • databases holding customer details, purchase history and preferences, etc
  • telephone and online support.

Finding an answer to a problem with a product or its operation might be resolved speedily by searching online or ringing an out-of-hours support line but relationships can be made, maintained or broken by the technology. For example, misunderstandings due to language differences, listening to annoying music while queuing for a response and sometimes being charged high costs, do little to build positive relationships.

While businesses are trying to manage their costs, they may be driven to **outsource** services such as after sales, help desks, etc. and these can impact positively and negatively on their reputation. BT and British Gas both experienced such challenges.

Key term

Wholesale – the sale of goods on a larger scale at a lower price, usually sold direct to the retailer to sell on at a profit.

Key term

Outsource – buying services or products from outside suppliers, often overseas, to cut costs.

- Suppliers: all businesses rely on their suppliers and their ability to supply when required and at the agreed price. The external environment impacts on suppliers and subsequently the business being supplied. The process is known as **logistics**, and includes:
  - supplies being available at the cost agreed (materials to supplier may have increased)
  - transport (timescales interrupted due to road works, bad weather, ferry strikes, etc)
  - availability of personnel (interruptions due to holidays, sickness, strikes, shortages).
- Employees: external environmental factors impact on businesses, one example being loss of productivity due to sickness. While holidays are usually planned and businesses anticipate changes to schedules in advance, sickness is generally unpredictable.
- Other factors impact on the number of employees a business can afford and also the availability of potential employees when a business is seeking to recruit. Examples of businesses struggling to recruit include:
  - suitably skilled staff
  - graduates with appropriate qualifications.

What is the benefit to the business if they do manage to recruit suitably skilled staff? What happens if staff are not suitably skilled?

Key term

Logistics – the operation and management of getting supplies from one point to another.

Benefits and importance of establishing and maintaining a competitive advantage

Benefits include controlling costs, having an advantage over competitors, informing future plans such as structure, pricing, location of business, means of promoting and providing services or products.

Important features include anticipating business and job security, providing what the market demands or needs and anticipating areas for development.

Situational analysis

A situational analysis is an investigation into the state of the internal and external factors which affect a business, in order for managers/owners to determine plans for its future. This assessment requires an evaluation of potential customers and the competition in order to speculate on the financial future for the business and inform decision making. This analysis of a business underpins the marketing or a business plan which managers use to review the business aims and objectives. An assessment of the business environment is undertaken using various techniques which are outlined below.

PESTLE analysis

This is a framework for evaluating external factors and their impact on the business to inform business strategy. There are many ways to replicate a suitable template to use, such as that shown in Figure 1.6:

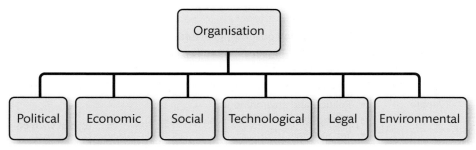

▸ **Figure 1.6:** Example template for PESTLE analysis

Each of the **PESTLE** categories is explored with regard to its impact on the business:

- political factors
- the economy
- sociological and cultural aspects
- potential technology developments
- current and potential legislation
- environmental considerations.

This analysis can, and possibly should, be combined with a SWOT analysis.

SWOT analysis

Key term

SWOT – strengths, weaknesses, opportunities and threats.

A **SWOT** analysis helps to examine the internal and external elements in a business. It is a useful approach to undertake in conjunction with, prior to or subsequent to carrying out a PESTLE analysis. The two can then be compared and challenged. A simple template can be used to undertake a SWOT analysis.

Evaluation judgements are listed in response to the heading in each box, as shown in Figure 1.7.

Strengths	Weaknesses
What are the strengths of the business, such as employees, product, etc.?	What are the weaknesses of the business?
Opportunities	**Threats**
What are the opportunities for the business based on the other responses?	What are the threats?

▶ **Figure 1.7:** Simple SWOT analysis template

5Cs analysis

Key term

5Cs – company, collaborators, customers, competitors, climate.

This type of analysis is used to inform the marketing of a business having undertaken other forms of situational analysis, such as PESTLE and SWOT. Each category is analysed by responding to questions which seek to identify, for example, the components that make up each of the **5Cs** (see Figure 1.8). This type of analysis is used to inform business operations as it focuses on current internal operations using data and statistics.

	Categories	Areas evaluated	Judgements
SWOT ANALYSIS	Company	• Product image and branding • Technology • Culture • Aims, vision	
	Collaborators	• Suppliers • Stakeholders • Distributors	
	Customers	• Demographic • Where, what and why they buy • Pricing • Frequency and quantity purchased	
	Competitors	• Current and potential • Market share • Strengths and weaknesses of competition	
	Climate	• Political and environmental • Financial: interest rates, exchange rates • Technology	

▶ **Figure 1.8:** Example template for 5Cs analysis

Porter's Five Forces

This is used to evaluate the position of a business in terms of its competition. Five categories are considered:

▶ existing competitive rivalry between suppliers
▶ threat of new market entrants
▶ bargaining power of buyers
▶ power of suppliers
▶ threat of substitute products (including technology change).

Each category is evaluated in relation to the impact of suppliers on the business, which might be replicated as shown in Figure 1.9.

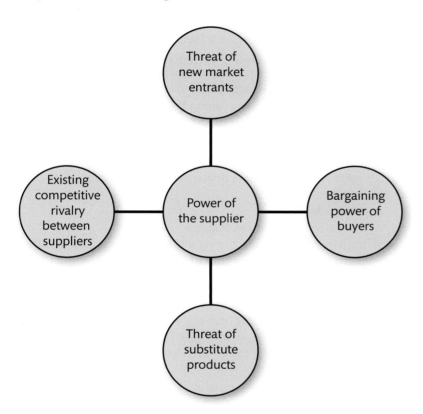

▶ **Figure 1.9:** Example template for Porter's Five Forces

Templates for undertaking **Porter's Five Forces** analysis also vary, placing each of Porter's Five Forces at the heart of the evaluation. This evaluation can also be undertaken in conjunction with SWOT and PESTLE analyses, by using the results of each analysis to evaluate each factor of Porter's Five Forces.

Key term

Porter's Five Forces – supplier power; threat of new entrants; threat of substitutes; buyer power; rivalry.

❚❚ PAUSE POINT   In what other ways could you structure a portfolio?

Hint   Look up the definition of portfolio – it does not have to be a folder containing paper. How else could you communicate your findings?

Extend   Using your results from your situational analyses or further analyses, evaluate how the business may react to future changes.

D Examining business markets

Different market structures

There are several different types of market structure which dictate the degree of risk to business operations. For example, the market structure determines the amount of power and competition in the market. A business will need to understand its market structure in order to plan strategically and operationally.

Market structures

You will focus on two types of market structure – perfect competition and imperfect competition (although there are at least four main types, including a monopoly).

Perfect competition

This concept refers to those businesses which all supply exactly the same product at the same price, such as newspapers and possibly basic food products. However, in reality, where suppliers can manufacture their own brands they become more competitive. Where the cost of products cannot be increased by individual businesses to increase their profits, the business has to find other ways to ensure they maintain or increase their market share, such as customer service or location.

There are no barriers to entry as the number of suppliers, producers and customers are unlimited. In summary, these criteria define perfect competition.
1 All firms sell an identical product.
2 All firms are **price takers**.
3 All firms have a relatively small **market share**.
4 Buyers know the nature of the product being sold and the prices charged by each firm.
5 The industry is characterised by **freedom of entry** and exit.

Imperfect competition

This type of market structure faces less competition than businesses fitting the perfect competition structure. While there may be many sellers, such as clothing shops, cafes, jewellers, etc. their product lines are not identical. Therefore businesses can determine their own prices, as seen in jewellery stores including Ernest Jones, H Samuel and Goldsmiths.

The differences between perfect and imperfect competition are based on:
▶ number and size of the producers of the products being sold
▶ number of customers buying the product or service the business offers
▶ type of products or services
▶ the effectiveness of communicating or marketing the products and services.

Features of different market structures

Each different market structure has similar and different features (see Table 1.7).

▶ **Table 1.7:** Features of different market structures

	Perfect competition	Imperfect competition
Number of sellers	Many	Variable, possibly not identical
Barriers to entry	None	Potentially significant
Type of substitute products	None	Many
Nature of competition	Price only	Price, quality, etc
Pricing power	None	Potentially significant

You will examine three main features which impact on business markets.

Key terms

Price taker – this is when a company has to accept the prevailing price of a product in the wider market.

Freedom of entry – a business has freedom of choice to enter or leave the market due to an unlimited number of buyers and sellers.

Number of firms

You have already considered how a business with a perfect competition structure can compete amongst other businesses offering the same product at a fixed price. Note how newspaper sellers can operate in a small locality yet still survive, although profits will be small. Yet they are not without risk and even the smallest retailer needs to understand their own strengths and weaknesses, and those of their competitors, to gain market share (albeit small in their sector).

Freedom of entry

You have looked at how perfect competition allows freedom of entry (and exit) to the market and the factors you have been learning about in this learning aim are crucial factors in making those decisions.

Freedom of entry differs when a business has an imperfect competition structure. The criteria for operating such a business are more flexible than perfect competition structures, for example there is flexibility in pricing. However, the business is unlikely to have unlimited customers and the cost to run the business will probably be quite high.

Nature of product

The product being offered determines the market structure. It also determines the freedom of entry, number of competitors offering similar products and whether the environment can sustain the market share or withstand further businesses entering the market.

For example, Currys, Comet and PC World all offered similar product lines with a few variances. Often they were situated in out-of-town retail parks competing against each other. When the businesses were no longer sustainable, Comet closed down and Currys merged with PC World. The nature of the products they offered was too similar for the demand – the products were not sufficiently different to remain competitively priced yet increase profits.

Relationship between demand, supply and price

You have started to explore the relationship between demand and price. Business markets rely on examining the relationship between demand, price and supply, represented here in a **Venn diagram** (Figure 1.10):

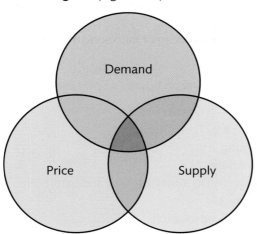

> **Figure 1.10:** Venn diagram representing the relationship between demand, supply and price

Key term

Venn diagram – a logical relationship diagram representing overlaps between categories.

45

Influences on demand

Five of the most common factors influencing demand for a product or service are explored here.

Affordability

Whether or not customers can afford or are willing to pay for the offer.

Competition

Demand can reduce significantly if the competition reduces its prices for like products, quality and service (think about Comet, Woolworths and the problems being faced by HMV and Jessops).

Availability of substitutes

If businesses are struggling to make sufficient profit to remain operating, they will seek alternative products or suppliers to keep their costs down and profits up. A business may resort to a substitute which is inferior or superior or seek out alternative and more competitively priced suppliers. Therefore alternatives depend on supply and demand from all sides of the operation. A business must consider all the external factors and undertake a situational analysis before taking the risk of bringing in a superior substitute product at a higher price.

Level of Gross Domestic Product (GDP)

The GDP is one of the most important indicators used by economists to calculate the state of the economy. The ONS (Office for National Statistics) produces these figures and relies on quarterly data gathered from:

▶ output – the value of goods and services produced from a sample of every type of business and sector

▶ expenditure – the value of all goods and services purchased by businesses, government and individuals, including all exported sales

▶ income – the value of money generated primarily through wages and profits.

Needs and aspirations of consumers

Consumers influence demand by their needs and aspirations. Our needs include basic requirements such as food, warmth, water and safety. These are common to everyone. Consumers also have other and varying needs which are those products and services they are used to and believe they cannot, or do not want to, live without. These might include:

▶ mobile phones
▶ technology and multimedia
▶ entertainment
▶ beauty treatments
▶ own transport.

These examples increase demand on businesses and also influence price, which may go up as well as down.

We also have aspirations which may include:

▶ latest trends in clothing
▶ technology improvements
▶ home improvements such as luxury kitchens and bathrooms
▶ home or garden projects
▶ larger housing or improved location
▶ newer, faster or bigger transport
▶ holidays (more frequent and luxurious).

Link

You will learn more about Maslow's hierarchy of needs in *Unit 14: Investigating Customer Service.*

Influences on supply

Whether supply can meet demand relies on being able to anticipate current and future demands based on GDP data and other statistical information such as UK consumer spending and Consumer Price Index, both available from the ONS. Crucial to meeting demand is the ability of the business to meet supply needs. For example, if an unexpected spell of hot weather increases consumer demand for BBQ charcoal, business is lost if the supplies are not available. Other influences on supply are outlined below.

Availability of raw materials and labour

Raw materials and labour influence supply, and raw materials also impact on the availability of products. Unseasonable weather conditions impact on food and livestock – in a particularly harsh winter when fewer live lambs are born than expected, the availability of lamb will be reduced and the price will therefore increase. Likewise, a very wet winter can ruin winter crops we rely on, especially around times of festivities when we traditionally eat particular foods. Ultimately, products made from these and other food stuffs will also be affected.

> **Key term**
>
> **Raw materials** – any material from which a product is made.

Examples of raw materials in short supply globally include:

- graphite
- platinum
- iron ore
- coal
- scrap iron
- Colombian emeralds.

Of course, a surplus of a raw material can also influence supply, for example the price suppliers can charge to manufacturers. The effects of availability are also reflected in the stock market.

Even if supplies of raw materials are readily available, labour availability influences supply. Businesses all rely on labour to supply their products or services – so if a supplier does not have enough labour to transport the raw materials to the manufacturer, the manufacturing process will be significantly interrupted. If this happens, the raw materials may be sourced from another supplier or an alternative means might be found for the logistics of obtaining the raw materials. Either way, there are likely to be cost implications.

Logistics

The process of ensuring smooth logistics is complex. As you learned, supply is influenced by logistics and the labour needed for a smooth operation. Imagine if the logistics company Eddie Stobart was unable to make any of its European deliveries which they claim occur every 20 seconds; consider the impact on the businesses involved. During the transport strike in 2008, the delivery of petrol to garages was heavily disrupted and many drivers were left stranded, unable to refill their vehicles with fuel.

Ability to produce profitably

As you have learned, all businesses rely on making some profit. Suppliers are controlled by the cost of raw materials and forecast their business plans based on the costs they are likely to incur to manufacture the product and then sell it to customers. Their customers will also have anticipated the cost of supply when they are forecasting their business needs to ensure they make sufficient profit to continue operating.

Competition for raw materials

When raw materials become scarce, for example some metals and fuel, prices will increase and this impacts on suppliers and their market share. Likewise, when raw materials become more readily available, there is competition between suppliers to maintain their profits and to keep their customers, who can choose where to take their business.

Government support

The government provides support for businesses if they feel there is a significant need to boost the UK economy. For example, in 2012 the Prime Minister announced considerable financial support for the UK **supply chain** to generate growth into the economy. Some of the businesses benefiting included:

▶ British Airways
▶ Jaguar Land Rover
▶ Sainsbury's
▶ Marks and Spencer
▶ O2
▶ Rolls Royce, and many others.

While this support directly affects these businesses, government grants, for example for central heating and insulation, also support other businesses indirectly by increasing demand and generating a need for supply.

Elasticity: price elasticity of demand

Economists use the term 'price **elasticity**' to measure the relationship between quantity in demand and change in pricing. The formula for this calculation is:

$$\text{price elasticity of demand} = \frac{\text{\% change in quantity demanded}}{\text{\% change in price}}$$

If a small change in price is accompanied by a large change in the quantity demanded, the product is said to be elastic (or responsive to price changes). Alternatively, a product is inelastic if a large change in price is accompanied by a small amount of change in the quantity demanded.

Pricing and output decisions

You have been learning about how market structures and pricing and **output decisions** relate to perfect and imperfect competition businesses in different ways.

Perfect competition businesses are usually so small that they are unable to affect price because the prices for the products they sell are predetermined and therefore the price they pay to suppliers is also unlikely to be negotiable.

However, imperfect competitive businesses may have more influence over both pricing and output decision making. Businesses can use a range of strategies to increase their profits based on either the price they charge for their products and services or the price they are willing to pay for output such as goods, services and labour. Depending on the type of business, what is output to one can be input to another depending on whether goods are coming in or out. Some of the strategies businesses use are outlined below.

Loss leaders

Businesses may introduce **loss leaders**, for example:

▶ estate agents, especially those selling large numbers of new housing for developers, may offer one house as a loss leader, especially if house sales have been slow or non-existent

Key term

Supply chain – the stages that goods pass through between the producer that makes them and the retailer that sells them.

Key term

Elasticity – responsive to price changes.

Key term

Output decisions – an economist term relating to maximising profit.

Key term

Loss leader – a product or service offered at a knock down price, possibly even at a loss to the business. This is done to attract additional sales and increase profits and market share.

▶ retailers may offer bargains on product lines which are slow to move

▶ the travel industry, for example, airlines will sell cheap flights or train companies may promote bargain prices for first class seats rather than run empty carriages

▶ restaurants and bars promote happy hour to attract customers at quiet times or to shift excess stock.

As you know, businesses need to keep their eye on the competition to make informed decisions.

Responses by business to pricing and output decisions of competitors in different market structures

Businesses with a perfect competition structure are too small to influence changes to prices as they hold a small share of the market.

Imperfect competitive structures can influence pricing by forcing suppliers to reduce costs when demand increases or the cost of raw materials decreases. Factors which contribute to their ability to influence output decisions include the:

▶ cost of production

▶ environment

▶ market power.

Assessment practice 1.2

C.P4   C.P5   C.M3   D.P6   D.M4   C.D2   D.D3

You are progressing towards realising your business idea. For future success you need to convince people who have shown an interest that you have considered your business environment and market. Provide a report that shows that you understand the effects of internal and external environments and how a large business can respond to change.

Your report should begin with an overview of the environment in which your chosen business operates. Consider the internal, external and competitive environment. Complete a situational analysis for your chosen business, using several techniques. Ensure that you choose appropriate techniques. Using this research, provide an analysis of how and how much the business environment has affected your chosen business.

You should then explore the business market in which your chosen business operates. Evaluate how the market structures influence supply and demand, which subsequently affect the pricing and output decisions for one business. While examining the operations of this business, evaluate how the business has reacted to changes and how they may react to future changes, for example, if demand changes or legislation restrictions develop further. Take into account any ethical or environmental issues.

Plan

* How will I structure my report so it is interesting and informative?
* Where will I undertake my research?
* How will I check if the information is accurate? How will I ensure I can find the information again?
* How will I ensure that I have chosen the most appropriate situational analysis techniques?

Do

* Produce a draft of my report and self-critique it for accuracy and content, improving where relevant.
* Ask someone I trust for critical feedback.
* Reflect and learn from the feedback given to me and amend my report as necessary.

Review

* I can identify what I have learned from this activity.
* I can explain how I would tackle a similar exercise differently next time and why.
* I can explain why I chose the situational analysis techniques I did and how they were successful.
* I am confident that the research I have conducted justifies my conclusions.

Investigate the role and contribution of innovation and enterprise to business success

Role of innovation and enterprise

For a business to retain or grow its market share, the role of innovation and enterprise is vitally important.

Innovation

You explored one example of innovation earlier when you looked at the CASA case study and their approach to providing care for vulnerable adults and children. Other ways in which a business can be innovative are outlined below.

▶ Creative process – a staged approach to creativity which does not occur by accident and involves a set of distinct processes as shown in Table 1.8.

▶ **Table 1.8:** Example of a staged creative process

Preparation	Such as research or reviewing current processes
Incubation	A period of reflection and working through ideas both consciously and subconsciously
Illumination	The light bulb moment when ideas become crystallised
Implementation	When the ideas or process are put into action

▶ Theoretical models exist in a variety of formats, stages and terminology, for example Graham Wallas' 1926 four stages of creativity model, where implementation is a verification stage, testing out the process for suitability.

▶ Product or service development require both innovation and logical steps to the process. While refining a current product or service might appear to take a less formal approach, there are theoretical models for new product development (NPD) developed by Booz, Allen and Hamilton. However, any business needs to establish a strategy for development to avoid compromising the existing business.

▶ New ways of increasing business efficiency or improving profitability are another way a business can be innovative. Improvements to business efficiency can increase productivity, cut costs and improve profitability.

▶ Successfully exploiting a new idea is both innovative and enterprising and may be the start of a new business or development of an existing business. Examples of recent success stories include:
  • Innocent drinks
  • Moneysupermarket.com
  • Tyrells Potato Crisps
  • Dyson and the bagless vacuum cleaner.

▶ Adding value to products has become an expectation, especially as we are technologically dependent. Examples of digital and non-digital products include:
  • adding cameras to mobile phones
  • internet-enabled phones
  • sandwich packaging which also serves as a temporary tray
  • The Saucy Fish Co., where the packaging is used for the cooking process.

▶ Services are added and new markets are exploited to differentiate a business from its competitors, such as:
  • the introduction of tablets transforming the popularity of desktop computers
  • Reactolite rapide glasses enabling prescription glasses to react to light changes

- Velcro providing alternative fastening to traditional methods such as press studs or hooks and eyes and which can be used on a wider range of products such as trainers
- Virgin, from the humble beginnings as a record shop in the 1960s, to record company diversifying into airlines, trains, telecommunications and finance
- online banking and mobile banking, first introduced in the US in the early 1980s
- standard broadband to fibre optic
- multi-car insurance offering discounts for families with more than one car.

Enterprise

Identifying opportunities to develop business activities

▶ Creativity is sought by employers and it is required if a business is to thrive. Organisations exist to support the research and development of creative enterprise. Project teams explore ways to develop exciting and creative commercial enterprises into subjects such as music, fashion, computing and cooking.

> **Research**
>
> Explore how creativity and innovation has made Heston Blumenthal OBE a household name in the world of cooking.

▶ **Lateral** thinking is a concept originally created by Edward de Bono to encourage creativity. You might know this approach as the currently popular term of 'thinking outside the box'. De Bono also introduced his 'Six Hats' concept which means considering an idea from the perspective of how others might view it. His metaphor of wearing someone else's hat is deemed to be extremely powerful.

▶ **'Blue sky' thinking** represents a no holds barred approach to thinking creatively. Consider it as giving permission for anything to be possible – the sky's the limit to expand individual and group ideas beyond any constraints which may appear to exist.

▶ Chance and **serendipity** are valuable ideas that occur out of the blue. They could relate to business which is unexpected, perhaps due to a misdialled phone number. For example, much like the serendipitous circumstances that led to the development of penicillin, James Schlatter discovered the artificial sweetener NutraSweet through unrelated work with amino acids. Of course, not all examples will result in a positive outcome, but one very famous example of a discovery by chance and serendipity was made by Alan Turing's team. Their discoveries ultimately saved thousands of lives, ending the Second World War earlier than expected. Their work also led to the production of the world's first electronic computer. Other serendipity products include Kellogg's Corn Flakes which were developed due to a delayed cooking process. The medical sector have also known several serendipity moments. The discovery of penicillin, and the discovery in 1998 that Viagra had additional uses other than its intended use as a heart remedy, were regarded by many as very happy accidents.

▶ Intuition can also lead to viable business opportunities. It can be considered to be something that happens by accident but theories exist that intuition occurs naturally as a result of complex thought processes and decision making. Many suggest that Steve Jobs showed great insight with his creation for Apple – he famously did little market research but, rather, offered the market what he felt they wanted, with obvious success.

> **Key term**
>
> **Lateral** – approaching subjects from alternative perspectives.
>
> **'Blue sky' thinking** – approaching subjects with no restrictions on perspectives.
>
> **Serendipity** – a pleasant discovery that occurs unexpectedly or by accident.

The Philips' story

Compact discs (CDs) were first introduced in November 1982 by UK electronics company Philips. CDs are the forerunner of today's extensive family of optical discs used in a wide range of devices and used universally.

The Philips family established their company in 1891 in the Netherlands, 14 years after Thomas Edison accidentally discovered how to record sounds, in 1877, while experimenting with recording Morse signals. They began their business manufacturing carbon-filament lamps, swiftly becoming Europe's largest supplier of light bulbs. In the early 20th century, they set up their first research laboratory, stimulated by the industrial revolution, and their diverse inventions continue to enrich our everyday lives. Famous inventions include radio technology, televisions, electric shavers and X-ray machines.

However, while the Philips brand has a worldwide reputation for being revolutionary, not all their innovations have been an immediate success. While they had major breakthroughs with the storage of digital data, images and sounds, some of their products are seen as too restrictive because they are too exclusive. Therefore, while some of their products were unique they were also likely to be more expensive than mass produced products. For example, when they introduced their first ever domestic video recorder (VCR) in the early 1970s, it required a Philips' video tape which was not compatible with other makes or later versions and it became obsolete. However, the technology lived on, leading to the inventions of the LaserVision optical disc, DVDs and optical telecommunication systems.

Check your knowledge

1   How does Philips maintain its market share?
2   What risks have Philips taken and what are the outcomes?
3   Name at least two functional/operational areas in the organisation which contribute to its survival.
4   Give examples of the affects between demand, supply and price.

 PAUSE POINT   What contribution has Philips made to consumers?

 Hint   How has Philips responded to changes in the market?

 Extend   Compare and evaluate the reasons for the success of two contrasting businesses. Evaluate how changes in the market have influenced business decisions and how successful they have been.

Benefits and risks associated with innovation and enterprise

To implement innovative and enterprising ideas requires considerable strategic thinking about the impact of the ideas. The benefits and risks to the business need to be carefully considered.

Benefits

Improvements to products

Businesses need to consider if:

▶ there will be sufficient improvements to existing products which will ultimately increase profits by reducing production costs or increasing prices

▶ there is a demand for these improvements or if they are really necessary. For example, it would not be sensible to only manufacture combination microwave ovens and to neglect the need for basic microwave ovens, or believe there is no longer a demand for mobile phones without a built-in camera.

Processes

Processes can be too cumbersome or bureaucratic to be efficient and you may be able to think of an example where you have found a process that has 'got in the way'. Overly bureaucratic processes are often blamed in the public sector leading to a duplication of work or delayed results.

Ultimately, such processes cost money to implement and so finding other ways to achieve the same result could benefit the business and its customers.

Services and customer experience

Innovation and enterprise can greatly improve services and the customer experience. For example, developments which will provide less painful dental treatment could revolutionise patients' experience. Similarly, when Virgin Atlantic first introduced flat beds in 1998 to their business class cabins, passengers could arrive feeling much more rested after long flights.

Business growth

Business growth is an important consideration of innovation and enterprise. Businesses are looking to increase profits, market share and possibly strive to become a market leader. To grow, the business needs to find ways to move with the times to meet consumer demand. Lego provided an example of business growth as a result of innovation and enterprise when they introduced a range linked to the latest Jurassic Park film success.

Development of new and niche markets

New and niche markets mean developing an entirely new product or an addition to a line of products. For example, Apple have introduced the iPhone, iPod and associated family of products to an existing line of products.

A new niche means a specialist market, for example organic or vegetarian food products. An example of a specific niche market is LoveThoseShoes which was set up by entrepreneur Glenys Berd. She introduced a range of healthy footwear in 2003 which was targeted at consumers with conditions such as arthritis and back pain.

Offering unique selling points (USP)

USPs can benefit a business providing they are based on solid research which confirms demand. You may find it difficult to identify a unique product but there may be something about the product or service that is unique only to that one business.

A German man calling himself Professor Shoelace realised there were enormous numbers of children who struggled to tie their shoelaces. Numbers increase when they are due to start school and many parents of the same generation grew up not wearing shoes with laces. To address this need, he has written hugely successful books bringing fun and excitement into lacing methods and also developed an iPhone App.

While this example might be viewed as a niche market, the business has extended its range to include shoelaces to attract different age groups, purposes and even promote charitable causes.

Well known USPs include:

▶ Burger King and their promise to respond to customer changes in their fast food 'have it your way'
▶ Avis cars offering customer pick up services
▶ John Lewis department store's slogan 'never knowingly undersold'
▶ Amazon – 'Earth's biggest bookstore'
▶ BMW – 'the ultimate driving machine'.

> **Key term**
>
> **Unique selling point (USP)**
> – an original or individual concept, service or product that is exclusive to your business.

Improved recognition and reputation

Businesses seek the benefits of recognition and reputation and these can be achieved if customers have a good experience which they then promote to others, such as friends and family. Businesses need to be recognised and are prepared to invest large of sums of money in rebranding if they believe the service or product they offer is not recognised clearly by the way it is promoted.

Branding

The **branding** of a product or organisation can make or break a business and should represent what it is offering so that it is easily recognisable.

> **Key term**
>
> **Branding** – producing a unique name or image for a business or product.

Smarter working

Smarter working involves businesses allowing their employees to work in different locations. It uses technology to enable communication between employees. This can benefit by businesses by:

▶ cutting costs
▶ speeding up production
▶ reducing customer waiting time
▶ increasing profits
▶ reducing unnecessary bureaucracy
▶ increasing staff motivation.

Risks

To make strategic decisions requires considering the risks as well as the benefits. Considerations are outlined below.

▶ Failing to meet operational and commercial requirements, for example legislative requirements such as health and safety. Businesses have to comply with commercial requirements; these could be variable depending on the type of business. For example the construction industry (such as plumbing) will have to comply with specific legislation when working with gas. Therefore a business could not extend its services by providing gas installations without relevantly skilled and qualified gas engineers.

▶ On a lesser but still important scale, the decision not to go ahead with an innovative idea might be due to an interruption in the process which impacts on the quality of a product or service. An example could be where a shelf stacker is rushing to restock products by stacking the front of the shelf instead of moving old stock forward and placing new stock at the back of the shelves.

▶ Failing to achieve a return on investment is a massive risk associated with innovation and enterprise. Consider the research and development team working on a project for many years at significant cost which, at its outset, is cutting edge and innovative. However, by the time it is refined, tested and comes to market, the demand may have been met by a competitor or an alternative product or service.

▶ Clive Sinclair is an example of an entrepreneur and inventor for whom some ideas never came to market. He is best known his for inventions of miniature pocket TVs, ZX80 and ZX81 computers and the C5 battery operated single-person car.

▶ DeLorean's invention, the DMC-12 car, failed mainly due to cost, the time it took to produce and product quality.

▶ An invention which never came to market is the 1926 Ford 'Flying Fivver' single seat plane.

▶ Cultural problems can prevent an idea or product coming to market. These include:
  • resistance to change, for example customers who prefer to stick with what they use already or employees who refuse to change or adapt to new processes: Samsung's introduction of a mobile phone with a curved screen in 2013 has so far not been revolutionary nor has Microsoft's range of curved keyboards

- unsupportive systems and processes – the distinction between the two is that the process represents a concept and the system is what actually occurs when carrying out the process. Therefore a process can get in the way of the system by being ineffective, for example if there is too much repetition for a system to be efficient. Another example is that of a telephone help service where the operator appears to read from a script rather than respond to the specific nature of a customer's enquiry
- insufficient support from leadership and management which might include financial support, time or additional resources and expertise to develop an idea or product. The majority of ideas do not receive sufficient support from management.

Case study

The beauty in the skies

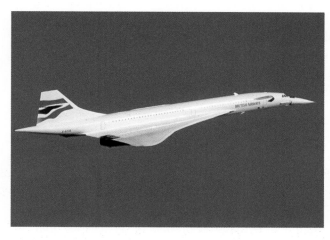

British Airways revolutionised air travel with the introduction of supersonic passenger air travel when Concorde first took to the skies in 1976. Travelling at twice the speed of sound, Concorde reduced the flight time from London to New York from around eight hours to about three and a half hours or less at a cruising speed of 1350 mph. To ensure safety on board, it required a team of 250 engineers and 5000 hours of testing before being certified for its first passenger flight.

Concorde took over 25 years to produce just 20 aircraft from initial project stage to first passenger flight, jointly between UK and France, supported by manufacturer

Airbus. Only 14 Concorde were in operation at enormous economic losses and considerable government subsidies. Despite having received considerable interest from other airlines to purchase 74 planes in the 1960s, these were cancelled during the early 1970s making production unprofitable. Reasons given included environmental concerns and spiralling costs of manufacture. At the same time, budget airlines started to appear and competition for reducing passenger air travel was rife.

Over time, the cost of operating Concorde became uneconomical; with rising costs of fuel as oil prices increased creating a downturn in passengers being able to afford its ticket prices. Concorde was withdrawn in 2003. This may have been influenced by a fatal crash which occurred in 2000.

Check your knowledge

1 What was the aim of this venture?

2 Who were the stakeholders?

3 What impact did the environment have on the demise of Concorde?

4 What relationships can you suggest between demand, supply and price?

5 What was the role and contribution of innovation and enterprise?

 PAUSE POINT What do you think had the greatest impact on Concorde's failure?

> Hint Refer back to the assessment criteria and the requirements for merit and distinction grades.

> Extend Undertake a situational analysis using one of the methods you were introduced to earlier such as PESTLE or SWOT.

You have been in business for a year and are happy with your business' progress. You know, however, that businesses often have to stay innovative and exciting to stay successful, particularly if the market or environment changes. Your friend thinks the business is going well and does not need to change. You decide to produce a presentation that shows how useful innovation and enterprise can be to a chosen business in the face of a changing market or environment.

You need to show how innovation and enterprise can contribute to the success of a business. Evaluate how successful innovation and enterprise has been for your chosen business, in particular, and how they have used this to be successful in the face of a changing market and environment. Justify your evaluations.

Plan

- Where am I going to start? Which business am I going to choose?
- How will I gather and interpret my evidence?
- How will I make my presentation engaging and informative?
- Do I need any help with interpreting or analysing data?

Do

- I have planned my presentation carefully so that the amount of time on each point is appropriate.
- I avoid shortcuts and ensure that I check my research from sources other than the internet.
- I enjoy researching, reading and exploring other people's opinions.
- I do not avoid seeking data and statistics to justify my evaluations.
- I practise my presentation so that I am confident in presenting.

Review

- I can explain why I structured my presentation the way I did.
- I can explain what skills I used throughout this activity.
- I can use this experience in future presentations to improve my approach.

PAUSE POINT

How have your own ethical principles or preferences influenced your choice of business for this task?

 Hint

Look back at all the businesses you have examined. Is there a common factor such as business type, size or structure or perhaps the product or service they offer? Why did you choose these businesses and not others?

 Extend

Carry out one or more of these assessment activities with a very different type of business.

Further reading and resources

Gilmour, K., Matthews, D. and Holden, G. *Starting and Running an Online Business For Dummies.* John Wiley & Sons (2011).

Gorman, T. *Complete Idiot's Guide to Economics.* Alpha Books (2013).

Smith, J. *Start an Online Business in easy steps: Practical Help for Entrepreneurs.* In Easy Steps Ltd (2011).

THINK ▶FUTURE

Andrew Churchill

Landscaping business owner

Andrew Churchill set up his garden landscaping business in 2004 offering a professional range of services. As owner, he is responsible for guaranteeing the work and ensuring all employees are suitably skilled to undertake work to the design specification.

When working with customers to discuss their requirements and their design ideas, Andrew calls on the support of his team members. For example, if the customer wants complex lighting arrangements or water features, the relevant skilled representative will accompany him on-site to discuss requirements.

Due to the success of his company, Andrew entered into a merger with Chiltern Fencing in June 2011 to form Chiltern Churchill. The new company has an even larger client base, including both landscaping and fencing solutions. As the business continues to grow with more customers and larger jobs, Andrew may have to consider taking on additional assistance to help deal with customers, suppliers, sourcing materials and ensuring processes and systems are fit-for-purpose for a growing business.

Focusing your skills

Preparing yourself

As a SME, the expectations are that any new employee will have responsibility for a range of business activities which would otherwise be spread amongst several members of staff or even departments in a macro-sized organisation. Here are some tips regarding the skills any business is likely to seek in an employee.

- How effective are your interpersonal skills? Can you communicate clearly with different people from different backgrounds?
- Would you be able to interpret customer enquiries and convey accurate messages to others? You may have to speak to suppliers and find out costs of materials or source different types of material for customers.
- How numerate are you? Would you be confident at calculating materials, quantities and sizes for producing quotations? Could you calculate VAT and any discounts to be applied?
- You would need to be able to follow processes and systems, book appointments for site visits and coordinate arrangements with other team members. If you feel you need to improve these skills, you might be able to get some

work experience even if it is voluntary.
- Your employer will rely on you to make sure the business runs smoothly. What would you do if you made a mistake? Everyone makes mistakes and can learn from them. Being honest about our mistakes is not only respected but can also help prevent problems later on.
- How good is your timekeeping? Employers will not tolerate lateness as it costs them money and loses them business. If you need to improve your timekeeping, set an alarm or two alarms in case you sleep through one. Set your alarm earlier so you don't miss your transport to work.
- If you have to visit a customer, would you promote the right image for the business? Is your clothing and appearance appropriate?
- What could you do to ensure that you were ready for the unexpected?
- It is likely you will need to file information such as customer quotations, invoices, customer orders, etc. You may be experienced at filing electronic files but not everything will be electronic. Few businesses are completely paperless. If you need to gain experience in manual filing, undertaking part-time or voluntary work or create your own filing system for your studies and personal records.

Getting ready for assessment

Josh is working towards a merit in his BTEC National Diploma in Business and is pushing himself to achieve a distinction. He was given an assignment about a large not-for-profit business covering learning aims C and D. He had to produce a report which represented how the business had adapted to changes in environmental factors over the years. He had to consider all angles that had impacted on the business and informed the decisions and then analyse the strengths and weaknesses of the decisions made and anticipate how the business will respond to future changes.

How I got started

First I created a plan. Next I underlined all the key elements of the assessment and checked against the learning aims to make sure I didn't miss anything. I created a file for all my research sources and used the references suggested in this unit. I searched for the books I thought would be useful and ordered them from the library early. I made a list of not-for-profit businesses and then reduced the list according to their size. I asked family and friends for any suggestions in case I had missed any. I didn't rely on just one business as I wanted to get the most out of this assignment. I was challenged to think about my reasons for selecting certain businesses in a previous activity. I set aside quiet time to undertake my research and enquired about business report writing and how to produce an executive summary.

What I learned from the experience

▶ I thought what I had written made sense and was accurate, but found even I make mistakes!

▶ Write the executive summary last after you know what you have written about.

▶ It's quite hard to write the conclusion.

▶ Check against the assessment criteria to make sure everything is covered, not only the merit and distinction but also the pass criteria.

▶ I'm glad I kept all my notes as some of them were better than when I tried to improve them (because I had made it too complicated). I also found it motivating to see how much I had learned and achieved especially at times when I thought I wasn't getting anywhere.

▶ Build in extra time to do assignments, I had a cold so my brain was woolly for a couple of days.

▶ The plan and order may change, especially when you need more books or your internet is down.

▶ I must always save my files – and often! I lost a whole page when we had a power cut.

▶ Don't just check the spelling and other obvious things but how the whole report looks. Sometimes the sections were just a sea of words and I lost interest in reading it.

How I brought it all together

I started my report by creating an outline to make sure it had the main headings, page numbers and, most importantly, my name and student number. We had been given a format which told us what type and size of font to use and the approximate length of the report. This is how I went about producing my report.

▶ I typed up my findings while the information was fresh and buzzing around in my head.

▶ I went back over my work many times to check it made sense, was in the right order and I hadn't missed anything.

▶ I used diagrams or models to explain.

▶ I kept all stages of my work, including doodles and notes, just in case.

▶ To choose my business to examine, I went back over the examples in this unit and especially the case studies. As I want to get a merit at least, I thought it would be better to find one of my own. I also felt quite proud as if I had discovered something new.

Think about it

▶ What method will you use to plan your assignment?

▶ Where will you work so you won't get interrupted or lose focus?

▶ What will you do to maintain your interest and enthusiasm?

▶ How will you know when you have finished?

Developing a Marketing Campaign 2

Getting to know your unit

Assessment

You will be assessed by a supervised assessment task.

Marketing is a dynamic field and is integral to a business' success. During this unit you will have the opportunity to create your own marketing campaign. This will allow you to understand every step of the process and give you the opportunity to develop the skills and knowledge you will need to be successful in the field of marketing. You will gain an insight into the importance of marketing to a business' success and, at the end of this unit, you will be able to make an informed choice about whether marketing is the field for you.

How you will be assessed

This unit is assessed under supervised conditions. You will be provided with a research topic before a supervised assessment period in order to carry out research.

The supervised assessment period can be arranged over a number of sessions. During these periods you will have to complete a task requiring you to prepare a rationale and then create a plan for a marketing campaign for a given product or service. Your responses will be marked externally.

As the guidelines for assessment can change, you should refer to the official assessment guidance on the Pearson Qualifications website for the latest definitive guidance.

This table contains the areas of essential content that learners must be familiar with prior to assessment.

Essential content	
A	Introduction to the principles and purposes of marketing that underpin the creation of a rationale for a marketing campaign
B	Using information to develop the rationale for a marketing campaign
C	Planning and developing a marketing campaign

Getting started

To generate customer interest and awareness businesses must market their products and services. List your recent purchases and identify the reasons why you chose them. List the reasons why you did not choose other businesses or services from which to purchase the same types of products. During this unit, expand your list by adding the different marketing methods used and whether categories of businesses choose the same marketing techniques.

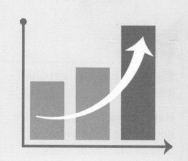

 # Introduction to the principles and purposes of marketing that underpin the creation of a rationale for a marketing campaign

Marketing is a means of promoting a business and what it offers, whether this is telecommunications, value food products, properties for sale or rent or a service such as car maintenance. Marketing is closely linked to sales with the intention that a successful marketing campaign will pay dividends in sales generated, for example the John Lewis Christmas adverts and those for M&S food.

The role of marketing

Without marketing, customers will not be aware of the product or service the business offers. The oldest form of marketing is by word of mouth which can be extremely effective but cannot be controlled by a business. Marketing aims to spread the word to potential customers and turn them into paying customers.

Principles and purposes of marketing

The principles of marketing are to generate customer satisfaction by:

▸ identifying needs

▸ promoting products (or services) or contributing to **brand** development

▸ pricing of the brand

▸ promoting the brand by various means

▸ distributing the brand in the right locations or by the appropriate means (such as online).

The purpose of marketing is to generate interest in a product or service resulting in a sale, by:

▸ anticipating demand – an ice cream manufacturer will expect marketing staff to study long range weather forecasts to anticipate demand on sales, just as a lettuce farmer will need to anticipate the demands for salad during hot weather and a department store will be be prepared for Christmas sales of the latest toy craze generated by blockbuster films such as Star Wars and Frozen

▸ recognising demand – keeping up to date with what competitors are selling is one way to recognise demand for products and trends in consumer behaviour (for example, Lego kits after the release of the latest Jurassic Park film)

> **Key term**
>
> **Brand** – the identification eg logo of a product or service which is instantly recognisable without explanation (such as the Kellogg's cornflake cockerel).

Key terms

BOGOF – buy one, get one free.

Happy hour – reduced price items at a predetermined time of the day or week.

- stimulating demand – finding ways to promote the brand such as:
  - advertising on billboards, in newspapers and online
  - offering **BOGOFs**, such as cinema tickets, pre-packed oranges or packs of socks or washing powder
  - **happy hour** which sells products at reduced prices, perhaps to fill empty tables in a restaurant or to encourage customers to stay and eat when buying a cheaper drink
  - offering vouchers for product lines which are poor sellers or where the business is over-stocked
- satisfying demand – ensuring stocks or capacity to deliver a service are sufficiently available to meet any demand generated, for example making sure there is enough stock to cover popular toys in the lead up to Christmas.

Marketing aims and objectives

Effective marketing strategies require careful planning and structuring into overall aims to identify the purpose, followed by the objectives to identify how the aim(s) will be achieved. Successful marketing is made up of the following aspects.

- Understanding customer wants and needs (which are not necessarily the same thing) – customers may think they know what they want but in fact need something different. For example, a customer may think they want a tablet when they might actually need a laptop to play their collection of DVDs. Therefore the person doing the marketing (the marketer) will need to differentiate between needs and wants in order to promote their products effectively and identify the key features they should be marketing.
- Developing new products – marketing can provide a business with customer ideas to help them expand their range. A business could do this by asking for customer feedback; such as Walkers Crisps did to generate new flavours. Once a business has developed a new product to sell to existing customers, for example a PlayStation, the business will develop new games and accessories to increase their sales.
- Improving profitability by reducing costs – for example by reducing costs a Lincolnshire baker delivers fresh baked bread to predetermined central locations such as schools, for customers to purchase and collect. This not only reduces transport costs for the baker but also reduces his **carbon footprint**.
- Increasing **market share** – businesses strive to become market leaders and start to achieve this by increasing their market share. Market share can be measured by either the volume of goods sold or the value of those goods. For example, in early 2015 Tesco was reported as having the greatest market share in the UK supermarket marketplace in terms of value of goods sold despite reports of losses during 2015, whereas Sainsbury's overtook Asda in terms of their market share held previously. Similarly, market leadership is the position of a business with the largest market share in a given market for goods and services. Pedigree Petfoods is the market leader in the pet food market with successful brands such as Whiskas cat food.
- Diversification – where a business markets new products which differ from its usual offering to new customers. This can work in two ways – the business may produce a new product in an area that it understands, for example a hybrid version of a mobile phone with a tablet such as the Sony Xperia. Or a business may enter a completely new, unrelated area such as supermarket banking.

Key terms

Carbon footprint – the amount of carbon dioxide and other gases emitted through fuel consumption.

Market share – the percentage of a given market that a business holds.

▶ Increased brand awareness and loyalty – this might relate to a business' overall brand (for example BMW) or to a product brand within the company (for example Mini). Successful raising of brand awareness can increase sales because customers will subconsciously or consciously seek out a brand when purchasing an item or service, perhaps due to loyalty or confidence in similar products or services. It is clear that a high level of brand awareness exists when consumers start to use the brand name in place of the product type. For example, if you were to talk about domestic appliances, would you say 'vacuum cleaner' or 'Hoover'? Other common brand names include Sellotape, Biro and Jacuzzi.

PAUSE POINT   What examples can you identify where you have been influenced to make a purchase based on brand loyalty?

> Hint   Refer to the list you created in Getting Started.

> Extend   Consider those products or services that failed to attract you and suggest ways to improve their marketing.

Types of market

There are two types of market – mass, the general population, and niche meaning more specialist.

Mass

Examples of mass markets include:

▶ spectacles and sunglasses

▶ cars

▶ tissues

▶ telecommunications.

Each of these examples is likely to be of interest to the mass market as they cover different age groups and locations when in their generic form. The choice of which car or pair of glasses, for example, will be made depending on other factors, perhaps style or price.

Niche

These markets are restricted to specialist interests or needs such as agricultural farmers who need tractors or a prosthetic limb for a paraplegic individual. Other examples include specialist suppliers of Kosher and Halal food or restaurants specialising in international food such as Polish, Nepalese and Korean which represent the local demographic.

Market segmentation

Any business needs to segment its market in order to develop a marketing strategy and avoid a 'scatter-gun' approach. In other words, it has to identify the purpose of its products or services in order to establish its target market. For example, if a business mined stones and promoted its products as just 'stones' their potential customers would not know what types of stones they were selling and in what state. These stones could be for paving or walls, could be polished or in their raw state or perhaps be diamonds ready to inset into jewellery.

> **Discussion**
>
> Discuss your suggestions with another learner or in a small group.

Another type of segmentation apart from product segmentation is by age, gender and ethnicity, for example hairdressing salons which specialise in Afro hairstyles, barbers for men and stylists for elderly customers. There are even stylists and makeup artists who specialise purely in applying their skills to the deceased for loved ones to pay their last respects. Other examples include sports goods, health-food stores and clothing stores such as Mothercare and PumpkinPatch, which target their products at those purchasing clothing and accessories for young children.

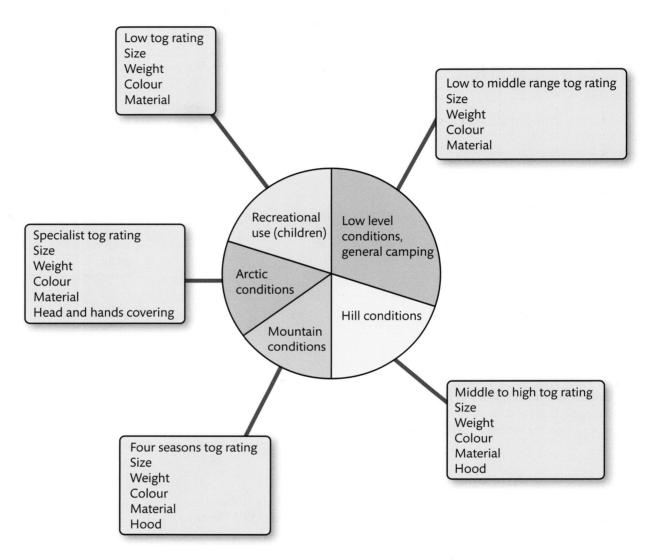

▶ **Figure 2.1:** Example of market segmentation for a manufacturer of sleeping bags

Branding

Branding often consists of a brand name (such as Nike), a logo (the Nike 'swoosh'), a slogan ('Just Do It') and guidelines for how the branding can be used. Some or all of these elements may be trademarked to prevent competitors from using similar branding. In some instances the branding will dictate colours and shapes that should be used. In other instances the brand can be used more flexibly.

A brand can be a powerful selling tool and can help achieve marketing objectives such as gaining market leadership and raising customer awareness.

Brand personality

Branding can exert a considerable influence over what the customer buys, especially if it displays **brand personality**. For example, think of the sophisticated and professional look of L'Oreal or the glittery, fun looking branding of Maybelline.

Brand image

A strong brand can stick in a customer's mind and help to link products with a particular supplier or manufacturer. For example, Maurice Drake's 1967 slogan 'beanz meanz Heinz' is credited as being one of the most successful advertising campaigns ever.

A strong brand can portray an image. This might be one of success or affluence, for example think of clothing brands such as Dolce & Gabbana, Calvin Klein, Ralph Lauren and Christian Dior. Younger-type brands which portray a casual, trendy image include SuperDry, Jack Wills and Juicy Couture.

Once a brand gets stronger, it can help a business to either enter new markets or sell into existing markets with less risk of failure. If a customer has a good experience of a specific brand, they are likely to purchase something else from the same brand.

Unique selling point (USP)

A brand can portray a USP to gain market share over their competitors and stand out from the crowd. For example, Velvet toilet tissue which promotes its products as being environmentally friendly by replacing trees and a Japanese factory which grows its vegetables using robots. Both of these examples are generic products sold to the mass market which trade on their USP.

Airlines offering a USP include Virgin when they promoted the first business class flat bed in their Upper Class cabins and the giant A380 which announced its personal shower facilities in business class cabins in 2008.

Implications of business size on marketing activity

There are many implications for marketing that are influenced by business size such as:

▶ product development to meet customer needs and feasibility according to employee capacity

▶ elimination of products or services which no longer meet requirements and are not financially viable

▶ marketing methods for promoting branding which are cost effective for maximum return and in the shortest time

▶ changes to branding which make excessive demands on a limited workforce.

Budgetary constraints

All marketing plans should be based on a budget to ensure the business does not overspend and can justify its expenditure based on the impact on its sales. For example, large businesses such as Coca Cola can afford to advertise extensively using multi-media whereas a local sandwich shop might need to rely on local newspaper advertising or a board on the pavement outside their premises.

Availability of specialist staff

If a business does not have the specialist staff in-house to successfully market their brand they might need to either change their intentions or source external support from specialists. This may place considerable pressure on the budget and may also take much longer than anticipated.

Key term

Brand personality – human characteristics to which a customer can relate, especially if similar to their own.

Tip

A unique selling point is now often known as a unique selling proposition.

Influences on marketing activity

In summary, there are two main influences on marketing activity – internal and external factors.

Internal influences

Marketers are not just interested in external influences but also those generated internally to the organisation, as outlined below.

▶ Cost of the campaign – marketing campaigns can cost as much or as little as you want to pay depending on the methods used. Every business should allow sufficient cost within its budget for marketing but, like most projects, a contingency is usually required for unexpected events. A business overspending on their budget will need to make cuts elsewhere – this might be by reducing their workforce.

▶ Availability of finance – a business may have difficulties with their **cash flow**, possibly due to suppliers demanding early payment, overspend or customers on account not paying their invoices within the specified time. If any of these factors are the case then the business may not have sufficient available funds to fulfil a planned marketing campaign.

▶ Staff expertise – internal staff might not have sufficient expertise to deliver the marketing strategy, whether this is negotiating advertising costs, producing professional artwork or writing **straplines** to attract attention. The business may have to seek external specialist support and increase their budget.

▶ Size and **culture** of the business – a small business with a culture which expresses traditional values, such as a family business of hand made, tailored suits, might implement a marketing strategy which relies solely on personal recommendation. However, London's oldest tailor, Ede & Ravenscroft, also promote their 327 year expertise in ceremonial wear through their website. This demonstrates their willingness to embrace modern techniques while still maintaining their professional and traditional culture.

External influences

External influences are less controllable than internal influences. Although businesses will assess risk and anticipate need, they cannot prepare for every eventuality. Some examples are outlined opposite.

Key terms

Cash flow – the money that goes into and out of a business.

Strapline – a caption or heading often providing a brief and snappy overview of a product, service or news story.

Culture – behaviours, habits and values of groups or individuals.

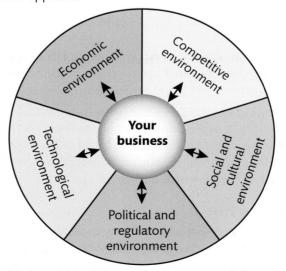

▶ **Figure 2.2:** External factors which will have an influence on marketing activity

▶ Social factors – a manufacturer of baby foods may not be prepared for a sudden and long term demand on their products perhaps due to health scares in dairy foods or an unexpected baby boom. While a tennis ball manufacturer might anticipate a rise in demand around the time of Wimbledon, Halford's may not have predicted the demand for bikes following the success of Bradley Wiggins in the 2012 Olympics followed by the Tour de France. Suppliers of wicker baskets were quick to promote celebrities riding women's vintage-style bikes complete with these baskets following Victoria Pendleton's Olympic triumph which resulted in significantly increased sales of both bikes and baskets.

▶ Technological factors can influence marketing activity, not only in terms of how businesses market their services and products (such as Ede & Ravenscroft) but also the speed and extent to which marketing can become **viral**. Marketing activities can be instantly promoted globally through social media, or by pop-ups when you go online. Before the internet, businesses mostly relied on newspaper adverts and knocking on doors (cold calling). Technological factors can have both positive and negative outcomes, such as the:

- extent of the global marketing reach

- ability to update or alter marketing materials quickly and with little expertise or specialist equipment required

- opportunity to replicate what competitors are doing.

▶ Economic factors – if projected sales are not realised due to unsuccessful marketing then a business may have to reduce its costs in other ways such as reducing the workforce like Rockwell Collins in late 2015. Most recently, projected sales have been affected by the recession as this has changed people's spending habits. This is further evidenced by the reported successes of pound shops and pawnbrokers. This change in spending habits needs to be anticipated by marketers as it influences marketing activities – how much and what type is needed to attract purchasers. If a business advertises solely or mainly in cinemas and there are fewer cinema-goers due to limited **disposable income**, then their adverts have reduced exposure.

▶ Environmental factors can have significant influence on marketing activity. For example, the travel industry has had to act rapidly at times such as the 2015 Paris bombings, the plane crash in Fox Glacier in New Zealand and volcanic activity in Equador. Each of these are desirable tourist destinations promoted for their beauty or culture. Some environmental factors can have a positive impact on developing existing or creating new business ideas such as conservation holidays.

▶ Political factors – legislation such as that prohibiting advertising cigarettes. This has had an impact on manufacturers and suppliers, because they are not able to promote smoking at sports events such as Formula 1 and football matches, and has restricted advertising in television programmes and films. In order to market their offers during the recession, supermarkets Lidl, Aldi, Morrisons and Asda started promoting value products; whereas M&S and Waitrose put greater emphasis on quality, both of which have reported increased sales and improved market share.

▶ Legal factors affect marketing activities – for example disallowing religious advertising such as the Lord's Prayer example in the early winter of 2015. Despite the efforts of the marketing specialists of JustPray.uk and the regulators such as the Cinema Advertising Authority, the advert will not be aired in public cinemas due to its religious status and potential breach of the 2010 Equality Act. Guidance on marketing and advertising law is available from the UK government website.

Key terms

Viral (advertising/ marketing) – unsolicited and infectious marketing tactics using social media to attract interest.

Disposable income – the amount of residual money available for non-essentials after paying bills and creditors, such as credit cards and store cards.

Link

Other legislation which affects marketing activities includes that listed in *Unit 1: Exploring Business* and *Unit 14: Investigating Customer Service.*

▶ Ethical factors mean the principles, values and standards people believe are acceptable practice. Each business should agree what they mean as behaving ethically in conjunction with legislation such as the Equality Act and that found in the Ethics Resource Centre. Everyone has their own ethical views shaped by their upbringing and culture. Marketing activities should be influenced by external ethical factors such as:

- usage and type of human images in any advertising
- not making invalid claims about value, quality and pricing
- not making promises which the product or service cannot deliver
- avoidance of breaches in legislation and regulations.

Businesses which compromise ethical practices can damage their reputation and may never recover.

Case study

Simply Nature – the brand

People are probably more conscious about body image than ever before and manufacturers of beauty products are at risk of inadvertently promoting images which display unethical practice. It is impossible to claim a business is completely ethical or unethical due to ethics being subjective.

Simply Nature wants to run an advertising campaign featuring models from a local modelling agency. Their products are designed for niche markets, segmented by:

- skin colour
- skin type
- external conditions
  (the natural elements – wind, air, water)
- age.

Their first attempt at advertising did not generate the amount of interest they hoped. They advertised in the regional commuter paper and at teatime on the radio. They undertook a survey on their website to ask for comments. However, despite the advertisement promoting positive body images regardless of shape, size or age, the feedback was negative. Comments such as 'if only I could look like that' and 'are you a miracle worker?' did nothing to increase their sales. One of the major factors Simply Nature had completely overlooked was to think like a potential customer, ask the questions they

would ask and answer those questions in advance in their advertising – questions such as price, distributor, quantity and benefit. They have yet to establish their USP.

While Simply Nature tried hard with their first marketing campaign, and had the best of intentions in trying to project an ethical image and segmenting their market according to age and ethnicity, they realised they needed to relate to the public in a more realistic way. Importantly, they have realised that they need to find out what their customers like about their products so they can build on something positive. They have started to gather testimonials which they are permitted to use and have changed their website so users can upload their photographs and comments to share with others.

Nevertheless, what Simply Nature are especially proud of is the ethical practice they apply to manufacturing their product, using all natural ingredients. These are sourced by working closely with tribal groups and ensuring they are not exploited, and testing on animals is also banned. They ensure the manufacturing process involves under-developed nations, employing the locals and paying a decent wage. Their business values all those involved and promises to continue donating a percentage of all profits to support local needs such as educational materials, medication and improving sanitary conditions.

Check your knowledge

1 What factors influenced the Simply Nature marketing campaign?

2 How has Simply Nature adapted their marketing strategy to stimulate demand?

3 What are the aims and objectives of the Simply Nature campaign?

4 How would you develop the brand image of Simply Nature?

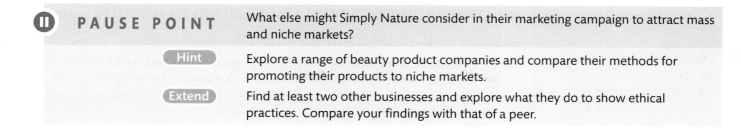

⏸ PAUSE POINT   What else might Simply Nature consider in their marketing campaign to attract mass and niche markets?

Hint   Explore a range of beauty product companies and compare their methods for promoting their products to niche markets.

Extend   Find at least two other businesses and explore what they do to show ethical practices. Compare your findings with that of a peer.

Assessment practice 2.1   A01

Kathy is convinced she wants to buy a steam oven. Her husband, Philippe, is worried about the cost – over £1000. It has many fancy features he does not think they will use and neither have ever cooked using steam.

Philippe has asked Kathy what sorts of things she will use the oven for, apart from their daily breakfasts, lunches and dinners.

Finances are tight as they will be adding to their family with twins in three months time. Philippe is concerned the steam oven might not be what they really need for family catering. He also wants to make sure they do not buy something in haste and later regret it, especially as Kathy enjoys cooking.

Kathy has been enticed by the promotional literature. She has read all about the benefits on their website and read testimonials from users. She downloaded the manual and checked out the recipes they included, along with her own recipes to make sure the oven would be compatible. Although she has never actually tried one out and does not know anyone who uses one, she explained to Philippe that she wanted her cooking to stand out from the crowd. All the promotional material makes it sound like that's exactly what this steam oven would enable her to do.

Philippe has asked you to assess whether they are being tricked into buying something which is not actually right for them. He has also asked for your opinion about how to evaluate promotional material, what pitfalls to consider and where to get extra information.

Plan
- I know what I am being asked to do.
- I shall check that I have sufficient knowledge about the task and product being marketed.
- I know where I can find out more information about this task.
- I know how to present my findings.

Do
- I can explain the features of the marketing campaign.
- I can make suggestions to Kathy and Philippe on how to make the right decision.
- I can justify my recommendations.
- I have documented all my sources and cited them in my report.

Review
- I can identify what went well and where I need to improve.
- I can explain how I would approach this differently another time.
- I can recognise the gaps in my knowledge and understanding.
- I have learned where to find sources of useful information.

B | Using information to develop the rationale for a marketing campaign

Information is required to develop the purpose for any marketing campaign and this is known as **market intelligence**. Without reliable intelligence using information from research on existing and past business performance, which is compared with the competition, any marketing campaign can go wrong. Subsequent sales forecasts can be inaccurate and could result in a business going bust. One example of where businesses missed a golden opportunity was when a Kodak engineer invented a digital camera in 1975 but received a cold response from management. Another possible overlooked opportunity is that of Direct Line who refuse to engage with comparison websites.

Key term

Market intelligence – gathering data from different sources which is analysed and evaluated to identify trends.

Purpose of researching information to identify the needs and wants of customers

One way to gather market intelligence is through **market research** which informs a business' decisions by helping it to understand the changing dynamics of its market. This involves finding out more about customers, competitors and the overall marketing environment.

To identify target markets

To launch a successful marketing campaign a business needs to be sure they are marketing their product or service to the right people. Businesses ensure they are marketing to the correct audience by, as one of the first steps in the process, undertaking work to identify their target market. A marketing campaign targeting the wrong market will cost a business time, money and possibly even reputation. Target markets can be defined at a narrow or broad level. Jamie Oliver identified a target market when he set up his Food Foundation in 2002, initially to redress the poor eating habits of school children. His target market was primary schools but he has extended his educational programme to communities and an apprenticeship programme. This broad market of primary schools could have been narrowed further – for example he might have wanted to start his campaign aiming at only 6 to 9 year olds in primary schools in Leicestershire. Target markets are often defined by age, gender, location and/or salary level as well as segmented by interests, wants and needs.

A business promoting a **consumer** dining magazine would need to know about its audience's interests – it would need to know the kind of dining experiences its customers are used to. These could be anything from Pizza Hut to Heston Blumenthal's Berkshire restaurant The Fat Duck.

The magazine would also need to understand its competitors – if there was a similar magazine catering for the kind of consumer who goes to The Fat Duck, how could the business differentiate its product? Finally, the overall environment would allow the business to test the size of the market, for example whether the product would be better as an online subscription site – and whether anything beyond the control of the business might affect the business plan.

To identify size, structure and trends in the market

For an effective marketing campaign, it is important to identify the target market by its size, structure and trends.

▸ Size – to determine whether the campaign needs to attract a mass or niche market, this will then inform the budget which needs to be sustained as a result of the sales generated.

▸ Structure – the demographic of your customers, which will help define where to advertise and the language and tone to use. For example, a business selling commodities for elderly people might rely on advertising in leisure magazines or travel brochures such as Saga.

▸ Trends – knowing how, when and by what means customers are likely to buy your products, based on previous performance, is useful when planning a campaign. This type of information contributes to market intelligence.

Reliable market intelligence relies on the analyses of trends in the market and the size or structure of those trends. For example, if consumers change their eating habits such as they did following the outbreak of 'Mad Cow Disease' in 1986 then a business selling or manufacturing beef burgers will rely on this information to develop new or alternative

<aside>

Key terms

Market research – systematic gathering, recording and analysis of data about issues relating to marketing products and services.

Consumer – someone who purchases and uses a produce or service.

</aside>

products. As the risk from BSE was diminishing, marketing campaigns targeted the re-building of customer confidence either to re-introduce beef or alternative products. Recent examples of businesses needing to regain customer confidence include Hotpoint and Indesit washing machines and the Vauxhall Zafira, which presented a fire risk.

To identify competition

Marketing campaigns rely on intelligence to assess threats from competitors, such as Netscape losing out to the Microsoft web browser. Unless a business is aware of potential threats and the risk to sales of their products or services, their marketing strategies may not be sufficiently effective in combating any threat. The major supermarkets actively promote the benefits to customers of buying from their stores such as Asda's catchphrase 'more for you for less'; Waitrose, Tesco and other supermarkets promise to price match their competitors and Lidl's challenge to customers to taste test products and guess which is a major brand versus which is Lidl's.

▶ When you visit a major supermarket, how aware are you that they are working hard to secure your loyalty as a customer?

> **Theory into practice**
>
> Next time you are shopping, check out the competition and make notes of those competitors and the reason why they might be a risk.

> **Research**
>
> Seek out information about each of these competitive businesses and compare trends on their performance based on data from Companies House.

Market research methods and use

There are two types of research – primary and secondary. The difference between them relates to whether the research is original to the organisation conducting the research (they gathered the data) or whether it came from another source (the data had already been gathered). Within these categories, information can either be internal – from inside the organisation, or external – from another organisation or source outside the organisation.

Primary research

Primary research is data and information that the business has gathered first-hand and has not been gathered before. Internal primary research data sources include:

▶ sales figures for the business' own products

▶ customer data held on a central database.

External primary research methods include:

▶ questionnaires and surveys such as online feedback forms

▶ interviews and focus groups

▶ mystery shoppers and other observation techniques

▶ trials of **prototypes** or new products for gathering feedback.

Key term

Prototype – an initial version or mock-up of a concept for further development.

Link

Information on customer service can be found in *Unit 14: Investigating Customer Service* and further information on research methods can be found in *Unit 22: Market Research.*

It is more cost-effective for a business to conduct secondary research before it starts conducting primary research. This allows it to build an understanding of the market and identify any major barriers before committing to expensive research. It also allows the business to develop some assumptions (for example, people interested in Sky may also be tempted by Sky bundles and other packages), which means the business can use the primary research to test its assumptions. This helps to restrict the scope of the primary research, which can be expensive and is rarely able to answer all questions about a particular market.

Theory into practice

Next time you are asked to contribute to primary research, keep a copy (perhaps a photograph or scan) of the survey or questionnaire used. Make a list of the advantages and disadvantages of collecting data using this method and also of the questions asked. Evaluate how the data being gathered will be analysed. In a small group discuss how the method or content for gathering primary research might be improved and why.

Secondary research

Secondary research uses data and information that has been collected before, either from within the organisation (internal) or by another organisation (external). Secondary research is sometimes referred to as 'desk research' and sources include those shown in Table 2.1.

▶ **Table 2.1:** Types of secondary research

Types	Internal	External
Reports from sales and regional representatives	✓	
Previous market research	✓	
Trade journals and websites		✓
Books and newspapers		✓
Industry reports from industry associations and government departments		✓
Census data and public records		✓

▶ Internal examples include business data on customers and financial records which can be obtained from loyalty cards such as those used by Tesco, Superdrug and Waitrose. Loyalty cards capture sales records which identify customer preferences. These enable a business to market similar products to those a customer frequently purchases, or issue vouchers to regain sales which may have lapsed.

▶ External examples include commercially published reports such as those produced by Thomson Reuters on market data around the world, government statistics which provide information about market trends, UK population and demographic data to inform ethical decisions.

Other examples include trade journals such as *Which?* magazine providing information on consumer rights and expert advice about products and services, and media sources such as news articles and consumer voices via social networking sites.

However, businesses need to be aware of the limitations of secondary research. For example:

▶ information may be old

▶ information may be biased to promote a particular cause

▶ collection methods may have been unreliable.

⏸ PAUSE POINT

Which research methods and information sources do you use when considering a purchase?

Hint   Comparing before taking out a mobile phone contract. Using information to decide on your course or institution to study at.

Extend   How would you undertake your research differently in future? How could you be sure your sources were reliable?

Importance of validity, reliability, appropriateness, currency, cost

Research methods can be qualitative, quantitative or include elements of both (see Table 2.2). Well-planned market research often involves a combination as they can reveal different things about the same market.

No matter how small or large a market research project may be, any type of research performed poorly will not give relevant results. All research, no matter how well controlled, carries the potential to be wrong which is why stringent tests are necessary to ensure claims are not made without rigorous testing.

There are many reasons why research may not provide trustworthy results and one example is whether the research is really measuring what it claims to be measuring. To ensure the integrity of the data, certain measures must be put in place to carry out suitable checks. Each of these following measures needs to be applied in conjunction with one another.

Validity

This is the process of ensuring data are valid by using original sources or tracing sources back to their original point. For example, information taken from websites such as Wikipedia cannot be assumed to be valid. Always check whether the source is cited and then read the data and information contained in that source. Information taken from data is an interpretation. Your interpretation and someone else's may be quite different. To check validity the results need to be tested to check if similar results would be obtained if another group containing different respondents or a different set of data points were used.

Key terms

Validity – the process of ensuring data are valid by using original sources or tracing sources back to their original point.

For example, if 50 holidaymakers participate in a research study focusing on customer satisfaction regarding a tour, is the information obtained from these 50 tourists sufficient to conclude how all customers feel about the tour? What if the same study was done again with 50 different tourists – would the responses be similar?

Key terms

Reliability – making sure the method of data gathering leads to consistent results when the input is consistent.

Reliability

Validity questions whether the research measured what it intended to measure and must be reliable. **Reliability** does not necessarily imply validity; a reliable measure need not be valid. Reliability is chiefly concerned with making sure the method of data gathering leads to consistent results.

▶ Reliability estimates the degree to which an instrument measures the same way each time it is used under the same conditions with the same subjects.

▶ Validity involves the degree of accuracy of your measurement and the methods you use.

Appropriateness

The question to ask of a research project is whether the collection of data and methods are appropriate. This means asking yourself the following questions.

▶ Is the data collection ethical, ie is it unlikely to cause harm or distress? Has permission been sought from all those involved? Is the data being used for the purposes described? Ethical committees exist for all types of research in different sectors and research is regulated by bodies such as the Association for Research Ethics (AfRE).

▶ Are the methods the most appropriate for the research, study, collection, analysis and distribution of data? For example, a study about the pictures children draw would not necessarily need to involve photographs or videos being taken or observing children on their own. Each of these methods might be entirely inappropriate and permission may not be granted. However, collecting the children's pictures and analysing the drawings and what they portray may be deemed more appropriate. These types of factors need to be considered in relation to the research purpose and rationale. Researchers are also required to conduct themselves appropriately, for example when preparing for and undertaking research. Researchers would need to be certain their research activities are ethical and there is no risk of harm to anyone involved. Those involved would need to give their permission and the topic being researched must meet ethical approval by regulatory bodies such as the AfRE.

Discussion

In a small group, identify the methods your organisation uses when involving you in any form of research such as learner satisfaction surveys or course feedback.

Currency

You may have heard this term in relation to research, especially if you have taken a vocational course where you collect evidence of your performance. The term currency refers to whether the data are up to date to ensure your results are both valid and reliable. Currency does not mean that research excludes data gathered in the past – it may be essential to provide evidence of trends over a period of time to prove a point. It may also be that the research is fairly unusual and no other similar studies have been undertaken before or not for many years.

If a study is attempting to demonstrate how consumers rate a new instant noodle flavour, they might choose to compare what customers say about the new flavour compared with existing flavours. However, using only customer ratings of old flavours will not produce valid results for the purpose of the research.

Cost

Any form of research carries a cost regardless of whether any materials are required. You may choose to interview your subjects and record the responses on your phone. You may transcribe the interviews and type onto an existing laptop and word process the results. However, the time it takes and any travel involved all attracts a cost. For a business, the cost is not only people's time but also the potential loss of any revenue while the research is undertaken. If the business intending to mass produce the new instant noodle flavour has invested heavily in the product and its packaging, made promises to suppliers etc, but the market research returns negative results, then the cost could be significant.

Types of data

The type of data collected for any research project is also fundamental to the study. The research tools such as questionnaires, surveys, interview questions, observation checklists etc should be examined to make sure they are appropriate for the methods used. For example, an observation checklist is not relevant unless observations are undertaken. There are two types of data used in research: quantitative data and qualitative data.

Quantitative data

Quantitative data is comprised of numbers which can be analysed mathematically and/or presented graphically. This data can include sales figures, market values and so on. Examples of tools for collecting quantitative data include questionnaires and surveys such as those used in your place of study or for conducting customer research in shopping centres or online. Gathering and interpreting quantitative data is a quicker process than using qualitative data methods.

The analysis of quantitative data can be validated and therefore produce **objective** results. However, any questions asked to produce quantitative data can produce skewed results because they can be interpreted differently, as can the method of asking the questions such as via an interview. For example, 200 surveys which all return a satisfaction level of 5 can be checked easily, whereas 200 interview responses might have been influenced by the interviewer.

Qualitative data

Qualitative data are **subjective** and often open-ended. It can involve interviews with customers or focus groups or invite respondents to add reasons or comments to surveys. Results usually provide a wide range of answers based on personal experience, feelings and expectations. A qualitative question might ask you why you bought a specific product and allow you to provide an open answer.

This kind of research can be used to:

▸ find out how customers perceive an organisation or brand

▸ understand how changes in price, or other variables, might affect consumer spending decisions

▸ investigate customer preferences, interests, aspirations, tastes and other variables.

Key terms

Objective – a judgement which is not influenced by personal opinions or points of view, neither biased nor prejudiced, and can be validated.

Subjective – based on personal opinions and interpretations. Analyses are not possible to validate.

▸ How do you think this person's response could be influenced by the woman asking the questions?

▶ Quantative data can provide clear, visual feedback for a business

▶ **Table 2.2:** The differences between quantitative and qualitative research

Quantitative	Qualitative
Objective	Subjective
Research questions: eg How many? What percentage?	Research questions: eg What? Why?
Tests theory	Develops theory
Focus is concise and narrow	Focus is complex and broad
Measurable	Interpretive
Basic element of analysis is numbers	Basic element of analysis is words/ideas
Reasoning is logical and deductive (concluding)	Reasoning is dialectic (for example, involving opinions) and inductive (leading)
Establishes relationships, causation	Describes meaning, discovery
Highly controlled setting: experimental setting (outcome oriented)	Flexible approach: natural setting (process oriented)

Research

Identify the type of data and methods used in studies to which you have contributed, such as learner or customer satisfaction surveys. Try to work out how the data are analysed and how the results might be presented.

PAUSE POINT   How would you create a questionnaire to collect both data types?

Hint   Evaluate two different types of questionnaires or surveys and identify what works well and what could be improved.

Extend   What improvement would you make to each type of data collection tool and why?

Sufficiency and focus of the research

The types of data gathered and the methods or tools used can skew research results. For example, a customer satisfaction survey which claims that customers are extremely satisfied but lacks any detail about the aspects of their satisfaction or what they like less, can be misleading. Frequently publicised examples include statements such as '84% of all customers using this skin product say they would recommend it to a friend'. The small print might add something like 'out of 67 users surveyed during the month of August'. Research findings should be based on sufficiency of data collection, such as the example of skin care products. For example, you may be convinced to purchase a product based on the views of 84 per cent of 67 customers but the results only portray a minority of the views of the population. You might also ask questions such as:

▶ How were the customers selected?
▶ Why did other customers not respond?
▶ What would customers say at other times of the year?
▶ How many customers chose not to respond?
▶ What did they like about it?

All research should have a focus which is related to the purpose for conducting the research and what you want from the study. Research is not valid if it arrives at a result but is unable to prove anything. However, research outcomes can occur as a result of chance, such as some of the discoveries by Stephen Hawking, for example that black holes should emit radiation.

▶ To what extent do you feel manipulated by the claims made by businesses about products?

Theory into practice

Consider the following:

'84% of all customers using this skin product would recommend it to a friend*'

*out of 67 users surveyed during the month of August

Check the sufficiency of the results from the example given by calculating:

- the number of people who would recommend the product to a friend out of those who responded
- the proportion of respondents in relation to the UK's population of (about) 62 million.

Tip

Explore where the surveys are situated, eg deliberately directed to their main consumer through the magazines, television programmes or websites that they are most likely to favour.

 PAUSE POINT   What would you consider to be a sufficient number of respondents to convince consumers to buy a product?

 Hint   Explore examples of market research findings such as those from *Which?* or other trade sites.

Extend   How representative of the population is the sample surveyed? What methods might you choose for a market research project?

Selection and extraction

You have been exploring some of the methods which can be selected for collecting and gathering data but the results from analysis also undergo a selection process. For example, in the skin product example showing the limitations of the information presented to the public, questions should be asked about the data not being used and how it can also skew results. When undertaking any form of research, considerable amounts of data are often collected and a decision needs to be made about which to use and what to leave out and why. The clearer the focus of the research and the comprehensiveness of the planning, the less likelihood there is of become overly bogged down in data. This is particularly so when trying to analyse qualitative data.

Extracting meaning from data relies on time and possibly the use of various tools to help with the process. Again it is important to plan for these activities. For larger scale studies, such as a dissertation or PhD thesis, researchers might purchase computer-assisted qualitative data analysis software. Although such software helps identify trends and patterns in responses, the analysis still relies on human interpretation to extract meaning from the data.

Developing the rationale

All research requires a rationale, whether it is to compare car insurance for the best deal which suits you, or to save money on travel costs to and from work or your place of study.

In addition to the Association of Research Ethics and the Ethics Research Council, the UK government also provides advice to businesses on how to conduct market research.

The rationale should include the focus, methods and means for conducting the study and the outcome being sought. This does not mean you make the research findings fit what you want to promote, but that you have a well thought out plan which supports the reason for conducting any form of research.

Research

Read about the different types of research methods depending on the rationale, such as testing a theory or finding a theory. For example, those described by Alzheimer Europe.

Interpretation, analysis and use of data and other information to make valid marketing decisions

You have started to explore the interpretation and use of data. Interpreting data is subjective, therefore rigorous steps for checking the validity etc must be planned and implemented. To analyse the data, it must be interpreted to find its meaning. For example, if a customer states they like the taste of a new instant noodle flavour, what does that actually mean? A customer who likes a flavour might not like the product enough to buy it. They might have other preferences or feel compelled to give a positive response. They might even prefer a competitor's product or flavour. Without asking the right questions the meaning can offer little of value.

Analysis requires a detailed examination of the data in preparation for interpretation. Data come in many forms, not just numbers, such as:

▶ images
▶ observations
▶ audio and video recordings
▶ reports
▶ case studies.

To analyse numbers, you can use software such as spreadsheets and apply formulae or, on a much smaller scale, it may be sufficient to use manual calculations. Whatever data type, analysis involves breaking down the data into smaller and smaller particles to explore meaning and find patterns and trends to establish the headline information.

The use of the data must inform the rationale for the research. When town planners are considering ways to develop shopping centres, they may seek the views of the public and other businesses and possibly those of specialist agencies, about improvements to facilities such as public transport links and disability access. Planning applications, even for private residences, are accompanied by invitations to the public to respond with queries and views.

To make a valid marketing decision a business may want to explore customer reasons for upgrading, equipment such as their mobile phone. Some customers may change mainly for the quality of the camera while another may need a larger display for reading messages. Other information such as amount of use or capacity may be irrelevant to the business at this moment in time.

Identification of any further sources of information that may be required

To support the market research and validate its results, the market research may require additional sources of information to satisfy the reliability or sufficiency of the data gathered. Depending on the type of research undertaken, further sources might include:

▶ government statistics
▶ national economic statistics such as from the Office for National Statistics (ONS)
▶ global statistics such as from the Organisation for Economic Co-operation and Development (OECD)
▶ environmental factors such as those related to food, environment or rural communities
▶ academic research articles and journals, which may contain more current information than that found in books – it takes a longer time to produce and publish a book.

In the case of a major government project such as the High Speed 2 Rail Route (HS2), market research has been ongoing since its inception. The public and various bodies have contributed their views and arguments both for and against its implementation on a massive scale.

Evaluation of the reliability and validity of the information obtained

The information obtained should be evaluated for its reliability and validity by, for example, finding other sources or further information to support or discredit the data or findings. A thorough evaluation aims to find holes in the research by rigorously testing the robustness of the entire study. To evaluate information obtained, methods include:

▶ involving others and asking them to critique the findings
▶ questioning its sufficiency, accuracy etc
▶ assessing the pluses and minuses (what works well and what needs improving)
▶ questioning what the information does not tell you
▶ identifying improvements.

> **Tip**
>
> If you have an employer, ask what methods of market research they use and what works best and what not so well. If you do not have a job, contact some local businesses for a mentor or ask at your place of study. Perhaps you have had a guest speaker who would be willing to mentor you.

⏸ PAUSE POINT   What examples can you identify where you have used similar questions to consider what further information is required, or to evaluate the information?

       Hint   Reflect on previous assignments, interviews or tasks you have undertaken.

       Extend   What can you do to improve further? What are your strengths and weaknesses?

Product life cycle

The product life cycle concept reflects the theory that products or services follow a cycle, just like people. They are born, grow up, mature and eventually die. It is a useful concept for thinking about what a product has achieved and where it is heading in the future.

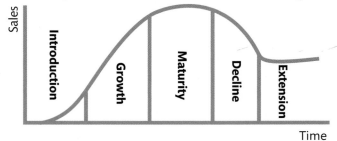

▶ **Figure 2.3:** The stages of the product lifecycle

A rationale for market research is to seek opinions about consumer preferences, the products or services they value and why, where improvements might be made and the reasons why some products lose favour when others do not.

▶ Introduction – in the introductory stage a product takes time to find acceptance by purchasers and there is slow growth in sales, just as market research takes time to plan, evolve and receive approval. With a new product only a few organisations are likely to be operating in the market, each experiencing high cost because output is low. A business may charge high prices to cover research, development and the initial promotional costs, but even then profitability may be difficult to achieve.

▶ Growth – if the product achieves market acceptance then sales grow rapidly. In this growth stage, profits begin to materialise as higher production levels reduce unit costs. However, the growing market attracts competition and soon producers have to invest in building a brand image, product improvements and sales promotions to obtain a dominant market position.

▶ Maturity – the maturity stage follows when a product experiences stable sales. This is generally the longest period of a successful product's life. But eventually sales fall and the market finds itself with too many producers who begin to suffer poor sales and falling profits.

▶ Most products reach the saturation stage when sales begin to fall. During this period, some brands will leave the market. The same is true of market research and the length of time the findings remain current, and therefore of value, is variable.

▶ Decline – products reach a stage of decline when sales fall significantly. Organisations progressively abandon the market, sometimes leaving a few producers who are able to trade profitably on low sales totals. Organisations use the product life cycle to devise new product plans. An organisation will look to introduce new products to coincide with the decline of the established ones or introduce product extensions by adding to the line – using the brand to provide credibility or imply necessity or need. Two examples are outlined below.

▶ A line extension is where a product is extended by adding a new colour, or perhaps flavour or size of packet. An example would be Cadbury and Mars who introduced fun size bags – these are line extensions because the product in the bag is a smaller version of their popular snack bars.

▶ A brand extension is where a well-known brand extends its range to a different product, such as Next Homeware, or the extension by Richard Branson of the Virgin Records Label brand into transport and telecommunications. M&S extended their well known brand into financial services, as have several other brands. Globally known Dutch giant Philips have been extending their brand since inception in 1891.

Case study

Evaluation of market research

The UK government runs a scheme for qualifying businesses which engage in research and development (R&D) that provides tax relief from HMRC for large businesses and tax credits for small and medium-sized enterprises (SMEs) (www.gov.uk/guidance/corporation-tax-research-and-development-rd-relief). As with any project, government or otherwise, the success and usefulness of the scheme is evaluated and reviewed for its effectiveness, and recommendations for improvements are identified.

R&D tax credits are a tax relief designed to encourage greater R&D spending, leading in turn to greater investment in innovation. They work by reducing a company's taxable income by an amount equal to a percentage of the company's allowable R&D expenditure. SMEs can also claim a payable credit if they are loss-making.

Since the inception of the schemes, companies have been able to claim R&D tax credits against qualifying R&D expenditure each year. By the end of 2012–13, more than 28,500 different companies had made claims under the SME scheme since it began in 2000–01, and over 7000 companies had claimed under the large company scheme, which launched in 2002–03. Overall more than 100,000 claims had been made up to 2012–13.

The government uses information and data from the Office for National Statistics which conducts the annual Business Enterprise Research and Development (BERD) survey of 400 of the largest R&D spenders and a sample of approximately 4600 other companies. This provides an estimate of total revenue expenditure on R&D by businesses.

An analysis of trends in average claim sizes over time and between regular, sporadic and repeat claimants is presented. The trend in the proportion of total UK revenue expenditure on R&D on which claims for R&D relief are made is then shown, followed by an industry

breakdown of claims and cost to the Exchequer in 2012-13. An analysis is then provided of trends in the numbers of 'high tech' companies (as defined by the OECD) claiming R&D relief. Finally, a geographical breakdown of the number and cost of claims in 2012-13 is presented.

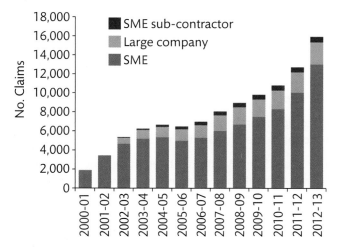

▶ **Figure 2.4:** Number of claims received for R&D tax credits by scheme (Contains public sector information licensed under the Open Government Licence v3.00)

The graph shows a marked increase in the number of claims in 2012–13, which most likely reflects the changes to R&D tax credit policy that came into effect on 1 April 2012. Between 2008-09 and 2012-13, the number of claims increased at an average rate of 16 per cent per annum, while the total value of claims rose at an average rate of 8 per cent a year. This adds up to 15,930 claims in 2012-13, with a tax cost of £1.4 billion and qualifying R&D expenditure of over £13.2 billion.

Check your understanding

1 What is the purpose of the HMRC tax relief scheme?

2 What is the rationale for this research?

3 What sources of primary and secondary data are used for the research?

4 How does the review provide meaning to the data presented?

5 What patterns or trends can you identify from the data presented in the graph?

What information provided in the case study did you select and extract and which did you choose to discard and why?

Hint   Highlight or underline what you believe to be the key information to answer the questions.

Extend   Compare the numbers in the case study with those in the graph. What else do they tell you about tax credit take-up and what further information might you need?

Assessment practice 2.2   A01 A02 A03

In the winter of 1979, a raid took place on the premises of a prestigious Birmingham company which prided itself on the safety of its deposit boxes where people could store their valuables, including jewellery, cash, precious metals and fine art. The haul was estimated at £4 million, a stunning figure at the time, and the robbery was marked down as one of the most notorious in the UK's history.

The company promoted its services as amongst the most secure in the country. Their marketing material claimed:

'New Street Safety Vaults has been in existence since 1947 and is a leading UK family-owned company offering safety deposit facilities that you can depend on. We can provide you with a secure method of storing your precious and irreplaceable items at a very reasonable price. Our high security systems are cutting edge, while also offering flexible access six days per week. One hour's notice is all we require for you to gain access to your safe. Rental length is negotiable, ranging from one month to long-term, and a variety of safe sizes is available to meet all needs. Our clients are assured of a discreet, reliable and secure service at all times.'

Your task is to:
- review and evaluate the marketing material
- identify the influencing factors for introducing an alternative strategy
- identify target markets and competition
- recommend methods and a rationale for an alternative marketing campaign.

Plan
- I know where I am going to begin.
- I know where I shall find my research sources for this task.
- I know how I shall manage my time.
- I know which aspects of the task will take the most and least time.

Do
- I am approaching this task in a rational manner and can explain my reasons for doing so.
- I can adjust my thinking and approach when I lose concentration or momentum.
- I am prepared for critical feedback to help me improve.

Review
- I can explain the methods and tools I used to carry out my research for this task.
- I can describe where I struggled and what I found easy, and why.
- I can recognise progress in my knowledge and the way I learn.
- I feel I am gaining in maturity in market research.

C Planning and developing a marketing campaign

A marketing campaign involves considerable thought and planning. Depending on the size of the business, the campaign may involve several people at different levels within the organisation apart from those who may be employed in dedicated marketing or advertising roles. Advertising is just one means of marketing although the term 'advertising' can be interpreted as any activity which promotes a product or service.

The purpose of a marketing campaign is to increase the business' positioning in the marketplace. That means to increase its market share and become a recognisable brand. Familiar, recognisable brands are identified by straplines or **slogans**, logos and images,

Discussion

In two groups, identify all the straplines you can within a set amount of time and then compare your list with those of your peer group. What are the common features? What is it about each of the straplines that made the brands so memorable?

A winning strapline or recognisable image turns a business into a household name. It also needs to say something about the product or service offered. The AO.com strapline 'we deliver when you're in, not when you're out' reacts to a common consumer complaint about businesses wanting to deliver goods when it suits them and not when convenient to the customer. The ongoing saga of the meerkats is a clever play on words for promoting the comparison website comparethemarket.com and when baby Oleg entered the scene, it became a series in its own right for that and subsequent episodes.

Key term

Slogan – a short, punchy phrase which conveys a memorable message, often used by companies to market their products or services. For example, 'Red Bull gives you wings'.

Marketing campaign activity

A marketing campaign can be planned by starting with a thought shower to capture ideas around the product or service to be promoted. The key features need to be explicit, such as value, price, USP, who you are intending to target, where and why they should buy it. The campaign is aimed at increasing sales. How, when and where the message is communicated will impact on the outcome.

Selection of appropriate marketing aims and objectives to suit business goals

Central to the marketing campaign are the aims and objectives appropriate to the overall business goals. To avoid the 'scatter gun approach' referred to a little earlier, the marketing aims are selected in response to the business goals set out in the business plan. Imagine that one of Apple's goals was to increase the sales of their Apple watches by 75 per cent compared to last year's sales. Their marketing aims and objectives would focus on the watch rather than promoting all Apple products together (see Table 2.3).

▶ **Table 2.3:** Outline of new marketing plan

Aim: to increase sales of Apple Watch by 75% on 2014-15 sales								
Objectives (SMART)	Promotional method	People involved	Lead person	Resources	Milestones	Deadline	Budget	Success factors

A marketing plan can be devised in many different formats, for example as a Gantt chart and supporting documents, so long as it has the key components. The titles used for each column in a marketing plan might vary, along with their order, and some might include much more detail. Where the plan involves more than one aim then a separate plan may be used, each one linking to the other. Plans might also be broken down into more detail against each resource perhaps in order to monitor and measure progress. An example of a marketing campaign plan is shown in Table 2.4.

▶ **Table 2.4:** Example of an outline for a marketing plan layout

Marketing campaign plan	
Campaign name and type =	
Planned launch date =	
Primary aim/objective (What is the main outcome you want to achieve? Tie it back to a relevant marketing objective.)	
Intended result/desired outcome	
Specific activities	
Materials required (eg printed materials, email design, etc)	
Key messaging (The points you want to communicate. How do you want your buyer to feel when they see your campaign?)	
Call to action (What do you want your buyer to do after seeing the campaign?)	
Follow up (What will you do about those who do respond? What will you do about those who do not?)	
Timing (for each activity)	
Overall campaign budget	
Measures of success (For example, new clients, new sales, etc)	

In the 1980s, NIKE, Inc.'s goal was to gain a larger share of the sports shoes market. To accomplish this it needed a campaign which would take it from selling almost exclusively to marathon runners to becoming a household name. As result of its 1980s campaign 'Just Do It' it increased its market share from $877 million to more than $9.2 billion in just 10 years.

Table 2.5 shows the next stage of the marketing campaign plan which is to define the aims and objectives of the campaign and how they will be implemented. The key performance indicators (KPIs) are necessary to provide a measure of progress made since they represent the success criteria for each stage.

▶ **Table 2.5:** Forming SMART objectives for a marketing campaign

Aims	SMART objectives	Strategies	Key performance indicators
Increase brand awareness and visits to the company's social media pages.	Increase new monthly visits to social media pages by +30% in 6 months.	Implement weekly updates of social media pages with interactive content, targeted at audience.	New visits to site (%).
Increase number of online sales through the dedicated company website, rather than third-party suppliers.	Increase sales volume +25% in 12 months.	Implement direct email marketing campaign using list of past purchasers from third-party websites.	Sales volume (units).

Research

If you have a part-time job or are undertaking work experience, ask the employer if you can study their marketing plan. Alternatively perhaps a family member, business mentor or your place of study will show you their plan.

Situational analysis

Undertaking a situational analysis requires investigating the state of the internal and external factors affecting a business. This allows marketers to formulate strategies relating to business goals. The business environment is assessed using various methods as described next.

Link

You can find out more about situational analysis in *Unit 5: International Business*.

SWOT

A SWOT analysis looks at the relationship between a business and its marketing environment. SWOT stands for:

▶ **Strengths** – the internal features of an organisation which may provide competitive advantages. One example could be highly efficient IT systems and processes.

▶ **Weaknesses** – internal aspects of the organisation which may not work as well as those of the competition or are not performing effectively. An example might be ineffective training on systems and procedures for new and existing staff.

▶ **Opportunities** – events and developments external to an organisation. This might include product or service extensions, or a new segment of a market opening up.

▶ **Threats** – developments external to the organisation which could damage overall performance. These threats can originate from governmental policy or legislation, such as an increase in corporation tax or new laws.

Link

You can find out more about SWOT analysis in *Unit 8: Recruitment and Selection Processes*.

Strengths and weaknesses are both internal to the business (such as the buildings, staff skills and experience, product and service quality etc) and external (meaning the opportunities and threats in the environment in which the organisation operates).

Carrying out a SWOT analysis requires you to research into an organisation's current and future position. Trends based on past performance and factors which influenced outcomes are also important. The idea is to match an organisation's strengths and weaknesses with the external forces (opportunities and threats). A SWOT analysis draws together all the evidence from the various analytical techniques used. It is a way of producing a summary which then provides the basis for developing marketing objectives or aims and ultimately strategies or plans.

Once key issues have been identified with your SWOT analysis, they feed into marketing objectives. The results of a SWOT analysis can be used together with a PESTLE analysis. The two can then be compared and challenged.

PESTLE

As part of the marketing planning process a business has to analyse its external environment. One useful way of analysing the external environment is by grouping external forces into six areas using a PESTLE analysis. PESTLE stands for political, economic, social, technological, legal and environmental.

▶ **Political** factors that affect a business are usually beyond its control, for example restrictions on advertising prescription-only medicines to the general public. However, the business needs to anticipate changes that are coming and decide what it should do to either make the most of an opportunity or reduce a threat. If licensing laws changed again, then associated businesses would have to come up with strategies to mitigate or fight the anticipated impact to the business and their customers.

- **Economic** factors can affect the performance of a business. These relate to the national or international economy, which goes through periods of prosperity (when high employment and income drives demand), recession (when demand falls, leading to lower income and employment) and recovery (when demand, income and employment rise gradually). During and following a recession, businesses must consider potential rises in taxes and interest rates and the effect they will have on both business decisions and customers' spending abilities and decisions.
- **Social** factors relate to the values and beliefs of society, which includes the population's demographic (for example, age, gender, ethnicity, income, education, occupation and population number). This information from sources such as newspapers and magazines helps businesses to target their services at broad segments of the population. For example, increased use of e-readers has had a significant impact on paper manufacturers and printers who have had to consider the threat to their businesses carefully.
- **Technological** developments can affect businesses in many ways. For example, the development of e-commerce benefited Amazon.co.uk, but eventually took business away from traditional bookshops that developed e-commerce websites later. By contrast, music downloads are facing increased competition from producers of vinyl records as retro and vintage products enjoy a revival.
- **Legal** developments affect businesses in a range of ways. For example, any changes to the Data Protection Act would affect any business that holds customer data. Similarly, businesses have to accommodate ongoing changes to equality laws in the way they market their products and services. For example, businesses might produce promotional literature in the different languages used by their target audience. They also need to ensure that images do not portray stereotypes and that their business goals do not discriminate against minority groups.
- **Environmental** factors can relate to the social, political and legal aspects affecting a business. For example, a business may decide to package their food products in recyclable packaging. This may prove to be popular with consumers if there is a growing level of concern over waste. Similarly, the government may put pressure on farmers to increase the amount of organic food grown and further reduce use of pesticides.

▶ How concerned are you about the amount of packaging that is used for a product?

Ⅱ PAUSE POINT What examples can you identify of successful marketing campaigns?

> Hint   Look for examples from different business sectors and business sizes. Explore this using sources other than the internet.

> Extend   What examples can you find of less successful marketing campaigns? Why were they less successful?

Use of research data to determine target market

A marketing campaign will be more successful if you have determined which market to target, as the same marketing approach may not attract or be suitable for everyone. This does not mean excluding anyone by making assumptions but does mean relying on primary or secondary data from market research to justify the target market. For example, it would not be the best plan for a manufacturer of the 'Rolls Royce' of prams and pushchairs to only target young women.

A marketing campaign needs to have focus. Therefore the manufacturer of high-end prams and pushchairs might target all adults over the age of 16 who could be expected to afford their high cost products. They could find out about the suitable demographic using secondary data sources such as those from the census statistics produced by ONS. These can be filtered by, for example people and society, income and lifestyles then by adults and income levels.

The usefulness of this and other data reports depends on the range of the market to be targeted, for example local, regional, national or global. Multi-national businesses are likely to employ people to examine economic, financial and forecast data, such as those produced by:

▸ the National Bureau of Economic Research in the USA

▸ Global Economic Data and Forecasts

▸ Global Financial Data

▸ Global Economic Prospects

▸ National Statistics.

Table 2.6 shows an extract from the UK government's website in which 'Her Majesty's Treasury publishes monthly statistical data containing major economic indicators'.

▸ **Table 2.6:** Extract from HM Treasury statistics showing growth over last 10 years (Contains public sector information licensed under the Open Government Licence v3.0).

	China	India	Australia	UK	Russia	USA	World
2005	11.3	9.3	3.2	3.0	6.4	3.3	4.9
2006	12.7	9.3	2.7	2.7	8.2	2.7	5.5
2007	14.2	9.8	4.5	2.6	8.5	1.8	5.7
2008	9.6	3.9	2.7	−0.5	5.2	−0.3	3.1
2009	9.2	8.5	1.6	−4.2	−7.8	−2.8	0.0
2010	10.6	10.3	2.3	1.5	4.5	2.5	5.4
2011	9.5	6.6	2.7	2.0	4.3	1.6	4.2
2012	7.7	5.1	3.6	1.2	3.4	2.2	3.4
2013	7.7	6.9	2.1	2.2	1.3	1.5	3.3
2014	7.3	7.3	2.7	2.9	0.6	2.4	3.4
[3] Source: IMF, World Ecomolo_Outloook Database. [4] Source: OECD							

Link

Find out more about SWOT and PESTLE by referring to *Unit 1: Exploring Business.*

Reflect

How does the UK compare with the other countries? How does it compare with the world year on year?

Tip

You might find it useful to present your results as a graph as well as a table. Explain your findings to a peer.

Smaller businesses also rely on data relating to the economy from news reports, financial articles or periodicals. This is so they can anticipate what the market can sustain. For example, an architect producing plans for large scale building projects may have decided to diversify the business model during the recession to promote regeneration projects, plans for building extensions or commercial property conversions.

Many businesses use the information extracted from analyses of primary data collected by:

▸ customer feedback

▸ mystery shoppers

▸ surveys and questionnaires

▸ businesses such as Nielsen and TTMC.co.uk, which undertake research on behalf of other organisations.

Use of research data to conduct competitor analysis

Businesses need to be aware of what their competitors are doing, as well as technological giants such Apple, Samsung, Sony and Microsoft.

Depending on the nature and size of the organisation, business intelligence databases can be purchased from companies such as Hoovers while a business with a niche market such as nuclear energy, will rely on numerous sources for intelligence to provide a comprehensive overview.

The Department of Business, Innovation and Skills (BIS) provides reports on business growth and performance such as how the UK performs as a competitor internationally as a research nation.

Other sources of business performance information are through organisations such as the Chamber of Commerce and Employer Business Partnership where employers network with competitors, suppliers and other businesses to develop contacts and promote their services. Local authorities use data gathered by the ONS, OECD and other sources to evaluate performances of local businesses and make decisions about market needs in relation to the local demographic. A construction business might extract useful information to establish their medium and long term aims to market residential or commercial development projects.

A UK umbrella manufacturer might use data from the Met Office to predict sales relating to long term weather forecasts.

Competitor analysis data are used to assess the strengths and weaknesses of your competitors as well as your own. Rigorous analysis and evaluation can help businesses to make informed decisions about product development and marketing strategies.

Tip

For a business or individual, try signing up for Really Simple Syndication (RSS) feeds which will automatically send alerts when changes have been made to that specific website to save time trawling for fresh information prematurely.

❚❚ PAUSE POINT   Have you been involved in a marketing campaign? Remember a marketing campaign is just a way of promoting something.

      Hint   If you have not been involved in any, ask your tutor about their experiences or about being involved at your place of study.

      Extend   Initiate a marketing campaign for your local 'corner shop' or to promote your favourite item of clothing.

Marketing mix

The **marketing mix** provides an excellent framework for developing marketing plans. The marketing mix for a product is generally accepted as being made up of four parts (the four Ps), which are product, place, price and promotion.

Key term

Marketing mix – factors that a company can control and which will persuade or influence customers to buy its products or services.

▶ **Figure 2.5:** The marketing mix

Once the marketing objectives have been agreed, marketing plans must be developed to provide a structure for how the goals will be achieved and the indicators for measuring progress.

Product development

A product is anything that can be offered to a market to satisfy a want or need. Products include:
▶ physical goods
▶ services
▶ experiences
▶ events
▶ persons
▶ places
▶ properties
▶ organisations
▶ information and ideas.

Therefore a combination of goods and services are offered to the target consumer. For example, you might buy a camera and receive a significant amount of added after-sales service to help you get the most from its features. These two aspects together make up the product being offered to the consumer.

Form and function

These terms derive from architecture where a design results in something being either:

▶ designed for form, for example a beautiful chair which can be admired but which is not comfortable to sit on, and therefore not particularly functional

▶ or designed for function as opposed to form, for example a pair of ordinary Wellington boots designed for walking through wet and muddy fields.

Packaging

Packaging can refer to how a product (or service) is promoted and is not just the physical wrapper around a product. How a product is packaged or labelled can make or break a sale. Some examples of poor physical packaging which make opening difficult, include:

▶ childproof medicine bottle caps

▶ sardine cans

▶ cellophane wrapped items.

Plain packaging, or that which does not represent the product, such as that used for medicines and sandwich packaging, can be a disadvantage because it is confusing to the customer. However the re-design of sandwich packaging used by Pret a Manger was not only creative but also functional – following a revamp, the packaging could be used as a tray as well as a receptacle. Another example of ineffectiveness or inappropriately labelled products is shown in this photo.

▶ Can you think of an example of a product you would purchase regardless of how it is packaged?

Some packaging is purely functional as the product says it all, such as net bags for satsumas.

Branding

There are many examples of really effective branding which has become synonymous with the product. Animals are often used to represent products even though seemingly unrelated and with considerable success, such as the:

▶ Andrex puppy

▶ Duracell bunny

▶ Freeview TV cat and budgie.

Developing a Marketing Campaign

Followers of the meerkats and baby Oleg story generated revenue not only for the website, comparethemarket.com, but also for the products associated with the brand, by capturing the public's imagination and tugging at heart strings.

▶ How many other businesses use similar tactics to entice sales?

The use of animals in marketing campaigns is recognised as a successful psychological tactic.

More than ever before, marketing campaigns are seeking global attention and so the branding of products must be carefully considered to prevent offence or misrepresentation. Mistakes do occur, where cultural differences do not readily transfer globally, and there are many examples to be found online.

These instances can cost businesses enormous sums of money to correct the branding without having to alter the product. One such example is when Oil of Olay changed the brand name in 1999 to Oil of Olaz supposedly due to some nationalities registering their objections about the name. It continues to be known as Oil of Olaz in parts of Europe while retaining the Oil of Olay name as a global brand.

Pricing strategies

Price is the amount of money consumers are charged to buy a product and can vary considerably. Marketing campaigns may focus on promoting special offers or BOGOFs.

Supermarkets used the BOGOF slogan successfully to encourage shoppers to bulk buy. However they were criticised subsequently for encouraging food waste.

Price is the one element of the marketing mix that produces revenue, the others generate costs.

▶ Penetration – a product is sold into a market at a low initial price in order to generate sales before the price is increased. You may have seen examples advertised as 'introductory offer' such as on online shops, subscription services and telecommunication contracts. This helps break down any barriers to the market and generates sales volume, but not necessarily **profit**, so it can be used as a short-term strategy to gain market share.

> **Key terms**
>
> **Profit** – the percentage of margin mark-up over the unit cost.

- Skimming – at the launch of a new product there will be less competition in the marketplace. Skimming involves setting a reasonably high initial price in order to get high initial returns from those consumers willing to buy the new product. Examples include latest technology such as TVs, music systems, cameras, mobile phones and other devices.

  As other similar products or upgraded models enter the marketplace, the price is lowered to remain competitive. This strategy is often adopted by technology companies that benefit from 'early adopters'.

- Competitor based – businesses need to remain aware of their competitors' pricing strategies otherwise they are likely to lose their market share by appearing to overcharge for similar products. You will be aware of price wars between supermarkets and it is difficult for consumers to make direct comparisons between products based on price alone.

  While brand items stipulate the **RRP**, some manufacturers restrict businesses to reduced prices so the product is offered at a consistent price across stores. Such examples include items in pre-priced packaging such as some Cadbury chocolate bars, cereals and promotional merchandise. It is illegal to make claims about substantial savings based only on the RRP.

- Cost plus – this is a pricing strategy which is used to determine the retail or wholesale price of products or services. Businesses apply a simple formula as a guideline for determining a sale price which still enables the business to make a reasonable profit:

Key terms

RRP – recommended retail price.

Unit cost – all expenses incurred to manufacture a product or deliver a service including transport, raw materials, labour, premises etc divided by the number of items manufactured.

Sale price LESS **unit cost** = gross profit

Unit profit is determined by the amount of mark-up the business adds to each unit. The mark-up is determined by looking at competitor pricing in order to remain competitive in the marketplace. Competitor pricing can vary depending on the geographic location of the business. For example, the cost of fuel can vary considerably in garages, even when situated opposite each other. This might be related to the cost from the supplier of the fuel, such as Shell, Texaco, or Esso, which is reflected in the mark-up. By contrast retail outlets selling identical goods will wish to remain competitive and might find themselves engaged in price wars such as the major supermarkets.

Research

Explore your local area for examples of price wars and cost pricing. Compare with examples your peers find.

Promotional advertising

Promotion is made up of various ways of communicating products or services of the business. The purpose of promotion is to raise awareness of a business and generate sales.

Promotion should inform, persuade and influence consumers to purchase a product or service and promote the reason why the purchase should be made from their business as opposed to another. For example, although the product differs, KFC, Burger King and McDonald's compete to persuade customers to purchase their fast food rather than go to one of their competitors.

A marketing model known as **AIDA**, defines promotion as a four-step process:

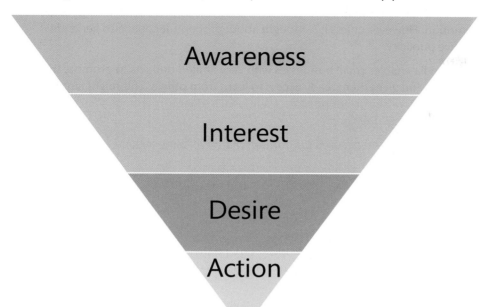

Key term

AIDA – Attention of the customer, Interest to learn more about the product, Desire for the product, Action to purchase when the opportunity arises.

▶ **Figure 2.6:** The marketing model AIDA

You might question why some businesses continue to advertise even though they appear to be extremely successful and are household names. One such business is Coca-Cola, a global brand dominating the market. It is claimed to be the world's third biggest global brand valued at around $80 billion. Around 94 per cent of the world's population recognise the brand and it is the world's favourite soft drink. However, they need to remain an active market presence to ensure that competitors do not gain advantage.

Public relations (PR)

Public relations relates to business communications and relationships with the public. This includes customers, suppliers, stockholders, employees, the government, the general public and the society in which the organisation operates. Public relations programmes can be either formal, such as a professional advertising campaign, or informal, for example promoting the business by word of mouth.

Sponsorship

In order for businesses to be more creative with their finances, particularly in relation to their marketing budget, they may seek sponsorship (input of money) from other businesses such as manufacturers and suppliers or celebrities. Sponsorship has become more popular during times of austerity and can be highly successful. Examples include:

▶ Santander: Olympic medallists, golfer Rory McIlroy.

▶ Formula 1 racing teams: oil companies, banks, airlines, luxury watch brands. The livery of sponsors has been adopted since the 1960s.

▶ Football clubs: Manchester United has several sponsors including Adidas, Apollo Tyres, DHL and Chevrolet.

Some businesses which rely on sponsorship are also sponsors themselves – Santander. is an example. Formula 1 driver Jenson Button appears in Santander advertisements (so he helps generate money for them), while his team McLaren-Honda is sponsored by them.

Use of social and other media

The media has opened up opportunities to promote businesses, enabling rapid promotion. However unless it is thought about properly, it could also generate negative publicity.

Social media enables small businesses with very limited budgets to promote their businesses and gives them ready access to learn from others. This might also be the case with businesses favouring more traditional marketing methods such as a routine advert in the local press.

Methods of online media used for promotional advertising include:

▶ Google
▶ YouTube
▶ Facebook
▶ Twitter.

Using social media enables businesses to expand their promotional range and therefore could lead to them being unable to fulfil the demand generated.

Guerrilla marketing

This approach refers to low cost, creative and unconventional methods used to maximise return. It can include using tactics such as flash mobs or graffiti, or, as in the case of a Unicef campaign around clean water, creative placement next to vending machines. The aim of this marketing is to keep the budget low but maximise the impact, particularly if the campaign goes viral through social media.

▶ How effective do you think this campaign was?

Personal selling

This is a skilled task which may require training a sales team. It is considered to be one of the more expensive aspects of the promotional mix. A seller presents a product direct to a consumer, often face to face, but it can also be over the telephone and through video-conferencing and instant messaging.

Personal selling may reach a relatively small number of people (compared with TV advertising, for example), but it is generally more effective as potential customers can ask questions relating to their own personal circumstances which may result in a sale, even an unlikely one.

Product placement

Product placement is when TV programmes and movies display recognisable brands. Examples include:

▶ Apple computers – 'Mission Impossible' and 'Independence Day'

▶ Mercedes Benz – 'The Lost World: Jurassic Park'

▶ Pepsi – 'Back to the Future'.

Prior to early 2011, product placement was not permitted in TV programmes made for UK audiences. Recent examples include:

▶ Nokia – 'Hollyoaks'

▶ Nationwide cash machine – 'Coronation Street', outside the corner shop.

Digital marketing

This is the promotion of products or services using multi-media. The place where you study probably uses digital marketing, as do many businesses, via means such as: websites, Facebook, Linkedin, texting.

Government departments and agencies also use digital marketing to promote their services, eg online services for vehicle road tax and to file tax returns. Some NHS services are promoted by text messaging such as clinics, flu jabs etc. The government's digital marketing strategy is available publicly.

Corporate image

Part of the marketing mix is the way in which the business promotes its corporate image to the world. For example, some technology companies promote a creative, friendly and almost family image such as those portrayed by Google and Microsoft. Apple's corporate image is often perceived by consumers as displaying success and bucking the trend, just by owning one of their products. Similarly, corporate image is reflected in the clothing people wear.

If a business wants to project a corporate image as the place to buy hiking gear then they would be unlikely to want a corporate image represented by Day-Glo clothing and footwear, advertised via gossip magazines.

A corporate image can be compromised if, for example, there is a change to their logo as consumers are likely to become confused about its identity. Over the years, McDonald's has made changes to its logo's typeface to represent a more modern look, and in mid–late 2000 parts of Europe adopted a green background to its recognisable yellow logo to represent an ecological image. Imagine if Coca Cola changed their logo or even the typeface for their name and how it might lead to confusion or even product rejection by some customers. When British Airways changed their livery in 1997, many considered it to represent a more down-market image of the airline and to not reflect British values.

 **PAUSE POINT** What examples can you identify of businesses with a successful marketing strategy and what makes them successful?

Hint   Explore examples from different sectors and sizes of business.

Extend   Compare how businesses have adapted their marketing campaign to embrace technological developments.

Place, distribution channels

The marketing mix includes developing a strategy for promoting the product in accordance with where it can be purchased and how it is distributed. For example, most consumers of confectionery will buy products from a shop. However, in order to sell confectionery at these stores, a manufacturer needs to sell and distribute the products to wholesalers who will then sell to the retailers, or sell direct to the retailers. Some wholesalers such as Costco and CKB Products sell direct to the public as long as certain criteria are met.

Businesses therefore need to adapt their marketing mix depending on the end customer – that is, whether they are a consumer or reseller. Each end customer will seek different benefits from the same product.

Direct to end users (mail/online/auction)

Direct distribution is where the business sells and distributes direct to the customer. For example, Apple sells products to customers via their e-commerce website and delivers direct to the consumer. In contrast, purchases made from Amazon and eBay may also be distributed indirectly when ordered through their websites on behalf of the retailer.

Many businesses continue to promote their products via a brochure such as Littlewoods, Screwfix, Park, Webb Ivory and Wickes. Customers can place their order over the phone or by completing a form.

Businesses might also sell via auction houses or websites. Examples include property and land agents or websites such as eBay.

Retailers

Marketing strategies also vary depending on whether consumers purchase from retailers or wholesalers. Retailers usually operate on a greater profit margin and can exploit savings to market their business and what they offer.

Wholesalers

As wholesalers rely on a quick turnaround of their products at prices which already have a low profit margin, they are likely to focus their campaigns on bulk buying, purchasers' convenience and out of town locations. They might include in their marketing mix the reasons why they can sell at lower margins and possibly advertise the benefits to the environment of their use of less packaging on the products they sell.

Extended marketing mix

This model extends the standard four 'P' model to seven 'Ps' by including the following parts: people, physical environment, processes.

People

Successful businesses recognise the need to constantly improve the service they offer alongside their products to benefit from repeat business. Even for low-price repeat-purchase items, it is now standard for companies to offer a level of customer care after the initial purchase. For example, snacks and sweets will have dedicated customer service to resolve any product queries or complaints.

Successful businesses also invest in training for their workforce to ensure employees have the right skills to represent the culture of the business.

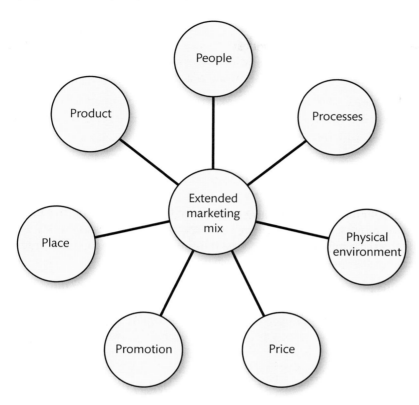

▶ **Figure 2.7:** All the elements of the extended marketing mix

▶ Have you ever had to complain about a product? How satisfied were you with the response you received? What impression did it give you of the company?

Physical environment

Businesses can reinforce their image and culture by means of the environment used by customers. For example, high-end vehicle manufacturers such as Porsche and Mercedes-Benz have plush, contemporary showrooms which accommodate both new and returning customers. When customers visit such showrooms for servicing or vehicle maintenance they can enjoy facilities such as WiFi-enabled quiet working areas, leisure areas with TVs, quality refreshments and child friendly play areas.

Customers of bargain shops are likely to experience fairly cramped conditions. This is because the retailer needs to maximise every inch of space to return maximum profit where the goods generate small profit margins.

Processes

Any business should recognise the importance of creating and maintaining a positive image because the purchasing process for a particular product or service can be a key part of the promotional mix. Many companies use technology to improve the service they offer customers. They might help customers to create accounts quickly (to avoid providing the same information each time they buy something) and track orders so customers can see when their purchase will be delivered.

Virgin Atlantic portray a friendly and relaxed yet professional identity through their marketing. The process of booking a flight, holiday or any one of their brands models that image. Customers checking in online for a forthcoming flight are able to recognise the Virgin brand in the same way as customers purchasing a rail ticket. They can identify with their ethos by the way the website is structured, its language and usage. When on board a Virgin flight that image continues with a cartoon safety video which attracts attention, unlike the more generic version used by many airlines. Customers' safety is paramount to airlines and passengers are more likely to pay attention when they engage with the corporate identity.

 PAUSE POINT   What are your experiences of the extended marketing mix?

 Hint   Reflect on your last major and minor purchases.

Extend   Create a SWOT analysis of both examples and evaluate each example in relation to the product's value.

> **Discussion**
>
> In a small group compare evaluations. Analyse their strengths and weaknesses and make recommendations for improving their marketing strategies. Justify your recommendations.

The marketing campaign

The marketing campaign involves planning a series of strategies and events which result in the marketing activities. For example, your place of study will have a marketing plan which identifies a series of strategies over the coming 12 months, or maybe longer, so that their courses can be 'drip fed' to entice potential learners to study with them. The strategies will relate to these events to identify where, when and how they will take place. The campaign will require resources and a budget, all of which have to link together.

While the initial ideas may appear fairly informal, such as asking a working group to jot down random ideas, the plan will develop into a timeline of some sort, possibly using a Gantt chart:

ID	Task Name	Duration (weeks)	Nov 2016 1W	Dec 2016 1W	2W	3W	4W	Jan 2017 1W	2W	3W	4W	Feb 2017 1W	2W	3W	4W	Mar 2017 1W	2W	3W	4W	Apr 2017 1W	2W	3W	4W	May 2017 1W	2W	3W	4W
1	Situation Analysis																										
1.1	Company Analysis	2	▓	▓																							
1.2	Customer Analysis	3	▓	▓	▓																						
1.3	Competition Analysis	5	▓	▓	▓	▓	▓																				
2	Ventures	3							▓	▓	▓																
3	SWOT and PESTLE	4					▓	▓	▓	▓																	
4	Market segmentation	6										▓	▓	▓	▓	▓	▓										
5.1	Product	2																▓	▓								
5.2	Price	2																		▓	▓						
5.3	Promotion	4																				▓	▓	▓	▓		
6	Execute	4																						▓	▓	▓	▓

▶ **Figure 2.8:** An example of a Gantt chart

Content of the marketing message

This should convey the key message and be the core of the marketing campaign. In other words, to identify the message you want to communicate to your target audience.

Marketing messages are designed to become second thoughts, so that when you think of something associated with the product (such as an energy drink) your next thought is to buy that product (for example Red Bull) and no other.

The content of the marketing message must attract attention within the first few seconds. If the message is being conveyed by a TV advert, the business may have less than 10 seconds to get the message across. A billboard advertisement may only be a fleeting sight to passers-by therefore it must be clear and uncluttered.

> **Research**
>
> Identify at least three examples of marketing campaigns which deliver a confusing message, for example an advert which leaves you unsure of the message being portrayed. In small groups, try and think of a way the business could make their message clearer.

Business to business (B2B) and business to consumer (B2C) marketers suggest content marketing has significant and rapid impact on sales.

Examples of particularly effective marketing content are those in which slogans become everyday phrases or require little if any explanation such as Ronseal's 'it does what is says on the tin'. Whereas when Hive first introduced their marketing campaign, customers may have been confused by the message or how to purchase it. You have probably been irritated by an advert, yet some might view this as clever marketing as it remains memorable and gets people talking about it.

Selecting an appropriate marketing mix

The next stage of a successful marketing campaign is selecting the right mix. A marketing campaign that does not respond to each aspect of the mix is likely to be unsuccessful. For example, a supplier of lawn turf might plan their campaign by considering the following mix:

- product – species of grass according to function; length of individual turf; USP or brand
- pricing – wholesale and retail charges; discounts for quantity
- promotion – adverts and samples in garden centres; developing relationships with landscape gardeners and corporate clients including local authorities; website testimonials and photos of projects; advertisements televised to coincide with gardening programmes and seasonally relevant
- place – purchase and delivery arrangements for retailers and wholesalers; direct sales to customers if permitted; terms and conditions; guarantees if relevant
- people – knowledgeable workforce; clear product information for wholesalers and retailers; capacity of staff to meet potential demand
- physical environment – conditions for storing the turf; arrangements for supply as demand increases
- process – ordering online; post cards with order form; free phone sales line; app; through distributors.

Selecting appropriate media

Identifying the right media is crucial not only to the success of the campaign but also to working within budgetary constraints. The mix, and in particular knowledge about potential customers, determines the appropriate and relevant ways to promote the business' products and services. If, for example the product is targeted at school children, then a TV advert should be scheduled at a time when children are not in school. Products targeted at young people might find greater success using social media sites, whereas services aimed at a mass market such as vehicle fuel, might select other methods such as TV, banners on commercial vehicles, leaflets in supermarkets etc.

A local theatre company might text previous customers, send mailshots via leaflet drops around the community with the regular post, place brochures in information centres and public places like surgeries, commission regional TV adverts and encourage website visitors to sign up for regular alerts.

Allocation of the campaign budget

The budget is set to prevent overspending. With so many options available for promoting the services and products of any business the budget must be agreed in advance and monitored closely. Calculations for determining any budget need to be based on the potential return for the investment. Therefore, if the product or service has a limited life span, such as the latest craze in electronic games or child's toy, it may be sensible to concentrate on a quick series of advertising over a very limited period of time. This avoids being left with stock after, for example the Christmas period.

Manufacturers of food products associated with religious festivals (for example, Easter eggs) are mindful of being left with products they cannot sell or have to sell off at considerably reduced prices and therefore at a reduced profit or even at a loss.

 **PAUSE POINT**   What other examples can you identify of where marketing campaigns are seasonal?

Hint   Identify businesses which are also affected by environmental factors.

Extend   Select one example and apply a situational analysis to inform a marketing campaign.

Timelines for the campaign including monitoring

The timelines for the entire marketing campaign should be set before starting the campaign as a whole. Timelines should be set for every activity. If possible milestones will also be identified, especially where activities cover a fairly long period of time. Each of the timelines (and milestones) should have a success measure or key performance indicator (KPI) attached to them, otherwise you cannot measure whether or not progress has been made.

Just as you have timelines set for any action plans negotiated with your tutor, these timelines might need to change if unanticipated factors occur, such as severe weather conditions affecting food crops, or perhaps unexpected volcanic activity affecting travel operators.

Each timeline provides a trigger for monitoring and reviewing the plan against the progress made, and that monitoring process also includes an evaluation of its success to date.

How the campaign is to be evaluated

Although a campaign requires a debrief at the end to evaluate its successes and learn from any errors, the evaluative process should be 'ongoing'. However, when planning the monitoring, review and evaluation (MRE) process, you should schedule in dates and times and not simply refer to it as 'ongoing' as this is unhelpful and unproductive. By coordinating the MRE process in alignment with the SMART timelines, the campaign is more likely to result in a successful and rigorous foundation for subsequent campaigns.

The sort of questions you might ask during the evaluation process are shown in Figure 2.9.

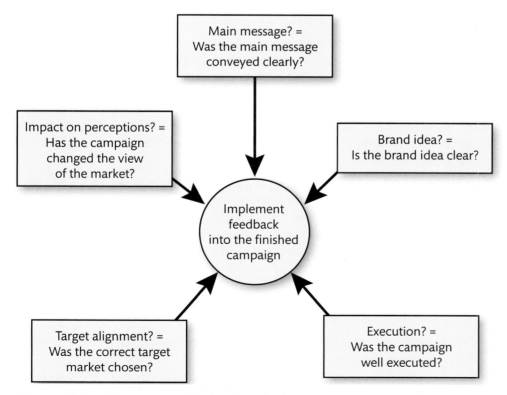

▶ **Figure 2.9:** Questions you can ask during the evaluation process

Appropriateness of marketing campaign

Just as seasonal influences have to be considered when planning a marketing campaign, so other aspects of the mix which can be evaluated and reviewed need to be examined, such as:

▶ product – aligning the product to the target group, for example Afro hair products to those customers and service providers matching the demographic, verified against public records

▶ pricing – high-end products targeted towards more affluent areas or bargain prices to areas of high deprivation, informed by census data

▶ promotion – PR events to corporate clients and digital marketing to prevalent IT users, checking online visitor numbers and impact relating to volume of sales

▶ place – reviewing the appropriateness of advertising and promotion placement by measuring public interest, perhaps by surveys and interest generated, and placement of product eg location on supermarket shelves or announcement of future lines, with advantageous positioning and size in magazines

▶ people – analysing feedback gathered by workforce and suppliers on the campaign itself and the product or service

▶ physical environment – anticipating and evaluating relationships between product, people, price etc and the environment such as economic, climate and cultural conditions

▶ process – aligning promotion with process for supplying it and meeting demand, and amending process if needed.

How far the marketing activity reinforces and supports brand value

Aggressive marketing activity does not automatically result in increased sales or profits. The aim of the marketing campaign might be to launch a brand, for example when Victoria Beckham launched her clothing brand VB. Subsequently the brand has been extended to include perfumes and other beauty products.

The main purpose of a marketing campaign might be to build its brand by generating customer expectations. An example is the hype created by Apple in anticipation of the new version of its iPhone. This marketing strategy is so successful that eager consumers have queued for hours and even days to be one of the first to purchase the latest version. Purchasers who buy a product when it is a relatively new concept to the market are called early adopters and are often used as a means of testing out the product and identifying its faults for manufacturers and designers to produce upgrades and new versions.

There are examples where a marketing campaign has tried to generate a brand and been criticised for attempting it. One such example is in politics where political parties are promoted as brands and the marketing campaigns attempt to convince the public to vote for a concept. There are examples where companies associated with brands might wish to be temporarily disassociated if, for example news reports are aimed at discrediting them for poor practice or problems with quality.

PAUSE POINT Have you or anyone you know been caught in the hype and queued for a new product launch? What enticed you to do so?

Hint Explore advertising and promotional literature for examples which generated similar extreme customer behaviours.

Extend Which campaigns have not made you purchase a new line or brand? Why not? What might they have done to interest you?

The sustainability of marketing activities

Consumers are at the centre of every marketing activity as without them businesses will not survive. With the cost of marketing having no limit, businesses need to ensure marketing strategies result in sustainable activities. Take for example a tried and tested set of activities which appear to suit the target market as sales continue to roll in, such as tattooing or body piercing. What if the trend for extensive and creative body art suddenly declined due to a further increase in government legislation or perhaps a health alert? The usual means of advertising will no longer be sustainable against the return in income and a whole new strategy would need to be considered.

Imagine that a major marketing activity might promote children's earrings as an additional service to the body art industry, and an advertising contract has been secured as part of those marketing activities. The government then introduces legislation restricting the age limit for children's body piercing, with or without permission, to above the age of 16. The business is still committed to a contract with several children's magazines, and relies on partnerships with jewellery manufacturers and beauty salons. This would have a huge impact on the businesses involved on both sides of the issue. The business promoting children's earrings would lose money because it could no longer market its product, and the magazines could be faced with empty spaces due to adverts not being filled. The jewellery manufacturers may even have marketed themselves as providers of this jewellery, showing the impact across different businesses.

Flexibility of the campaign to enable response to both internal and external changes

One of the many benefits of frequent monitoring and evaluation of a marketing campaign is being able to adapt to unexpected changes which influence its success. It is important to consider the knock on effects of changing any plan when so many factors are involved. There may be penalties to pay, such as wasted advertising space or printing costs.

Marketers are required to remain aware of internal and external changes which affect the relevancy of the campaign. For example, if a business employed an ageing sales force and retirement was looming, then the marketing plan would need to accommodate training replacement staff and possibly periods of reduced productivity.

External changes are influenced by global forces. For example if a specialist travel company promoted climbing holidays along the Ecuadorian and Colombian border their marketing activity would have been affected when volcanic activity was detected as in August 2015. The marketing campaign would need to be flexible to accommodate government restrictions on accessing areas considered dangerous, and marketers would need to be aware of information reported by the Foreign and Commonwealth Office (FCO) and other reliable sources.

Relevance to organisational goals

While marketing campaigns must be flexible there are limits according to the goals of the organisation. A business which prides itself on complying with its environmental sustainability policy, such as the values promoted by Brompton Bikes, would be unlikely to adopt a marketing campaign promoting a new line in combustion engine powered bicycles. A marketing campaign will also need to balance how relevant they appear to the goals of the business. For example, a campaign might be created to meet a business' goal of increasing their sales in the first six months of the year. However, the campaign would not directly refer to this goal as that is unlikely to sit well with customers.

Appropriateness to target market

We have already discussed how the target market for a product, and so their marketing campaign, varies from business to business. The target market for Brompton Bikes is predominantly commuters to or from urban environments. A similar business would be likely to consider their target market as learners, graduates and young to middle-aged professionals. Marketing activities might include targeting universities and Blue Chip companies based in cities, or targetting employees who travel to and from their offices on a frequent basis, such as those working in local authorities and government departments.

The types of media would be representative of their target groups, such as social network sites, professional periodicals and billboards at train stations or on buses. A similar business would probably consider it less lucrative or sustainable to engage in marketing activities aimed at senior citizens and remote or rural areas due to **economies of scale**.

Key term

Economies of scale – a term relating to the cost benefit in return for output such as the income return after deducting the cost of a marketing campaign aimed at a mass market.

Legal and ethical considerations

Finally, there are many legal and ethical considerations which may impact on marketing activities such as:

▸ suitability of air-time when advertising adult-only products or services

▸ easy ways to borrow money

▸ hard-to-interpret messages such as excessively high interest rates for loan repayments

▸ misrepresentation such as claims or promises of longer life or increased happiness or percentages of satisfied customers

▸ use of stereotypes to promote services such as hairdressers, builders or professionals

▸ adverts for charitable donations which attack consciences or bombard vulnerable people with excessive requests

▸ opt-out clauses for future purchases such as repeat magazine subscriptions which automatically take payment unless the (sometimes unknowing) customer cancels in advance.

There are many laws and regulations which govern the world of advertising and consumer marketing such as the Advertising Standards Authority. These rules are in place to investigate any potential misrepresentation, such as claims made in late 2015 about misleading packaging on Nurofen products in Australia.

An example of a possibly unethical practice was the withdrawal by a major UK high street retailer of a range of children's clothing that included items such as a padded bikini bra, due to complaints about inappropriateness.

Assessment practice 2.3

Cupid's Cakes is a SME manufacturing cup cakes for couples looking for love. They have decided to introduce speciality line extensions to represent key yearly events. Their recipe has been trialled in-house and they have developed a small range of gluten-free, vegetarian and savoury cakes. Their packaging is generic. They aim to become an instantly recognisable brand and need help to progress their organisational goal to become the UK's market leader in supplying speciality cup cakes. They currently sell through their website and have regular customers including:

- two national supermarkets, one high-end
- a hundred or so bakery shops mainly around the South East
- four corporate clients.

They have gathered the views of internal staff who really like the new flavours but are keen to see these new lines in packaging which somehow reflects its contents. A small number of staff members have mentioned something about a 'sharing' cup cake as it is more romantic.

Family members who work for Cupid's Cakes have managed to persuade management to ask for your help in putting together a marketing campaign. You will be working directly for the MD, Sophie Armitage, and her finance officer, Alonso Khu, who have asked that you provide a thorough plan and include any supporting ideas and rough work as they want to learn from your expertise. They may use your rough notes in the order you produced them as a training resource for developing a marketing team.

Your task is to undertake the following activities.

1 Plan and develop a marketing campaign based on a situational analysis.
2 Suggest appropriate ways to undertake market research to assess an extended range of relevant packaging.
3 Draft out at least two different tools for gathering data.
4 Explain how the data will be analysed and used.
5 Identify areas where there is potential to extend target markets, based on government data.
6 Produce a 12 month marketing plan based on a marketing mix.
7 Justify your marketing campaign activities.
8 Describe the procedure for extending the marketing campaign.

Plan

- I know how I will break down the task and prioritise each component.
- I know what resources I will need to help me to complete this task.
- I have planned what strategies I will deploy to manage my time effectively.
- I have worked out how I will know when I have finished.

Do

- I am flexible in my approach and have analysed which ways work best for me.
- I can identify when I've gone wrong and learn from my mistakes.
- I am open to constructive criticism.
- I can celebrate my successes and explain why they worked well.

Review

- I can explain how I tackled this task.
- I can recognise the progress I have made since the last assessment practice task.
- I can relate my learning to the workplace.
- I can evaluate the usefulness of the sources I have used and know where to find them again.

THINK ▶FUTURE

Jemima Usher
Marketing graduate

I have recently been employed by a multi-national company as a member of their marketing team. There are 15 of us at Head Office and smaller teams based in offices around the world. My direct boss is the Marketing Director and she reports to the Board but also works with the other Marketing Directors around the world. Our company manufactures widgets that are placed in cans of drink so they fizz when opened. I admit it's not the most exciting of products but that makes my job even more rewarding as I have to think laterally.

After I achieved my Level 3 BTEC qualification I was offered a place at university to study for a degree in Marketing which I achieved three months ago. This company offers lots of prospects and apart from ongoing training they have said that if I show promise they may be prepared to sponsor me to study for a Master's Degree part-time. I also have the opportunity to spend some time at some of their other offices overseas and although very excited, know I have to work very hard and prove myself as a valuable and reliable member of the organisation.

Focusing your skills

Having the skills

To impress any organisation sufficiently to offer you employment you need to demonstrate the skills you will bring to their business. In the case of a marketing executive, such as Jemima, you will need to prove you can:

- work effectively in a team
- communicate with others at all levels
- use your initiative
- negotiate your ideas
- be flexible and reliable
- learn from your mistakes
- seek out, analyse and evaluate data
- pay attention to detail.

Planning for the future

If like Jemima, you are planning to go to university or possibly think it is out of reach, carry out a SWOT analysis during or towards the end of this qualification and compare with any earlier versions. These questions might also help with your development.

- Which skills have I improved since starting this course?
- Where do I wish to see myself in 5, 10 and 15 years time?
- How will I get there?
- What have I got to lose by not applying to university?
- What will I gain?
- What does my personal marketing campaign look like?

Getting ready for assessment

This section has been written to help you to do your best when you take the external examination. Read through it carefully and ask your tutor if there is anything you are not sure about.

About the test

Before your supervised assessment you will be issued with Part A of your assessment, which contains material for the completion of the preparatory work for the set task.

- Read all of Part A carefully.
- Highlight or underline key words.
- You will have a set period of time to complete independent research around this. Make sure you put time aside in your diary for this well in advance.
- You can take research notes into the supervised assessment so make sure your notes are clear and concise. Check with your tutor how long these notes can be.
- Decide on where you will carry out this preparatory work so you are not disturbed.
- Get together everything you might need, including:
  - laptop
  - reliable internet connection
  - text books and other useful resources
  - pens (and spares), scrap paper, pencils and sharpeners, highlighters, calculator, dictionary and thesaurus, maybe a ruler and rubber.
- Do not forget anything else you might need such as glasses, laptop lead, etc.
- Avoid any distractions from a mobile phone!

Preparing for the test

This unit is assessed under supervised conditions. Pearson sets and marks the task. As mentioned, you will be provided with a topic to research prior to a supervised assessment period in order to carry out research.
The external assessment can be completed over a number of sessions.
You will need to prepare

- a rationale
- a plan for a marketing campaign for a given product or service.

Make sure that you arrive in good time for your test and make sure that you leave yourself enough time at the end to check through your work. Listen to, and read carefully, any instructions you are given. Marks are often lost through not reading instructions properly and misunderstanding what you are being asked to do. There are some key terms that may appear in your assessment. Understanding what these words mean will help you understand what you are being asked to do.

As the guidelines for assessment can change, you should refer to the official assessment guidance on the Pearson Qualifications website for the latest definitive guidance.

Key term	Definition
Primary research	Research compiled directly from the original source, which may not have been compiled before. Learners are expected to understand the advantages and disadvantages of different primary research methods.
Qualitative research	Descriptive data, such as data drawn from open-ended questions in questionnaires, interviews or focus groups.
Quantitative research	Data in numerical form which can be categorised and used to construct graphs or tables of raw data.
Secondary sources/research	Published research reports and data, likely to be based on analysis of primary research.

Sample answers

Look at the sample questions which follow and the tips on how to answer them well.

Worked example

Set task brief

- You are required to research the events management market independently prior to the supervised assessment window.
- You should research and analyse at least one marketing campaign related to the events management market and its associated costs.

Task information from Part B

Events Management

The number of UK businesses organising events is growing year on year having increased by 500 per cent over the last 10 years. The events market is now worth £1 billion. Events include corporate team days, civil ceremonies, religious festivals and prom celebrations.

Your research should have covered examples of similar businesses and how they use the marketing mix to produce their campaign.

The average event generates 75 per cent gross profit. Events range from £10,000 for a teenage birthday party for 50 to £1,000,000+ for corporate events such as weekends on a yacht in the Mediterranean for 80 guests.

Clients are increasingly generating repeat business having been introduced either through word of mouth or by adverts placed in local media or brochures usually found at events such as corporate conferences, fairs (such as craft or wedding fairs). An increasing number of wealthier private clients are those with second homes in the UK which they visit occasionally.

Circle or highlight the key information you might need to support a marketing campaign.

Part B of your assessment will be held under supervised conditions. You will be provided with information relating to the subject of your preparatory work for Part A.

Worked example

Activity 1

Prepare a rationale for the Sussex Events marketing campaign and re-branding. This should include:

- marketing aims and objectives
- research data on the market and competition
- justification for your rationale.

(Total for Activity 1 = 34 marks)

> Make sure that you understand everything being asked of you in the activity instructions so that you can be sure your answer is clear and focused on exactly what you have been asked to do.

Activity 2

Based on your rationale from Activity 1, develop a budgeted plan with a timescale for your marketing campaign. You need to present this in an appropriate format which enables SMART planning and monitoring.

(Total for Activity 2 = 36 marks)

> Always make a plan for your answer before you start and remember to include an introduction and a conclusion and think about the key points you want to mention in your answer. Think about setting yourself some timeframes so that you have time to cover everything – and, importantly, have time to write the conclusion!

Set task information

Sussex Events is an SME specialising in events management. They have been in business for eight years and expanded from two partners to become a limited company with 40 employees. Their turnover has increased year on year to £12.2 million but they have noticed a slight decline in the number of corporate clients and an increase in overseas clients with second homes, especially those from Russia, China and India.

MD Evangelo Ezra wants to develop a brand which represents what they actually do. In discussions with his partner, Sharma, they recognise they also need to better promote their goal which is to increase the market share of events management for private customers. Although the return is greater from corporate clients they cannot risk further decline as the impact on their turnover is too significant. They are also concerned about the impact on their business due to declining oil prices. Several of their repeat clients are from the UAE and there is potential that clients will have less money to spend on elaborate events.

Evangelo and Sharma recognise a gap in the market specialising in birthday parties, graduation parties, stag and hen do events and might expand into christenings and engagement parties in the future.

Their initial marketing budget is £75,000 although they could be flexible by 10 per cent but prefer to keep that as a contingency.

> Keep in mind what the activity has asked you to do. You need to discuss the aims and objectives of the campaign and so should highlight them here.

> Make use of the research you have already completed for Part A. You will have some information on these types of events already.

> Always make a note of any figures that are mentioned in the set task information - you will need to make sure that your answers take into account this sort of information.

Activity 1 Answer:

▶ **Marketing aim**

- To expand Sussex Events as the Events Management Specialist for non-corporate clients.

▶ **Objectives**

- Identify our USP.
- Brand our business as the private party specialist.
- Develop a marketing campaign which:
  - identifies our target market
  - spreads our message through a variety of media
  - plans for sustainability and growth.

> The marketing aim states the overall intention and the objectives begin to break down how the aim will be achieved. You might find it useful to keep breaking down the objectives into sub-levels, as the third objective begins to show.

> Notice how the objectives all start with verbs and remember that each should be SMART when replicated in your marketing plan.

▶ **Research data on the market and competition**

I recognise that four other companies operate in the Sussex area. Specialist activities are also available such as go-karting and firework displays, which are important to note as they provide additional options for activities at celebratory events such as birthday parties.

Although there are several event organisers offering party planning outside of Sussex, such as Collection26, I chose to focus on the local competition due to the logistics of travelling distances to plan and execute the party arrangements which would impact on the profits of Sussex Events.

As Sussex covers a wide area, I also narrowed my search to within 30 miles of the offices for Sussex Events to identify any local competition and found there was one business operating but which specialises in corporate team building events…

> You can find listings of businesses such as events organisers, on the internet but make sure that you are specific with your searches to ensure you can make direct comparisons with other businesses offering the same type of business as the one in your case study. In this case, you would have concentrated on businesses offering private parties rather than major businesses providing corporate events.

> Try and keep your answer as focused on your key points as possible. If you find your answer drifting away from that main point, refer back to your plan.

> Do not just rely on the internet for your sources. Explore free newspapers and parish magazines in the local area where smaller businesses will promote their services, especially those just starting up. Check the government website for any businesses which are registered limited companies. In this case, you would search for companies registered as private party planners.

▶ **Justification for your rationale**

The re-branding of Sussex Events is crucial if the business intends to change direction by specialising in private parties. Although the current brand provides an instant indication of the purpose of the business it does have a corporate image and is unlikely to attract local attention as…

…The branding should reflect the party and celebratory aspect of the business and its aim to take the stress out of private event planning. If Sussex Events intends to extend its market lines the branding will also need to reflect events which are associated with more sober occasions such as funerals…

When deciding upon a new branding, the current branding will provide a starting point so that current clients can recognise a connection between Sussex Events and its new proposed name of… Corporate clients are likely to hold private events and know others who might do so, therefore there are opportunities to retain clients although for different purposes.

…The logo to promote the brand should use colours which are… and the logo itself should be meaningful enough to represent all elements of the business: fun or sombre and professional…

> You will be able to pick up new ideas by looking at how the competition promotes their services through their website and other media.

> This answer shows how you would start to form your marketing plan and includes some key areas you should consider covering.

Activity 2 Answer:

Aim: To expand Sussex Events as the Events Management Specialist for non-corporate clients											
Sussex Events Marketing Campaign [year]											
	April		May		June		July		August		
USP											
Target market											
Branding											
Strapline											

> Note how the actions on the left hand side are taken from the objectives. These are just some of the actions that comprise a marketing campaign – you will add more detail in your example.

> The example shown in Gantt chart format just shows an extract of a one year campaign.

The second plan starts to show how the objectives will be met by identifying responsibility, milestones and costs etc.

Aim: To expand Sussex Events as the Events Management Specialist for non-corporate clients

Sussex Events Marketing Campaign [year]							
	How	Who	Lead	Cost £	Milestone	Success measure	Progress
USP	Identify competitors	MM	SD	500.00	06 June	Limited competition	
	Compare offer	MM	MD	500.00	10 June	USP identified	
Target market	Research	Outsource	SD	7500.00	01 May	Sales growth of 50%	

Legend

Sales Director: SD
Marketing Manager: MM
Managing Director: MD

Note how the plan includes a legend (a key) to identify who is taking responsibility as the lead person on each part of the campaign and who is responsible for carrying out the work.

These Gantt charts are one example of how you might start your answer in Activity 2. There are other tools that you could use to develop your budgeted plan. From this initial point you would need to expand your answer, including details of how you would plan and monitor the implementation of your marketing plan.

Further reading and resources

Mortimer, R., Brooks, G., Smith, C. and Hiam, A. (2012) *Marketing for Dummies*, New Jersey: John Wiley & Sons

Websites

www.cityindex.co.uk/

Information on spread betting and Forex trading in the UK.

http://www.worldwideerc.org

Worldwide ERC is an association of professionals in workforce mobility.

www.ft.com/global-economy/uk

The *Financial Times* offers information about UK businesses and their positioning in the global economy.

www.gov.uk/government/organisations/companies-house

Information about limited companies including their trading, profit and loss accounts.

http://smallbusiness.chron.com/

Information, news, features and advice for small businesses.

http://www.thisismoney.co.uk/money/news/article-2908159/Sainsbury-s-beats-Asda-2nd-biggest-supermarket.html

News article from January 2015 on supermarket rankings.

Personal and Business Finance 3

Getting to know your unit

Assessment

This unit is externally assessed using an unseen paper-based examination, and marked by Pearson.

The ability to manage money is crucial to keep both yourself, as an individual, out of future difficulties and also to keep businesses out of difficulties. If you are not able to manage your money effectively, then all sorts of problems may lie ahead. Managing your money will help you achieve future objectives and dreams. Similarly, if a business cannot manage its money it is not likely to survive.

How you will be assessed

This unit is externally assessed by an unseen paper-based examination. The examination is set and marked by Pearson. Throughout this unit you will find practice activities that will help you prepare for the examination. At the end of the unit, you will also find help and advice on how to prepare for and approach the examination. The examination must be taken under examination conditions so it is important that you are fully prepared and confident with key terminology and accounting techniques. You will also need to learn key formulas and be confident with carrying out calculations accurately. A calculator will be essential.

The examination is made up of questions that require short answers, calculations and extended writing. You will need a calculator in the examination and throughout your study of this unit.

As the guidelines for assessment can change, you should refer to the official assessment guidance on the Pearson Qualifications website for the latest definitive guidance.

This table contains the areas of essential content that learners must be familiar with prior to assessment.

Essential content	
A	Understand the importance of managing personal finance
B	Explore the personal finance sector
C	Understand the purpose of accounting
D	Select and evaluate different sources of business finance
E	Break-even and cash flow forecasts
F	Complete statements of comprehensive income and financial postition and evaluate a business's performance

Getting started

Personal finance involves understanding why money is important and how managing your money can help prevent future financial difficulties. Write down a list of future medium- and long-term wants. Discuss why you will need to be able to manage your money to achieve these goals.

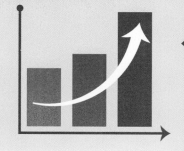

A Understand the importance of managing personal finance

You will make important financial decisions throughout your life. The choices you make will not be without some risk and need to be taken very carefully. This unit will help you understand how to manage your personal finances and make informed decisions to help prevent future financial difficulties.

Functions and role of money

Money flows in two directions, into your ownership and out. Money comes in from various sources including wages, gifts and savings. Money goes out to pay for necessities and wants. The same is true in business – money comes in from sources, including sales and bank loans, and goes out to pay day-to-day expenses and fund expansion. Therefore the ability to handle money received, and to control money paid, is a fundamental requirement for personal and business success. The starting point is to understand what 'money' is.

▶ What do you think are the three biggest financial decisions you will ever make in your life?

Discussion

What is money? Can you write a definition? What forms can money take? In small groups, discuss what you think money is. Write a definition of money and produce a spider diagram showing the different forms that money can take. Feed back to the rest of the class and discuss your results. Can you all agree on the best definition of money?

The functions of money

The functions of money are the jobs that it performs. These are outlined below.
▶ Unit of account
  • It allows us to place a monetary value on goods and services.
  • The price of goods and services show the unit of account, for example a chocolate bar is 60p or a new car is £30,000.
▶ Means of exchange
  • It allows us to trade.
  • Businesses and customers can buy and sell goods and services using money, for example when you purchased your lunch yesterday or paid to go to the cinema.
▶ Store of value
  • It allows us to use it in the future as it keeps its value.
  • You might have money saved in a bank account or 'piggy bank' which you can then use to buy goods and services in the future.

▶ Legal tender
  • It is a legaly recognised form of payment.
  • Money is widely recognised and used for all sorts of transactions from buying an ice cream or getting a haircut to paying a deposit on a house and receiving your wages.

Research

Did you know that the Royal Mint sets rules on what is legal tender? If you owed £100 and wanted to pay off your debt in 2p pieces would this be legal tender? Take a look at the guidelines on the Royal Mint website. Why do you think these guidelines exist?

Role of money

Different people will have different attitudes to money. An individual may also change their attitude to money based on the situation they find themselves in. The role of money is affected by a wide number of factors, including those outlined below.

▶ Personal attitudes
  Individuals will vary in their attitude to risk and reward as well as saving and borrowing. You may be risk averse so you will try to avoid risk, or you may be willing to take more risks and may even enjoy risk taking as you are incentivised by the potential rewards. Equally, you may be more or less likely than others to save your money rather than spend it. This can, in part, depend on your family's attitude to money, for example whether you were brought up being told savings were good and encouraged to save for a rainy day. You will also be influenced by your attitude to borrowing. You might like to live within your own means and only buy what you can afford. Alternatively, you might be happy to buy goods and services on credit or to borrow money in order to get what you want sooner rather than later.

▶ Life stages
  As you grow up from childhood to adulthood, your financial needs change. Each stage of your life has different implications that will affect not just your needs but also your attitude to money, as discussed above. Table 3.1 shows the common financial needs and implications of each stage.

▶ Culture
  Different cultures, affected by tradition, religion and ethical beliefs, will have different attitudes to money. The older generation of Chinese people, for example, have a culture of saving. However, as the country becomes wealthier, young people are more willing to spend and even buy on credit.

▶ Life events
  Events throughout your life will impact on your attitude to money. These events may be within your control, for example going to university, travelling abroad, getting married or starting a family, or may be outside your control, for example illness, financial gains or losses.

▶ External influences
  Factors outside your control, including the state of the economy, will have an impact. For example, the state of the economy will impact on wages, availability of jobs and the prices of goods and services. Decisions by the government will affect the amount of tax you pay or the amount you receive in benefits. These all directly affect your ability to spend and save.

▶ Interest rates
  When **interest rates** are low you may be more willing to borrow money or spend on credit. When interest rates are high there is more of an incentive to save.

Key term

Interest rate – the proportion of an amount that is charged as interest to the borrower.

Table 3.1: Financial needs and implications at different life stages

Life stage	Financial needs	Implications
Childhood	• Limited needs • Mainly reliant on parents • May want to buy sweets or toys	Money received from presents may be spent as attitude will be that this is to buy things you want May be encouraged to save or parents or grandparents may set up a savings account for you into which they make regular payments May rely on pocket money
Adolescence	• Want to be more independent • Slightly less reliant on parents as want to socialise away from family	May look for a part-time job Still partially reliant on pocket money More likely to receive cash as gifts and may be willing to save up smaller amounts in order to make bigger purchases
Young adult (This is a very big stage which can encompass a wide range of different scenarios depending upon life choices)	• University or starting a career • Looking to be more independent • Buying a car and buying or renting a flat or house • Looking to settle down and maybe get married or start a family	May take a student loan if going to university Borrow money to pay for a car or purchase one on a finance deal May be looking at taking out a mortgage Need to earn money to support self and others Eligible for credit and debit cards
Middle age	• Support family • Start saving for children's futures, e.g. university, weddings, etc. • Look to improve own lifestyle, e.g. new car or move house • Enjoy having access to additional money to spend on luxuries such as foreign holidays	Savings accounts for specific purposes Paying a mortgage Planning for own future through pensions and retirement plans Likely to be the stage of life when income peaks but matched with high expenditure
Old age	• Fewer dependents • May downsize, e.g. move from family home to a smaller retirement home • Fewer financial needs for assets but may be higher for services such as health care	Mortgage payments stop or become lower Less income as reliant on a pension rather than a salary

Planning expenditure

When planning expenditure, that is, money paid out, it is important to consider a number of common principles. These are important to ensure that you avoid over spending which will put you at risk of financial difficulties both now and in the future. You should look to control costs in order to avoid getting into **debt** in the future. If your spending is too high, this may mean more money is going out than coming in which will lead to the build-up of debt. Debt is expensive as interest will be charged on money owed. If debts are not paid or not paid on time, this will affect your **credit rating**. A poor credit rating will affect your ability to borrow in the future. In extreme cases, an individual may be declared **bankrupt** if their debts have spiralled out of control.

To remain **solvent**, you should set financial targets and goals. These should consider how much money you want to earn and place limits on how much you will spend. If you save some of your income, this can help generate future income as money saved will earn interest. Savings will also help provide a safety net for the future, for example to provide insurance against loss or injury. What would happen if you could not work in the future? Sometimes you will also want to save to fund future purchases, for example to buy a car or pay a deposit on a house.

Inflation is a general rise in prices. This leads to the value of money falling, that is, £10 today is worth less than £10 ten years ago. Expenditure now can help counter the effects

> **Key terms**
>
> **Debt** – money owed.
>
> **Credit rating** – a score given to individuals on how likely they are to repay debts based upon their previous actions.
>
> **Bankrupt** – when an individual or organisation legally states its inability to repay debts.
>
> **Solvent** – the ability to meet day-to-day expenditure and repay debts.

In pairs discuss:

- How would you rate your own attitude to money?
- Do you take risks?
- Can you think of a time when your attitude to money was irresponsible?
- How could you have behaved differently?
- What factors influence your attitude to risk?

As a group draw a spider diagram of factors influencing people's attitudes to risk.

of inflation. For example if you spent £150,000 buying a house today the value of the house would increase. If you left £150,000 in a savings account the amount would go up because of inflation but the spending power of your savings would go down.

The common principles to be considered in planning personal finance are summarised in Figure 3.1.

▶ **Figure 3.1:** How important are each of these principles in planning your own personal finances?

PAUSE POINT Can you explain the functions and role of money?

Hint Close the book and draw a concept map about the factors affecting the role of money. Think about both personal factors and external factors.

Extend What do you think are the short- and long-term consequences of bankruptcy?

Different ways to pay

One of the functions of money is as a means of exchange. This means you can use it to pay for things. There are, however, a number of ways of paying for things – not just with notes and coins. Therefore any method of payment is classed as money. Table 3.2 shows methods of payments.

▶ If you wanted to buy a car what are the different ways you could pay for it?

▶ **Table 3.2:** Methods of payment

Method of payment	Explanation/features	Advantages	Disadvantages
Cash	Notes and coins in a wide range of denominations	Most widely accepted form of exchange Physical not virtual Consumers feel confident when using Makes budgeting easier	Can be lost or stolen Threat of counterfeit Only really appropriate on purchases up to a certain amount Cannot be used online
Debit card	Issued by banks with payments for goods and services being deducted directly from a current account	No need to carry cash Secure method of payment with low risk of theft Widely accepted Offers a degree of protection on purchases Suitable for online transactions	Short time lapse between making the transaction and the money being withdrawn from the customer's account may result in overspending Not accepted or appropriate for small transactions
Credit card	Issued by financial institutions allowing customers to delay payments for goods and services	Allows a period of credit that is interest free, e.g. one month Most cards are widely accepted Loyalty schemes are often offered, e.g. collect points or cash back Offers a degree of protection on purchases Suitable for online transactions	Interest is charged on balances not paid off within a month Can encourage a customer to overspend and get into debt Interest is charged on cash withdrawals A limit will be set on the amount of credit allowed
Cheque	A written order to a bank to make a payment for a specific amount of money from one person's account to another account	Low risk form of payment as the cheque can only be cashed by the named payee Widely accepted for face-to-face and postal transactions No need to provide change as can be written for an exact amount	Expensive for the consumer if the bank refuses to clear the cheque, i.e. it 'bounces' The time delay between writing the cheque and it being cashed could cause a consumer to go overdrawn Viewed as old fashioned Easy for the consumer to make errors when writing the cheque which will create problems for both the consumer and the recipient
Electronic transfer	Payment is transferred directly from one bank account to another	Almost instantaneous Provides a record of payment No additional costs incurred Easy to use for one-off and more frequent transactions	Risk of loss if the transfer is incorrectly set up Not appropriate for face-to-face transactions
Direct debit	An agreement made with a bank allowing a third party to withdraw money from an account on a set day to pay for goods or services received, e.g. pay a gas bill	An easy way to make regular payments, e.g. utility bills Amount paid can vary to ensure the payment matches the amount required by the vendor Quick and easy to set up	If the payer makes a mistake and takes too much it is the payee's responsibility to claim back the money The payer determines the amount paid each time making it difficult for the payee to plan and budget
Standing order	An agreement made with a bank to transfer a fixed sum of money to a third party account on a set date on a regular basis, e.g. pay £30 for a phone contract each month	The same amount is paid each time making it easier for the payee to plan and budget Easy both to set up and to cancel No need to remember to make regular, standard payments	Payments are taken regardless of the customer's balance which could lead to the unplanned use of an overdraft facility Payments will continue to be made unless cancelled

▶ **Table 3.2:** – *continued*

Method of payment	Explanation/features	Advantages	Disadvantages
Pre-paid card	Money is uploaded onto a card with transactions then being withdrawn to reduce the balance	Can set a budget in advance to avoid overspending If lost or stolen the loss is limited to the remaining balance An effective way of controlling the amount spent by children and where money is spent, e.g. upload money for school lunches or transport	No protection if lost Sometimes requires an initial fee to purchase or set up the card, e.g. Oyster travelcards
Contactless card	Cards containing antennae allow money to be transferred when the card touches a contactless terminal	Gaining in popularity Secure method of making payments	Often only accepted for relatively small transactions Still not widely accepted as seen as new technology
Charge card	Issued by financial institutions allowing customers to delay payments for goods and services for a short period of time; the balance must be paid off in full when a statement is issued	Reduces risk of running up debts Allows a short period of credit Avoids the need to carry cash Often offers additional perks	Must be paid in full each month Often an annual fixed fee is applied
Store card	Issued by a retail outlet so that customers can delay payments for goods and services (similar to a credit card but only accepted by stores specified)	Allows a short period of credit that is interest free, e.g. one month Often offer loyalty schemes, discounts and special promotions or privileges	Only accepted in issuing store or linked associations Interest is paid on outstanding balances Can encourage overspending and result in a consumer getting into debt – particularly if they hold multiple cards
Mobile banking	The ability to carry out financial transactions using mobile devices such as phones or tablets	Convenient as can be used at any time and place Secure	Features are still limited and hence mobile banking does not offer all of the functionality of Internet banking
Banker's Automated Clearing Service (BACS) Faster Payment	A system that allows the transfer of payments directly from one bank account to another	Faster payment allows almost instant transfers that are guaranteed within 2 hours Can be accessed in a number of ways including in a branch, over the telephone and online No additional costs	Faster payment is not offered by all banks or branches and the customer may therefore have to default to BACs which can take three days to transfer payments A limit is set on the amount that can be transferred in any single transaction
Clearing House Automated Payment Systems (CHAPS)	A system that allows the transfer of payments directly from one bank account to another	Transfers can be made the same day assuming instructions are received prior to a set time, e.g. 2 pm at Barclays There is no limit on the amount that can be transferred in a single transaction	Normally, there is a fixed charge per transaction regardless of the amount transferred

Discussion

In pairs discuss:

- Which of the payment methods in Table 3.2 do you use regularly or semi-regularly?
- Which of these methods do your parents use regularly or semi-regularly?
- Does your payment method depend upon the product you are buying?

As a class, draw a mind map to show when each method of payment is suitable. Justify your decisions.

Current accounts

A **current account** is an account with a bank or building society that is designed for frequent use. Money can be paid in and withdrawn on a daily basis without the need to give notice. Most people will use a current account to get wages paid into, to pay cheques into and out of, pay bills and other frequent expenses, and to withdraw cash.

In the same way as a business changes the features of its products to try and be competitive and attract customers, banks will try to attract customers by changing the features of their accounts. The features of a current account will include:

▸ rate of interest paid on any positive balance
▸ rate of interest charged on a negative balance
▸ **overdraft** limit
▸ charges on unauthorised overdrafts
▸ additional incentives.

> **Key terms**
>
> **Current account** – an account with a bank or building society designed for frequent use, e.g. regular deposits and withdrawals.
>
> **Overdraft** – the ability to withdraw money that you do not have from a current account.

▸ What would you look for when choosing a bank to open a current account with?

Types of current account are outlined below.

▸ Standard
  This is the normal account offered to customers with a reasonable credit rating. It includes standard features such as the ability to pay and withdraw money, cheque book, debit card, interest payments on positive balances and a pre-agreed overdraft limit.
▸ Packaged, premium
  This account offers additional features to a standard account, for example car and house insurance, credit card protection, breakdown cover and cash back on certain transactions. The bank may have additional charges for these accounts so it is important that you check whether you are being offered a good deal or not.
▸ Basic
  This account offers only limited features designed for those customers who may otherwise find it difficult to open a bank account due to poor credit ratings. A basic account will not offer an overdraft and will not pay interest on positive balances.
▸ Student
  This account is designed specifically to meet the needs of learners. Common features include an agreed overdraft limit and incentives to join the bank, for example free rail cards or cash. Banks are keen to attract learners because once a young person has joined a bank they tend to stay with that bank for life. However, this is less often the case now due to the availability of information on the Internet and the ease with which banks can be changed.

The advantages and drawbacks of different account types are summarised in Table 3.3.

▶ **Table 3.3:** Advantages and disadvantages of different types of current account

Type of current account	Advantages	Disadvantages
Standard	No charges on credit balances Offers the holder a wide range of facilities including a cheque book, debit/cash card and possibly an overdraft facility Convenient for receiving regular payments, e.g. wages and making regular withdrawals	Potentially high charges on the use of an overdraft facility Standard features only, i.e. no additional perks
Packaged, premium	No charges on credit balances Offers the holder a wide range of facilities including a cheque book, debit/cash card and possibly an overdraft facility Convenient for receiving regular payments, e.g. wages and making regular withdrawals Offers the holder additional perks at a packaged price cheaper than acquiring them individually (standard additional features include things such as holiday/travel insurance, break down cover and phone protection)	Additional monthly charge is frequently applied The package offered may not offer value for money or meet the needs of the individual account holder
Basic	Available to customers with a low credit rating Offers an easy first step for individuals to gain access to basic banking facilities, i.e. the ability to pay in and withdraw cash	Limited facilities, e.g. no debit card or overdraft facility
Student	Course fees and student loans can be easily handled Bonuses offered are designed to meet the needs of learners, e.g. discounts on travel or small lump sum cash payment	Overdraft facilities could encourage overspending Charges for overspending are high Limited facilities

Research

Look at the student accounts currently being offered by banks. As well as visiting individual bank websites, you could also look at comparison websites. Which bank do you think is currently offering the best deal to learners?

Case study

Which account?

Gabriella has just finished sixth form and is looking forward to starting at Birmingham University in October. During the summer, she starts to look at which student accounts are available. She is surprised to see that they vary so much between different high street banks. To help her decide which account is best, she summarises her findings in a table

Account name	Interest paid on credit (positive balances)	Interest free overdraft and additional overdraft	Charges for unauthorised overdraft	Conditions	Other
Student first	3% on balances between £500 and £3000	Up to £500 in first year increasing to up to £1500 in subsequent years (terms and conditions apply) No additional overdraft	£25 administration £5 daily charge	None	£100 Waterstones voucher Ability to apply for a student credit card
Varsity account	None	Up to £1000 in first 3 years Up to £3000 if studying for a fourth and fifth year	£10 a month penalty plus 8% on outstanding balance	Must pay £250 a month into account	Four year student rail card plus 10% discount on national coach travel
Student sense	1% up to £200 1.5% up to £1000 2% up to £3000	Up to £1500 per year	£35 administration £5 daily charge	Must register for online banking	Three year student rail card Debit card 10% discount on student insurance with same provider
Student ABC	0.5% no upper limit	Up to £1000 in year 1 and £3000 in year 2 and beyond		Must register for online banking Must pay £100 per month into account	£60 cash deposit

Check your knowledge

1 Outline why you think Gabriella should open a student current account.
2 Can you identify which student account is best for Gabriella? Justify your answer.
3 What would be your priorities when choosing a student account?
4 What do you think are the benefits to the banks of offering student accounts?

Managing personal finance

Few businesses have just one product. They have a range of products to meet the needs of different customers. A car manufacturer, such as Ford, will have cars to match different incomes, lifestyles, family size and preferences. This is also true of banks, building societies and other providers of financial services. They will all offer a range of products to match the needs of different individuals. Financial services will include borrowing.

Different types of borrowing

These are outlined below.

▶ Overdraft
  - This allows you to withdraw money that you do not have from a current account.
  - It may be suitable to meet short term needs, for example a shortage of cash just before payday.

▶ Personal loan
  - This gives you the ability to borrow a set amount of money, normally for a specific purpose, to be repaid in regular instalments with interest.
  - It may be suitable to fund the purchase of a high price item such as a car or to make home improvements.

▶ Hire purchase
  - This allows you to have use of an item immediately but pay for it in regular instalments. The item remains the property of the seller until all instalments have been made.
  - It may be suitable for one-off or infrequent purchases, for example a TV or fridge freezer.

▶ Mortgage
  - This is a long-term loan to fund the purchase of assets, normally paid back over a long time, for example 25 years. It is secured against an item, for example a house.
  - It is suitable for assets that will maintain value for a long time and cannot normally be paid for outright.

▶ Credit card
  - Goods are paid for by card and can be paid for either at the end of a set period, normally a month, when a statement is issued or over time with the card provider stating a minimum payment each month. The minimum payment will be a percentage of the balance on the credit card.
  - It may be suitable when buying high price goods or services, for example a holiday, or at times when expenses are higher than usual, for example Christmas, to spread the costs of spending.
  - It may also just be used for convenience and safety as an alternative to using cash.

▶ Payday loan
  - This is a short term source of finance used to bridge the gap between now and next receiving a wage. It will normally only available for relatively small amounts at very high rates.
  - It may be suitable in an emergency to meet cash shortages.

The advantages and drawbacks of the various types of borrowing are summarised in Table 3.4.

▶ **Table 3.4:** Advantages and disadvantages of different types of borrowing

Type of borrowing	Advantages	Disadvantages
Overdraft	Interest is charged only on the amount outstanding Can be paid off without penalties An overdraft facility can be prearranged and only used if needed Provides a short term solution to cash flow problems	When used, interest charges are often high Additional penalty charges for going over a pre-arranged limit are often very high Not the cheapest form of borrowing The ease with which these can be obtained could encourage overspending
Personal loans	Regular, pre-agreed payments make planning and budgeting easy As a general rule these would only be issued to individuals who can prove their ability to make the repayments Useful when looking to purchase a specific item of medium to high value, e.g. a car or home improvement	May have to be secured against an asset which means if payments are missed the asset may be taken to cover the outstanding debt Not really suitable for short term loans
Hire purchase	Spreads the cost of an expensive item over a period of time Credit is secured against a specific item Often allows a customer to afford something now that they could not otherwise afford, e.g. four years' interest free on furniture	Interest charges may be higher than other traditional loans Ownership of the asset may legally be kept by the seller until the final payment is made Agreements can be manipulated to make a purchase seem deceptively appealing
Mortgages	Allows the customer to spread the cost of expensive items over a long period of time, e.g. the purchase of a house is often spread over 25 years Interest rates, depending upon the mortgage deal, can sometimes be fixed or tracked against a standard rate of interest reducing the risk of fluctuations	Interest payments, although sometimes fixed for a short period of time, can vary – this seriously affects the borrower's ability to repay or meet other expenses Failure to meet repayments may lead to a loss of a home and seriously affect an individual's future credit rating Penalties may be applied to early repayment
Credit cards	The credit card holder can pay above the minimum rate if they wish and hence speed up the rate of repayment and reduce interest incurred Can be used for items of multiple sizes and value, to a limit, without the need to secure against an asset Provides some protection on purchases	Can encourage overspending, sometimes on unnecessary purchases, and can lead to debt problems Interest rates are often higher than on a personal loan
Payday loans	Help solve immediate short term cash flow problems Relatively easy to secure	Interest rates are very high and the cumulative amount to be repaid can quickly spiral out of control

Different types of saving and investment

Managing personal finance can also include saving and investment. These options are open to you when you are earning or receiving more money than you need to cover your **expenditure**. Even when income and expenditure are the same or similar, it can be wise to take advantage of opportunities to save and invest to increase future wealth. Different types of investments are outlined below.

▶ Individual savings accounts (ISA)
  This is a type of saving account where the holder is not charged income tax on the interest received.
▶ Deposit and savings accounts
  These are accounts where interest is paid on the balance and normally the holder needs to give notice before withdrawing funds.

▶ In what ways might a new business pay for its office equipment?

Key terms

Expenditure – the amount of money you need to cover all your expenses/outgoings, e.g. your mortgage and bills.

Shareholder – someone who has invested in a company in return for equity, i.e. a share of the business.

▶ Premium bonds
A government sheme that allows individuals to save up to a set amount by buying bonds. The bond holder does not receive interest on their savings but each bond is placed into a regular draw for cash prizes.

▶ Bonds and gilts
These are fixed term securities where the lender (the individual) lends money to companies and governments in return for interest payments. The money is invested for a specified period of time.

▶ Shares
Shares involve investment in a business in return for equity, i.e. the **shareholder** becomes a part owner of the business. The shareholder will receive dividends from the company's profits and will also want the value of the shares to increase.

▶ Pensions
These are long-term savings plans where individuals make regular contributions, called premium payments, throughout their working life. This is then repaid as either a lump sum, regular payments or a combination of the two upon retirement. Pensions can be state, company or private.

The advantages and drawbacks of the different types of savings and investment are summarised in Table 3.5.

▶ **Table 3.5:** Advantages and disadvantages of different types of saving and investment

Type of saving and investment	Advantages	Disadvantages
Individual savings accounts (ISAs)	Tax is not charged on interest earned allowing the saver to keep all of the rewards for saving Interest rates are sometimes slightly higher than in alternative savings accounts	Notice is often required to make withdrawals and according to the agreement there may be a limit set on the number of withdrawals made If the saver makes more withdrawals than set out in the agreement then the penalty may cancel out the tax savings There is a limit set on the annual amount that can be placed in an ISA
Deposit and savings accounts	Interest is earned on positive balances Accounts sometimes require regular deposits of a set amount forcing the saver to follow a savings plan	Interest earned is taxed The percentage rate of interest paid on savings is likely to be lower than interest to be paid on borrowing, therefore the benefits of savings are lost if the customer is borrowing at the same time
Premium bonds	Chance of winning substantially more than could be earned in interest Can be easily withdrawn with no loss or penalty	No guaranteed return on investment Maximum amount reviewed annually by the government The amount invested, assuming zero or low returns, loses value due to inflation
Bonds and gilts	Regular fixed returns Spreads risk across a range of markets	Risk of losing some or all of the value of the investment if the bond or guilt value falls Interest payments may not be received if the issuer is unable to make payments
Shares	Share prices fluctuate offering a potential high reward Shareholders' returns can include dividend payments and an increase in share value As part owners in a business there may be additional benefits including discounts and special offers For some investors share ownership is more than just a way of saving – it is a pastime and creates interest	Share prices fluctuate offering a potential high risk There is no guarantee of any reward or return as all of an investment can be lost

▶ **Table 3.5:** – continued

Pensions	Encourages individuals to save throughout their working life for retirement	Movement between jobs may mean that one policy stops and another starts, thus reducing the overall cumulative value of the savings
	Depending upon the policy, an individual's savings may be boosted by an employer's contributions increasing the final value of the saving	Final outcome is difficult to predict
	Regular payments are deducted, sometimes at source, meaning the individual is tied into making the regular contributions	If compulsory payments are deducted this may affect short-term living standards

PAUSE POINT   Can you explain the difference between saving and investment?

> **Hint**   Draw a concept map about different methods of saving and investment. For each method, weigh up the risk versus the reward and award the method a mark out of with 10, 10 being highest risk and 1 lowest risk.

> **Extend**   Which method of saving or investment do you think offers the lowest risk at the highest reward? Justify your answer.

Risks and rewards of saving versus investment

Saving and investment both involve forfeiting current spending in the hope of gaining greater wealth in the future. **Saving** involves placing any extra money in a secure place where it will hopefully grow as it gains interest. If you are saving your money, it is often with a view to buying a specific good in the future or to support a planned future lifestyle. Many parents will start to save when a child is born to pay future college fees or to support the child as he or she grows up. **Investment** involves making a commitment to a project in the hope that it is successful and a healthy return is made on the investment. This could involve investing in the shares of a business.

The risks and rewards of saving versus investment are summarised in Table 3.6.

Key terms

Saving – placing money in a secure place so that it grows in value and can be used in the future.

Investment – speculative commitment to a business venture in the hope that it generates a financial reward in the future.

▶ **Table 3.6:** Risks and rewards of saving versus investment

	Risks	Rewards
Saving	• Low or zero risk as money saved is guaranteed to be available in the future • Inflation can reduce the spending power of money saved	• Interest payments • Financial security/peace of mind
Investment	• Investments can go wrong and all or some of the value may be lost • No guarantee of a return	• If successful, there is potential for a high financial return (significantly higher than could be earned in interest) • Can be exciting! Some people will invest in shares, antiques, art or foreign currencies, for example, in the hope of high returns

Research

Work in pairs. You have £2500 and must invest or save it for at least five years.

• Mind map all the options – showing risk versus potential rewards.
• Identify your preferred saving method. Find an account that offers the highest return.

How much would your savings be worth in five years?

You read about a new form of investment called crowd funding. Visit one of these websites as part of your research.

• Choose one or more businesses to invest in. Calculate your expected return on your £2500 in five years' time.
• Present your saving and investment options to the rest of the class.
• As a class, try to reach an agreement on what would be the best use of the money.

Key terms

Insurance – an agreement with a third party to provide compensation against financial loss in line with the conditions laid down in the policy agreement.

Premiums – regular payments made by an individual or company to an insurance provider in return for protection.

Different types of insurance products: their features, advantages and disadvantages

Insurance is a form of protection. Specific items as well as individuals and pets can be insured. Insurance policies cover the cost of loss, damage or illness up to prearranged levels in return for regular payments called **premiums**. Figure 3.2 illustrates some of the different types of insurance that are available.

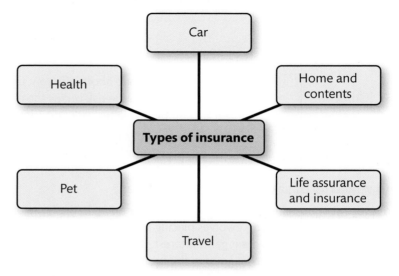

▶ **Figure 3.2:** What items of worth do you have insured? Is your mobile phone insured?

Insurance can be taken out against anything deemed to have a worth or where there is a risk of financial loss. A common type of insurance now is against mobile devices such as your mobile phone. The premium paid will vary depending upon the amount of cover provided and the amount of risk as assessed by the insurance provider. Types of insurance are outlined below.

▶ Car
  - It is a legal requirement to insure any car that is on the road – this covers theft as well as accidents.
  - The degree of cover will vary depending upon whether the policy is third party or fully comprehensive.
  - It protects the driver, passengers and other road users.

▶ Home and contents
  - Home insurance covers the physical building, for example against fire.
  - Contents insurance covers the physical items in the house including electrical equipment, furniture and personal items. If there are individual items of high value, for example a diamond ring, then they may need to be specified on the policy.
  - Items can be insured when a person is using them away from home as well as when inside the house.

▶ Life assurance and insurance
  - Life assurance is an ongoing policy to pay a lump sum upon death.
  - Life insurance is a policy for a set period of time to pay a lump sum if you die within that time period.
  - Mortgage lenders often insist upon life insurance for the same period as the mortgage to secure repayment of the mortgage if the holder dies while monies are still owed.

- ▶ Travel
  - This protects individuals or groups while abroad. Policies can be purchased to cover a specific trip, multiple trips or for all trips within a year.
  - Cover will generally include loss or theft of property, illness, cancellation and emergencies up to predetermined limits.
  - Specific types of holiday or activities, for example skiing or extreme sports, will require additional cover due to the high level of risk associated.
- ▶ Pet
  - This protects the owners of pets against some or all of the expenses associated with treating ill or injured pets, i.e. vets' fees.
- ▶ Health
  - This covers individuals, families or employees against medical expenses including assessments, treatments and loss of earnings.
  - In the UK the National Health Service provides free medical care but individuals may wish to take out insurance to receive payments if, for example, time is spent in hospital, or to receive private treatment.
  - Health insurance can include payment plans to cover routine visits such as to the dentist or optician with a percentage of expenses paid.

The pros and cons of different types of insurance are summarised in Table 3.7.

▶ **Table 3.7:** Advantages and disadvantages of different types of insurance

Type of insurance	Advantages	Disadvantages
Car	Meets legal requirements Protects self against theft or damage Protects against damage caused to a third party	Premiums can be high depending upon assessed level of risk, e.g. expensive for young drivers Normally there is an excess that must be paid, e.g. first £500 of all damages is still the responsibility of the car owner
Home and contents	Protects against damage which may otherwise be too expensive to repair resulting in the loss of a home Contents are protected both when inside the house and outside	Premiums are an additional expense to home ownership Some items cannot be replaced due to a value beyond the financial worth, e.g. a painting or inherited piece of jewellery
Life assurance and insurance	Provides peace of mind to family following the bereavement of a homeowner	If the policy holder does not die within the period of life insurance no payment is made (could be seen as an advantage!)
Travel	Provides protection for personal belongings when away from home Covers medical costs when on holiday Protects against cancellation and sometimes delays	The person suffering the loss is likely to have to pay upfront to replace items or cover medical costs and then reclaim later An additional cost when travelling abroad
Pet	Avoids expensive vet fees If vet fees are too high, there may be no alternative to having the pet put down – insurance can avoid this	An additional monthly expense to protect against the unexpected
Health	Some compensation is provided when ill which can reduce the financial burden and stress allowing the patient to concentrate on recovery rather than financial worries If used to fund private care, this often results in quicker treatment and better facilities	Paying for something that you hope you will not use Premiums can be expensive depending upon the degree of cover required Will not cover pre-known conditions

Insurance is big business

Members of the general public are likely to protect their home, their home's contents, their car and maybe their health or pet. For celebrities, it seems they protect a whole lot more. Sporting stars can insure against damage to limbs which would ultimately lead to a huge loss of earnings. When Christiano Ronaldo played for

Real Madrid the club obviously felt his legs were an asset worth protecting and insured his legs for £90 million in 2013.

The music business also sees professionals insuring their voice, hands or other body parts. Jennifer Lopez, for example, insured her bottom to the sum of £180 million while Mariah Carey insured her legs for up to £1 billion. Following his role as James Bond, Daniel Craig insured his body for £6 million; not to be outdone, Joey Essex insured his hair for £1 million.

Check your knowledge

1   Outline why the general public are likely to insure their homes and content.

2   Outline why celebrities are willing to take out insurance policies worth such high amounts.

3   What would be the benefit to Real Madrid of Christian Ronaldo being insured?

4   Explain why insurance companies would be willing to issue these types of insurance policies.

Assessment practice 3.1

1   Identify **two** disadvantages of using a credit cards. (2 marks)

2   Describe **two** examples of a type of borrowing. (4 marks)

3   Describe the likely financial needs and implications of a person in the young adult stage of the life cycle. (6 marks)

Bethany and Mark have inherited some money from their grandfather. Bethany wants to save the money for future use so that she has something to rely on while Mark thinks that he will make the best use of his money if he invests it.

4   Assess the risks and rewards of saving versus investment. (12 marks)

 B   Explore the personal finance sector

Features of financial institutions

Financial institutions are organisations that offer financial services to individuals and/or businesses. These services include the ability to deposit or withdraw money, obtain credit and make investments, as well as offering advice on matters of personal and business finance.

Types of organisations and their advantages and disadvantages are outlined below.

▶ Bank of England
  - This is the UK's central bank with responsibility for maintaining a healthy level of financial stability for the UK as a whole.
  - Responsibilities include issuing legal tender, setting interest rates and controlling the national debt.

▶ Banks
  - A bank is an organisation that handles financial transactions and stores money on behalf of its customers.
  - Services offered will include holding deposits, making payments when instructed to do so and supplying credit.

▶ Building societies
  - These are organisations that handle financial transactions and store money on behalf of their members.
  - The members, or account holders, are part owners of the building society and have a right to vote and receive information on the running of the society.
  - Unlike banks they do not have shareholders on a stock exchange which allows costs to be kept down.

▶ Credit unions
  - These are not-for-profit organisations that handle financial transactions and store money on behalf of their members.
  - Often there is a responsibility or desire to support a community made up of its members.
  - Members are the owners and have a voting right.

▶ National Savings and Investments
  - This is a government-backed organisation that offers a secure saving option.
  - It offers a range of options including ISAs, premium bonds and gilts and bonds.

▶ Insurance companies
  - These are businesses that protect against the risk of loss in return for a premium.
  - They are profit-making organisations.

▶ Pension companies
  - These are businesses that sell policies to individuals, either privately or through employers, to allow them to save now to fund retirement in the future.
  - Pension companies normally invest the money paid to them in contributions in order to increase its value. However this is not risk free.

▶ Pawnbrokers
  - These are businesses or individuals who loan money against the security of a personal asset, for example an item of jewellery or piece of electronic equipment.
  - If the item is not bought back from the pawnbroker within a specified period of time then it will be sold on.

▶ Payday loans
  - These are organisations that offer a short-term source of finance used to bridge the gap between now and next receiving a wage; they are normally only available for relatively small amounts at very high rates.
  - They may be suitable in an emergency to meet cash shortages.

The pros and cons of different financial institutions are summarised in Table 3.8.

▶ Table 3.8: Advantages and disadvantages of types of financial institution

Type of organisation	Advantages	Disadvantages
Bank of England	Responsible for protecting the financial stability of the economy as a whole Sets interest rates at a level designed to help achieve a stable economy Lends to banks	Not a bank for members of the general public Can raise interest rates making borrowing more expensive
Banks	Offer a range of services and account types Provide a secure place to store money Pay interest on credit balances on most types of accounts	Savings are only protected up to the value of £75,000, so if a bank goes bankrupt savings above this would be lost Profit-making organisations owned by shareholders, therefore costs to individuals may be higher than necessary in order to fulfil shareholder objectives
Building societies	Offer a range of services and account types Provide a secure place to store money Pay interest on credit balances on most types of accounts Owned by members and therefore costs can be kept down allowing for higher interest payments	Savings are only protected up to the value of £75,000, so if a building society goes bankrupt savings above this would be lost May lack the business drive of a commercial bank
Credit unions	Offer a range of services and account types Provide a secure place to store money Owned by members and therefore costs can be kept down allowing for higher interest payments Often offer additional benefits to the community or a good cause	Savings are only protected up to the value of £75,000, so if a credit union goes bankrupt savings above this would be lost May lack the business drive of a commercial bank
National Savings and Investment	Government-backed, therefore offering security on 100% of savings with no upper limit Offers additional services/methods of savings, e.g. premium bonds	Rates are variable Not as easy to access due to lack of a high street presence Often required to give notice on withdrawals
Insurance companies	Protect against unexpected losses or financial expenses Easy and regular monthly payments make planning easy Wide range of services and levels of cover to suit the needs of individuals	Premiums are assessed on the estimated degree of risk which may be seen to penalise some members or groups of society too harshly Profit-making organisations, therefore premiums will be charged to ensure shareholder needs are met
Pension companies	Provides a structure to help plan for financial security after retirement Deductions can be taken directly from pay and be fully or partially matched by an employer's contribution Experts are employed to make investment decisions	Poor investment decisions by the pension company may result in a disappointing return Money already invested in a pension cannot be released prior to the dates agreed in the policy
Pawnbrokers	A quick way of acquiring cash needed for a short period of time The asset can be brought back within a set period of time Interest is not charged	The amount given for the asset is often substantially lower than its actual worth If the money is not repaid within the agreed period, the asset will be sold on
Payday loans	A quick way of acquiring cash needed for a short period of time	Interest charges are likely to be very high Often results in paying back a final sum substantially higher than the initial amount borrowed

▶ A pawnbroker's business can thrive during times of financial hardship. How do you feel about this?

Communicating with customers

Traditionally, banking was carried out face to face where there was a personal relationship between the bank manager and clerk and the customer. The bank manager was seen as a figure of authority in the community. Over time, this relationship has become less common and, as banking organisations have grown, the service has become less personal.

Changes in technology have also changed the way in which the banking industry operates.

Discussion

In small groups, discuss how technology changes have affected how banking operates. As a whole group, discuss whether these changes have had a positive or negative impact on banking. Consider this from the point of view of employees, banks, customers (of different ages) and other businesses. Think about whether this has affected other industries or just banking. Think of examples.

Methods of interacting with customers include:
▶ branch:
  • physical places where the customer will visit to carry out transactions which can be face to face, for example over the counter transactions or using computerised facilities, such as automatic teller machines (ATM)
  • offer additional facilities and services such as advice.
▶ online banking:
  • the use of the internet to carry out banking transactions.
▶ telephone banking:
  • when transactions are carried out over the telephone.
▶ mobile banking:
  • the use of mobile devices such as mobile phones and tablets to conduct financial transactions.
▶ postal banking:
  • the use of the postal service to carry out paper-based financial transactions.

The pros and cons of different ways of interacting with customers are summarised in Table 3.9.

▶ **Table 3.9:** The advantages and disadvantages of different methods of interacting with customers

Method	Advantages	Disadvantages
Branch	Opportunity to build a relationship developing trust and brand loyalty Transactions can be conducted there and then Additional services such as advice can be offered Gives the customer a high level of confidence	Need to travel to a branch which is likely to incur travel costs, e.g. parking or fares for public transport Restricted to bank opening hours May be long queues plus travel time, making the process time consuming
Online banking	Available 24/7 High degree of privacy Convenient	Takes time at the beginning to set up or apply for Not suitable for cash withdrawals Increased risk due to cyber crime If just an online account, the facilities may be limited
Telephone banking	Convenient, especially to access basic functions such as checking a balance No additional charges	Full access may be limited to set hours Call centres and automated telephone systems can frustrate customers Higher risk of fraud and identity theft
Mobile banking	Convenient Available 24/7 No additional charges	May need to download specific apps to access mobile banking for a particular bank Higher security risk due to increased risk of loss or theft of mobile devices Can be prone to hackers sending texts asking for bank details
Postal banking	Traditional method that many customers will feel comfortable with Does not require any additional technology or devices	Can be slow due to the postal system Post can get lost

Consumer protection in relation to personal finance

There are laws and organisations responsible for protecting the rights of consumers. In relation to personal finance, they are there to help ensure that the consumer is not treated unfairly or exploited. The following organisations and laws are concerned with protecting consumer rights.

▶ Financial Conduct Authority (FCA)
  - The FCA is an independent organisation with a remit to regulate the actions of providers of financial services.
  - It is funded by membership fees charged to financial service providers.
  - The organisation's work focuses on three key areas:
    - authorisation – permitting financial service providers to trade
    - supervision – ensuring procedures and practices are in the interest of the consumer
    - enforcement – using powers to ensure standards are maintained.
▶ Financial Ombudsmen Service (FOS)
  - The FOS is an organisation appointed by the government to represent the interests of the consumer in disputes with financial service providers.
  - It is funded by compulsory fees charged to all regulated financial institutions plus additional fees when actions are taken against an institution.
  - The FOS becomes involved in disputes only if they cannot be satisfactorily sorted between the consumer and the financial institution prior to involving the FOS.

▶ Financial Services Compensation Scheme (FSCS)
- The FSCS is the organisation in the UK that will pay compensation to a consumer of financial services if the service provider is unable to.
- The FSCS, for example, protects all savers in banks and building societies up to £5,000, i.e. if the financial institution goes bankrupt the savings will be refunded by the FSCS.

▶ Office of Fair Trading (OFT)
- The OFT is a government organisation that was established to regulate all markets, including financial markets.
- The OFT's aim was to encourage fair practices and healthy competition between financial institutions.
- Since 2014 responsibility for financial institutions has been passed to the FCA.

▶ Legislation: consumer credit
- These are laws passed by the UK government to enforce the regulation of any firm offering credit to consumers.
- Any firm offering credit, for example leasing, hire purchase agreements or credit cards, must be registered with the FCA.

▶ How confident are you that your savings are safe in the bank?

Research

Visit the websites below to carry out research on the roles and responsibilities of these organisations and consumer credit laws.

www.fca.org.uk/

www.financial-ombudsman.org.uk/

www.fscs.org.uk/

www.gov.uk/offering-credit-consumers-law

Do you think that it is necessary for the government and other organisations to regulate financial institutions? Or should they be trusted to self-regulate?

Information guidance and advice

Personal finance is a complicated matter and it is important to all individuals. There are a number of government-funded and independent organisations which offer guidance and advice to individuals on personal finance. These are outlined below.

▶ Citizens Advice
- This is an organisation, run by charities, that offers advice on a wide range of issues both financial and non-financial.
- Advice is offered at physical centres as well as online and via email and telephones.
- Financial advice covers areas including, debt, benefits, banking, pensions and insurance.

- Independent financial advisor (IFA)
  - IFAs are professionals who offer independent advice to their clients on financial matters including savings, investments, mortgages and pensions.
- Price comparison websites
  - These websites collate prices for similar goods and services within an industry allowing consumers to make comparisons easily and find the best deals.
- Money advice service
  - This is a government organisation set up to offer free and impartial financial advice in the UK.
- Debt counsellors
  - This is a professional who offers independent advice on how best to manage debt.
- Individual Voluntary Arrangements (IVAs) bankruptcy
  - This is a government organisation that allows an individual to declare themselves bankrupt while agreeing to pay all or part of the money they owe to creditors through an insolvency practitioner.
  - Regular payments are made to the insolvency practitioner who then spreads this across the creditors deciding how much to pay each one.

The pros and cons of different providers of financial information and guidance are summarised in Table 3.10.

▶ **Table 3.10:** Advantages and disadvantages of different providers of financial information and guidance

Provider	Advantages	Disadvantages
Citizens Advice	Free service Offers face to face as well as online and telephone advice Wide range of areas covered	Trained volunteers are not necessarily professionals in financial issues and therefore knowledge may be limited
Independent financial advisor (IFA)	Advice is offered by professionals in the field Services offered are regulated by the FCA and FOS Advisers will take time to understand an individual's full financial situation	Services will be charged for Advice offered is not guaranteed to be 100% up to date or unbiased
Price comparison websites	Easy to access 24/7 Free service	Not guaranteed to be 100% up to date, accurate or unbiased Do not always cover all of the available options Potential for bias
Money advice service	Government-funded therefore advice is free and impartial Covers a wide range of financial matters	Advice is only available online or over the telephone – no physical presence Can take time to find and understand the exact advice that is being searched for Advice can be generic rather than personal
Debt counsellors	Advice is offered by a professional who specialises in debt management Services offered are regulated by the FCA and FOS	Services will be charged for Advice will focus just on debt management rather than the whole package of financial concerns
Individual Voluntary Arrangements (IVAs) bankruptcy	Helps manage debt repayment with regular payments making budgeting easier Independent advice, without bias	Set up and handling fees are charged for the service Will affect future credit ratings

Assessment practice 3.2

1 Describe the role of the Financial Conduct Authority.   (2 marks)

2 Identify **two** disadvantages of online banking.   (2 marks)

3 Explain **two** advantages of building societies.   (4 marks)

Bethany is still not sure what to do with her inheritance money. She has tried researching online but is overwhelmed by the amount of information available.

4 Discuss the different sources of financial information and guidance that Bethany could use.   (12 marks)

 C # Understand the purpose of accounting

It is impossible to truly understand how a business operates without some knowledge of the accounting process. You may be familiar with the expression 'a picture paints a thousand words' – in business you can adapt this to 'numbers paint a thousand words'. Anyone who wants to understand how well a business is performing – such as the owner, an employee or a potential investor – is likely to turn straight to its accounts. However good a business idea might be, if the owner does not keep a careful eye on the business's accounts, it is almost certain to be doomed to failure.

Purpose of accounting

Accounting involves the recording of **financial transactions**, planned or actual, and the use of these figures to produce financial information. In this first section, you will look at a number of reasons why accounting is important to business success.

Record transactions

Keeping business records accurate and up to date is important for the smooth running of a business. The business owner or a bookkeeper must record all of the money coming into the business (from sales) and all of the money going out, such as expenses. If a business fails to do this it may find itself not chasing payments, forgetting to pay bills or, even more seriously, in trouble with **HM Revenue & Customs (HMRC)**. If the business does not record its transactions correctly, it cannot report its financial performance accurately and therefore tax payments may be wrong.

Management of the business

A manager is responsible for the planning, monitoring and controlling of the resources for which they are responsible. A manager who clearly understands the business's accounts will be better able to make informed decisions and plan for the future. Management of a business involves careful coordination of resources including staff, materials, stock and money. The manager must ensure there are sufficient funds to pay wages, order new stock, pay bills and meet other demands for cash outflows by balancing this with the money coming in from sales.

Compliance

Financial reporting is governed by laws and regulations. This is to ensure that any financial records give a fair and accurate picture of the business. It is important that businesses comply with these laws and regulations in order to ensure that investors

Key terms

Financial transactions – actions by a business that involve money either going into or out of a business – for example, making a sale or paying a bill.

HM Revenue & Customs (HMRC) – HM is an abbreviation for Her (or His) Majesty's, and the HMRC is a British government department responsible for the collection of all types of taxes.

Key term

Fraud – when an individual acquires company money for personal gain, through illegal actions.

Key terms

Profit – surplus achieved when total revenue (income) from sales is higher than the total costs of a business.

Loss – shortfall suffered when total revenue from sales is lower than the total costs of a business.

Gross profit – sales revenue minus cost of goods sold (the cost of the actual materials used to produce the quantity of goods sold).

Sales revenue – quantity sold multiplied by the selling price.

Net profit – gross profit minus other expenses, for example, rent and advertising.

and other stakeholders are not misinformed. Compliance will also help protect against fraud. **Fraud** is when company monies are used inappropriately or acquired by the wrong person for personal gain.

▸ What are the main purposes of these laws and regulations?

▸ How do the reporting requirements vary between organisations?

▸ Why do you think it is important for financial reporting to be regulated?

Research

In pairs research the laws and regulations that govern financial reporting in the UK. Some useful websites to get you started are:

www.gov.uk/guidance/audit-accounting-and-reporting-guidance-for-uk-companies

www.frc.org.uk/

www.icaew.com/en/technical/financial-reporting/other-reporting-issues/other-uk-regulation.

Measuring performance

Without financial records it would be impossible to know if the business was making a **profit** or a **loss**, or whether or not the business was owed money or was in debt to others.

Throughout this unit, you will consider how a business can measure its financial performance and what actions it can take to improve its performance. Key indicators of financial performance include:

▸ **gross profit** – this is the amount of profit left after the cost of producing the good or service is deducted from the amount of **sales revenue**

▸ **net profit** – this is the smaller amount of profit made after all other expenses are deducted from the gross profit

▸ value owed to the business – this is the amount of money owed to the business from sales that have not yet been paid for

▸ value owed by the business – this is the amount of money the business owes to others for goods or services purchased but not yet paid for.

▸ Why is it important to keep a close eye on a business's financial affairs?

Control

Accounting will control the flow of money into and out of the business by maintaining accurate records and monitoring performance. This should mean that any unusual activity is spotted, helping to prevent fraud. It will also, therefore, track the amount of money the business is owed, **trade receivables**, from the sale of goods and the amount the business owes, **trade payables**. This will help ensure that the business can meet its day-to-day expenses. If trade receivables and payables are not carefully controlled, there is a danger that the business may not be able to survive. This will also involve credit control which aims to ensure that all money owed to the business is paid on time.

Types of income

Income is money coming into the business. There are two categories of income:

▶ capital income

▶ revenue income.

Capital income

Capital income is the money invested by the owners or other investors that is used to set up a business or buy additional equipment. It tends to be used to buy things that will stay in the business for a medium-to-long period of time – for example, premises, vehicles or equipment. These are called **fixed assets**. When setting up a business, capital income might also be used to buy opening stock, but, as the business develops, stock should be paid for by sales income. The sources of capital income available to business owners are influenced by the type of business.

Loans

A loan is an amount of money lent to the business or business owner(s) from a bank or other financial institution. It is a lump sum that then has to be paid back at a set amount per month over the period of the loan, often five years, although longer-term loans can be agreed. As well as the repayment of the loan, there will be a monthly interest repayment. This is the amount of money the bank is charging for the loan as a percentage of the amount borrowed. The interest rate can be fixed or it may vary with changes in the economy. It is the interest payable on top of the loan that makes a loan a relatively expensive source of capital income. Monthly payments have to be made even if the business is not making a profit.

Banks are not guaranteed to lend money to a business, so the business would have to justify how the money borrowed would be spent and, more importantly, how they can afford to repay it. Often bank loans have to be secured against an **asset** (for example, the entrepreneur's home or the company's vehicles) to convince the bank that the risk being taken is not too great. This means that if the business fails to meet payments, the bank can claim the asset.

Mortgages

A mortgage is similar to a bank loan, but it tends to be for a larger sum of money and over a longer period of time (typically 25 years). Mortgages are always secured on an asset, normally a property. Individuals will take out a mortgage to buy a house. Businesses might take out a mortgage to buy their premises – for example, a factory, retail store or warehouse.

Shares

A business becomes a company when it is registered with Companies House and issues shares to its shareholders. The shareholders are the owners of the business and all contribute towards the capital income. Shareholders normally receive a voting right

Key terms

Trade receivables – money owed to the business from sales made but not yet paid for.

Trade payables – money the business owes from supplies purchased but not yet paid for.

Key term

Fixed assets – items of value owned by a business that are likely to stay in the business for more than one year – for example, machinery. Also known as non-current assets.

Key term

Asset – any item of value owned by an individual or firm.

and the more shares they own, the greater their ability to influence decision making. Shareholders are rewarded for their investment by the payment of a dividend; this is a share of the profits.

Owner's capital

Owner's capital is money invested in a business from the owner's personal savings. A sole trader is a person who owns a business on their own; they therefore have to find all of the capital income from their own sources or personal loans. Sole traders often invest their personal savings into the business or borrow from the bank using their personal assets, such as their house, to secure the loan. This investment is a big risk for a sole trader, as they are ultimately responsible for the debts of the business. Being a sole trader can also limit the amount of money available and can therefore restrict the size of the business. However, if successful, the sole trader can keep all of the profits for themselves.

A partnership is when two or more people join together to set up a business as partners. Each partner would be expected to contribute towards the capital income, so increasing the potential amount of money available. Partners also share decision making and the profit. In most partnerships, any loans taken out are still secured by the partners' own assets, so this is still quite a high-risk option.

Debentures

Debentures are medium- to long-term sources of capital income. Large companies often use them to secure income. Interest is payable, normally at a fixed rate, and the debenture is repaid as a lump sum, normally on a pre-agreed date. Debentures can be secured against an asset.

Revenue income

As you have already seen, capital income is the money invested in the business to set it up or later buy additional assets; it is a long-term investment. Revenue income is the money that comes into the business from performing its day-to-day function – selling goods or providing a service. The nature of the revenue income depends on the activities that the business does to bring in money.

Sales

Sales, or sales turnover, is money coming in from the sales of goods or services. For example, a jeans shop has money coming in each time a customer buys a pair of jeans, or a hairdresser receives money each time a customer has a haircut. Sales turnover is therefore determined by the prices charged and the number of customers.

Sales can be either: cash sales (the customer pays there and then) or credit sales (the customer buys then but pays at a later date).

The significance of the difference between cash and credit sales will become clear later on when you learn about cash flow.

Rent received

A business that owns property and charges others for use of all or part of that property will receive rent as their main source of income. If a business owns a house and rents out three rooms, then it will receive rent from each of these renters. Similarly, a business may own land or offices which it rents out to other businesses.

Commission received

A business may sell products or services as an agent of another business. They sell another business's products on their behalf and, for each sale they make, they get paid a percentage on that sale. This percentage is called **commission**.

Key term

Commission – A commission is a fee paid to a salesperson in exchange for services in facilitating or completing a sales transaction. Commission could be a flat fee or a percentage of the revenue, gross margin or profit generated by the sale. It could also be charged by brokers to assist in the sale of security, properties, etc.

If, for example, you were to buy tickets for a concert from www.ticketmaster.co.uk, then Ticketmaster would receive a percentage payment for that ticket from whichever company was hosting the concert.

Interest received

Interest received is money earned on savings or lending. If, for example, a business has a positive bank balance it will receive interest on this. This acts as revenue coming into the business. Equally a business may lend money to another person or business. Interest will be charged to the lender and the business lending the money will receive interest as a form of revenue.

Discount received

Discount received is when a business is given a percentage off a sale, normally in return for quick payment or a bulk order. This reduces the costs to the business.

❙❙ PAUSE POINT

Can you explain, with the use of examples, the difference between capital income and revenue income?

Hint — Close the book and draw a concept map about the classifications of income. Think about how often income is coming into the business and what it is likely to be used for.

Extend — Can you explain how capital income can lead to revenue income in a number of scenarios?

Types of expenditure

Expenditure is money spent by a business and can be split into two categories: capital expenditure and revenue expenditure. You are going to start by looking at capital expenditure. This is used to buy **capital items**, which are assets that will stay in the business for a long period of time. Capital items are non-current assets and intangible assets, as explained below.

Capital expenditure

Non-current assets

Non-current assets are items owned by a business that will remain in the business for a reasonable period of time. These are shown on a business's **statement of financial position** (or balance sheet) and include land and premises, machinery and equipment, vehicles, and fixtures and fittings. These are sometimes referred to as 'tangible assets' because they can be touched.

Most fixed assets lose value over time and for this reason they are depreciated. This means that each year their value on the balance sheet is reduced in order to give a fair value of the asset.

Intangibles

An intangible asset is something owned by the business that cannot be touched but adds value to the business. Here are four common intangibles that exist within businesses.

▶ Goodwill – when you buy an existing business, its name and reputation will already be known, and it may already have an established customer base or set of clients. This increases the value of the business and therefore increases the selling price of the business. A sum of money is added to the value of the business to reflect the value of this goodwill. However, goodwill is difficult to place a figure on – how much would you pay for a recognised brand business name?

Key terms

Capital items – assets bought from capital expenditure such as machinery and vehicles that will stay in the business for more than a year.

Statement of financial situation – a financial document that shows the net worth of a business by balancing its assets against its liabilities. It is often called a balance sheet.

- ▶ Patents – a patent is the legal protection of an invention, such as a unique feature of a product or a new process. An entrepreneur or business may patent their idea to stop others from copying the idea. Having a patent allows the business to exploit this in the future by launching an innovative product at a premium (more expensive) selling price. The patent itself must, therefore, be worth something, but again it is difficult to know exactly how much value to place on it.
- ▶ Trademarks – a trademark is a symbol, logo, brand name, words or even colour that sets apart one business's goods or services from those of its competitors. Trademarks can be a key influence on consumer choice and build a strong brand loyalty. A trademark, therefore, is of value to a business and consequently recorded as an intangible asset.
- ▶ Brand name – a feature of a business that is recognised by customers and distinguishes the business from competitors. Customers will link the brand name to expectations based on previous experiences with the brand. It is sometimes said that a brand name is a promise of what to expect.

Case study

Colour wars

When Stelios Haji-Ioannou, founder of easyJet, launched easyMobile in 2004 he planned to launch the brand with their signature colour of orange. However, Orange, a competitor in the mobile phone market, had already trademarked the colour orange in relation to 'telecommunications products and services'.

Orange, the company, felt that two mobile phone companies using the same colour would cause confusion to customers and wanted to protect their

customers' best interests. Orange had trademarked a specific shade of orange, but Haji-Ioannou felt that Orange had no case and that easyMobile had the right to use any colour they wished.

The case eventually went to court, but easyMobile ended mobile phone service in 2006 and so it was never brought to a resolution.

The European Court of Justice confirmed in 2003 that colours could be trademarked but that they had to be identified by a colour code (such as Pantone), not just a sample of colour. Other colour trademarks include Heinz's distinctive turquoise cans and Cadbury Schweppes plc's famous shade of purple.

Check your knowledge

1 Should Orange be able to stop a competitor from using a specific colour? Justify your answer.

2 Why might it be important to show a value for these trademarks in a business's accounts?

3 How would you go about attaching a monetary value to these trademarks?

Revenue expenditure

Revenue expenditure is spending on items on a day-to-day or regular basis. These are the expenses incurred by a business that are shown on the profit and loss account (also known as a statement of comprehensive income). The types of costs incurred vary from business to business.

Inventory

Most businesses providing a good or service will require some sort of inventory, whether it is raw materials, finished goods to sell on or supplies to provide the service

– for example, shampoo and conditioner for a hairdresser. When a business is first set up, it is likely to have to buy inventory with cash as it will not have built a reputation as being trustworthy and able to pay. As a business becomes more established, it may be able to buy inventory on credit (such as receiving the inventory and paying 30 days later). Bigger and more established businesses may also be able to drive the cost of inventory down as they will buy in larger quantities. There are other costs related to inventory, such as insurance and storage costs.

Rent

This is the cost of using premises not owned by the business. These are regular payments, usually monthly, for the use of premises.

Rates

In the same way as private residents pay council tax to the local authority, businesses pay non-domestic rates. This is a sum of money paid to the local council to go towards services such as street lights and refuse collection. This is not a set amount, but is calculated by the council based on the size and location of the premises and the nature of the business.

Heating and lighting

This covers payments for services such as gas and electricity. The business will receive regular bills, often quarterly (every three months) for the provision and use of these services.

Water

This involves payment for the supply of water to premises and use of water. This can be a fixed rate or based upon usage if a water meter is fitted.

Insurance

A business is legally required to take out a number of types of insurance to protect itself from the possibility of serious losses. These include:

▶ buildings insurance – to protect the physical building from damage that may be caused by events such as fire

▶ contents insurance – to protect what is inside the building in terms of machinery, fixtures and fittings and stock from damage that may be caused by events such as flooding

▶ public liability insurance – to protect people within the building who may be harmed or injured from an event such as an accident

▶ employers' liability insurance – this means that if the employee is injured at work, the business is protected against any claims for compensation or any legal costs incurred.

Administration

Administration refers to the paperwork that goes on within a business either internally between employees or externally with suppliers and customers. Administrative costs include items such as postage, printing and stationery, which might include items such as business cards, headed paper and order books.

Telephone charges are also classed as an administrative cost and are slightly unusual from an accounting point of view. For a landline, these costs are split into two: there is the line rental cost, which is paid quarterly in advance and then the call charges, which are paid quarterly after use.

Salaries

A salary is an annual figure paid to an employee divided into equal monthly payments. For example, a trainee accountant may have a salary of £18,000 per year, meaning their gross pay is £1500 per month. The employee will then have to pay National Insurance, tax and maybe pension contributions on this figure, so the amount they actually take home will be quite a bit less. For the business, however, the actual amount they have to pay (the real cost to the business) is higher. On a salary of £18,000 the business also has to pay employers' National Insurance of 12.8 per cent, (an additional £2304) plus any pension and other benefits.

Wages

A wage is an hourly rate paid to an employee, meaning there is a direct link between the number of hours worked and the amount of money paid. Paying a wage rather than a salary allows greater flexibility for both the employer and the employee, but also creates greater uncertainty.

Link

The minimum wage is covered in more detail in *Unit 8: Recruitment and Selection Process.*

> **Research**
>
> Employers in the UK, by law, have to pay a minimum wage to all employees over 16. From April 2016 a National Living Wage will be introduced for workers over 25.
>
> What is the current minimum wage in the UK?
>
> Should business pay a National living wage? Debate the arguments for and against introducing the living wage.

Marketing

This covers a whole range of costs associated with attracting the customer and convincing them to make a purchase. Possible marketing costs might include advertisements, promotional literature, promotional events, point of sale materials and so on.

Bank charges

Unlike personal banking, which is generally free, banks charge businesses for each transaction that takes place, for example, every time a cheque is paid in or written, whenever cash is deposited, and so on. Banks might offer free banking to businesses for the first year as a marketing technique, but, once the first year is over, bank charges can soon start to add up to quite a large amount of money.

Interest paid

If the business has a bank loan or a mortgage, then interest will be charged on this. Banks may offer big businesses preferential rates if they are confident that the money will be paid back and if they want to keep that particular business as a loyal customer. Big businesses will carry out a lot of transactions and pay high bank charges, so, for the bank, it may be worth offering lower interest rates to keep them happy.

Key term

Depreciation – an accounting technique used to spread the cost of an asset over its useful life.

Depreciation

Assets lose value over time. Accountants use depreciation to spread out the cost of an asset over its useful life. **Depreciation** is a paper exercise to match the cost of an asset against the time it is used within a business. For example, if a machine is purchased at a cost of £50,000 this would not be shown as a one-off expense at the time of purchase but in the accounts shown as an expense of £10,000 per year. You will learn about two types of depreciation in more detail later in this unit:

▸ straight-line depreciation: an asset is depreciated by a set amount each year

▸ reducing balance depreciation: an asset is depreciated by a set percentage of its remaining value each year.

Discount allowed

Reductions offered to customers are an expense to a business as it reduces the amount of cash flowing into the business. Discounts may be allowed to attract customers, for bulk purchases or to gain a competitive advantage.

▸ When a business offers a discount on its products, are you encouraged to buy?

 PAUSE POINT   Can you explain, with the use of examples, the difference between capital expenditure and revenue expenditure? Close the book and draw a concept map about the classifications of expenditure.

> Hint   Think about the frequency with which the expenditure is going out of the business and what it is being used for.

> Extend   Can you think of any examples where short-term capital expenditure may reduce long-term revenue expenditure?

Assessment practice 3.3

1 Identify **one** intangible asset.   (1 mark)
2 Identify **two** sources of revenue income.   (2 marks)
3 Outline what is meant by 'depreciation'.   (2 marks)

D | Select and evaluate different sources of business finance

Sources of finance

As discussed earlier, businesses need finance for a wide number of reasons, both to fund capital and revenue expenditure. The source of finance is where this money comes from. What the money will be used for will determine which source is the most suitable. For example, you might look for a long-term bank loan or mortgage to fund capital expenditure such as buying a factory, but this would not be appropriate for replenishing stock. Sources of finance can be short term or long term. Short term means they have to be paid back in one year, and long term means in a period of time greater than one year.

Internal sources of finance are those available from within a business. These include:
▸ retained profit
  • profit (sales revenue minus total costs) kept in the business to fund future expenditure.
▸ net current assets
  • current assets minus current liabilities shows the money available in the business to fund day-to-day expenditure.
▸ sale of assets
  • selling an item of worth owned by a business in order to achieve an immediate cash injection.

> **Key term**
>
> **Internal sources of finance** – money available to fund expenditure from within the business.

The pros and cons of internal sources of finance are summarised in Table 3.11.

▶ **Table 3.11:** Advantages and disadvantages of internal sources of finance

Internal source of finance	Advantages	Disadvantages
Retained profit	No interest charges Available immediately Only available up to the amount already accumulated by the business and therefore avoids debt No loss of ownership (control)	Amount available may be limited Reduces payments to shareholders which may cause dissatisfaction Once used it is not available for alternative purposes
Net current assets	Encourages the business to manage cash flow effectively	Can put pressure on customers as shorter credit terms are offered and this negatively affects relationships with suppliers if longer credit terms are negotiated Lower stock holdings can affect the firm's ability to meet customer needs
Sale of assets	No interest charges Reduces **capital** tied up in assets, releasing it for other purposes Can mean disposing of an asset no longer of use to the business	It is likely that the amount received is not a true reflection of the value of the asset Can increase costs in the long run if an asset needs to be leased back

External sources of finance are those available from outside the business. They are outlined below.

▶ Owner's capital
  • This is money invested in the business from the owner's personal savings.
▶ Loans
  • Loans are money borrowed from a financial institution normally for a set period of time and for a specific purpose.
  • Interest will be payable on the loan.
▶ Crowd-funding
  • This involves attracting investment from a large number of speculative investors many of whom may invest relatively small amounts. If cumulatively this matches the required amount then the investments are collected together.
  • Normally makes use of the internet to attract investors.
▶ Mortgages
  • These are long-term loans, normally around 25 years, that are secured against a specific asset, for example a building.
  • Interest will be payable on the mortgage.
▶ Venture capital
  • This is investment from an experienced entrepreneur in return for a stake (equity) in the business.
▶ Debt factoring
  • This involves the selling on of a business's debts to a third party in order to receive the cash quickly.
  • The factor company pays the business a percentage of the money owed and takes on the responsibility to chase the debts which need to be repaid.

Personal and Business Finance

▶ Hire purchase
  • This involves paying to use an asset in instalments to spread the cost over its useful life and hence provide a source of finance.
  • The asset will remain the property of the seller until the final instalment has been paid.
▶ Leasing
  • This involves paying to use an asset in instalments to spread the cost over its useful life and hence providing a source of finance.
  • Ownership of the asset stays with the supplier throughout the length of the lease agreement.
▶ Trade credit
  • This is a period of time offered by suppliers to allow the customer to purchase a good or service now and pay at a later date, for example 30 days after purchase.
▶ Grants
  • This is a lump sum provided to a business by the government or another organisation to be used for a specific purpose. For example, it could be used to provide employment in a deprived area or invest in the research and development of an environmentally friendly alternative to fossil fuels.
▶ Donations
  • These are sums of money given voluntarily to a charity or social enterprise.
▶ Peer-to-peer lending
  • This involves one business person lending money to another business person in return for interest payments.
▶ Invoice discounting
  • These are reductions offered to customers making a product or service cheaper, often applied as a percentage.

The pros and cons of external sources of finance are summarised in Table 3.12.

▶ If you had enough money, what would encourage you to invest in someone else's business?

▶ **Table 3.12:** Advantages and disadvantages of external sources of finance

	Advantages	**Disadvantages**
Owner's capital	No interest payments or need to repay High level of commitment from the owner	Amount available is likely to be limited If there is more than one owner this could cause friction if everyone is not able to contribute the same amount
Loans	Regular pre-agreed repayments make planning and budgeting relatively easy Ownership or control is not lost	Interest is charged on the amount borrowed Interest rates can fluctuate Often secured against an asset which can be seized if repayments are missed Interest has to be paid regardless of whether a profit is being made
Crowd-funding	Offers the ability to raise finance from a large number of investors No interest is paid as investors will only be rewarded if the business is successfully sold on at a later date	Partial loss of ownership No guarantee that the crowd fund will attract sufficient investment to meet the proposal
Mortgages	Large amounts of finance can be raised and repaid over a prolonged period of time Ownership or control is not lost	Interest is charged on the amount borrowed Interest rates can fluctuate Often secured against an asset which can be seized if repayments are missed Interest has to be paid regardless of whether a profit is being made Not suitable for small amounts or as a short-term source of finance

	Advantages	Disadvantages
Venture capital	Finance is provided by a business professional who will often offer advice and mentoring alongside the investment Venture capitalists are often risk takers and may see the potential in a high risk investment that other investors including banks may not be willing to invest in	Partial loss of ownership and control Conflict can arise between the entrepreneur and venture capitalist regarding the direction and day-to-day running of the business
Debt factoring	Speeds up the flow of cash into the business from debts The factor company takes on the risk of bad debt	Only receive a percentage of the amount owed, therefore reducing profits Can give the wrong impression or alienate customers
Hire purchase	Avoids the need to pay a lump sum for the use of an asset Regular instalments make planning and budgeting easier Spreads the cost of an asset over its useful life	Overall amount paid for the use of an asset is likely to be higher than if purchased outright Only really suitable for relatively low cost assets, e.g. vehicles and not premises
Leasing	Responsibility for maintaining and repairing the asset stays with the supplier Spreads the cost of an asset over its life to avoid paying a lump sum up front	Overall amount paid for the use of an asset is likely to be higher than if purchased outright Never actually own the asset and therefore payments are ongoing
Trade credit	Delays the need to pay for goods and services purchased, therefore aiding cash flow No loss of ownership or control	Potential loss of discounts offered for cash payments Only suitable as a short-term source of finance
Grants	No need to repay and no interest charges No loss of ownership or control	Often require a lengthy application process Might only be awarded if certain conditions are met affecting the way the business operates on a day-to-day basis
Donations	No need to repay and no interest charges No loss of ownership or control	Likely to be small amounts only Unpredictable
Peer to peer lending	Interest rates can be lower than lending from more traditional financial institutions Fixed rate of interest can be agreed making it easier to plan and budget	Amounts available may be limited and provided for a short period of time only
Invoice discounting	No need to repay and no interest charges No loss of ownership or control Reduces costs to the business so increases profit	Often only available if purchases are paid in cash which affects cash flow

Assessment practice 3.4

1   Give **two** examples of external finance.   (2 marks)

2   Outline **two** advantages of net current assets as an internal source of finance.   (4 marks)

Ahmed wants to open a small business selling custom bikes, and is looking at ways of raising money. He owns his own house and is considering acquiring a second mortgage. He is also speaking to his bank about a loan and is looking at crowd-funding sites, as he thinks his product is innovative and could attract investors.

3   Assess a mortgage, a loan and crowd-funding as sources of finance for Ahmed.   (8 marks)

Break-even and cash flow forecasts

Cash flow forecasts

Cash flows into and out of a business on a regular basis. A **cash flow forecast** tries to predict in advance what and when these cash flows will be. Having a healthy cash flow is crucial to the survival of a business. A healthy cash flow means that a business will have enough cash at any one point in time to be able to meet demand for short-term cash outflows. Imagine what would happen if at the end of the week a manager turned to the business's employees and said, 'Sorry, I haven't got enough cash to pay your wages this week.'

By forecasting cash flow in advance, a business can identify where there might be shortages and either try to prevent this from happening or put plans in place to deal with it.

Inflows/receipts

Cash inflows or receipts are the money coming into the business from various sources, which include:

▶ cash sales – the customer pays at the time of purchase

▶ credit sales – the customer pays in a pre-agreed period after the sale, for example 30 days

▶ loans – bank loans to fund the purchase of assets such as machinery and vehicles

▶ capital introduced – money invested from entrepreneurs or shareholders when a business is first set up or looks to expand

▶ sale of assets – the sale of items owned by the business which are no longer needed in order to bring a short-term cash injection into the business

▶ bank interest received – interest paid by the bank on credit balances.

Outflows/payments

Cash outflows or payments are the money going out of the business for various purposes, which include:

▶ cash purchase – items purchased by a business and paid for at the time of purchase

▶ credit purchases – items purchased by a business and paid for at a later point in time

▶ purchase of assets – non-current assets that a business is likely to keep for more than one year such as machinery and vehicles

▶ Value Added Tax (VAT) – businesses that are VAT registered must pay VAT to HM Revenue & Customs (HMRC), and this should be shown in the cash flow forecast

▶ bank interest paid

▶ rent

▶ rates

▶ salaries

▶ wages

▶ utilities.

A business with sales in excess of the VAT threshold, £82,000 in 2015, must register itself with HMRC and then record VAT received on sales and paid on purchases. A business must then work out whether it has paid or received more money in VAT, then claim a refund or make a payment as appropriate.

Key term

Cash flow forecast – a document that shows the predicted flow of cash into and out of a business over a given period of time, normally 12 months.

Tip

Formulas used in this topic will not be given to you in the examination. It is therefore important that you learn them.

Worked Example

Paddington Games sells £10,000, excluding VAT, of games per month and purchases supplies of £6000, excluding VAT. The tables below show the cash in and the cash out for Paddington Games.

Cash in	January	February	March
Sales	£10,000	£10,000	£10,000
VAT on sales	£2000	£2000	£2000
Refund from HMRC			
Total cash in	£12,000	£12,000	£12,000

Cash out	January	February	March
Purchases	£6000	£6000	£6000
VAT paid	£1200	£1200	£1200
Payment to HMRC			
Total cash out	£7200	£7200	£7200

Over the three months of January to March:

- the total VAT received was £2000 × 3 = £6000
- the total VAT paid was £1200 × 3 = £3600.

The net VAT is therefore £6000 − £3600 = £2400

This means that the business has received more in VAT than it has paid and therefore must make a payment of £2400 to HMRC.

Key terms

Opening balance – amount of cash available in a business at the start of a set time period, for example a month.

Closing balance – amount of cash available in a business at the end of a set time period, for example a month.

Prepare, complete, analyse, revise and evaluate cash flow

A cash flow forecast is a simple statement showing opening balance, cash in, cash out and closing balance. It is normally shown on a monthly basis and drawn up for a 12-month period. The **opening balance** is how much money the business has at the start of the month and the **closing balance** shows how much money it has at the end of the month. For example, the closing balance at the end of January becomes the opening balance at the start of February.

Case study

Carla's Cycles

Carla owns a small bicycle store in Sheffield, called Carla's Cycles. She opened the business three years ago with a friend who had a finance degree, but has recently had to start completing the finances for the business herself. The illustration below shows the cash flow forecast for Carla's Cycles.

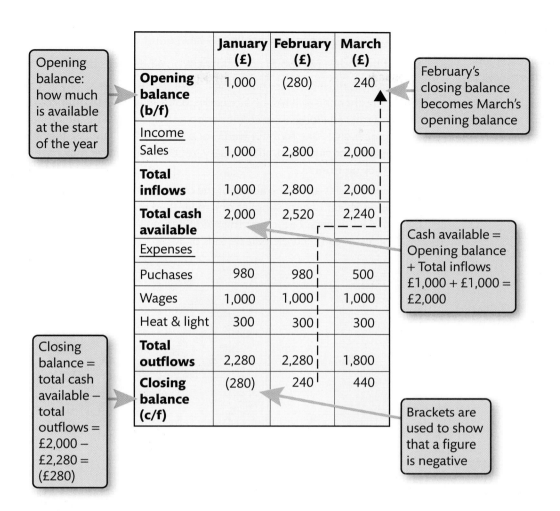

Opening balance: how much is available at the start of the year

February's closing balance becomes March's opening balance

Cash available = Opening balance + Total inflows £1,000 + £1,000 = £2,000

Closing balance = total cash available – total outflows = £2,000 – £2,280 = (£280)

Brackets are used to show that a figure is negative

	January (£)	February (£)	March (£)
Opening balance (b/f)	1,000	(280)	240
Income Sales	1,000	2,800	2,000
Total inflows	1,000	2,800	2,000
Total cash available	2,000	2,520	2,240
Expenses			
Puchases	980	980	500
Wages	1,000	1,000	1,000
Heat & light	300	300	300
Total outflows	2,280	2,280	1,800
Closing balance (c/f)	(280)	240	440

▶ **Figure 3.3:** Cash flow forecast for bicycle shop, Carla's Cycles

Carla's Cycles has £1000 available at the start of the year; Carla then predicts the following sales:

- £1000 in January
- £2800 in February
- £2000 in March.

In this case, total inflows and sales are the same, showing that Carla only makes cash sales and not credit sales. The total cash available is opening balance plus total inflows. Carla predicts the following:

- her purchases will be £980 in both January and February, and £500 in March
- wages will be £1000 per month
- heating and lighting will be £300 per month.

Total outflows are all of Carla's expenses added together. The closing balance is calculated by deducting the total outflows from the cash available. Remember that one month's closing balance becomes the next month's opening balance.

The timing of the cash inflows and outflows is important. At the end of three months Carla has a positive balance of £440, but in January she had a negative balance of £280. This means that, although her cash flow was healthy at the end of three months, she had problems earlier and would have had an overdraft of £280 in her bank or been unable to pay one of her expenses, which could stop her from operating successfully in the following months.

Check your knowledge

1   What problems might Carla experience as a result of cash flow in January and February?

2   Outline three reasons why cash flow forecasts are so important to businesses.

3   Can you think of any actions Carla should take in light of her cash flow forecast?

You will need to learn the formula to calculate the closing balance:

opening balance + cash inflows – cash outflows = closing balance

Credit periods have two major influences on a business's cash flow.

The business must consider how long it gives its customers to pay. If it accepts cash sales only, then this will not be a concern, but it may have to offer credit in order to ensure a sale. The longer the credit period, the slower will be the money coming in. If a greengrocer gives one month's credit for a sale made in January, they will not see cash flowing into the business until February. Yet the greengrocer may have had to pay for their stock up front.

▶ Credit periods affect the ability of the business to gain credit from its suppliers. If a business can secure supplies on credit, then this will slow down the flow of cash out of a business. The longer the credit period, the later the cash flows out. Some businesses can secure credit periods of 30, 60 or even 90 days..

▶ Why is it important to keep a close eye on a business's financial affairs?

If a business both sells on credit to its customers and buys on credit from its suppliers, it needs the first to have a shorter credit period than the second.

Opening and closing cash/bank balances

The opening balance at the start of the year will be a true reflection of the business's bank balance, whereas the closing balance will be based upon the predicted incomes and expenditures over the period of the cash flow forecast, normally a year. One of the key purposes of the cash flow forecast is to highlight, in advance, any months where there is a risk of a negative cash flow, as this allows the business to make arrangements – for example, a prearranged overdraft with the bank – or to try to take actions to avoid this.

A business with a negative closing balance is often said to have **liquidity** problems and is in danger of becoming **insolvent**. In the next section on cash flow management, you will look in more detail at methods available to try to avoid these negative closing balances.

Figure 3.4 illustrates a sample cash flow forecast for the first four months of a sole trader.

Key terms

Liquidity – measures a firm's ability to meet short-term cash payments.

Insolvent – when a firm is unable to meet short-term cash payments.

	January £	February £	March £	April £	Total £
Opening balance (b/f)	0	(3,500)	(1,520)	2,500	
Income owner's capital	10,000				10,000
Bank loan	15,000				15,000
Cash sales	5,000	7,000	8,000	7,000	27,000
Credit sales	0	9,000	11,000	12,000	32,000
Commission received	0	800	950	950	2,700
Total inflows	30,000	16,800	19,950	19,950	86,700
Total cash available	30,000	13,300	18,430	22,450	
Expenses					
Cash purchases	8,000	9,500	9,500	3,500	30,500
Credit purchases	0	0	0	7,000	7,000
Heat and light	0	0	0	200	200
Fixtures and fittings	5,000	600	0	0	5,600
Equipment	5,000	0	0	0	5,000
Drawings	0	2,000	2,000	2,000	6,000
Marketing	3,000	0	1,200	0	4,200
Premises costs	10,000	0	0	0	10,000
Insurance	500	0	0	0	500
Wages	1,000	1,500	2,000	2,000	6,500
Administrative costs	1,000	750	800	1,250	3,800
Overdraft interest	0	70	30	0	100
Loan repayments	0	400	400	400	1,200
Total outflows	33,500	14,820	15,930	16,350	80,600
Closing balance (c/f)	(3,500)	(1,520)	2,500	6,100	

▶ **Figure 3.4:** Why might a new business experience cash flow problems in the first few months of trading?

Celina's cleaning services

Celina is setting up a small business providing cleaning services to offices on a trading estate in Scarborough. She has asked you to help her prepare a cash flow forecast for her first 12 months of trading.

You should produce a forecast from January to December based on the information provided below.

Sales and purchases for the 12 months are expected to be as follows.

Month	Sales	Purchases
January	£5000	£600
February	£5000	£600
March	£5000	£600
April	£5000	£600
May	£5000	£600
June	£5000	£600
July	£4000	£500
August	£4000	£500
September	£5000	£600
October	£6000	£650
November	£6000	£650
December	£6000	£650

At the beginning of January, Celina will buy two small cars, to drive herself and staff to the offices, each costing £10,000. She will invest £15,000 of her own money and has agreed a bank loan of £7000. Celina will receive the loan in January and start repayments the following month at a fixed rate of £250 per month. When meeting with her bank manager, she also agreed a business overdraft that will be charged at a rate of 1 per cent on any negative closing balances.

In order to start trading in January, she buys £4000 worth of cleaning equipment, including vacuum cleaners and floor buffers. In addition, she spends £150 on less durable (not as long-lasting) products such as dusters and mops, which she plans to replace every second month.

Celina plans to offer 30 days' credit terms to two of her bigger cleaning contracts. These two combined will account for £2200 of her monthly sales.

Celina has rented a small lock-up to store her equipment and materials at a cost of £600 per month. She will employ four cleaners, each earning £400 per month, and a cleaning supervisor earning an annual salary of £7200. She will withdraw £1000 a month for herself, and hopes to be able to increase this to £1200 per month after six months.

Additional monthly costs include:
- £300 car insurance
- £20 advertising
- £100 fuel.

Check your knowledge

1 Use a spreadsheet to produce a 12-month cash flow forecast for Celina.

2 Identify and explain any potential cash flow problems she may face.

3 Do you think Celina was right to offer her two biggest customers 30 days' credit? Justify your answer.

Use of cash flow forecasts for planning, monitoring, control and target setting

A cash flow forecast can help to identify where there are potential shortfalls but might also indicate where there are large amounts of cash left at the end of a month or year. Although you may think this is a good thing, if the cash balance at the end of each month is high, it might be an indication that the business is not taking advantage of opportunities. For example, could it use this cash surplus to improve or expand the business?

Cash flow forecasts are just that, a forecast, and therefore the actual cash flow of the business should be monitored alongside the forecast to see if inflows and outflows are as expected, better or worse.

Problems within the cash flow forecast

Problems occur with cash flows when the business's outflows are greater than the opening balance plus the inflows, as this will result in a negative closing balance. This means that the business will not have enough cash to meet payments that are due.

Very few businesses have consistent cash flows throughout the year; they are likely to experience busy times and quiet times. These fluctuations are known as the cash flow cycle. For some businesses, particularly those in a seasonal industry, these fluctuations can be quite severe. Someone who owns a small bed and breakfast in a seaside town will have to pay costs like rent, heat and light, insurance and bank charges throughout the year. In season, they will also have additional costs like wages and stock, but it might only be in the summer months where there are any cash inflows.

Solutions to cash flow problems

If a business has predicted cash flow problems in advance, then there are a number of possible solutions. These are outlined below.

▶ **Overdraft arrangements** – a business with a fluctuating cash flow cycle should be able to show the forecast to the bank and make arrangements for periods of negative cash flows. Banks sometimes offer free overdraft facilities to help businesses through these periods, but only if pre-agreed. Going overdrawn on a bank account without an agreement with the bank can be a very expensive option.

▶ **Negotiating terms with creditors** – creditors are people or businesses that a business owes money to, normally because goods or services have been bought on credit as opposed to cash purchases. A business with cash flow problems could try to negotiate a longer payment term with its suppliers – for example, an increase from 30 days to 60 days. This would slow down the flow of cash out of the business. A negative effect of this, however, may be the loss of any discounts offered for prompt or early payment.

▶ **Reviewing and rescheduling capital expenditure** – having identified cash flow problems, the owner or manager could review what cash outflows were being spent on. Such a review might identify areas of expenditure that could be cut or postponed. It is difficult to do this if the expenditure is on revenue items – for example, replacement stock – but more achievable if it is capital expenditure. A business could, for example, postpone plans to replace machinery or buy a new van.

An alternative action here could be to consider leasing an item of capital equipment rather than buying it outright. This can prove expensive in the long run, but means that rather than paying one lump sum, the business can pay to use it on a monthly basis.

Theory into practice

Draw a cash flow table to show your personal finances for the next month. Think about what money will be coming in from wages, presents, parents, as appropriate, and what expenses you will have. These might include food and drink, presents, trips, travel, etc.

1 What is your opening balance at the start of the month?

2 What is your closing balance at the end of the month?

3 Are there any points during the month where you may have a cash flow problem?

4 What actions can you take to ensure that any cash flow problems are solved?

Benefits and limitations of cash flow forecasts

Cash flow forecasts are a very useful tool for many businesses. Table 3.13 outlines the benefits and limitations of using them.

▶ **Table 3.13:** Benefits and limitations of cash flow forecasts

Benefits	Limitations
• Encourages planning for cash inflows and outflows • Enables cash flow to be monitored and corrective action taken if necessary • Can be used as part of a business plan to help raise finance • Identifies in advance times of negative closing balances allowing the business to plan for these	• Based on forecasts and therefore may be inaccurate • Cannot plan for unexpected events such as a rise in the cost of raw materials • Time taken to produce a cash flow forecast could have been spent on other tasks

 **PAUSE POINT**

Draw a flow diagram showing how cash can flow into and out of a business. Identify whether each cash flow is a regular or one-off (less frequent) occurrence.

Hint

Think about your own cash flow table. Are there any similarities between your cash flow and a business?

Extend

'It is possible for a successful business to go out of business because it has cash flow problems.' Can you explain this statement?

Discussion

Work in small groups. Each group takes a different local business – a retailer, leisure provider, manufacturer, service provider, etc.

Produce a diagram to show fixed, semi-variable and variable costs for each business.

How easy was it to classify each cost? What are the similarities and differences between different types of business? Why might there be similarities between businesses that are different?

Break-even analysis

Break-even is the point at which a business is not making a profit or a loss, i.e. it is just breaking even. This means that the money being received from sales is the same as the money being spent on costs.

Costs to a business can be categorised as follows:

▶ variable costs – vary with the level of output, for example raw materials

▶ semi-variable – part of the cost stays the same and part varies in relation to the degree of business activity, for example a worker may be paid a fixed rate of pay but at busy times earn additional payments for working overtime

▶ fixed costs – do not vary with output, for example rent

▶ total costs – fixed costs + variable costs.

Sales by a business generate revenue; this is cash coming into the business. Important terms are:

▶ total revenue – the total amount of money coming in from sales, calculated as quantity sold multiplied by selling price

▶ total sales – the amount of sales made in a set time period, for example a year; this can be expressed as value or volume

▶ selling price per unit – the amount a customer pays for each unit bought

▶ sales in value – sales expressed in monetary value, for example £s, calculated as quantity sold multiplied by selling price per unit

▶ sales in volume – sales expressed as a quantity, for example tons or units.

Break-even is the point where total revenue (TR) = total costs (TC).

This can be calculated using the formula below:

$$\text{break-even point} = \frac{\text{fixed costs}}{\text{contribution per unit}}$$

Contribution per unit is calculated as:

selling price – variable costs per unit

Total contribution is calculated as:

sales revenue – total variable costs

Total variable cost is calculated as:

variable cost per unit × quantity

or

contribution per unit × number of units sold

Worked Example

Fay makes celebration cakes from a rented kitchen. She has fixed costs of £20,000. Her variable cost per cake is £10 and her selling price is £26.

contribution per unit = selling price – variable cost

contribution per unit = £26 – £10 = £16

$$\text{break-even point} = \frac{\text{fixed costs}}{\text{contribution per unit}}$$

$$\text{break-even point} = \frac{£20,000}{£16} = 1250 \text{ cakes}$$

Fay must sell 1250 cakes to achieve break-even. If she sells fewer than this she will make a loss. If she sells more she will make a profit.

If Fay sells 1251 cakes she will make £16 profit, because after break-even has been reached, the contribution per unit no longer has to contribute towards fixed costs and therefore becomes profit.

How much profit would Fay make if she sold 1500 cakes?

Margin of safety is the actual number of units sold over and above the break-even point. This is calculated as:

actual sales in units – break-even level of output

To work out the break even level you need to calculate:

break-even point = fixed costs / contribution per unit

contribution per unit = selling price – variable costs

then

margin of safety = actual sales – break-even level of output

Worked Example

Assume Fay sold 1500 cakes.

margin of safety = actual sales in units – break-even level of output

margin of safety = 1500 cakes – 1250 cakes = 250 cakes

Drawing a break-even chart

Break-even can also be shown on a break-even chart. This plots the costs and revenues at each unit of output. The break-even point is where the total cost line crosses the total revenue line. A break-even chart can also be used to calculate margin of safety and profit or loss at different levels of output.

Step by step: drawing a break even chart

6 Steps

1 Draw your axes, adding labels 'Cost/sales' on the vertical axis and 'Output' on the horizontal axis.

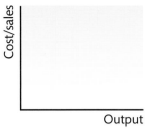

2 Draw your fixed cost line.
- Remember this stays the same regardless of output and is therefore a horizontal straight line.

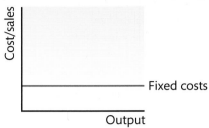

3 Draw your variable cost line.
- At 0 output variable costs will be £0.
- As output increases variable costs will increase.
- The variable cost line therefore slopes upwards from 0.

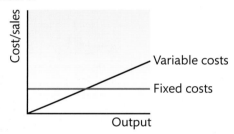

4 Draw your total cost line.
- Remember total costs are fixed costs plus variable costs.
- The total cost line therefore starts at the fixed cost point and slopes upwards.
- Notice the total cost line is parallel to the variable cost line.

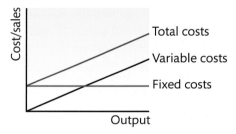

5 Draw your total revenue line.
- If no units are sold, total revenue will be £0.
- As sales increase, total revenue will increase.
- The total revenue line therefore slopes upwards from 0.

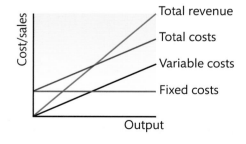

6 Identify the break-even point.
- Identify where the total cost line crosses the total revenue line.
- Draw a line downwards to the Output axis.
- Read off the break-even level of output.

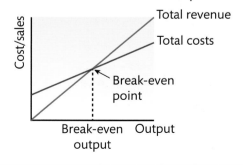

▶ **Figure 3.5:** Completing a break-even chart

> ## Theory into practice
>
> You are the finance assistant at Deluxe Car Washing Services. Produce a break-even chart and check your workings against the break-even formula for the following:
>
> - car wash price = £12.50 per car
> - overhead costs = £175 per week
> - labour costs per wash = £4.50 per car
> - materials and water cost = £1 per car.
>
> **1** Label your graph in full and include the break-even formula to show you are right.
>
> **2** The business averaged 30 cars per week during July – work out the margin for safety.
>
> **3** How much profit would they make if they washed 20 cars during one week, and what recommendations would you make to them about this?

Identification of area of profit and area of loss

Break-even level of output is the level of output where the business is making neither a profit nor a loss. If the business sells less than the break-even level of output, then it is making a loss. For every item sold above the break-even level it is making a profit.

Worked Example

Kenji imports silk dresses from Vietnam which he then sells through his online shop. He has imported 100 dresses at a cost of £1000. In addition to the cost of the dresses, it costs him £3 per dress postage and packaging. His fixed costs are £1105. He sells the dresses for £35 with free postage and packaging offered to the customer.

First calculate Kenji's break-even level of output.

   contribution = selling price – variable cost

His variable cost per dress is (£1000/100) + £3 postage and packaging = £13

   contribution = £35 – £13 = £17

break-even = fixed costs/contribution

$$\text{break-even} = \frac{£1105}{£17} = 65 \text{ dresses}$$

Kenji must sell 65 dresses to reach his break-even point.

If he sells 50 dresses he makes a loss.

   sales revenue = 50 × £35 = £1750

   total costs = £1105 + £1000 = £2105

   loss of £2105 – £1750 = £355

If he sells 66 dresses he will make a profit of £17 as the contribution from the one dress over his break-even now becomes profit.

If he sells all 100 dresses he will make a profit of £595.

Carry out a calculation to show how he will make a profit of £595.

Profit and loss can also be shown on a break-even chart, as demonstrated by Figure 3.6.

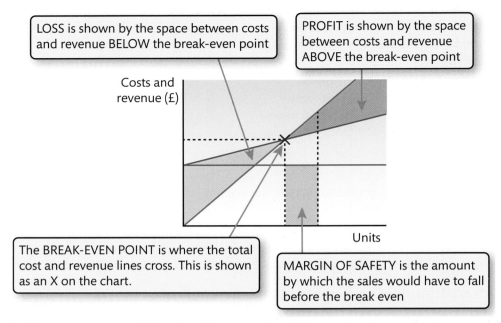

LOSS is shown by the space between costs and revenue BELOW the break-even point

PROFIT is shown by the space between costs and revenue ABOVE the break-even point

Costs and revenue (£)

Units

The BREAK-EVEN POINT is where the total cost and revenue lines cross. This is shown as an X on the chart.

MARGIN OF SAFETY is the amount by which the sales would have to fall before the break even

▶ **Figure 3.6:** What are the benefits of showing profit and loss on a break-even chart?

Contribution per unit benefits and limitations

Contribution per unit is used by businesses to help inform decision making. There are benefits and limitations to it as a decision-making tool, as shown in Table 3.14.

▶ **Table 3.14:** Benefits and limitations of contribution per unit

Benefits	Limitations
• Straightforward to calculate • Allows for the calculation of break-even level of output • Can be used to inform decisions, e.g. what price to charge • Can be used to carry out what-if analysis	• Does not take into account fixed costs • Assumes that prices remain constant • Does not take into account any unexpected changes to variables, e.g. selling price and variable costs can fluctuate

Use of break-even for planning, monitoring, control and target setting

Break-even can be used as a management tool for planning, monitoring, control and target setting.

▶ Planning
  • Set budgets for the amount of sales necessary and costs.
  • Forms part of a business plan to show at what point the business will start to make a profit.
  • Informs pricing decisions.
▶ Monitoring
  • Monitor progress towards achieving break-even point.
  • Identify changes to selling price of costs.
  • Take corrective action if targets look unlikely to be met.
▶ Control
  • Keep costs within budget.
  • Motivate employees.
  • Manage sales accounts.

▸ Target setting
- Set sales targets for individual employees, teams or products.
- Set expenditure budgets.
- Set profit budgets based upon sales targets and cost targets.

Prepare, complete, analyse, revise and evaluate break-even

You should now be able to prepare a break-even chart, calculate the break-even level of output and analyse the effect on break-even and margin of safety if any of the variables, i.e. costs or selling prices, vary.

Case study

Cheltenham Coffee

Faizal is looking to set up a mobile coffee van in the centre of Cheltenham. He has calculated that his fixed costs will be £24,000 per year. Each cup of coffee will cost him 40p to make. He has decided on a selling price of £1.60 per cup to undercut major competitors such as Costa and Starbucks who have stores nearby. He plans

to trade 250 days a year and estimates he can sell 120 cups of coffee each day.

1. Calculate Faizal's break-even level of output.
2. What is Faizal's margin of safety?
3. Draw a break-even chart to show:
   - break-even point
   - margin of safety
   - loss if he sells just 60 cups per day
   - profit if he sells 120 cups per day.

Unfortunately, Faizal had forgotten about some of the cheaper competitors in the local area including Wetherspoons who charge just £1.20 per cup of coffee with unlimited refills.

4. Draw a new total revenue line to show what would happen if Faizal lowered his selling price to match Wetherspoons.

Break-even is a useful management tool. Table 3.15 shows the advantages and disadvantages of break-even.

▸ **Table 3.15:** The advantages and disadvantages of break-even

Advantages	Disadvantages
• The business knows how many items it must sell in order to break-even • Informs decisions on what price to charge • Can set targets • Identifies fixed and variable costs • Can identify if costs are too high allowing the business to look for ways of lowering costs • Can set targets which will motivate employees • Easy way to calculate profit or loss at different levels of output	• Does not take account of variations in costs or selling price • Forecast sales may not be achieved and hence, even though the break-even point is known, it may not be achieved • Targets set may be too high, creating stress

Ⅱ PAUSE POINT   Do you know how and why a business should use break-even analysis?

    Hint   Think back over the case studies and identify what they needed to know from the analysis.

    Extend   What actions do you think businesses might take from the results of their break-even analysis?

Assessment practice 3.5

1   Give **two** examples of inflows or receipts that might come into a business. **(2 marks)**

2   State **three** uses of break-even. **(3 marks)**

3   Outline two benefits to a business of using contribution per unit. **(4 marks)**

Dominic has started his own bread-making business. So far, he has been just checking his finances month-to-month. A friend recommends he complete a cash flow forecast for his business. Dominic isn't sure that completing a forecast will be worth his time.

4   Assess the benefits and limitations of cash flow forecasts for Dominic. **(8 marks)**

Complete statements of comprehensive income and financial position and evaluate business performance

Until now, you have focused on whether or not a business has enough cash to survive on a day-to-day basis and whether it can achieve break-even. As part of this you have already learned a number of formulas including costs, revenues, contribution and break-even. Beyond survival, a business is also likely to have an objective of profit. Here you will look at the financial documents that a business produces at the end of a financial year (or mid-year, called interim accounts). There are two key documents that a firm will produce, and these are:

▶ a **statement of comprehensive income**, which calculates whether the firm has made a profit or a loss by deducting all expenses from sales revenue

▶ a **statement of financial position**, which calculates the net worth of a business by balancing what the business owns against what it owes.

Statement of comprehensive income

Purpose and use

A statement of comprehensive income, if produced correctly, will give an accurate calculation showing how much profit or loss the business has made. It records sales, costs and profit over a period of time (normally a year).

Calculation of gross profit

The first part of the statement of comprehensive income is made up of three components.

▶ Sales revenue is the money coming into the business from providing a trade – for example, selling goods, manufacturing goods, or providing a service. The calculation for sales turnover is quantity sold × selling price.

▶ **Cost of goods sold** includes the costs directly linked to providing that trade, for example, the cost of buying in the goods or the raw materials used to produce the goods. To work out the cost of goods sold, a simple calculation is done to ensure that the figure recorded for cost of goods sold can be directly linked to the goods actually sold and not just all the materials purchased.

Key terms

Statement of comprehensive income – shows the trading position of the business which is used to calculate gross profit. It then takes into account all other expenses to calculate the profit or loss for the year.

Statement of financial position – a snapshot of a business's net worth at a particular moment in time, normally the end of a financial year.

Cost of goods sold – the actual value of inventory used to generate sales.

If, for example, you bought 12 balls of wool and knitted a jumper, is the cost of wool for that jumper 12 balls? What if you had three spare balls to start with or two balls left at the end?

The calculation for cost of goods sold is:

opening inventories + purchases – **closing inventories**

▶ Gross profit is the amount of money left or the surplus after the cost of goods sold has been deducted from the sales turnover. This is not, however, the business's final profit as there are still other expenses to deduct in the next part of the account. The calculation for gross profit is:

sales turnover – cost of goods sold.

> **Key terms**
>
> **Opening inventory** – the value of inventory in a business at the start of a financial year.
>
> **Closing inventory** – the value of inventory at the end of a financial year.

Section 1 of a statement of comprehensive income for the year ended 30 April 2015	£000s	£000s
Sales		411,529
Less cost of goods sold		
Opening inventory	34,993	
Purchases	128,129	
Closing inventory	21,445	
		141,677
Gross profit		269,852

▶ **Figure 3.7:** Why is it important to calculate the actual cost of goods sold rather than just use the purchases for the year?

Calculation of profit or loss for the year

Profit is the money after all other expenses have been deducted from gross profit and any other revenue income has been added. Revenue income is non-capital income that is received by the business from sources other than sales, for example, discounts received and interest on positive bank balances.

Depreciation appears as an expense in the statement of comprehensive income, as this is a way that accountants can spread the cost of a fixed asset over its lifetime. Depreciation will be explained in more detail under the fixed asset heading when you look at a balance sheet.

The calculation for profit for the year is:

gross profit – expenses + other revenue income

gross profit = sales revenue – cost of goods sold

cost of goods sold = opening inventory + purchases – closing inventory

profit or loss for the year = gross profit – expenses + other income

Figure 3.8 shows a statement of comprehensive income for the year ended 30 April 2015. What expenses do you think a business might include under the heading 'miscellaneous'?

Statement of comprehensive income for the year ended 30 April 2015		
	£000s	£000s
Sales		411,529
Less cost of goods sold		
Opening inventory	34,993	
Purchases	128,129	
Closing inventory	21,445	
		141,672
Gross profit		269,852
Less expenses		
Rent and rates		37,554
Wages and salaries		96,221
Telephone and postage		1,359
Distribution		31,593
Advertising		15,579
Miscellaneous expenses		28,452
Depreciation		17,848
Total expenses		228,696
Revenue income		0
Net profit before tax		41,246

▶ **Figure 3.8:** Statement of comprehensive income for year ended 30 April 2015

Reflect

Assume that Celina's cash flow forecast for year 1 was accurate and at the end of the year she holds one month's worth of purchases. Produce a statement of comprehensive income for Celina's cleaning business. Swap your work with another learner and check each other's work. Did you remember all the information you needed? Is there anything you need to remember for future activities?

Transfer of profit to a statement of comprehensive income

Tax is to be deducted from the profit: this is a percentage of the profit that is to be paid to HM Revenue & Customs (HMRC). This then gives profit after tax.

The business then has to decide how to use this profit. In the case of a company, a proportion of it may be issued to shareholders in the form of dividends. For a sole trader or partnership, it could be taken out of the business as drawings. Either some or all of it is likely, however, to be ploughed back into the business – this is called retained profit. Retained profits are transferred from the statement of comprehensive income to the statement of financial position.

Adjustments for depreciation (straight-line and reducing balance)

Depreciation is an accountancy concept used to spread the cost of an asset over its useful life. It is important that when fixed assets are shown in the statement of financial position, they are given a realistic value. For this reason, they are depreciated on an annual basis. The annual amount by which the assets are depreciated is therefore included as an expense in the statement of comprehensive income. If, for example, a business bought a delivery van for £30,000 and three years later still showed its value as £30,000, this would be unrealistic and inaccurate accounting. The statement of financial position should therefore show the historic cost of an asset, the amount by which it has depreciated over its life and then a current value for the asset. This final figure is called the net book value and this represents what the asset is thought to be worth at that moment in time.

There are two ways in which depreciation can be calculated. These are:

▸ straight-line depreciation: an asset is depreciated by a set amount each year

▸ reducing balance depreciation: an asset is depreciated by a set percentage of its remaining value each year.

The straight line method involves reducing the value of an asset, from the price paid, i.e. its **historic cost**, by a fixed amount each year. To calculate the amount, the accountant must, first of all, make two decisions:

▸ how long the asset is expected to be useful to the business, i.e. its **expected life**

▸ at the end of its useful life, how much it might be worth if sold on or sold for scrap, i.e. its **residual value**.

Once these decisions have been made, the following formula can be applied.

$$\frac{\text{historic value} - \text{residual value}}{\text{expected life}}$$

If, therefore, a Ford transit van cost £16,000 and it was expected to be used by the business for four years with a resale value of £4000, the calculation of depreciation would be shown as follows.

$$\frac{£16,000 - £4,000}{4 \text{ years}} = \frac{£12,000}{4} = £3,000 \text{ depreciation per year}$$

The £3000 would be shown as an expense on the statement of comprehensive income.

The reducing balance method involves reducing the value of the asset by a set percentage each year. The percentage is decided by a senior accountant and stated in the financial reports. This method depreciates an asset by a lower amount as the asset ages.

If, therefore, a Ford transit cost £16,000 and a decision was made to depreciate it by 20 per cent per year the depreciation would be calculated as:

Historic cost = £16,000

Year 1 depreciation = £16,000 × 0.20 = £3200
    Net book value = £16,000 – £3200 = £12,800

Year 2 depreciation = £12,800 × 0.20 = £2560
    Net book value = £12,800 – £2560 = £10,240

Year 3 depreciation = £10,240 × 0.20 = £2480
    Net book value = £10,240 – £2480 = £7760

▸ Why do new cars depreciate as soon as they are driven out of a car showroom? Can you list five possible factors that might explain it?

Adjustments for prepayments, accruals

It is important that the financial records are a true and fair record of the business's activities. For this reason, adjustments will be made to a statement of comprehensive income so that the expenditure shown matches the period in which the good or service is used. For example, if rent is paid quarterly in advance, the expense may be incurred in one financial year but the premises are actually used in the next financial year. To take account of such timing differences, two types of adjustment are made.

> **Key terms**
>
> **Historic cost** – the cost of an asset when it was first purchased.
>
> **Expected life** – how long an asset is expected to be used within a business.
>
> **Residual value** – the value of an asset when it is disposed of by the business, for example, resale value.

These are outlined below.

▶ Prepayments
  - A prepayment is when an expense is made in advance of the periods to which it relates.
  - The expense is therefore taken out of expenses in the statement of comprehensive income and shown as a current asset in the statement of financial position.
  - An example would be rental on a phone line paid quarterly in advance.

▶ Accruals
  - An accrual is when an expense is paid after the periods to which it relates.
  - The expense is therefore added as an expense in the statement of comprehensive income and shown as a current liability in the statement of financial position.
  - An example would be electricity paid quarterly in arrears.

Interpretation, analysis and evaluation of statements

Once produced, the statement of comprehensive income can be used internally by management to help measure the performance of the business and inform future decision making. It can also be used externally by potential investors and creditors. A creditor, for example, might look at the business's statement of comprehensive income when deciding whether or not to offer trade credit.

The statement of comprehensive income may be analysed in a number of ways including making:

▶ comparisons between figures within the statement of comprehensive income, e.g. profit as a percentage of sales revenue

▶ comparisons between years, i.e. gross profit this year as compared with gross profit for last year

▶ intrafirm comparisons to see how different aspects of the business are performing, e.g. revenue for one product or branch compared with another profit or branch

▶ interfirm comparisons to see how the business is performing in relation to its competitors.

When interpreting and analysing a statement of comprehensive income, it is also useful to consider profit quality. Profit quality is how sustainable the profit is. If profits have increased, but this is because of a one-off event, such as selling an asset, then this cannot be repeated the following year and profit quality may therefore be seen as poor. However, if the increase in profit is as a result of increased sales or lower costs, then this may be seen as achievable in future years and therefore profit quality is seen as good.

Profit quality can be used to evaluate the statement of comprehensive income. Anyone looking at the accounts may also want to consider the accuracy of the information. Accounts must be accurate to meet legal requirements but it is possible to manipulate data to make it look more favourable. This is called window dressing.

 PAUSE POINT

Write out a list of all the headings shown on a statement of comprehensive income. Write a short explanation or formula next to each heading.

 Hint

Remember to include the adjustments you have just read about.

Extend

What are the benefits of comparing a statement of comprehensive income between different years for the same business?

Statement of financial position

Purpose and use

A statement of financial position is a snapshot of a business's net worth at a particular moment in time, normally the end of a financial. It is a summary of everything that the business owns (its assets) and owes (its liabilities). A statement of financial position therefore states the value of a business.

Statement of financial position

Statements of financial position can be shown in a vertical or horizontal format, vertical being the most common, and therefore the style of presentation you will use in this unit. A vertically presented balance sheet is presented as:

non-current assets
- intangible assets
- tangible assets

+ current assets

– current liabilities

= non-current assets/liabilities

– non-current liabilities

= net assets.

This is the first half of the balance sheet that calculates the net assets – that is, the worth of the business. Imagine if the business were to close today and you sold all of its assets, then paid off all of its liabilities. This is the amount you would be left with.

Non-current assets

Non-current assets are those items of value that are owned by the business and likely to stay within the business for more than one year. These can be:

▶ tangible assets
- i.e. they can be touched, for example a machine or premises.
▶ intangible assets
- i.e. they cannot be touched, for example a trademark or recognised name.

Tangible assets include premises, fixtures and fittings, equipment and vehicles. It is important that when these are shown in the statement of financial position, they are given a realistic value. For this reason, they are depreciated on an annual basis. As you have already learned, if a business buys a delivery van for £30,000 and three years later still shows its value as £30,000, this is unrealistic and inaccurate accounting. The statement of financial position should therefore show the historic cost of an asset, the amount by which it has depreciated over its life and then a current value for the asset. This final figure is called the net book value and this represents what the asset is thought to be worth at that moment in time.

You have already looked at how to calculate depreciation using the straight-line method. The Ford transit van that cost £16,000, with a residual value of £4000, was to be depreciated by £3000 per year.

In the balance sheet, the net book value (the cost of an asset minus depreciation) would therefore be shown as in Table 3.6.

▶ **Table 3.16:** Example net book value for a Ford transit van

Year	Cost	Accumulated depreciation	Net book value
1	£16,000	£3000	£13,000 [1]
2	£16,000	£6000	£10,000
3	£16,000	£9000	£7000
4	£16,000	£12,000	£4000 [2]
[1] The value of the van at the end of 1 year: £16,000 – £3000 = £13,000.			
[2] The value of the van at the end of 4 years matches the residual value used in the calculation above.			

An intangible asset is something that adds value to the business but does not have a physical presence. One example of this that you might see on a balance sheet is 'goodwill'. This means when someone buys an already-established business, they are also buying the goodwill that the business has built up, such as brand recognition or a loyal customer base.

The value of an intangible asset can change over time. If a decision is made to decrease the value of an intangible asset, a principle similar to depreciation is applied. This is called 'amortisation' where a one-off change is made to the value of the intangible asset. This will be shown in the statement of financial position to record the cost, amortisation and net book value of the intangible asset.

▶ Why is it important for this business to put a realistic value on its office equipment?

Current assets

Current assets are those items of value owned by a business whose value is likely to fluctuate on a regular basis. Every time a business makes a transaction, the value of its current assets will fluctuate. Current assets include:
▶ inventories
▶ trade receivables
▶ prepayments
▶ cash in the bank
▶ cash in hand.

Inventory is the value of stock held at that moment in time. Depending upon the nature of the business, it can take three different forms: raw materials, work in progress and finished goods. A business must be careful to give stock a realistic value and not overvalue stock – for example, inventory which they are unlikely to sell because it has gone out of fashion or is damaged.

Key term

Current assets – items owned by the business that change in value on a regular basis, such as stock.

Trade receivables are people who owe the business money. Although the business does not yet physically have the money, it is, in effect, owned by the business. Trade receivables are customers who have not yet paid for the good or service provided by the business and must be monitored to ensure that they do make the payment by the due date.

Prepayments are when an expense is made in advance of the period to which it relates. Therefore it is classed as an asset and transferred from the statement of comprehensive income.

Current assets are listed in order of how easy it is to turn them into cash quickly. For example, if a business has liquidity problems, it may find it difficult to turn inventory into cash quickly. In addition, in trying to do so, it may not receive its true value. In contrast, cash in hand is just that – cash!

Current liabilities

A current liability is something owed by the business that should be paid back in under one year. Examples of current liabilities are outlined below.

▶ Overdrafts
  - The ability to withdraw money from a current account that you do not have.
▶ Accruals
  - This is when an expense is paid after the period to which it relates.
▶ Trade payables
  - These are people or businesses the business owes money to because it has received a good or service but has not yet paid for it.

Net current assets/liabilities

Net current assets/liabilities is a very important figure for a business; it represents the business's ability to meet short-term debts. A business with insufficient net current assets, also called working capital, does not have enough current assets to meet its current liabilities. This is potentially disastrous because, if the liabilities have to be paid for now, and the business cannot meet these demands from its current assets, then it will have to find the cash elsewhere. This could mean being forced to sell a fixed asset without which the business cannot operate. Net current assets/liabilities is calculated as current assets minus current liabilities.

▶ Current assets are greater than current liabilities = net current assets.
▶ Current assets are less than current liabilities = net current liabilities.

Non-current liabilities

A liability is something that the business owes. If it is classed as non-current, this means the business will pay it back in more than one year. Examples of non-current liabilities include bank loans and mortgages. These are likely to be used to buy fixed assets or to set up the business initially.

Net assets

Net assets are the figure that represents the total value of all the assets minus the value of the liabilities. Net assets are calculated as follows.

Non-current assets + current assets – (current liabilities + long term liabilities)

Capital

The second half of the statement of financial position then asks how this has been financed. This shows the **capital employed** and is presented as:

owners' or shareholders' capital
  + retained profit
  – drawings
  = capital employed.

> **Key term**
>
> **Capital employed** – the total amount of capital tied up in a business at a point in time. It is calculated as owners' or shareholders' capital + retained profit – drawings.

Opening capital is the capital in the business at the start of trading. This is the money invested in the business from the owners. Owners may be a sole trader, partners or shareholders.

Retained profit is the profits kept from previous years plus the net profit from the current year. This will be transferred from the statement of financial position.

Drawings are withdrawals made by owners from the business. For a statement of financial position to balance, net assets must be equal to capital employed.

	Cost	Accumulated depreciation	Net book value
	£	£	£
Non-current assets			
Premises	218,000	28,880	189,120
Fixtures and fittings	38,500	15,800	22,700
Vehicles	19,500	19,500	0
Current assets			
Stock			34,294
Debtors			21,455
Cash at bank			0
Cash in hand			381
			56,130
Less current liabilities			
Creditors			17,881
Overdraft			12,389
			30,270
Working capital			25,860
Non-current liabilities			
Bank loans			50,998
Net assets			186,682
Financed by			
Capital			60,000
Retained profit			126,682
Capital employed			**186,682**

▶ **Figure 3.9:** Example of a statement of financial position

Adjustments

Adjustments will be made between the statement of comprehensive income and the statement of financial position to ensure that both records are showing a true and fair picture of the business's activity. These adjustments are outlined below.

▶ Depreciation, straight line or reducing balance
  - Annual depreciation is shown as an expense on the statement of comprehensive income.
  - Each year depreciation is deducted from the net book value of an asset to show the value of the asset at the end of the year; this is the value of the asset recorded in the statement of financial position.
▶ Prepayments
  - A prepayment is when an expense is made in advance of the periods to which it relates.
  - The expense is therefore taken out of expenses in the statement of comprehensive income and shown as a current asset in the statement of financial position.
  - If, for example, broadband is paid for 12 months in advance, and the accounts are produced half way through this 12 month period, half of the total payment would be recorded as a prepayment under the current asset heading on the statement of financial position.
▶ Accruals
  - An accrual is when an expense is paid after the periods to which it relates.
  - The expense is therefore added as an expense in the statement of comprehensive income and shown as a current liability in the statement of financial position.
  - An example would be electricity paid quarterly in arrears; a figure would be shown in the statement of financial position to account for the value of electricity already consumed.
▶ Interpretation, analysis and evaluation of statements.

Once produced, the statement of financial position can be used internally by management to help measure the financial health of the business and inform future decision making. It can also be used externally by potential investors and creditors. An investor, for example, might look at the business's statement of financial position when deciding whether or not to offer capital to the business.

The statement of financial position may be analysed in a number of ways. These include making:
▶ comparisons between figures within the statement of financial position, e.g. current assets in relation to current liabilities
▶ comparisons between years, i.e. value of fixed assets or current liabilities in one year compared with previous years
▶ intrafirm comparisons to see how different aspects of the business are performing, e.g. debtors for one branch compared with another branch to identify any potential concerns regarding bad debts
▶ interfirm comparisons to see how the business is performing in relation to its competitors.

When interpreting and analysing a statement of financial position, it is also useful to consider working capital because this is a measure of the firm's ability to meet day-to-day expenses. The statement of financial position is a useful indicator of how effectively management are running the business.

Both statements of financial position and statements of comprehensive income are interpreted with the use of ratios.

Write out a list of all the headings shown on a statement of financial position. Write a short explanation or formula next to each heading.

Hint   Remember to include the adjustments you have just read about.

Extend Explain the relationship between a statement of financial position and a statement of comprehensive income.

Measuring profitability

You should now be familiar with the basic language of accounts and the key financial accounts produced by businesses. You will now look at what these accounts actually tell us and how an accountant can use or interpret them. Ratio analysis allows for a more meaningful interpretation of published accounts by comparing one figure with another. Ratio analysis also allows for both **interfirm** and **intrafirm** comparisons.

Ratios will be used by internal **stakeholders** such as managers and employees, as well as external stakeholders such as investors and creditors.

Profitability is a measure of the profit of a firm in relation to another factor. It allows for a more comprehensive assessment of the performance of a firm by comparing one figure to another. Imagine that there are two firms, A and B, both with a profit of £750,000 per year – how would you be able to tell which one was performing better? If, however, you were told that Firm A has sales revenue of £1.5 million and Firm B has sales revenue of £3 million, then it is clear that Firm A has greater profitability as it is generating the same amount of profit from a lower level of sales. This indicates it is more efficient and better at controlling its costs.

There are four profitability ratios you will look at here:

▶ gross profit margin
▶ mark-up
▶ net profit margin
▶ return on capital employed (ROCE).

Key terms

Interfirm – between different firms, for example, comparing the performance of two different house builders.

Intrafirm – within the firm, for example, comparing this year's results with last year's, or the performance of the York branch with the Leicester branch of a retail store.

Stakeholder – anyone with an interest in the activities of a business, whether directly or indirectly involved.

▶ What sort of information will the investors in this business need to be given about the company's finances?

Gross profit margin

This is calculated using the following formula: $\frac{\text{gross profit}}{\text{revenue}} \times 100$

This ratio looks at gross profit as a percentage of sales turnover. It shows us, for every £1 made in sales, how much is left as gross profit after the cost of goods sold has been deducted. A gross profit of 88 per cent therefore means that, for every £1 of sales made, 88p is left as gross profit.

If gross profit margin falls from one year to the next or is thought to be too low, a firm may try to reduce the cost of its purchases. This may involve looking for a cheaper supplier, but the firm must try to ensure that this does not affect the quality of the product. Alternatively, it may try to increase sales without increasing the cost of goods sold.

Mark-up

This is calculated using the following formula: $\frac{\text{gross profit}}{\text{cost of sales}} \times 100$

This ratio looks at profit as a percentage of cost of sales. It shows what percentage of cost of sales is added to reach selling price. For example, a mark-up of 25 per cent would mean that if the cost of raw materials used to produce a good were £1, it has been sold for £1.25.

Net profit margin

This is calculated using the following formula: $\frac{\text{net profit}}{\text{revenue}} \times 100$

This ratio looks at net profit as a percentage of sales turnover. It shows, for every £1 made in sales, how much of it is left as net profit after all expenses have been deducted. A net profit of 31 per cent therefore means that, for every £1 of sales made, 31p is left as net profit.

If net profit margin falls from one year to the next or is thought to be too low, a firm may look to reduce its expenses, for example, by moving to cheaper premises or cutting staffing costs. Before taking any action, however, the accountant must try to identify the cause of a falling figure – whether it is related to sales, cost of goods sold or expenses – as all of these factors will impact upon the net profit margin.

Worked Example – Freedom Designs Ltd

Sales turnover = £411,529

Gross profit = £269,792

Net profit = £41,246

Gross profit percentage of sales = £269,852 / £411,529 × 100 = 65.5 per cent

For every £1 Freedom Designs Ltd makes in sales, 65p is left as gross profit. A fashion retailer is likely to have reasonably high costs of sales due to the nature of their product. If it was a service industry then you might expect this percentage to be higher.

$$\text{net profit percentage of sales} = \frac{£41,246}{£411,529} \times 100 = 10 \text{ per cent}$$

For every £1 Freedom Designs Ltd makes in sales, just 10p is left as net profit. A fashion retailer is likely to have reasonably high expenses due to the nature of their business. A retail business with a physical location (as opposed to e-commerce) may have high overhead costs such as premises and heat and light.

Return on capital employed (ROCE)

This is calculated using the following formula:

$$\frac{\text{net profit before interest and tax}}{\text{capital employed}} \times 100$$

This ratio shows the percentage return a business is achieving from the capital (or money) being used to generate that return. It shows, for every £1 invested in the business in owners' capital or retained profits, what per cent is being generated in profit. A ROCE of 5 per cent means that, for every £1 tied up in the business, 5p is being generated in net profit.

Investors will often compare ROCE to the interest rate being offered in a bank or building society to see if their investment is working effectively for them in generating a return.

Worked Example – Freedom Designs Ltd

Net profit before interest and tax = £41,246

Capital employed = £186,682

$$\text{ROCE} = \frac{£41,246}{186,682} \times 100 = 22 \text{ per cent}$$

This means that, for every £1 being used within the business, there is a return of 22p. This is certainly higher than you could expect from a bank.

Measuring liquidity

Liquidity ratios measure how solvent a business is – that is, how able it is to meet short-term debts. There are two liquidity ratios you will look at here:

▶ current ratio
▶ acid test ratio/liquidity ratio (liquid capital ratio).

Current ratio

This is calculated using the following formula:

$$\frac{\text{current assets}}{\text{current liabilities}}$$

This ratio shows the amount of current assets in relation to current liabilities and is expressed as x:1. If a firm had a current ratio of 2:1, this would mean that, for every £2 it owned in current assets, it owed £1 in current liabilities, and this would generally be considered acceptable. If, however, a firm had a current ratio of 0.5:1, this would mean that, for every 50p it owned in current assets, it owed £1 in current liabilities. This means if the firm's bank demanded that it repaid its overdraft immediately and creditors demanded payment, the firm would not be able to cover these demands from current assets. This is therefore a dangerous position to be in.

Worked Example – Freedom Designs Ltd

Current assets = £56,130

Current liabilities = £30,270

$$\text{Current ratio} = \frac{£56{,}130}{£30{,}270} = £1.85$$

This means that, for every £1 the business owes in short-term debt (that is, its current liabilities), it owns £1.85 in current assets. The business therefore has sufficient liquidity to meet short-term debts.

Liquid capital ratio

This is calculated using the following formula:

$$\frac{\text{current assets – inventory}}{\text{current liabilities}}$$

The liquid capital ratio is thought to be a tougher measure of a firm's liquidity. Like the current ratio, it shows the amount of current assets in relation to current liabilities, but it does not include inventory. This is because inventory is considered to be the hardest current asset to turn into cash quickly. The result is expressed as x:1.

Worked Example – Freedom Designs Ltd

Current assets = £56,130

Stock = £34,294

Current liabilities = £30,270

$$\text{Acid test} = \frac{£56{,}130 - £34{,}294}{£30{,}270}$$

$$= \frac{£21{,}826}{£30{,}270} = 0.72$$

This means that, for every £1 the business owes in short-term debts, it only has 72p in liquid assets (current assets excluding stock). This figure shows the firm to be **illiquid**, as it could not meet its short-term debts if immediate repayment was demanded. A fashion retailer is likely to have a large amount of its current assets in the form of stock, due to the nature of the firm.

Research

Select a business that you are interested in (or you could use the one you studied in *Unit 1: Exploring Business*). Compare the profitability and liquidity of your chosen business to that of Freedom Designs Ltd.

Which one do you think is performing best? Justify your answer..

Key term

Illiquid – not easily converted into cash.

Measuring efficiency

Efficiency ratios tend to be used to assess how well management is controlling key aspects of the business, primarily stock and finances. There are three efficiency ratios you will look at here:

▸ trade receivable days

▸ trade payable days

▸ inventory turnover.

Trade receivable days

This is calculated using the following formula:

$$\left(\frac{\text{trade receivables}}{\text{credit sales}}\right) \times 365$$

If you do not know what percentage of sales were made on credit, then it is acceptable to use the sales figure as given in the statement of comprehensive income. The ratio measures, on average, how long it takes for debtors to pay; it is expressed as a number of days. For example, if a business has a debtors' payment period of 60 days, this means, on average, it takes debtors two months to pay for goods or services purchased on credit. A business with cash flow problems will try to reduce its debtors' payment period.

Worked Example – Freedom Designs Ltd

Debtors' trade receivables = £21,455

Sales = £411,529

$$\text{Trade receivables days} = \frac{£21,445}{£411,529} \times 365 = 19 \text{ days}$$

This means that, on average, it takes a customer 19 days to pay for their purchases. A fashion retailer is unlikely to offer long payment terms.

Trade receivable days will vary from firm to firm, depending upon the nature and price of items sold and whether the business deals in **business-to-business** or **business-to-consumer** sales. If it is business-to-business, longer payment terms may be given. One business may also give different payment terms to different customers depending upon the size and importance of a customer's business, reliability of payment and discounts offered.

Trade payable days

This is calculated using the following formula:

$$\left(\frac{\text{trade payables}}{\text{credit purchases}}\right) \times 365$$

If you do not know what percentage of purchases were made on credit, then it is acceptable to use the purchases figure as given in the statement of comprehensive income. The ratio measures, on average, how long it takes a firm to pay for goods and services bought on credit; it is expressed as a number of days. For example, if a business has trade payable days of 30 days, this means that, on average that there is a one month gap between the business buying the good or service and paying for it. A business with cash flow problems will try to lengthen its trade payables days.

Key terms

Business-to-business – B2B refers to when one business sells to another business – for example, a stationery business selling to a firm of accountants.

Business-to-consumer – B2C refers to when one business sells to an individual – for example, a stationery business selling wedding stationery to a bride and groom.

Worked Example – Freedom Designs Ltd

Trade payables = £17,881

Purchases = £128,129

$$\text{Trade payables days} = \frac{£17,881}{£128,129} \times 365 = 51 \text{ days}$$

This means that, on average, the firm pays its suppliers in 51 days. This may mean that some suppliers offer one month's credit and others two months.

Inventory turnover

This is calculated using the following formula:

$$\left(\frac{\text{average inventory}}{\text{cost of sales}}\right) \times 365$$

Average inventory is calculated as follows:

$$\frac{\text{opening inventory + closing inventory}}{2}$$

This ratio measures the average amount of time an item of stock is held by a business, and is expressed as a number of days. If a business has an inventory turnover of 7, this means that, on average, it holds each item of stock for one week. The rate of inventory turnover is very much dependent upon the nature of the firm. For example, you could expect a florist or fishmonger to have a much lower inventory turnover than a fashion store or car showroom. However, if the rate of inventory turnover appears high for the nature of the product, this might result in stock going out of date or out of fashion.

Worked Example – Freedom Designs Ltd

Opening inventory = £34,993

Closing inventory = £21,445

Cost of goods sold = £141,737

$$\text{Average inventory} = \frac{£34,993 + £21,445}{2}$$

$$= \frac{£56,438}{2} = £28,219$$

$$\text{Inventory turnover} = \frac{£28,219}{£141,737} \times 365 = 73 \text{ days}$$

This means that, on average, the business turns its stock over, or sells its stock, every 73 days. This is just over every two months, which is what you might expect from a fashion retailer with approximately six new lines per year.

Limitations of ratios

Although ratios are very useful there are also a few limitations. These are described below.

- They are calculated on past data and therefore may not be a true reflection of the business's current performance.
- Financial records may have been manipulated and therefore the ratios will be based on potentially misleading data.
- Ratios do not consider qualitative factors.
- A ratio can indicate that there is a problem in a business but does not directly identify the cause of the problem or the solution.
- Interfirm comparisons can be difficult as not all firms report their performance in the same way or generate their accounts in the same way.

Ratios only report on the financial performance at a set point in time; the statement of financial position is a snapshot of the business at a point in time. At other times of year the picture may be different.

Assessment practice 3.6

1   Identify **two** components that make up the first part of the statement of comprehensive income.   (2 marks)

2   A business purchases 20 new laptops for £11,500. They expect each laptop to last around 3 years and hope to resell nine of the laptops at the end of this time.

Calculate the straight line depreciation value of the laptops.   (2 marks)

3   It costs Dominic 85p to make a loaf of sourdough bread. He sells the bread for £1.25. He is thinking of increasing the price to £1.50.

Calculate the following.

(a) The mark up on the bread when sold for £1.25.   (2 marks)

(b) The mark up on the bread when sold for £1.50.   (2 marks)

THINK ▶FUTURE

Charlotte Donaldson

Assistant Management Accountant

I've been working in accounts for four years since finishing in the sixth form at school. I started as an apprentice which meant I was being paid to work at the same time as gaining professional qualifications. I am now AAT qualified and studying for CIMA. At the end of this I will be a fully qualified accountant. When I first started, I was responsible for everything from raising invoices for customers and processing invoices from suppliers, to keeping a register of fixed assets, including controlling company cars. Since I started, the company has grown and I now manage two junior clerks who have taken responsibility for raising and processing invoices. Managing and training other members of staff has given me a real sense of responsibility. I have even been sent on two management courses to help me develop my management skills. This has been a great experience.

Focusing your skills

It is important to take care and ensure that everything I do is accurate. I have to check everything I do because it has a knock-on effect on the final management accounts.

- Company records have to be up to date and correct in preparation for any VAT inspections.
- Employees' benefits need to be recorded otherwise they may be taxed incorrectly.
- The information I pass on to the management accountant has to be correct in order for her to produce accurate reports to HMRC and the company directors.
- The accounts we produce have to meet legal requirements.

Looking ahead

After four years, I have learned so much and was lucky to be in a company that was growing. This meant my job role was constantly growing and evolving with the company, allowing me to take on more responsibility. I have now been successful in gaining a new job in a different company, which is a promotion. I am looking forward to learning new skills and continuing with my studies to become fully qualified as a management accountant in my new job.

- Once Charlotte had decided she was ready for a new challenge, what do you think she had to do to get ready for a promotion?
- Do you think she was right to look for a new job with a new company?
- What might the advantages be of moving to a new company?

Getting ready for assessment

This section has been written to help you to do your best when you take the external examination. Read through it carefully and ask your tutor if there is anything you are not sure about.

About the test

This unit is externally assessed using an unseen paper-based examination. Pearson sets and marks the examination. The assessment must be taken under examination conditions.
The test is in two sections:
- Part A: personal finance
- Part B: business finance.

There are three types of questions:
- short answer questions
- calculation questions
- longer answer questions.

Sitting the test

Listen to, and read carefully, any instructions you are given. Lots of marks are often lost through not reading questions properly and misunderstanding what the question is asking.
Most questions contain command words. Understanding what these words mean will help you understand what the question is asking you to do.
As the guidelines for assessment can change, you should refer to the official assessment guidance on the Pearson Qualifications website for the latest definitive guidance.

Command word	Definition – what it is asking you to do
Give	You can provide: • examples • justifications.
Outline	Your work, performance or practice provides a summary or overview or a brief description of something.
Identify	Indicate the main features or purpose of something by recognising it and/or being able to discern and understand facts or qualities.
Illustrate	Include examples, images or diagrams to show what is meant within a specific context.
Calculate	Work out an answer, usually by adding, multiplying, subtracting or dividing. Can involve the use of formulas.
Explain	Your work shows clear details and gives reasons and/or evidence to support an opinion, view or argument. It could show how conclusions are drawn (arrived at). You are able to show that you understand the origins, functions and objectives of a subject, and its suitability for purpose.
Discuss	Consider different aspects of: • a theme or topic • how they interrelate • the extent to which they are important. A conclusion is not required.
Analyse	Present the outcome of methodical and detailed examination either by breaking down: a theme, topic or situation in order to interpret and study the relationships between the parts and/or information or data to interpret and study key trends and interrelationships.
Assess	Present a careful consideration of varied factors or events that apply to a specific situation or identify those which are the most important or relevant and arrive at a conclusion.
Evaluate	Your work draws on varied information, themes or concepts to consider aspects such as: • strengths or weaknesses • advantages or disadvantages • alternative actions • relevance or significance. Your inquiries should lead to a supported judgement showing relationship to its context. This will often be in a conclusion.

Sample answers

For some of the questions you will be given some background information on which the questions are based.

Look at the sample questions which follow and the tips on how to answer them well.

Answering short answer questions – give, state and identify

- [ ] Read the question carefully.
- [ ] Highlight or underline key words.
- [ ] Note the number of marks available which will match the number of points asked for in the question, e.g. 'state one' = 1 mark or 'give two' = 2 marks.

Make sure that you make the same number of statements as there are marks available. Take care that if you are making two or more points that these are sufficiently different points (not the same one made in a slightly different way).

Worked example

State **two** functions of money. [2]

Answer: Unit of account. Store of value.

Two accurate and different points are made gaining full marks.

Command words 'give', 'state' or 'identify' can be answered in single words or statements. There is no need to write in full sentences as the examiner is only testing your knowledge, i.e. your ability to recall information.

Answering short answer questions – describe

Note the number of marks available. If 2 marks are available you will be required to describe one concept. 'Describe' requires two linked sentences where the second sentence adds a development to the first. If the question is worth 4 marks, you would repeat this process of making a point and then adding a development a second time.

Worked example

Describe **one** benefit of producing a cash flow forecast. [2]

Answer: One benefit of producing a cash flow forecast is it will identify months where there is a potential cash shortage. It can also be shown to a bank manager as part of a business plan.

The first point is correct, as is the second. However, the candidate would only be awarded 1 mark as these are two separate points rather than one point which has been described or developed. A better response would have made the first point: 'One benefit of producing a cash flow forecast is it will identify months were there is a potential cash shortage'. This statement would then have been developed, gaining a second mark: 'This would allow the business to make plans for these months, maybe by arranging an overdraft'.

Answering calculation questions

Write down the formula.

☐ Identify the numbers provided in the additional information given within the question.

☐ Put numbers into the formula.

☐ Show all your working.

☐ Express the answer in the correct way, e.g. £, units.

☐ Check your working.

Worked example

Jack has provided you with the following information from his statement of financial position.

Revenue	£250,000
Cost of goods sold	£130,000
Expenses	£80,000

Calculate Jack's net profit margin. [5]

$$\text{Net profit margin} = \frac{\text{net profit}}{\text{sales revenue}} \times 100$$

Net profit = revenue – cost of goods sold – expenses

Net profit = £250 000 – £130 000 – £80 000 = £40 000

$$\text{Net profit margin} = \frac{£40\ 000}{£250\ 000} = 0.16$$

The candidate has written down all of the information, including the formulas, correctly. Working is well laid out, making it easy for the examiner to see what they have done. Unfortunately, they have forgotten to multiply by 100 at the end to gain the correct answer of 16%. However, because everything else is correct, only 1 mark would be lost for this error.

Answering extended answer questions – explain

You are required to develop a line of argument using linking words such as therefore, so that, because. Start your answer by making a relevant point and expand on this using two or three steps in a line of argument.

☐ Avoid moving on to new points until the point you have made has been fully developed.

Worked example

Example:

Explain the benefits of an individual taking out travel insurance before travelling abroad. [6]

Travel insurance protects the holder from financial losses incurred while away from home.

One benefit of this is that if personal belongings are lost or stolen they will be covered by the insurance policy. Therefore, the holder will be able to make a claim so that they can get back the cost of replacing the lost items, e.g. money or a camera. This means that the person travelling has not lost a lot of money because they had taken out protection in advance.

A second benefit is that the traveller may be protected if the holiday is cancelled or other changes are made, such as flight delays. This means that, although the inconvenience will still exist, the traveller could be compensated for this. This would allow them to cover additional expenses incurred while waiting for flights, etc.

A third benefit is the traveller would be insured if they fell sick. This would mean that they could receive treatment without having to worry about big medical bills. These would be paid for by the insurance company or paid for and then reclaimed. This means that the traveller will feel more confident while away and be happy that if they need medical care that they can seek this.

> It is a good idea to start by identifying the key term in the question. Here the answer starts by showing the examiner that the candidate understands what travel insurance is. It is important here that the candidate has said 'while away from home', so they are not just talking about insurance in general but the answer is specific to travel insurance.

> A number of steps have then been given in a logical line of argument, e.g. covered – claim – get back the cost – not lost money. Three different aspects of travel insurance have been identified and explained in context.

Answering extended answer questions – discuss, analyse, assess, evaluate

☐ Read the question carefully.

☐ Highlight or underline key words.

☐ Look at the number of marks available as an indication of how many arguments are required and the depth of arguments.

☐ You are required to develop a line of argument using linking words such as therefore, so that, because.

☐ Start your answer by making a relevant point and expand on this using two or three steps in a line of argument.

☐ Avoid moving on to new points until the point you have made has been fully developed.

☐ You will need to present two arguments from different viewpoints, e.g. one advantage and one disadvantage or one argument for and one argument against.

☐ You do not need to make judgements and write a conclusion.

Worked example

Example:

Karen runs a road haulage business. She is looking to expand the business and wants to purchase two more lorries.

Assess the use of external sources of finance to Karren. [10]

External sources of finance are from outside the business, e.g. bank loans and leasing.

Karren could use a bank loan. This would involve receiving a lump sum from the bank. She could use this to buy the lorries. However, it is expensive.

Karren could lease the lorries rather than buy them. The advantage of this is that she would be able to expand the business as she would have the lorries now. However, she would not be paying a lump sum for them but paying in smaller amounts on a regular basis to the lease company. This helps spread out the payment for the lorries and could help Karren's cash flow. She would also avoid potentially high interest payments. However, although this is a good source of finance in the short run, in the long run it is likely to be more expensive as Karren will have to keep paying to lease the lorries for as long as she wants to use them. She will never actually own them. Therefore, this may have a negative effect on her profit margins in the long run.

Overall, a bank loan may be the better option as Karren wants to expand the business and she will therefore benefit from owning the lorries rather than leasing them. Or she could look at asking friends and family or a venture capitalist to invest money into the business to help her expand.

This answer shows a good understanding of the topic, i.e. external sources of finance, and uses technical language throughout the answer. The first paragraph makes a relevant point and some judgement but lacks development. It is rather descriptive. The second paragraph is much better, discussing the issues related to leasing in a more developed way. It also provides a balanced argument.

The conclusion tries to weigh up the two options but then moves on to bring in new points/ideas. It is not a good idea to bring in new points in the conclusion. This should be a judgement made based on the arguments that have already been presented. The candidate would have gained more marks if they had brought in additional sources of finance earlier and discussed the advantages and disadvantages of these to help present a more balanced argument.

Managing an Event 4

Getting to know your unit

Assessment
You will be assessed by a series of assignments set by your tutor.

Managing an event is a really exciting part of working in business. Huge numbers of events happen every day, from small events that raise money for charity as part of corporate social responsibility, through to corporate events such as sporting sponsorship events. This unit gives you the chance to analyse and make judgements about business events. You will also have the chance to create your own event and test your practical skills.

How you will be assessed

This unit will be assessed internally through a series of tasks set by your tutor. Throughout this unit, you will find assessment practices that will help you to practise and to develop your knowledge and skills ready for assessment. Completing these activities will help you to be fully prepared for assessment as you will have practised the activities before you complete your final assessment.

In order for you to successfully pass this unit, you must make sure that you have met the requirements of all the Pass grading criteria. You can do this by checking yourself against the criteria.

To gain a Merit or a Distinction, you must extend your work further. For Merit criteria you must analyse different elements of the unit. For Distinction you must evaluate. Evaluate means make judgements about different criteria in the unit.

The assignment(s) set by your tutor will consist of a number of tasks designed to meet the criteria in the table. This is likely to consist of activities such as:

▶ writing an individual report identifying tasks that need to be carried out for an event with a summary of skills needed by an event organiser
▶ an individual summary report and group presentation of an investigation with a detailed plan of an event
▶ taking an active part in staging and managing an event
▶ writing a report which records and evaluates the success of the event.

Assessment criteria

This table shows you what you must do in order to achieve a **Pass, Merit** or **Distinction** grade, and where you can find activities to help you.

Pass	Merit	Distinction
Learning aim A Explore the role of an event organiser		
A.P1 Explain the role and skills required to be an effective events organiser. **Assessment practice 4.1**	**A.M1** Analyse own skills with those required by an event organiser, highlighting areas for development. **Assessment practice 4.1**	**AB.D1** Fully justify how own skills match those of an event organiser. **Assessment practice 4.1**
A.P2 Investigate own skills in the form of a skills audit. **Assessment practice 4.1**		
Learning aim B Investigate the feasibility a proposed event		
B.P3 Investigate the staging of several events to determine common success factors. **Assessment practice 4.2**	**B.M2** Assess the feasibility of the event proposal. **Assessment practice 4.2**	**BC.D2** Evaluate and justify, feasibility plan, tools, budget and risk, making any required contingency adjustments. **Assessment practice 4.2**
B.P4 Explain the chosen event idea, including reasons for choice. **Assessment practice 4.2**		
Learning aim C Develop a detailed plan for a business or social enterprise event		
C.P5 Explain factors that need to be considered when producing a detailed plan for the proposed event. **Assessment practice 4.2**	**C.M3** Analyse the key factors that need to be considered when producing a plan for an event. **Assessment practice 4.2**	
C.P6 Produce a detailed plan for your chosen event using planning tools, including a detailed budget and consideration of risk assessment and contingency planning. **Assessment practice 4.2**		
Learning aim D Stage and manage a business or social enterprise event		
D.P7 Stage an event, demonstrating some relevant management skills. **Assessment practice 4.3**	**D.M4** Demonstrate effective and safe event-management skills when organising and staging an event. **Assessment practice 4.3**	**DE.D3** Justify how own contribution has contributed to a successful outcome of the event by the demonstration of outstanding management skills throughout the arranging and staging of an event. **Assessment practice 4.3**
Learning aim E Reflect on the running of the event and evaluate own skills development		
E.P8 Review the success of the event in meeting aims and objectives, achieving targets and receiving good feedback from stakeholders. **Assessment practice 4.3**	**E.M5** Analyse the planning and running of the event, how risks and contingencies were managed, making recommendations for future improvements. **Assessment practice 4.3**	

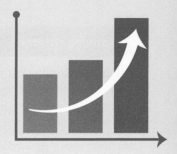

Getting started

Events management is an exciting part of business activity. There are many events every year from local charitable events through to national and international events. List any events you have been to in the last year. At the end of the unit, review your list and see how many you had forgotten.

A Explore the role of an event organiser

In this section, you will explore the very important skills that are required by successful event organisers, including tasks that they need to complete individually or as a team, planning skills and the tools that they use to audit activities that have taken place.

Tasks to be completed

If you think about events that you may have helped to organise or have attended yourself, there are lots of different tasks that need to take place including:
▶ organising where, when and how the event is going to take place
▶ the legal requirements to hold an event
▶ organisational procedures that need to be applied, such as policies on how risk assessments are completed or security controls.

Discussion

Before you start working on the elements that need to be organised when you hold an event such as a special occasion party, draw up a list of those elements and discuss the importance of each one, in small groups. What would happen if any of those elements was missing?

Organising

Ensuring that an event is organised properly means ensuring that all elements of an event are suitable for its purpose. Each of these seven elements (see Figure 4.1) are outlined below.

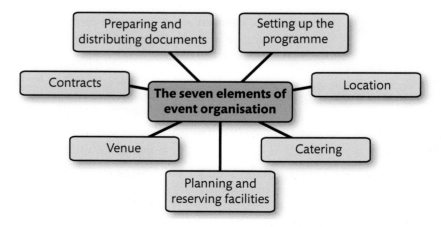

▶ **Figure 4.1:** The seven essential elements of any event

Venue

The first part of organising an event is to find the venue where the event is going to take place. The venue will set the scene for the type of event that is going to happen and will influence whether or not people want to attend. It will also help to identify the costs that will be involved. Small venues may be offered without cost. Other larger venues may charge fees which will need to be paid for or recovered through the event.

When thinking about a venue, an event organiser needs to consider:
▸ the type of people coming (business people, students etc)
▸ the number of people that can be seated or can stand
▸ the travel method used to get to the location (car, minibus or public transport such as trains or coaches)
▸ any ethical or belief considerations, for example it would be inappropriate to have an event for vegetarians in a location where the main focus of activity is the production or selling of meat or fish.

▸ The type and location of a business event has a big impact. Can you think of a local venue that would not be suitable for an event such as a business meeting?

The size of the venue will have a big influence on the event. A large venue will be able to accommodate larger numbers of people and may have a greater range of facilities, such as restaurants and leisure facilities.

However, smaller venues may have the advantage of being able to offer a more relaxed and friendly atmosphere if fewer people are in attendance. Some venues, for example hotels, have a number of different meeting room options that can accommodate from two to a thousand people. Other venues are specifically designed to have thousands of people, such as conference or convention centres.

Location

The location of a venue will influence the success of a business event. The target market should influence the location. For example, if an event was trying to sell upmarket products, it would need to be held in an upmarket area where the visitors are likely to have higher incomes and, therefore, be able to afford to buy the products.

The location can also be influenced by the type of participants, for example local business people or the public. For local participants, the event organiser needs to think of the best location in a local area. If the event is planned with regional participation in mind, the organiser needs to pick a location based on geography so that all the people attending the event will travel approximately the same distance to get there.

Knowing a bit about the type of people that will be attending and the theme of the event will also influence the suitability of the location. For example, if the event is focusing on green issues, it should be at a location with easy access to public transport rather than a venue that can only be reached by car. If the event is linked to an activity that requires specific facilities, such as water for a boat trade show, then the location needs to have those facilities.

Some business events are organised at a location such as a tourist destination, so event participants can combine visiting the business event with the attractions. Event organisers may even plan afternoon excursions for participants. With any venue, it is important to consider the **ambience** of its location.

Key term

Ambience – the atmosphere at the event.

Research

> The Irish Maritime Festival is the largest maritime, food and family festival in Ireland. In 2014, it attracted 40,000 visitors. Find out about the different excursions and activities that are available at the festival and discuss how local businesses benefit from being associated with this event.

Key term

Outside catering – when the business or organisation providing the venue does not also provide the catering.

Catering

Catering may also be an important aspect of organising an event. The type of catering may influence where you decide to hold it. A three-course lunch is most likely to need a hotel with facilities, while sandwich delivery may have less strict location requirements. Some venues offer catering and others require **outside catering** to be brought to the venue.

Discussion

> A company in Manchester provide a variety of catering services, including outside catering, throughout the north-west. They offer a wide range of menus and use local suppliers. In small groups, discuss the advantages and disadvantages of using an outside catering company when organising an event. What are the advantages and disadvantages to a business of providing this service?

Some event organisers might decide to provide their own catering, for example by making cakes or other foods to be given away or sold. It is important that any catering provided at events follows guidelines issued by the Food Standards Agency to avoid people falling ill. The local authority environmental health team also gives advice about making sure that food is safe and investigates complaints if anyone should fall ill after an event. It is essential that event organisers are clear about their responsibilities.

PAUSE POINT

Can you explain why it is important to ensure that the venue, location and catering are correctly matched to an event?

Hint

What would happen if an event had the wrong venue, location or catering – what would be the impact on the success?

Extend

To what extent do you think good or bad catering arrangements influence the success of any event? Explain your answer.

Planning and reserving facilities

An event organiser must also ensure that everything goes to plan so that the event is a success. Planning does not just include the event itself, but also needs to take into account other events that are happening at around the same time. Too many similar events happening in the same week may result in poor attendance at your event.

The time of year will also influence the planning of an event and the organiser needs to think about whether:

▶ the event needs to be inside or outside – it is usually more appropriate to run outside events in the summer
▶ the event is linked to a particular festival or tradition – if so, it will need to happen at the same time
▶ the event depends on other factors such as supplies that are only available at certain times of year or are cheaper in a particular month.

The organiser will need to plan whether physical equipment or facilities are required to run an event. This may include the buildings, IT equipment, a special feature of entertainment or display that is brought in for the event or toilets or car parking attendants if an event is outdoors.

Discussion

Free WiFi is available as a facility at many events and activities, both indoor and outdoor. What are the benefits and concerns of offering free WiFi at a business event? In groups, debate whether you think free WiFi is now critical for all business events. One group should present the case for free WiFi and another group against.

Very large events might take much planning and require a lot of facilities. These may include:

▶ cash machines (available for a charge if the event organisers want people to buy goods during the event)
▶ first aid facilities (in case anyone requires medical attention)
▶ special assistance (for example for anyone who uses a wheelchair or has other mobility needs)
▶ baby changing facilities (if large numbers of parents are expected with young children)
▶ policing or stewarding to control large numbers of people
▶ facilities for animals
▶ power
▶ signs or banners showing people where to go and that the event is happening
▶ bunting or other decorative materials to highlight where the event is happening
▶ arrangements for parking, if needed
▶ facilities for rubbish collection during and after the event
▶ refreshments including drinking water, where necessary
▶ cleaning companies or volunteers for after the event has finished.

Research

Many business events now rely not only on physical facilities such as toilets or refreshments but also on digital facilities. The Brighton Digital Festival takes place annually and provides digital and virtual facilities. Research the facilities used at the 2015 festival and in previous years. How important do you think digital facilities are now? Provide reasons for your answer.

 **PAUSE POINT**   How might fundraising event arrangements be affected by the weather? What impact would this have on event planning?

Hint   Compare organising the event in June with organising it in December.

Extend   Give a judgement on the best time to organise an outside fundraising event and other influences that might affect it.

Setting up the programme

The programme is the list of what will happen at the event and the order in which it will happen. It guides the organisation of the event and will be used by **attendees**. The programme's quality and content will help to guide people's interest as well as give them an outline of what is going to happen during the day. The programme will also give details of any special guests, speeches, entertainment, prize-giving or free gifts that might be part of the event. Sometimes, having a guest speaker may encourage more people to attend and this will need to be highlighted in the programme.

There are several different types of programme that may be used for an event. These may include programmes that have various activities that attendees can choose from or programmes where everyone is following the same structure for the event.

The length of time for the event will also influence the programme. All-day events need more time for people to travel to the event and for coffee and lunch breaks. Events that take place over a few days may require arrangements for accommodation, including breakfast.

Case study

Norfolk Network

Norfolk Network brings together different enterprises throughout the whole of Norfolk into a membership community. The network was set up to bring together business people throughout Norfolk with the purpose of satisfying five strategic objectives:

- to stimulate, champion and circulate the stories coming out of the Norfolk innovation community
- to facilitate intelligent introductions and recommendations
- to grow the existing knowledge base
- to remain as the 'go-to' authority on what is happening in the SME innovation community in Norfolk
- to nurture emerging talent.

The network regularly holds events that are free for its members and also for the wider business community.

Go to their website www.norfolknetwork.com and then check your knowledge.

The programmes for these events are important to ensure that they have the right focus for those who may wish to attend and that they are attracting the right people.

Check your knowledge

1 Why do you think Norfolk Network holds free events?
2 What are the advantages of holding free events?
3 Are there any potential disadvantages?
4 Carry out research on the internet to find free events that are happening in your area. In small groups, consider why these organisations are holding these events.

PAUSE POINT

Which facilities would you need to organise a mini food festival locally? How would they influence the event programme?

Hint — Write a list of all the facilities that you need to think about for a mini food festival and list their availability and cost.

Extend — Make a judgement on the impact on the festival if any one of those facilities was missing.

Preparing and distributing documents

Key term

Soft copy – a version of a document, such as a pdf, that can be emailed or uploaded to a website.

Most events require some form of documentation in hard copy or **soft copy** that can be distributed before, during or even after the event. For environmental and cost reasons, soft copies are often preferred. Sometimes documents may be supplied on a USB stick or in a free wallet or bag that is given out by the event organiser. Alternatively, they can be uploaded to a website or other secure online storage area with passwords given to users so that they can be accessed.

The main documents that might be needed for an event are listed in Table 4.1. A number of different documents may be needed to support an event. These may be more traditional paper documents or other methods that organisations are increasingly using to distribute information about events, such as websites with a secure username and password, email or social networking websites.

▶ **Table 4.1:** The main documents needed for an event

Document	What is included
Background	• The event's purpose. • The target audience. • The cost of attending the event and any discounts that might be available. • Details of how much tickets are and where they can be purchased, if required. • Any permission or authorisation needed to hold the event from the local authority, police or other agencies.
Agenda or schedule	• Information about what is happening and the times involved. • May also include the deadline for submitting any papers or items that people want to put forward for discussion at the event.
Event papers	• Minutes of previous meetings. • Biographies of previous speakers. • Information about organisations involved with the event.
Communication plan	• Contacts for further information. • Website link or launch. • Social media plan, for example through Twitter or Facebook. • Information to be given out during the event – event brochure, flyers for publicity and posters or other sources of information.
Travel arrangements	• How to get to the event by train, car or even by plane. • Signs to the event, including arrangements for parking. • Banners to publicise the event's location.
Accommodation	• Arrangements for hotels that are close to where the event is being held.
Additional needs or special arrangements	• Arrangements for people with disabilities or those who have special dietary needs need to be considered as well and where possible adjustments need to be made to accommodate everyone.
Risk assessment	• Organisers need to have considered the health and safety risks of events and this is completed using a risk assessment. You will learn more about this assessment later in the unit.

Distributing documents prior to a business event is an important step. It may be a formal business meeting and, therefore, an agenda needs to be sent out in advance so that people attending know what will be discussed. Some agendas are regularly published on the internet so that people who may be interested can see what will be discussed.

Sometimes, it is important to send out other paperwork before the event so that participants can be prepared. The type of paperwork depends on the audience and the level of discussion. Many organisations will publish biographies of people who are speaking at the event. Larger events, such as conferences, usually publish a list of all the abstracts of submitted papers and distribute this before the event. Another type of meeting paper that might be published and sent out prior to the event would be a list of the different workshops, demonstrations or other activities available.

Discussion

The Mayor of London organises many different consultations and events each year. Topics and events are published in advance and social media are used to give responses and pose questions at www.london.gov.uk. In small groups, discuss the benefits of using social media for planning and distributing documents.

The organiser will need to find out if people are likely to want to attend, and consultation before the event will help to highlight any issues that may affect the quality and success of the business event. For example, if the event is organised at the same time as another similar event, attendance may be poor. Planning ahead will help to solve this problem. Consultation may also generate ideas for a very different event.

Consulting the different groups that are likely to be interested in the event may also lead to further ideas or extra items being added to an agenda. During the planning stages of a formal meeting, there is usually an opportunity for prospective participants to add items or issues that they would like to cover to the agenda.

When planning a business event, such as staff training or team building, the organiser needs to ask the following questions.

▶ What do the staff expect to get out of the event?
▶ How will the business benefit from this event?
▶ How much time do staff have available for the event?
▶ When would it be best to hold this event so that it does not affect the business's operations?

▶ Consulting different groups of people is a very important part of event planning

Information on any business event should include:

▶ the time the event starts
▶ the cost of attendance
▶ the specific programme of the event
▶ how to get there
▶ any prior knowledge that the event participants need before the event.

The event organiser must be able to communicate this information in a clear and accurate manner. Many organisations use websites to communicate this information easily and cheaply. Some organisations now also use social media to advertise and promote events and this may be done using text or video on different social and business networking sites. Individuals are asked to pass on the information to their friends and families or other business associates, to increase numbers.

Once people have signed up for the event, the organiser will need to send them joining instructions and, if necessary, notify them of any alterations to the arrangements.

Sometimes, for various reasons, events have to be changed. This may be because:
▶ the event is growing too large for the chosen venue
▶ the event cannot take place because of illness
▶ of changes in the weather
▶ of lack of funding
▶ of lack of interest
▶ of a concern by authorities that the event should not go ahead, for example due to security or health and safety concerns.

It is very important that records of all participants or ticket-holders are kept so that information or changes can be communicated. It is also useful to make contingency arrangements so that if a time or location change needs to be made, the event will still be able to take place.

 PAUSE POINT   Name three documents that are required when planning a small business conference.

 Hint   Think back to documents required before, during and after the event. Refer to Table 4.7.

Extend   Make a judgement about which documents are most important when planning a small business conference and why.

Contracts

Most events will require contractual agreement that will be agreed either verbally or in writing. The contract sets out the offer and prices for the individual elements of the event including:
▶ venue
▶ catering
▶ insurance
▶ advertising/promotion.

Separate agreements can be made with outside suppliers and may include those used for booking a hotel venue or hiring equipment.

The *Supply of Goods and Services Act 1982* ensures that the event organiser is supplied with goods and services as part of a contract and it also protects suppliers and customers. The Act sets out requirements for ticketing that protect both the event organiser and attendees, and also protects consumers from faulty equipment.

Investigating current legal requirements including consumer protection

There are a number of important legal requirements that need to be considered when organising an event. These include:
▶ contractual
▶ health and safety, including public liability insurance
▶ age restrictions
▶ licensing
▶ consumer protection.

Contractual

As previously mentioned, the *Supply of Goods and Services Act 1982* is very important to event organisers. As an event organiser, you should always ensure that you have a contract with any suppliers you are using. This includes suppliers offering intangible goods such as the venue owners supplying the venue, as well as those offering tangible goods, for example, the caterers. The *Supply of Goods and Services Act 1982* ensures that you are protected if there are any issues with any of the suppliers. It also protects the suppliers themselves if the event organiser has any issues, such as with payment.

There are also contracts between the event organiser and the attendees. If an attendee has purchased a ticket to the event, then they have entered into a contract with the event organiser to receive the event, as advertised. The *Supply of Goods and Services Act 1982* protects customers from anything that may go wrong with an event.

Health and safety requirements

There are stringent health and safety requirements for all events. Making sure that people organising and attending events are aware of these is very important to ensure that everyone is kept safe.

The *Health and Safety at Work Act 1974*, and subsequent updates and regulations, highlights that everyone has a responsibility for their own health and safety and has a duty of care for others. When organisers put together an event, they need to contact different agencies and authorities to ensure that all health and safety requirements can be met. These include contacting:

▶ police, fire, ambulance

▶ environmental health/food standards agency

▶ highways

▶ local authority licensing team.

Event organisers, are ultimately, responsible for the health and safety of everyone taking part in an event. They must ensure that a nominated person has the responsibility for health and safety. Many different aspects need to be considered, including arrangements for first aid, insurance and food hygiene.

If anything goes wrong at the event, for example if someone is injured or even dies, there could be serious consequences for the organiser, under criminal law. It is possible to be prosecuted for corporate manslaughter and go to prison if found guilty.

Venues must have **public liability insurance**, which ensures that money is paid out in the event that a member of the public has an accident at that venue.

Event organisers will also need to ensure that any stallholders or businesses offering services at the event also have their own insurance against loss or damage.

Link

You will learn more about legal requirements in *Unit 23: The English Legal System*.

Key term

Public liability insurance – insurance cover required to hold an event; cover is usually needed for up to £5 million.

Research

The SURGE Festival takes place in Glasgow during the summer. This is a festival of street arts, physical theatre and circus and offers masterclasses and workshops to the public. Research the SURGE Festival and list the potential health and safety issues that could arise. Describe how the SURGE Festival organisers look after the health and safety of everyone that attends.

Age restrictions

Any organised event needs to meet age requirements. For example, at a music event or festival, it must be ensured that young people are aged 18 or over if they are going to buy any alcohol or tobacco products that are on sale. There are also strict rules about selling raffle or lottery tickets to, or by young people under the age of 18.

Licensing

For many events, it is necessary to have a licence. The licence may be for holding the event itself and be required by the council, or it might be for the purposes of entertainment. It is not necessary to have a licence for:

▶ live unamplified music

▶ live amplified music for up to 200 people

▶ performances of plays and dance for up to 500 people

▶ indoor sporting events for up to 1000 people (as long as the event yakes place between 8 a.m. and 11 p.m.).

For other events, it may be necessary to close or block a road and, again, a licence from the Highways Agency is needed before this can happen. It can take four to six weeks to get permission so you need to plan ahead.

Research

Regulations for organising charitable events are less strict, although organisers must still be careful about licence requirements for raffles, lotteries, some types of entertainment and alcohol. Not following regulations risks a fine of up to £1000.

Read the Can Do Guide to organising and running a voluntary or community event on www.gov.uk. Write down three pieces of information and discuss these with your class.

⏸ PAUSE POINT   Can you explain why health and safety is extremely important when planning an event?

       Hint   Think about what would happen if something went wrong at an event and someone was injured.

       Extend   To what extent can all health and safety concerns be planned for by an event organiser?

Consumer protection

From 1 October 2015, the *Consumer Rights Act 2015* was brought into force and replaced other pieces of legislation including the Sale of Goods Act, Unfair Terms in Consumer Contracts Regulations and the Supply of Goods and Services Act. The *Consumer Rights Act 2015* provides protection for event organisers, suppliers and customers.

The Act brought into force changes to the rights of consumers, including those that relate to different types of services and events. These include:

▶ digital content such as apps, e-books and movies

▶ additional protection for faulty goods

▶ additional protection for unfair terms such as hidden charges or fees.

Consumers can, ultimately, take event organisers to court. This is both expensive and time consuming. Alternative Dispute Resolution (ADR) may be used instead. An ADR will be used to negotiate between the two parties involved to avoid the time and costs of a lengthy court procedure.

Link

You will learn more about legal matters in *Unit 23: The English Legal System*.

Research

Find out more about the *Consumer Rights Act 2015*. Compare the Act to previous legislation. What has improved and why is this good for event organisers, suppliers and attendees?

Discussion

Access the Citizens Advice Bureau website and research their advice regarding selling and purchasing of tickets for an event. In pairs or small groups, discuss what this guidance would mean for a small business event selling tickets in your area.

Setting up organisational procedures

Organisations will usually have a set of procedures that they follow for events, and these procedures will change depending on the size of the organisation, the type of event that is taking place and who is involved.

▶ A business meeting may only require an employee to let their line manager know that it is taking place as part of the organisation's procedures.

▶ A business conference may need to be agreed by the chief executive or managing director.

Procedures for signing off events will depend on the purpose of the event and the potential effect of the event on the organisation's reputation. If there are a number of expenses involved, the finance manager or director may need to authorise the event and confirm that there is money available for this purpose.

As the organiser of the event, you will need to know who must give authority for any event and the forms that need to be completed. You should follow organisational procedures or you may get into serious trouble, especially if something goes wrong.

Risk assessments will highlight any issues found while organising an event, and help the organiser to take steps to reduce the likelihood of anything untoward happening.

To make sure all the risks are assessed correctly and steps are put in place to minimise risk, the event organiser should carry out a risk assessment for the event. There are lots of different ways of doing risk assessments but examples of how a hazard can be identified and the controls that should be put in place is provided in Table 4.2.

▶ **Table 4.2:** Risk assessment for an indooor business fair

Hazard identified	People at risk	Likelihood	Severity	Controls	Further action
Tripping or falling on the steps in the entrance	Visitors Exhibitors Employees	Low	Low	Keep the steps clear during the event	Not needed
Too many people attending the event	Visitors Exhibitors Employees	Low	Low	Make sure that visitor numbers are controlled at the entrance	Not needed
Trailing wires from stands may cause someone to trip	Visitors Exhibitors Employees	Low	Low	Wires should be taped to the floor	Not needed

Security procedures are also important when organising an event, depending on the type of event and the activities involved. The event organisers must be aware of the emergency procedures that are used by the venue where the event is being held. They will need to talk to the venue's manager or coordinator to find out:

▶ what happens in an emergency

▶ where the nearest fire exits are

▶ what kind of sound indicates that there is an emergency

▶ what happens if someone needs to be searched.

Materials and equipment must be kept secure before, during and after the event, from the time they are placed in the venue until they have been picked up. Some equipment is extremely expensive and would be costly to replace, so it must be secured, monitored and returned to its owners at the end of the event. For some events and venues, it may be possible to have a security officer or guard who takes charge of looking after valuable items.

Organisational procedures may also change depending on the type of event and the people involved. For example, if a celebrity is coming to an event, organisations may have a different set of procedures applied. If a member of the Royal Family is attending an event, procedures for security will be managed by the Royal Protection Branch of police and can require a year's notice when planning an event.

⏸ PAUSE POINT	How do organisational procedures help organisations to plan events most effectively?	
Hint	Think about what could happen if they were not in place.	
Extend	To what extent can organisational procedures help or restrict an organiser when planning an event?	

Planning skills

There is a common expression that says 'failing to plan is planning to fail'. Organising and running events is very important and has an impact on others. This means that planning is very important and event organisers must use the six planning skills carefully and to the benefit of the event. These skills are:

▶ organising

▶ problem solving

▶ time managing

▶ negotiating

▶ communicating

▶ interpersonal.

Organisational

During the event, it is important to make sure that everything runs smoothly. Being organised means making sure that everything is running to time, notes are taken, documents distributed, rooms are easily accessible and arrivals or cancellations are noted.

▶ Note taking – it is usual for someone to be appointed to take notes. This service may be arranged by the event organiser or volunteers might be asked to do this during the event. The extent to which note taking is required will depend on the type of business event. For formal meetings, an assistant is usually appointed to take notes and then write them up into formal minutes.

- Document distribution – it is the event organiser's job to make sure that delegates receive the correct documents for the business event. The type and number of papers will depend on the event itself. Formal governing body meetings such as those at a school, college or university may have a large number of papers that must be read in advance of the meeting. For conferences or less formal meetings, there may be a pack of information that is given out to delegates at the event. Some conference organisers, for example CRAC, give delegates online access to all the papers from its conferences so that they can use them after the event.

- Location of rooms and facilities – at any event, delegates may get lost. There should be support available to help them find their way. In large hotels, a key point of contact is often the reception. In other event locations, there may be a sign-in table that is constantly staffed and delegates can come here to ask about room locations and facilities. It may be a good idea to set out a location map of the venue and facilities at this table.

- Recording attendance and cancellations – recording attendance must be done for any business event. Not only is this important for health and safety reasons, but it also provides proof for an employer or trainer that the person actually attended the event. Often the record of attendance will include extra information such as telephone numbers or email addresses so that the delegates may be contacted again after the event. This is particularly important if names are not given in advance.

  It is also very important to monitor cancellations. Some organisers offering free events now only charge if an organisation does not turn up rather than if they do. In some instances, there is a £50 charge for non-attendance, which helps to ensure that people do go when they have booked a place. If an organisation keeps on cancelling places, the event organiser may decide not to offer them a place in the future.

To organise the different elements happening at the same time, event organisers need to have good enough personal skills to be able to manage all the different elements simultaneously. The skills they need to demonstrate are shown in Figure 4.2.

▶ **Figure 4.2:** Event organisers need good personal skills to be able to organise several elements at the same time

These were the personal skills an event organiser needs to have.

- Prioritising tasks is very important as it ensures that tasks are carried out in a correct and efficient order.

- Following procedures ensures that the event organiser is following the organisation's requirements when running the event.

▶ Being detailed and not forgetting any elements of the event will ensure that it runs smoothly.

▶ Keeping files (either physical or electronic) securely and in order makes it easier and quicker for the event organiser if they need to look back at their notes. For some files, it is a legal requirement to ensure that quick reference can be made (for example risk assessments).

▶ Do not make assumptions about what is happening. Doing this may lead to mistakes. It is important, as an event planner, to check and then double-check arrangements so that you are in control rather than out of control.

> ⏸ **PAUSE POINT**   Why are good organisational skills so important when planning an event?
>
> ⬤ Hint   What would be the consequences if the event was poorly organised?
>
> ⬤ Extend   To what extent do you agree that good note taking is the most important organisational skill for an event organiser?

Problem solving

An event organiser must try to resolve any issues so that there is a positive outcome for everyone. Problem solving means talking to attendees to find out any concerns, monitoring outcomes of the event and dealing with anything else unexpected.

▶ Liaison with attendees – during the event, the organiser needs to talk to the delegates regularly. The event organiser needs to make attendees feel that they are being well looked after and that, if there are any issues, these can be resolved before they turn into a complaint. They can talk to attendees through formal introductions at different times during the event or during refreshment breaks such as coffee or lunch.

Attendees must be told who they should go to if there is an issue or problem. During the event, it may be appropriate to get feedback directly from them through surveys or questionnaires. Any issues raised at that time can then be dealt with straight away. Whether or not it is possible to gain such feedback during the day will depend on the type of event, the people involved and any technology that may be necessary to do this. For example, at the entrance to the event, it may be possible to have an event feedback form that is available online throughout the event and is checked regularly. It may also be possible to get event feedback immediately by setting up a hashtag for the event, for example, '#event', and then feedback can be taken through Twitter.

▶ Potential revision/rearrangements of event outcomes – even the best events have things that go wrong and require rearrangement. There are a number of reasons why an event may need to change its outcomes. How an issue is dealt with depends on the type of issue, for example, if a speaker is delayed, it may be possible to rearrange the time that they were due to talk by moving another speaker to an earlier point in the day.

If something has happened with the location, it may be possible to move the event to another location. Sometimes there will be problems that cannot be overcome so it may be necessary to cancel the event or postpone it until another time. The event organiser will need to have access to the right people and funds to get additional resources, if this is necessary. This may involve having an amount of cash or a debit/credit card available for the event organiser's use.

▶ Arising issues – these are anything or everything that happens which was not expected. These issues may happen at the beginning, middle or even towards the end of the event. Issues may be categorised into two types – those that can be controlled by the event organiser and those that cannot, as shown in Table 4.3.

▶ **Table 4.3:** Issues that are within, and beyond, the control of an event organiser

Issues that can be controlled by the event organiser	Issues that cannot be controlled by the event organiser directly
• Facilities available in the venue • Resources available in the venue • Catering arrangements • Schedules • Non-attendance of delegates	• Bad weather • Transport issues such as problems on motorways or public transport • A major incident such as a fire in the area around the venue • Fraud promotion or selling associated with the event, eg scam ticket sales • Publishing of event details incorrectly by a third party • Worldwide issues such as the Icelandic volcanic ash crisis in April 2010 which grounded all UK flights

The most important aspect of dealing with arising issues is to make sure that there is good communication. If delegates do not know what is happening, they are more likely to be unhappy. If they are kept informed, they can make decisions about what to do next.

Even if something cannot be controlled by the organiser, it is important to consider how the impact of that issue could be minimised. For example, if there is extreme weather on the day of the event, the organiser can just accept that there is a problem or make a back-up arrangement to move the event to a different location or provide other facilities. Of course, any event that takes place should already have had a risk assessment so that any possible hazards and steps to avoid those hazards should have been assessed.

For problem solving, event organisers need to be:
▶ creative
▶ quick to respond
▶ sympathetic to any situations
▶ assertive enough to make changes
▶ knowledgeable about alternative options available.

PAUSE POINT

Think of all the possible reasons why a business conference might need to be postponed or rescheduled.

 Hint

What could go wrong and mean that the event could not run?

Extend

To what extent do you agree that good event organisation is more about luck than planning?

Time management

Good time management means that event organisers focus on what is important and keep everything on track. The most common time management mistakes made are:
▶ wasting time doing activities that are not relevant to the event, such as checking personal emails or text messages
▶ waiting for someone else to do something before being able to progress on another aspect of the event
▶ not being organised, for example spending time looking for paperwork or going over tasks that you have done before
▶ not focusing on doing a task well through **multi-tasking**.

Key term

Multi-tasking – when more than one task is being performed at the same time.

Discussion

In small groups, think of all the activities that you waste time on or avoid doing. What are the consequences of wasting time on these activities or avoiding them on a daily basis? Now think of suggestions for how you could avoid wasting time on these activities.

Good time management skills involve:

▶ having and using a diary or schedule

▶ planning each day

▶ allowing some time for interruptions

▶ avoiding distractions like Facebook/Twitter/emails

▶ setting goals or priorities

▶ delegating to others where possible

▶ avoiding wasting time by waiting for others.

▶ Good time management skills are essential for an event organiser to ensure that the event runs smoothly

Negotiation

Event organisers need to be able to negotiate. This means that they need to be able to reach agreement with others without argument and through compromise. Negotiating requires:

▶ looking for mutual benefit

▶ being fair

▶ developing relationships.

Event organisers need to be able to negotiate with others when they are working on an event, for example by working on arrangements with suppliers or discussing services or facilities available. Through negotiating, an event organiser may be able to get a better price or higher level of service for their money. This means that they need to be:

▶ clear

▶ prepared

▶ confident when discussing terms

▶ good at listening

▶ able to reflect on what they think they have heard to clarify it.

Theory into practice

In groups, allocate the following roles – event organiser, supplier and observer – and use the following scenario.

- The event organiser wishes to pay £50 for the catering suppliers.
- The supplier wishes to charge £75 for these supplies and is willing to walk away, if necessary.

The observer should write notes on how the two different parties carry out the role play.

For 10 minutes, the event organiser and the supplier negotiate the contract. Add extra details to make the role-play realistic.

After the role-play, the observer should give feedback to the others and measure the negotiation skills demonstrated, using the criteria above.

Communication

Good communication is an essential skill for any event organiser. There are different methods of communication, including using the phone, text messaging, emailing and in person. When communicating, the event organiser needs to make sure that they are able to communicate to others effectively but also are able to listen well, so that they can understand what is communicated to them.

When communicating verbally, event organisers need to:

▶ be clear in their language

▶ speak at an appropriate pace (not too fast or slow)

▶ leave suitable pauses

▶ speak at an appropriate volume.

When communicating in writing, event organisers need to ensure that:

▶ grammar and spelling are good

▶ documents have a clear structure

▶ handwriting is legible (where used)

▶ they make appropriate use of salutations, for example Dear Sir and Yours faithfully in letters and emails

▶ jargon is avoided (complicated terms that others will not understand).

▶ Communication is important in an event. Think how you can improve on your own communication skills.

Different communication styles are explored in Table 4.4.

▶ **Table 4.4:** Benefits and drawbacks of different communication styles

Communication style	The benefit or damage to event planning
Communicating positively	People are more likely to want to work with you if you are positive, and this should lead to your event being successful.
Communicating regularly and often	If people know what is happening they are less likely to be anxious and will put all of their energy into the event.
Listening to what others are telling you	If someone more experienced is able to give good advice or recommendations, make sure that you give it serious consideration. They may be able to help you think of something that you have not thought of yourself.
Asking others for help when you need it	Communicating that you need some help means that you will be more likely to be successful than if you try to do everything on your own.

Interpersonal

Interpersonal communication means the skills that event organisers need when working with others. This may include times when you are working in a team or when communicating with suppliers and customers. Good interpersonal skills mean that the event organiser is:

▶ optimistic

▶ calm

▶ confident

▶ relaxed

▶ positive.

A good event organiser will also demonstrate:

▶ **rapport** with others

▶ appropriate levels of **empathy**.

Skills auditing

In this unit, you have learned about the tasks that have to be completed and the different planning skills required when an event is being organised. It is important that the event organiser gets feedback on all the elements of that process. Event organisers can use lots of different methods to get feedback. These include ratings using different scales, observations, questionnaires and through appraisals (often used for internal events).

Likert scale

Likert scaling asks respondents to tick the box which they think accurately describes their response to the statement.

Event organisers can get feedback on how they performed using this scale. Asking **respondents** to make judgements helps the event organiser to make improvements in the future. An example of Likert scaling is shown in Table 4.5.

Key terms

Rapport – a good relationship between people, with good communication and an understanding of the way each other is working.

Empathy – being able to understand the feelings of others.

Respondent – someone who is giving the feedback, i.e. the person answering the questions.

▶ **Table 4.5:** An example of Likert scaling

	Strongly Agree	Agree	Have no opinion	Disagree	Strongly Disagree
The event organiser communicated well verbally.					
I received all the information that I needed for the event.					

Semantic differential scale

Semantic differential scaling is another way that questions can be asked of an event's attendees about the performance of the organiser. An example is shown in Table 4.6.

▶ **Table 4.6:** A semantic differential scale

Indicate your opinion of the organiser of the event by putting a cross or tick in the relevant box based on the relevant scale of 1 to 8.									
	1	2	3	4	5	6	7	8	
Organised									Disorganised
Well managed									Badly managed
Excellent communicator									Poor communicator
Well presented									Badly presented

Discussion

Conduct research into different types of questionnaire and feedback forms. Compare the types of question used and discuss, in pairs, the strengths and weaknesses of the different styles of form.

Observation

Observation is another way of gaining feedback. An observation is when a person is asked to watch what the event organiser is doing and make judgements about their performance.

Observation is a good way to see how someone is performing in real time. The **observer** will write down what the event organiser is doing well and also where they need to improve. Observation can be carried out by a person that is known to the event organiser but it also can be carried out without the **observee** knowing until after they have been observed. This sort of observation is known as mystery shopping and, immediately after the organiser has been observed, they are given feedback.

Key terms

Observer – the person that watches the event organiser.

Observee – the event organiser, the person being watched.

▶ Observing at an event is a good way of capturing first hand evidence of how an event is running

Questionnaire

After an event, attendees are often sent questionnaires asking them to give feedback on the event. This data may be collected by paper or online. Paper-based questionnaires are less common now as they can be expensive to collect and analyse. Online surveys may have low **response rates** but they are very easy to complete. Sometimes prizes are offered as an incentive to encourage people to complete the questionnaire.

> **Key term**
>
> **Response rate** – the number of people that have responded to a questionnaire either on paper or online. The more people that reply, generally, the more accurate the results are likely to be.

> **Link**
>
> You will learn more about questionnaire design in *Unit 22: Market Research*.

Questionnaire design is very important. You have already learned about some of the ways that questions can be asked through likert or semantic scaling. Feedback may also be gained through questionnaires by ranking aspects of the event in order, with 1 being the most influential to 5 the least.

When writing questions to gain feedback, it is very important that they are:

▶ not leading
▶ easily understood
▶ balanced in their approach, for example yes/no
▶ asking for the correct feedback
▶ clear
▶ tested before they are used at the event
▶ aware of cultural differences that may influence the responses.

Testing questionnaires before they are used is very important to avoid mistakes being made. The quality of the data that comes from questionnaires is directly linked to the quality of the questions asked. Poor questions lead to poor responses.

 **PAUSE POINT**   What are the different methods that can be used by event organisers to make judgements about their skills?

Hint   Think about the different types of scale and format that you have learned about.

Extend   To what extent do the questions influence the outcomes of the skills analysis performed by any event organiser?

Appraisal

Appraisal is another way to review an event organiser's performance after the event has finished. Performance appraisal lets the event organiser know what went well and whether their skills have been used effectively. A performance appraisal may be carried out after each event or on a regular basis, such as six monthly or annually. Appraisals identify short and medium term goals that event organisers can work towards to improve their skills for the future.

> **Research**
>
> There are many different ways to conduct appraisals. The timing, content and whether or not they are linked to bonuses or other rewards are very different for every business. Find three examples of appraisals from your research online. Compare the strengths and weaknesses of each type.

As an events assistant for a local hotel chain, you must show your manager that you understand what skills an event planner requires. To do this, you will write a report describing the event organiser role and the skills needed to be an effective events planner.

You have also been asked to assess your own skills against the skills that you have learned about in this unit. Prepare a report that considers the skills that you have already developed on your BTEC National course with those required by an event manager.

Prepare a detailed skills audit showing your existing skills and prepare a list of the types of skills that are required by an event organiser in the hotel industry.

Compare the sets of skills. Explain in detail the skills that you already have and those you need to develop. Analyse your own skills compared to those required by an events planner and develop plans for any areas where you need to improve. Justify fully how your skills match those of an event organiser and your plans for improvement.

Plan

- I will review skills audit definition and categories associated with it.
- I will research what skills an event manager requires.
- I will find different sources from which to do my research.
- I know my deadlines.

Do

- I will review different types of skills audit.
- I have a deadline for my first draft.
- I will reference the website and research material that I have used.
- I will check that I have kept to your interim targets.

Review

- I evaluated the production and presentation of the skills audit.
- I checked the accuracy of my spelling and grammar.
- I know what I would do differently next time to make sure that I improve in future assignments.

B   Investigate the feasibility of a proposed event

In this unit, you have learned about the skills that are required by an event organiser and the documentation and initial plans that are needed for an event to go ahead. The type of event that is proposed and whether or not it is likely to be able to go ahead is also important. There are lots of different types of event and the likelihood of an event going ahead very much depends on the type of event.

Different types of event

The type of event has a huge impact on the skills that organisers need to use.

Business events

Business events can take a huge variety of forms. The type of event will depend on its purpose and the likely outcomes. Examples of various business events are shown in Table 4.7.

▶ **Table 4.7:** There is a wide variety of business events

Conference	Business conferences can take place on a small or large scale. They often have speakers available to talk about chosen topics.
Exhibition	Business exhibitions usually take place in a meeting hall or exhibition centre like the NEC (National Exhibition Centre) where businesses are given stands to present their businesses. Visitors are invited to go round and get information from each stand.
Product launch	Business organisations that manufacture products often have a specific date and time when they officially unveil a new product, for example a new model of a car.
Trade show	A trade show is a business event that is open to a particular type of business, for example the solar energy trade show.
Shareholders' meeting	Shareholders own shares in either private limited companies (Ltd) or public limited companies (plc). Shareholders need to meet regularly to get updates on how the company is doing and the size of the dividend (share of the profits) that they are likely to get. At the shareholders' meeting, the directors will also make other decisions, such as voting on policies or key personnel.
Press conference	Press conferences are often held by organisations for important news or other information to be given to the media. Press conferences may be held when there is bad news or may be used to launch something new that the organisation is trying to promote.
Awards evening	Awards evenings can take place for a variety of reasons, including for academic achievement, music or bravery. You may have had awards evenings during your time at school or college.
Team building	Team building events can take different forms. They can be indoor or outdoor, for example they may involve teams being put together to answer quizzes, business problems or challenges. They can also be more physical activities where teams are asked to compete on assault courses or take part in activities such as blindfold driving! The main purpose of the event is to bring people together and help them to work better as a team.
Seminar	Seminars bring together groups of people with a theme. Guest speakers are often asked to host the event and then attendees get together and discuss suggested topics. Business seminars commonly have themes, for example, how to set up your own business or finance.

Sport and recreation events

The most common types of event that you have probably been involved in are those that relate to sport and recreation. These events can happen on a huge scale or be much more local and organised by charities or other voluntary organisations. Some events involve huge sponsorship deals by companies and are shown on television throughout the UK and worldwide.

▶ The Olympics – there are two types of Olympic Games: summer and winter. Each takes place every four years. The Olympics enable top athletes from different countries to compete against each other. As the event involves world-wide participation, it moves around the world and to different time zones. In 2012, the summer Olympics were held in London and 51.9 million people watched some of the Olympics in the UK – representing 90 per cent of the population.

Research

Find out where the summer and winter Olympics are being held over the next 12 years. Find out about the planning and investment that are involved for such a large event. Do you think different locations will have different considerations? If so, what might they be?

- The Commonwealth Games, like the Olympics, involve lots of different countries and athletes competing in different sports. There are 71 different countries that take part in the Commonwealth Games which happen every four years, like the Olympics. The Commonwealth is a group of countries that voluntarily associate together to help each other.
- Sports tournaments and matches are available for a huge number of different sports across the UK and the world. Many are covered by television companies such as BT or Sky. The Rugby World Cup in 2015 took place in England. Like many other sports, rugby has a variety of types of event so, as well as the World Cup, there are other large-scale events, such as the Six Nations which involves six countries competing in rugby matches. This event has taken place for more than 120 years so has a long tradition. Football matches are also common events both individual matches and also competitions.
- Motorsport events happen on a huge scale with high numbers of people involved and large costs. Motorsport involves different types of motor vehicle racing, and includes Formula 1, Nascar, rally and motorbike racing. These events take place all over the world and have high health and safety requirements as they are often dangerous and, occasionally, participants are injured or killed. However, these incidents have reduced in number more recently as there are very strict health and safety restrictions in place.
- Racing – there are many different types of racing including horse and greyhound racing. Stadiums are located around the country and people attend events to watch different horses compete. The Grand National is one of the most famous horse races that takes place in the UK.
- Equestrian events are those that involve horses. As well as horse racing in stadiums or across courses, there are also a variety of other events such as jumping events, polo matches or dressage. Smaller events are also possible locally, such as gymkhanas where horse riders compete with each other in different categories.
- Country fairs are common throughout the UK, particularly during the summer months when the weather is warmer. Country fairs bring together different suppliers from a particular area. There are often competitions and displays that take place and local producers are able to sell goods.

Research

Find out if there is a country fair held near where you live. Research and think about the different types of suppliers that take part in country fairs each year.

- Food festivals are popular and range from outside festivals that involve stall holders setting up and cooking or displaying produce to those that, in the winter months, might be associated with festivals or celebrations, such as Christmas.

Case study

Aldeburgh Food Festival

Aldeburgh Food and Drink Festival takes place each year in Suffolk and has done so for the past 10 years. The event involves bringing together chefs, suppliers and sponsors to promote the best food available in the Suffolk area. It also allows different people working in the food industry to share ideas and thinking. The aim of the event is to help bring together people who produce the food with those that eat it and to celebrate the variety of food available in the local area. It also encourages people to visit the area.

The event itself takes place over two days and involves:

- demonstrations from visiting and local chefs
- talks
- master classes
- tastings
- competitions.

In 2015, there were over 120 suppliers at the festival, ranging from charities to restaurants to well-known breweries. They had a 'festival bakery', which was an opportunity for various bakers to conduct workshops and was an also an opportunity for flour suppliers' goods to be showcased. There was also a separate, ticketed event called the 'Festival feast' that offered attendees the opportunity to eat dishes made with local produce, and enjoy drinks produced by local suppliers.

Check your knowledge

1 What is a food festival?

2 What are the advantages and disadvantages to local producers of being part of a food festival such as Aldeburgh?

3 Make a judgement about whether or not food festivals have the biggest impact on small or large food suppliers. Give reasons for your judgement.

▶ Fun runs take place all over the country on a regular basis and can involve people dressing up before they take part. They are commonly 5 or 10 km in length and can be used to raise money for charity. There are many websites that promote access to these events all over the UK. Fun runs have become even more 'fun' in recent years with events such as the Colour Run, Cancer Research's Pretty Muddy and the Glow in the Park Run.

▶ Village fetes regularly take place all over the UK, especially during warmer weather. They can have themes relating to traditions, such as the Cuckoo Fair at Downton, or they can be used to raise money for local causes.

▶ Sailing regattas, like fun runs and fetes, are regular local events. Sailing can take place at seaside locations on a large scale. For example, the Isle of Wight has a sailing regatta called Cowes Week. Other smaller regattas also take place inland such as the Wroxham Broads Regatta in Norfolk.

▶ Dog shows take place all over the UK according to location and breed of animal. One of the most famous dog shows is Crufts, which takes place each year. Some events centre around a breed of dog such as those held by the Bernese Mountain Dog Club of Britain or the British Samoyed Club, while others cater for any breed and have a variety of activities taking place, such as the All About Dogs event.

▶ Collectors' fairs are extremely varied and can cover any collectible item such as:
  - antiques
  - stamps
  - toys.

They can be specialist or more general depending on the type of people expected to attend.

Entertainment

Events that entertain people can be a good way to generate interest in a topic or type of activity. Entertaining people at events can include music festivals, concerts or plays.

▶ Music festivals take place all over the UK. Some festivals, such as Glastonbury, are very large and are shown on television or broadcast on the radio. Music festivals may be outside and include camping, such as Reading or Leeds or the Big Reunion Festival that takes place in Skegness at the Butlins Holiday Park. Music festivals range from one or two days to almost a week depending on the time of year and whether or not there is camping available or included in the ticket.

▶ Concerts – like music festivals there are many different **genres** of concert. Concerts may include popular groups or singers that are commonly played on radio or TV. Classical musicians often play concerts on a local or national basis. Concerts may be performed in large locations, such as the O2 Arena in London or smaller locations such as a local town or village hall. The size of the location and the level of fame of the people performing will affect ticket availability and prices.

▶ Plays – a play is a show or story that is performed by actors. The writer of the play has a big influence on where it is performed. Shakespeare's plays are regularly performed in Stratford-Upon-Avon or in London at the Globe. Plays may also be performed at a more local level or in a festival format such as a drama festival.

Key term

Genre – styles or types.

Celebrations

Christmas, weddings, prom nights and birthdays are also examples of events that can take place at any time of the year. Businesses often decide to celebrate milestones in their history, for example being open for five or ten years. They may also accompany this with special offers or discounts.

Religious celebrations such as Christmas, Eid, Hanukkah or Diwali also encourage celebrations and a variety of events may be held for them.

Social enterprise events

Some events are designed to support others by raising money or by improving the lives of others. Organisations that seek to do this are known as **social enterprises**.

Social enterprises often hold fundraising and charity events to raise money for their particular cause. Social enterprises hold two main types of events.

▶ Charity sports events include:
  • fun runs
  • sponsored walks
  • guided cycling.

The purpose of each is to raise the profile of the social enterprise and also raise money.

▶ Charity fundraising events which can take many forms and very much depend on the amount of money being raised and the people involved, as shown in Table 4.8.

Key term

Social enterprise – an enterprise that has a social or environmental mission and seeks to have a positive impact on communities or people by investing the majority of the profits made into the cause that they want to help or improve.

▶ **Table 4.8:** Different types of charity fundraising events

Dinners	Dinners may be held to raise funds through sponsorship by organisations or by social enterprises holding the events themselves to raise money for their cause.
Coffee mornings	Macmillan Cancer Support hold the World's Biggest Coffee morning each year to raise awareness of the charity and raise additional funds to support people with cancer.
Galas	The Lowestoft Lions hold a Gala Day each year at Oulton Broad to raise money. The Gala day includes a variety of events from dog agility competitions to raft racing.
Auctions	Charity auctions can be used with physical products, for example, the auctioning of paintings or other sporting memorabilia, or can be used to auction activities, for example, an auction of promises. An auction of promises asks someone to donate their time and then bids are made by people attending the auction for that service.
Quizzes	Quizzes raise money for the social enterprise by asking teams or individuals to pay an entrance fee to the quiz. Some of the money raised may be used for a prize for the winners and additional money may be raised through, for example, selling raffle tickets or food or drink.

Feasibility of event proposal

When you are planning your event, it is really important to make sure that it is **feasible**. This is because any event needs to be successful and to have positive outcomes. Making sure that an event is feasible requires the event organiser to think about the idea behind the event, its purpose, aims and objectives. The constraints stopping the event going ahead and the success factors to show if it has been successful also need to be outlined during the planning stages.

Key term

Feasible – likely or probable that something will succeed.

Mind map event ideas

A mind map is a diagram that is used to help to structure your thinking about an event. It provides a way of seeing, instantly, all the different types of activity that could happen and the ideas that have been developed. An example is shown in Figure 4.4.

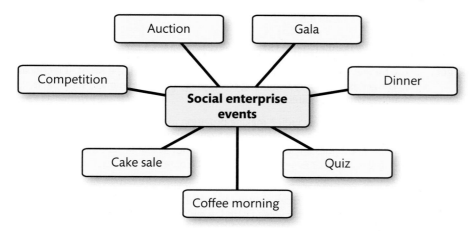

▶ **Figure 4.4:** Mind maps can help you to structure your thinking about an event

Purpose of event

The purpose of the event is very important and influences how and when the event is held and also the amount of income generated from the event. Events can be held for many different reasons and the purpose of the event influences the planning at every stage. To help you learn and think about your ideas for your event, consider some of the reasons why events take place including:

▶ profit making

▶ charity fundraising

▶ general awareness

▶ **networking** amongst professional or other groups

▶ sharing of good practice or ideas

▶ promotion, discount or selling opportunities

▶ training for staff

▶ reward for staff

▶ **stakeholder** support.

Aims and objectives

The purpose of the event also influences the aims and objectives of that event.

Aims and objectives are central to most aspects of business as they are the driving force behind what happens with the business.

Key terms

Networking – the process of connecting groups of people together, for example business professionals.

Stakeholder – anyone who is affected by a business, including internal stakeholders such as members of staff and external stakeholders such as customers.

Link

Unit 1: Exploring Business discussed business aims and objectives.

- The aims are the overall goals – for example raising a certain amount of money for charity, a particular number of sales or a specific event such as a dinner taking place.
- Objectives are the list of plans that help achieve those aims – for example selling a number of tickets by a specific date or organising a specific amount of advertising with a radio station by a certain date.

Aims and objectives should be SMART (specific, measurable, achievable, realistic and time-constrained).

Constraints

- Constraints are the parameters or boundaries within which the event needs to be held. Events like the Olympics involve millions of pounds being spent on different aspects of their promotion and organisation. Sponsors get involved and the funds are raised. For most events, there are restrictions on what can be achieved. Some of these are outlined in Table 4.8.

▶ **Table 4.8:** Some of the restrictions on events organisation

Budget	The budget is the amount of money that can be spent on the event. It is critical to know this at the very beginning of the event planning to make sure that it matches what is required.
Venue	The type of venue, including making provision for poor weather, is also critical. Making sure that the chosen venue is available on the specific date can ensure that the event goes ahead or is moved if it is not available. Some venues require booking months, or even years, ahead of the date of the event.
Human resources	Time and expertise are both critical when thinking about the amount of time and energy that people can contribute to the process. The level of skill and time available of the people involved with the event will have a significant impact on the event. Time required is nearly always underestimated so it is important to allow more.
Physical resources	These are the items that are required during the event, such as the furniture and catering equipment, but also the resources required for advertising before the event.

Success factors

What makes an event successful is the extent to which it achieves what it set out to do, ie the extent to which it achieve its purpose, aims and objectives. Smaller goals and targets are often set at the planning stages of any event so that, after the event has happened, you should be able to look back and see if you achieved what you set out to do. Some goals and targets that you could use to review your event include:

- sales of tickets to exceed 200
- attendance at the event to be 50 or more people
- amount of money raised for charity after expenses is £250
- costs and income are equal (known as break-even)
- 500 new followers on Facebook and Twitter achieved.

Notice that all these goals and targets are SMART.

C Develop a detailed plan for a business or social enterprise event

You have learned, throughout this unit, about the role of the event organiser and how to investigate whether or not an event is feasible. Now you are going to learn about the planning tools that you can use to help you organise your own business or social enterprise event and the other factors that you need to consider when planning an event.

Use of planning tools

There are three key types of planning tool that you will learn about and practise using ready for your assessment – Gantt charts, critical path analysis and online planning tools.

Gantt charts

On a Gantt chart, each stage of the planning of an event is represented by a horizontal bar, allowing the event organiser to work out how long an event will take to plan and the critical elements of each stage.

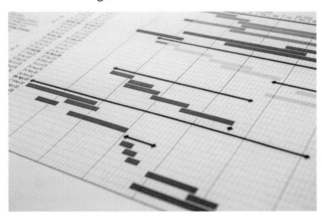

▶ What are the other benefits for using a Gantt chart for an event?

Critical path analysis

Critical path analysis is a business tool that allows you to plan an event. It requires the event organiser to draw out the set of stages that the event needs to go through in order to get to the end. The length of time for each stage is included. By doing this it is possible to see the minimum amount of time needed, known as the critical path. (See Figure 4.5.)

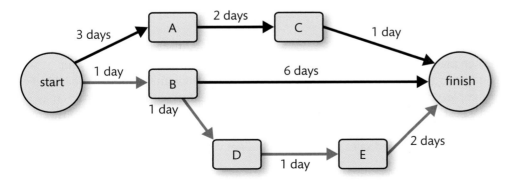

▶ **Figure 4.5:** A plan for an event showing the critical path

Online planning tools

As well as the more traditional event planning tools such as Gantt charts and critical path analysis, it is also possible to use online software and tracking tools to plan and organise events. Websites such as Eventbrite give planning guides and access to online services such as e-ticketing and marketing that help with event planning and delivery.

Apps may also be used to help with online event planning, for example Doodle (a scheduling tool) can be used to put speakers, event hosts and attendees in touch with each other for free.

> **Research**
>
> Find out the apps that are available for free to help organise events online. Compare the advantages and disadvantages of each. Discuss in pairs, which app would be best for organising a charity dinner for a social enterprise.

Other factors to be considered

When you are planning your business or social enterprise event, it is important that you consider all the elements of the plan carefully and in detail to ensure that the event is a success.

Aims and objectives

You know how important it is to be clear about the purpose and goals of the event. When writing your detailed business plan you need to make sure that these aims and objectives are written clearly and the objectives are SMART.

> **Theory into practice**
>
> You have been asked to organise a coffee morning to raise funds for a local charity. Before you begin organising the event, the charity has asked you to help them to understand the different planning elements that go into organising this event including its:
>
> * purpose
> * aims and objectives
> * goals and steps.
>
> Think back to the purpose, the goals and steps that need to be achieved and the specific actions that must be put into place for this event to happen.
>
> List your ideas and share them with another member of your class. Give each other feedback.

Budget

When planning your event, you will need to know how much you have in your budget so that you can plan the most appropriate event with the money available. For example, you may decide to organise a business breakfast with training which may only cost a few hundred pounds rather than a large conference in a prestigious venue that might cost thousands. You need to learn about how the type of event, available finance and expected sales influence the budget you need.

There are various ways to budget. One way is zero budgeting, where you, as the event organiser, need to work out how much you think an event will cost and then put in a proposal for the money needed. Alternatively, you may be given a specific allocated budget and therefore know exactly how much you can spend. Either way, a good way to budget for an event is by producing a spreadsheet.

Once a budget is set, it can be used to work out any income that may come in for the event. For example, consider the budget for a business breakfast event (Figure 4.6).

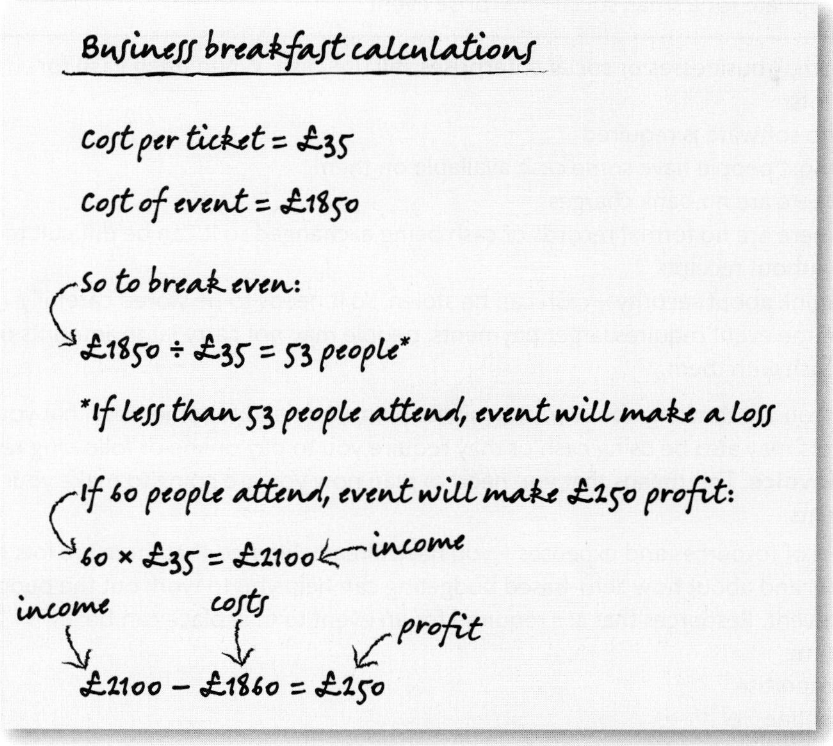

Link

Working out break-even points are covered in more detail in *Unit 3: Personal and Business Finance*.

> **Business breakfast calculations**
>
> Cost per ticket = £35
>
> Cost of event = £1850
>
> So to break even:
>
> £1850 ÷ £35 = 53 people*
>
> *If less than 53 people attend, event will make a loss
>
> If 60 people attend, event will make £250 profit:
>
> 60 × £35 = £2100 ← income
>
> income   costs   profit
>
> £2100 − £1850 = £250

▶ **Figure 4.6:** Working out the break-even point and the profit for an event

▶ Available finance – the amount of money that is available in the planning stages of the event. It is often necessary to have some money in advance of the event to pay suppliers and for advertising and tickets. Knowing how and when money is likely to be available and on what basis will influence how you run your event.

▶ Expected sales figures – for example, the number of tickets to be sold, the number of donations to be received on the day or even the number of attendees expecting to purchase items at the event, for example if it is an auction or sale with free entry. Working out the expected sales compared to expenses is critical when working out if your event is going to break even. Many businesses or social enterprises will want to make a profit so that the money can be reinvested or donated to their charity or social cause.

▶ Banking – thinking about the banking arrangements for any event is very important. Banking relates to cash and also to any electronic payments. Many businesses, including social enterprises, take payments by debit card, mobile phone or by other mechanisms such as PayPal. You will need to be clear when organising your event which methods are most suitable. If you are taking mobile payments you will need to organise:

• the bank account into which payments will be made
• the PayPal or mobile phone account that you will use
• any other online resources such as a website or event planner to book tickets or to provide additional information.

You will also need to take into account any payments that may need to be made to the bank or PayPal for using this service.

Many small businesses or social enterprises still use cash. When using cash for payments:

- no software is required
- most people have some cash available on them
- there are no bank charges
- there are no formal records of cash being exchanged so it can be difficult to track without receipts
- think about security – cash can be stolen, so it needs to be stored carefully
- if the event requires larger payments, people may not carry large amounts of cash with them.

When you are thinking about your business plan, you need to remember that your suppliers may also be using cash or may require you to pay online or following receipt of an **invoice**. This means that you need to plan how you are going to make your payments.

▶ Cost of resources and expenses – you have already learned that there are lots of costs and about how zero-based budgeting can help you to work out the budget for an event. Resources that are required for an event to take place can be:
- time
- expertise
- online.

You will also need to think about the **opportunity cost** of using one resource rather than another to make sure that you make the best use of the resources available to you for your event.

You will need to work out the total cost of the resources that you require for your event and then compare it against your expected income. You will need to work out the expenses that you need to pay such as:

- venue
- catering
- staff
- travel.

You will learn more, in this unit, about how to choose your venue and catering. Remember that, when you are planning your event, you need to ensure that you have enough staff involved to make the event run smoothly. You may need staff to:

- take payments
- show people around
- organise activities
- act as marshals to help people park their vehicles
- answer questions and give advice or directions.

It is very important to plan the number of staff required in advance so that you can get the right amount of help. For a social enterprise event, it may be possible to get volunteers to help to raise money for free but, for a business event, this is less likely.

When you are choosing your event, you should also take into account the travelling involved to host the event. As the event organiser, consider how you will get there: if

Key terms

Invoice – a document that is sent by the supplier to the person purchasing goods with terms of reference for payment, eg within 30 days. Sometimes invoices can be sent after an event but, for smaller businesses, are often required to be paid in advance or on delivery.

Opportunity cost – the cost of making one decision over another. For example, the cost of the missed opportunity if you spend your money on one venue which means that you cannot spend it at another.

you can go by public transport or whether you need to drive or be driven. If driving is involved, who can do this for you and is payment required? If there is equipment needed for the event, how will it be transported to the venue?

Resources

Depending on the type of event that you are organising, there will a number of other resources that you might need, some of which are shown in Table 4.10.

▶ **Table 4.10:** Resources that you will need to run an event

Flip chart, whiteboard, smartboard or noticeboard	It is important to have access to display boards, either paper-based or electronic, before, during and after the event. Flip charts, whiteboards and smartboards are often important during your event for your speakers to use or to give extra information. Noticeboards around the venue can also show people where they need to go or be used to advertise in advance. Signs to get to your event are very important too.
WiFi	Some locations offer free WiFi and others charge. When planning your event, you need to think about the speed and signal for the WiFi in your area. Poor WiFi signal can sometimes be worse than none at all as your attendees may get a bad impression of your event.
Telephone	Access to phones during the event may be important – this could be a landline or mobile phone. As the event organiser, you may wish to give updates on social media, such as Facebook or Twitter, so it may be important to have access to a smartphone to do this.
Ability to take money	You have already learned about the importance of choosing how to pay at or before an event so, if you do opt for cash, where will it be stored and how will it be kept secure? If you are opting for any form of online payment, how will this be achieved?
Chairs and tables	Chairs and tables are often supplied at venues for events but it is important to review what is on offer and check that they are suitable for the event being held. For business conferences, for example, suppliers coming to talk to your attendees may want to book a particular size of stand or bring resources with them. Planning the layout and size of your chairs and tables will help to ensure that your event runs smoothly.
Computer or tablet	At the event, you may require access to online resources for emailing updates, providing information on social media or even for tracking attendees. Having access to a computer, laptop or tablet may be necessary and should be reviewed as part of your plan.
Giveaways	At the event, you may decide to give away packs or bags to attendees so that they can take something away from the event, including extra advertising or information.
Wrist bands or stickers on entrance	You may also need to have some form of identification in place, if people are going to come and go from the event. How will you know that they have paid? Are you going to require a payment on entry to your event or a donation to the charity that you are supporting, if you are setting up as a social enterprise?

Venue

You have already considered some of the resourcing requirements that you need to think about when choosing your venue. You have already learned about making sure that you can travel easily to the event, but you also need to find out about:

▶ the size of the room

▶ facilities available

▶ car parking

▶ access arrangements.

Theory into practice

Find out about a venue in a small city, town or village that is near you and complete the following checklist by finding out more about that venue.

How is the venue booked?	
Who is the venue keyholder/caretaker and how are they contacted?	
How many people are allowed in the venue at one time?	
How many rooms does it have?	
How many people can fit into each room at one time?	
Does it have toilets?	
Does it have tea and coffee making facilities?	
Does it have a sink or other washing facilities?	
Is there access to a kitchen including facilities to chill things, eg a fridge?	
Is it possible to cook there?	
Are cleaning materials available?	
Are there bins available for rubbish to be taken away after an event?	
Is it possible to park a car there?	
Is parking free and for how many people?	
Is it near a bus/train/tram stop?	
How accessible is it for people who use a wheelchair?	
How accessible is it for attendees with young children?	
How far is it for people to walk to if they have mobility problems?	
Any other relevant information	

Catering

You have already learned, in this unit, about the different types of catering that may be on offer and about the difference between in-house and external catering arrangements. When planning an event, the first question you need to think about is whether or not catering is required at all. If you decide that you do wish to cater for your attendees, you need to think about all the different elements involved (Figure 4.7).

When thinking about catering as a whole, you need to think about how to inform your attendees about:

▶ any ingredients that may cause concerns for people with allergies or intolerances, for example peanut allergies or gluten intolerance
▶ any ingredients that may be suitable/not suitable for those following vegetarian or vegan diets

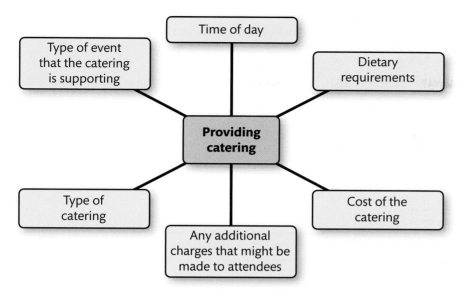

▶ **Figure 4.7:** Different elements involved when thinking about providing catering for an event

▶ any preparation of the food that needs to take into account religions or beliefs, for example making sure that meat is halal or kosher.

When using an external caterer, these questions should be asked and acted on.

Legal constraints

As the event organiser, you have already learned about some of the legal constraints that you need to consider when an event is planned, but here is a reminder of some of the key areas that you need to think about.

▶ Contracts need to be drawn up with clear terms and conditions for suppliers. Contracts may be agreed in writing or verbally. Either way, they are legally binding when an offer has been made to supply goods or a service and it has been accepted.

It is not always possible for a person under the age of 18 to enter into a contract so it may be important, when running your event, to check if this is possible. If it is not possible, then a person aged 18 or over will need to help you with your event planning.

▶ Health and safety including risk assessments – remember that you will need to ensure that your event is carried out safely and you will need to produce a risk assessment that includes **hazards** in the venue and the **risk** to people attending your event. Health and safety is very important, and there is a lot of guidance available from the Health and Safety Executive (HSE) to help you when you are planning an event.

When you are planning your event, you need to think about any hazards that might affect attendees and anything that you can do to lower the risk of this happening – to lower the likelihood that harm will be done.

For example, if you are expecting large crowds to come to your event you need to think about the possible hazards of:

• people getting crushed against each other
• people getting crushed against physical features of the venue such as walls or fences
• people pushing each other
• people throwing things.

> **Key terms**
>
> **Hazard** – the HSE define a hazard as anything that may cause harm.
>
> **Risk** – the likelihood that harm will be done as a result of a hazard.

The risk assessment then considers the likelihood of these hazards happening and what can be done to reduce the risk of harm, as shown in Table 4.11.

▶ **Table 4.11:** An example of a risk assessment

Hazard	Risk	Likelihood	What can be done to limit the risk
People getting crushed against each other	People being injured or trampled	Low	The number of people entering the event could be restricted using marshals.
People throwing things	People being injured by items hitting them	Medium	Ensure that bags are checked for items that may be thrown.

Research

Using the HSE website, carry out research into the health and safety requirements for running a plant sale at a hall near where you live. Think of all the possible hazards and risks and then produce a risk assessment using the tips and guidance from the HSE.

▶ Negligence liability – you learned earlier in this unit about the need for public liability insurance when running any event. This insurance is required in case anyone has an injury or accident caused by the negligence of the event organiser at an event. Public liability insurance often covers injuries or accidents up to millions of pounds. Negligence liability insurance, like public liability insurance, is often required at large events.

Negligence is when someone has not taken reasonable care and another person is harmed by this carelessness. Having a risk assessment helps to show that reasonable care has been taken as long as the actions of that risk assessment have been taken. Making sure that everyone involved in the organisation and planning of your event takes reasonable care of others also helps to reduce the likelihood of negligent decisions being made.

If negligence is found, there are serious consequences for the event organiser, particularly if someone has died. Prison sentences may be given, so taking care of health and safety to a high level is very important.

Team working

It is very rare to have just one person organising an event, due to the amount of work involved. It is much more common for a team of people to get together so that they can develop and share out the tasks. Responsibilities of the different organisations and groups need to be worked out with the organiser well in advance of any event. This means that each team member can ensure that they make the event a success. Some of the roles that have specific responsibilities include:

▶ media and marketing
▶ customer service
▶ health and safety
▶ administration
▶ finance.

Having a good team in place which knows how its tasks have been allocated should ensure that everything runs properly and that the right decisions are made. There needs to be a set of procedures to follow, including who will authorise invoices and who has authority to make decisions.

For some events, the whole team may need to agree on every aspect of the arrangements. For other events, authority may be delegated to different team members. Having regular planning meetings, with updates and notes or minutes, keeps the event on track and ensures that communication is clear between team members.

PAUSE POINT   How does having a good team who have been allocated specific responsibilities help an event to run smoothly?

Hint   What could happen if communication was poor or team members did not know what they were expected to do for an event.

Extend   'Failing to plan is planning to fail' – to what extent do you agree with this view?

Insurance

You have learned a lot about the different types of insurance needed when running your event – negligence liability and public liability. It is also good to have insurance covering equipment and resources at the event. For some resources such as vehicles, business insurance may be needed. Insurance may also be required to cover the cost of replacing any resources, especially equipment such as microphones or speakers if these are used.

Research

Research the cost of insurance to run one of the following in your area:

- dog show
- coffee morning
- mini marathon
- firework display
- flower show.

Is the public liability insurance needed? How much does it cost? Are there any excesses offered?

Compare your results with other members of your class for different events. How similar or different are the costs and excesses?

Methods of communication

It is very important to share information about the business event, including the time the event starts, the cost of attendance, the specific programme of the event and how to get there. The event organising team must be able to communicate this information in a clear and accurate manner.

Many organisations use websites to communicate this information easily and cheaply. Other **communication channels** include email, posters, advertising in magazines or newspapers, flyers or letters. Some organisations now also use social media to advertise and promote events and this may be done using text or video on different social and business networking sites. Individuals are asked to pass the information to their friends and families, or other business associates, to increase numbers.

Key term

Communication channel – the method which is used to communicate.

Once people have signed up for the event, the organiser will need to send them joining instructions and, if necessary, notify them of any alterations to the arrangements.

| Hint | Think back to what you learned at the beginning of this unit about reasons for an event being changed or cancelled. |
| Extend | Communication is more important when cancelling an event than when it is going ahead as planned. Discuss this view. |

Contingency planning

Key term

Contingency plan – a back-up plan in case something goes wrong.

The final part of planning an event is called **contingency planning**. This is the planning for some of the 'what if' scenarios. 'What if' scenarios are used to think about many of the possible things that could go wrong and to plan for them accordingly.

Contingency questions can be asked in advance and back-up plans can be put into place for an event, as shown in Table 4.12.

▶ **Table 4.12:** Contingency questions and their back-up plans

What if?	Back-up plan
The keynote speaker does not turn up for the event.	A back-up speaker is in place to take over if necessary and a note has been added to the invitation stating that this will happen if necessary.
The venue is closed due to bad weather.	An alternative venue is on stand-by. Shelters are available nearby.
The catering company does not turn up.	A local supermarket is within a very short distance of the venue and alternative arrangements can be made.
The IT equipment required is not working.	Back-up IT systems are in place. Suitable IT trained staff will be available on the day to fix any problems if they occur.

Not every possible eventuality can be planned for with 'what if' scenarios but many can be!

Discussion

Write a list of all the 'what if' questions for a quiz evening at your centre involving 50 people, a quiz master, a prize of £50 and a donation of £10 per team to enter the quiz.

Work in small groups and discuss which of your 'what if' questions has the biggest potential impact on that event.

PAUSE POINT

Investigating the idea behind an event and coming to conclusions about the best choices are critical for the event's success.

| Hint | It is important to think of plenty of ideas to choose from when planning an event. Come up with as many ideas as you can. |
| Extend | Carefully consider and make a judgement about each of those ideas. |

Assessment practice 4.2

You are an events organiser and must write a business plan and feasibility report for a proposed business or social enterprise event to demonstrate the knowledge gained from your BTEC course.

As preparation, work in groups to present an investigation into a range of successful events (both large and small). Produce an individual summary report of this research. Determine the common success factors for these events and use this research to develop your event proposal and assess its feasibility. Your group's presentation will need to justify your chosen event, backed by research.

Your plan should cover why the event has been chosen. Explain the reasons why some events are chosen over others. Using tools to make a judgement about the best event is very important.

Explain how the planning of an event needs to be well executed. Include a plan that sets out all the relevant details required for the event. You should include critical success factors. Also include the relevant planning tools that consider budgets, legal constraints, risk assessments and contingency planning. You should explain and analyse all the key factors that need to be considered when producing a detailed business plan for an event.

Make sure that, throughout your plan, you include evaluation and justification of why different options have been chosen, referring to your research. These need to include the risks associated with the plan and any contingency arrangements. Evaluate and justify your feasibility plan, the tools you used, the budget and risks. Make any contingency adjustments that may be required.

Plan
- I should think of as many different event ideas as I can.
- I should make judgements about each of those ideas.
- I should consider the strengths and weaknesses of each.
- I shall make a judgement about the best idea to take forward.

Do
- I should take my best idea and now plan my event.
- I shall remember all the tools and techniques that I have learned.
- I shall consider how I can use tools to ensure that my event runs to time.

Review
- I shall make judgements about the best way to measure my event's success.
- I shall review planning and the execution of the event.
- I know what I would do differently next time I run an event.

D   Stage and manage a business or social enterprise event

The next part of your learning for this unit is staging and managing the business or social enterprise event itself. This means running the event alongside the management and problem solving that needs to take place during the event.

Management of the event

Management of the event is the way that you run the event and ensure that the event runs smoothly. You will do this either individually or, more likely, as part of a team.

Contracts

When managing the contracts for the event, it is very important that the event team ensures that the suppliers and staff working at the event do so in a way that actively supports the event's success. Suppliers need careful management to ensure that they turn up on time and that the quality of the products or services that are being offered is as requested. Any problems during the event need to be sorted out quickly and efficiently to avoid a negative impact on the smooth running of the event. Likewise, procedures for checking the participation and behaviour of personnel working either directly for the event or for organisations associated with the event need to be monitored.

Marketing of the event

You have already learned that the marketing of events is very important for an event to be successful. Having the correct number of attendees can make the difference between an event making a profit or surplus, or breaking even, or even running at a loss (think back to budgeting earlier in this unit). Making sure that marketing is carried out effectively and with the correct level of impact is very important.

▶ Publicity for any event is very important and can be undertaken in many different ways, as shown in Table 4.13.

Link

Think about all of the marketing techniques you covered in *Unit 2: Developing a Marketing Campaign*.

▶ **Table 4.13:** Planning the publicity for an event

Method	Use and impact
Press release	Press releases can be sent to all local print and online media to let potential attendees know that the event is happening.
Promotional video release	Video releases can be placed on YouTube and then linked to your website and social media to highlight that the event is taking place.
Stunt or activity that is newsworthy	Flashmobs and mini staging can all highlight that the event is about to take place and to generate social media and press interest.
Social media hashtag, tweet or Facebook invitation	Using Twitter, setting up hashtags or Facebook can all be used to generate publicity for the event. Encouraging people to retweet and share the information means that it gets to more people cheaply and quickly.
Blogs	Bloggers often have large followings so try asking a blogger to mention your event. Writing a blog and then sharing its content with others may also raise awareness of your event.
Competitions	Competitions associated with the event offering prizes may stimulate interest and can be sent out via email, poster or other methods.
Promotions and discounts	Events sometimes offer special discounts or offers that are only available on that day. Having a promotion that is limited encourages attendance.

▶ Advertising comes in many forms, both on and offline. Online advertising has become very popular and targeted advertising is relatively cheap to buy through websites such as Facebook and Google ads. This type of advertising works on a pay per click basis so anyone going onto the advertisement and then clicking through to the event would generate a charge. Using online targeted advertising such as Facebook can generate a lot of additional information for event planners, including the types of people looking at the online advertising and the likely chances of them attending.

▶ Advertising online is a much more modern way of attracting attendees but sometimes it is best to stick with the older methods such as billboards, advertising in newspapers or even by the roadside. For example, many smaller village events are still advertised regularly on signs along roadsides as this is the most effective form of advertising. Even if offline advertising is used, most events will still have a website so that potential attendees can find out more.

Case study

FlipSide Festival

FlipSide Festival was launched in 2013 as the offspring to FLIP in Brazil, and brings Latin American culture to Suffolk.

The festival itself brings together writers, musicians, dancers, chefs and sports people. In 2014 they partnered with the charity Street Child World Cup. The event takes place over three days at Snape Maltings.

FlipSide Festival uses lots of different ways to get publicity and to advertise that the festival is happening including:

- distribution of leaflets and printed guides
- working with schools
- a live drawing festival
- inviting famous writers to speak at the event
- advertising on signs by the road
- promotion through the website
- a writing competition.

Check your knowledge

1 What is the difference between publicity generation and advertising?

2 What are the advantages and disadvantages of using a competition to generate interest in an event compared with only providing advertising for that event?

3 Websites are the best way to promote any event. Discuss this view.

▶ Sponsorship – some events are sponsored and are held in conjunction with third parties. Each year, Helen & Douglas House Hospice holds a 'Santas on the Run' fun run in Oxford, which is sponsored by businesses. In 2015, they were sponsored by Element Six, Holiday Inn, TripAdvisor and Withy King (a law firm). Entrants to the two mile race pay to take part and, in exchange, receive a santa suit. All the money raised goes to the hospice. If you choose to use a sponsor for your event, make sure that they are looked after and managed carefully before, during and after the event so they are happy that their sponsorship money is used wisely and to the best effect.

 PAUSE POINT   Why might a local company sponsor an event like the 'Santas on the Run'?

Hint   What are the advantages to a local company of being associated with a good cause?

Extend   The reputation of a sponsor for an event is more important than the event itself. Discuss this view.

▶ Guest lists need to be managed carefully before and during an event to ensure that the right people have been invited and are attending. When guests are invited to events, it is important to make sure that they are given plenty of notice and that they have replied to confirm their attendance.

Some guests might also be considered to be very important people (VIPs) attendees so they need to be treated even more favourably than other guests and may need a special area to sit in or special treatment during the event. Sometimes local dignitaries, such as members of the council or the mayor, are invited to events. Members of the Royal Family may also be asked to attend events which must be organised with sufficient notice.

When you are managing the guest list, you need to think carefully about the types of guest that you want to invite to the event and how they will mix with each other. For example, if your event is a dinner, you will want to make sure that tables are set up so that attendees can mix and make friends. If your event is a quiz, teams need to be organised. If you are organising an art auction, you need to ensure that attendees have an interest in art and will want to buy.

▸ Invitations are also very important and create an impression of the event. They may be sent by email or be printed and sent through the post. Invitations may also be sent through social media and through event planning websites such as Eventbrite. The type of invitation will have an influence on how many people decide to attend the event. When choosing or making invitations, it is very important to consider:
  • design – it needs to be appropriate for the type of event
  • the type of event, for example charity or for profit
  • how to give a donation to the charity (if applicable)
  • date, time and address of the event
  • the details of the event including any dietary arrangements
  • style of the event including any dress code
  • any other relevant information such as additional stalls, competitions or fundraising activities that are happening at the event
  • who to reply to (RSVP).

Customer service

Customer service needs to be carefully managed during any event. Looking after all the needs of all the people attending the event can make the difference between an event being a success or a failure. Here are some top tips for making sure that people who attend the event are looked after by the event team and have a good time.

▸ Smile.
▸ Make people feel welcome by saying hello to them when they arrive.
▸ Respond to the needs of people by listening to them and answering questions.
▸ Use appropriate language.
▸ Be polite.
▸ Be on time.
▸ Apologise if something is not going to plan.

Link

You will learn more about customer service in *Unit 14: Investigating Customer Service.*

Monitoring procedures to ensure that allocated tasks have been completed

As the event organiser, you need to continually keep track of how the event is progressing. You need to learn ways to ensure that everything is checked and double-checked. Monitoring takes many different forms and involves checking things such as:

▸ bookings
▸ deliveries
▸ advertising and publicity
▸ staffing
▸ security.

Monitoring may also involve taking into account aspects of the event which are outside the organiser's control. This may be done on a daily, monthly or annual basis depending on the type of event. Some monitoring takes place during the planning stage of the event, while further monitoring will take place during the event to ensure that everything is running smoothly. A good event organiser will need to be able to monitor many different things at the same time to ensure that all the parts come together to make a successful business event. Monitoring procedures may include using:

▶ shared notes
▶ checklists
▶ action points in minutes
▶ event plans with SMART targets.

Security and health and safety

Matters relating to health, safety and security need to be considered during the planning and running of the event because they are very important and are required by both civil and criminal law.

Event organisers must be aware of the emergency procedures that are used by the venue where the event is being held. They will need to talk to the venue's manager or coordinator to find out what happens in an emergency, where the nearest fire exits are, and what kind of sound indicates that there is an emergency. This information will need to be made available to delegates and other attendees.

At the beginning of the event, a verbal or written notification must be given to those attending to let them know what to do if there is an emergency during it.

Security procedures for vehicles and for individuals also need to be followed.

Methods of communication

During the planning and staging of your event you need to think carefully about how you communicate with your business team. There are two main forms of communication – internal and external.

▶ Internal communication means within the team or enterprise where you are working. Communicating between team members may be less formal and could be through:
  • instant messenger
  • text messaging
  • emailing
  • mobile phone
  • meetings or briefings
  • posters
  • two way radios
  • closed circuit television
  • intercoms.

  Internal communication is usually much less formal and quicker to communicate important information. Making sure that everyone on the team knows what is happening is vital to make sure the the event runs smoothly. Radios are often used by key staff during events so that others can hear key messages. Different radio channels are used by different teams.

▶ External communications are those that are going on outside the event or enterprise that the event is being staged for. These are the communications that are going out to the wider public. Attendees may be encouraged to give feedback on the event while they are attending by:
  • signing in to the event
  • using #hashtag links
  • using Twitter – tweeting

- other social media, such as videos being posted to YouTube
- posting comments and images of the event to websites for sharing
- sending out press releases to the media for following up online or in print
- giving out newsletters, information or other packs to attendees at the event and to other parties post-event
- giving out freebies with post-event advertising such as bags, pens or t-shirts.

Making sure that communications are monitored and providing responses where necessary is very important. External communications make sure that the event is fully publicised. External communications are frequently picked up by the media and shared. Sharing can go a long way and with social media you can create large audiences.

Attendee evaluation

Evaluating an event is a very important stage of running a business event that is sometimes not completed in as much detail as other elements of the event. This often happens because, at the end of the event, organisers may be relieved that it has finished or immediately start thinking about their next project. Event planning can be very hard work. However, it is critical that an event evaluation is made so that the event can be improved if it is held again. Notes or minutes of this meeting should be kept and filed so that they may be referred to.

If possible, ask delegates to complete a short questionnaire asking them to give feedback on their thoughts about the event and any ways that they think it should be improved. This could be on a paper that is handed out and completed by hand or by an email which is sent soon after the event.

⏸ **PAUSE POINT**	What is the difference between internal and external communication? Give examples of each.
Hint	How do you communicate within a business or to other stakeholders not working in the business?
Extend	Divide into two groups, and debate whether 'External communication is more important than internal communication.' Each group should take an opposing view.

Problem solving

During the running of an event it is very important that actions are taken to solve any problems that occur. These problems include taking forward any contingency plans, any customer service concerns and health and safety issues.

Research

Carry out research online or in your local papers to identify two local events that are happening near you. Now think of the different problems that event organisers could face when running those events. Make a list and compare with someone from your class.

Implementation of the contingency plan

The contingency plan, as you have already learned, is there only to be used in the event of an emergency. There are few events that do not have any problems at all. To help the event run smoothly, the organiser will need to have already thought about what possible problems might occur and have made contingency plans. For example, if the event is to include computer presentations or DVDs, the organiser may want to check the services provided at the venue and also take along their own laptop and projector as a back-up. Some problems cannot be anticipated, therefore quick thinking is necessary. Good event organisers have this quality and are able to sort out solutions.

Contingency plans can be used for almost any aspect of running the event, from entertainers or catering staff not turning up, through to not enough chairs and tables at the venue. What is extremely important is that plans are put into place and can be easily followed if something should go wrong.

Customer service issues

During an event, it is very important that any problems with customer service are faced and dealt with. If customers are not having a good time, it is important that their concerns are heard and that steps are taken to address the problems. Social media can be used to highlight customer service issues very quickly, by bringing them to the attention of other participants at the event, people outside the event and, ultimately, into the media spotlight to the detriment of the event organiser.

When dealing with customer service issues it is important that:

▶ customers are listened to
▶ apologies are given where the service has been below expectations
▶ empathy and appreciation of the customers situation is shown
▶ actions are taken to address the issue or concern, where possible, and are taken quickly.

Some customer service issues are more common than others. Some issues are relatively easy to prevent or solve at a very early stage, as demonstrated in Table 4.14.

Link

You will learn more about customer service in *Unit 14: Investigating Customer Service*.

▶ **Table 4.14:** Customer service issues and ways they can be avoided or resolved

Issue	Avoidance and resolution
Staff having a lack of knowledge about what is happening at the event	• Ensure that good training and guides are given out before the event. • Have senior staff available to support and give out information. • Supervisors or the event organiser must check the information being given out.
Staff being rude to customers	• Staff should be trained in customer service approaches before the event. • During the event, staff should be moved to duties or placed in pairs or small groups to assist each other. • Apologies to customers should be given by more senior staff or the event organiser.
Food service being too slow	• Check service standards and arrangements in advance of the event. • Additional staff may need to be drafted in on the day to help out.
Car parking being difficult	• Find out alternative parking arrangements before the event. • During the event, provide suggestions for other places to park for later arrivals. • Place staff outside the venue to support attendees who are arriving so they do not need to come to the venue to get additional information. • Put out a text message or email to attendees on their way to the venue giving additional important information.

During the event, the key concern is to make sure that customers are listened to, that staff are happy and able to answer any complaints and that actions are taken.

PAUSE POINT   Which types of complaints might be received by an event organiser holding a quiz night?

Hint   What could go wrong during a quiz night that could negatively affect a customer?

Extend   Customer complaints should be welcome. Give a judgement about this view.

Health and safety issues

During the event it is very important that all health and safety matters are dealt with appropriately. This means that any low level concerns that are emerging should be dealt with quickly and safely. This will minimise distress to the attendees and make sure that the event continues positively.

Health and safety issues at an event may be prevented by having good plans and procedures in place before the event. However, it is not always possible to predict all the possible health and safety issues that can occur. What is important is to ensure that, if there is an emergency or any health and safety issues arise, they are dealt with calmly and effectively.

Health and safety issues may be controlled by:
▶ good communication through different channels
▶ competent and well-trained staff being used at the event
▶ clear coordination of the event team working with the venue team
▶ management of the team and monitoring of what is happening.

Reflect on the running of the event and evaluate own skills development

The final part of running an event is the review and evaluation of the event itself after it has finished. Sometimes, to an organiser forgets to evaluate what has happened and learn from any challenges that have happened during the course of the event.

Evaluation of the event

As an event organiser, you need to learn about:
▶ the different ways to review the success of an event
▶ how to analyse the feedback on evaluation forms
▶ how to collect feedback on suggestions for improvement in the future.

Review of success

Measuring whether or not an event has been a success can take place in lots of different ways, but there are four key success measures that are commonly used. These are outlined below.

Meeting aims and objectives

You learned about aims and objectives earlier in this unit. Here is a quick reminder.
▶ Aims are overarching goals for an event.
▶ Objectives are the plans to achieve those goals.

PAUSE POINT   What are SMART objectives?

Hint   Remember that each part of SMART represents a word that you learned earlier in this unit.

Extend   There is little point in setting objectives unless they are SMART. Discuss this view.

Measuring whether or not aims and objectives have been met is a very important part of event planning. There are different ways to measure the success, as shown in Figures 4.8 and 4.9.

Overall aim: to organise a BTEC Business Workshop Day for Level 3 learners to work with local employers on 5 December		
Objective	**Owner**	**Review and update 8 December**
To organise three speakers to attend the BTEC Business Workshop Day by the end of October	Jade Smith	Speakers organised: • Browns Accounting • Webb Administration Ltd • Brisbane Sales Ltd All confirmed by 31 October.
To book and pay the deposit for the Conference Suite at the High Cliff Hotel by 18 September	Sara Niddrie	Booking was made on 15 September. Deposit was 50% of the cost, which was quite high, but funds were organised.

▶ **Figure 4.8:** Monitoring objectives

If an event is very large and involves lots of people, there is likely to be lots of planning required and objectives may need to be monitored more regularly. At meetings which track the progress of the event, you may find it useful to RAG rate the achievement of the event objectives at regular intervals. This can also be used at the end of the event planning.

RAG rating means:
▶ red
▶ amber
▶ green.

Each of the colours can be used by you to measure and evaluate the progress of the event while it is still being planned or to measure the success of the event in achieving objectives afterwards.

In Figure 4.9, the objective of having three speakers was not met due to a date clash with another event. When reviewing objectives using the RAG rating system, it is quick and easy to review the success of chosen objectives and notes can be added to the review for future events.

Overall aim: to organise a BTEC Business Workshop Day for Level 3 learners to work with local employers on 5 December		
Objective	**Owner**	**Review and update 8 December**
To organise three speakers to attend the BTEC Business Workshop Day by the end of October	Jade Smith	Only two speakers organised: • Browns Accounting • Webb Administration Ltd There was a clash with another event and an alternative speaker was not available. *If we organise this event again we need to ensure that we research other events during December to avoid this happening again.*
To book and pay the deposit for the Conference Suite at the High Cliff Hotel by 18 September	Sara Niddrie	Booking was made on 15 September. Deposit was 50% of the cost, which was quite high, but funds were organised.
50 students to attend the workshops to find out more about the chosen businesses	Jade Smith	52 students attended on the day so the target was exceeded.

▶ **Figure 4.9:** Monitoring objectives using the RAG system

The objectives of an event can cover a number of different elements, as shown in Table 4.15.

▶ **Table 4.15:** Objectives of an event

Element	The objective you set
Attendee satisfaction	• To have 92% of people attending your event to recommend it to a friend. • To have 95% of people attending your event say it was a good or outstanding experience.
Fundraising	• To have raised £100 for charity after all income has been checked and all expenses deducted. • To have encouraged 20 more people to donate to the charity or social enterprise.
Media	• To have 100 new followers on Facebook. • To have 50 people retweet the event and an increase of 40 followers on Twitter. • To have had five articles about the event published about the event or refer to it in online and print media.
Marketing and sales	• To have 100 new customer email addresses for follow up after the event. • To collect 100 mobile phone numbers that can be used to send promotional material via text or other information such as events or general information about the business. • To have 10 new photos for the website to promote the organisation and other business events. • To have 20 additional bookings for the next event through promotion and discounts during the event. • To sell 150 products or items during the event through promotions and discounts. • To sell 50 tickets for the event to show a film or listen to a speaker.
Celebration or recognition	• To have presented an award to recognise the efforts of a particular person. • To have given certificates or prizes to a group or individuals.
Information and training	• To have increased awareness of a particular concern, cause, issue or campaign, for example diabetes awareness or supporting the homeless. • To have trained 50 people in how to use social media. • To have hosted a debate on the use of social media with two teams and 40 people attending.

Reflect

Looking at Table 4.15, can you identify how the objectives are SMART?

Timing

Making a judgement about the timing of your event is also very important. Timing of an event can be measured in different ways:

▶ the time of year that the event was held
▶ the length of time for the whole event to take place
▶ the time of day the event was held
▶ the timings for the start, middle and end of the event.

You will need to review whether or not the timing of the event had an impact on your event. You need to consider the impact of the timing on the:

▶ weather at your event (warm, cold, rain, sunshine, any other concerns such as flooding or snowfall)
▶ attendance during the whole event (same throughout the event or better at the beginning, middle or end)
▶ catering of the event, if applicable (breakfast, morning coffee/tea, lunch, afternoon tea, dinner)
▶ technology used at the event (were sufficient facilities available on that day/at that time?).

Keeping to budget

The budget has a huge impact on the success of the event.

▶ Over-budget means that the event may have made a loss unless more attendees turned up than expected.

▶ Under-budget may mean that savings have been made but what has the impact been on the event – negative or positive?

▶ After the event it is important to review all types of expenditure and sales to see how the plan compares with what actually happened, as shown in Figure 4.10.

Expense	Estimated cost	Actual cost	Difference
Hire of hall	£30 per hour × 5 hours = £150	£25.50 × 6 hours = £153	+£3.00
Catering, including tea/coffee and bottles of water	£100	£89.60	−£10.40
Advertising in the local paper	£300	£100	−£200
Leaflets, including distribution	£200	£250	+£50
Hire of IT equipment, including WiFi charge	£200	£200 (no charge for WiFi)	=
Appearance fee for the speaker	£500	Agreed half-price as a one-off £250	−£250
Total	£1450	£1042.60	−£407.40

▶ **Figure 4.10:** Look back over all types of expenditure and sales and compare them with the plan to see what actually happened

It is also important to check the budgets relating to income to see if the number of people attending matched the number expected and the impact of the number of people attending the event (see Figure 4.10).

Item	Estimated sales	Actual sales	Difference
Tickets on entry	100 × £2 = £200	120 × £2 = £240	+£40
Programmes	100 × £1 = £100	75 × £1 = £75	−£25
Total	£300	£315	+£15

▶ **Figure 4.11:** Do the budgets relating to income match the estimated and actual numbers of attendees?

As well as writing up the expenses and any income, at this stage, it is also important to make notes about any special discounts or arrangements that were negotiated for the event. Sometimes, it is possible to get big discounts on a first event, for example a discounted rate on the venue, because the owners hope that you will organise a second event there. Note down these discounts or promotional offers so that, if you do plan a second event, you can take it into account in your planning.

Effectiveness of contingency plan

When you are planning your event, you will always hope that your contingency plan is not needed because the event runs to time and in the location that you expected. However, if you do need to use your plan, or something happens during your event, it is important to review what happened.

▸ How well written was the plan?

▸ Did it have all the necessary steps to avoid problems or concerns?

▸ Was there anything that you had not included on the plan that affected the event?

▸ Did the plan include any unnecessary information?

▸ Was there anything that could have been done in the main event planning to avoid using the contingency plan?

Analysis of evaluation forms

You learned, at the beginning of this unit, about different ways to evaluate an event and the types of feedback that can be used to find out the opinion of your attendees about your event.

There are lots of different ways that you can evaluate the feedback of your event with your attendees and also with the other members of the team who are organising the event with you by using:

▸ delegate questionnaires (online or paper-based)

▸ event debrief forms

▸ feedback forms (online or paper-based)

▸ voting schemes (such as using coloured balls or booths)

▸ electronic feedback through video or audio recording

▸ noted interviews or meetings after the event.

Delegate questionnaires (see Figure 4.12) are one of the most popular ways to collect feedback from people attending an event. They are often given out on paper during the event and collected at the end. This means that the information about the event is collected quickly and the response rate is often good.

It is also possible to collect immediate feedback at the event using a tablet device or mobile phone to ask questions.

Questionnaires can be sent out by email after the event but these often have lower response rates as people do not fill them in when they are at home. Sometimes prizes or other incentives are used to encourage people to fill them in.

PAUSE POINT Compare a paper evaluation form with one on a tablet or smartphone for taking feedback at an event.

Hint Think about the technology, processing of answers and time needed at the event.

Extend The response rate for a questionnaire or evaluation form is the most critical part of collecting feedback. Discuss this view.

Event debrief forms are really used by the team members to review what happened at the event, what worked well and what not so well (see Figure 4.13). Debriefing of the event may also take place at a meeting where notes are taken. The notes or forms can then be analysed to find out if there are learning points that need to be considered when planning the next event.

DELEGATE FEEDBACK QUESTIONNAIRE				
Name of delegate				
Delegate's email address				
Name of event				
Date and location				
Please rate the event using the scales provided (1 being very good; 4 being very poor). Please circle.				
How useful was the pre-event information?	1	2	3	4
How easy was the location to find?	1	2	3	4
How good was the registration process?	1	2	3	4
What did you think of the refreshments?	1	2	3	4
What did you think of the facilities on offer?	1	2	3	4
How did you find the equipment provided ?	1	2	3	4
How did you find the presentations given?	1	2	3	4
How good was the event overall?	1	2	3	4
General comments about the event				
Suggestions for other events or ways to further enhance the event				
Would you recommend this event to a colleague or friend?	Yes		No	
Can we contact you about future events?	Yes		No	

▶ **Figure 4.12:** An example of a delegate questionnaire

What do you need to remember when writing a questionnaire or feedback form? How does this impact on your evaluation?

Hint   Think about the types of question that you choose – qualitative and quantitative.

Extend   To what extent do evaluation forms influence the perceived success or failure of an event?

EVENT DEBRIEF FORM
Name of the event
Date, time and location
Event organiser
How did the event run overall, including what was particularly good about it (if anything)?
Were there any accidents/emergencies/major issues?
Was anything missing on the risk assessment?
Were there any problems with the venue or facilities, including catering if applicable?
Any other issues or notes from the event that other event organisers should be aware of?
Would you recommend using this venue again?

▶ **Figure 4.13:** An event debrief form

Suggestions for improvement

After the event, any problems that arose should be investigated and their source identified. For example, if too many or too few delegates turned up, the event organiser will need to consider which factors contributed to this.

A good organiser will also make a note of lessons learned. This should be for all outcomes, whether they are positive or negative. If something has worked really well, you will need to remember it, but if it has not worked well you will need to try to ensure that it does not happen again.

Remember that you will need to think about all the different ways to review and analyse suggestions for improvement and all the elements that might need improving from the very beginning to the end, including:

▶ choosing the idea

▶ planning

▶ pre-event materials

▶ materials for the event

▶ running the event

▶ feedback and changes to plans during the event

▶ feedback after the event

▶ materials given out after the event.

Above all, you need to be thinking at all times – what was the impact of my event?

Assessment of personal skills development in running the event

During the running and reviewing of your event, it is easy to think only of the feedback from delegates and your team members on the event itself and what has worked well and less well. Running an event involves lots of different skills and thinking about the skills that you have developed through the process, including those that you need to work on more, is very important.

Events involve a lot of people, activities and planning so being able to plan events well will help you to develop your skills and make your event more useful in the workplace in the future.

When you are reflecting back on the event, you need to think about the skills you gained:

▶ before the event

▶ during the event

▶ after the event.

You also need to think about the skills you still need to develop after the event and ways in which you are going to develop them in the future.

Event management

You have already learned that managing an event is not about just one thing – it is about many different elements. Making a judgement about each of these elements will help you to think about your own performance when managing an event (see Table 4.16).

> ▶ **Table 4.16:** A table like this will help you to make a judgement on your own performance

Event management skill	Evidence for how well I am doing in that skill	Judgement
Knowledge	Awareness of different venues for where events could be held and knowledge of the prices, using contacts given to me by my aunt.	Good knowledge of event planning and good use of link to family member.
Delegation		
Budget planning and monitoring		
Organisation		
Supporting others		
Training others		
Motivating others		

<aside>

Key term

Delegation – to give a task to someone else, usually a member of the team, and trust them to do it on your behalf.

</aside>

Employability

Another way to make an assessment of your personal skills in running events is to rate yourself according to different skills (see Figure 4.14).

Element	Rating (1 very good to 4 very poor)			
Reliable	1	2	3	4
Creative	1	2	3	4
Flexible	1	2	3	4
Optimistic	1	2	3	4
Confident	1	2	3	4
Calm	1	2	3	4
Self-motivated	1	2	3	4
Self-awareness	1	2	3	4
Able to cope under pressure	1	2	3	4

> ▶ **Figure 4.13:** An example of a self-evaluation sheet

For any areas marked 3 or 4, you should consider how you would improve your skills in this area and produce an action plan, with a timescale, for how this could be done.

Asking for feedback from other team members, and thinking about the evidence for your rating, will also help you to think about the skills you already have and those you will learn in the future.

Ⅱ PAUSE POINT

Why do you think it is so critical for an event organiser to be honest about their skills in event planning?

Hint — Think about what would happen if they over- or underestimated their own skills.

Extend — An experienced event organiser is critical to the success of any event. Discuss this view.

Communication

Think back to events where you have been able to practise your communication skills. Ask yourself how well you communicated during these events in preparation for your assessed event. Use these questions as a guide and think of others to help you make judgements about how well you communicate.

▶ In writing:
- Was my presentation suitable?
- Were my spelling and grammar correct?
- Did I use the appropriate formal language required for the event rather than 'text speak language'?
- Was my communication timely?
- Was my communication clear and easily understood by everyone?

▶ In person:
- Was I clear?
- Did I speak at an appropriate pace (not too fast or slow)?
- Did I leave suitable pauses?
- Did I speak at an appropriate volume?
- Was I specific?
- Did I greet people correctly at the event?
- Was I clear in giving and receiving instructions to and from other team members?
- How well did I listen?

Negotiation

Making an assessment of your negotiation skills can be carried out in lots of different ways. One way is to use the semantic scaling you learned about earlier in this unit (see Table 4.17).

▶ **Table 4.17:** A semantic scale to help you to assess your skills

	1	2	3	4	5	6	7	8	
Prepared									Unprepared
Good questioning									Bad questioning
Excellent communicator									Poor communicator
Good at summarising									Poor at summarising
Good at giving feedback									Poor at giving feedback
Good at mediating									Poor at mediating

Time management

Time management is about making the best use of time and ensuring that events run smoothly and that attendees, the event team and the organiser are happy with the way the event runs.

To measure your time management skills, you need to ask yourself about the following elements:

▶ diaries
▶ scheduling
▶ to do list
▶ punctuality
▶ time wasting/distractions

- focusing attention
- getting tasks completed on time
- prioritising
- taking breaks
- managing emails and other communications
- running and participating in meetings.

Reflect

Consider all the time management elements that are you learning about on your BTEC course. How many of these elements do you use when producing your coursework, studying for your exams or other studies at your centre? Discuss which of the elements helps you the most.

Problem solving

Problem-solving skills require quick solutions to be made using judgement and creativity (to ensure that something that is going wrong is put right). Being good at problem solving requires calmness and being able to act quickly. Think back to an event you have been involved with as part of your learning, and look at the qualities in Table 4.18. Think about your own skills and those you need to develop.

▶ **Table 4.18:** Assessing your skills

Problem-solving skill	Evidence and approach
Being quick to respond	
Being sympathetic	
Being calm	
Ensuring that changes are made when required	
Demonstrating sympathy	
Demonstrating empathy	
Knowing alternative options	
Adapting to new circumstances or information	
Being flexible	
Ensuring that the pace of solving the problem is appropriate	
Responding to urgent or challenging information	
Listening and understanding the problem in hand	

 **PAUSE POINT**   What would happen if an event organiser had poor problem-solving skills?

Hint   Think about what would happen if an event continued without change/contingency activity.

Extend   Consider the differences between the problem-solving skills you would need for a small-scale event versus a large-scale event.

Team working

When you are reviewing your team-working skills, you may find it useful to ask for feedback from other people. You can ask for 360 degree feedback from your tutor, from other event organisers in your class and then from team members that you were working with as the event organiser. 360 degree feedback is given to provide feedback from lots of different perspectives. Team working skills can be rated as you have done before for employability (see Table 4.19).

▶ **Table 4.19:** A table to help you to rate your own team-working skills

Element	Rating (1 very good to 4 very poor)			
Respects others	1	2	3	4
Values others	1	2	3	4
Collaborator	1	2	3	4
Shares ideas	1	2	3	4
Helps others	1	2	3	4
Shows commitment to the event/task	1	2	3	4
Decision making	1	2	3	4
Keeps trying to improve the event for everyone	1	2	3	4
Doesn't give up	1	2	3	4

Analysis of own skills

The final part of this unit asks you to think about an overall analysis of your skills as a whole. You have already learned about the different personal skills that you can develop before, during and after an event. You have also reflected on different events that you have been involved with in the past. Summarising all those skills into one main document will help you to think about how you have contributed to events in the past and to reflect on the skills that you need to learn and develop in preparation for your assessment for this unit.

A useful tool is to give an analysis of all of the different aspects of personal skills development using the questions, questionnaires and scaling activities that you have used in this unit. You can then apply them to a single SWOT analysis like the one shown in Figure 4.15. A SWOT analysis shows your areas of strength and weakness. It also allows you to consider areas of learning that you need to think about as opportunities and also to see that what is stopping you taking your learning forward, i.e. may be a threat.

Strengths	Weaknesses
Team player based on rating from other members of my team	Disorganised, as materials I was asked to produce were not printed on time
Opportunities	**Threats**
Develop time management skills Develop IT skills in design to improve my work rate.	Completing my learning and research for other units on my BTEC National Level 3

▶ **Figure 4.15:** An example of a SWOT analysis

Assessment practice 4.3

You will now manage the event which you planned earlier. You will need to provide evidence of your active participation in staging and managing the event and write a report evaluating the event's success. Your report should include a witness testimony *or* photographic evidence *or* records from your assessor to show the event happening

Event planning has many different elements to it. You need to consider every type of situation you can think of, monitor circumstances during the event, adjust things where necessary and demonstrate the management skills required of you during the event.

Demonstrating that the event has been conducted safely and positively is important when staging an event. When staging your event, throughout each element, you will need to think of how your actions have been effective and where you need to improve.

Your written report, which will record and evaluate the success of the event, analyse the planning and running of the event, and analyse how risks and contingencies were managed, should include:

- how effectively your skills have helped to meet the aims, objectives and targets of the event, through your own evaluation and through feedback from the people affected by your event
- feedback from stakeholders, including attendees, team members and suppliers, possibly including a satisfaction survey
- recommendations for future improvements
- judgements about how you have performed and how your contribution has led to a well-planned and effective event through planning, demonstration, management skills and checking the arrangements recommendations for future improvements.

Throughout your review, analyse all the elements of your performance, show how the different actions and elements of the event were managed and make judgements about the skills that you have developed or need to develop further. Consider how well your initial plan contributed to the event's success.

Plan

- I shall reflect back on what I have learned – which skills did I develop and should include.
- I shall plan how to get feedback from my stakeholders.
- I shall decide how to compare my results to my original aims and objectives.
- I shall decide how to make judgements about my work. I shall identify which command words will help me.

Do

- I shall decide how to write my report. I shall consider an introduction and headings.
- I shall check that my spelling and grammar are accurate.
- I shall think about how I can check that my report makes sense to a third party.

Review

- I have evaluated my proof reading skills.
- I have evaluated how professionally I presented my work.
- I have analysed what I could do differently next time to make sure that I improve in future assignments.

Further reading and resources

Capell L. *Event management for Dummies,* John Wiley & Sons. (2013)

Johnson N. *Event Planning Tips: The Straight Scoop On How To Run A Successful Event,* (CreateSpace Independent Publishing Platform) (2015)

Lindsey K. *Planning and Managing A Corporate Event,* How to Books (2011)

www.eventmanagerblog.com

A community-based blog offering advice and tips on event planning and new initiatives.

www.nonprofitpeople.monster.com/training/articles/94-tips-for-successful-event-planning

A non-profit business people offer hints and tips on ways to plan events for not-for-profit causes.

www.smallbusinesscan.com/how-to-plan-a-successful-business-event/

A small business website with hints and tips on how to run successful events.

THINK ▶FUTURE

Samantha Pierce

Event planner

I have been working in marketing and events for more than 10 years. This means that when I am organising an event I am not only thinking about the planning of the event itself but also about ensuring that the marketing is right to get lots of interest from people wanting to come to the event.

The most challenging part of my role is being organised. Nothing can be left to chance and I need to make sure that every possible problem that could go wrong is thought about in advance. In my role, I have planned very small events for up to 30 people including private dinners with exclusive speakers. I have also run events at a premiership football club which were much more complicated. Communication was needed with all sorts of people from the media, including television and radio and also social media Twitter.

Sometimes, people ask me for the best piece of advice that I can give them when planning an event. I tell them: organisation, organisation, organisation. If you are organised and plan well ahead, you can never go wrong as you have thought of every possible problem or concern and have made arrangements to deal with it. It is also really important to have your own set of reminders and tips when planning your event.

Focusing your skills

The role of the event planner

The role of event planner is very important for an event, and the skills that they have in terms of planning, interpersonal and communications are critical.

- What are good communication skills?
- Which are the most important skills when negotiating?
- How can the skills of empathy and rapport be used when planning an event?
- Think about the impact of poor time management on the running of an event.

Tips to remember when planning an event

- What are the objectives of the event?
- How will your event create a positive impact?
- Which risks need the most careful management during the event?

Think carefully and detail all the elements of the event into a single plan by writing everything down and keeping good records.

Getting ready for assessment

Emilia is working towards a BTEC National in Business. She was given an assignment that asked her to stage and manage a business event and write an evaluation review to highlight the skills that she developed for learning aims D and E. She had run the event demonstrating her skills and then reviewed the success of the event by writing an evaluation that showed the extent to which she:

▶ achieved her aims and objectives
▶ achieved her targets and received feedback from her stakeholders
▶ analysed the event and how risks and contingencies were managed, making recommendations for future improvements
▶ justified the contribution she made and demonstrated outstanding management skills throughout the arranging and staging of the event.

How I got started

▶ First, I reviewed all of my notes from my classes and I re-read sections of the unit again. I had not learned about insurance or risk assessments before so, during the running of the event, I made sure that I regularly reviewed the unit and what I needed to do.

▶ I made sure, when I was running my event (which was a mini business conference held in my centre), that I kept notes on what was working well and what was working less well. This meant that I was able to make judgements about my performance as I went along.

▶ It was important for me to make sure I had a note book to jot down all the different aspects of the event as I went through. I also compared the staging and arranging of my event to others that I have been to as part of the course and from when I was younger. I noted how complicated the staging and arranging of an event was, and how much work goes on behind the scenes to make sure it is successful.

How I brought it all together.

▶ The event itself worked well. My group held a one-day conference where three speakers came in to talk about their businesses, and to pass on hints and tips to learners in my class. The speakers were all excellent. One of them turned up late as he was delayed by an accident when he was driving to the conference. This helped me to use our contingency planning, and I was able to give a short talk on what we were learning on our BTEC National course.

What I learned from the experience

▶ I found that we had much less time to stage and arrange the conference than I thought. I thought we had weeks to get everything organised but it went really quickly. I also learned, on the day, that it is good to have as many different people helping as possible. We didn't remember to give out any extra paper or pens during the conference, so this is something that I will remember if I organise a conference again in the future.

▶ After the event, I was very tired but started to write out my notes and information about what had worked well and what had worked less well. I learned that this was a useful thing to do. My friend didn't do this and she soon forgot some of the skills that she needed to use during the event. This made it harder for her to write up her evaluation.

Think about it

▶ Have you used different ways to make judgements about your performance during the event, making sure that you have asked different stakeholders?

▶ Do you know how to analyse feedback from questionnaires or forms to draw conclusions and justify your own contribution when event planning?

▶ Is your evaluation written in a way that clearly gives judgements and draws conclusions together, so that you can demonstrate your management skills, including showing that your skills are outstanding?

Recruitment and Selection Process 8

Getting to know your unit

Assessment

You will be assessed by a series of assignments set by your tutor.

Employees are the most important resource in most businesses. This is because their work has a big influence on the success of a business. Businesses need to attract and select people to work for them in a legal and ethical way. Different online and offline processes are used by businesses from planning the workforce through to advertising, selecting and finally offering the job to the successful candidate.

How you will be assessed

This unit will be assessed through a series of internally assessed tasks set by your tutor. Throughout this unit you will find assessment activities that will help you to practise and to develop your knowledge and skills ready for assessment. Completing these activities will help you to feel fully prepared for your final assessment. In order for you to successfully pass this unit, you must make sure that you have met the requirements of all the Pass grading criteria. You can do this yourself by checking against the criteria.

To gain a Merit or a Distinction, you must extend your work further. For Merit criteria, you must analyse different elements of the unit. For a Distinction, you will need to be able to provide an evaluation, meaning that you will need to make judgements about different content.

The assignments set by your tutor will consist of a number of tasks designed to meet the criteria in the table. These are likely to consist of the following activities such as:

▶ writing a report that examines recruitment processes in a large business
▶ taking part in recruitment and selection practical activities as an interviewer and as a person interviewing a candidate
▶ producing all the documents that are needed for recruitment and selection processes
▶ writing reviews, including judgements about your own performance, outlining what you did well and areas where you could have done better, along with an action plan.

Assessment criteria

This table shows you what you must do in order to achieve a **Pass, Merit** or **Distinction** grade, and where you can find activities to help you.

Pass	Merit	Distinction

Learning aim **A** Examine how effective selection and recruitment contribute to business success

Pass	Merit	Distinction
A.P1 Explain how a large business recruits and selects giving reasons for their processes. **Assessment practice 8.1**	**A.M1** Analyse the different recruitment methods used in a selected business. **Assessment practice 8.1**	**A.D1** Evaluate the recruitment processes used and how they contribute to the success of the selected business. **Assessment practice 8.1**
A.P2 Explain how and why a business adheres to recruitment processes which are ethical and comply with current employment law. **Assessment practice 8.1**		

Learning aim **B** Undertake a recruitment activity to demonstrate the processes leading to a successful job offer

Pass	Merit	Distinction
B.P3 Prepare appropriate documentation for use in selection and recruitment activities. **Assessment practice 8.2**	**B.M2** In recruitment interviews demonstrate analytical responses and questioning to allow assessment of skills and knowledge. **Assessment practice 8.2**	**B.D2** Evaluate how well the documents prepared and participation in the interview activities supported the process for a job offer. **Assessment practice 8.2**
B.P4 Participate in the selection interviews, as an interviewer and interviewee. **Assessment practice 8.2**		

Learning aim **C** Reflect on the recruitment and selection process and your individual performance

Pass	Merit	Distinction
C.P5 Complete a SWOT analysis on your performance in role in the interviewing activities. **Assessment practice 8.2**	**C.M3** Analyse the results of the process and how your skills development will contribute to your future success. **Assessment practice 8.2**	**C.D3** Evaluate how well the recruitment and selection process complied with best practice, drawing reasoned conclusions as to how it will support your future career. **Assessment practice 8.2**
C.P56 Prepare a personal skills development plan for future interview situations. **Assessment practice 8.2**		

Getting started

Part of recruitment and selection is making people aware that a vacancy exists. Write down as many ways as you can think of that an employer could use to make people aware of a vacancy. When you have completed this unit, see how many ways you missed.

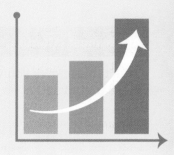

 # A Examine how effective recruitment and selection contribute to business success

In this section, you will consider the reasons why a vacancy exists in the first place, the processes that happen to attract and choose new staff and the ethical and legal considerations that influence those processes.

Recruitment of staff

There are lots of different reasons why an organisation may decide to recruit someone to a position (see Table 8.1). One of the most common that you may have heard of is that someone is leaving to go and work for another organisation and their position needs to be filled. Large businesses carry out **workforce** planning to find out if they need to recruit anyone at all.

▶ Before looking at Table 8.1, how many different reasons for recruitment can you think of?

Workforce planning

Businesses need to match the skills, knowledge and number of employees to their current and future needs. To work out their needs, they need to review the number and skills of employees they have now, what they think will happen in the future and the number that they will need in the future.

Discussion

ICT has changed the skills, knowledge and number of employees that are required in the workplace. How do you think the following advances in technology have affected the way that businesses plan their workforces: mobile phones, laptops and video conferencing? Does the use of IT decrease employee numbers? If so, why? What are the advantages and disadvantages of relying on IT?

In large organisations with more than 250 employees, the types of skills required will depend on the industry that they work in. For example, a retail business may need staff to put out stock and to serve customers face-to-face. A production company may need staff to work in packing or on the production line. A financial organisation may need staff with specialist experience and qualifications to offer advice and maybe telephone skills.

There are lots of reasons why businesses will need to recruit staff. Businesses often recruit due to a mixture of some, or all, of the reasons that are shown in Table 8.1.

Research

Find out and compare the staff turnover rates in different industries. Find out which industries have high rates of turnover and which have lower. Choose two businesses (one in each industry) and examine the impact of their rate of turnover on the recruitment of staff.

Table 8.1: There are many varied reasons why businesses recruit staff

Reasons for recruiting staff	
The business is growing	If the number of customers or sales is increasing, the business will need to recruit. Employees may be needed locally, nationally or even globally.
Job roles are changing	Advances in technology influence the way jobs are performed. For example, self-service tills were introduced in the UK in 2002. This did not lead to fewer staff being recruited by supermarkets but, instead of having staff on the tills waiting for customers, they are able to stock the shelves and increase sales.
Systems are changing	If customers use systems in new ways, the skills and number of employees needed changes too. For example, many people book hotels and flights online so staff taking telephone bookings only are reduced.
New vacancies are being created by more space or product development	Staff may be needed to operate in new gaps in the market or environment. For example, Facebook was effectively launched to the general public from 2004. Now there are vacancies to work at Facebook all over the world for the people with the right skills and expertise. Businesses launching new products may need new staff to promote and sell them.
Vacancies caused by leavers/**staff turnover**	Staff leave for many different reasons and may or may not need to be replaced. Staff may leave due to personal reasons such as moving house, for promotions outside the organisation or for higher wages/salaries.
Staff are being internally promoted	If an employee gets a promotion to a higher job within the business, this is called an internal promotion. A new person will need to be recruited to cover their former role.
New offices or branches are being opened	Businesses often start small and then need more staff as they start to expand.
Seasonal fluctuations lead to a need for temporary staff	For some businesses, there are huge variations in staff, for example businesses working in the tourist industry often see large increases in the number of staff needed in the summer compared with the winter. Hotels, holiday parks and entertainment businesses will all see high increases in the demand during the summer months. Other businesses have large increases in the winter, for example retailers during the run up to festivals such as Christmas, Hanukkah or Eid.

Job centres and agencies

An organisation may not able to manage the process of recruiting themselves because they are too busy or feel they do not have suitably qualified staff to run the recruitment process. They may use job centres or other agencies. Job centres are popular places for employers to advertise vacancies as this is where people go to get advice on different jobs and benefits. Job centres work with employers to provide additional training and support to local areas so that employees can be found to fill vacancies. Job centres are also able to offer employers extra training and support so that they can recruit employees, for example, by giving advice on recruitment or on different training opportunities such as apprenticeships. Recruitment agencies such as Reed or Office Angels are also popular but, unlike the job centre, they charge commission for finding suitable people for employers on a temporary or permanent basis.

Key term

Staff turnover – this calculation takes the number of employees that left in a given amount of time (usually a year) as a percentage of all employees. For example, ten employees leaving in one year from 100 employees would be 10/100 = 10% turnover. The average UK staff turnover is 15%.

Research

Many vacancies are available online so it is a popular method of recruitment. In small groups, research the type and variety of vacancies available. Consider splitting your research into regions. Can you see any differences between the types of job available? Why are there regional differences?

Can you find examples of off- and online advertising at your local job centre?

Key terms

Fixed-term contract – an employment contract between employee and employer with a defined end date.

Probationary period – a defined 'trial' period where employee and employer can work out if the employee is a good fit for the role and the business.

Recruitment agencies provide employers with details about potential applicants. Often recruitment agencies will provide staff on a temporary or permanent basis. This means that an employer may have a chance to see how an employee is likely to work out by putting them on a three-, six- or twelve-month **fixed-term contract** initially. This is often a cost-effective option for employers, particularly if their business changes rapidly and they may not need to keep staff permanently. Also, almost all jobs, whether permanent or fixed-term contracts will have a **probationary period**. What do you think are the advantages for an employer and employee in using fixed-term contracts? What are the advantages of having a probationary period?

The advantages and disadvantages of using an agency are outlined in Table 8.2.

▶ **Table 8.2:** Advantages and disadvantages of using an agency or consultant

Advantages	Disadvantages
The organisation can concentrate on running the business and not looking for new employees.	The organisation must pay the agent and the new employee, adding to costs. These costs include a fee for finding the employee and often a percentage of their salary going forward.
The organisation does not have to employ a recruitment team.	The agency/consultant may not find the right person for the job as the agent does not know in detail the culture and values of the business. They also do not know if the person will work well with other members of the team.
The agency/consultant will have access to lots of different people and will screen out anyone who is unsuitable.	They may not care about employing the right person for the job as much as someone working in the organisation, as they will not be working directly with that person.
They will not tell competitor organisations that you are recruiting, but your own advertisements will.	
They can offer specialist support and expertise for the recruiting team, for example a finance specialist when recruiting to the finance team.	
They can offer advice about what is happening in the employment area.	

Case study

Bartley Major

Bartley Major is a **headhunting** agency based in Cheshire. They recruit employees for leading companies throughout the British Isles.

They were approached recently by a leading cosmetics retailer, Live Beauty, to help them recruit a new Brand Communications Director. To ensure they got the right person for the job, the agency spoke extensively with their contact at Live Beauty and made sure they had as full a job description as possible. Making sure they knew the deadlines for the role, the recruiter at Bartley Major then researched suitable candidates, providing Live Beauty with an appropriate shortlist. The recruiter then helped prepare the candidates for interview and, when a successful candidate was chosen, the recruiter managed much of the administrative detail between the new employee and their new employer.

For all roles like the above, Bartley Major's activities include:

- targeting high achievers to form a pool of applicants
- presenting candidates to clients after initial screening and selection
- interviewing candidates and preparing them for interview with the employer
- negotiating salary packages
- helping candidates to resign from their current employer.

They also conduct assessment days so that employers can receive details about applicants' previous knowledge, experience and ability before the recruitment process starts.

Check your knowledge

1 What is a recruitment agency?

2 What were the advantages to Live Beauty of using Bartley Major?

3 Do you think there may have been any disadvantages?

4 'Headhunters are only useful to recruit the most senior employees.' Discuss.

5 What sort of information do you think the recruiter needed from Live Beauty to make sure their search was successful? Create a list, and share with a peer to see how many you have both thought of.

Internal advertising compared to external advertising

Jobs can be advertised internally or externally. Internal advertising means that the advertising of the job will only be done inside the organisation. This means that the person will already have an idea of the type of organisation that they are working for and the skills needed to work there. Sometimes, this type of advertising and recruitment will also give current employees the chance for promotion or additional responsibility, so it can be motivating for them.

Organisations will sometimes decide to advertise a vacancy internally first. If no suitable employees apply for this job, they will advertise outside as well. Of course, if a vacancy is advertised internally and someone changes jobs to fill the role, somebody new may be needed to replace them, in turn. This may extend the recruitment process and may be a problem for the organisation if they need to recruit quickly. The advantages and disadvantages of internal advertising are outlined in Table 8.3.

> **Key term**

Headhunter – an organisation that finds and approaches individuals already employed by a business to ask them if they wish to work for another business.

▶ **Table 8.3:** Advantages and disadvantages of advertising internally

Advantages	Disadvantages
Cheap to advertise	Limited choice of candidates
All candidates known to the organisation	May cause problems amongst employees due to the change
Candidates also already know the organisation	Employees may be stuck in their ways
More likely to have a smaller number of applicants	May not generate new ideas
Can encourage career progression	The successful candidate will need to be replaced, needing another recruitment plan

External advertising is the opposite of internal and is the process of recruiting from outside the organisation. There are a number of ways this can be done and these include the organisation itself doing the recruiting or making use of job centres and agencies. The advantages and disadvantages of external advertising are outlined in Table 8.4.

> **Table 8.4:** Advantages and disadvantages of external advertising

Advantages	Disadvantages
Higher number of candidates	Takes longer
Candidates may have new ideas	Person appointed may not be as good as they appear
Potential for new skills to be brought into the organisation	More expensive to advertise

Online recruitment and traditional methods

Many businesses now make use of online methods to recruit staff rather than traditional advertising such as shop windows or in the local newspaper. Online methods include:

- social media such as Facebook and Twitter
- websites
- online application forms to be filled in onscreen
- emailing completed forms or curriculum vitae (CV).

Traditional methods are those that have been used for many years including:

- calling in for a discussion or informal chat
- sending in a paper application form
- writing a letter of application to be sent in by post with a CV.

Case study

Debenhams

Debenhams use their website to provide information for applicants. The site uses online questions to help potential applicants search for job vacancies that might be relevant to them. They then set up a user name and password as well as giving their email address to Debenhams and starting the online application. This means that Debenhams have contact information from the earliest stage and can monitor who is interested in their vacancies.

The online application form screens applications by asking questions about aspects such as:

- whether the applicant has the correct legal documents to work in the UK
- whether they are at least 16 years of age and therefore of school leaving age in the UK
- qualifications relevant to the role
- skills relevant to the role
- previous criminal convictions.

Check your knowledge

1 How do Debenhams use online applications as part of recruitment?

2 What are the advantages of using such a system?

3 Are there any disadvantages?

4 Compare and contrast the online application process for three different organisations that you are aware of. To what extent do these processes have common features? How important is conformity in recruitment?

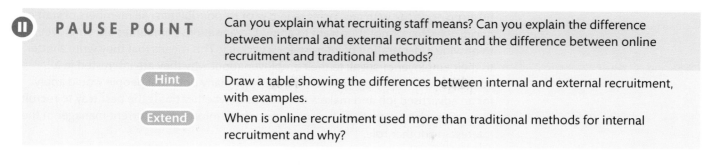

Can you explain what recruiting staff means? Can you explain the difference between internal and external recruitment and the difference between online recruitment and traditional methods?

Hint   Draw a table showing the differences between internal and external recruitment, with examples.

Extend   When is online recruitment used more than traditional methods for internal recruitment and why?

Recruitment and business success

Recruiting the right staff is very important for the success of a business. Often people are the most expensive assets in a business and employing the wrong people can be costly if customers are unhappy or receive poor service. Each time a business recruits a new member of staff there is a cost to the business. This is called an **opportunity cost**. This is the cost of the advertising and recruitment process itself but also the cost of the opportunity (because the time that the hiring manager spent on recruiting could have been used elsewhere in the business). Good recruitment leads to high numbers of applicants and, ultimately, a good choice of people to work for the business. Poor recruitment has the opposite effect and can lead to the business being short of staff and unable to work effectively.

> **Key term**
>
> **Opportunity cost** – the cost to the business of making one decision over another, choosing one alternative compared to the next best.

Professional recruitment leading to efficient staff integration

Recruiting staff in a professional way is also critical to businesses and helps their success. This is because professional recruitment means that the reputation of the business continues to be good so more people will be attracted to work there.

Professional recruitment also ensures that new staff fit into the **culture** of that business and quickly have a positive impact on the business because they are aware of what is required by the business at the very start of the process. This means that staff become integrated more quickly, leading to efficient working practices. What do you think the impact of recruiting the right people is on the business?

> **Key term**
>
> **Culture** – this means 'the way we do things around here': the values and expectations of people in a business that are not written down.

Recruitment and selection process

The two elements of the recruitment and selection process are:
- producing the documents that are needed for recruitment from the advertisement, including arrangements for applicants to send in their information to the business
- selection of the candidates once applications have been received.

The recruitment process

You have already learned that advertising can be internal or external and the same is true of all other elements of the recruitment process. Businesses often use different documents for internal recruitment compared to external. This is because they already know the employees that are involved. Some businesses may ask employees to write a letter rather than fill in an application form for an internal vacancy.

Job advertisement

Internal advertising is the simpler of the two types of advertising for a vacancy. This is because it only needs to be shown to employees who currently work for the organisation. It may be placed on the staff noticeboard, web page, company magazine or mentioned in a staff meeting or through a mass email. The details of the job need to be given, together with any increase in pay or responsibilities. All members of staff can decide whether or not they want to apply. Organisations sometimes ask employees to provide a 'declaration of interest' for a vacancy. This means that they write a letter to their employer or speak to their employer about why they are interested in a particular job. The employer can then see how many potential people would apply for an advertised job and make a decision as to whether this is the best way to recruit. They often also ask that any potential candidates inform their current manager of their interest in another role.

External advertising is more complicated as it can be achieved in a number of different ways. Some organisations use newspapers or radio, others a poster in a window, some keep an up-to-date list of interested people to email and others rely on industry-related journals or magazines. Online advertising through websites is becoming increasingly popular. In short, the most suitable place to advertise a post is where potential applicants will read it, so this can vary by sector depending upon who your likely pool of candidates is. Advertising, as you have already learned, may also be done by using an agency or job centre.

One of the cheapest methods of advertising a position is a poster in the window of a business or on a noticeboard. You may have seen this type of notice when you were looking for a part-time job. Employers will put it in the window and anyone in the local area will see it and then may decide to apply. Any applicants will already have some information about the company. This type of advertising does limit the number of possible people applying, because only those who have been past or into the organisation will see it. This type of advertisement may seem old fashioned but it is still relevant for certain types of work.

Job analysis

The job advertisement is one of several documents needed for the recruitment process. As soon as an advertisement is placed, potential applicants will want to know more about the job role so a job description needs to be written. Before businesses write this description, they often analyse the job to review all the different parts of it and the type of person that would be able to perform the role effectively. Job analysis considers the:

▶ tasks (including difficulty and impact of errors)
▶ competencies
▶ attributes.

Job analysis is used to create the job description and person specification that are required.

Job description

Job descriptions give information to prospective employees about what the job actually involves by giving the purpose of the job and the types of responsibilities and duties that will be expected as part of that job. Different organisations have their own particular extra information, but there are a set of key elements that are always included and they are shown in Table 8.5.

Person specification

The job description essentially concentrates on providing information about the job. The **person specification** is a direct contrast. It provides information about the type of person that the organisation is looking for to do the job. The elements of a job specification are shown in Figure 8.1.

> **Key term**
>
> **Person specification** – the list of requirements that a person needs to have in order to meet the expectations of the job.

▶ **Table 8.5:** Elements of a job description

Element	Description
Title of the job	This is really important as it is used to give a person an idea of what the job involves and an indication of the level of responsibility, for example, Finance Manager.
Department and location	A job description will be written for a particular department in an organisation, especially if the organisation is very large.
Broad terms	This gives a very rough idea of what is involved in the post. Many job vacancies have open-ended terms, meaning that they can change slightly to take into account the needs of the business or employee.
Responsible to whom	This tells the applicant to whom they must report with any problems or queries.
Responsibilities	This tells the applicant about any people or resources they are responsible for.
Scope of post	This gives the applicant guidance on how far reaching their post is, for example, whether or not there is a possibility to supervise others or make management changes.
Education and qualifications	Some organisations will also include details about the level of qualifications and experience that the job requires, for example, 'graduate required'. Such information may also be included in the person specification.
Name of compiler and approver	This is the person who designed and agreed the job.
Date of issue	This is when the description was issued. In a fast-changing business world, it is important to know when the last changes were made to the job.

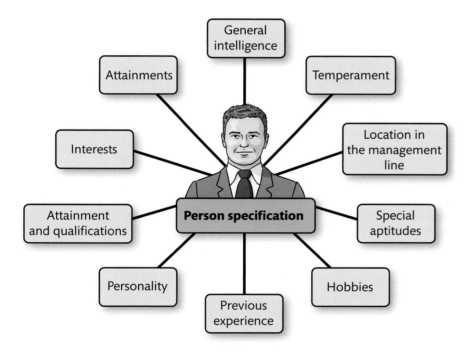

▶ **Figure 8.1:** Elements of a person specification

The person specification gives a list of requirements, but these relate to the person doing the job. It will have an introduction at the start giving details about the job, such as job title, post reference number and management responsibilities (including who the employee needs to report to and is responsible for). It will then detail attributes that the organisation wants that person to have, for example, their type of personality or intelligence level. Often person specifications have a list of attributes that are considered to be **essential** or **desirable elements**. The elements of a person specification are outlined in Table 8.6 and an example of a brief person specification is shown in Figure 8.2.

Reflect

What elements do you currently have if you applied for a job now? What elements are you working towards and want to achieve? How will you gain these elements.

▶ **Table 8.6:** Elements of a person specification

Element	Description
Title of the job and reference number	This is really important as it gives a person an idea of what the job involves. The reference number makes it easier for the organisation to send out details and keep information on file.
Location in management line	A person specification will give clear details about how senior the post holder will be. This helps a potential applicant to work out whether they are suitable for the job.
Essential and desirable characteristics	The person specification will list characteristics that a person needs in order to perform the role, for example, excellent communication skills or the ability to speak an additional language.
Attainments, qualifications and general intelligence	This information details the education level and qualifications that the person should have. Employers will sometimes write 'must have degree-level education' or 'Level 3 education'.
Previous experience	The level of experience needed for the job should be outlined. This must be done in a way that does not discriminate against older or younger employees, so should not state a number or years but could say 'extensive experience'.
Special aptitudes	These are special skills that a person doing this job needs to have, for example, ability to use IT or minimum typing speed.
Temperament and personality	Someone applying for this job needs to be able to demonstrate a certain type of personality so indicators will be provided to help applicants understand what is required, for example, 'able to work under pressure' or 'good sense of humour needed'.
Any other relevant information	Without discriminating against any applicants, it may be possible to list other relevant information on the person specification, for example, 'must be willing to undertake extensive overnight travel'. This is indicating that such work will be needed and therefore should be prepared for.

Person Specification
Post Title: Finance and Administrative Officer
Grade: Clerical 3/4

Criteria	Essential	Desirable
Qualifications/Knowledge	• BTEC National Diploma in Business • GCSEs in Maths and English plus 3 others at Grade C or above or equivalent • ICT skills, particularly spreadsheets and databases	
Work-related Experience	• 1 or 2 years general office and/or financial experience • Good level of numeracy	• Experience in higher education
Skills/Abilities and Special Attributes	• Good organisational skills • Able to prioritise workloads • Good communication skills • Team-working ability	• Previous experience or willingness to work in an open-plan environment

▶ **Figure 8.2:** An example of a brief person specification

Some organisations will also use ratings in their specification (see Figure 8.3). This means that they will rate how important a part of the person specification is to a job, with 10 meaning that this attribute is very important and 1 not important.

Person Specification
Post Title: Business Assistant
Grade: 4

Criteria	Essential	Desirable	Rating
Qualifications and knowledge	BTEC National in Business (Merit)		10
	Maths and English GCSE Grade 5 or above		10
		Good working knowledge of word processing software	8
		Good working knowledge of spreadsheets	5
Work-related experience		Experience of working in an office	5
Skills	Good organisational skills		10
	Able to prioritise workload		10
	Good communication skills		10
	Able to work well in a team		10
		Experience of working in a sales environment	3

▶ **Figure 8.3:** Applicants must have the essential skills to be selected but having desirable ratings ensures that the correct emphasis is placed on the skills required for the job

 PAUSE POINT   What is the difference between a person specification and a job description?

Hint   Think about the purposes of each document to help you remember.

Extend   What would happen in the recruitment process if one of these documents was missing? What would the implications be for the business?

Research

Imagine you have a degree in Business Studies following your BTEC National Business course. Find three job descriptions, with person specifications for a Business Assistant/Executive, to compare. Use job websites to help you and make a note of the similarities and differences. Which would you apply for? What skills would you need to develop to apply for that role?

Write your own CV using the examples listed to help you with your design. Now share your CV with two other learners in your class. Ask them to give you feedback on your CV and how you could improve it. Once you have made the requested changes, repeat the process.

Did you find any common mistakes or errors?

Were there any areas where everyone could improve their CVs?

If you, as a manager, received a CV with mistakes in it, what would you do? Would you still consider the applicant for the vacancy? Why?

CV or application form

A CV (curriculum vitae) requires applicants to write all their details including education and history on a two-page sheet, including referees. The organisation can immediately see everything about an applicant. CVs only focus on positive aspects of an applicant, so it may be difficult to compare candidates. CVs may also have been used to apply for lots of jobs so may not be specific to a particular role. It is important to review a CV regularly or to adapt it for each individual job if an applicant really wants that job. An extract from a CV is shown in Figure 8.4.

Curriculum Vitae

Personal Details
Name — Gita Powell

Address — 18 Hill Lane
Southampton
SO15 5RL

Telephone — 023 80511822

Education
2015–2017 — Topton College
2010–2015 — Besthampton School

Academic Qualifications
BTEC National Extended Diploma in Business — MMP Awarded including Maths and English
Eight GCSEs

Work Experience
2015–2017 — Part-time employment at Next using the till, pricing stock and stock management as well as dealing with customers

Personal Statement
I am a really outgoing person who likes to play sport. I am a member of the Badminton Team at College and also play at the weekend for my local team. I enjoy computing and am able to use a number of different software packages including Microsoft Office XP. I am hardworking and always on time.

Referee
Kate Sharp
76 Laxford Avenue
Southampton
SO26 8PU
Tel: 02380 876233

▶ **Figure 8.4:** Example of a CV

Research

Find a job online that you want to apply for. Think about the skills needed and how to display them in your CV. Have you chosen the best format? Look online. Are there other ways of presenting your CV, e.g. a skills-based CV? Write your CV into a different template, thinking about the skills you need for the role you researched.

Employment Application Form

Section 1 Contact and personal details

PLEASE PRINT CLEARLY USING BLOCK CAPITALS

Please circle one:
Mr   Mrs   Miss   Ms

Surname

Forenames

Address

Home tel. No.

Mobile No.

Postcode

Nationality

Date of birth

Age

National Insurance No.

If you have answered yes to any of these, please give details

Do you have a family member or friend employed here?   Yes   No

Have you worked here before?   Yes   No

Do you have a criminal record?   Yes   No

Do you have any police proceedings pending?   Yes   No

Please note: Applicants may be subject to a Criminal Records Bureau check.

Section 2 Employment & Availability

Shift systems and pay scales are uniform across all departments as is our commitment to good customer service. Once you have completed this form, you may be contacted by a manager for any department to arrange an interview.

Do you require   FULL TIME / PART TIME   work

Do you have any holidays booked?   Yes   No

If yes, please give details:

Are you available to work Bank Holidays?   Yes   No

Section 3 Education

Please give information of schools and colleges attended and dates of leaving if applicable

From .... to ....

From .... to ....

From .... to ....

Section 4 Qualifications

Please give details of any qualifications (GCSE, BTEC) etc:

Are you still at school and studying for GCSEs?

Yes   No

Subject	grade	date

Please note that if the answer is yes to the above question, we cannot employ you until you officially leave school on the last Friday in June. However, we would like you to continue and complete this form so that we can keep your name on file for the Summer Holidays.

Any other qualifications?

Section 5 Social Activities

Are you a member of any clubs or sporting associations?

How do you like to spend your free time?

Briefly describe your personality

Section 6 Work History

Please give details of previous employers, company name, address, dates of employment and reason for leaving

Company

Address

Postcode

Employed from .... to ....

General Duties

Reason for leaving

Are references available?   Yes   No

Company

Address

Postcode

Employed from .... to ....

General Duties

Reason for leaving

Are references available?   Yes   No

Section 7 Personal Reference

Please supply name, address and contact number of a person, not family, who has known you for at least three years so that we may contact them for a character reference if required.

Name

Address

Tel. No.

How long has this person known you?

Years .... months ....

Section 8 Additional Information

Why did you choose us as a potential employer?

What relevant skills do you feel you have to offer?

Section 9 Questionnaire

Please circle one

How did you learn of this vacancy?   Radio   Newspaper   Internet   Friend/Family   Other

Section 10 Declaration

I confirm that the information I have submitted is true

Print Name .... signed .... date ....

▶ **Figure 8.5:** Have you ever used sample application forms?

Application forms also require applicants to give their details but in a standard format that makes it easier for employers to compare applicants (see Figure 8.5). They can be completed online or in paper form. The information in the questions can be directly related to the individual business needs, meaning that they can sometimes be of more use to a business to ensure they are getting the right candidate for that specific job role. Paper application forms are sent out and this means there are often additional time and postage costs. Online application forms can save processing and postage time as part of online recruitment.

Letter of application

Letters are used by applicants to outline why they are suitable for a job. Applicants can use a letter (see Figure 8.6) to highlight any special skills and attributes they feel they have that make them suitable for the job. Applicants should use the job description and person specification when highlighting their particular strengths so that an employer can match them to the job.

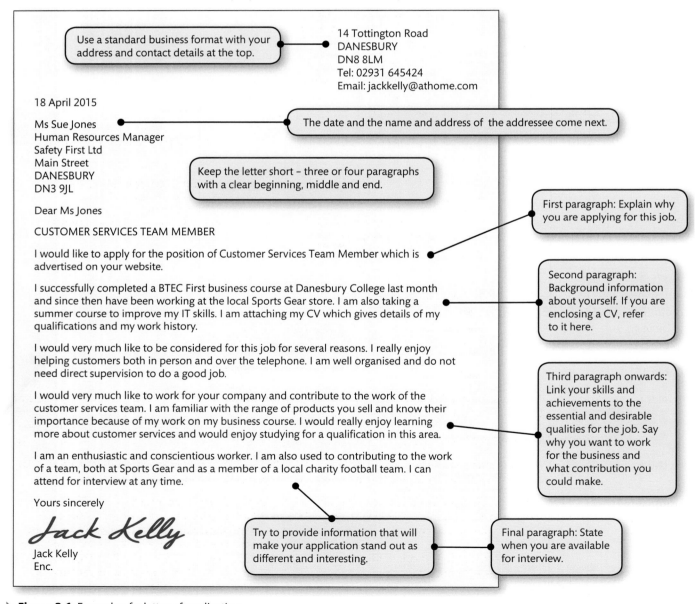

▶ **Figure 8.6:** Example of a letter of application

Online recruitment

Online applications are very popular. They take two main forms: the email application and the online application form.

▶ Email applications are very similar to the letter application but, instead of sending the information through the post, it is emailed, which is quicker. An email application may have the letter of application within the body text of the email or attached as a separate document.

▶ Some employers ask for CVs by email.

▶ Applicants may need to download and fill in an application form that can be sent as an attachment by email.

All these methods save time and postage costs, allowing businesses to make use of technology to become more cost-effective. Online applications mean that, rather than filling in an application to send in, the application is online so the information is sent to an online database and stored immediately. This method of application is very cost-effective for employers as data can be filtered automatically, reducing processing costs. It also reduces time spent on the process, for example, by not having to use agencies or staff members sifting through CVs. A time-saving example might be an employer asking that potential applications have a Merit for BTEC National Business. When the online application reaches the online database, those details will be automatically checked and, if the information provided does not match the specification required, then that application is immediately discounted.

⏸ PAUSE POINT   What are the advantages and disadvantages of using application forms and CVs online and offline?

          Hint   Compare the different types of paper applications and then online applications. Consider creating a table.

          Extend   Consider one business and decide which application documents and methods would suit their needs best.

Selection

The selection part of the recruitment and selection process refers to the methods used to actually choose the right person for the job. There are lots of different methods that can be used. A summary of each of these methods is given in Table 8.7 and each is explored in more detail throughout this unit.

▶ **Table 8.7:** Summary table of selection methods

Assessment centre	Assessment centres involve candidates being asked to go to a location for one or two days where they take part in lots of different activities. These activities may include role plays, tests, group interviews or presentations. The purpose of an assessment centre is to see candidates perform over a longer period of time. Assessment centres are commonly used for graduate or senior management positions.
Psychometric tests	Psychometric tests try to measure intelligence or personality type to assess how good a person will be at a job. These may be multiple-choice tests that are paper-based or completed online.
Group/team activity interviews	Group/team interviews involve a number of candidates being invited to visit the organisation, talk to other candidates and ask questions about the job. They take place if large numbers of staff are needed. Group interviews may be used as the first stage of the process to select candidates who seem more interested in the job or who ask suitable questions. It can be a good opportunity for a candidate to decide whether or not they wish to go forward with their application and for an employer to get a first impression of the candidates. In a group interview, it is important for candidates to stand out from the rest of the applicants and this may be difficult to do. Employers may give candidates a task to complete as part of a smaller group to monitor how well they work with each other.

Table 8.7: – *continued*

Individual face to face interview	This type of interview is very intense and expensive as the candidates are expected to meet in a one-to-one situation to talk about why they want the job. Each candidate is spoken to individually. It is likely that only very promising candidates will be picked to go through to this stage. Sometimes, candidates will need to have more than one interview and will need to be called back for a second interview that might be on the same day or at a later date.
Telephone interview	Telephone interviews are often conducted with candidates who are applying to work in a customer service environment such as in a retail store or in a call centre. The telephone interview can take place at any time and the interviewer chats to the candidate to judge whether or not they have the right skills to work for their organisation. The interviewer may ask all sorts of questions about organisational skills or other information to make decisions about the suitability of the candidate. Telephone interviews can be a useful way of screening out unsuitable candidates at an early stage as they do not require the candidates to travel to a location, or if they live a long distance from the employer. As part of the interview, candidates may be asked a number of different questions including calculations, so they should be prepared for this.
Panel interviews	Sometimes interviews are carried out by a group or panel of people from the organisation who will have different backgrounds and who will be looking for different skills and characteristics in the candidates. A Chairperson will be appointed and each member of the panel will be able to ask questions.
Presentations at interview	Some employers require candidates to give a presentation at interview. A presentation may require a candidate to talk to the panel about a pre-prepared particular topic, and can be a good way to choose a person for the job. Some employers give time during the interview process for candidates to prepare. Candidates are given instructions about the amount of time they are allowed to use and if they can have technology or other aids to help them, for example, slides or handouts.
Tests at interview	Tests can also be used at interview to select the best candidate. The results of the test may be discussed during the interview with the candidates to find out their thinking or can be used towards the end of the process to choose between candidates. The type of test will depend on the role. It is common in jobs related to finance or data for candidates to be given a piece of data to analyse and then talk about at interview.

Research

Find out about the use of technology in selection interviews by researching video conferencing during selection. How many organisations do you know that use this type of interviewing? What are the advantages and disadvantages of interviewing in this way?

Interview protocol and the selection process used

Interviews need to follow interview protocols. Protocols are expected rules and guidelines that are not written down but the candidate(s) and the interviewer(s) are expected to follow. These may be things like:

▶ candidates arriving at the interview early
▶ the need to dress smartly with a clean and tidy appearance
▶ the interviewers shaking hands with candidates when they enter the room
▶ the candidate speaking highly of their last or current employer and not saying bad things about them
▶ candidates not eating during the interview including chewing gum
▶ at the end of the interview, the candidate thanking the employer for the interview.

For different types of interview the protocols are slightly different and this does have an impact on the way that the process is run. The type of interview and process used is very important to make sure that the organisation recruits the right person and that the candidates are given the right impression of the organisation. The best selection processes give candidates the opportunity to demonstrate their suitability for the job as well as ensuring that they leave the process with the very best impression of the organisation. You have already learned about different types of selection and each has its own set of protocols.

Assessment centre

At assessment centres, candidates are usually given their meals throughout the day and overnight accommodation and breakfast if the event goes over two days. Candidates are assessed during the formal stages of the two days, for example during the interview, but also during the less formal stages such as during dinner or coffee breaks. Candidates need to be aware that they are being monitored and judgements are being made throughout all activities and they should be professional at all times.

▶ **Advantages**

- Assessment centres allow employers to see candidates for longer and can form a better view.
- Candidates also spend longer with the employer to find out if they wish to work for that business.
- Different tests and activities can give the employer a more rounded view of the candidates.
- Large numbers of candidates can be screened quickly as they can all be invited together.
- Agencies may be used to carry out the process on behalf of the employer and this avoids them wasting their own time when looking for the right candidate.

▶ **Disadvantages**

- It can be costly particularly when using an agency.
- It can take a lot of time to carry out.
- Sometimes candidates may not turn up if they think that the process is too difficult or they have to travel from far away.

Psychometric tests

Psychometric tests may be completed in a test centre, for example with the employer or with an agency, or many organisations are now asking candidates to complete them online at home. Psychometric tests can be used to test for different types of skills. Some psychometric tests make judgements about levels of skill, for example in literacy or numeracy. Other types of psychometric test give information about the type of personality and working practices that a person has.

▶ **Advantages**

- Psychometric tests for literacy and numeracy can help to work out if a person is suitable for a role, for example, if they have to use numeracy a lot in their role it can be critical.
- The tests may help to predict if a candidate is going to fit well into a team or a job role.

▶ **Disadvantages**

- Candidates may get nervous and not perform as well.
- Good candidates may be rejected if online tests are used before they arrive for interview.
- It may be possible to cheat in an online test if it is completed at home.

> **Key term**
>
> **Psychometic tests** – a series of tests that measure personality, skills or behaviour types of prospective employees and are used to compare applicants as part of recruitment and selection.

▶ What are psychometric tests used for?

Research

Research the use of psychometric testing in your area. You could use online research or interviews/questionnaires.
- Which companies are using it?
- How are they using it?
- How do you think they benefit from it?

Share your findings. Can you see any similarities with the type of businesses that have chosen to use psychometric testing? Why do you think this is? Discuss as a group.

Group or team activity interviews

The protocols for group or team interviews will vary significantly depending on the type of business that is recruiting. This is because the skills that are required for those businesses will also vary significantly. If a person is being recruited to work in an office, for example in finance, the type of activity that is conducted will be very different compared with a group interview for a role in a customer service environment such as in a retail shop.

▶ **Advantages**
- Many candidates can be seen quickly.
- It can be a good way of screening candidates initially.
- There is less chance of the interview not taking place as many candidates are invited.
- Discussion and debate can be generated which helps the employer make decisions about the best candidates.

▶ **Disadvantages**
- Candidates may be shy in larger groups and behave differently.
- Conflicts may occur between candidates if not managed correctly.
- Peer pressure between candidates may make them behave differently.

PAUSE POINT	How would you feel as an interviewee during a group interview or team activity?
Hint	Think about the types of activities you might be asked to do.
Extend	What would you find out as an employer?

Individual face to face interview

Face to face interviews carried out one to one are still one of the most common forms of interview. This type of interview will usually take place in the workplace. Candidates will usually wear business dress such as a suit.

▶ **Advantages**
- There is a single focus on the person being interviewed.
- Detailed and confidential information can be shared between the interviewer and interviewee.
- A good rapport can build between interview and interviewee allowing the candidate to do their best.

▶ **Disadvantages**
- It can be time consuming.
- It may involve several one to one interviews which takes time.
- If candidates fail to turn up then the time is lost.

Telephone interview

Telephone interviews are commonly used when large numbers of applications have been received. Telephone interviewing enables communication skills to be assessed. Sometimes telephone interviews will include scenarios that candidates have to complete, including mini tests.

▶ **Advantages**

- The interviewer gets to talk to the interviewee in person.
- There is no travelling involved for either party.
- The interview can be carried out by an inexperienced person or be automated, making it cheaper.

▶ **Disadvantages**

- It is not possible to give a judgement about body language or other characteristics of the applicant.
- Questions may be too basic by telephone and not provide sufficient information about candidates.

Panel interviews

The protocols for panel interviews are again very different depending on the organisation. Often panel interviews only consist of three panel members but, on occasion, it can be as many as ten different people depending on the job role and organisation involved. Panel interviews, particularly when they are large panels usually adopt formal procedures.

▶ **Advantages**

- Candidates can be met by more than one person up to large groups of people.
- Different panel members are able to look for different aspects or skills of the candidates.
- Candidates are put under some pressure and this can test their communication skills.
- Different departments in a business can be involved.

▶ **Disadvantages**

- Panel members can only ask a limited number of questions.
- Candidates may be nervous and not perform correctly.
- It can take time to organise.

Presentations and tests at interview

There are no set protocols for presentations and tests at interview. Each business will decide how and when presentations and tests are used. Sometimes candidates are asked to prepare a presentation in advance of the interview day and then be prepared to give that presentation. For other recruitment processes candidates are given the topic when they arrive. Tests may also be done in advance, usually online, or on the day, and candidates are then often asked to discuss what they have found and be asked further questions about their results.

▶ **Advantages**

- Gives another perspective to the candidates that can be used to compare good candidates.
- Identifies any weaknesses that candidates may have, for example when testing literacy and numeracy.
- Can test the skills that may be essential for the role, for example presentations.
- Research presentations can provide good ideas for the organisation that can be used later even if candidates are unsuccessful.

▶ **Disadvantages**

- It needs organising in advance.
- Questions and model answers need to be prepared for tests.
- It takes up time during the interview.

PAUSE POINT   What are the benefits of a telephone interview compared to a face to face one?

Hint   Think about the different skills of communication required for each. Are telephone interviews ever not appropriate? Justify your answer.

Extend   What type of interview would be most suitable when employing a senior member of staff to work in a large finance organisation, and why?

Initial selection processes using screening

Selecting the right person for the job from the candidates shortlisted is a very lengthy process so this means it costs businesses time. Some organisations will use initial selection processes to screen candidates first before they take them through to be selected for interview. The screening will check skills, for example organisational skills or other information, to make decisions about the suitability of the candidate to go forward.

▶ Telephone interviews cut out time and costs for both parties by avoiding travel. Telephone interviewers often have a set of standardised questions so the process may be completed by less experienced interviewers and is more cost-effective for the organisation. As part of the interview, candidates may be asked a number of questions including calculations.

▶ Short online tests also ensure that candidates are screened. These tests may be completed within strict timed deadlines to see how candidates work under pressure. They may test English, maths or other types of skills such as attention to detail or awareness.

It is really important that all selection processes meet the needs of the business that is recruiting, especially the initial selection, or the organisation may lose very good candidates at the early stages of the process who may have been good for the role. This is even more important in areas of industry where there are not enough skilled people in a particular field. An organisation will want to encourage as many people as possible to be interested in their role and not be put off or excluded at the first stage.

Use of technology in the process

Technology has transformed the way that employees are recruited, as you have already learned. It reduces costs and makes the process much faster through the use of online application forms and CVs being uploaded to websites, compared with waiting for the post. Even traditional methods of application can be enhanced using technology. For example, if an employer wishes to see an example of a candidate's handwriting, this can be scanned and then emailed or uploaded. It is important that technology is used carefully and appropriately for the role but, because technology is used in many roles, using it in the process of application can, in itself, test the skills of the applicants at the initial stage.

PAUSE POINT   What are the benefits of a telephone interview compared with a face to face one?

Hint   Think about the different skills of communication required for each. Are telephone interviews ever not appropriate? Justify your answer.

Extend   What type of interview would be most suitable when employing a senior member of staff to work in a large finance organisation, and why?

Communication with prospective employees

Communication during the selection process is also very important and this can be done easily through a variety of different methods:

- letter
- telephone
- email
- text
- social media.

It is really important that the communication is good, clear and that applicants/ candidates are kept up to date at each stage of the process. While letters are an excellent way of having a record of something that is sent out, they take longer to send than an email.

On the flip side, a letter is often viewed as an official and important document compared to an email, which may get lost in a junk inbox or go unnoticed if the applicant receives a lot of emails on a daily basis. Most methods using online or paper provide a record of the communication that can be reviewed at a later date, if necessary. Telephone communication through voice rather than text does not always provide a record unless the organisation uses voice recording as part of their protocols. It is very important that the quality of any selection process can be monitored to ensure that the organisation is providing the very best service possible and that, if any improvements need to be made, these can be identified and actions be put into place.

Quality of the process and the documents

Recruitment and selection is very important to businesses because a good quality process using good quality documents should lead to good quality employees that join and stay with the business. If the process is weak and the documents are poor, it is likely that the best employees will not be recruited and that some employees may not stay.

Linking the process to efficiency and business success

Having the best process that requires the least amount of time necessary to recruit the best employees should lead to business success. Often employees are the biggest expense for a business so having an efficient selection process ensures that the correct amount of money is spent on the process and also ensures that the right people are selected.

Ethical and legal considerations in the recruitment process

There are a number of ethical and legal issues that you must consider in relation to the recruitment and selection process. Ethical issues are those not governed by law but which are considered as the right processes to follow to be fair and equal to all.

It is important that employers are aware of the latest equal opportunities legislation and ensure that they comply with it or risk prosecution. Most employers have a very clear equal opportunities policy to help them comply with the legislation, and also to ensure that they make changes to help prospective employees from different groups to be successful in their applications. Try to think of the benefits to employers of hiring a diverse workforce.

Research

Carry out research into Equal Opportunities Policies by either researching online or visiting employers to ask for a copy. Your school or college will have a policy too. Review the content of the policy and discuss what you have found, in small groups or pairs. How does this influence recruitment and selection in an organisation?

Ethical considerations

Ethical considerations are slightly different to legal ones in that they include elements that are not required by law but, when implemented, they ensure that the process is fair, even if legal action could not be taken. These include considering:

▶ being honest in an advertisement
▶ maintaining confidentiality throughout the process
▶ ensuring the same questions are asked at interview to all candidates
▶ using the same criteria for all applicants
▶ asking applicants to disclose if family or friends work for the same business.

PAUSE POINT What would the consequences be if an employer did not follow any of the above ethical considerations?

Hint Think how you would feel if any of these ethical considerations affected you.

Extend What could the consequences be for an employer that was found to be acting legally but not ethically?

Equal opportunities legislation

Link

More information on equal opportunity legislation can be found in *Unit 23: The English Legal System*.

Equal opportunities legislation ensures that all prospective employees are supported to do their best and that they are not disadvantaged. The law that relates to equal opportunity changes regularly and is updated. The *Equality Act 2010* ensures that different groups of prospective employees are not discriminated against when applying for jobs due to any of the following reasons:

▶ age
▶ being or becoming a transsexual person
▶ being married or in a civil partnership
▶ being pregnant or having a child
▶ disability
▶ race including colour, nationality, ethnic or national origin
▶ religion, belief or lack of religion/belief
▶ gender
▶ sexual orientation.

These reasons are also called 'protected characteristics' and, if discrimination does take place, a prospective employee can take action against an employer.

It is also important that employers offer the minimum wage when advertising a vacancy. The National Minimum Wage is the amount of money set by the government as recommended by the Low Pay Commission. Each year the amount goes up, but it is the minimum amount that workers aged 16 or over must be paid for doing a job. There are very few exceptions to this amount of money and specific rates are given for workers aged 16 and 17, as well as 18 to 21 and 22 or over. These amounts are the minimum rates that must be paid, but, of course, employers can choose to pay more if they wish.

In 2015, the rates were increased to:

▸ £6.70 an hour for adults (aged 21 and over)
▸ £5.30 an hour for workers aged 18 to 20 inclusive
▸ £3.87 an hour for young people (16 to 17 years old)
▸ £3.30 for apprentices.

If employees are not being paid the minimum wage, they can ring the Pay and Work Rights Helpline to report their employer and either give their name or call anonymously.

Employers must always ensure they are using the latest legislation and minimum wage rates during the recruitment process. If any of the above is not adhered to, then employers can face prosecution. This is obviously damaging to a business, not only due to the financial impact, but also to their reputation as a reliable and honest business.

Right to work legislation

Employers must also make sure when they are recruiting a person that they have the right to live and work in the UK. The law relating to working in the UK is complicated and changes frequently. Employers must make sure that they are aware of the law and that they ask for the right documents and information to avoid employing a person that does not have the right to work in the UK.

The government's website has lots of information about the latest legislation but, essentially, the most critical information is to ensure that prospective employees have the correct paperwork such as letters from Her Majesty's Revenue & Customs (HMRC) or a British or an EU passport, or documents from the Home Office proving their right to work in the UK. Employers must check these documents and ensure that prospective employees are allowed to work in their businesses. Employers must keep a copy of the documents and ensure that they are still within the required dates. If they do not check these documents, and employ someone illegally, they risk a fine of up to £20,000 per person (as of August 2015).

> **Research**
>
> Go on to the gov.uk website and find out the latest legislation relating to documents and the right to work in the UK. Consider how this legislation would affect a hiring manager in a small business.

> **Case study**
>
> ### Birmingham City Council
>
> Birmingham City Council are an equal opportunities employer. They have an equality statement that is given to every applicant for employment with them. They also carry out equal opportunity monitoring as shown below.
>
> ### Equality Statement
>
> Birmingham City Council is committed to equal opportunities in employment and we positively welcome your application irrespective of your gender, race, disability, colour, ethnic or national origin, nationality, sexuality, gender identity, marital status, responsibility for dependants, religion, trade union activity and age.
>
> ### Equal Opportunities Monitoring
>
> Monitoring is an essential and integral element of the City Council's Equal Opportunities in Employment Policy. The City Council will develop a comprehensive monitoring system in order to examine the effective implementation of its policy and to assess whether it is achieving its aims and objectives, and to plan future priorities and strategies.
>
> #### Check your knowledge
>
> 1 What is the purpose of an equality statement?
> 2 Why do you think Birmingham City Council (BCC) monitors the success of its equal opportunities policy?
> 3 What benefits do you think BCC gain by having an equal opportunity policy?
> 4 To what extent can an organisation remove both indirect and direct discrimination from the organisation through its equal opportunities policies?

Businesses rely on effective and efficient recruitment to contribute to their success. There are many different methods that can be used.

Consider how large businesses manage their recruitment and selection process to ensure that they recruit the best candidate both for the job and their overall business success. Consider a business with at least 250 employees, perhaps choose one that you already know something about. You may want to use a business that has a local office you can contact or visit for information.

Prepare a report looking at the recruitment and selection process of your selected business. In your report you should analyse the different recruitment processes used, and evaluate these processes and how they contribute to the business's success. When preparing your report you should explain:

- the recruitment and selection process of your chosen business and why these have chosen by the business, including the different recruitment methods used
- how the business's recruitment processes are ethical and adhere to current employment law.

Plan
- What should the focus of my report be?
- What do the command words explain, analyse and evaluate mean?
- Will I need to speak to anyone at my chosen business to conduct my research?

Do
- Am I on track to meet my deadline?
- Is there any part of the report I am struggling to find information about?

Review
- Did I complete the task in a way that I am happy with?
- Did I ask for assistance when it was needed?
- Is there anything I would do differently in future assignments?

B   Undertake a recruitment activity to demonstrate the processes leading to a successful job offers

During this unit you have learned all about the different documents that are required for the recruitment and selection process. For your BTEC assessment, you will need to prepare relevant documents that will be assessed and you will also have to demonstrate your skills by participating in a selection interview in different roles and completing the required paperwork for the process. To get higher grades in your BTEC, you will need to show analytical responses and make judgements about the documents you have produced.

Job applications

When preparing for recruitment and selection for any job role in a business, there are a number of relevant documents that you should consider for the process:
- job advertisement, including where it could be placed
- job analysis
- job description
- person specification
- application form
- personal CV
- letter of application.

Reflect

Review the learning that you have completed throughout this unit and remind yourself about the elements required for each of the different documents and stages.

PAUSE POINT   Try to remember each stage of the process and match a document to that stage.

> Hint   See if you can remember the different elements of each of the documents.
>
> Extend   Consider the weaknesses in each document that you can remember and, when designing your own document, consider how you could overcome these weaknesses.

Interviews and skills

You have already learned in this unit that there are key documents that are required before and during the recruitment process to ensure that the right applicants are attracted to and selected for interview and assessment. The next key part of the recruitment selection process is the demonstration by candidates of their performance during the interview and any association tests or other practical assessments.

Communication skills required for interview situations

A common phrase that is very true of interview situations is 'it's not what you say that matters, but how you say it'. This is really important in the interview and assessment situation. Your communication skills can make the difference between giving an employer a good or bad impression. Being able to communicate clearly is very important to an employer who must be able to understand what you are saying. However, communication is about more than just speaking – it is also about other elements such as how you stand, the language you use and your ability to respond to what is being said to you.

Body language and listening skills

You will learn about the impact of the way you present yourself as you go through this unit. Listening skills and body language are very important as you can use your body to show that you are listening. This is called **active listening**. Active listening means that you give signals that you are listening such as nodding or shaking your head when someone is talking, that you are leaning forward slightly rather than back to show that you are interested in what the person or panel is saying and that you are showing you are listening by not fidgeting or looking at your watch.

Professional approaches

It is very important in an interview situation that you are professional. This means that you act in a way that shows you are serious about the job and that you can act in a way that the profession requires. If you are applying for a job in an office, you must show that you are able to behave like an office worker and that you will fit into the team. Being professional means that you can fulfil all the expectations of what someone would do if they were working in that role in all aspects of how you behave.

Formal language

Formal language means being clear in your speech when you are talking, and avoiding language which is slang or which is not appropriate in a business situation. Table 8.8 shows some examples of language that is formal and informal (language that you might use with your friends but not during an interview).

> **Key term**
>
> **Active listening** – when a person gives physical signals that they are listening to the other person such as nodding their head.

▶ **Table 8.8:** Formal and informal language

Formal language examples for interview	Informal language examples
Sir or Madam	Mate
Please explain…	You know,
Thank you for coming	Like I said
May I?	Innit
Could you?	Whatever

Skills and attitudes of interview and interviewee

To get the best outcome from an interview situation, it is very important that the **interviewer** and **interviewee** have the best possible attitudes to the situation. If they are both positive about the interview, both parties can get the all the information they need from the interview so that a decision can be made about whether or not someone is suitable for the job. Both parties also need to use their skills during the interview. The interviewer needs to use their skills to ask the right questions, and to make sure the interviewee is feeling relaxed so that they get as much information as possible from them. The interviewee needs to make sure that they use their skills to show that they are the best person for the job.

Role play

As part of your assessment for this unit, you will take part in an observed role play exercise. Sometimes, in interview situations, candidates are asked to take part in a role play as part of their assessment or interview. A role play can take place at interview in all sorts of ways, either individually or as a member of a group.

▶ Individual role play – this is a one to one role play where the person interviewing you is also involved. They may be assessing the way that you deal with a situation: for example, they may take the role of an angry customer and then ask you to role play your response.

▶ Group role play – these are often carried out in assessment centres and do not usually involve the interviewer taking part. They are often watching how you perform your role as part of a team that might be made up of existing employees or other candidates.

In both situations, your interviewer will be looking at all the elements of your behaviour and performance that you are learning about in this unit.

Body language

Eye contact and smiling are extremely important and help to communicate that you are open and trustworthy. A firm handshake is also a way of showing that you are confident and a suitable person for the job. However, being overconfident is as bad as being shy and nervous, because that may make the interviewer perceive you as big-headed. The way you sit in the interview chair can also give signals to the interviewer. If you slouch backwards during the interview or tap your foot, you may appear not to be interested in the position.

Dress

There are other non-verbal barriers that may affect how you communicate. Dress is an extremely important issue within recruitment and selection. How you dress will communicate to your interviewer something about whether or not you will fit into the organisation. It is usual within the business world to wear smart clothes in an interview for example, a suit, and, for men, a tie. Your choice of dress may be a barrier to communication if you dress in a way that the interviewer does not expect. Wearing clean clothing, being washed with combed hair and appropriate general body hygiene also influences the interviewer subconsciously.

Link

Ensuring you use the right type of language for the situation is covered in *Unit 1: Exploring Business*.

▶ During an interview you should also be aware of your body language.

Interview questions

Interview questions used throughout the process are the last part of interview. You will learn about how these questions are designed in this unit but what is also important is the way that questions are communicated. Questions should be asked in ways that help candidates to do their best. They should be:

▶ clearly communicated and allow time for the interviewee to have a very short pause before they answer if they need to

▶ repeated if necessary if an interviewee does not understand the first time (sometimes interviewees are very nervous)

▶ short enough for the interviewee to understand the question but long enough for them to be able to give a good answer

▶ asked in a way that supports the interviewee to give their best answer.

Designing interview questions

The use of effective questioning techniques is also very important. Asking the right questions will help the candidate to give the right answers. Questions often start with more general questions about the person, for example why they want the job and any other background information. They then often go through questions that relate to specific aspects of the job before they conclude with any other relevant information that might be needed.

Open questions	Closed questions
These are questions that give the candidate the opportunity to give an open answer, for example: • What is your biggest strength? • How would you deal with this problem? They may also be used to check information given.	These are questions that only allow a candidate to give a limited answer, for example: • How long did you work at ABC Ltd? • How many GCSEs do you have? • Have you got a driving licence?

Using a variety of types of question will allow the interviewer(s) to get a good idea about the candidate, so it is essential that the questions are prepared before the interview, especially if the interview is going to be conducted by a team or panel. Questions need to be fair and appropriate so that all candidates can do their best.

If a panel is being used as part of the interview process, they will need to meet to check and agree the questions. This also gives the panel an opportunity to think about what is recorded on the interview feedback form that is often used by organisations to record what interviewees say during interview. You will learn more about interview feedback forms in this unit.

At the end of the interview candidates usually have the opportunity to clarify or ask questions about the post so it is often a good idea to have a question ready that you might want to ask.

Interview feedback form

During the interview, detailed records need to be made so that candidates can be compared. These records are also used so that if there are any questions after the interview (about whether or not the process was fair and accurate), they can be answered.

Interview feedback forms are very important, particularly on panel interviews, as members of the interview panel will complete their own forms and then compare their answers as part of the discussion after the interviews have been finished.

Like interview questions, there are lots of ways to design interview feedback forms. Often the forms will allow enough space for the questions to be listed and scores to be given. An example of some questions that could be on a feedback form are shown in Figure 8.7.

Question	Interview notes	Score (circle)
Why are you interested in this job?	Clear reasons given for wanting the office junior role Has learned about offices during the BTEC National Course	⑤ 4 3 2 1
What experience do you have of working in an office?	Weekly work experience as part of Cassie's study programme at college Experience of working with other people through her part-time job working in a restaurant	5 4 ③ 2 1

▶ **Figure 8.7:** Example of a feedback form

At the end of the form there is usually a total number of possible points scored, for example 20. The scores for the individual are then added up to see who has the highest total. Interview panels will use the scores to compare answers where members of the panel thought candidates did better or worse than each other to finally agree who is the best person to offer the job to.

Sometimes, businesses will use a different type of form to make judgements about candidates without using the questions. This type of form makes judgements about different aspects of the presentation and conduct of a person during the interview process. An example of this type of form is shown in Figure 8.8.

Appearance	Excellent	Good	Fair	Poor
Dress				
Body language				
Eye contact				
Reasons for applying for the job				
Knowledge of the business				
Knowledge of the industry				
Commitment to the role				

▶ **Figure 8.8:** Example of a form used to make judgements about a candidate during interview

In the example shown in Figure 8.8, you will notice that there is no middle option called 'average'. Sometimes businesses do have a middle point or average score but by avoiding this, panel members or interviewers are forced to choose whether or not they think someone is better or worse than average.

Observation form

Observation forms (see Figure 8.9), like interview forms, are a record of how a person has performed during a particular part of the process.

Observation form

Candidate name ....

Date ....

Presentation title ....

Rating   **5**-Excellent,   **4**-Above average,   **3**-Average,   **2**-Fair,   **1**-Poor

Timing	1	2	3	4	5
Content	1	2	3	4	5
Delivery	1	2	3	4	5
Response to questions	1	2	3	4	5

Any other comments ....

....

Name and signature of person completing the form:

Name (Print) .... **Signature** ....

▶ **Figure 8.9:** Example of an observation form

Observation forms can be used for role plays, during the interview, presentations or any other practical activities. Like interview feedback forms, the observation form will have a way of recording what has happened during assessment. Observations forms are usually in addition to the interview feedback form, so they provide another way of measuring how different candidates have done.

Reviewing applications from peer group

In some organisations, working in teams is absolutely essential and so applications from prospective employees may be reviewed by the people with whom they will be working. By asking fellow employees (also known as their peer group) to be involved with the selection of new employees, they become responsible for ensuring that the new employee settles in well and become more accountable for the decision. The business might decide to use this part of the process to allow employees to choose who is selected to come for interview. This type of interview style is often used with senior positions in organisations. As Table 8.9 demonstrates, it has advantages and drawbacks.

▶ **Table 8.9:** Advantages and disadvantages of peer group reviewing

Advantages	Disadvantages
Peer group employees help select the new employees and therefore should help them to settle into their new job role.	Employees may not always be aware of the future skills required by the business and may not support the right choice of candidate.
Employees will be able to judge whether or not the new person will fit into the organisation well by helping to assess all the skills of the employee, such as body language.	Employees might have to spend a lot of time preparing and reviewing applications when they should be doing their existing job.
New employees will have been tested in front of their peer group so their reactions to different situations will already have been judged by their peer group.	The peer group may disagree about who is the best person for the job and this may make it more difficult when the person starts.
New employees will be known to the team before they start in terms of their background, experience and skills, so may become more effective more quickly in their role.	Training needs to be given to the peer group employees and leaders on how to make this type of review work effectively.

Submitting applications to peer group

Using a peer group process can be a very effective way to select future employees but it is important for this process to take place extremely carefully. Some businesses ask prospective employees to confirm that they are happy with the core values and mission of the organisation before their application is submitted to a peer group for review. Sometimes, an employee may have decided to work towards a promotion and their peer group may also be part of the process that is choosing them: for example, a member of a finance team in a business may decide to submit an application to become the line manager if their manager leaves. Members of their peer group may be used as part of the application process for the new role, and therefore their application will need to be submitted to their peer group.

Many jobs are advertised externally in the UK to make sure that ethical and legal considerations are taken into account. This means that a peer group may be reviewing external and internal applications, which can be challenging as some of those applicants are known to peers and others are not. It is very important, like any part of the selection and interviewing process, that staff are well trained and clear about their roles when involved in the recruitment and selection process.

Discuss

In pairs, think about how you would feel being involved in peer group reviewing.

What do you think would need to be included in the training?

⏸ **PAUSE POINT**   Think back to when you might use open and closed interview questions.

> **Hint**   Try to remember the meaning of each and the type of answers each is likely to receive.

> **Extend**   What are the advantages and disadvantages of each type of question, giving examples of the different types of question?

Work-related competence analysis

At the end of the process, and after the interviews have taken place and the appropriate person has been chosen, analysis of the impact of the process takes place. This is where the team that was involved in the recruitment process look at the key elements to ask if the process has worked.

▶ Were the correct questions asked to recruit the right person? Did the recruiter at the agency not know to ask a certain question that would have helped the business to select the right candidate?

▶ Was the job description completed with the right level of information? This could be too much or too little information – both can be problematic.

▶ Did the person specification lead to the application form being completed with the right level of information? For example, if the right skills were not highlighted in the person specification, then they can not be asked for in the application form.

▶ Did the person specification and job description lead to the right level of information being completed in the letter of application?

▶ Did the process adhere to equal opportunities legislation? You have already looked at how this is essential for both ethical and legal requirements. If a new employee was found to have been hired illegally due to oversights in the process, then that would cause major problems for a business.

It is really important that there is a review of each of the documents to check if they were fit for purpose, and that the right person with the appropriate skills and knowledge has been recruited to the post. The questions above highlight how a failure of one piece of documentation can lead to problems with others. For example, if the person specification is not thorough enough, the right information cannot be sought in the application form or letter of application. It is also important to ensure that all the activities were conducted taking into account equal opportunities law. If not, the business risks being taken to court, which could not only cost them money in terms of paying compensation to a prospective employee but it could also damage their reputation.

> **Reflect**
>
> Think back to your role play practice and perform a work-related competence analysis. Does everyone in your group agree? Why do you think it is important that everyone can agree on the outcome of this analysis?

Evaluation of documentation produced for the process

As for the work-related competence through the documentation produced before interview, after the process has taken place, the team, often including the human resource team, will check that the documentation meets the needs of the process by asking the following questions.

▶ Did the documentation ensure the right candidate was selected? For example, did the application form provided highlight the right skills and qualities that the business actually needed in the candidate for the role? Were the letters of application reviewed appropriately to select the right pool of candidates for interview?

▶ Did the interview process form and questions ensure that candidates demonstrated their skills effectively? For example, was a question asked that might have seemed like a good idea when writing but actually didn't reveal anything useful about the candidate? This might be a case of needing a question similar to the one asked, but avoiding phrasing which led to the candidate being unclear about what they needed to provide (or avoiding the focus of the question).

- ▶ Could the process have been improved? Any actions that come from this evaluation should always be SMART. The business needs to ensure that they can implement any improvements to be more effective at recruitment in the future.

Sometimes, businesses forget the very important last stage of the process but this is essential to make sure that the process is improved each time and ensures that the right people are selected to work at that business in future.

> **Discussion**
>
> In small groups, think about what actions might be implemented after both these processes. Make sure you think about how any actions would need to be SMART (specific, measurable, achievable, relevant and time constrained).

C Reflect on the recruitment and selection process and your individual performance

You have already learned that the last stage of the recruitment and selection process is about reviewing and making judgements about how the process has worked. For this unit, you will be taking part in a recruitment and selection process yourself and you will need to review your own individual performance. There are three parts to this process:

- ▶ reviewing and making judgements about your own performance
- ▶ reviewing your personal strengths and weaknesses
- ▶ writing an action plan with ways for you to improve in future.

Review and evaluation

The review and evaluation needed for this unit requires you to look back over the activities you have completed for this unit and make judgements about:

- ▶ your individual performance in the role play activity during interviews as interviewer and interviewee
- ▶ your communication skills
- ▶ your organisational skills
- ▶ the skills you have acquired (including the employability skills you have developed).

Role play activity

Think back to the role play activity you have already completed in this unit. For the final part of this unit, you need to review the role play activity and make judgements about your own performance.

For this unit, you need to review yourself but it can also be helpful to have someone else review you, so ask one of the learners from your role play group to give you some feedback on your performance by answering the questions shown in the table below. Ask members of your group to complete this activity with you but don't look at the feedback until after you have completed your own individual appraisal of your roles, as shown in this unit a little later. This will make sure that you get accurate feedback and don't influence their views.

Name of person being reviewed:	
Name of person carrying out the review:	
How well did they listen?	
What was their body language like during the role play?	
How professional was their language?	
What was their dress like?	
How did they ask questions?	
How did they answer questions?	
What was their attitude like during the role play?	
Any other relevant information	

To help you get an even better idea of how you have performed from another person's perspective, you may wish to add more questions of your own to the role play activity review and also give it to more than one person. The feedback that you receive will help you to make judgements about your own performance.

Appraisal of your role being interviewed, interviewing and observing

Without looking at the feedback you have received from your peers, think about your own performance in the role plays when you were:

▶ being interviewed
▶ interviewing someone else
▶ observing.

Use the prompts in the box below to guide you.

Being interviewed	Interviewing someone else	Observing
Body language	Body language	Skills of observation
Listening skills	Listening skills	Note taking
Professional approach	Professional approach	Organisation
Skills	Skills, including control	Giving feedback
Attitudes	Attitudes	
Dress	Dress	
Answers to questions	Asking questions	
Asking questions	Listening to responses	
	Making notes	

Review of communication skills

As part of your review of your performance, you also need to think about how you communicated in each of the roles and when producing your documents. There are many ways to review your communication skills but the checklist below is a good way to start reviewing your performance. Remember that, in order to develop your skills for the workplace to their highest level, you need to analyse and evaluate your performance. This means that you really need to outline what you did well and less well.

Communication skill	Rating 1–4 (4 is highest)	Why do I think this? What evidence do I have?
Did I communicate clearly when I was speaking?		
Was my handwriting legible when I was making notes?		
Did I communicate everything that was needed?		
Was I accurate in my communication?		
Was I certain about what I was communicating?		
Did I remember to include everything I needed to?		
Did others understand me when I was communicating?		
Was I polite and professional when communicating?		
Did I use business terms and professional language throughout my performance?		
Did I make sure that I was thinking about legal and ethical considerations when I was communicating?		

You may think of other aspects of communication that you want to add to your checklist and compare your work with that of other learners in your class. By rating yourself and collecting evidence, you can reflect on your performance and highlight areas where you want to improve.

Review of organisational ability

During this unit you have learned that organisation is very important during the recruitment and selection process. You need to be organised in lots of different ways. You need to be organised when you are:

▶ producing documents
▶ choosing deadlines for applications and notifying applicants
▶ running an interview process
▶ being an interviewee.

To help you review your organisational ability, another checklist has been produced for you to complete and review your skills.

Organisational skill	Rating 1–4 (4 is highest)	Why do I think this? What evidence do I have?
Did I always plan what I was going to do in advance of the activity?		
Did I keep to the agreed deadlines for producing my documents?		
Did I ensure that all the activities were detailed to the right level?		
As interviewer, did I publish a schedule in advance of starting the interview with all the necessary information?		
As interviewer, did I ensure the interview(s) started and finished on time?		
As interviewer, did I prepare my questions in advance?		
Did I make sure that other panel members (where appropriate) were aware of what they were doing?		
As interviewer, did I make sure that I had all the required paperwork ready and materials such as pens/pencils?		
As interviewee, did I arrive on time?		
As interviewee, did I have all the materials I needed?		
As interviewee, did I prepare answers to questions that might come up in the interview in advance?		

Now using the checklist, have a look at where you rated yourself the highest and the areas for development. (You will need to add these to the SWOT and action plan that you will learn more about later in this unit.)

> **Reflect**
>
> Think back to interview situations you have attended for work, for education or any other purposes. Think about what you did well and how you could have behaved differently to improve your performance.

Assessment of how the skills acquired support the development of your employability skills

During this unit, you have learned that recruitment and selection is about making sure that the right person is chosen to work in a particular role. Employers look for qualifications and experience as part of the shortlisting process before interview; during interview they then ask candidates about the way that they work, often testing these skills with interview questions or assessments. All of these recruitment and selection processes are being used to test the overall employability skills of a candidate. Employability skills are those skills that show that you can become an effective team member in the workplace and are not necessarily related to qualifications or experience.

The skills you will have developed through the role play activity in this unit, and indeed throughout your entire course, will have helped you develop the employability skills that an employer will seek. These skills include:

▶ cognitive and problem-solving skills – using critical thinking, solving problems with interesting and creative solutions, using systems and technology

▶ intrapersonal skills – communicating with others, working collaboratively, negotiating and influencing other people, presenting yourself well

▶ interpersonal skills – self-management, being able to adapt to different situations, being able to reflect on your behaviour and change it as necessary.

During the review stage of this unit, you will find yourself thinking about these types of skills. It is important that you consider the role play activity, and your behaviour, to think about how you are developing them.

 **PAUSE POINT** Identify how employability skills are developed in interview situations you have experienced. Review the employability skills and work out which are your biggest strengths and weaknesses.

 Hint   Think about each skill in turn and the behaviour that would be associated with it.

Extend   For each skill, think of ways that it will be seen in a real job situation.

The UK Commission for Employment and Skills suggests that the most common gaps in employability skills that employers find young people have when going into the work place are:

1 lack of life experience

2 poor attitude or motivation

3 lack of skills or competencies

4 lack of common sense

5 poor literacy/numeracy skills

6 poor results from education.

Some of these employability skills are more challenging to gain than others. Looking at each of these areas, consider which ones, you, yourself, can improve.

▶ What can you do to improve these skills?

▶ Who do you need to ask for help?

▶ Think about how you could gain skills or competencies in a voluntary or work experience capacity.

▶ How can you make sure that you get the best results on your BTEC National Business course?

SWOT and action plan

A SWOT analysis is a very useful business tool that you will have already come across in your BTEC National Studies. SWOT stands for strengths, weaknesses, opportunities and threats. A SWOT analysis can be applied to many different situations and can provide an at-a-glance look at actions that could be taken in the future to make improvements.

For this unit, a SWOT analysis and action plan are going to be applied to your performance in the role play activities and the documents you produced, as well as considering overall judgements about your work on this unit and making a plan for the future.

SWOT of role play performance

During the role plays you have taken the roles of interviewer and interviewee. A SWOT analysis is a good way of summarising your performance into one easy format that can help you identify what you need to improve on in future. SWOT, as you have already learned, means the following.

▶ Strengths – what are you really good at?
▶ Weaknesses – which areas did you not perform well at?
▶ Opportunities – what could you do to improve your performance, especially in areas where you did not do well?
▶ Threats – what is stopping you get better?

A SWOT diagram is a good way to review your skills at a glance and the SWOT itself is usually written as shown in Figure 8.10 .

It is really important that you use a judgement word with each of the areas in your SWOT to show why you think something is really a strength and also if it really is a weakness. If you think that as the interviewer you were very good at something, then you should give the reason why. For example, if you were good at asking questions you may explain that this meant, that candidates gave clear answers: 'good questioning as interviewer as candidates gave clear answers to the questions asked'.

> **Link**
>
> You learned about SWOT analysis in *Unit 1: Exploring Business*.

S	W
• Good questioning as interviewer as candidates gave clear answers to the questions asked • Good timekeeping as interviewer as the schedule ran on time	• Poor handwriting as other members of the panel could not read my handwriting • Lack of knowledge of some business terms as I did not understand what was meant by business culture
O	T
• Practise note taking and reviewing my handwriting • Read more business books to learn more business terms and write a list of new ones to learn for interview and work purposes	• Allowing time to practise my handwriting and reviewing it • Planning to be organised and research business terms

▶ **Figure 8.10:** An example of a completed SWOT analysis

You may find it useful, in the first instance, to complete a SWOT of your role as an interviewer and then complete a separate one as the interviewee.

⏸ PAUSE POINT	Compare the SWOT for your role as an interviewer and interviewee, and review differences and similarities between the two.
Hint	Use different coloured text in a document or different coloured pens to compare your performance as interviewer and interviewee.
Extend	Make judgements about why you are better at some elements than others.

Self-critique of the events and documentation prepared and how it supported the activity

Like the SWOT analysis of your performance in the role plays, it is also important for you to review and be self-critical of the events that you planned as part of recruitment and selection, and of the documentation that you prepared.

When you are writing a self-critique, you are really thinking about your own performance. You may wish to review the sections that you completed on communication and organisational skills earlier in this unit.

▶ For events, you should think about timing, smooth running, keeping to schedule, outcomes and results and more.

▶ For documentation, you should think about presentation, spelling, grammar, completion by candidates and more.

You need to ask yourself the following questions.

▶ What went well?

▶ What went less well?

▶ What would you do differently in future?

Review of the effectiveness of the recruitment and selection process

Reviewing the overall effectiveness of a recruitment and selection process is very important. When businesses are thinking about the overall effectiveness of recruitment and selection, there are several elements that they need to analyse and evaluate.

▶ Was the advertising effective?

▶ Did the process attract suitable interest/enquiries?

▶ Did the process attract suitable numbers of applications?

▶ Were the right number of candidates brought in for interview and assessment?

▶ Did the schedule work?

▶ Were the notes/records sufficient?

▶ Did the process give enough information to make a decision about the best person to appoint for the role?

▶ Did the process follow best practice for legal and ethical considerations?

▶ Did a suitable person get appointed to the role?

Throughout this unit, you will need to think about which of these elements apply to the recruitment and selection role play activity that you have just been through. You will need to analyse the results of your process and think about how your skills development will contribute to your future success. For higher achievement, you will also need to evaluate the process and compare it with best practice, including conclusions about how it will support your future career.

Action planning

A very important part of reviewing a process and making judgements about it is taking actions as a result of that the review. You have already worked on ways to review processes and events, including completing a self-critique and SWOT. All review processes should be followed by action planning. There are lots of different ways to action, but a common way is to use SMART targets to plan actions for the future. SMART targets are:

- ▶ **S**pecific
- ▶ **M**easurable
- ▶ **A**chievable
- ▶ **R**elevant
- ▶ **T**ime constrained.

Action plans usually make use of SMART targets to make sure that individuals are clear about what they need to do and when.

Action plans are usually based on areas that you have previously identified as weaknesses in your personal skills, but they can also be areas where you were good but would like to get even better! (See Figure 8.11.)

Date	Personal skill to be developed	How will it be developed?	What will the outcome be	By whom and when?	Resources and help I need?	Review and monitoring
18 November	Time management	Completing an online MOOC course on time management	Course completed	Person A 30 March	Access online Registration online	

▶ **Figure 8.11:** An example of an action plan

The best action plans are known as 'living documents' – this means that they are reviewed regularly and updated. By adding a date column, it is possible for actions to be updated and removed and others added.

By preparing a personal skills development plan and keeping it as an updated document, it will help you to continually improve your skills for interview situations immediately after your course and into the future.

▶ Think about a time when you have had to change a plan due to things changing.

Assessment practice 8.2

You have been invited to take part in a recruitment and selection activity by the business you studied earlier. You have a job role to advertise. Create appropriate documentation for selection and recruitment activities. Produce a report at the end of the activity, to evaluate your own performance. During the activity, you will participate in selection interviews as both the interviewer and the interviewee.

Make sure that you understand best practice in recruitment and selection. Ensure that you have all the information you need about the skills and qualities required for the job role.

Produce appropriate documentation as both interviewer and interviewee, including:
- a job advertisement, job description and person specification
- an application form, CV and a letter of application.

As interviewer, design appropriate interview questions and ensure that they allow assessment of skills and knowledge. Conduct role play selection interviews and participate in them, as an interviewer and interviewee. As an interviewee, you should provide analytical responses that allow for assessment of skills and knowledge.

Ensure that you keep evidence throughout the activity.

Throughout the activity, evaluate how both the documentation you have provided and your own behaviour in the interviews support the process for a job offer.

Complete:
- a SWOT analysis on your performance in role in the interviewing activities
- a personal skills development plan for future interview situations.

After completing these, you should analyse the results of the process and how your skills development will contribute to your future success. Provide an evaluation of how the recruitment and selection process complied with best practice, and draw reasoned conclusions as to how this will support your future career. Be honest about your own performance and ensure that your evaluation considers the entire process and the documentation that you have completed throughout.

Plan
- When are my deadlines?
- How will I ensure that I have detailed conclusions showing judgements for how I have done well and where I need to improve?
- How will I link my report to my future career?

Do
- Am I recording enough information during the activity to be able to make the right evaluations and conclusions in my report?
- Have I completed enough planning for the activity to run smoothly?

Review
- Did I seek enough feedback from others to correctly identify areas of improvement?
- Can I refer my behaviour during the activity back to the employability skills I need to develop?
- Did I observe any behaviour of my peers that I should copy in the future?

THINK ▶FUTURE

George Richards

Human Resources
Manager of a Finance
Business

I have been working in human resources for the past 15 years. Over this time, I have been part of many different recruitment and selection processes. Each year, we select lots of young people to come and work with us on apprenticeships or to join us after they have finished university.

Candidates always ask for feedback after the recruitment and selection process and I am happy to help them. The most common feedback that I give them is how they can improve their performance in the process by presenting themselves as professionally as possible, ideally wearing a suit. Men should always wear a tie as this shows they are serious about working for us. Preparation is everything. I always ask candidates why they want to come and work for us and what they know about our company. If they do not have good answers for these questions, I get the wrong impression from the start.

Sometimes people say to me that going for interviews is good practice even if you don't get the job. This is true, but what makes me really annoyed is when I offer a job to a candidate and they say they need to think about it. I always think why don't they find out more about the job, make that decision before and during the process and then let me know at the end of the interview. Offering a job to a candidate that does not want the job wastes my time and their time!

Focusing your skills

The role of the interviewer

The role of the interviewer is very important in the recruitment process. It is essential that any interviewer is well trained and knows what they are doing, to ensure that the right candidate is chosen to work at the organisation. Here are some simple tips to help you when interviewing.

- What are the timescales involved in the recruitment activity?
- Which types of questions are required?
- How many applications are likely to be generated?
- How many candidates will be selected to go forward for interview?
- Think about the level of the role and the team that the candidate will need to work with.

Preparing for an interview

When you are shortlisted for interview in the future, how should you prepare?

- Find out how much time you have until the interview.
- Prepare by finding out as much as possible about the organisation that is interviewing you.
- Try to think of as many questions as possible that you might be asked and think through your answers.

Think of questions that you have for the organisation – if you can find out any of the answers before interview this can avoid any problems. For example, if you need to find out more about the salary offered it is usually not good practice to ask during the interview.

Getting ready for assessment

Alex is working towards a BTEC National in Business. For learning aim A, he was given an assignment that asked him to write a report detailing how a business recruits and selects its employees. He had to write a report and make sure that he covered:

▶ how and why the business recruits

▶ how and why the business makes sure that it operates ethically and within the law

▶ an analysis, with judgements, about the different methods the businesses uses and how these methods help the business to be successful.

Alex shares his experience below.

How I got started

First, I looked back over all the different recruitment methods that I had learned about in class. I decided to review the advantages and disadvantages of each to help me think about the different possible ways that any business could recruit.

I then wrote a list of all the different ways that my chosen business recruits and reviewed the advantages and disadvantages of each for that business. My chosen business was a local retail company, so it was very important for me to make sure that I applied the recruitment methods to my chosen business and thought about what methods suited my retail business and which ones did not. I learned that my local retail business used online and offline methods depending on the type of role that was being recruited.

It was important for me to also look back over my notes and think more about the ethics of recruitment and also the influence of the law on recruitment. I remembered that the *Equality Act 2010* was important and that I needed to reference this legislation in my work.

How I brought it all together

I decided to write a detailed report including different sections. I wrote an introduction to the retail business and the reasons why the business needs to recruit. I then included a section called 'Recruitment methods' that gave the advantages and disadvantages of each. My next section was called 'Ethical and legal recruitment' and in this section I wrote about all the relevant legislation and applied it to my business. I then provided a section that gave judgements about the extent to which I thought that the methods used were helping the business to be successful. This gave me an opportunity to do more research on the retail sector as a whole, and I found that there are good opportunities for career development in retailing. At the end of my report, I made sure that all the sources of information, including my BTEC National textbook, were referenced.

What I learned from the experience

I found researching and investigating different recruitment methods to be really interesting. I found out that a retail career is something that I may be interested in after I have finished my BTEC National Business course.

During the work on my report, I learned some useful skills. I learned it was important to make sure I noted carefully where I got my information from. For one source, I forgot the online reference and it took me ages to find it again, which wasted my time. Now, in future assignments and other work, I know I need to note down my sources really carefully. I also learned that it is useful to start a bibliography during the early stages of my research and build it up as I go along rather than waiting to list all my sources at the end.

Think about it

▶ Have you included a bibliography in your work to make sure that you reference your sources at the end of your work?

▶ Do you know how to reference quotes and other material clearly?

▶ Is your report written in your own words to make sure that you have not included any information that has not been written by you (unless it has been referenced correctly as a direct quote)?

Investigating Customer Service 14

Getting to know your unit

Assessment
You will be assessed by a series of assignments set by your tutor.

In this unit, you will study how excellent customer service contributes to business success.

You will also learn that it costs a business more to attract new customers than it does to keep existing customers, so it is important that existing customers are kept happy. You can do this by building relationships with internal and external customers and giving them excellent service that exceeds their needs and expectations.

When working in a customer service role, you also need to know how to deal with customer requests and complaints. This unit will help you to develop the communication and interpersonal skills that you will need to do this, and to understand the importance of having good product or service knowledge. You will explore how a business builds effective relationships with customers by identifying and confirming their needs. You will examine how businesses monitor and evaluate their level of customer service provision by asking for feedback and how this is used to improve the level of service provided.

This unit will enable you to evaluate your own customer service skills and to create a development plan for improvement. This unit also supports further training, study or employment in a business environment.

How you will be assessed

This unit is assessed by a maximum of two internally assessed tasks set by your tutor. Throughout, you will find assessment practices to help you work towards your assignment.

Make sure that you have met all the grading criteria. These criteria require clear explanations in your own words, for example covering approaches that businesses take to customer service and recommending improvements. You will identify skills required to deliver quality customer service, including effective communication. You must assess your own skills and demonstrate them in order to produce a further development plan.

For a Merit, you will need to analyse examples of how legislation and regulation impact on customer service. You will also need to recommend improvements, including ways to monitor performance, provide examples of good practice and analyse different types of data.

For a Distinction, in addition to the Merit criteria, your accounts and reports will need to be based on wider research, examples of good practice and your evaluations of their effectiveness. Your reports will refer to legislative requirements for businesses to ensure that customer service expectations are exceeded. These reports should be creative, original and should include realistic ways for you to develop skills based on feedback from role-play and self-evaluation.

The assignments will consist of tasks designed to meet the criteria in the table. You will be required to:
▶ prepare a training pack providing practical information on delivering customer service to ensure business success
▶ take part in role-play scenarios
▶ identify your own strengths and weaknesses relating to customer service skills
▶ produce a plan for your personal skills development
▶ write a report.

Assessment criteria

This table shows you what you must do in order to achieve a **Pass**, **Merit** or **Distinction** grade, and where you can find activities to help you.

Pass	Merit	Distinction
Learning aim A Explore how effective customer service contributes to business success		
A.P1 Describe the different approaches to customer service delivery in contrasting businesses. **Assessment practice 14.1**	**A.M1** Analyse how legislation and regulation impact on customer service provision in a selected business. **Assessment practice 14.1**	**A.D1** Evaluate the importance for a selected business of providing excellent customer service and adhering to relevant current legislation and regulations. **Assessment practice 14.1**
A.P2 Examine ways that customer service in a selected business can meet the expectations and satisfaction of customers and adhere to relevant current legislation and regulations. **Assessment practice 14.1**		
Learning aim B Investigate the methods used to improve customer service in a business		
B.P3 Research methods a business can use to make improvements to the customer service provision. **Assessment practice 14.1**	**B.M2** Analyse different methods of monitoring customer service for a product or service in contrasting businesses. **Assessment practice 14.1**	**B.D2** Evaluate the benefits of improvements to customer service performance for the business, the customer, and the employee. **Assessment practice 14.1**
Learning aim C Demonstrate customer service in different situations, using appropriate behaviours to meet expectations		
C.P4 Demonstrate communication and interpersonal skills appropriate to meet customer needs in different situations. **Assessment practice 14.2**	**C.M3** Assess how the development plan has improved the performance of customer service skills. **Assessment practice 14.2**	**C.D3** Demonstrate initiative in making high-quality justified recommendations to develop own communication and interpersonal skills to meet customer needs. **Assessment practice 14.2**
C.P5 Review own customer service skills, identifying gaps where improvements could be made. **Assessment practice 14.2**		
C.P6 Present a clear, effective development plan for own customer service skills. **Assessment practice 14.2**		

Getting started

Customers' experiences influence decisions about where they shop. List some businesses that you have used recently. Rate your satisfaction with each one using a scale of 1 to 5 with 5 being the best. Reflect on what influenced your rating and identify skills influencing your decision. Develop this list as you work through this unit, noting any changes.

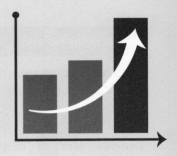

A Explore how effective customer service contributes to business success

Customer service in business

Customer service is part of everyone's job regardless of whether the business is in the private or public sector, a sole trader or a large organisation. Satisfied customers are more likely to continue taking their business back to the same company or individual, whether they are buying a meal, a drink, a mobile phone contract, clothing, a holiday etc.

Definition of customer service

Customer service is about relationships – it relates to the assistance and advice provided by a business to those people who buy or use its products or services. Without customers, there is no business.

In *Unit 1: Exploring Business* you learned about the different types of customers in an organisation and how the quality of the customer service experience contributes to the effectiveness of the business, whether its customers are internal or external. The larger the business the more likely it is to have a dedicated customer service team, for example Virgin Atlantic has specialist customer service departments according to the nature of an inquiry, as do Ford and Apple. Whatever the size of a business, and whether or not it has customer service departments, it is everyone's responsibility to ensure that customers are a priority and given the best service possible.

Customer service roles and importance of teamwork

Customer service roles vary according to the type of business, as demonstrated in Table 14.1.

▶ **Table 14.1:** Examples of different customer service roles, duties and methods for dealing with customers

Type of business	Role	Customer service duties	
Beauty salon	Receptionist	Take bookings; respond to queries; manage diaries for stylists; greet clients; provide refreshments; take payments; order supplies etc.	Ensure that all customers know they are valued and listened to and that their expectations are met or exceeded
Garage	Mechanic	Liaise with individual customers or businesses with fleets of vehicles; explain diagnosis, remedies and timeframes; communicate price and availability of any required parts; schedule work and keep to deadlines.	
Retail	Sales assistant	Ensure that customers are served in sequence and that they receive assistance where and when they need it; communicate size, quantity and price clearly, ensuring that exchange of payment is understood and accurate.	
Construction	Painter and decorator	Respect customer premises; do not smoke on-site; remove all rubbish; don't take or make personal phone calls; use dust sheets to keep mess to a minimum; be punctual; communicate clearly with customer about progress, timeframe and price for work.	

In each example given in Table 14.1, the methods for dealing with customers could include face-to-face, telephone, emails, and even text messages (for example, if you need to remind a customer about an appointment or provide an update on the progress of a repair).

Each of these roles relies on effective teamwork as each individual's role impacts on another's role in the team.

Reflect

Think about the occasions when you have been part of a team. Consider what worked well and less well. Why was this?

Discussion

Discuss examples of teamwork in different businesses and roles with your peers. Can you identify any similarities or differences between the examples?

Different types of role will require appropriate means of communication and language and you will learn more about them during this unit. Each job will provide a list of duties specific to the role and these often vary.

Importance of following organisational rules and procedures

Organisations have rules and procedures and, as you learned in *Unit 1: Exploring Business*, they may be **formal** or **informal**. They may also have legal requirements, for example following legal guidelines when disposing of toxic waste.

Key terms

Informal – less business-like, friendlier and could also mean *ad hoc*. Informal can refer to information given verbally.

Formal – business-like, factual, technical and professional, providing a record. It can refer to writing, such as formal written feedback.

Link

You can learn more about legislation and regulations in the business world in *Unit 1: Exploring Business, Unit 8: Recruitment and Selection Process* and *Unit 23: The English Legal System*.

Without proper procedures in place, employees would be unclear about their roles and some jobs would be duplicated while others maybe overlooked. Sometimes, there are legal requirements, for example paying taxes forms the basis for accounts procedures to ensure that the correct amounts are deducted from salaries or when completing a self-assessment tax return.

Some people find it hard to comply with rules, but they are there for a reason, very often to provide protection. Everyone needs rules, not only to protect them but also to bring some order to how they behave. Although you may not agree with every rule, rules are needed so as to know your limits and boundaries.

Of course, there are exceptions, for example when rules are not properly thought through, they are wrongly conveyed or misinterpreted, or there are simply too many.

Different approaches to customer service across industries need different skills and knowledge

You have started to explore the different types of customer service roles that exist in different businesses and a few examples of the different skills required, such as communication. This section examines in more depth both the approaches and the skills required for roles in different industries.

Retail shops selling tangible goods, need for detailed product knowledge and effective selling skills

Sales assistants need to be able to give customers information about the products they want to buy. The purpose of an assistant is to sell products so that the business makes a profit but customers might need information about a product in order to make a decision. Information and specialist product knowledge might include details such as the price and availability of products or, for example in certain stores such as car dealerships or electrical goods stores, the specifications of the products they are selling.

▶ Can you think of an example when you have found rules too complicated and confusing?

▶ Staff need training on product knowledge and their knowledge must be updated when they work in fast-moving industries such as technology. In some stores, staff are trained to be specialists in a niche range of products.

▶ Can you think of a time when a sales assistant's knowledge of a product has persuaded you to buy it?

▶ The ultimate goal of a sales assistant is to sell a given product. The of skills to be effective in any role are called **interpersonal** skills, such as those identified in Figure 14.1.

> **Key term**
>
> **Interpersonal** – the ability to build and maintain positive relationships.

▶ **Figure 14.1:** Examples of interpersonal skills which would be essential in a sales role

Discussion

In a group, discuss the skills you need to be an effective sales person. Can you rank the skills in order of the most important for a sales role? What are your reasons? Do you all agree?

From a customer's perspective, it is important to have confidence in the information you are given. Therefore **credibility** and **integrity** are important skills as well as being persuasive. Other important skills include:

▶ the ability to understand the customer's needs and wants

▶ patience – customers are entitled to change their minds

▶ the ability to articulate clearly

▶ non-verbal communication (NVC) – watch for body language and unspoken signals that will help you to anticipate what the customer wants and does not want

▶ politeness and good manners – these show respect and courtesy, which pay dividends when demonstrated between staff as well as towards customers

▶ smiling – but avoid being over-zealous or pushy

▶ mindfulness of language barriers and cultural differences

▶ communicating responses and information clearly and accurately

▶ resisting making promises that cannot be kept

▶ good time management, which includes punctuality and ability to work to tight deadlines.

Key terms

Credibility – when something or someone can be believed in and trusted.

Integrity – being trustworthy and honest.

Key term

Non-tangible – not able to be touched.

Offices such as those offering a non-tangible service

Some businesses never meet the customer face-to-face, for example those providing information about utilities such as gas or electricity will generally be over the phone or online, perhaps through a comparison website. There are many types of businesses where sales personnel are selling something that is **non-tangible**, such as advice from a solicitor or services of a bank. The different methods of communication used in offices include:

▸ face-to-face customer contact – for example, solicitors often meet with customers personally and are less likely to communicate by email due to the sensitive nature of enquiries

▸ online – for example, banks such as Natwest now have a strong online presence as well as high street branches, but there are also purely online banks such as First Direct; banks also make online customer contact through web chats

▸ written – solicitors, for example mostly rely on sending letters, producing legal documentation as hard copy, however, as with most professions, specialist terminology is used internally which can be difficult to interpret as a customer

▸ telephone – for example, Apple provide customers with a case number which they can refer to in the future to help resolve outstanding queries; the travel industry continues to use telephone sales, in particular, tailor-made travel such as that provided by businesses like Trailfinders and other tour operators.

As a result of the 2013 consultation, HMRC devised new methods for their service, such as face-to-face and telephone support, tailored to help customers complete their tax returns.

Banks are a good example of how customer service has changed for a non-tangible product. Traditionally, banks were run by a bank manager who met with customers and had responsibility for their accounts. Bank tellers managed over-the-counter transactions. Cash machines (ATMs) were then introduced in 1967 by Barclays, cutting down on human contact. Online banking was the next step, introduced in the early 1980s.

▸ Reg Varney, a popular actor, using the world's first cash machine in Enfield Town, North London on 27 June 1967

Discussion

Discuss, with a peer, or in a group the similarities and differences between the effectiveness of customer services in the private and public sector.

Link

Look back to *Unit 1: Exploring Business* for a reminder of the difference between private and public sectors.

Case study

Recruitment services

Charter Selection is a recruitment agency specialising in placing skilled applicants into marketing and sales positions in a range of industries.

Marketing and sales is traditionally considered to be a joint role but businesses are also seeking highly effective individuals with specialist skills for each role. The types of skills they seek are outlined in the table below.

Generic skills	Marketing	Sales
Effective communicator using different media	Creative	Knowledgeable about product
Has integrity	Innovative	Personable
Relationship builder	Highly literate	Reliable
Team player	Able to work to tight deadlines	Able to cope in a pressurised environment
Uses initiative	Able to work within tight budgets	Meets and exceeds targets
Follows procedures	Skilled at identifying new business opportunities	Numerate and literate
Responsible	Able to maintain and build customer confidence	Identifies new business
Punctual	Aware of competitors' activities	Closes sales
Complies with legislation		Builds repeat business
IT literate		Maximises profit
Diligent		

As a family owned business, Charter Selection are also on the lookout for skilled individuals to join their company. As their reputation promises professionalism and highly experienced and knowledgeable staff, they are selective about whom they employ. Just as they carefully scrutinise the applicants they put forward to employers, potential applicants will be expected to bring well-honed skills to the business and have the ability to interact positively and effectively with both external and internal customers.

Check your knowledge

1 What skills are required to work in marketing or sales?

2 What types of communication skills are necessary to liaise with customers?

3 Why is time management important to each type of role?

4 What are the possible rules and procedures you would be required to follow in these roles?

5 With at least three different audiences to impress, how will you ensure that you stand out from the crowd?

 **PAUSE POINT**   How do the skills required in marketing or sales roles differ from those needed to work for a recruitment agency?

Hint   Take an online tour of recruitment agencies to explore job opportunities on offer. Look at the skills listed in different job descriptions.

Extend   What are the lessons you have learned from examining how others interact with internal and external customers?

Contact centres

Contact centres employ staff who make telephone contact with customers. These staff require a number of specific skills, many of which were listed in Figure 14.1. Staff often follow a script but should still ensure that they use listening skills to fully understand each customer's needs.

An unusual example is that of the Good Samaritans who demand a wide range of specialist skills, such as coaching, listening and knowing what to say and what not to say, while being careful about the level of dependency developed between the caller and the listener.

Time limitations

Businesses have to operate within time limitations. Staff working in contact centres will be expected to respond to a call within a given time, just as they will be expected to respond to the customer's enquiry within a certain time. Consider the impact this has on both the customer and the call operative in situations such as:

▸ reporting a gas leak

▸ seeking software and technological support

▸ calling emergency services.

Reflect

Imagine making or receiving such a call. If the details are not relayed clearly or understood accurately, lives may be put at risk. The necessary services may also be delayed and subsequently could be put at risk while dealing with the emergency.

Discussion

Discuss, with a peer or in a small group, the skills required by an employee in two different types of contact centre and compare them with each other.

Hospitality industry, for example, serving food or drinks

Employees in the hospitality industry often work long hours and are also governed by deadlines. For example, people serving in fast food restaurants are expected to identify and make up the customer order, take payment and be courteous, all within a very restricted timeframe. Customer service skills in the hospitality industry include remaining courteous at all times and being well organised, regardless of whether you are working in a fast food restaurant or a Michelin-starred restaurant.

Additional skills will be required in more upmarket restaurants which often operate silver service, where specially trained staff follow specific codes of etiquette.

▸ Having reviewed the skills needed in various customer service roles, how do you think you do?

Theory into practice

Next time you are in a café or restaurant, pay attention to the skills of the person who is serving you. What did they do well? What difficulties did they encounter and how did they overcome them? Who else did they involve with your service and what skills did that require?

Customer expectations and satisfaction

Different types of customer

Internal and external customers

Link

The different types of customer are also discussed in *Unit 1: Exploring Business.*

There are two types of customer that a business has to deal with – internal and external. You are an external customer when you enquire about or purchase a product or service and you are an internal customer if you work for the company. In each example you are part of a team and every team relies on the relationship between customers to maintain the chain for business success.

▶ Internal customers also include employees in different departments. For example, in a college you will find a variety of different job roles, such as receptionists and those working in student services, finance, learning support and maintenance. All these employees are considered customers of the college. Each department cannot operate successfully without the others. People who work very closely with a business but are employed by another company providing products or services are also customers.

▶ External customers are what we typically think of as customers, for example someone buying a ticket for the cinema, a meal or a pair of shoes. Table 14.2 suggests some of the customers involved in a veterinary practice. Both internal and external customers make up the team and all rely on each other to ensure business success.

▶ **Table 14.2:** Examples of internal and external customers of a veterinary practice

Internal customer	External customer
Receptionists/administrative support	Animal owner/handler
Veterinary surgeon/practice owner	Animal (ie the patient)
Stationery supplier	
Suppliers of equipment	
Landlord of premises	

Customer personalities

We all have different personalities and experiences. Some people are much easier to relate to than others but, in business, you have to make the effort to get along with everyone.

Whatever your role in a business, you will encounter customers, whether internal or external, with different personality types including those who act defensively, arrogantly, in a menacing fashion or in a **passive-aggressive** manner. Demanding customers are the most challenging and need to be handled with care. Aggressiveness is unhelpful and disruptive and can cost businesses money and lose them customers. Other customers may be very quiet. This may be because they are thinking about what they need or because they are shy or may even have a learning difficulty. Whatever the reason, it is important that you show respect.

Key term

Passive-aggressive – stubborn and/or sulky (digging in your heels and refusing to do something which is your responsibility).

PAUSE POINT

Consider your own behaviour. Look at a customer service situation you have been in and think about how it could have been improved.

Hint What happened before the customer reacted? Was there anything in your language or tone that led to this response?

Extend What actions do you think you could take to try and stop the situation happening again?

Reflect

There may be good reasons why a customer is demanding. Try to think of some reasons why.

Discussion

Discuss, with a peer or in a small group, a recent experience as a customer. How did you feel? Were your expectations met or exceeded in that experience? Why was this? What else could have been done to improve your experience?

Customers with special requirements

Some customers that you encounter may have special requirements that you should be aware of and respect.

▶ Language – it can be challenging to understand someone whose first language is not the same as your own and it can be equally challenging for them to understand you. Different accents and dialects can also lead to confusion and misunderstanding.

▶ Culture – different cultures have their own etiquette. It is important to respect this without falling into the trap of **stereotyping** people from other cultures.

▶ Ageism – the 2009 Equality Bill was passed in the UK to combat ageism. Care needs to be taken when asking someone's age in a delicate situation, for example a cinema ticket seller requesting evidence for a ticket concession.

▶ Gender – existing legislation aims to stop discrimination on the basis of gender. Regardless of the sector you are working in, customers (whatever their gender) should always be treated with respect.

▶ Family friendly – while many businesses promote their family-friendly policies (such as Travelodge, McDonalds and Pizza Hut), some businesses are not so welcoming. For example, furniture and electrical stores promote their products for families but are not necessarily suitable for shoppers with young children.

▶ Customers with particular needs, for example visual, hearing or mobility conditions, may require assistance, for example with:
  - reading small print
  - hearing in a noisy environment
  - avoiding obstacles
  - carrying purchases to a vehicle
  - packing at the checkout.

Key term

Stereotyping – assumptions about someone or something which may be held by many people and which may be simplified without full thought being given to them.

Tip

Disabilities can be referred to as conditions rather than issues.

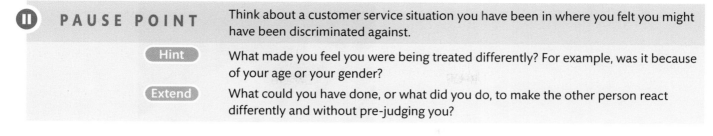

PAUSE POINT   Think about a customer service situation you have been in where you felt you might have been discriminated against.

Hint   What made you feel you were being treated differently? For example, was it because of your age or your gender?

Extend   What could you have done, or what did you do, to make the other person react differently and without pre-judging you?

Customer complaints

The **Ombudsman** reported that, in the first ten months of 2015, there were more than 15,500 complaints about communications providers alone made by the British public.

The way in which customer complaints are managed can defuse a situation and prevent the complaint from getting out of hand. Simple approaches can lead to a satisfactory and speedy resolution. This resolution can often be reached by talking to the person and listening to them, just as you might talk to your tutor if you were unhappy about your course.

In most cases, the customer is more likely to complain when they are not kept informed about what is happening.

Below are two examples of situations where businesses did not meet customer expectations, leading to complaints.

▸ In the summer of 2015, many households in the north-west of England had to boil water for drinking after parasites were found to be contaminating water supplies.

▸ In the summer of 2012, RBS-Natwest experienced problems with their online services for several days, leaving 12 million customers unable to withdraw money or make transactions.

> **Key term**
>
> **Ombudsman** – a not-for-profit service, founded in 2002 to provide independent dispute resolution.

> **Research**
>
> Statistics based on analyses of customer satisfaction data in the telecommunications sector are produced by **Ofcom**. Look at the trends of complaints in this sector. What can you identify? What reasons can you think of for this?

> **Key term**
>
> **Ofcom** – Office of Communications, a regulatory body supervising the communications industry.

Customer expectations and satisfaction

We know that customer expectations and satisfaction are not always matched by the service or products they receive. However, there are many examples where customers are satisfied and their expectations are met or even exceeded.

▸ Anticipation of good service – customers anticipate and generally receive good service from retailers such as Waitrose, John Lewis and M&S which are renowned for exchanging or replacing goods that do not meet expectations. It could be fair to assume that a business which survives is meeting its customers' expectations.

▸ Reliable information or service – customers expect to receive reliable information about products and services. However, Ronseal, which has traded on their promise 'Does exactly what it says on the tin' for more than 20 years, is rethinking its **strapline** with the introduction of different containers. Claims such as these can leave a business open to complaints if they do not live up to the promise.

> **Key term**
>
> **Strapline** – a caption or heading often providing a brief and snappy overview of a product, service or news story.

▶ The quality of a product also adds to a business's brand and reputation

▶ Offering different options – customers may not always know what they need, although they usually know what they do or do not want. A retail sales assistant may be asked for their opinion on a dress and may need to give their response in a tactful way. An assistant in an electrical goods store may offer a different product to a customer if they feel it would better fit the customer's needs.

▶ Impact of advertisements – customers expect products to fulfil the promises made in their straplines. Straplines are a form of advertising and all advertising must try to reach a balance between selling the product and ensuring that it meets customers expectations. An advert for a car, for example, should only list those features in the car that a customer would receive for the price advertised, and not the additional non-standard features that will cost more. There are examples where the actual product does not match the expectations raised by its adverts, for example fast food.

▶ Reputation – the most effective way of keeping existing customers and gaining new ones is through a good reputation. Business reputation can be spread rapidly and widely by posting online comments, for example on websites such as TripAdvisor. By mid-2015, more than 250 million reviews had been posted on TripAdvisor about more than 5.2 million businesses and properties.

 **PAUSE POINT** Imagine how quickly business reputations can spread through social media and the different ways in which this can happen.

Hint Social media can 'spread the word' about a new business, whether it is good or bad. What avenues have you seen for this?

Extend Is it always a good thing that someone's opinion about a business can be broadcast so widely? Is it always fair?

▶ Word of mouth/recommendations from others – this is a longstanding means of spreading a business's reputation and means that people are more likely to rely on the word of others, especially personal recommendations, when deciding which business to use. This might be a tradesman, for example an electrician, or a restaurant, hotel, beauty salon or garage.

Discussion

With a peer or in a group, discuss which products and services you have chosen based on recommendations? Did your expectation match with satisfaction gained?

- Importance of responding to customer needs – You should always try to respond to customers' needs appropriately – try to be polite, respectful and keep calm. Unfortunately, many businesses promise a great product but do not always supply it, for example telecommunications and retail. Public transport is often seen to let down customers, especially rail transport. Unfortunately, if alternative means of transport are limited, passengers might have little choice but to put up with poor service. Delayed deadlines in the construction industry can impact on future business. For example, the new Wembley Stadium and the Millennium Dome projects both exceeded their deadlines which reduced ticket sales and bookings. Conversely, when customers' needs are met, these experiences are shared with other potential or existing customers and can increase sales or secure ongoing business.

- Exceeding customer expectations through providing additional help and assistance – Some supermarkets provide exceptional customer service and exceed expectations, leaving a positive and lasting impression. High-end businesses such as Claridge's and Harrods are also known for dealing promptly with problems. Customers require follow-through and, if the matter continues to be unresolved, there is a greater chance of other people becoming involved and the customer having to repeatedly state the problem or keep chasing for a satisfactory conclusion. Consequently, customer satisfaction levels are unlikely to be positive and this is the message that will be conveyed to others.

- Offering discounts – Most customers enjoy a bargain and discounts are a good way for businesses to gain extra business. Customers may expect the discount to be calculated prior to purchase by an employee and rely on them to have accurate numeracy skills. Unfortunately, it is not unusual for discounts to be inaccurately calculated or promoted. For example, any sign promoting 20% discount as equivalent to VAT-free is incorrect as the actual calculation are not the same. Supermarkets also offer **BOGOFs** and buy one get one half price (although they have been criticised for encouraging shoppers to buy additional food they may, ultimately, throw away).

> **Key term**
>
> **BOGOF** – buy one get one free.

- Offering additional products or services – Some businesses promote additional products or services as a means of enticing customers to spend more or buy from their business more often. For example:

  - bars and restaurants offer cheaper drinks or food during a happy hour as a means of attracting customers during periods which are normally quiet

  - businesses sometimes offer free components such as batteries, accessories or similar related products to persuade customers who are hesitating about making a purchase

  - additional services or products might also be offered as a sweetener to customers who have been dissatisfied with a product, perhaps a food item or service such as a car valet when vehicle servicing has been delayed.

- Providing exceptional help and assistance for customers with special requirements – Local authorities provide mobility scooters and some supermarkets (for example, Tesco) also make them available for a very small charge, or provide specially adapted shopping trolleys to accommodate wheelchair users. Some supermarkets often have staff available to escort shoppers whatever their specific needs or disabilities.

Although Sainsbury's became the first UK supermarket to introduce Braille signage in late 2011, there is little evidence of other supermarkets and retailers following. However, in some areas of the UK, local authorities have introduced tactile signage for walkways and alternative alert methods at road crossings.

▶ Balancing customer satisfaction with business goals, aims and objectives – it can be difficult to balance the needs and wants of customers with business expectations. For example, customers may expect discounts or sale offers on certain products, such as sofas or cars, but this expectation, and the desire to ensure customer satisfaction, must be balanced against a business's goal of making a profit. Another example could be a contact centre staff member trying to reach a set target of resolved calls while also ensuring that customers feel that their problem has been dealt with appropriately and to their satisfaction.

The risks of not dealing with complaints

While it might be tempting to avoid complaints, they should be seen as an opportunity for the business or employee to make improvements. In learning aim B, you will see that asking the right questions to elicit a meaningful response about customer satisfaction is key.

A complaining customer needs time to get the problem 'off their chest'. Don't interrupt them – it will not speed up the solution. By listening, you are also showing **empathy** with the customer.

Businesses need to listen and respond to their customers. In the 1980s, Coca Cola announced it was changing the famous formula of their beverage, leading to numerous complaints and a rapid reinstatement of the original formula.

Key term

Empathy – share in another's feelings; demonstrate an understanding.

Case study

'We are sailing'

Cruise company Cunard are world famous for their luxury ships and their flagship is the passenger liner Queen Mary 2 (QM2), hailed as the most magnificent ocean liner ever built. Cunard celebrated their 175th anniversary in 2015 and pride themselves on providing high-quality service which more than meets customer expectations. Their vessels sail all over the world and the QM2 is probably most famous for its transatlantic crossings. As well as luxury cruising, it is also used as a means of transport for many migrants, distinguishing it from other passenger cruise ships.

There are 1238 officers and crew and they are responsible for up to 3090 passengers and 1310 cabins. Every crew member and officer has a specific role to fulfil, and within tight deadlines. Their work hours are long, free time is limited and they often spend many months at sea before going home to spend a couple of months with family and friends. The crew represent a cross-section of nationalities and cultures and all live and work very closely together, sharing cabins, meals, washing facilities and leisure time. While a certain level of English is required to be considered as a member of the crew, they must work hard at their interpersonal skills as many of them are in contact with passengers undertaking duties such as:

- cleaning and servicing cabins and main areas, and providing room service
- cooking, preparing, serving meals and drinks, waiting at tables
- maintaining the engines
- painting and decorating, maintenance
- religious services and marriage ceremonies
- attending to and walking passengers' dogs
- producing daily newsletters and daily TV shows, as well as capturing guests' memories by photography and videos.

What is especially striking is how well the crew appear to get on with each other and their professionalism. They readily help others to fulfil their duties and always ensure that they are busy. They are discreet, eager to please and smile. All officers and crew evidently practise the Cunard values through the respect they show to passengers and each other.

Check your knowledge

1 How do Cunard maintain high levels of customer satisfaction?

2 What different types of customer do Cunard have on the QM2?

3 Give examples of where ineffective teamwork could affect customer expectations.

4 Identify the types of communication skills required by the crew.

5 Consider what special requirements would need accommodating and suggest ways to fulfil customer needs.

PAUSE POINT   What might your expectations as a passenger on the QM2 be? How might they compare with a crew member's expectations?

Hint   Make a spidergram of your expectations as a passenger. Then select a specific crew member role and make a comparison.

Extend   What did you learn from this activity? What will change as a result?

Benefits of building customer relationships

Building effective relationships with internal and external customers is crucial to business success. Customers need to be sure that any guarantees against problematic purchases or monetary commitments made against future purchases, such as deposits or vouchers, will be honoured by the business. They also need to feel confident that they will be treated well by the business, whether they are making a complaint or visiting the store.

Enhanced reputation of business

Some businesses have always enjoyed a positive reputation, such as John Lewis (JLP) and M&S, although not without occasional glitches. Businesses like this ask themselves 'What are we doing that is right?' and more importantly 'How can we find out what we need to do better?'. Virgin continue to work hard at satisfying customers and certain segments of their business, such as media and air travel, have developed a reputation for supporting customers well. This reputation means that customers are likely to speak positively of a business, whether this is through word of mouth or via online forums and feedback. Increasingly, customers review online feedback prior to making a purchase or booking – a good reputation will be reflected in this feedback and is likely to lead to repeat business and new customers.

Repeat business

The best way to succeed in business is through repeat business. It costs more to generate new business than it does to retain what has already been gained. If customers feel that a business will invest in building a good relationship with them, they are more likely to return to that business. For example, Virgin Atlantic Airways offer Airmiles to frequent flyers, providing an incentive for customers to return. Several retail businesses also build brand loyalty by offering reward schemes, such as Boot's Advantage points and Superdrug's Beautycard. On a smaller scale, the owner of a local corner shop can build personal relationships with local customers to encourage repeat business.

Customer confidence in business

No business is totally infallible, no matter how much they try – but learning from mistakes gives them the opportunity to improve. Businesses that have developed confidence by admitting their errors, include:

▶ Toyota, who voluntarily recalled vehicles when they had issues with programming software in a new line of vehicles

▶ Asda, M&S, Boots, Sainsbury's and Tesco's who admitted issues with suspect food products, for example when horse meat was discovered in packaged meat products

▶ Fujitsu, who voluntarily recalled laptop battery packs due to a fire risk.

Some businesses offer additional free services to maintain customer confidence in their product, such as Mercedes, who offer annual winter checks, and Toyota, who offer a free service with its voluntary recalls.

Job satisfaction for employees

By building positive customer relationships, employees are rewarded with greater job satisfaction. For example, the local newsagent is likely to look forward to visits from local customers with whom they have developed a good relationship. Other examples might include a JLP employee who helps a couple set up their wedding registry or a personal shopper who helps a customer to find their perfect outfit – both of these situations are likely to lead to happy customers and a rewarded employee.

Of course, if you work or intend to work in the voluntary sector you might give your time for free, which may feel rewarding in itself. But you will have the opportunity to develop transferrable skills by building relationships with a diverse range of customers, including some who may have specialist needs.

Customer service legislation and regulations

Customer service is controlled by legislation and regulations to protect businesses and, most importantly, their customers. As with many professions, a professional body exists for customer service. Some pieces of legislation are common to all types of business, while others are sector specific.

To ensure that businesses comply with legislation, they must have policies and procedures in place. Employees must be aware of them and how to implement them. Businesses need to monitor their practices to ensure compliance and to ensure that their knowledge and practices are up to date and in line with new developments. Failure to do so can result in serious consequences, such as serious injury, death and major fines or imprisonment for the perpetrator or employer. You are also responsible for ensuring that your understanding is current.

Discussion

In a small group, discuss the legislation and regulations of your place of study. Compare these with business legislation, perhaps from places where you or your peers work. Search for legislation associated with businesses where you aspire to work when you have completed your studies.

Industry and sector-specific codes of practice, ethical issues and standards

There are many codes of practice including:

▶ health sector requirements for the presence of additional adults during medical examinations

- Health and safety guidance on the risks of lone working which is relevant to any sector – the risk can be easily overlooked by, for example, teachers of courses at outreach centres, codes of conduct also exist for home visits by professionals such as social workers
- the construction industry has multiple codes of practice. These are based on guidance from the BMA (British Medical Association).

Codes of practice for ethical issues and standards also exist. Businesses paying particular attention to internal codes of practice include:

- care homes for the elderly, infirm or vulnerable
- hospitals
- private health clinics
- hospices
- doctors' surgeries.

Advertising and marketing campaigns must also comply with legislation and codes of practice such as those set out by the Advertising Standards Agency.

Failing to meet legal and regulatory requirements

There are a number of implications if businesses do not meet the legal and regulatory requirements discussed earlier.

- Consumer protection – this exists to help consumers during the buying process. Customers are also protected in other ways, for example purchasing with a credit card provides a time-bound insurance against loss or damage.
  - *The Consumer Credit Act* of 1974 regulates and provides protection for loans and hire agreements and provides a cooling off period to protect customers from making rash decisions (possibly due to excessive pressure).
  - *Consumer Protection from Unfair Trading Regulations 2008* protects customers against unfair or misleading trading practices which include omissions and aggressive sales tactics.
  - *The Data Protection Act 1998* entitles you to know what information is held about you and how it is used.
- Distance selling – regulations exist to protect customers purchasing from a distance. The law changed from Distance Selling Regulations in 2014 to Consumer Contracts Regulations and applies to all purchases made at a distance, for example via the telephone, online or shopping channels, such as IdealWorld and QVC. Businesses are required by law to provide information about the goods, services and seller.

Research

The Government Deparment for Business, Innovation & Skills provides examples of successful prosecutions by its Criminal Enforcement Team. Research some of these cases and report the details back to the class. Do you see any similarities between the cases?

Sale of goods – the *Consumer Rights Act 2015* is reported to be the biggest shake up in consumer rights law for many years and aims to simplify the rules by combining previously separate legislation including:

- Sale of Goods Act
- Unfair Terms in Consumer Contracts Regulations
- Supply of Goods and Services Act.

This Act came into force from 1 October 2015 and protects customers by imposing set rules for:

- refunds and timeframes
- remediation options
- replacements and repairs
- additional items sold or provided with the item of interest
- pre-contract information.

▶ Health and safety – breaches of health and safety are a criminal offence. Therefore the consequences can include prosecution, fines or prison. The HSE or health and safety officers from local authorities inspect and regulate compliance with health and safety rules. Businesses are responsible for ensuring that their processes and systems comply with legislation. If they do not, there are consequences other than prison. For example, the CEO of Volkswagen resigned in the autumn of 2015 due to fraud regarding vehicle emissions and the impact on the company's reputation has yet to be measured.

▶ Non-complience with health and safety can have serious consequences

Discussion

The phrase 'health and safety gone mad' has become popular in recent years. In small groups, can you think of any examples? What do you think the instigators of these policies were trying to achieve?

▶ Data protection – personal data must not be shared without that individual's permission, dependent upon characteristics such as age, vulnerability, mental health etc. However, businesses are discovering the value of having data-sharing policies, because they have found that the over-protection of data can impact on supporting the customer in the best way. For example, in the NHS data was not shared between Trusts and relevant customer data was not passed between relevant departments. Information regarding police crime hotspots is also now shared online to help combat vehicle licensing tax evasion.

▶ Equal opportunities – legislation exists to protect people from being discriminated against on the basis of the following protected characteristics:

- age
- disability
- gender reassignment
- marriage and civil partnership
- pregnancy and maternity
- race
- religion and belief (including non-belief)
- gender
- sexual orientation.

▶ The implications of a business not meeting all legal and regulatory requirements can be costly and lead to failure of the business. Examples of where businesses have been sued for non-compliance include:

- General Electric in 2010 for racial discrimination and harassment
- Thames Valley Police in 2014 for referring to Romany gypsies as travellers
- an employment tribunal case in 2014 against the police force for age discrimination.

> **Key term**
>
> **Liquidate** – terminate/close down a business.

> **Link**
>
> Equal opportunity legislation is discussed in more detail in *Unit 8: Recruitment and Selection Process.*

Case study

'Keeping abreast of legislation'

In 2011, French company Poly Implant Prothèse (PIP) was found to have been illegally manufacturing and selling breast implants made from cheaper industrial-grade silicone since 2001 (instead of the medical-grade silicone they had previously used).

Hundreds of thousands of unapproved implants were sold globally by PIP from 2001 to 2010, the firm having since been **liquidated**. The implants were found to have a 500 per cent higher risk of rupturing or leaking than approved models, as well as being implicated in several deaths.

In the UK, reports claimed that at least 50,000 women had PIP implants and many had to have urgent replacements. The NHS and some private clinics offered the removal of PIP implants free of charge.

In 2013, the British Association of Aesthetic Plastic Surgeons (BAAPS) proposed much tighter monitoring of all medical devices, including breast implants, and all cosmetic injectables via compulsory, regular reporting of adverse effects.

The Department of Health commissioned a review of regulations and a report was issued calling for much tighter and rigorous regulations including:

- EU regulations on medical devices to include all cosmetic implants, with urgent action to be taken in the UK
- standards to be set by the Royal College of Surgeons including formal and certificated training
- the sharing of patient records with their GPs and themselves, with individual outcomes for surgeons reported on the NHS website
- a registry of patients having breast implant surgery and other cosmetic devices to be developed.

The British Association of Plastic, Reconstructive and Aesthetic Surgeons keeps a register of well-established and reputable members. The Committees of Advertising Practice write and maintain the UK Advertising Codes, which are administered by the Advertising Standards Authority.

Legislation and regulations which exist in the UK do not automatically extend to overseas. However, due to the seriousness of poor business practice, new rules and regulations are now in place and customers are becoming better informed and critical. However, reports continue to appear in the media about the marked increase of children aspiring to cosmetic surgery or change of body image.

Check your knowledge

1 What legislation changed as a result of this scandal?

2 How can the cosmetic surgery industry rebuild customer confidence?

3 What are the likely consequences to business reputation as a result of similar cases?

4 How do customer expectations influence the cosmetic surgery industry?

5 How important is it for businesses such as these to follow rules and procedures?

What ethical issues are likely to arise within the cosmetic surgery industry?

Explore the influences which might be associated with trying to provide customer satisfaction.

How does the latest legislation endeavour to better regulate similar businesses?

Investigate the methods used to improve customer service in a business

Monitoring and evaluating customer service provision

In this section, you are going to explore the ways in which businesses find out about their customers' satisfaction levels, both internal and external. Businesses can and do make claims about customers' reactions which lack credibility and integrity. By finding out about customers' real impressions, businesses can make improvements, change their business models or extend their products to meet current needs. More importantly, they can also learn what it is they do well and then do more of it.

You have probably been asked to complete satisfaction surveys at your place of study. Sometimes this can be online or via a paper form and it can be a nuisance if you are busy or not motivated to complete it. In this section, you will learn about other ways to gather this information (data) and then what happens to the data once it has been gathered.

Using research from customers to identify improvements and monitor complaints

In *Unit 1: Exploring Business* you were introduced to the Office of National Statistics (ONS) and using demographic trends as a means for businesses to better meet local customer needs. Using this data only provides a small portion of the picture; **primary research** is also often an invaluable resource.

Monitoring

Businesses can get an idea of what customers like about products or their preferences by what they buy and do not buy. However, not every customer buys something. They may make enquiries of a business, in person or by other means, but that does not necessarily tell the business why they did not make a purchase. You can use the following information to fill in the gaps in your knowledge.

▶ Customer profiles – it is vital for any business to know their customers, in other words, their customers' characteristics. They use this information to build a customer profile which includes characteristics such as gender, income and/or age group.

▶ Data, eg types of customer, products or services provided, customer care and service – customers' characteristics help inform businesses about their specialist needs as well as general needs. For example, simple questionnaires often ask for your gender or perhaps your age group. More complex and lengthy surveys request information about your ethnic group, financial status and other personal information. All these details are then analysed and the evaluations provide valuable sources of information to businesses.

> **Key term**
>
> **Primary research** – new research which aims to answer specific issues or questions. It can involve interviews, questionnaires or surveys of individuals or small groups.

> **Link**
>
> Social responsibility requirements were looked at in *Unit 1: Exploring Business*.

Supermarkets and other large businesses collect customer data by offering loyalty cards and via payment methods. They can then target groups or individuals with information, offers, vouchers and other enticements to encourage spending/visits to stores.

Completing the National Census survey is compulsory. The ONS relies on this collection of data in the UK every 10 years to produce statistics about our habits, movements, population etc. The government can then plan and predict for the future. As the statistics are in the **public domain**, businesses can use them to find out about their local, regional and national market opportunities.

The UK Customer Satisfaction Index (UKCSI) exists as a national measure of customer satisfaction based on analyses from six-monthly online consumer surveys. Data is gathered based on several categories including quality and complaints.

Non-government organisations exist for the purpose of gathering data, which they sell to other businesses. These businesses use the data to monitor customer preferences and evaluate provision by, for example, making assumptions about the area in which customers live in relation to their likely purchasing power and suitability of products.

Some businesses request email addresses, sometimes with offers of discounts or other enticements, to gather customer data.

▸ Sources of information, eg customers, colleagues, management – some businesses gather information from colleagues and management about their customer experiences. These experiences could provide information about internal customers as well as external customers. For example:
  • McDonald's rewards employees for their customer service qualities, relying on gathering feedback from internal and external customers
  • Cunard and several other cruise companies, collect nominations from passengers, colleagues and management in recognition of quality service. Crew and officers alike are then recognised by their photographs, which are displayed in key public areas.

▸ Methods – feedback tools need to be created carefully so that you can find out what you want to know.

  Invitations for customers to provide data can appear in different forms such as:
  • questionnaires, eg household paper surveys or in magazines
  • online comments and feedback requests
  • comment cards inviting feedback and offering incentives
  • telephone surveys
  • compliments, suggestions and complaints boxes

> **Key term**
>
> **Public domain** – if information is in the public domain it can be accessed by anyone and there are no copyright or legal restrictions on it.

▸ Comment boxes also effective for understanding the customer experience

- quality circles where staff members, normally in similar roles, meet to discuss ways of making improvements and resolving problems
- staff surveys which are used to gather the views from all staff and, when analysed, can be compared with the feedback received from customers
- mystery shoppers who are employed to portray a customer over a period of time and in different circumstances to gather data on their experiences – business staff are unaware of the true intentions of these shoppers or the timing of their visits to better replicate realistic situations
- recording and sharing information by telephone – this is used frequently by businesses, especially in customer service or call centres; there are legal guidelines about recording communications, in any form, to protect both sides of the communication, such as:
  - The Regulation of Investigatory Powers Act 2000
  - Data Protection Act 1998
  - Human Rights Act 1998

▶ You have probably experienced a taped message at the start of a phone call advising you that a recording will be made, usually for training purposes. Businesses can then analyse the contents of calls to improve services and resolve complaints. The *Financial Services Act 2012* requires recorded communications when related to specific instructions.

Evaluating customer service

Once feedback is collected, the results need to be analysed. This can be a time-consuming and highly skilled job and relies heavily on the quality of the feedback mechanisms and the way in which the methods, such as questionnaires, are structured.

For example, the way in which questions are phrased can produce unreliable or unhelpful responses, while providing quick-to-complete questionnaires with smiley faces can produce hurried reactions. Similarly, if odd numbers of options are given, the middle is usually seen as the safe (but not always helpful) option. There are two types of data which can be generated: **quantitative** and **qualitative**.

▶ Analyse responses – the areas businesses usually want to explore include:
  1. level of customer satisfaction
  2. quality of product or service
  3. meeting regulatory requirements
  4. balancing cost and benefits.

  Most types of survey seek to analyse satisfaction levels and quality. Businesses also seek confirmation of compliance (item 3 above) but, when it comes to item 4, businesses are striving to find more creative ways to gather feedback which can be analysed simply, quickly and more cheaply with maximum impact.

  A pitfall of presenting responses by percentages is that they can be misleading. For example, saying that 89 per cent of survey participants would recommend a product appears impressive to a customer but there may have only been 100 respondents. Eighty nine people is not many when you consider the whole population.

▶ Planning for change, resolving problems/complaints – businesses also use analysis of feedback to plan for change by resolving problems, responding to complaints or finding ways to do more of what they already do well. Microsoft does this by gathering and analysing data from users of their software to improve and refine their products and develop new software. For example, when computers crash or programs close during operation, the information can be fed back to Microsoft, helping them to improve the coding of the software for future updates.

Key terms

Quantitative – numbers, responding to the what, when, where and why questions.

Qualitative – data providing context and information about how or details about why (customer comments).

First Direct's online banking services' methods of gathering feedback (including Twitter) and trustworthiness have helped them to trade on customer recommendation above any other bank by being more **customer-centric**.

An apparently minor complaint might become more serious according to the number of times similar complaints are lodged.

Indicators of improved performance

Successful businesses identify key performance indicators (KPIs) to measure improvements. They do this to focus on what needs improving by identifying current performance. For example, your place of study will use the results from previous satisfaction measures as a **benchmark** to evaluate the successfulness of planned improvements based on complaints and feedback.

Reduction in numbers of complaints

We know it is important to identify customer complaints in order to target improvements. When corrected, the smallest problems can result in significant impact. Consider the factors outlined below.

▶ Major complaints often take longer to put right.

▶ Simple or small problems can often become quick wins.

▶ What appears to be a small problem might be significant when repeatedly complained about.

▶ Complaints cost businesses money and reputation.

Citigroup identified that, on the vast majority of occasions, customers mistakenly contacted the wrong help line with a simple question. Citigroup decided that the quickest and simplest remedy was to give contact centre staff a crib sheet of responses to the most frequently asked questions. In 2007, Tesco were faced with complaints about contaminated fuel. They apologised publicly and promised to pay for repairs to damage caused by it.

Increase in profits

Resolving complaints leads to increased profits and is a key indicator for monitoring and evaluation. When Apple had a problem with the antenna on its iPhone 5, complaints from customers were rapidly resolved, leading to increased sales and enhanced profits. Subsequent developments to its 's' generation with promises of improved software performance meant that, when they launched the new tablet sized 6 series, it sold millions of units leading to record-breaking financial results.

Businesses will report their profits to stakeholders at set points in the year. This is used as a benchmark for the success of the business and analysts will review the accounts of a business to determine its success. Improved profits for a business might be due to a variety of reasons, many of which we have looked at previously in this unit, and an increase in profits is generally viewed as a key indicator of success.

Reduction in turnover of staff

Staff turnover is reduced if businesses find out what their employees (their internal customers) like about them and what they can do to improve their job satisfaction. Businesses that collect customer satisfaction data also use the results to monitor employee performance. Some firms reward employees with bonuses, while others might pay their staff large bonuses but little if any salary. Either way, businesses set targets for employee performance and use them to inform training plans which are usually discussed at annual employee **appraisals** and half-yearly reviews.

Key term

Customer-centric – putting the customer at the centre of operations.

Tip

An apparently minor complaint might become more serious according to the number of times similar complaints are lodged.

Key term

Benchmark – a standard to compare things against.

Key term

Appraisal – an assessment of performance.

Appraisals are usually valued by employees as this is their time to reflect on their progress and achievements and any additional training they might need. Opportunities for further progression within the business might also be discussed, providing employees with goals. A good appraisal will make an employee feel valued and less likely to leave the organisation. Productivity increases as employees remain motivated and loyal to the business.

Repeat business from loyal customers

Loyal customers bring repeat business and retaining customers is the most cost effective and efficient way to run a business. Many businesses provide loyalty cards, a progression from very early loyalty systems such as Green Shield Stamps, which began in the late 1950s. By collecting stamps which were issued by retailers, customers could save up for unrelated products. Although withdrawn in the early 1990s, other similar systems exist today, such as Nectar cards, Airmiles and Avios points.

These methods vary in the rewards they offer and other associated services, such as credit and payment facilities. Some airlines also subscribe to loyalty schemes where customers can earn points towards future travel, gifts or activities. These systems also provide retailers with intelligence about their customers. By reviewing customer feedback and, particularly for online retailers, reviewing customer lists, businesses can make sure that they are doing all they can to ensure that customers return to their business.

Key term

Dividend – a sum of money paid regularly (usually once a year) by a company to its shareholders. The money usually comes out of profits.

Case study

Successful UK department store John Lewis (JLP) was established in 1864 and has built a reputation for high quality and excellent customer service.

The partnership philosophy lies behind their success. Every employee owns a share of the business and each one benefits from its success. Depending on reported annual profits, employees, known as partners, receive bonus **dividends**, are involved in quality circles and have the power to make changes.

The integrity of the partnership relies on reminding themselves of their roots and business values which include:

- embracing diversity
- acting with integrity and courtesy and sharing the rewards and responsibilities of co-ownership
- applying principles which underpin environmental policies and responsible sourcing and trading.

In addition to bonus payments, which have exceeded 12 per cent since 2004–05, employees have access to an extensive range of social events and benefits such as:

- large country estates and hotels
- sailing clubs and other sports activities
- subsidised staff dining room.

JLP is involved with many charities and staff continue to be paid when engaging in charitable work. Employee retention is high, with many partners continuing in service for most or all of their working lives.

JLP posts weekly news and updates on their financial status regularly through their website and constantly strives for customer feedback using various formal methods, such as online feedback forms and regular mystery shopping.

More informal means of gathering feedback include:

- high visibility of management in stores, talking to customers
- a desire to know what customers want by always listening to them and being open to feedback
- acting quickly on what customers say and letting them know the outcome.

While JLP has a reputation for appealing to middle- and upper-class shoppers, the partnership promises that their goods are 'never knowingly be undersold' and offers price matches and extended guarantees on products such as electrical goods, encouraging new shoppers to enjoy the JLP experience.

The business extends its high quality customer service to the grocery arm of the business, Waitrose and online food home delivery supplier Ocado. The extended value and essential ranges attract an even greater market share and customer demographic.

Like several other major department stores and supermarkets, JLP branched out into finance services and loyalty schemes. More than 40 years ago, customers could open store accounts and the JLP loyalty partnership card offers a small discount, which was introduced in the 1970's on purchases. Vouchers are also issued to customers, who are viewed as the major stakeholders

in the business, based on attractive discount enticements to try new products or online food shopping.

Check your knowledge

1   What factors contribute to the success of JLP?
2   List the different ways in which customer feedback is sought.
3   What does JLP do to encourage repeat business?
4   How does JLP strive to attract new customers?
5   How does JLP demonstrate its ethical standards?

 PAUSE POINT   What benefits do you think partners bring to JLP's success?

> Hint   You might find it helpful to start with a list of skills that partners require to be successful in their roles.

> Extend   What other businesses can you identify which operate in a similar way?

Assessment practice 14.1

A.P1 **A.P2** **A.M1** **A.D1** **B.P3** **B.M2** **B.D2**

You are a customer service representative. Your manager is concerned about the business's customer service levels.

You are asked to produce a report for the business owner comparing current customer service provision and processes with that of a previous employer. Your report should consider both businesses and include:

- a description of their approach to customer service delivery, how they meet the expectations and satisfaction of customers and how important this is to the business
- a description and evaluation of the benefits that a business, the customers and the employees might find with improved customer service
- a description of how the businesses adhere to current legislation and regulations and the impact and importance of this to the business
- a description and analysis of at least three methods for monitoring customer service, using qualitative and quantitative research, you should consider how effective these are.

Produce a customer service training handbook that includes relevant legislation and regulations and can be used in practical situations. Your training handbook should evaluate the importance of providing excellent customer service and adhering to relevant current legislation and regulations.

Plan

- I shall identify the customer service skills which will be the focus for the training handbook.
- I shall seek extra support for any skills that I need to develop to achieve this assessment, such as analysing quantitative or qualitative data.
- I shall read the learning aims and assessment criteria to help me plan my outcomes.
- I shall allocate time and a plan for visiting different businesses to learn about how they monitor customer service. I shall try and find out their process for analysing the data and what they do with the results.

Do

- I shall keep focused and be realistic about how much I can do in a short amount of time.
- I shall ask other businesses if they would be willing to show me an example of a training handbook.
- I shall focus on something quite small for the training handbook, perhaps training on a new policy or procedure.
- I shall test out my training handbook on a peer, friend or mentor for ease of use.

Review

- I shall reflect how I could have tackled this activity differently and what I would do again.
- I shall evaluate whether the training handbook would be accessible to someone with a particular impairment, such as colour blindness, dyslexia, etc.
- I shall consider what legislation I have looked at (or possibly overlooked) when undertaking this activity.

Demonstrate customer service in different situations, using appropriate behaviours to meet expectations

Customer service skills and behaviours

Customer service extends well beyond the world of retail and external customers. As you have been learning, the interaction between internal customers and those involved with the business in ways other than as consumers is crucial to business success.

Communication skills

Effective communication is made up of a range of complex skills.

▸ Face-to-face communication requires multiple skills, apart from speaking or listening. At least 60 per cent of what people process is through non-verbal communication (NVC). The way you communicate face-to-face will vary depending on the situation, such as whether you are in a library, with friends or in a careers office.

▸ Written communication generally refers to letters. Protocols around how you write letters differ according to trends, businesses, opinions and cultures. Many businesses will provide standard templates for their regular documents, such as invoices and other accounting documents. Many businesses, for example solicitors, still use letters. Figure 14.2 shows some simple examples of the etiquette that should be followed when writing letters.

A

Dear Sir (or Dear Madam)

~~~~~~~~~~~~~~~~~
~~~~~~~~~~~~~~~~~
~~~~~~~~~~~~~~~~~

Yours faithfully

T. Brown

Tom Brown

B

Dear Mr Smith (or Mrs Smith or Ms Smith)

~~~~~~~~~~~~~~~~~
~~~~~~~~~~~~~~~~~
~~~~~~~~~~~~~~~~~

Yours sincerely

T. Brown

Tom Brown

C

Dear Paul

~~~~~~~~~~~~~~~~~
~~~~~~~~~~~~~~~~~
~~~~~~~~~~~~~~~~~

Yours sincerely (or Kind regards)

Tom

Tom Brown

▸ **Figure 14.2:** Etiquette for addressing and then ending different types of letters: A is formal and unfamiliar; B is formal but personal; C is informal

Key term

Memo – short for memorandum, meaning a brief note about something that needs to be documented, but for internal customer use only.

▸ Emails and other electronic media have replaced much of the need to write letters and even send **memos**, although not entirely. Emails were once considered an informal means of communication. There are rules on how to write business-appropriate emails.

▸ Telephone – effective telephone skills include the speed and volume of your voice and ensuring that you are as articulate as possible – so avoid 'erring' and coughing or giggling. Ensure that you are making the call in a suitable location – if it is a private call, no one should be able to overhear. Do not forget your body language as this can have an impact, even on the telephone. Smiling when you are on the telephone will affect the pitch of your voice.

▶ Verbal – many of the skills required for dealing with telephone calls are required for any verbal communication, such as pitch and tone of voice. Prepare to communicate by asking the right sorts of question and ensuring that the information you receive is accurate. You may have to pass it on or repeat it later. Two types of questions you will need to use are:

- open – used to find out more information by asking questions which avoid yes/no answers, such as: What style are you looking for? How many would you like? When would you like delivery?
- closed – used to confirm information by asking questions which result in yes or no answers, such as: Do you like...? Would you prefer...?

▶ Non-verbal, eg sign and body language, listening skills – regardless of whether you are speaking to an internal or external customer, whether face-to-face or over the telephone, your body language will have an impact on how you appear to the other person and can affect the entire conversation. For example, slouching or avoiding eye contact will give a bad impression.

Sign language is another form of NVC and someone with a hearing impairment may rely on it as their first or only form of language. Sign or hand language is also used as a form of communication in some business situations, for example stock market dealers, turf accountants and divers.

EAT   DRINK   MORE   PLEASE   THANK YOU   SORRY

▶ Sign language for common words and phrases

Link

Communication skills are also covered in *Unit 8: Recruitment and Selection Process.*

Active listening skills are probably the most important part of communicating effectively. This means remaining focused by devoting your whole attention to what is being said and ensuring that you are able to recall the key facts of a conversation at a later stage.

Paraphrasing, or translating a customer's needs into your own words, is an effective way of ensuring that you have understood what they want. You may need to ask questions to gain a better understanding.

▶ Barriers to communication – certain attitudes and behaviours may affect how you treat customers or how they treat you, including:

- assumptions made on first impressions
- negative facial expressions and body language
- apparent shyness or a lack of interest
- impatience
- low self-esteem and lack of confidence
- sloppiness
- poor manners
- limited product or service knowledge.

▶ Undeveloped skills can impede the clarity of communication, for example:

- being unable to articulate clearly
- having weak literacy and numeracy skills
- not being able to apply active listening skills.

▶ There may also be barriers, such as language or cultural differences, that can cause communication difficulties.

PAUSE POINT

How would you communicate with a person who could not hear you? How would you interpret their response to you?

Hint   Exaggerating the way you normally communicate is not an effective strategy.

Extend   Produce training guidance. Include effective tips for communicating with customers with three different specialist needs.

Interpersonal skills

Personal presentation is of prime importance but it can be overlooked easily. A smart appearance need not be costly and first impressions really do count. Some businesses provide a uniform which enables employers to have a certain control over their employees' presentation and means that they can be easily identified by external customers. A clean and well-pressed outfit with clean and appropriate footwear helps form a professional impression. Consider these factors about personal presentation.

▶ Attitude – how you approach and interact with a customer, the interest you show in helping them feel valued and the time you allocate to meet their needs.

▶ Behaviour – you are representing the organisation and your behaviour should reflect its values.

▶ Hygiene – nothing is more likely to put off a customer and alienate colleagues than poor hygiene. You and your clothing should always be free from odours.

▶ Personality – customers are more likely to respond positively to anyone with a good personality and are more likely to make a purchase from someone they like.

▶ Conversation skills – knowing what not to say is just as important as knowing what to say. While it is not uncommon for employees to bluff their way through a conversation, respect can soon be lost, making it hard to regain customer trust.

▶ Giving a consistent and reliable response – customers want an honest response but this does not give you a licence to be blunt or cruel. However, many sales have been made as a result of honest and direct responses.

PAUSE POINT

Think about your ideal job. Would you suit it? How might your manner or behaviour impact on customers and colleagues?

Hint   If you have a job, what could you do to change your behaviour to better meet the expectations of others?

Extend   Do you think customers need time to browse, think, make up their minds and respond to your questions?

Theory into practice

What impresses you? Make a point of observing how others present themselves and how you are influenced by the different aspects you have been considering. Select a range of situations, businesses, employee roles and even your place of study. Make notes about your first impressions and compare with any subsequent thoughts.

Make a list of your biases or prejudices as they reveal themselves. Reflect upon what you can do to manage them.

Behaviours

There are many characteristics which affect your behaviour. A positive attitude is more productive than a negative approach and will be reflected in your actions and communication. If you offer assistance or show respect, it reflects well on you and the organisation you work for. The benefits and potential pitfalls of each behaviour are shown in Table 14.3.

Theory into practice

Practise your communication skills with a peer or in a small group. Choose a simple scenario and each take a different role. When you have finished, each make notes of what worked well and why, and what could be improved. Take turns to try out each of the roles.

▶ **Table 14.3:** Examples of possible benefits and drawbacks of different behaviours

	Benefits to self and others	**Potential impact on others**
Being positive	Willing to give anything a go Problem solver Cheerful disposition Keen to learn Ambitious Confident	Unrealistic Irritating Over-ambitious Over-zealous Patronising Overly-sensitive **Egotistic**
Offering assistance	Meeting or exceeding customer expectations Customer-centric Willing Team player **Altruistic**	Overbearing Invading personal space Patronising
Showing respect	Personable Builder of relationships Conscientious Altruistic	Patronising Egotistic Over-zealous

Key terms

Egotistic – self-important, striving for favourable impressions, conceited.

Altruistic – selfless, concern for others.

Attrition – the rate at which employees leave a business.

Client retention – ensuring that customers stay with the business and do not take their custom elsewhere.

Case study

'Healthcare provider'

A healthcare provider has been helping people access affordable healthcare for 140 years, through a variety of health cash plans, dental plans, private medical insurance, and mobility and living aids.

The company follows mutual values so does not have shareholders. It is completely focused on providing excellent personal customer service. This customer-centric approach has brought huge commercial success. Some 3 million customers and 20,000 corporate health schemes have taken the group's turnover to almost £340 million.

'Private medical insurance is a complicated business and training takes time – so reducing staff **attrition** is very important to us.' Employees put forward their own project proposals for improving service. The 'ideas produced have not only improved empowerment, but noticeable, incremental performance gains by collaborating better' by 'developing new ways of updating and understanding internal customers – which has had a real impact on the frontline service our external customers receive... and our people get to feel that they're making a difference,' says their Customer Quality Manager.

The business finds creative ways of evaluating their strengths and weaker areas by engaging with external customers to compare its customer service performance with others. They use data from the financial sector, but recognise that they also need to look further afield by analysing what other successful businesses do in different sectors, such as M&S.

In late 2014, the company was awarded with the title of Best Healthcare Trust Provider in recognition of excellence across the health insurance sector. As one of the UK's largest providers of self-funded trusts it boasts an outstanding track record for **client retention** with corporate clients staying, on average, for 10 years.

Check your knowledge

1 What creative approaches does the company use to gather data?

2 To what does the company attribute its success?

3 How does the company look after its internal customers?

4 What customer service skills and behaviours are likely to be important to the company?

PAUSE POINT   How would you define the healthcare provider in the case study in a strapline?

 Explore what other private and public healthcare businesses do to respond to customers' needs.

 Compare the monitoring strategies of your chosen healthcare businesses and evaluate their effectiveness.

Dealing with customer service requests and complaints

Customer service situations

Customer service happens throughout business. Below you will consider some of the occasions when it is needed.

Providing information

Internal and external customers require information, for example price or product availability. The way you provide that information can vary, in format and method. Some business transactions require documentation, such as invoices, credit and delivery notes. A customer supplier may be chasing payment of an outstanding invoice and require a rapid verbal response, whereas a consumer may have a serious complaint which needs to be followed up in writing.

Never be afraid to admit it if you do not know something. Reassure the customer that you will find the answer and come back them and always ensure that you do get back to them. If a customer is left without information after being promised a response, they are likely to take their business elsewhere. This applies to internal, as well as external, customers.

Products or services

Customers are likely to enquire about the availability, cost and specifications of a product or service and the means by which they enquire will vary according to the type of business and its location, for example:

1 face-to-face, for example in a supermarket, department store or garage

2 over the telephone, for example to check availability for a dentist or doctor's appointment or seek an insurance quotation

3 by email or online, possibly to enquire about information which is not clearly described on the seller's website or which is specific to the customer's needs

4 by form, such as a tear-off slip from a magazine or an application for a loft insulation grant or planning permission.

In situations such as 3 and 4, the process for managing customer enquiries should be made clear at the outset. In each case, try to anticipate a customer's needs by giving them information which they might have forgotten to ask for. This will help them to make an informed decision.

Promoting additional products and services

There is often an opportunity to offer customers additional products and services, such as travel insurance with a holiday, or a helmet with a new bicycle. However, you should always be mindful of your customer's needs. It may be that a product, such as a helmet, is a vital addition to the original sale and should be encouraged. In other instances the additional product or service may not be as welcome, for example if the customer is in a rush or if they have a limited budget. You must balance your personal goal (eg commission) and the business goals (eg to make a profit) against your customer's needs.

Giving advice

Customers may seek your advice, particularly if you work in retail. Depending on the training you have received and the nature of the business, you may be confident to do this and be expected to do so by your employer. The **caveat** is that you must know your limitations and remember that some advice can only be given by experts.

Key terms

Caveat – conditions or limitations.

Verbatim – repeating the message exactly as it was originally given.

Taking and relaying messages

Hearing something is different to actually listening. An interaction may need you to take and pass on a message so you need to be accurate. However, taking and relaying a message does not just involve passing it on **verbatim** – it may require action. For example, you may need to answer the customer's query or simply let them know an item is no longer available and offer an alternative.

Safety tip

Employees in hotel restaurants sometimes need to request residents' room numbers. This can be overheard in public areas, especially if a receptionist repeats the room number in front of other guests and visitors.

Tip

You might find it useful to prepare a short crib list of questions which are most commonly asked, so that you have the answers at your fingertips.

Limitations of role and authority

It is crucial to know and operate within the limitations of your role and your authority. Table 14.4 considers the relationship between these points and a number of job roles.

▶ **Table 14.4:** Suggested limitations and authority in a variety of business sectors and roles

Type of role	Example of limitation	Example of authority
Marketing	Information offered to public and competitors, eg by editorials Future plans and strategies which may restrict current opportunities Business secrets, eg about future products or services or product secrets such as recipes or components	Promoting business to existing and potential clients Resolving customer dissatisfaction Building relationships Sharing information with sales team Knowing competitors
Sales	Unrealistic claims about product or service to get a sale	Accurate information including specification and pricing Resolving customer issues Keeping all parties informed
Travel agent	Giving unrealistic information Passing information around third hand about ideal places to travel or restrictions that may not be true Not pushing one tour operator over another purely for profit	Distinguishing between recommendation and advice for clients' travel plans Knowing geography
Chef	Knowing how much variation is possible in food preparation Not best-guessing recipe contents	Knowing contents of food, especially that which can cause allergic reactions Accommodating diners' special requests, within reason Sticking to deadlines

In addition to limitations, there are also expectations that you will deal with customer requests and complaints. Your job description will outline your responsibilities and the expectations that your employer has of you.

Keeping records

Records need to be kept as 'evidence' of transactions or interactions. Keeping up-to-date, accurate records is fundamental to ensuring that information can be found and shared with appropriate parties. There are also laws regulating how long different records must be kept. A simple and logical system is vital, whether it is paper-based or electronic. You must also ensure that records are in an appropriate format – a scribbled post-it note containing someone's personal information would not be an appropriate record.

Dealing with problems

Some jobs exist solely to deal with customers' problems and people are employed with special skills who can remain unflappable and get the best possible result for all parties. Some businesses, such as JLP, Microsoft or Apple, view problems as an opportunity to refine systems and products or devise new ones.

Handling complaints

Large businesses are likely to have whole departments that are dedicated purely to handling complaints, although, often, they are disguised under positive names, such as Customer Relations.

Businesses should have a clear procedure for dealing with complaints which all employees are made aware of. A complaints procedure provides the steps that an employee needs to take when dealing with a complaint and should be shared with the customer if the complaint becomes more serious and cannot be resolved simply and quickly. In a more serious situation, you may need to suggest to a customer that, if they are not fully satisfied, they should put their complaint in writing, and advise them where and how to submit it and how it will be handled.

Remedial measures

Most complaints can be resolved fairly swiftly and painlessly while others require more attention and customers may need to be offered incentives to resolve their complaint. For example, a business such as M&S may give a customer a small bunch of flowers in addition to resolving a food complaint, which may be in addition to a refund or replacement. By contrast, an insurance company might be called upon to repair damage to a car and remedial measures will need to be taken to ensure that the guilty party contributes to the cost (for example, by increasing the cost of their insurance when they renew their policy). As an interim measure, the owner of the damaged vehicle might be given a courtesy vehicle while their repairs are carried out.

Emergency situations

A complaint may be raised which is deemed an emergency, for example a gas odour, a fire or an accident. It is also important to know how to report a case of an injury or disease in the workplace.

You may be asked to deal with a customer who has inadvertently spilt some toxic substance on their clothing or body and this must be reported immediately and assistance must be called. In accordance with legislation, records must also be kept and, depending on the type of business sector where you work, you would need to be very familiar with the rules and regulations of this legislation. This could be a matter of life or death.

Organisational policy

All businesses need to have policies and procedures in place and sometimes these might be shared with external customers. They should always be very well understood by internal customers.

Policies are usually a summary of legislation or external regulation and relate to how the business conducts itself. Every policy should identify how the implementation and impact of the policy will be monitored. Policies are usually reviewed on a regular basis by management who use data to analyse and evaluate the outcomes of each policy, just as the government reviews its policies and updates legislation.

Individual skills audit and development plan

You have explored how customer service needs can be met and the skills associated with meeting those needs. You will practise these skills through role-plays and it would be useful to complete a self-assessment similar to those which businesses use. This is oftern referred to as a skills audit.

When applying for a job, you might be asked to undertake some kind of assessment. Many job descriptions also include a list of suggested essential and desirable skills which help to match well-suited applicants with appropriate job roles. Here are some approaches for assessing your skills and attributes.

Skills audit of customer service skills

Customer service is part of every job role and the skills required to fulfil the role successfully are extensive. Table 14.5 is an example of a skills audit which you can use to identify your areas for development.

▶ **Table 14.5:** Suggested example for a generic skills audit

Skill	Skill level			
	Struggle unless very familiar situations	Fairly able in routine situations	Effective in more complex situations most of the time	Can apply very effectively in wide variety of situations
Confidence				
Receiving and passing on messages				
Resolving problems				
Developing relationships				
Attention to detail				
Record keeping				
Following written and verbal instructions				
Meeting deadlines				

Research

It might be useful to seek the views of someone who knows you well in a business situation. If you have a part-time job or a business mentor, ask for their input and compare it with your own evaluation.

Link

Guidance on reviewing your communication and organisational skills can be found in *Unit 8: Recruitment and Selection Process*.

Link

More information on SWOT analysis can be found in *Unit 8: Recruitment and Selection Process*.

Skills audits should generally include four options. This avoids a 'middle of the road option' which is fairly meaningless. Audits should also avoid words like 'good' which are hard to define. The important thing is to be honest so that you get a clear picture for your development plan.

Personal SWOT analysis to assess any gaps

Carrying out a SWOT analysis is another way of assessing your gaps. Carrying out the skills audit could provide a basis for a SWOT analysis if you list the skills from each skill level in each square. Below is an example of how you might combine the outcome from a skills audit with a personal SWOT analysis.

Strengths List the skills identified as: **Can apply very effectively in wide variety of situations**	**Weaknesses** List the skills identified as: **Fairly able in routine situations**
Opportunities List the skills identified as: **Effective in more complex situations most of the time**	**Threats** List the skills identified as: **Struggle unless very familiar situations**

The example portrayed above is only one way you might choose to use the outcome from a skills audit. You might carry out the SWOT analysis with individual skills to identify a focus for a development plan. For example, if you know that you can be overly talkative, you might decide that in a business situation it could be a weakness to overcome or even a threat to how discreet you might be with customer information. Your SWOT analysis could focus on individual interpersonal and communication skills, such as:

▶ body language, for example facial expressions, gestures, inappropriate touching, slouching
▶ listening skills, particularly how well you are able to recall details of conversations and relay messages accurately
▶ handling complaints, such as the ability to diffuse potentially difficult situations, retain customers or maintain composure
▶ working with others, including the ability to be an effective team player, adapt to different roles and maintain relationships.

Set objectives to meet skills development goals for a specified customer services role

Once you have identified what you can do, how well you do it and what you need to work on, you can produce a development plan which identifies your goals. This plan provides a useful framework for working out how to improve on each of the skills and who or what might be involved.

▶ Identify resources and support needed to meet the objectives of your plan – the important aspect in each case is to have a goal, which can and may change, enabling you to focus on what you want to achieve. To do this, carry out some research into the job roles or business sectors that you find interesting. A useful starting point is to trawl the local newspapers and internet sites, and visit some businesses and recruitment agencies to get job descriptions, which will give you a better idea of what is required.

▶ Set review dates – every plan should have an overall goal which is broken down into more manageable steps which can be monitored against pre-set deadlines or milestones. Review dates should be carefully considered.

▶ Monitor the plan to assess progress against targets – you need a monitoring procedure to ensure that you meet your targets. If you don't attach dates to targets, it will be hard to measure progress. However, your targets and their dates might need to change, particularly if your original plan overlooked the complexity of each task or if you have limited access to resources.

Case study

Vetfone™ Hosted Call Centre Helpline

VetsDirect provide veterinary advice and welfare services to some of the biggest names in pet services and welfare in the UK. The Vetfone™ service is provided to pet owners as a membership or Pet Insurance policy benefit, and is used by owners who need advice about their sick pets. This can sometimes be advice on how to care for their pet at home, or they may be directed to the nearest emergency vet.

In accordance with VetsDirect quality procedures, telephone calls are processed by experienced RCVS qualified and registered veterinary nurses. The virtual call centre means nurses can work flexibly from home offices using remote IT systems. This allows VetsDirect to attract and retain the highest quality veterinary nurses, regardless of where they live.

VetsDirect are passionate about delivering the highest quality services for pets. Veterinary nurses take calls 24/7 about a variety of pet problems from worried pet owners. The urgent nature of their work requires them to think very seriously about who is providing their telephone services. The company they use have proved that they can deliver a financially acceptable solution and also the quality and availability of service required for such an emergency service. On the rare occasions when things go wrong, they react professionally to correct any shortcomings.

The latest call centre technology distributes calls to the veterinary nurses and is supported by online information resources, databases and veterinary decision support processes, including voice call recording and skills-based routing. Skills-based call routing ensures that the call is answered by the person with the most appropriate skill set.

Nurses can use a web interface to control their availability by logging in and out ensuring that only available nurses are called, improving the efficiency of call throughput. Nurses can easily transfer calls to colleagues, or other destinations, or call the customer back later. Overflow operatives can stand by if needed and be quickly drafted into the pool of available nurses when demand is exceptionally high. Supervisors and managers can remotely access real time and historical reports to fully analyse the workforce and their efficiency.

Check your knowledge

1 What is the purpose of VetsDirect?

2 What is the role of their call centre staff?

3 How does VetsDirect compare with the services offered by traditional, local veterinary surgeries?

4 What specialist skills are required by the nurses?

5 How has the call centre contributed to the success of VetsDirect?

PAUSE POINT

What are the key skills that call centre staff require to be effective? How do these skills compare with those needed in other job roles?

Hint

Read the book recommended at the end of this chapter. Look at call centre job descriptions to find skills that employers seek.

Extend

What skills are you going to develop further and where will you gain additional experience and valuable feedback?

Assessment practice 14.2

C.P4   C.P5   C.P6   C.M3   C.D3

Show your customer service skills in three different situations – through role-play or evidence from part-time work.

The aim is to test your customer service skills, identify gaps and measure your progress against a development plan. Start with your own assessment, which should be similar to the skills audit that you completed previously. As the business you identified will have their own idea of what they want, you may undertake another assessment to use as a benchmark to measure your performance and plan for development.

You will need to practise your skills on several occasions and may choose to do this over several days or weeks. Produce your own development plan and put milestones in place to measure progress. You should demonstrate product or service knowledge when dealing with customers' queries, requests and problems. You may find that you encounter other customer service skills through this activity as well.

Write an evaluative report with an assessment of your progress, reflecting on what went well and what was more challenging and why, including details of where you need to work on your individual communication and interpersonal skills. Justify your account with testimonials from others, which may include customer feedback and analyses of data. Assess how the development plan has improved your performance in customer service skills. Consider how you have demonstrated initiative in making high-quality, justified recommendations to develop your own communication and interpersonal skills to meet customer needs. Consider any potential breaches to confidentiality and other policies when you gather evidence.

Plan

- I shall try approaching a business to offer my services for real-life experience in this assessment, perhaps as a volunteer (eg a charity shop, CAB or college marketing events).
- I shall decide how I will keep reflective notes and gather feedback.
- I shall identify how my performance will be assessed and the skills that I am measuring.
- I shall decide what I hope to get out of this activity, perhaps by carrying out another SWOT analysis.

Do

- I shall pace myself by keeping within my plan and avoid being over-ambitious.
- I shall measure my progress against my development plan.
- I shall read about developing interpersonal skills, body language and the business sector that I am engaging with.
- I shall remember to celebrate my successes as well as identifying development areas.

Review

- I shall assess what progress I have made.
- I shall identify the problem solving techniques that I have developed.
- I shall evaluate the usefulness of a personal development plan and how I might use a similar approach to help me through my studies, preparing for further and higher studies or employment.

Further reading and resources

Knapp D. *A Guide to Customer Service Skills for the Help Desk Professional*, Boston: Cengage (1999).
Pease A. and Pease B. *The Definitive Book of Body Language*, Orion (2006).
Rumsey D. *Statistics for Dummies*, John Wiley & Sons (2011).
www.fsb.org.uk/stats
Statistics from the Federation of Small Businesses.
www.gov.uk/government/organisations/companies-house
Information about limited companies including their trading, profit and loss accounts.
http://www.tradingstandards.uk/
Professional body for protecting consumers.

THINK ▶FUTURE

Jess Bolton

Receptionist and administrator at Let us find your castle

Having just achieved my BTEC National in Business I got a job working for 'Let us find your castle'. This is a small estate agency employing just four negotiators and is managed by its owner, a former estate agent of a large, national agency. Initially, they relied on the owner's son to provide administrative support to the negotiating team, but he was promoted to trainee negotiator.

The owner advertised for a replacement and was quite willing to take on a college leaver as he wanted the business to shape the new employee around their values and principles. The advert offered training in estate agency protocols and it included a list of skills that the owner wanted to see in the applicant. I thought I would be a good fit for the role, but wanted to make sure that I was fully prepared for the interview and could show that I had everything he was looking for.

To prepare, I produced a SWOT analysis and skills audit so that I could assess my suitability against the job advert. I made sure that I was totally honest and even asked some colleagues at my Saturday job for their opinion about my strengths. Once I'd done this, I felt much more confident about my ability to respond to the interview questions and ask my own prepared questions.

Focusing your skills

Preparing yourself

Imagine you are applying for Jess's job and prepare a SWOT analysis and skills audit to assess your suitability in:

- presenting a friendly yet professional face to clients visiting the agency
- efficiently identifying customers' requirements when making contact personally, by telephone, email and via internet searches
- diligence in keeping diaries of viewings and valuations for all negotiators and owners
- monitoring and ordering stationery and other supplies
- signing for deliveries and keeping accurate records
- making drinks for the team
- acting as linchpin for all customers including conveyancing solicitors, mortgage lenders, sale board manufacturers and erecters

- adhering to relevant legislation, such as confidentiality and data protection
- working to demanding deadlines to produce property details
- ensuring that copy is accurate and timely for advertising properties in newspapers and online
- updating records, advertising and window displays with new properties, changes to price, under offer stickers
- producing mailshots, solicitor information, dealing with incoming and outgoing post
- running errands
- ability to keep calm.

Getting ready for assessment

Since joining this course, Kamilla has increased in confidence and enjoys being able to use skills developed from part-time work in her assignments and activities. She wants to achieve a distinction for her coursework and is considering applying to university to take a business degree.

Kamilla's latest assignment, covering learning aims A and B, is to produce a customer service training handbook in accordance with relevant legislation and regulations. To gain a distinction, she has to investigate the methods used to improve customer service in business, analyse data and evaluate the benefits and impact on the business, customers and employees. The assignment also requires a report which Kamilla decided would include the reasons for the training handbook, based on research she will undertake.

How I got started

First I chose a business and job role. I picked one I was interested in as the work I do now might help me develop sector knowledge and perhaps lead to a job.

I listed everything I needed to do and put it into a Gantt chart with deadlines, milestones and details of how I planned to go about each task, including what I would need. This is my draft list, which I changed slightly as I couldn't achieve some items in the order planned.

▶ Research the business to understand their mission, values and how they gathered customer feedback and complaints.
▶ Identify relevant legislation for the business sector and the job role selected.
▶ Gather a collection of job descriptions for a similar role to compare and identify the main characteristics required.
▶ Research a collection of customer feedback mechanisms using at least three different methods.
▶ Compare a selection of training handbooks.
▶ Decide upon one aspect to include in the training handbook.

How I brought it all together

I produced my report first, using my research and my evaluations of customer service. Because I had researched several businesses, I was able to compare each of them and decide what constitutes excellent customer service. This is one of the distinction criteria.

I searched for different customer feedback methods and found it really useful to pay attention when I visited many businesses and retailers. I then started to think about missed opportunities for gathering feedback, especially when I, my family or friends talked about our experiences as customers. Every time the phone rang, I was eager to see if it was a business and how they could improve; this helped me decide upon a skill as a focus for my training handbook.

What I learned from the experience

I didn't want to rely on the internet unless I was confident about the source of information. I made a massive error when I discovered part way through my report that I was using the wrong legislation – it was for Australian businesses and not the UK. I also forgot to keep accurate records of my sources and had to go back through everything to produce my bibliography. I now know that I need to keep a source list which is foolproof by not relying on deep weblinks which I can't find again and to keep full references of books and newspaper articles, such as title, page numbers, dates and author.

I also overestimated my own ability to analyse data. I thought my numeracy skills were reasonable but my reliance on spreadsheet formulas almost let me down. It was only because I got my dad to check my report that a glaring error was spotted. So I had to go back over the formulas and check my calculations using a calculator after improving my estimating skills. I now know to check that the answer is what I would expect rather than assume it must be right.

Think about it

▶ How will you organise yourself to fulfil the assignment criteria?
▶ What extra training will help you to achieve a merit or distinction?
▶ How will you manage distractions?
▶ What methods will you use to critique your work and identify improvements?

Visual Merchandising 16

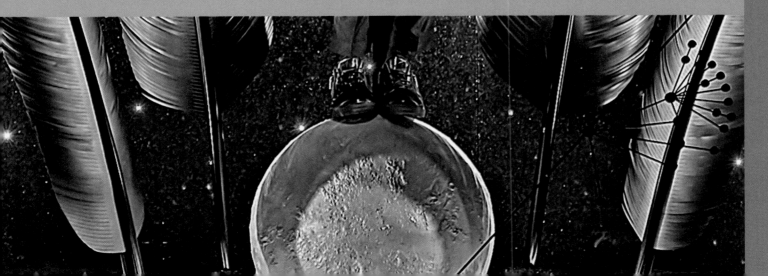

Getting to know your unit

Assessment
You will be assessed by a series of assignments set by your tutor.

Visual merchandising is used to increase store traffic and sales volume by using stimulating and energising displays to make products attractive and appealing to customers. Many techniques, including digital technology, colour, light, space and sound are used depending on the type and size of the retail business and the products it sells. It is important to ensure that all displays are safe and meet legislative requirements. Through completion of this unit, you will discover the most effective ways to use these different techniques in a variety of settings. You will then be able to go on to put what you have learned into practice by demonstrating your visual merchandising skills in a practical assessment.

How you will be assessed

This unit will be assessed internally by two tasks set by your tutor. Throughout this unit, you will find assessment practices that will help you work towards your assessment. Completing these activities will not mean that you have achieved a particular grade, but you will have carried out useful research or preparation that will be relevant when it comes to your final assignment.

In order for you to achieve the tasks in your assignment, it is important to check that you have met all of the Pass grading criteria. You can do this as you work your way through the assignment.

If you are hoping to gain a Merit or Distinction, you should also make sure that you present the information in your assignment in the style that is required by the relevant assessment criterion. For example, Merit criteria require you to analyse and discuss, and Distinction criteria require you to assess and evaluate.

The assignment set by your tutor will consist of a number of tasks designed to meet the criteria in the table. This is likely to consist of a written assignment but may also include activities such as the following:

- a presentation
- a practical task
- a discussion.

Assessment criteria

This table shows you what you must do in order to achieve a **Pass**, **Merit** or **Distinction** grade, and where you can find activities to help you.

Pass	Merit	Distinction

Learning aim **A**

Pass	Merit	Distinction
A.P1 Investigate the visual merchandising and display techniques that can be used in retail outlets. **Assessment practice 16.1**	**A.M1** Analyse the different approaches to visual merchandising used by contrasting business, supported by independent research. **Assessment practice 16.1**	**A.D1** Evaluate the extent to which different visual merchandising and display techniques contribute to the success of two contrasting businesses. **Assessment practice 16.1**
A.P2 Explain how visual merchandising is affected by legal and safety regulations. **Assessment practice 16.1**		

Learning aim **B**

Pass	Merit	Distinction
B.P3 Explain how psychological techniques are used by two contrasting retail outlets. **Assessment practice 16.1**	**B.M2** Analyse how psychological and technological techniques are used to increase business success. **Assessment practice 16.1**	**B.D2** Evaluate how psychological and technological techniques are used to increase business success. **Assessment practice 16.1**
B.P3 Explain how technological techniques are used by two contrasting retail outlets. **Assessment practice 16.1**		

Learning aim **C**

Pass	Merit	Distinction
C.P5 Produce a realistic plan for a visual merchandising display for a product or service in a retail outlet. **Assessment practice 16.2**	**C.M3** Plan and create an individual visual merchandising display, using recommendations and feedback to assess the success of the project. **Assessment practice 16.2**	**C.D3** Demonstrate individual self-management and initiative in the presentation of a high quality successful display for a retail outlet through the creative use of visual merchandising. **Assessment practice 16.2**
C.P6 Create a successful visual merchandising display for a product or service in a retail outlet. **Assessment practice 16.2**		

Getting started

Retailers use visual merchandising techniques to attract customers' attention and create a desire for their product. Think about the retailers you have visited most recently and write a brief description of the different displays (in-store and in the window) that you have seen, and who the display was aimed at.

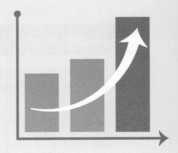

Explore how retail outlets apply visual merchandising and display techniques in line with legislation and safety considerations

Displays and the way products are placed within a store do not happen 'by chance'. They are carefully planned and designed by the retailer to attract customers' attention and encourage them to 'stop and buy'. Retailers consider many factors by using different display and product placement techniques.

Visual merchandising

Key term

Visual merchandising – displaying products and services in a way designed to attract customers' attention.

The way products and services are displayed will depend on the retailer's business structure and the objectives they have set out to achieve. Physically displaying goods by setting them out in the most attractive manner possible can be achieved by combining the product, environment and space into stimulating and engaging displays. This encourages the sale of products or services. For instance, a high end retailer's display is likely to be spacious, with the display projecting luxury, whereas a budget retailer is likely to display many products in a small, crowded space projecting an image of 'finding a bargain'.

Display techniques

Product placement

Retailers will display and place their products where they are most likely to attract the customer's attention. The window is an obvious place for display but other areas can be just as effective. For example, you will often find promotional items at the entrance of a store or at the end of an aisle. Other effective areas include the bottom of stairs and escalators or in high traffic aisles, or placed near complementary merchandise. On the other hand, quite often, you will see products on promotion placed out of context away from other similar products to encourage sales. Some customers may be surprised to see the product at the end of the aisle, and so this attracts their attention. Other customers will be used to this kind of product placement and will expect promotions and special offers to be placed out of context. Nevertheless, they are still drawn to the possibility of a bargain or special deal.

Discussion

Compare and contrast the display techniques used in supermarkets and department stores. Which similar display techniques do they both use and which do they use that are different? What do you think are the reasons for the differences?

Product segmentation

Product segmentation is another important factor for retailers. There may be one or several things to consider when creating a visual display or placing products, such as the theme, the season, whether there is a specific promotion or event to be used, or if the promotion is across the business.

In fashion outlets, products are segmented by categories such as outdoor, casual, workwear or sportswear clothing, whereas in a bedding shop the product segmentation is more likely to be in size of bedding, for example single, double or king size, and in a cook shop the display might be brand or colour themed.

In a department store, there may be a promotion across the business where there is a percentage amount off a certain brand's products. These brands may have products across different retail areas such as clothing, homeware, gardening and stationery.

Table 16.1 provides a quick recap of product placement and segmentation.

▶ **Table 16.1:** Product placement and segmentation have to be considered carefully by retailers

Product placement	Product segmentation
• Window • Front end • Aisle ends • Near stairs • At entrance • Near escalators/lifts • High traffic aisles • Complementary merchandise placement	By: • theme • promotion • event • season. Across the business

❚❚ PAUSE POINT   What is the difference between produce placement and product segmentation? Write a paragraph on the differences.

Hint   Close the book and draw on your experiences of when you have visited different retailers.

Extend   Why should a retailer consider product placement and product segmentation when planning visual merchandising displays?

Techniques of visual merchandising – what to look out for

Here are some key techniques and terms used in visual merchandising.

▶ Using a story or theme – these can be used for events such as the World Cup or for seasonal events such as pumpkins at Halloween or strawberries in the summer for Wimbledon.

▶ What theme do you think is used here?

- Coordination – whatever other technique is being used, coordination is a vital part of visual merchandising. A good example is colour coordination which can be used to assist in the story being told. For example, a colour coordinated theme using opposite ends of the colour wheel will work well for clothing where whole outfits are being displayed. By contrast, using a variety of shades of one colour will work well in a floristry display where texture is creating the interest.

- Colour or style blocks – this is when items are displayed by colour, texture or shape to create a mass effect, such as a whole denim display of different articles of clothing, or a display of vases of many shapes, but all in the same colour. Products such as bedding work well with this technique and it offers opportunities to sell complementary products alongside.

▷ Can you think of the types of items likely to be displayed in colour blocks?

- Complementary or contrasting colours – this works well when shoppers are being encouraged to buy a whole collection, for example for a special occasion, when accessories to the main outfit can be purchased, such as shoes, belts and jewellery, or for furnishing a room, when coordinating curtains, lamps and rugs are displayed with a three piece suite.

▷ Showing complementary colours is an effective way to show the full range in a collection

- Repetition – this is most effective when used sparingly, such as in spas or beauty salons, where small product displays are repeated on different shelves, using the same colour schemes and brands. It also works well in boutique-style displays such as handbags, shoes or clothing in a department store or small shop.

▶ Mirror image and triangular formulation – table top displays work well here where the same items are displayed on each side of a triangular formation, having the highest items in the centre and the lower items on the outside edge.

▶ Triangular formation can be effective when displaying small food or items

▶ Focal points – these can be created in many different contexts according to the retailer, for example, a garden centre creating a 'BBQ party' display, or a fashion outlet using mannequins in the centre of their store.

▶ Branding/signage – displays using a variety of products, all from the same brand, become effective when there is a strong branding message which encourages the customer to purchase matching items. Alternatively, displaying the same products of a brand in one area, with signage of that brand within or above the display, adds to its effectiveness.

▶ Signage – is important to guide customers to different departments and to identify key locations such as tills and customer service.

Key term

Micro-merchandising – getting the right products, sizes and colours at the right prices to meet local customer demands.

▸ Mass display – displays such as vintage sewing machines or cartoon characters filling a whole shop window create attention, interest and a desire for the shopper to explore further. The same applies to internal displays of whole walls of jewellery or colour coordinated footwear, which will attract the customer.

▸ **Micro-merchandising** – this is when stores customise their retail offering to meet the local needs of their customers by selling locally produced products such as food, clothing and pottery, or items that would be required by the local population, for example souvenirs in a holiday destination or walking boots and outdoor equipment in or near a national park.

Discussion

What display techniques do retailers use in your nearest high street? Who are their displays aimed at? How well do you think they reach their targeted customers?

Key term

Furnishing enhancements – props that are used to make displayed items more attractive and eye-catching. They may also be for sale, but not always.

Props, fixtures and free-standing displays

Props are used to make displays and product placement within a store more attractive and inviting to customers. Sometimes, these props are available to purchase and therefore used by the retailer to help the customer to coordinate and accessorise their purchase. At other times, the props are not for sale but are used to attract the customer's attention to make the product more interesting, for example food products arranged around tableware. These are known as **furnishing enhancements.**

▸ **Table 16.2:** Types of props, fixtures and free-standing displays used as display techniques

Display	How it can be used effectively
Mannequins, busts and forms	Mannequins are regularly used in shop windows. However they are just as effective when used inside a store. For lower level displays, mannequins can be in a sitting position, or you could just use a bust.
Product demonstration	An effective way for customers to get to know if a product is right for them is to try it. Product demonstrations can be carried out in many different ways including: • showing a film on a screen in-store • having a live demonstration of a product • offering free food samples for customers to try.
Gondolas	These are bespoke display stands that are designed for specific products. The placement of products within the gondola is very important. Customers like shopping to be easy and are likely to choose products that are at eye level as they often buy the first thing they see. After this, the customer will look above eye level, before looking below. The retailer will, therefore, put the product that they wish to sell the most of at eye level. Higher priced products will be placed just above eye level, and lower priced products will be below eye level.
End caps	At the end of aisles, end caps are used to add an element of surprise by positioning products that are out of context with the rest of the aisle. This will attract the customer and encourage them to investigate further.
Dump tables, bins and counters	Items on promotion or which are reduced are often displayed in bins or on counters. Using a table for a low level display of kitchenware or clothing can allow different themed displays using a combination of other techniques, such as block colouring or mirror imaging, to be created.
Garment rails, slat walls and shelves	Garment rails can be placed on the wall, or be free standing depending on the layout of the store and the space available. Slat walls can be used for hanging rails or shelving, However, the products on sale should be in reach of the customer. Only items that are not for sale should be displayed out of reach.
Free-standing displays	These include the use of stacks or islands that can be found in the centre of a shopping area. They can create an impressive impact when used effectively, for example as the centrepiece of a themed display for a special event.

▶ How many techniques can you see in this display?

 PAUSE POINT   Can you explain the different display techniques and when they are used?

Hint   Close the book and write down all that you can remember.

Extend   Why are the display techniques so important to the retailer's business success?

Case study

Improving sales through visual merchandising

The owner of a fashion retailer read an article on how visual merchandising can increase sales within a business. The owner had never paid much attention to displays as business was steady with plenty of customers. However, a national fashion retailer was opening opposite her shop and, on reading this article, she decided she needed someone who could help to create a better look for the shop and ensure that she was ready for any competition. She decided it was time to employ somebody who was trained in visual merchandising.

Claire, who had just completed a course in visual merchandising, applied for, and got the job.

The first thing Claire did was to look at the products on sale and brand them into four categories.

1   Coordinated outfits.

2   Styles such as work wear and casual wear.

3   Outerwear.

4   Accessories.

She then looked at the sales floor and considered the windows and doors, before deciding where each of the four categories should be placed.

The coordinated outfits were made into a feature by using mannequins to display a full outfit. Next to the mannequins, racks of clothing were placed in garment type (skirts, trousers, tops) and size order so that the customers could easily locate every part of the outfit, in

the colour and size that they required. On top of the racks, coordinated shoes and bags were placed sparingly.

Claire decided on a summer display of casual clothing because of the season they were in and put the workwear further towards the back of the store. The summer display was used to attract attention and encourage customers to enter the store.

She created an accessories section in the store which was arranged by colour so customers could easily choose their accessories to match the outfits they were buying, or had bought already.

Once Claire had completed the displays, she walked through the shop as if looking at it for the first time to experience the 'customer journey' and asked her manager to do the same thing.

Over the next few days the store remained as busy as it had been, but customers appeared to be buying more items and sales increased over the next few months by 5 per cent.

Check your knowledge

1   Why did Claire place the shoes and bags on top of the garment racks?

2   What other techniques could Claire have used to display the coordinated outfits?

3   Which techniques could Claire use to display the outerwear?

4   Why did Claire do a 'walk' of the shop floor?

5   What were the main factors contributing to the increase in sales?

Research

Find out what the experts say about visual merchandising, using at least two different sources, for example, *International Visual* or *Retail Focus*.

What common themes run between the website pages? Are there any differing opinions or ideas? Which displays do you find most appealing and why?

Legislation and safety considerations

Point of sale (POS) and ticketing

Many retailers across many different sectors display the prices of their products on the actual product. However, department stores and other retailers will show prices on the display if it is not possible to display the price on the product, or if it will not be easily seen by the customer. An example of this would be a washing machine display where the retailer has a POS next to the washing machine displaying the price. Supermarkets use the shelf edge to display prices as it is not practical to individually price every item on their shelves. Ticket positioning is very important to ensure that the retailer is operating legally as well as making it easy for the customer to find the price. Customers are less likely to make a purchase if they cannot see the price of the item.

Product labelling

The label on a product gives the customer information about the product, which may have a direct influence on whether or not they will buy it. The main types of information include:

▶ quantity – this could be the number of items in a packet, the weight or the volume
▶ size – this could be the dress size, shoe size, dimensions of a piece of furniture etc. – in fact any measurement that states the size of the product, enabling the customer to decide whether it will meet their requirements
▶ composition – what an item is made of can be very important for a customer – they may want to know what an item of clothing is made of in order to determine if it is suitable for its intended use, for example whether it is waterproof or washable
▶ origin – this will tell the customer where the product has come from – customers may choose their purchase based on the item's origin, for example, food labels state where the food product has come from; a customer concerned about the environment may only wish to buy local produce and the same can be applied to items of clothing or furniture.

Display safety

When placing products within a retail environment and arranging displays, you must consider health and safety. The safety factor should be part of the planning stage when deciding on the layout of the store or of the display area.

Merchandise must be displayed at a safe height, for example items that need to be lifted with two hands should not be displayed on a wall, or placed on a shelf above waist height. Items that can be lifted with one hand can be displayed higher. However, the visual merchandiser must ensure that it will still be safe if the customer wants to pick up and inspect the item.

The display must be made stable by ensuring that any weight is distributed evenly and any parts that are likely to move are securely anchored down. The space that the display is in must be large enough to ensure that there cannot be any injury to the person putting the display in place, or the customer.

If food makes up part of the display, you must ensure that it is kept at the correct temperature and meets the hygiene requirements of food health and safety.

Items that have special storage requirements, such as fireworks, must be kept locked away, although you will see them in the shops displayed in glass cabinets.

When constructing displays, the visual merchandiser must ensure that they do not create any trip hazards or other health and safety issues, for example by leaving sharp tools lying around or glass items that could get broken. Ladders or step-ups provided by the employer should be used if high areas need to be reached.

Safety tip

Ensure that any item which a customer is likely to want to touch, pick up and inspect is comfortably within their reach.

▶ Visual merchandisers must respect health and safety guidelines

Legislation in visual merchandising

Table 16.3 gives a summary of current legislation which applies to visual merchandising.

▶ **Table 16.3:** TLegislation linked to visual merchandisings

Legislation	Details
Price Marking Order 2004	There is an obligation to indicate the selling price of all products in pounds sterling and it must be easy for the customer to see. Other information that must be displayed on the ticket includes quantity (such as items in a packet), size, composition and origin.
Trade Descriptions Acts 1968 and 1972	Under this Act, retailers must not mislead customers in the way they describe their products for sale. All information given on a product must be accurate and up to date.

Research

Further information on these acts can be found online.

What must the retailer consider in terms of this legislation when:
* planning and deciding on the layout of a retail area
* constructing the display
* dismantling the display?

What are the consequences if these considerations are not put in place?

Link

Go to *Unit 16, : Visual Merchandising topic C* to find more information about health and safety, risk assessment and ticketing legislation.

B Examine the psychological and technological merchandising techniques used to influence customers

Key term

Psychology – the scientific study of the human mind and its functions, especially those affecting behaviour in a given context (for example, when buying something).

The retail industry is very competitive and visual marketing can allow brands and organisations to differentiate themselves from one another. As customers often make buying decisions based on emotion, retailers use the **psychology** of visual merchandising to connect with their customers. To enable the retailer to do this, they must be sure of their target market and be aware of how their customers think and feel.

Psychology of visual merchandising

There are a number of methods that businesses use to influence their customers – these include psychological and technological techniques. These can be broken down into the two areas explored below.

How customers are influenced by the use of visual merchandising

By knowing the customer well, retailers can use visual merchandising to influence what they might buy. This involves undertaking plenty of market research to establish what customers are looking for and what they want from a retailer. Customers are often categorised according to the products or services being sold. This might be by age, hobbies or interests, gender, families and so on. For example, a store like Toys "R" Us will have a very different visual merchandising style compared with a store like Abercrombie & Fitch and this will have been influenced by looking at different customer groups, who are likely to be families and small children for Toys "R" Us compared with young adults for Abercrombie & Fitch.

Discussion

Can you think of other examples of different retailers and how their customers vary? What products do they offer and what category or type of customer are they looking to attract? What is their merchandising style?

As well as wanting or needing the product or service, many customers like to enjoy the buying experience and a feeling of buying into a certain lifestyle. There are retailers who are expert at connecting with their customers in this way, such as niche computer retailers (Apple), luxury department stores (Harvey Nichols) or high-end home entertainment specialists (Bang & Olufsen).

Key term

Opulence – an impression of wealth and luxury and possibly glamour.

For example, the Apple Store offers a sleek buying and browsing experience, with displays and decoration that match the style of their products. A luxury department store such as Harvey Nichols will give the impression of **opulence** in their displays and decoration. How a store displays its merchandise and the signage etc. it uses has an impact on customers – they can recognise the type of shop from the way merchandise is displayed. For example, a high-end clothing store is instantly recognisable as such to customers, compared to a low-end store, such as Primark. The latter store is likely to be more cluttered, while a high-end store may choose to only display a few choice pieces of their merchandise.

Discussion

In small groups, discuss how you think you may have been influenced by retailers to purchase certain items. Which retailers are good at influencing you? How do they do it? Which retailers do not influence you? Why is this?

Effective use of an environment's design

Retailers make the best use of the environment available to them through a variety of different methods, some of which are outlined below.

▶ Visual communication – such as signage or the use of images (the brain can process images much faster than written text). Supermarkets will use the image of a shopping trolley to tell shoppers where they are located, whereas other retailers use an image for recognition of their brand, such as the 'apple' logo for Apple.

▶ Lighting – this can vary from store to store and can even vary between parts of the store, for example recessed lighting on shelves that hold shoes.

▶ Colours – some retailers have distinct colour schemes that are instantly recognisable (think of IKEA's blue and yellow) while other retailers go for muted tones (such as Muji's brown and white design).

▶ Music – retailers use music to create a certain mood in a store, for example H&M's in-house DJ versus the ambient music you might hear in a department store.

▶ Scent – certain retailers might use scent to encourage purchases, for example health and beauty retailers like Lush or The Body Shop, or a supermarket piping through the smell of freshly baked bread.

All these influences are used to stimulate customers' perceptual and emotional responses, and, ultimately, to affect their purchasing behaviour. The following case studies provide some examples of how retailers use the above to influence customers' purchasing behaviour.

Case study

Hollister

Hollister is a fashion retailer that uses the scent of its own distinctive perfume, low lighting and loud music to create a unique atmosphere as part of the buying experience. This is aimed at heightening the buying desire of the customer, who is likely to be making purchases for their imminent night out.

Molton Brown

Molton Brown is a retailer that describes itself as a 'bath and body connoisseur'. Its displays are colour coordinated, using glass shelving and bright lighting to create a luxury spa feel. There are modern wash basins available, with soft white towels, where customers are able to use the products. This encourages the customer to treat themselves to an 'affordable luxury' or to buy as a gift for a special friend.

IKEA

IKEA prides itself on offering a range of home furnishing products that are affordable and displays its products by creating different room scenarios through product placement, lighting and colour coordination. Although the store is very large, it is broken down into smaller themed areas, using 'pathways', props and temporary walls so that the customer can only see one theme at a time, which allows them to concentrate on that area and not be distracted. The retailer creates yet another shopping experience, the 'market place' by displaying smaller household items in compartmentalised areas, bins and mass displays that are colour coded and all signposted. The store uses two concepts, using different visual merchandising techniques, which are brought together through their corporate signage. The first concept encourages the customer to purchase whole room concepts and the second concept gives a 'market place' feel where the customer can expect to find bargains as well as expected and unique items to purchase for their home.

Check your knowledge

1 What is the target age group for Hollister?

2 Thinking of Molton Brown, what is the link between the display and the desired effect it wants to establish on the customer?

3 Who are IKEA's customers likely to be?

4 What do the examples above have in common, and what are the differences?

Key terms

Tangible – items that have a physical presence and can be touched.

Intangible – items that do not have a physical presence and cannot be touched.

Psychological techniques

The psychological techniques that are used by retailers can be seen in the different types of display and product placement that we explored earlier in this unit and in the three examples given in the case study above. These techniques are either **tangible** or **intangible**.

Tangible

Tangible techniques come in many forms, shapes and sizes (see Table 16.4) and it will depend on the products or services being displayed as to which would be the most appropriate and effective.

▶ **Table 16.4:** Tangible techniques used by retailers to encourage sales

Tangible technique	Description
Store location	Location can mean the success or the failure of a business. A business that is average, but in the right location, is more likely to succeed than an excellent business in a poor location. This may change over time – for example, the popularity of out-of-town retail parks has grown in recent years to the detriment of the traditional high street.
Design and aesthetics	The design and aesthetics must be appropriate to the goods or services being sold and to the customers who are going to buy. For example, the difference in the store design and aesthetics between low- and high-end clothing stores reflect the likely wealth of their customers.
Store windows	This is what is going to entice the customer into the store – how many times have you entered a store based on what you saw in the window? Store window displays can be used as a talking point. For example, the Christmas windows at Harrods are 'unveiled' each year and customers come to view them and, possibly, shop in-store.
Transition zones	These are the areas directly inside the front door of the store. They can be put to good use with visual merchandising displays following the theme of the store, or by having their own dedicated theme for maximum impact. This can be a bad place for important signage as customers often walk straight through without noticing them. Also, by pausing to read signage, other customers might get stuck behind them.
Use of company and/or brand names	Some businesses rely on their company or brand name. Clever use reinforces the message and perceived importance of the company or brand to the customer. For example, Coca Cola. In 2011 Coca Cola launched a promotion to encourage the general public to share their product and were so confident in their brand that they replaced the Coca Cola logo on the bottle with a first name from a list of the most popular first names.
Fixtures positioning	Height and depth of fixtures are important. Customers quite often buy the first thing they see, which is likely to be at eye level. Retailers will therefore place products that they wish to sell more of, such as those that have higher profit margins, at eye level. This can also serve a practical purpose – some retailers place smaller-sized shoes on a lower shelf, correctly guessing that those customers are less likely to be able to reach higher shelves.
Signage	Retailers need to make it easy for customers to: • find products • pay for products • eg in clothes stores, find the fitting rooms. Signage needs to be easy to see with clear messaging using a minimum number of words. The position of signage is also important – in many stores with multiple levels there are clear signs for what is on each floor, positioned by the escalators or stairs.
Promotions	Promotional messages must get to the customer in the clearest and quickest possible way in order for the promotion to be effective. This can be done through displaying the products themselves or through the use of signage and other point of sale materials. Promotional products will often be grouped together – for example, promotional products in a supermarket are often of a type and positioned together so that customers are more likely to pick one up and consider another.

▶ **Table 16.4:** – *continued*

Odd versus even pricing	£4.99 can appear more attractive than £5, depending on the goods and services being sold. Retailers decide on the pricing policy for the goods they are selling and the expectations of their customers. Some retailers, such as Tiger, use even pricing – this can appear more 'honest' to a customer.
Fitting rooms	There are a variety of different kinds of fitting room and they usually mirror the image and quality of the products being sold. In all cases, fitting rooms should be clean and tidy, with unsold products put away as quickly as possible. The number of fitting rooms is also something the retailer must consider to ensure meeting customer needs. Some larger fitting rooms may have a display in a communal area of the fitting room.
Packaging design	Much time and research goes into the packaging design of most products. Packaging can be part of the buying experience: • expensive perfume or clothing will raise the customer's expectation of the packaging, eg paper carrier bags tied with colour coordinated ribbon • a plastic bag is satisfactory for items purchased from a discount store.
Angles and sight-lines	When the customer walks through the door, what is it that their eye is drawn to? This is where best-selling products or important messages should be placed.
Composition (vertical and horizontal)	Which is going to be easier for the customer to read? This has to be taken into consideration along with the design and layout of the display.
Point of sale (POS)	This is the place where the sale is made and completed. Thinking big picture, this could be a shopping mall; thinking smaller picture, this could be the area around the shop counter.
Displays	Physical objects will be used in displays such as mannequins, props and the actual goods. These vary depending on the type of store and the products to be displayed. An electronic goods retailer may just have a display of one single laptop, while a gift store might group together a number and variety of different products into one display.
In-store announcements	These are used to give messages to the customers, for example about: • items that have just been reduced • special offers or promotions • new products that have arrived in-store.

▶ Retailers use a variety of techniques that encourage us to buy their products

Intangible

Although not so many in number, intangible psychological techniques (Table 16.5) are just as important to visual merchandising as tangible techniques. This is what creates the atmosphere for the customer. It taps into the customer's feelings, perceptions and subconscious mind. It can reach out to all of the customer's senses beyond touch to create innovative and creative displays that are effective and increase the customer's buying desire.

Intangible technique	Description
Atmospherics	The following techniques can help to create an atmosphere that fits with the brand image of the retailer and the products or services it sells. • Music – when used appropriately, this is a good way to create an atmosphere, for example a health spa will play calming music to set a relaxing backdrop for their customers, whereas a retailer selling fashion clothing will want to energise their customers by playing upbeat music. • Mirrors – a clever way of making a display look larger than it is or to help reflect the light of sparkling products. Jewellery retailers use spotlights to enhance their displays and small boutique shops may line their walls with mirrors to give the impression that the shop is larger than it really is. • Lighting – good, bright lighting is used by many retailers when customers want to be able to identify the products they wish to purchase quickly or be able to read the labelling or see the colour. However, there are other retailers such as Hollister who use lighting to create a unique shopping experience through the use of low lighting. Spotlights are used to 'showcase' individual items – think of luxury goods displayed in glass cases in a department store, or hot food displays where lighting is combined with heat as part of the display.
Sensual environment	Our senses are a direct route to our feelings, emotions and memories which will have a direct impact on our buying behaviour. • Sight and touch are used as part of the buying experience. How often have you touched articles of clothing that you have been drawn to because of the colour or texture? Images of attractive people also play a part in the buying desire, known as the 'halo effect'. This means that, although we may not admit to it, when a product is adorned by an attractive image (such as an animal or person), we are likely to be more impressed by the product. • Scent and taste can be used directly and indirectly as part of the display. For example, food and drink displays will often have samples available for the customer to try, whereas other non-food retailers might have chocolates or drinks available as part of a wider promotion using a celebration theme. The same applies to scent when samples are available to try at perfumeries, or it can also be used to enhance the buying experience, such as a coconut scent being used in a travel agency. • Sound can be used to influence sales of products, for example playing French music when promoting French products. Sound can also be used to slow us down or speed us up, for example soft, slower music creates a more relaxed atmosphere, whereas loud up tempo music will create energy. • Temperature needs to be just right! Shoppers are coming into stores from outside, where it is likely to be colder and they will be dressed accordingly. If the store is too hot or too cold, the customer is more likely to leave quickly.
Visual effects	Visual effects are an important part of the display and will have an impact on the way in which the customer views the products. • Light can change the colour of a product, which can have a direct impact on the impression it leaves on the customer. Clothing and fashion stores will be promoting the latest colour schemes and so the lighting must not detract from, but should enhance, the product. • Colour is used by retailers to make them and their products/services easily identifiable. Colours will influence customers' choices, for instance, bright colours such as red and orange stand out, so, if a retailer wishes to attract the attention of their customers, they will use these colours. Cool colours such as blues and greens will create a feeling of calm and so retailers will use these colours when they want to create a feeling of relaxation. Think of Laura Ashley's green colour scheme branding, which sets the scene for home decoration, versus the fast food retailer KFC's red and white branding. A colour rebranding can be confusing for customers – consider McDonald's change to a more muted earth-tones colour scheme from their instantly recognisable red and yellow scheme. Background colour also needs to be considered to ensure that it does not clash with the items on display. • Texture creates interest and can be used abstractly to attract attention by either complementing or contrasting. Think of Apple stores, where texture is used to complement, ie the sleek products for sale displayed on equally sleek high benches with a minimalistic approach versus DFS furniture stores where the products and props are displayed to contrast with each other to make up a whole room effect. • Shape and dimension help to draw the customer's eye to the display, for instance, beauty retailers use triangular displays because the eye is drawn to the centre of the display. An odd number of products in a display will always be more attractive as the eye keeps moving around to look at each item, rather than seeing them as a whole. Displays should be uncluttered, and the principle 'less is more' really does apply here. Displaying fewer items at different heights and levels will add dimension.

▶ Lighting, music and display colours are all examples of intangible techniques

Discussion

Can you think of more examples of retailers who use psychological techniques, both tangible and intangible, in visual merchandising?

What techniques are they using? What products are they selling? How well have they demonstrated that they know their target market?

PAUSE POINT   How many of the tangible and intangible techniques can you list?

Hint   Close the book and write down all that you can remember.

Extend   Why do retailers use these techniques? How can tangible/intangible techniques be used to increase a business's success?

Research

Retailers use psychological techniques on their websites to promote and advertise their businesses. Visit three different retailers' websites and look at the different psychological techniques used.
- List common themes.
- Who is the target audience?
- Which websites do you find most appealing and why?
- What differences do you see between website 'displays' and the high street?

Technological techniques

Retailers who use technology within their visual merchandising displays do it to attract their customers' attention and to give more information in an interactive way than can be given through signage and point of sale materials. This can be seen in different ways, as shown in Table 16.6.

▶ **Table 16.6:** The use of technology within visual merchandising displays

Technology	What is it?	How and where could it be used?
Electronic displays to broadcast in-store advertising messages and information on services	• These are set up to display key messages and information using TV screens. • The content can be set up to change throughout the day, to ensure that key messages are displayed at set times. Scrolling messages can be set up to be displayed at the bottom of the screen, all of which can be controlled, amended and updated from a separate computer. • As messages need to change, updating can take place immediately and there is no 'paper wastage' or risk of using out-of-date material.	• These types of electronic displays work well in areas where the customer is waiting or requiring specific information. • Shopping malls often use large plasma screens to display up-to-date information such as any special events that are scheduled or any special offers that retailers may have on that day. • Opticians' waiting areas will often use electronic displays to broadcast any messages or offers that may be available. They also use these to announce when the optician is ready to see you – doctor's surgeries often use this method too.
Demonstrations of new products and services	In-store demonstrations of products are used in stores for short periods of time to promote sales of specific goods.	These demonstrations are often used for 'new to the market' products that customers may not be aware of.
Interactive/ touchscreen/ windows, interactive points of sale	Electronic note pads and tablets are made available for customers' use. This could be for the customer to obtain more information about the product or even to call over a sales assistant.	• They are used by a variety of retailers where the customer is encouraged to interact with the buying experience. • Travel agencies have devices available in their high street stores for customers to be able to book their own holidays or travel arrangements. • Computer shops have demonstrator models for customers to try out before they buy. These demonstration models are usually pre-programmed with all the information that the customer requires. • In stores such as Argos, customers can use a touchscreen to check that an item is in stock in the store before they order it.
QR (quick response) codes	This is a 2D bar code that can store information horizontally and vertically meaning that it can hold a massive amount of information. This means that a customer can scan the QR code using their smart phone to obtain more information on a product, or even be taken to a specific website or webpage.	• QR codes can be found on packaging, brochures, leaflets, posters, museum displays – in fact on almost anything. • The QR code is used by those promoting their product, service or business to enable the customer to obtain more information. This could be a direct link to a website, or an interactive webpage dedicated to that particular product.
Digital media	Digital media can be audio, video or photographic media that are created electronically.	• Digital media are used to advertise products in many different ways such as posters, promotional films or audio advertising. • Car showrooms often have large TV screens playing promotional films of their newest cars – quite often these tie in with a TV advertising campaign. • Films are often advertised using posters displayed on the sides of commercial vehicles, such as local buses. • Department stores will advertise promotional products through audio messages across their loud-speaker system.

Research

Displays using technology take up less space than mannequins, props or the goods themselves. They are used in the same way – to tell a story and influence customer sales.

- Research which businesses, locally or nationally, use technology in visual merchandising.
- Explain how this technology is used.
- Evaluate how this technology is used to increase business success.

▶ How are customers likely to react after watching an in-store demonstration? What skills are required by the demonstrator?

Discussion

What stores have you been in that use technology in their visual merchandising? What are they using? How effective is it and how does it make you feel? Does it make you more likely to buy the product?

Assessment practice 16.1

A.P1   A.P2   A.M1   A.D1   B.P3   B.P4   B.M2   B.D2

As part of a job application for a visual merchandising position, you must complete a written report evaluating two contrasting retail businesses and put together a presentation on the impact of legislation on visual merchandising.

The report should consider the effectiveness of the visual merchandising used in each of the businesses and the different approaches taken in terms of the display, psychological and technological techniques. It should evaluate the extent to which different visual merchandising and display techniques contribute to the success of the businesses.

You should explain how psychological and technological techniques have been used by these retail businesses and you should analyse and evaluate of how these techniques have contributed to business success.

Your presentation should consider legislation and safety in relation to visual merchandising.

Plan
- I know what I am being asked to do.
- I feel confident that the businesses I have chosen are suitable for this task.
- I am clear about what I need to include in my report.

Do
- I know where to find all the information I need about the businesses I have chosen.
- I can identify when I've gone wrong and adjust my thinking to get myself back on course.
- I have a plan in place (including timescales) to complete the piece of work.

Review
- I can explain what the task was and how I approached it.
- I can explain what I would do differently if I were to approach the task again.
- I can see which assessment criteria I have met and identify any areas for development to improve my grade.

C Create a successful display for a retail outlet through the use of appropriate visual merchandising techniques

This is the practical part of the unit, where you will be required to create a successful display for a retail outlet, using all the visual merchandising techniques that you have learned about. This is your chance to put your creative skills and knowledge of creating effective visual merchandising displays together. You will be required to have a certain amount of self-management and initiative to make your display unique and to ensure that you meet the objectives of making your display successful. The construction, planning and structure of your display will depend on the:

▶ products you are looking to promote

▶ type of retail outlet

▶ success factors that you will need to consider.

Before you decide what you are going to base your display on, this final part of the unit will focus on the different retail outlets, the success factors and the legal and safety aspects that you must consider.

Retail outlets

▶ 'Pop-up' shops are increasingly popular with small and big businesses to capitalise on seasonal sales

There are many kinds of retail outlet and the most common are outlined below.

▶ Department stores such as House of Fraser, John Lewis, Debenhams and Harvey Nichols are all well known and have a national presence (although they do vary in the number of stores they each have). There are also independent family-owned department stores across the country, such as Banburys in Barnstable, Barkers of Northallerton and Hancock & Wood in Warrington.

▶ Discount stores come in many different guises, such as the Pound Shop, TK Maxx and Home Sense, offering a range of products for sale at 'bargain prices'.

▶ Supermarkets – the four recognised national chains are J Sainsbury plc, Tesco, Asda and Morrisons. However, there are others such as Waitrose, Lidl and the Co-operative, which target specific markets such as luxury and convenience, as well as individual supermarkets that are independently owned and quite often specialise in foods from certain countries to offer to their local community.

- Hypermarkets are found in out of town locations, Asda and Tesco being the two most recognised retailers. These are very large-scale stores that combine a supermarket and department store. They offer a wide range of products such as clothing, shoes, home appliances and groceries. The idea of these stores is to offer everything the customer requires under one roof.
  - Convenience tobacco newsagents (CTNs) tend to be run by small independent businesses, although there are national chains, such as McColls. CTNs have a presence in the high street, although they can also be found in residential areas to provide convenience items for local residents.
  - Factory outlets can be found across the country and vary in terms of what they offer. Factory outlets give retail businesses the opportunity to sell stock that may not pass the scrutiny of quality control, and which is then sold as 'seconds'. For example, items may have minor flaws in them, such as a crooked seam on a piece of clothing or a misaligned pattern on a piece of china, which mean they cannot be sold in a main high street store. Also, previous season's ranges are sold in such retail outlet stores. The stores can be stand-alone or they can be found in 'outlet villages' where many different retailers can be found in one dedicated location. Examples of outlet villages include Bicester Village in Oxfordshire and Boundary Mill Store at Colne, Lancashire.
  - Not-for-profit organisations include charities which have their own chain of retail outlets on the high street such as Oxfam, Cancer Research and Save the Children. There are also one-off shops in towns across the country that are run by local charities. Other organisations, such as the National Trust, raise money through shops attached to their historical properties, and the RNLI (Royal National Lifeboat Institution) may have a shop attached or close to a life boat station.
  - 'Pop-up' shops are used for seasonal and holiday occasions, such as at Christmas, Easter or the summer holidays as well as for special promotions. An example would be BMW promoting their Mini cars by opening a pop-up shop to promote their latest model in the main area of a shopping mall or a hypermarket. Another example would be a specialist retailer setting up a pop-up shop in a department store selling their seasonal goods such as Christmas foods or decorations.
  - Farm shops are situated away from large town or city centres and can be found in smaller market towns and on actual farms. They promote country lifestyles and quite often continue the theme by offering more than just farm-produced food products, for example, clothing, pottery and even a cafe.
  - Outdoor/indoor markets are popular in cities and towns throughout the country and can be a permanent fixture or a weekly feature. They promote an image of offering local, hand-crafted goods as well as bargains and unique products for sale.

- A fruit and vegetable stall is a very colourful display

Success factors

Effective displays encourage customers to enter a store and to maximise their purchases. It will not be down to just good luck, or just to the skills of the individual. The successful visual merchandiser will ask themselves questions like the ones shown in Figure 16.1.

> What is the appropriate merchandising style for the product/business or the type of outlet it is being sold in?
>
> What are the most appropriate props and displays to use?
>
> How can I ensure that the signage and graphics I use will be effective?

▶ **Figure 16.1:** A successful visual merchandiser will think hard about how they are going to tempt customers into their store and keep them there!

Table 16.7 looks at retail outlets in more detail in terms of their success factors.

> **Key term**
>
> **Visual standards** – retailers that have more than one outlet will want to ensure that each site has a visual consistency. The displays are likely to be identical in each of the outlets and they will have a consistent theme and be of the same quality.

▶ **Table 16.7:** Retail outlets and their success factors

Retail outlet	Success factors
Department stores	• Department stores have a high street location. • Their window displays aim to be 'on trend' offering the latest fashions and products. • The window displays are themed and changed regularly. • Inside, the use of mannequins and props are important to maintain the interest of the customer and to ensure that the products are displayed to meet the **visual standards** of the store.
Discount stores	• Discount stores use their windows to communicate to their customers using digitally produced posters and banners. • They use a combination of red and white in their graphics as these colours are often associated with sales and bargains. • Inside the stores, the products will be placed on racking and in bins, usually in a mass display.
Supermarkets	Supermarkets do not use their windows for displays. They use the inside of the store and the success factor here is to use the appropriate displays and product placements for the products they are selling. For instance, supermarkets that sell clothing will use mannequins (depending on the space available) and display their clothing using the techniques of fashion outlets. By contrast, food is displayed very differently, for instance, a 'market' style will be used for fresh fruit and vegetables, while ambient products will be displayed on shelves and at the end of aisles.
Hypermarkets	• Hypermarkets have a main body, which is the supermarket, and around this there are smaller outlets/retailers offering a variety of products and services. The other outlets could include sectors such as travel agencies, shoe repairers, key cutters or florists. • The success factors for the hypermarket will be similar to those of the supermarkets, but on a larger scale. Graphic images are used and corporate signage is positioned above the aisles to keep customers informed about what types of product they will find in each of them. • The outlets within the complex of the hypermarket will also need to ensure that they meet the visual standards of the hypermarket in order to complement the overall image.

▶ **Table 16.7:** – *continued*

Convenience, tobacco and newsagents stores	• These smaller retailers quite often have small windows used to display the goods that they are selling. • The suppliers they use will install points of sale within the shop, which gives a professional image that the retailer might not be able to afford. • Hand written promotions and posters may be used – these work well in this situation, giving the impression of a local personal service.
Not-for-profit organisations	• These businesses are created to raise money for a cause and any profits they make go towards this cause. Charity shops are a good example of this. • Some of the larger national charities have professional looking retail outlets, whereas more local charities will not. • The success factors are the way that the charity shops display their products using mannequins, props, signage and graphics.
Pop-up shops	• Pop-up shops are just that – they are created and designed to have a short life over a seasonal period, such as Christmas or the summer months. • They need a wow factor to attract the attention of customers and to make it inviting for the customer to walk into the shop. • Pop-up shops can be found in a variety of locations, such as shopping malls and the high street. • It depends on the products being sold as to the merchandising style being used.
Farm shops	• Farm shops are usually located away from the high street and can be found in villages, small towns or actually on or near a farm. • They will have a rustic, yet modern, theme which will start on the outside of the building, setting the scene of what the customer can expect inside. • They do not always have a window so rely heavily on in-store displays. • Many sell more than just food so use attractive displays to encourage impulse buying of sometimes quite abstract purchases, such as clothing and kitchen equipment.
Outdoor/indoor markets	• Outdoor and/or indoor markets can be static. This means they are set up on a permanent basis and the stall holder can leave their goods on the stall. Alternatively, they can be transient, meaning that the stall holder has to set up their stall with their goods each time there is a market and then pack up at the end of the day. • The stalls used are quite small and so the stall holder has to display their goods in a way that shows off the products, but without overcrowding, so that the customer can see what is actually for sale. The products will be the main focus of the display, with a limited amount of signage (which may be used to explain the origin of a product, or how to use it).
Factory outlet	• When grouped together in a factory outlet 'village', the factory outlet stores often have the same visual image as their high street mainstream stores so that they can be recognised instantly by their customers. • Alternatively, the stores may go for a 'bargain' or 'reduced price' visual display by blanking out the windows with giant posters stating that the goods inside are greatly reduced. • There are also stand-alone factory outlet stores that have a warehouse appearance, such as the retailer 'Factory Outlet' which can be found in the high street and out of town centre locations.

Discussion

What visual standards would you expect to see in each of the stores listed above? What are the benefits to the retailer in having visual standards? How does it have an impact on the overall business success?

Ⅱ PAUSE POINT   Which retail outlet will you base your display in or on? What will the success factors be and how will you measure them?

Hint   Use Table 16.7 to plan your ideas. Research by looking at displays in retail outlets. Plan how to achieve your end goal.

Extend   Seek and use feedback. Be imaginative in creating the display. Use your initiative and keep to the plan, using self-management.

Legal and safety aspects

Health and safety, risk assessment and ticketing legislation are all important aspects of visual merchandising. The safety of the customer and those working in the store needs to be considered and regular risk assessments should be carried out.

Health and safety

The employer and the employee each have a responsibility towards health and safety at work. Adequate and appropriate training must be given, where required, and personal protective equipment (PPE) must be supplied by the employer. In return, the employee must follow instructions given in training and wear the PPE supplied. The workplace must be maintained to ensure that it is a safe place to work and, in return, the employee must work in a way that ensures that personal safety and the safety of others whether they are customers or colleagues. The main causes of accidents in the workplace are summarised in Figure 16.2.

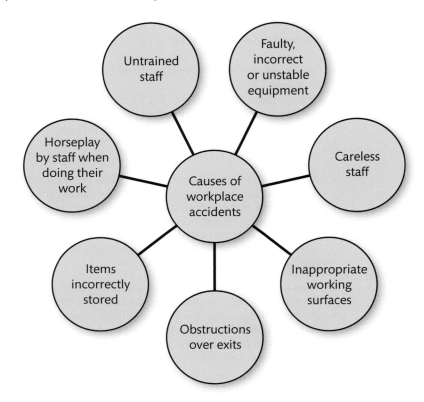

▶ **Figure 16.2:** The main causes of workplace accidents

Safety tip

Causes of workplace accidents:
- untrained staff
- faulty, incorrect or unstable equipment
- careless staff
- inappropriate working surfaces
- obstructions over exits
- items incorrectly stored
- horseplay by staff when doing their work.

Discussion

Can you think of other examples of how workplace accidents might be caused?
Can you think of any real-life examples?

Link

Go to *Unit 16: Visual Merchandising topic A* to find more information about point of
sale (POS), ticketing and display safety, and legislation in visual merchandising.

Risk assessment

Every task and process at work will have an element of **risk** to it, no matter how small.
For example, when a floor plan is designed, you must ensure that it does not have
any trip **hazards** where customers or members of staff could injure themselves. You
should be looking around the sales floor and display areas asking yourself questions,
like the ones shown in Figure 16.3.

Key terms

Risks – the risk is the chance, high or low, that somebody could be harmed by an
identified hazard, together with an indication of how serious the harm could be.

Hazards – a hazard is anything that may cause harm, such as chemicals, electricity,
working from ladders, an open drawer etc.

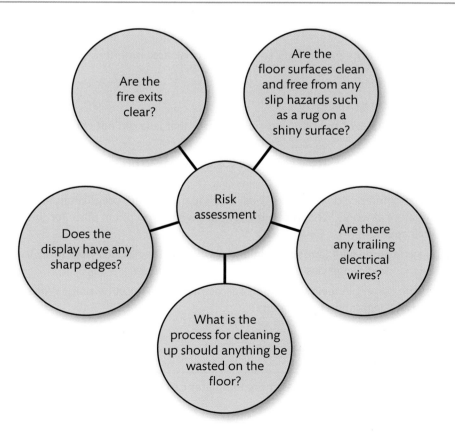

▶ **Figure 16.3:** Take a good look around the sales floor and ask yourself if everything is as safe as
it can be

Five steps to risk assessment.

`5 Steps`

Jane was put in charge of the risk assessment for her company which had concessions within a large department store in five different towns. After seeking advice from her manager, she downloaded the risk assessment template from the government website and decided to follow the five steps to risk assessment.

1 To find possible hazards, Jane checked the accident book and spoke to colleagues in each store, before inspecting the floor space of the concession, the actual displays and the display area. Risks identified included step-ups for reaching above shoulder areas, fire hazards and trailing wires.

2 Jane then looked at 'who' was at risk. She considered the ages, fitness and experience of her colleagues. There was one pregnant woman. Jane made a special note of this.

3 Jane set the level of each risk identified. She decided that the step-up was most hazardous, followed by the fire hazard – in this case keeping fire exits clear.

4 Jane recorded her findings on her risk assessment template, putting in sufficient detail about what hazards she had found and measures to reduce the likelihood of the hazard causing any harm.

5 Jane put a note in her diary to review her risk assessment in six months' time.

Check your knowledge

1 Can you think of any other possible hazards that Jane did not consider in step 1?

2 Why did Jane look in the accident book and speak to her colleagues in step 1?

3 What difference does it make to an individual if they are pregnant in terms of safety at work? What recommendations would you put in place for this colleague?

4 Do you agree with Jane's assessment of which of the hazards were likely to be the most dangerous? Give a reason for your answer.

5 Is Jane correct in reviewing the risk assessment in six months' time? What does the legislation recommend?

Tip

Health and safety and risk assessment templates can be downloaded from the government website:

www.hse.gov.uk/risk/risk-assessment-and-policy-template.doc

Ticketing legislation

It depends on the types of goods and/or services that are being sold and on display as to what the law says must be displayed on the label or ticket.

There are laws around food labelling and the retailer must ensure that the information on the label is:

▶ clear, easy to read and to understand

▶ permanent

▶ easily visible

▶ not misleading.

The name of the food must be displayed with a 'best before' or 'use by' date and there must be a list of ingredients with quantities showing.

For other goods and services, you don't have to show particular information on the label for every kind of product, but, if you include it, you must be accurate. There are special rules for some products and their retailers, such as precious metals, footwear, food and drink, and products for children. Labels must not be misleading about things like:

▶ quantity or size

▶ the price

▶ what it is made of

▶ how, where and when it was made

▶ what you say it can do

▶ the people or organisations that endorse it.

In all cases, you must include safety information for products that could be dangerous.

Research

Look at a number of different retailers' ticketing and labels. Can you see any trends when the same products are being sold, or when different products are sold? How does the information given by each retailer differ? What are the key pieces of information being given? Is each retailer meeting the legislation requirements?

If you are a retailer, you must display:

▶ the price of the products – this must be in pounds sterling and include VAT, where applicable

▶ the price of a single item (the unit price) for products that are sold loose

▶ metric measures (like kilograms, centimetres or litres) for unit pricing – except for some products (for example, beer is still sold in pints).

Ⅱ **PAUSE POINT**   What parts of the health and safety and ticketing legislation are going to apply to your display?

Hint   It is never a good idea to 'guess' what the law says, so do your research to ensure that you have the right information.

Extend   What are the implications if you do not meet the legislative requirements when displaying and selling goods?

Assessment practice 16.2

You are invited to the second stage of the interview and must create a display for the business, a retail outlet.

The employer is looking for someone who can demonstrate self-management and initiative in the presentation of a high-quality successful display through creative use of visual merchandising.

Plan and create an individual visual merchandising display, keeping all the planning documents and notes as evidence.

Keep records (including photographs, witness statements and observation records) throughout to show how you demonstrate individual self-management and initiative to present a high-quality, successful visual merchandising display.

When you have completed the display, obtain feedback and recommendations and use this information to assess your display's success.

Plan

- I have access to the resources I need to create my display.
- I know how much time to allocate to each part of the task.
- I will keep all my evidence in an organised way.

Do

- I have set myself milestones to ensure that I am on track.
- I am making the most of support available.
- I know how I can overcome things that I am struggling with.

Review

- If I have gone wrong anywhere, I can explain how and why.
- I can describe my thought process throughout both tasks.
- I was able to link the learning from both parts of the task

---

Further reading and resources

Bailey, S and Baker, J *Visual Merchandising for Fashion (Basics Fashion Management)*, Bloomsbury Publishing (2014)

Morgan, T *Visual Merchandising: Window and In-Store Displays for Retail*, 2nd edition Laurence King (2011)

Richards R. *Visual Merchandise Display*, The Business Education Centre (2013)

www.internationalvisual.com

A specialist visual merchandising company offering tips, recommendations and advice for visual displays, through a series of pictures.

www.retail-focus.co.uk

A retail specialist website with news and magazine-style articles for the retail industry.

www.drapersonline.com

Specialising in the fashion industry, a specialist website giving fashion business intelligence, seasonal and sector analysis, industry opinions and best practice.

www.retailstorewindows.com

A blog website where visual merchandising thoughts, ideas and observations are discussed.

THINK ▶FUTURE

Lauren Massey

Freelance visual merchandiser

I started my career working for a local fashion company, as a sales assistant. I then completed a course at the Fashion Retail Academy in London and got a job as an in-store visual merchandiser for a national fashion retailer (GAP). I was in charge of graphics and signage, so I was responsible for posters, point of sale and ticketing on hangers as well as ensuring that rack displays and mannequins were dressed to company standards. I then became a visual merchandiser for a fashion designer concession (Ossie Clark, London), where I was responsible for visual merchandising standards across six concessions, each based in different large department stores. I was expected to use my initiative to display new stock by creating a theme or fashion story building on the original ideas from the designer. I needed to know who our customers were and the surrounding retail climate. I sent a weekly report to head office including footfall, best sellers, events in the area, weather, in-store events and customer feedback, all of which could affect the business.

Being a visual merchandiser let me set up my own vintage range of clothing and accessories online. The experience and skills I have gained from working as a visual merchandiser means I understand how to present products in groupings. I style whole outfits which I advertise online, giving customers the option to buy the whole or part of the costume design.

Focusing your skills

Making a difference

You are a key asset to the retailer. As a visual merchandiser, you should consider the following.

- Fashion and trends – what are your interests? What products would you enjoy working with? Can you spot the latest trends?
- Creativity – can you put colour schemes together? Can you see themes and 'stories' to build into a display? Where do you get your inspiration?
- Attention to detail – can you see the finer points that make a display complete? Do you have an 'eye for style'?
- Stamina – visual merchandising can be physically demanding and is not just a one-off. Do you have the enthusiasm to keep displays fresh? Do you have the enthusiasm to 'start again' as the displays need to be changed?

Business skills

These are essential to ensure that the effectiveness of the visual display is transferred to the business' success.

- Identify what will sell – especially when given autonomy for what will be displayed. You must recognise what is selling well, or what will sell well to maximise the business opportunity.
- Stock control – there must be enough stock available to ensure that the store can meet the sales generated. If stocks run low, the display must change unless a quick re-order is possible.
- Communication – you cannot work alone. Communication with the sales team, peers and senior management is vital to ensure the company's visual standards are met.
- Report writing – capturing local information and passing it on to management is essential to ensure displays and product placement are kept up to date and meet customer needs.

Getting ready for assessment

Jacob is working towards a BTEC Level 3 National Extended Diploma in Business and has chosen visual merchandising as an optional unit. His first assignment entitled 'Applying for a job as a visual merchandiser' covers learning aims A and B. The task was to research two contrasting retail businesses and create a written report, presenting the findings as part of the 'job application'. The report and the presentation needed to cover:

▶ effectiveness of visual merchandising used in each business

▶ different approaches each business used in terms of the display, psychological and technological techniques

▶ an explanation of how visual merchandising is affected by legal and safety regulations.

How I got started

▶ I thought about the two contrasting businesses that I was going to use. It was important to choose two businesses that were local so that I could look around them. I thought about what criteria I was going to use to measure the effectiveness of each business. I went back over my notes on the different display techniques and why they are used and the psychological and technological techniques used in visual merchandising. This helped me decide the criteria to use.

▶ I kept my notes on health and safety and the legal issues in a separate folder because, although this was an important part of the assignment, what I was required to do was explain how visual merchandising is affected by legal and safety regulations. I planned to link this part of the assignment to the two businesses that I was researching.

▶ As I was aiming for a distinction, I focused on the relevant assessment criteria (A.D1 and B.D2). This meant I needed to evaluate my research findings within my report and presentation. There would be analysis and explanation too, but I needed to ensure that my work was weighted towards the evaluation.

How I brought it all together

We had been given a format to follow for the report. This is how I went about completing my work.

▶ I jotted down my findings, in no particular order, onto one sheet of A4 – a bit like a spidergram, so I could see everything on one page.

▶ I went back over this page, putting my points in order and ticking them off as I included them in the report.

▶ I created my presentation, based on the key points from my written work.

▶ I used diagrams or models to explain the points I was making.

▶ I checked the assignment brief to ensure that I had covered all aspects of the learning aims.

▶ I kept all stages of my work including doodles and notes, in case I needed to refer to them again.

▶ I studied the different images that we covered in our lessons and then searched the recommended websites to get ideas on what makes visual merchandising effective and which displays were likely to work well in the businesses that I had chosen.

What I learned from the experience

▶ I was pleased with my choice of businesses and I took lots of notes while visiting them. I wish now that I had taken photographs. This would have been useful to look back on and use in my presentation. It would have been much easier to have shown the photographs than trying to explain what I meant.

▶ It would have been useful to have had a detailed action plan with dates against each action to ensure that I was on target to complete by the deadline.

Think about it

▶ Have you thought about the different types of businesses you want to use in your report? Have you made sure that you can find out enough information about your chosen businesses?

▶ Have you created a plan for your assessment including times and dates, and milestones, for you to work against?

▶ Do you feel confident about delivering your presentation? What can you do to help if not? Are you happy with your level of writing for your written report?

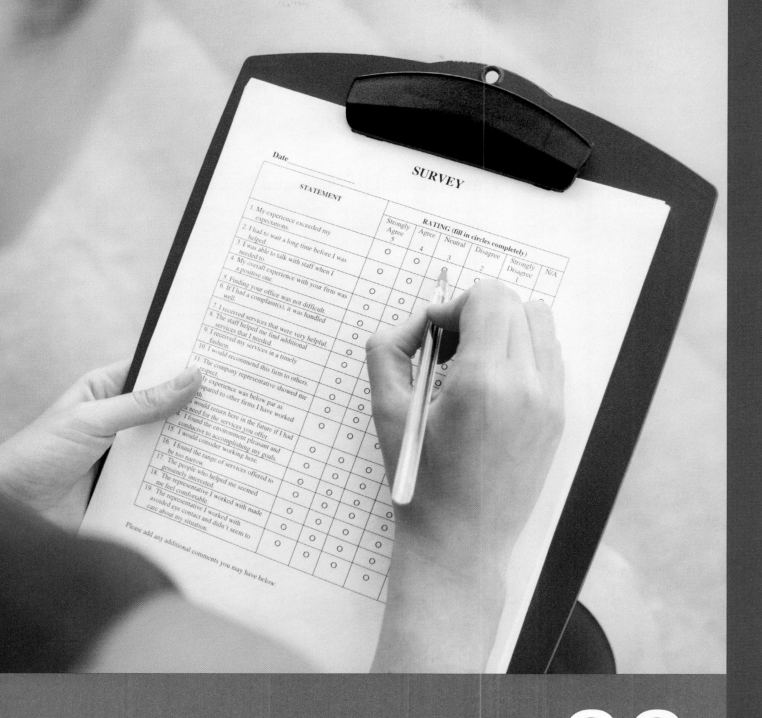

Market Research 22

Getting to know your unit

Assessment
You will be assessed by a series of assignments set by your tutor.

Marketing information plays an important role in identifying and satisfying customers' needs. To obtain this information, businesses follow certain processes and carry out research. Once the marketing information is collated, businesses analyse and interpret the data so they can improve their product or the service they supply, or so they can offer new products or services.

How you will be assessed

This unit will be assessed by a series of internally assessed tasks set by your tutor. Throughout this unit you will find assessment practices that will help you work towards your assessment. Completing these activities will not mean that you have achieved a particular grade, but you will have carried out useful research or preparation that will be relevant when it comes to your final assignment.

In order for you to achieve the tasks in your assignments, it is important to check that you have met all of the Pass grading criteria. You can do this as you work your way through the assignment.

If you are hoping to gain a Merit or Distinction, you should also make sure that you present the information in your assignment in the style that is required by the relevant assessment criterion. For example, Merit criteria require you to analyse and discuss, and Distinction criteria require you to assess and evaluate.

The assignments set by your tutor will consist of a number of tasks designed to meet the criteria in the table. This is likely to consist of a written assignment but may also include activities such as the following:

▶ a report explaining the different types of research used in a chosen business
▶ a practical task of drawing up a market research plan that you then implement
▶ an analysis and interpretation of your practical market research activity.

Assessment criteria

This table shows you what you must do in order to achieve a **Pass**, **Merit** or **Distinction** grade, and where you can find activities to help you.

Pass	Merit	Distinction

Learning aim **A** Examine the types of market research used by business

Pass	Merit	Distinction
A.P1 Explain the range of market research methods used by a selected business. **Assessment practice 22.1**	**A.M1** Assess, using suitable examples, how different market research methods are appropriate in helping to meet marketing objectives and inform decision making. **Assessment practice 22.1**	**A.D1** Justify the use of using specialist marketing agencies for carrying out original market research. **Assessment practice 22.1**

Learning aim B Plan and implement a market research activity to meet a specific marketing objective

Pass	Merit	Distinction
B.P2 Undertake secondary research for a selected marketing objective. **Assessment practice 22.2** **B.P3** Undertake pilot primary market research and collect sample data. **Assessment practice 22.2** **B.P4** Undertake the final market research activity using a detailed sampling plan to obtain a range of secondary and primary data. **Assessment practice 22.2**	**A.M1** Analyse the reasons for choosing particular research methods, the type of data to be collected and the sampling plan. **Assessment practice 22.2**	**B.D2** Evaluate the effectiveness of the pilot research recommending changes that should be made to the final market research activity. **Assessment practice 22.2**

Learning aim C Analyse and present market research findings and recommend process improvements

Pass	Merit	Distinction
C.P5 Interpret findings from the market research undertaken, presenting them in a range of different formats. **Assessment practice 22.3**	**C.M3** Analyse the findings of the market research using a wide range of statistical techniques and comment on confidence levels. **Assessment practice 22.3**	**C.D3** Assess the limitations of the data collected and justify research planning process improvements in light of the work undertaken. **Assessment practice 22.3**

Getting started

The purpose of market research is to obtain information that businesses can use to understand what their customers want and need. Techniques include questionnaires and interviews. Have you ever been asked survey questions in the street or by phone? Or received a questionnaire through the post? Watch for opportunities that businesses use to gather information. Keep a record of every time you come across any market research activity, noting what is being asked and through which medium

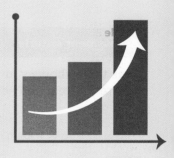

Examine the types of market research used by businesses

Purpose of market research

Businesses have many different reasons for undertaking market research and the outcome, or objectives, they wish to achieve will determine their main purpose for the research. In all cases, businesses want to gather data on their customers, potential customers, competitors and the general market place. This data will support the marketing and other business decisions that the organisation makes and reduce the risks involved in making those important decisions. Table 22.1 explores some of the reasons why a business might want to carry out market research.

▶ **Table 22.1:** Five reasons why businesses should undertake market research

Purpose	Explanation	Benefits and examples
Understanding customer behaviour	• Businesses need to understand who wants their products and/or services and why their customers want them. • They also need to establish how they can convince people to buy their products and services.	• Businesses can act on what drives their customers into making purchases and identify what customers are looking for in terms of benefits. • Marketing messages can then be used to encourage certain feelings in customers. For example insurance companies will often use fear in their marketing messages such as 'What will happen if you are not insured?', whereas an upmarket travel company will use exclusivity such as 'Private helicopter transfer is included from the airport to your hotel'.
Determining buying trends	• Identifying upward customer trends is important to the success of new and existing businesses. • Different generations will have unique buying patterns and many marketing budgets will be based on the spending habits and lifestyles of these different generations where trends can be identified.	• Businesses can understand how different types of customers use a product and where they are likely to purchase it. • For example the **millennial** generation is likely to purchase a mobile telephone online and use it for games, emails, social media and telephone calls. A phone company would need to determine what differences (if any) there would be between this generation and the **baby boomer** generation.
Investigating brand/advertising awareness	Brand awareness of a business and the effectiveness of its advertising can be tested through market research. This will ensure that marketing budgets are directed to areas where most impact can be made to promote the brand.	• By knowing how aware their customers are of advertising promotions and their brand, businesses can establish how effective their campaigns are and marketing budgets can be allocated to where most impact can be made for maximum effect. • Quite often customer surveys include specific questions which are related to an organisation's brand or a specific advertising campaign.

▶ **Table 22.1:** – *continued*

Aiding new product development	When developing a new product and/or service, businesses will seek the opinions and thoughts of customers and potential customers before taking it to market. This could include customers trying out products in store, being sent samples or the launch of pilot schemes in local areas.	• Using customer comments will help a business to make changes and adapt their products or services to ensure they meet the needs and desires of their present and future customers on a large scale. • For example, a large restaurant chain offered a 'sample menu' in key locations across the country. They then asked their customers in those restaurants what dishes they had ordered, what they thought of the menu and whether they would recommend the restaurant with its new menu to their friends and family. This helped to determine the menu that was rolled out in all of the restaurants.
Investigating feasibility of entry into new markets	• Before entering into a new market, a business needs to ensure that there is a demand for its product or service and that the market is not already saturated. • This will involve talking to key stakeholders inside and outside of the business, as well as potential and existing customers.	• A thorough feasibility study that involves all key players will ensure that a new product launch has a fair chance of success. Knowing what the current and predicted usage of a product will be is invaluable to a business as well as knowing what impact the product will have on the market. • This information will influence whether or not a business will go ahead into the new market or whether they need to make any changes to their plans.

Discussion

If you were going to start up your own business, which of the main purposes of market research in Table 22.1 would be most relevant? How would you prioritise the main purposes? Are there any that would not be relevant to you? Why would you make these decisions?

Research

Customers often use social media, such as Instagram or Facebook to communicate about a brand. For example, they may share pictures of meals or hotel rooms. Some organisations and businesses monitor their customers and reply to comments. This is a direct opportunity to pick up valuable market research data. Use the internet to check the Facebook pages of organisations you are familiar with and see what conversation topics are trending.

Which pages are most effective? Are they also the most popular? Is there anything that you would change to improve them? Give reasons for each of your answers.

Key terms

Baby boomers – a generation of the population born between 1946 and 1964.

Millennials – a generation of the population born between 1982 and 2000.

Types of research

Businesses use many different types of research as part of their market research. The appropriate method, or combination of methods, selected depends on the desired outcome and objectives of the research.

Here are some key types of market research used by businesses.

▶ **Qualitative research** – used to gain an understanding of what customers are thinking and what motivates them. It can provide an insight into a problem or it can help to develop ideas. Quite often qualitative research is gathered through face-to-face interviews or focus groups where **respondents** are encouraged to elaborate on their answers.

Key term

Respondent – person who replies to a questionnaire or survey to supply information.

Link

For the differences between quantitative and qualitative research, look at Table 2.2 in *Unit 2: Developing a Marketing Campaign*.

▶ **Quantitative research** – customers or potential customers are asked structured questions so that hard facts can be obtained. The questions are likely to be closed questions and do not allow the respondent to elaborate on their answers or give their opinions. From these replies, statistical data can be drawn up and analysed. Quantitative research is usually gathered through surveys or questionnaires. By asking a large group of people the same questions, a business can build up a picture of how customers behave.

▶ **Primary research** – research is carried out with the named objective, for the first time, to answer specific questions or as an exploratory exercise. Primary research can be carried out in many ways, including via surveys, observation, e-marketing, focus groups and pilot research. It can help to define a specific problem and will usually involve questionnaires as well as interviews or focus groups where detailed questioning can take place and lengthy answers can be obtained from a small group of respondents.

PAUSE POINT Outline the differences between qualitative and quantitative research.

Hint Try drawing a table and listing as many types of features of each of these types of research as you can.

Extend Are there any examples of qualitative and quantitative research you have been involved in? How did you find the process?

Research

Using the internet, undertake your own secondary research on a shopping centre near you. Find out the annual footfall, catchment population, details of customer profiles, average visiting frequency and age profiles of its visitors.

▶ **Secondary research** – existing research that has already been compiled and organised is used. A business might use sources such as the internet, newspapers or company reports to gather information. For example, if a retailer is considering opening a store in a particular shopping centre, they can undertake internet research to obtain information such as customer profiles or the annual footfall (by visiting the website of the shopping centre). It is quicker and more cost effective for the retailer to use this secondary research rather than undertaking their own (primary) research (for example, by going to the shopping centre).

Primary research

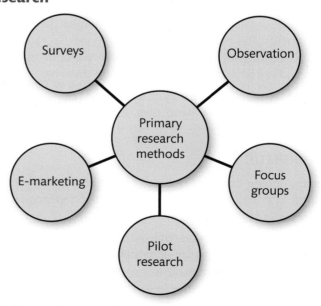

▶ **Figure 22.1:** Primary research methods

Figure 22.1 demonstrates some of the main methods of carrying out primary research.

▶ Surveys – used as a detailed study to obtain data on factors which include attitudes, impressions, opinions or satisfaction levels. This can be done by asking questions either face-to-face or through methods such as online or postal questionnaires.

▶ Observation – used to obtain primary research where customers or potential customers are observed. This could be footfall of shoppers, or their eye movements when looking at a display (to identify what attracts their attention), volume of traffic on a road or how drivers conform to the highway code.

▶ E-marketing – online consumer panels are used by small and large businesses to obtain information either as a one-off or as part of an ongoing project. Many people prefer to answer online questionnaires and these can be used alongside other research methods such as focus groups or face-to-face surveys in order to validate the online findings.

▶ Focus groups – a hand-picked group of people are brought together and questioned on their opinions of a specific product or service. This is a form of qualitative research where people are asked a variety of questions such as what they think of the packaging or size of a product.

▶ Pilot research – in this method, a control group of people try out a product or service and give feedback to the business about how they got on with the product or service and what they thought of it. This can give the business a better understanding of the market, including the customers' perceptions and expectations, as well as lead to a faster and smoother roll-out of the product or service.

Internal and external

Internal and external resources are also important types of research used by businesses regularly.

Internal

▶ Loyalty schemes – many retailers use loyalty schemes based on their customers' spending habits. These businesses can then track the spending behaviour of their customers. Think of loyalty cards that are used by supermarkets such as Sainsbury's Nectar Card or Tesco's Clubcard. Companies send their customers money off coupons or targeted emails, based on each customer's spending habits which have been identified through the use of the loyalty card.

▶ EPOS records (Electronic Point of Sale) – is a computerised system that records the sale of goods or services to customers. It is a self-contained system that can take all methods of payments including bank and credit card sales, verifying them as part of the purchase. It can also manage and report on other functions such as stock control. Businesses can gather historical data from an EPOS system, for example which are the most popular products and at what time of year sales are highest.

▶ Website monitoring – businesses use cookies to track how people are using their website. They can identify the amount of time a visitor spends on the website and which pages they go to. The number of visitors to a website can also be tracked. You are likely to have seen the pop-up message that appears when you go onto certain websites, advising you that they are using cookies.

▶ Accounting records – this historical data can be used by businesses to identify the spending and ordering habits of their customers. This will tell them when to expect busy times in order to ensure they are fully stocked and staffed to be able to deal with demand.

> **Link**
>
> Internal and external resources were introduced in *Unit 2: Developing a Marketing Campaign.*

External

- Internet – there is a vast amount of information concerning market research available on the internet. It is important that the information and data being used is reliable and up to date. It is a good idea to use other sources of market research as well as the internet, although using the internet effectively can cut down on the amount of time and money spent.
- Government statistics – these are available on government websites and cover a whole range of topics that would be useful in market research such as the population and **demographics** of regions across the country.
- Competitor reports – these are often available on the internet, for example the accounts that registered businesses must submit to Companies House. This information can then be purchased through a variety of websites.
- Specialist market research agencies, for example Mintel – some businesses buy in expertise such as the services of a market research company. This might be because they do not have the internal expertise or time to dedicate to a specific market research product. Communication is key when working with specialist market research agencies to ensure that they understand the objectives and purpose of the research.

Key term

Demographic – the statistical data of a population such as age, income, education, gender, race etc.

Appropriateness of the choice of research methods

Depending on the purpose of the research, some assessment methods are better than others. There are also other factors that need to be considered such as those outlined below.

- **Cost** – some methods of research are very expensive, while others can be undertaken with little cost attached. Gathering primary data by stopping people in the street to ask specific questions, or observing how many customers walk through a shop door is both time consuming and costly. By contrast, undertaking secondary research on the internet using data that has already been gathered from another source, is much quicker to obtain and does not tie up a member of staff for days at a time. However, if a business wanted to use a specialist market research agency, then there would be a significant cost involved. Businesses need to consider the scope of the research they wish to undertake to ensure that the best option is chosen, in relation to cost. Most market research will have a budget that must be considered.
- **Accuracy** – secondary research must be verified to ensure that the data are accurate. When using surveys and questionnaires, businesses must be aware of who is responding to their questions and be sure that the answers given by the respondents are an accurate reflection of what they are really thinking. For example, an online survey might seem less reliable than a focus group, but you would need to consider who else is involved in the focus group. People may be less inclined to speak their mind about sensitive topics in front of other people. In some instances anonymity, eg via an online survey, might produce more honest replies. Ensure that any survey questions will not result in ambiguous answers.
- **Timelines** – an adequate amount of time must be allowed to ensure that the data can be collected, collated and analysed for the research to be meaningful. When undertaking primary research, is there enough time to distribute surveys and then wait for the responses to come in, to conduct consumer interviews, or to set up a focus group? Timelines are also important when completing secondary research to ensure that there is sufficient time to browse the internet, newspapers or libraries. Many businesses will conduct market research to a specific schedule to ensure they get the result they need prior to their next action, for example a product proposal or new marketing campaign.

▶ **Response rates** – certain factors must be taken into consideration that could affect the response rate to any questionnaire or survey (see Figure 22.2).

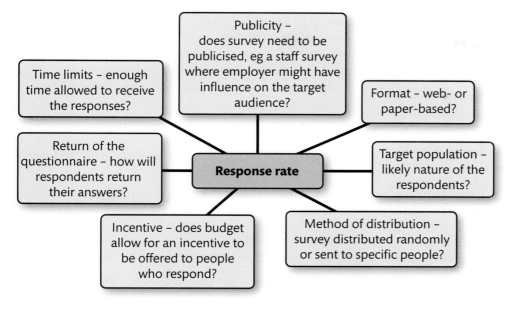

▶ **Figure 22.2:** Factors that could affect the response rate to a questionnaire or survey

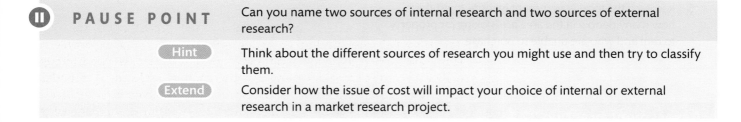

Ⅱ **PAUSE POINT** Can you name two sources of internal research and two sources of external research?

Hint Think about the different sources of research you might use and then try to classify them.

Extend Consider how the issue of cost will impact your choice of internal or external research in a market research project.

Case study

Making the appropriate choice of research

Melanie works for a successful estate agency which is looking to expand its services into the rental market. The estate agency was opened five years ago and they have steadily increased their customer base, selling houses in the local area. Melanie's manager, who is the owner of the business, has seen an opportunity to expand the business and feels offering a rental service is the obvious thing to do, although she is not 100 per cent sure about this.

There are already four estate agents in the town and two of them have had a rental side to their businesses for several years.

Melanie has been asked by her manager to undertake some primary and secondary market research that will contribute to the final decision on whether to go ahead with the expansion.

Melanie thought through her options and decided to draw up a list of the different methods of market research she could use to gather sufficient information. This was her list:

1 Trawl through the company customer history, looking for trends in purchasing activities, such as those who are purchasing several properties, and the types of people buying the properties, such as builders or local business people.

2 Speak to those identified in step 1 to establish if they are planning to rent out the properties they are buying and if so, would they consider allowing her company to handle the rental arrangements?

3 Carry out a competitor mystery shop (ie shop at other agencies) to experience the services offered and the types of rental properties they have available.

4 Look through the local paper to see how many houses are advertised for rent, paying particular attention to the size of the properties (number of bedrooms) and the rent being asked for each.

5 Research the local government website to establish how many people in the area are looking for property to rent and who are unable to purchase.

Melanie showed the list to her manager and they both agreed this would be a good starting point. Melanie drew up an action plan to prioritise which research she would complete first, and put a timeline in place. Once she had all the information, Melanie put a report together with a recommendation that there was a strong business case to support them going ahead with the expansion.

Check your knowledge

1 Which of the above methods that Melanie planned to use are primary research?

2 Which of the above methods are secondary research?

3 Can you think of any other web-based research that Melanie could have included in her research?

4 In which order would you prioritise the above tasks?

5 Which of the five points above do you think would cost the most in terms of time and money?

Assessment practice 22.1   A.P1   A.M1   A.D1

You have decided to apply for a start-up loan of £10,000 to fund your own business – a home delivery pizza and pasta food outlet. The start-up loan company has asked you to complete a written report examining the different types of market research that you plan to undertake. You will need to explain the different types of market research you intend to use, the purpose of using them and analyse how appropriate your choice will be in relation to the business you wish to develop and your marketing objectives. You need to analyse the reasons for choosing particular research methods, the type of data to be collected and the sampling plan.

You are hoping the start-up loan company will agree to you using a specialist marketing agency for carrying out some original market research. In order for the start-up loan company to agree to this, you must justify how using a specialist marketing agency will support your market research in meeting your objectives.

Plan

- I shall summarise what I know about the different types of market research.
- I shall decide how I shall write up my written report.
- I shall decide whether I need to consult anybody in order to put my assignment together.

Do

- I have a clear action plan of what I need to do.
- I have allowed sufficient time in order to gather the information required for the assignment.
- I know whether I need to make any visits, for example to a specialist marketing agency.

Review

- I have covered all aspects of the task.
- I can see any areas for improvement on this task.

B Plan and implement a market research activity to meet a specific marketing objective

For this unit you are required to plan and implement market research, with a specific marketing objective and purpose. This is an opportunity for you to put all the knowledge you have learned from learning aim A into practice and demonstrate the skills required for you to undertake market research successfully.

It is important that you understand what is required of you before you can start your market research activities. First of all you must think about how you will put a plan together and how much time you will need to ensure you have all the information you require.

Planning stage

Planning is a vital factor in the success of any research project. Table 22.2 below explores the essential areas that you should plan for.

▶ **Table 22.2:** Planning a research project

Planning	How can you do this?
Defining the problem	This is where you must be clear on the purpose of the research. Ask yourself these questions. • Why is the research needed? • How will the research inform me and be relevant to the purpose and objectives? • How will the information that is collected help to solve the problem?
Setting research objectives	The objective or objectives should be clearly set out so that everyone involved in the research has a point of reference and can focus on what the desired end result needs to be. Whether it is just you who is undertaking the research, or a team of people or even a whole department, it is important that the objectives are **SMART**.
Setting budget	Any meaningful market research will need a budget. The amount of money and time required will depend on how much work needs to be carried out, which can only be determined once: • the objectives have been written • the data which are to be collected has been identified • the methodology which is to be used has been chosen.
Determining the data to be collected	This will depend on the nature of the problem that has been defined and the objectives that have been set. The data to be collected can then be identified. This is most likely to be a combination of qualitative and quantitative data. It is at this point that you will also need to think about the methods you will use to collect this data.

> **Key term**
>
> **SMART** – an acronym used when talking about objectives to ensure that the objective set is specific, measurable, achievable, relevant and time-constrained.

> **Link**
>
> Find out more about SMART aims and objectives by referring to *Unit 1: Exploring Business.*

Choice of methods

Once you have considered each of these four areas shown in Table 22.2, you need to think about the amount of secondary and primary methods you will use and how much qualitative and/or qualitative data will be required.

> **Theory into practice**
>
> Consider your own research project and ask yourself:
> - What is the most useful way that I can use each research method?
> - How will I be able to implement them in my research project?
> - Are any of the methods more suitable than others for my research project?

> **Key terms**
>
> **Ambiguous** – words or phrases which could have more than one meaning or which could be interpreted differently.
>
> **Jargon** – specialist words used by a profession or group of people which not everyone will understand.
>
> **Non-biased** – the questions in the survey are not prejudiced towards or against a group of people, especially in a way that might be considered to be unfair.

Questionnaire design

To ensure your survey is effective you need to design and construct it carefully. Some guidelines are provided below.

▸ The questions should be specific and kept simple. Use language that is not **ambiguous** and avoids **jargon**.

▸ The questions should be relevant to the respondents, so be sure you know who your target audience is.

▸ The questions you ask must be directly linked to the purpose of your research, in other words the objectives.

▸ Ensure your questions are **non-biased**.

▸ The choices for the respondent to use can be evenly spaced or randomised when the questions are used for quantitative purposes. There should always be a neutral choice, or a n/a (not applicable) option.

▸ Limiting open-ended questions will reduce the amount of time needed to analyse the returned data. It is important that these types of questions are carefully constructed so you can obtain information which is strictly relevant to the objective.

> **Tip**
>
> The look and feel of your questionnaire must be visually appealing. A progress bar and clear navigation on a web-based survey will keep the respondent engaged.

> **Tip**
>
> Plan enough time for the statistical analysis of the data that are returned through the questionnaires.

Ⅱ PAUSE POINT List all the stages involved in planning a research project.

Hint Think about these in the order you would need to complete them – you could complete a flowchart.

Extend For each stage, think about the different considerations you will need to take into account.

Types of questions

The most commonly used types of questions are open and closed. However, there are other questioning techniques that can be used to gather information on a survey.

▸ **Open questions** – used when a detailed answer with a full explanation is required (used to obtain qualitative data).

▸ **Closed questions** – used when a one-word or direct answer is required without further explanation (used to obtain quantitative data).

▸ Probing questions – used to gather more information after the initial question. For example, the initial question might ask 'Do you drink coffee?' followed by a second question asking 'If yes, what type of coffee do you prefer?'. This type of questioning technique works well if you want to gain some understanding of a statement the respondent may have given on a questionnaire or within a focus group.

▸ Funnel questioning – this technique is most likely to be used in focus groups as it enables more information to be obtained about a specific point. It starts with open questions, then moves towards closed questions as more clarification or commitment is required. For example, if the focus group were brought together to give their opinions on a new kitchen food mixer, they might be asked 'How often did you use the mixer?', 'What did you make?', 'Did the mixer inspire you to make the food item, or have you made it before?', 'How easy was it to clean?', 'How did you find the weight of the mixer?', 'Would you recommend it to a friend?'. Far more information can be gathered using the funnel questioning technique than if the focus group had been asked 'What did you think of the food mixer?'

▸ Asking the right kinds of questions will help you to gather the information you need

Key terms

Open questions – questioning technique used to obtain a more detailed answer where the respondent can give their opinions and thoughts behind their answer.

Closed questions – questioning technique used to obtain a direct answer. For example, a supermarket might ask 'How often do you buy milk?' and the respondents would have to choose between several options, eg never, once a week, 1 to 3 times a week, 3 to 5 times a week, every day.

Sequencing

When you are designing your survey questions, you need to think about the order in which you place them. The answers given by the respondent are likely to be influenced by previous questions. The sequence of questions will have a direct impact on how they will be interpreted and answered by the respondent. Figure 22.3 demonstrates this.

This will be interpreted as excluding the food mixer because it has been asked after the question 'How often do you use the food mixer?'

Example 1

	Everyday	2 to 3 times a week	Once a week	Once a month	Never
How often do you use a food mixer?					
How often do you use kitchen equipment?					

This will be interpreted as including the food mixer because it has been asked before the question 'How often do you use the food mixer?'

Example 2

	Everyday	2 to 3 times a week	Once a week	Once a month	Never
How often do you use kitchen equipment?					
How often do you use a food mixer?					

▸ **Figure 22.3:** The order in which you place questions in a survey is very important and will make a difference to the responses you receive.

From Figure 22.3, you can see how you can influence the answers to your questions in a way that means you do not get an accurate picture of how often the food mixer is being used.

II PAUSE POINT   List as many different types of questions as possible.

Hint   Have you taken a survey recently? What type of questions did it include?

Extend   With your list of questions, think about the best order for the questions to appear in a survey.

Length of your questionnaire

The length of your questionnaire must suit your target audience and keep them engaged until they have completed it. The actual length will depend on many factors, from the difficulty of the questions through to the medium being used. Surveys with more complex, difficult questions will feel longer to complete than a survey with easy, quick answer questions. It might be a good idea to balance your survey between these two forms. You could check the length of your survey by testing it out on a few people and asking them how they feel about the length. Decide which medium you will use for your survey. Will it be paper-based or will it be online? If using an online survey, you could have a progress bar running at the bottom of the screen as well as stating at the beginning of the survey how long it is likely to take.

Avoiding bias

When designing your questions, be aware that respondents may not understand or read them in the way that you intended them to be read, or even answered. You should always be sure that the questions you are asking are applicable to the respondent, or at least give them an option to say that the question is not applicable. Asking more than one question within a question can also lead to bias as there is a strong possibility that you will confuse the respondent. Allow enough time to ensure that your questions are worded in a way that will avoid bias and that you test them before conducting the main survey.

Relevance of questions to objectives

> **Tip**
>
> Keep your questions focused and relevant to the objectives and purpose of your market research.

Remember to keep a focus on your objectives when constructing your questionnaire. This will help you to ensure your questions are relevant to your objectives. If you are not sure whether you are asking a relevant question, read through your objectives and ask yourself how the question is relevant and what it will achieve in terms of meeting your objectives.

Pilot sampling plan

Once you have drafted your survey or questionnaire, pilot it with a test group of people. Choose people whose opinions you value and who will give you honest, timely feedback. Make sure the pilot sampling plan is in your overall project plan so you can build in the time for it to be meaningful and informative. Think about the information you want from the sampling plan so that the answers and feedback can contribute to your final draft and overall success. Have clear guidelines about what you want to cover and on what you require feedback. Also, ensure that you communicate clearly with your pilot sample population so that they understand what is expected of them and the context in which they should respond to your questions. You might add some additional questions to obtain feedback on the questionnaire itself, as well as the topic or product being tested.

Probability sampling

This involves using a form of random sampling that ensures all of the different types of people in the area of population that you wish to sample have an equal chance of being chosen to complete the survey. For instance, if your market research objective was to inform a retailer how satisfied its customers were with its customer service, then all customers would need to have an equal chance of being selected to take part in the survey. Table 22.3 looks at the advantages and drawbacks of different types of sampling.

▶ **Table 22.3:** Types of sampling and their pros and cons

Type of sampling	Explanation	Advantages	Limitations
Random	When names are drawn out of a hat or a computer is used to generate a list of names randomly from a database.	• A simple of way of selecting a random list. • Cost effective and quick to organise.	• Because of the luck of the draw, you may not get a good representation of sub-groups within a population. For example, the random list may mean that nobody is chosen from a certain age group.
Systematic	You choose the first person to be sampled and then go on to select every fourth, fifth or sixth person (or whatever interval you choose) to be in the sample.	• This samples the population evenly, giving a good representation of all types.	• If the the interval you choose for sampling coincides with a trait within the population, then your sample will not be random or representative of the whole population.
Stratified	The whole group is divided into sub-groups according to its make-up. This might lead you to base your sub-group on, for example ethnicity or age groups. You would then take a random sample from each of the sub-groups.	• This ensures there is a representative sample from each of the sub-groups that you have identified within the whole group. • Even the smallest sub-groups can be reached and you can guard against having an unrepresentative sample. • You will have a higher success rate of reaching across all of the sub-groups. Therefore a smaller sample size can be used, saving time and money.	• Requires more effort in its administration than other simpler random techniques.
Cluster	The population to be sampled is divided into clusters, usually using geographical boundaries. Random samples are then taken from the chosen clusters.	• Cluster sampling is quick and easy to administer so you can allocate your time and resources to the clusters you have identified rather than across a larger geographical area.	• This gives the least representative sample of a whole population or area. There is a tendency for people in the same area to have the same characteristics, meaning that your sampling may be over or under representative of the whole population. • Because sampling does not come from across a whole population, this could lead to a sampling error as a significant proportion of the population will not be sampled.

Non-probability sampling

In non-probability sampling, samples are collected in a way that does not give all of the individuals within a population an equal chance of being selected for the market research. When using this technique, individuals are often chosen because they are easy to get to, or the individual undertaking the research has decided who they will have in their sample. The downside of using non-probability sampling is that you cannot be certain that you have a true representative sample of the population that you want to complete your market research. The pros and cons of different types of non-probability sampling are outlined in Table 22.4.

Type of sampling	Explanation	Advantages	Limitations
Quota	• Choose a trait on which to base your sampling, for example year groups in a school, or gender. • Then take an equal sample from the chosen trait group, regardless of how many are in each group.	• The basis of each quota can be whatever is suitable for the market research, such as age, gender, education, race, religion etc.	• Some groups may have larger numbers than others, meaning that your overall data collected may not be balanced.
Convenience	Probably the most used method of sampling, as those in the sample are chosen simply because they are easy to access.	• An easy way of obtaining a sample. • The cheapest and least time consuming method.	• There is a possibility that you will not have a true representation of the population that you wish to survey as you will be leaving your selection to sample to pure chance.
Observation	Involves going to a specific location to observe individuals in order to complete your market research.	• Everyone you observe will be captured.	• Dependant on the number of individuals who might be in the area at the time, so it is important to select an appropriate time of day or night.

⏸ PAUSE POINT   What are the differences between probability and non-probability sampling? List as many as you can.

Hint   It depends on the purpose of the research project, objectives and desired outcome as to whether probability or non-probability sampling is most appropriate.

Extend   When might you use probability and/or non-probability sampling and how will it affect the data collected?

Sample size and effect on confidence levels

There is no direct formula for the size of sample that you will want to use in your market research. A larger sample will bring back more responses and is more likely to be accurate than a smaller sample. However, if you choose a larger sample, you could be swamped with responses that you will have to find time to go through. Before deciding on your sample size, there are a few things about your target population that you should think about.

▶ Population size – how many people are there in the demographic of your target population? For example, if you wish to know about car drivers in the UK, your sample would be based on the number of car drivers in the UK, which you would be able to obtain from reliable sources such as the RAC or the DVLA. As there will be people giving up driving, while others will start to drive, it is difficult to have a totally accurate number. Therefore, the number does not need to be 100 per cent accurate and an approximation would be acceptable.

▶ Confidence level – the level that you wish to use as a benchmark to decide how accurate your data and results will be. Most market research reports state the confidence interval, or margin of error. You can make this decision, which is usually around 90 per cent or 95 per cent accurate.

▶ Confidence interval (margin of error) – this links to the confidence level above. As you cannot expect your sample to be perfect, you need to decide how much error you will allow. This means what percentage of error you will allow your sample results, ie to either fall below or be higher than. Think of poll results at election time, they will often give a result and next to this result you will see ±5 per cent.

The calculations are quite complicated and there are a number of websites that have dedicated calculators to help you decide on your sample size. You choose the confidence and interval levels on which you will base your survey and the calculator will tell you the minimum number of respondents needed to meet these levels. The more accurate you want your survey results to be, the higher the number of people you will need to sample.

> **⏸ PAUSE POINT** Two examples of websites with calculators can be found in the list of websites at the end of this unit.
>
> **Hint** Try putting in different figures and see the effect this has on the sample size.
>
> **Extend** Think about your own research project. What does the sample size and confidence level need to be in order for the data to provide effective information that meets the proper objectives?

Pilot research

Once you have completed the planning of your market research, the final stage is to undertake a pilot. This can be done by testing out your completed questionnaire with a small sample of your target population to see what reaction you get. The results of this may mean that you wish to change something in your questionnaire. Pilot research also enables you to carry out a pre-test to obtain an initial measurement, say of advertising awareness of your organisation or certain products, before undertaking the final survey.

Case study

Undertaking pilot research

Siham is working on a market research project to establish if there is a market for a Moroccan restaurant in her home town. Firstly, she wants to know if the local population is aware of the different types of cuisine available in the town. There are already four pubs offering food as well as two Chinese, an Indian, an Italian and a Spanish restaurant. She is also looking to establish what the local population think of what the current restaurants are offering.

Siham knows that the questions she asks must not be biased and that she must select the pilot group of respondents carefully, ensuring that the questions are appropriately constructed. She is not quite sure how to go about this so she has planned to spend some time with her manager who has more experience of writing and distributing surveys.

Once Siham has established how well informed her audience is about what is already available to them and what they think of the existing restaurants, she wants to extend her research to find out how popular a Moroccan restaurant would be.

Siham's plan includes selecting a focus group once she has received the results from her initial pilot research, in order to gather more detailed primary data.

Check your knowledge

1 Is there any secondary research that Siham could use to inform her pilot sample?

2 How can Siham be sure of having a true representative sample in her pilot sample?

3 Siham wants a 95 per cent accuracy once her questionnaire goes live following the pilot sample. Using a sample calculator, how many would you recommend she has in her sample size?

4 If you were Siham's manager, what advice would you give her to ensure her questions avoid bias?

5 Are there any other methods of research that Siham could use, other than a focus group, once it has been established that there is a market for a new Moroccan restaurant?

Implementation stage

Once you have gone through the planning stage for your market research, there are four areas that you should consider in the implementation stage.

▶ Review the pilot primary research – it is essential that you learn any lessons available by reviewing the outcomes of your pilot primary research. This is your opportunity to adjust and make amendments to your research to ensure that you receive the most informative and accurate results from your questionnaires and surveys.

▶ Final questionnaire design – be sure that in the final questionnaire design you have taken into consideration any feedback you may have received. Check and correct any spelling and grammar errors.

▶ Final sampling plan – revisit the sampling plan that you intend to use and be confident that it will yield the results you need to receive accurate and meaningful data. This is the data which you will then analyse as the final part of your market research.

▶ Data collection, primary and secondary – this is the final, practical stage of implementing your plan. You will collect the data to inform your market research through your questionnaires and other primary and secondary research.

Assessment practice 22.2

B.P2 | B.P3 | B.P4 | B.M2 | B.D2

The start-up loan company was impressed with your report and has decided to give you the £10,000 loan. In order for the money to be released, you must submit a plan detailing the research methods, which should include secondary research, that relate to your objectives, and pilot primary market research with details of the sample size.

You must also submit a copy of your pilot questionnaire and your pilot research.

Along with the plan and questionnaires, you should submit a piece of writing in which you analyse the reasons for choosing the research methods, the type of data you will collect and your overall sampling plan.

After submitting your 'evidence' and written work to the start-up company, you should evaluate the effectiveness of your pilot research. You know that making some changes might benefit your market research and so want to email the start-up loan company explaining the recommended changes you would like to make and why you want to make them.

You have now satisfied the start-up loan company's requirements and they have agreed to release the loan, meaning you can go ahead with the research. The start-up loan company would like to see your final questionnaire with your sampling plan and, when available, the evidence of the research data you have collected that reflects your original plan.

Plan

- I know how this task fits in with the task in assessment practice 22.1.
- I know what I need to organise for my primary and secondary research to ensure that I meet the deadline.
- I know what criteria I am going to use in my evaluation.

Do

- I know how I shall justify the reasons why I chose my research methods.
- I have saved my original questionnaire and my revised questionnaire, as well as the evidence of the research data that I have collected.

Review

- I know what aspects of the research went well during this assessment activity.
- I can identify the reasons why some aspects of my research did not go so well as others.

C   Analyse and present market research findings and recommend process improvements

This section covers the final stage of your market research, which is based on the data collected and findings completed in learning aim B.

Statistical analysis and interpretation of primary and secondary research

Before you can present your findings, you need to be sure that you understand the data you have obtained and that you can interpret it accurately.

Data analysis/interpretation

Arithmetic mean, mode and median

You will use either the mean, mode, median, range, or a combination of these, when interpreting your data. This will allow you to articulate (explain) your findings. For example, if your market research was based on a product that you were planning to sell, you would be able to give an average (**mean**) number of times that the product was used or the most common value (**mode**) or number of times that it was used. Using **median** you would be able to establish the middle value that the respondents would be prepared to pay for the product. The difference between the highest and lowest values in your data (**range**) would allow you to give the range in price that your respondents would be prepared to pay, which would be the difference between the highest price and the lowest price. Figure 22.4 demonstrates how to calculate the mean, mode, median and range.

▶ **Figure 22.4:** Calculating the mean, mode, median and range

Respondent	Number of times product is used	Amount prepared to pay for product
A	7	1
B	9	7
C	6	1
D	4	8
E	9	2
F	10	8
G	5	1
H	9	8
I	9	3
J	12	8
Mean To calculate the average number of times the product is used, add all the responses together and divide by the number of data sets: Number of times product is used = 80 Number of data sets (respondents) = 10 80 ÷ 10 = 8	8	
Mode To calculate the number of times the product is most commonly used, put the data in numerical order and identify the most commonly given number, so: 4 5 5 6 7 9 9 9 9 10 12 The most common number = 9	9	

Respondent	Number of times product is used	Amount prepared to pay for product
Median This is the median amount that the respondents would be prepared to pay. In an odd number data set, this would be the middle number. In an even number data set, this would be the sum of the two middle numbers divided by two. To calculate when using an odd or even number set, list the numbers in ascending numerical order to find the mid point: 1 1 1 2 3 7 8 8 8 8 Because there is an even number (10) in this data set, the two middle numbers, 3 and 7, are added together and divided by 2 to find the median. 1 1 1 2 ③ ⑦ 8 8 8 8 ③+⑦= 10 10 ÷ 2 = 5		5
Range This is the difference between the highest and the lowest number. Highest amount respondents would pay = 8 Lowest amount respondents would pay = 1 8 – 1 = 7		7

Key term

Quartile – a division of statistical data divided into four equal parts or defined areas. The first part or area is the first quartile, the second is the second quartile, the third is the third quartile and the fourth is the fourth quartile.

Range and interquartile range

The interquartile range is the difference between the lower and upper **quartiles**. Please follow the worked example below.

Standard deviation

This is a measurement of the variance from the expected mean (average) value of your data, or statistics of your market research. A low standard deviation means that your data are very close to the mean (average), whereas a high standard deviation means that your data are spread over a large range of values. For example, when using questionnaires in which you ask respondents to rate your product or service on a scale of, say, '1 to 10', you will calculate the mean (average). If the mean is close to the mid-range of your scale this would be a low standard deviation. If the mean is not close to the mid range, this would be a high standard deviation.

▶ **Figure 22.5:** Standard deviation

Respondent	Easy to use	Value for money
A	6	1
B	8	7
C	4	1
D	6	8
E	7	2
F	6	8
G	8	1
H	3	8
I	6	3
J	8	8
K	4	8
Mean	6	5
Standard deviation	1.65	3.31

Worked Example

If you have a set of data based on the price that your target population would be prepared to pay for your product, the figures might come in to you like this:

| 45 | 43 | 45 | 56 | 52 | 39 | 45 | 52 | 46 | 43 | 54 |

Step 1: Put your data/figures into ascending numerical order:

| 39 | 43 | 43 | 45 | 45 | 45 | 46 | 52 | 52 | 54 | 56 |

Step 2: Find the median, which is the 6th value = 45.

39	43	43	45	45	**45**	46	52	52	54	56
1st value		3rd value		5th value	6th value	7th value		9th value		11th value
	Lower quartile				Median		Upper quartile			

The median is found by taking the number of data sets, which is 11 in this case, and then always adding 1. Then divide by 2, so the sum looks like:

11 + 1 ÷ 2 = 6

Meaning you use the 6th value.

Step 3: Work out the lower and upper quartile values, which are the 3rd and 9th values. You do this by dividing each of the lower and upper quartiles into two halves.

For the lower quartile, take the number of data sets, which is 11 and then add 1. This time you divide by 4 to get the quartile value. The sum looks like this:

11 + 1 ÷ 4 = 3, meaning you use the 3rd value

For the upper quartile, repeat the process as above.

Step 4: To work out the interquartile range, find the difference between the upper and lower quartile by subtracting one from the other.

Upper quartile = 52

Lower quartile = 43

52 − 43 = interquartile range is 9

Looking at the example in Figure 22.5, where respondents were asked to score two features of a product at between 1 and 10, you can see that the mean for both areas is 5. Looking at just this fact, you could assume that both areas sampled were identical. However, when you look at the standard deviation figures, you can see that they are quite different. When at 0, the standard deviation is exactly on the mean (average), so you can see 'easy to use' 0.63 is very close to the middle range of the score, where most respondents scored either 4, 5 or 6, demonstrating that everyone in the sample had roughly the same opinion about how easy the product was to use.

The further away from the middle range of the score, the bigger the deviation number will be. When you look at the data set for 'value for money' the respondents scored between 1 and 8, meaning that some felt the product was value for money, whereas others did not.

When comparing these figures for data analysis, standard deviation can be quite an important factor, as shown in this example. A business could make an incorrect assumption if it only used the mean (average) score rating.

Discussion

When comparing figures for data analysis, standard deviation is an important
factor to consider. Looking at Figure 22.5, what incorrect assumptions could be
made if just using the mean? What does the standard deviation tell you about the
'value for money' response?

Calculating standard deviation is quite a complicated process. The worked example
below uses the data from Figure 22.5 to show how it is done.

Worked Example

Step 1: To calculate the standard deviation you take each data value and minus it by the mean, squared (see column 4).

Step 2: Total the numbers in column 4. This gives 30.

Step 3: Divide this by the number of data sets (in this case 11):
$30 \div 11 = 2.27$

Step 4: Then find the square root of $2.27 = 1.65$ This is the standard deviation.

A second example has been worked in columns 5 and 6.

Column 1 Respondent	Column 2 Easy to use	Column 3 Data value minus mean	Column 4 Data value – mean squared	Column 5 Value for money	Column 6 Data value minus mean squared
A	6	$6 - 6 = 0$	0	1	$1 - 5 = -4^2 = 16$
B	8	$8 - 6 = 2$	$2^2 = 4$	7	$7 - 5 = 2^2 = 4$
C	4	$4 - 6 = -2$	$(-2)^2 = 4$	1	$1 - 5 = -4^2 = 16$
D	6	$6 - 6 = 0$	0	8	$8 - 5 = 3^2 = 9$
E	7	$7 - 6 = 1$	1	2	$2 - 5 = 3^2 = 9$
F	6	$6 - 6 = 0$	0	8	$8 - 5 = 3^2 = 9$
G	8	$8 - 6 = 2$	4	1	$1 - 5 = -4^2 = 16$
H	3	$3 - 6 = -3$	9	8	$8 - 5 = 3^2 = 9$
I	6	$6 - 6 = 0$	0	3	$3 - 5 = -2 = 4$
J	8	$8 - 6 = 2$	4	8	$8 - 5 = 3^2 = 9$
K	4	$4 - 6 = 2$	4	8	$8 - 5 = 3^2 = 9$
Mean	6		$30 \div 11 = 2.27$ $\sqrt{2.27} = 1.65$	5	$110 \div 11 = 10$ $\sqrt{10} = 3.16$
Standard deviation			1.65		3.16

❚❚ PAUSE POINT Calculating standard deviation needs practice. Try some more examples. Google 'standard deviation'.

Hint Use a deviation calculator.

Extend Watch videos on video sharing websites such as YouTube, eg 'Standard Deviation –
Statistics' to see how standard deviation is calculated.

Calculate your own set of data following the examples above.

Time series

Time series refers to market research which is carried out over a period of time. Sales figures are often collected in this way so that an organisation can see how their figures compare over a one-year period against those of a competitor. Another example would be to collect data on the behaviours of customers over a period of time, for example booking summer holidays. The data from the market research would inform which weeks or months of the year customers were likely to book their summer holiday.

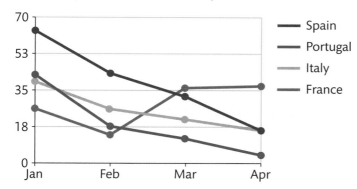

▶ **Figure 22.6:** A time series line graph

This time series data has been plotted onto a line graph shown in Figure 22.6. From the line graph you can see that Spain is the most popular destination overall and that most bookings are made in January, tailing off as the year progresses. Holiday companies can use this information to decide on the best time of year for their advertising promotions and to manage the business in terms of cash flow.

Discussion

Looking at the line graph in Figure 22.6, what else does it tell you about the behaviours of customers booking their summer holidays? Which is the least popular destination? Which destination has a different trend to the other destinations? What would be the benefit of plotting the rest of the year?

Scatter diagrams and trends

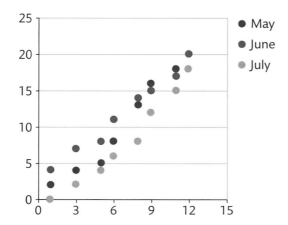

▶ **Figure 22.7:** A scatter diagram showing a positive correlation

Scatter diagrams are a good way to visually demonstrate any connections between values, which in turn will enable you to identify any trends in your data. The more spread out the points are on the graph, the less connection between the values.

Where there is a close connection, the points on the graph will be in a concentrated area, or in a straight line. Another word for connection is **correlation**.

The correlation is positive when the vertical variable increases as the horizontal variable decreases, as in Figure 22.7.

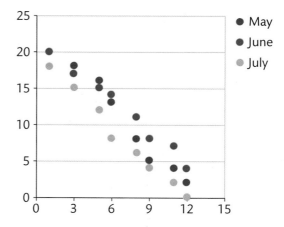

▶ **Figure 22.8:** This shows negative correlation

The correlation is negative when the vertical variable decreases as the horizontal variable increases, as in Figure 22.8.

Interpretation of secondary research

When using secondary research it is important to read the data in context and to interpret the information that it is giving you accurately. Triangulating the data or information found will confirm if it is up to date and relevant to your market research. For example, if you read a newspaper article claiming that one of your competitors has had a bumper year in terms of sales, and that they are planning to extend their premises in order to expand their business, further research would confirm the accuracy of the newspaper report. You could do this by checking with the local council to see if any planning applications have been received. When using websites or articles from the internet, check the date of the article to ensure it is current and then see if you can confirm what the website or article is telling you through a different source, either on the internet or elsewhere.

Tip

Use both primary and secondary research when collecting information and data for your market research.

Research

Identify what is already on the market for a certain product or service that could be used as secondary research. Look at local or national newspapers to identify businesses advertising a certain product and/or service and compare how the product or service is presented, the prices and reviews. You can research by looking at newspapers or going to the newspaper's website.

Once you have identified the product or service, visit other websites offering the same product/service.

Then undertake further research to find out what consumers say about the product by looking at the reviews on the seller's website and then looking at independent review websites.

Presentation of research results

Once you have collected all the information from your market research, and have analysed the data, the final stage is to present the results. The audience for your presentation is likely to be managers and/or colleagues. However, if you are working for a market research company, you could be presenting to the business who commissioned the market research, ie your customer. There are various ways of presenting the information and the most suitable style to use will depend on your audience and the data you are presenting. Your presentation should be structured with an introduction, content and conclusion. At the end of the report you will be expected to make recommendations based on the data you have presented and to refer back to the original objectives and the purpose of the market research project.

Below is a list of what to include.

▶ Report – a well organised document which will define and analyse the whole of your market research project and should include:

- the purpose and objectives of the research
- details of your planning
- method of data collection
- an analysis of the data
- conclusions and recommendations.

▶ You should organise your report into sections, with headings and sub-headings which are usually numbered for reference. Your presentation should highlight the key points of your report which you should have available in full so you can refer to it during your presentation. Depending on the circumstances, you could send your report to your audience in advance of your presentation so they can read it and prepare questions. Alternatively, it may be more appropriate to leave your audience with the full report at the end of the presentation.

▶ Graphs and tables – visual presentation works well and will help you to explain intricate details and/or complicated figures. Offering a handout of any visuals that you have used will help you to get your points across and leave your audience with something to take away and reflect upon. Besides the tables, line graph and scatter graphs that have been used to illustrate points earlier, other graphs that can be used are outlined below.

▶ Bar chart – useful when you wish to compare one set of data with another, or if you wish to track changes over a period of time. In Figure 22.9, two regions are being compared over four months.

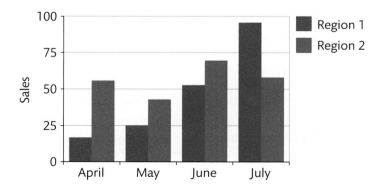

▶ **Figure 22.9:** A bar chart showing regional sales

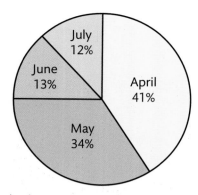

▶ **Figure 22.10:** A colour-coded pie chart

▶ Pie chart – useful when you wish to demonstrate percentages or proportions. In Figure 22.10, the chart has been colour coded against months of the year. This works well with up to about six data sets or less.

▶ Presenting conclusions and recommendations – the way in which you present your conclusions and recommendations will have an impact on the way they will be received by your audience. You are aiming for maximum effect, with accuracy and meaningful data, which will mean that your recommendations are seen as viable and can be taken seriously. There should be a detailed introduction where you outline what the presentation will cover, followed by the main points of the research project that will lead to your conclusions. The conclusions and recommendations should relate directly back to the purpose of your market research and the objectives that were set. You should also think about the way in which you are going to conduct your presentation:

- Are you going to use presentation software such as PowerPoint?
- Will you use any handouts?
- Will you put a presentation pack together for your audience?
- Will the presentation be formal or informal?

▶ Awareness of audience type – in order for your presentation to be received positively, it is important that you know who your audience is and the format in which they will expect your report to be presented. Will you be expected to present to a group of people using a visual aid, such as PowerPoint, or will you be submitting a PDF report without a personal presentation, or will you be required to do both? You can then tailor your presentation and/or report to their preferences and style. For example, if you are going to present to a board of directors, you need to keep your presentation formal, using visual aids. However, if you are going to present to your colleagues during their lunch break, a more informal approach will be better received. If you are submitting a PDF report without a personal presentation, then the report must cover fully all aspects of your research project with clear explanations of the results and recommendations. Remember that you will not be present to answer questions. You should spend time thinking about who your audience is and what their expectations of you and the presentation will be.

 **PAUSE POINT**

If you were creating a presentation for your classmates, what types of things would you need to take into account?

 Hint

Of the different considerations you have learned about, which do you think is the most important in this situation?

 Extend

If your audience was your tutors, instead of classmates, would your presentation look the same? What different things might you consider?

Value of the information

Before completing your final preparations for your presentation and report, you should spend time considering the value of the information you have been using. In all the research methods that we have looked at there will be limitations such as those outlined below.

▶ Sufficiency – have you enough data sets? Have you interviewed enough people? Have you received enough questionnaires back from your survey? Did you spend enough time observing traffic flows on a certain junction? It will depend on the nature of your research as to how big your sample needs to be. For example, if you are researching safety features, then you need to be sure you have a sufficient sample size to confirm a high percentage of accuracy, However, if you are researching preferences for a type of food, this will not be as important.

- Accuracy – have you used the correct sampling methodology? Has the data been entered onto the database accurately? Have you captured the appropriate target audience? Can you be sure the respondents have answered questionnaires honestly? The planning process should eliminate some inaccuracies but you should also check for accuracy as you gather the data, and as part of the data analysis.

- Bias – are your samples representative of the diversity of the population you have surveyed? Are you using leading questions which could make them biased? Are focus groups run in a way that includes everyone? Are your questions ordered in a way that reduces any influence on the respondents? It is difficult to eliminate bias totally in your research but you should be aware that your own attitude, behaviour and beliefs will have an impact on the research. Try to keep an open mind while carrying out research and be aware if you think any bias is 'creeping in'.

- Subjectivity – has your judgement been shaped by personal opinions and feelings rather than outside influences? In market research you must 'stick to the facts' in order for the data and information to be credible. What one person may like, another may not – this is subjectivity.

'Reliability of the sample' takes in all of the above, ie sufficiency, accuracy, bias and subjectivity. There also needs to be consistency in your approach and the way the market research is conducted. For example if you make changes to some of the questions on a survey then you will get a slightly different response to those from the original version. This will then make the data drawn from the sample unreliable. You should also consider the people who will give you feedback. Have you chosen the correct population to relate to your original objectives? Have you used a large enough sample size to give you sufficient data? These points need to be considered to avoid additional work where you may need to use follow up questionnaires.

Recommend improvements

Improvements to the process of any market research should be recommended once the process has been reflected upon and reviewed. There will be many different people involved in the process such as your managers and colleagues, outside agencies, suppliers to your business, customers and end users. This is not a finite list and different organisations will have different people involved in the process. Feedback from those involved in the process should be obtained and listened to as this will also inform any improvements to any future market research.

Tip

To reduce bias in your market research reporting ask another person to analyse the data to get a different view point.

Discussion

Can you think of any particular examples where research must not be biased and must remain subjective? What different areas is this market research conducted in? Are there any areas where people might have particularly strong opinions? Investigate a market research piece in an area that you think might be contentious. How has the research piece avoided bias and remained subjective?

PAUSE POINT   Who are the key people likely to be involved in your market research project?

Hint   What information will you want to get from these people to help you improve your market research processes?

Extend   How can you use this information to improve future research projects? How can you include this in your assignment?

Assessment practice 22.3

The start-up loan company is using your new business market research activity as a case study and has asked you to present the results of your research, including your statistical analysis and interpretation of your primary and secondary research, to their senior managers.

Your presentation should cover:

- a summary and explanation of your findings using different formats to illustrate each point which goes on to analyse these points using a wide range of statistical techniques
- the confidence levels and how they fit in with your results
- an assessment of the limitations of the data you have collected
- the improvements you would want to make in the planning process, justifying why.

Plan

- I know how I shall cover the main points in my presentation.
- I know how I shall structure my presentation.
- I know who can listen to my presentation that understands market research.
- I have taken into consideration my audience, ie senior managers.

Do

- I have used different formats to demonstrate my points within my presentation.
- The results of my research are collated, explained and analysed.

Review

- I covered all parts in sufficient depth to meet all of the criteria.
- I know what have been the most useful parts of this assessment activity to demonstrate my learning.

Further reading and resources

Bradley, N. (2013) *Marketing Research: Tools and Techniques*, Oxford: Oxford University Press.

Hague, P.N. and Hague, N. (2013) *Market Research in Practice: How to Get Greater Insight From Your Market*, 2nd edition, London: Kogan Page.

Hyman, M. and Sierra, J. (2010) *Market Research Kit For Dummies*, New Jersey: John Wiley & Sons.

Websites

http://businesscasestudies.co.uk/barclays

A case study of Barclays discovering customer needs through market research.

www.greenbook.org/marketing-research

A website dedicated to giving advice on marketing research, with related articles and case studies.

www.mymarketresearchmethods.com/survey-design-best-practices

Advice on how to write a good questionnaire and other market research methods.

www.quirks.com/index.aspx

A worldwide market research portal with articles and information about all areas of market research.

www.mrs.org.uk/careers/#features

A website offering advice about, and opportunities for, careers in market research.

www.checkmarket.com/market-research-resources/sample-size-calculator

www.macorr.com/sample-size-calculator.htm

Websites with calculators.

THINK ▶FUTURE

Jairam Alleyne

Market Research Manager

Jairam was recently promoted to market research manager, after starting his career as a market research assistant. Working on the 'client side' of market research rather than for a market research company means that Jairam is often the link between the customer and the department store he is employed by. His role is to find out what customers think of the products that his company sells, ranging from their levels of staisfaction through to how easily they can purchase the products (including in store and via the internet). Part of the job is 'getting to the bottom of things' and Jairam does this through his perserverance and the ability to 'keep asking questions' until he has enough information to build a whole picture of customers' thoughts and ideas.

Jairam enjoys the variety that his job brings and the fast pace of market research. As a manager, he gets involved in the different departments of his company and regularly helps his colleagues to understand their customers better. He enjoys the challenge of continuously juggling different pieces of work amongst the projects in which he is involved.

Focusing your skills

Knowing the job

In order to be effective as a market researcher it is important to build a foundation of knowledge that will be key in everything you do. This means building your own 'knowledge store' such as:

* being aware of the different research methods and when to use them, for example knowing when to use qualitative and quantitative methods as well as primary and secondary research
* knowing what your organisation wants to achieve so that the information you gather will feed into the objectives, and be part of it
* seeing the link between all of the different pieces of information you gather to build the bigger picture
* knowing who your key stakeholders are and making contact with the relevant people in your organisation and those within the agencies that you may use, to network and build professional relationships.

Having the skills

Having the right skills to use in market research will make the difference between whether a project is successful or not and whether you can make a difference to the success of your organisation. Essential skills are outlined below.

* Multitasking – this is a fast paced environment and the ability to manage having many jobs on the go at once is essential, as well as being able to think quickly.
* Communication – you need to be able to articulate and share the information you gather as part of your market research to the relevant people within your organisation.
* Flexibility – be prepared to be flexible with your approach. Deadlines will be moved, appointments changed, customers unavailable, colleagues will be in meetings – situations like these need to be built into your daily schedule.
* Self and time management – working to financial constraints and deadlines is essential to ensure projects are delivered on time and within budget.

Getting ready for assessment

Paul has decided to complete the market research unit in his BTEC Level 3 National Extended Diploma in Business. The assignment is based around a business start-up scenario and, as Paul hopes to start his own business one day, he can see how relevant and useful this assignment will be. The assignment has been divided into three sections.

▶ Planning the market research.

▶ Finalising the planning and undertaking the market research.

▶ Analysing and presenting the results of the market research.

Paul shares his experience below.

How I got started

First of all I thought about the business before thinking about the market research: Where would the business be located? What type of customers would use it? What prices could I charge? How busy would I be? How many staff would I need? I soon realised that only market research could answer these questions. I then came up with some objectives to focus the market research.

Next I looked at my notes about different types of market research and reminded myself what primary and secondary research were and when I would use them. I needed to be clear on the purpose of the research and that my choice of research methods would be appropriate.

The planning stage of market research was easy because I was in control of how I went about it. However, once I got to the implementation stage, I had to make sure I gave myself enough time to collect all the data I needed and that it would be meaningful.

I learned early on that I needed to write down how I was going to complete this assignment, what I had done so far, and any adjustments to timings when things didn't go to plan. I set up an action plan in the form of a table detailing what I needed to do, what part of the assignment it was going to contribute towards, and when I had to get it done by. I also had a column for when I needed to change things.

What I learned from the experience

I learned very quickly that being organised was key to my success. I created an action plan early on, but if I had done it sooner and put lots of detail in it, extracting the different parts of the assignment and putting them all onto the action plan, I would have been even more on top of my work.

I went straight in with the presentations and found that I wasn't always sure which slide was coming next. I should have printed off the presentation slide notes, so I could refer to them during the presentation, and I wish now that I had practised presenting to family members.

Get the questionnaires to the sample audience as soon as possible and send out more questionnaires than the number of responses that you need. Also, give a date by which the responses need to be returned. Some responses came back after I had collected my data, and this meant I either had to ignore the response, or start again with my analysis.

How I brought it all together

My action plan really helped me to bring my assignment together as there were so many parts to it and being organised was really important. This is how I completed my work:

▶ I jotted down every question I could think of in relation to the business and how I would know that it would be successful. This helped me to establish my objectives for the market research.

▶ I read through all my notes on the different aspects of market research (which really helped!).

▶ I put an action plan together of what I needed to do and by when.

▶ I used PowerPoint for my presentations. To avoid overcrowding, each slide covered just the main points relevant to the research.

▶ I read through my completed work and the assignment brief before submitting anything to ensure that I had covered every part of all of the learning aims.

▶ I kept all my notes and scribbles throughout the assignment in case I needed to go back over anything.

Think about it

▶ Have you written a plan with timings so you can complete your assignment by the agreed submission date?

▶ Do you have a full set of notes on the types of market research as well as on the planning, implementation and analysis of it all?

▶ Is your information written in your own words? Have you referenced clearly where you have used quotations or information from a book, journal or website?

Getting to know your unit

Assessment
You will be assessed by a series of assignments set by your tutor.

Law is a fascinating subject which affects all individuals and businesses. You have probably heard of terms like 'crime scene', 'investigation' and 'homicide', and you may have seen media presentations of court room dramas and watched programmes on policing, but these only give a tiny insight into the legal system. This unit provides useful information because individuals and business organisations will, at some point, need legal advice and it is important that they operate within the law to avoid adverse consequences. Note that this unit refers only to the English system of law, which only applies to England and Wales, not to Scotland and Northern Ireland.

In this unit you will examine criminal and civil law and how different courts deal with cases to resolve legal issues. You will explore the roles of members of the legal profession and others who participate in making decisions in court cases and dispute resolution. You will discover how individuals and businesses are protected by laws made in the UK and by the EU. You will also learn how the law changes and adapts to new situations through case law and the legislative process. You will develop relevant workplace skills, such as researching sources of law, to be able to provide accurate and independent legal advice related to coursework and assignments.

How you will be assessed

This unit will be assessed by assignments set and marked by your tutor. You will need to work independently on your assignments, so it is important to be well prepared. Collect your notes, research and class activities in a folder to help you with formal assignments and make use of the unit specification and assignment brief to plan your approach to this unit and to manage your time. You will also find it useful to create a glossary of legal terminology and of terminology related to assignments so that you are clear about what is required, in questions asking for explanation, analysis and evaluation. You need to practise the higher level skills required for merit and distinction grades so that you can develop the points you make in an assignment and make rational judgements and valid conclusions. This unit contains useful information and activities to help you prepare for your assignments.

The assignments set by your tutor will consist of a number of tasks designed to meet the criteria in the table. They are likely to include a written assignment but may also include activities such as:

▶ case studies where you make decisions about a case and provide legal advice
▶ presentations or role plays to illustrate legal practice and procedures.

Assessment criteria

This table shows you what you must do in order to achieve a **Pass**, **Merit** or **Distinction** grade, and where you can find activities to help you.

Pass	Merit	Distinction
Learning aim **A** Examine the jurisdiction of the courts, and their alternatives, in contributing to case outcomes		**A.D1** Evaluate how dispute solving in the courts compares with methods of alternative dispute resolution (ADR). **Assessment practice 23.1**
A.P1 Using case examples, accurately apply and explain the jurisdiction of civil courts. **Assessment practice 23.1**	**A.M1** Compare and contrast the criminal and civil court hierarchies and appeal routes, demonstrating accurate use of legal terminology, case law citation and application, to both civil and criminal law situations. **Assessment practice 23.1**	
A.P3 Using case examples, accurately apply and explain the jurisdiction of criminal courts. **Assessment practice 23.1**		
Learning aim B Investigate the role of the legal profession and lay people in contributing to case outcomes		
B.P3 Using case examples, accurately apply and explain the role in the civil courts and ADR of the legal profession and lay people. **Assessment practice 23.1**	**B.M2** Compare and contrast the role and function of lawyers and lay people within the English courts and ADR. **Assessment practice 23.1**	**B.D2** Evaluate the effectiveness of lay personnel in the English courts and ADR. **Assessment practice 23.1**
B.P4 Using case examples, accurately apply and explain the role in the criminal courts of the legal profession and lay people. **Assessment practice 23.1**		
Learning aim C Explore sources of law relevant for providing legal advice		**C.D3** Evaluate how far the sources of law provide certainty for lawyers providing legal advice. **Assessment practice 23.2**
C.P5 Demonstrate how the legislative process would apply in given scenarios. **Assessment practice 23.2**	**C.M3** Analyse the impact European law has had on domestic law in given situations. **Assessment practice 23.2**	
C.P6 Explain the rules of precedent and statutory interpretation through accurate application in given scenarios. **Assessment practice 23.2**		

Getting started

In small groups, list what you consider to be legal issues and key words related to the English legal system. Discuss what is law, why we have laws and how they affect individuals throughout their lives, and businesses throughout their existence. When you have completed this section you can return to your list to expand on the points you originally included.

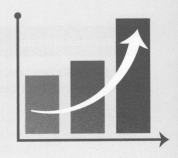

A Examine the jurisdiction of the courts, and their alternatives, in contributing to case outcomes

The English legal system has existed for hundreds of years and has developed and adapted over time. It is a system that operates to create and apply the law fairly and for the benefit of society. The English legal system applies to England and Wales. Scotland and Northern Ireland have legal systems which are quite different.

Meaning, purpose and terminology of the law

Studying law can sometimes be difficult because of the complicated legal terminology. It is important that you find legal definitions using a legal dictionary. The legal definition of a word can often be quite different from the everyday meaning. For example, in the **law of contract**, 'consideration' does not mean being kind and looking after someone, it means 'the element of exchange'. For example, when you buy a new mobile, the consideration is the money paid and the phone you receive.

Law consists of a set of legal rules aimed at governing behaviour and it encourages individuals and organisations to operate within the law or face consequences if they do not. Where legal rules appear to conflict, the legal system provides a forum for deciding legal arguments and settling disputes.

Rights and duties

The law provides us with rights and duties, for example an employee has a right to be safe in the workplace and the employer is under a duty to carry out risk assessments, provide health and safety training and a safe environment. When you go shopping, you have the right to buy items which are of satisfactory quality and the retailer is under a duty to replace or provide a refund for items which are faulty. Some of our fundamental rights are incorporated into the Human Rights Act 1998 from the European Convention on Human Rights.

> **Discussion**
>
> Deeply disturbing cases have been reported where victims have been kept as slaves or as captive in their own home or another person's house. Discuss the rights that the victim is being deprived of. What could happen to the person keeping the victim captive?

Law and morality

Moral behaviour is what society generally regards as acceptable behaviour, although opinions may differ on what is and is not acceptable. There is an overlap between law

> **Key term**
>
> **Law of contract** – the part of civil law protecting people and businesses who have made agreements, for example about buying and selling goods and services.

and morals – for example you would agree that murder is both illegal and immoral, but how would you categorise:

▸ cheating on a partner

▸ swearing

▸ spitting?

This 'grey area' between law and morals can be hard to navigate, for example some behaviour:

▸ is morally right and legal, for example looking after your family members

▸ may be considered as morally right but illegal, for example unplanned strike action due to a serious and contentious issue at work

▸ may be considered immoral but legal, for example smoking and drinking alcohol

▸ is both immoral and illegal, for example child neglect.

Discussion

In small groups think about the examples listed. Do you all agree on how they should be categorised? If not, what are your reasons?

▸ Why do you think some people consider unplanned strike action to be morally right in certain situations?

Law and rules

Discussion

In small groups imagine you have been asked to appear in a reality television show where the contestants share a house. Discuss the house rules you would introduce and the consequences for the rules being broken.

You will come across rules constantly – these may be imposed by your parent or guardian, by your school or college, by a sporting association or social club or by your local council. BTEC have rules about assessments which you will be familiar with – failing to meet a deadline could lead to failing a unit, which would be unacceptable. All of the rules mentioned here only affect part of society, while legal rules affect **all** of society. Rules are similar to laws as they aim to control behaviour but the consequences of breaking rules are less severe than the consequences of breaking the law.

Purpose of law

The law gives us some certainty about the way we expect to be treated, the activities we are allowed to take part in and the knowledge that there can be solutions to legal problems if things go wrong.

Fatal and non-fatal offences – fatal offences cause death such as murder and manslaughter, whereas non-fatal offences cause harm or injury but not death.

Constitutional law – this branch of law controls the government and how it operates.

The aims of the law are outlined below.

▶ Protect – you are protected from harmful treatment and the law recognises **fatal** and **non-fatal offences** against the person as crimes. Your belongings are protected because criminal damage and theft offences are also classed as criminal behaviour. The law provides a framework for businesses to carry out transactions with some certainty that they will be treated fairly otherwise the other party can be taken to court. The law also protects people by making provision for education and welfare.

▶ Uphold rights – if you are deprived of your legal rights this can lead to civil or criminal court action.

▶ Maintain order – allowing individuals and organisations to do whatever they liked without limits would lead to chaos and the abuse of weaker parties. The law aims to provide public order, thus peaceful demonstrations related to civil liberties and human rights are lawful but riots and violent disorder are against the law. The law also contributes to political and economic order by regulating **constitutional** arrangements and financial transactions. The law contributes to social order by recognising that people are all different, but at the same time promotes equality.

▶ Provide justice – this sounds quite simple but in practice it is very difficult for decisions in all cases to be considered as just and proper by all members of society. Everyone has a different interpretation of justice and different legal theories promote different views. Many would agree that like cases should be treated alike, but the circumstances surrounding every case will be unique.

▶ Evaluation of effectiveness of the legal system – the English legal system is complex and sophisticated, having been changed and adapted over the years. In many cases it fulfils its aims but it is not perfect and there are cases which clearly show injustice. There are areas of the law which need to be reformed and updated.

Categories of law

There are many ways of putting law into categories. One way of categorising it is according to the area being dealt with such as family law, company law, contract law and consumer law.

Sometimes law books define law as:

▶ common law, which refers to law which can be found from previous cases, or

▶ statute law, which is law found in acts of Parliament.

Public law and private law provide us with another distinction:

▶ public law involves the state or government and applies to everyone

▶ private law is concerned with sorting out disputes between individuals or businesses in the civil courts.

One of the most common ways of categorising law is by differentiating between criminal and civil law.

Differences between criminal law and civil law

The purpose of civil law is to provide a forum for settling disputes and providing remedies for the claimants. In some instances such as a traffic accident, a dispute might not be able to be resolved between the two parties. In this case the conflict will be taken to a civil court, where a decision will be made. Most civil claims are resolved by a sum of money, called **compensation**, being paid. Occasionally, a court may order a party to do something (this is called specific performance), or prevent them from doing something (this is a court order called an injunction).

Key term

Compensation – a sum of money which may be paid to someone (a claimant) who has successfully brought a case against someone else (a defendant).

The purpose of criminal law is to punish people who break the law, to maintain law and to keep order and protect the public. If a person commits a serious crime such as assault, they are likely to go to prison. For lesser offences, the punishment may be a fine or community sentence. Motorists who break the law may be given penalty points or banned from driving.

Sometimes behaviour cannot be distinguished easily as a crime or a civil wrong because one course of action can lead to criminal and civil court action. For example, a motorist who is speeding and driving erratically, crashes the car causing injury to a pedestrian and to property. The pedestrian who is injured and the owner of the damaged property could sue the motorist for being negligent and ask the civil court to order the payment of compensation. On the facts of the case, the Crown Prosecution Service (CPS) could prosecute in the criminal courts for speeding, driving without due care and attention or reckless driving. The motorist could be found guilty of a crime and liable for injury and damage. The main features of criminal law and civil law are outlined in Table 23.1.

> **Key terms**
>
> **Liable** – in terms of the law, this means someone is legally responsible for their actions.
>
> **Accused** – person accused of committing an offence.
>
> **Claimant** – the person or organisation complaining that they have suffered loss or damage.
>
> **Defendant** – the person alleged to have caused the loss or damage.
>
> **Tort law** – part of the civil law dealing with civil wrongs such as negligence and nuisance.

▶ **Table 23.1:** The differences between criminal and civil law

	Criminal law	Civil law
Purpose	If a person breaks the criminal law and they are taken to court and found guilty, the purpose of the case is to punish the offender.	If a civil wrong is committed and the party at fault is found to be **liable**, the purpose of the case is to find a solution or remedy for the injured party.
Outcome/ punishment/ remedies	The outcome for a guilty offender is a sanction or punishment, by imposing a fine, community service, a curfew or at worst, a prison sentence.	The outcome for the injured party is usually compensation or where compensation is insufficient, a court order such as an injunction.
Taking the case to court	The decision to take a matter to court is made by the CPS.	The decision to take the matter to court is made by the individual with the complaint.
Parties to an action	There are two sides presenting conflicting evidence – the prosecution who make the case that the **accused** is guilty of an offence and the defence who argue that the accused is innocent.	The two sides in a civil action are the **claimant** who is making a complaint against the other party to show that they are liable for injury, damage or death. The **defendant** will argue that they are not at fault.
Standard of proof	The decision in a criminal case is very serious as the accused may lose their freedom. The magistrates, judge or jury must be sure 'beyond reasonable doubt' that the accused is or is not guilty.	In a civil case the decision is made on a 'balance of probability' – in other words to make a decision the judge has to be over 50 per cent sure that the defendant is liable.
Case names for current and past cases	Criminal cases are referred to as R v Surname of the accused, for example, R v Smith. R stands for *Regina* which is the Latin word for the Queen.	Civil cases are referred to by the surname of the claimant and the surname of the defendant – Surname v Surname, eg Smith v Brown.
Terminology	Words such as 'prosecution', 'guilty', 'not guilty', 'verdict' and 'sentencing' relate to criminal law.	Words such as 'sue', 'liable', 'not liable' and 'remedies' relate to civil law.
Courts	If the accused pleads not guilty a trial will take place. This will be held in either a Magistrates' Court or a Crown Court.	If the parties cannot agree to an out of court settlement, a trial will take place in either the County Court or High Court.
Examples of offences or civil wrongs which could have an impact on businesses	Offences can include: • offences against property such as theft, fraud, robbery and burglary • offences against employees such as assault, battery, actual bodily or grievous bodily harm • motoring offences • breaches of health and safety laws and corporate manslaughter • breaches of environmental law such as pollution • being in breach of trading standards laws.	Civil wrongs can include: • being responsible for negligence or nuisance which are wrongs in the category of **tort law** • employment law cases such as unfair dismissal and discrimination • breach of contract leading to losses for a business, its customers or suppliers • rights relating to trademarks, copyright and intellectual property • disputes between partners or directors.

Hint

Highlight evidence to suggest that the case is criminal or civil. Use the table above to justify your identification of each case.

Extend

Examine each case report. Mind map all parties directly and indirectly affected. Explain the consequences for each party.

The role and jurisdiction of criminal first instance and appeal courts

A **first instance court** hears trials initially and **appeals** are made to a higher court.

Types of offences

There are thousands of different criminal offences. Crimes can be classified in different ways relating to the definition of the crime being found in **statute**, **case law** or **delegated law**. Crimes can also be classified according to the damage caused – against a person, against property or against public order. Another way of classifying crime is according to seriousness, as outlined below.

▶ Summary offences – these are minor offences which are tried in a Magistrates' Court where the maximum sentence for one offence is up to six months in prison and/or a fine of up to £5000.

▶ 'Either way offences' – these are semi-serious offences where the defendant pleading not guilty may have a choice to be tried in a Magistrates or Crown Court. Alternatively the Magistrates' Court may try an either way case and decide that its sentencing powers are insufficient. In such a case they would reach a verdict and send the case to the Crown Court for sentencing.

▶ Indictable offences – these are very serious cases which have to be tried in a Crown Court if the accused pleads not guilty. The sentence is discretionary and depends on the circumstances of the offence, unless the charge is murder when the judge must give a life sentence.

> **Key terms**
>
> **Jurisdiction** – to have the power to hear legal cases.
>
> **First instance court** – will hear trials. The trial process is adversarial which means the two opposing sides present their cases and cross examine each other's witnesses.
>
> **Appeal court** – reconsiders a decision made in a previous trial.
>
> **Case law** – cases which have been dealt with by the courts. The facts and decision may have been reported so that they can be referred to again in other similar cases.
>
> **Delegated law** – Parliament gives some person or body the authority to make laws on their behalf.
>
> **Statute law or legislation** – another name for an act of Parliament, a written law which affects everyone.

Verdicts and potential consequences

When a criminal case comes to court, the magistrates or jury will decide whether the accused person is guilty or not guilty and that decision is known as the verdict. If the accused person is found not guilty, they are acquitted which means they are free to leave the court. If the accused is found to be guilty, the magistrates or the judge will pass sentence. The punishment could range from a fine to community service or a prison sentence, depending on the type of crime committed by the accused.

The role and function of courts (criminal)

The role and functions of courts are outlined in Table 23.2 and in the text which follows.

▶ **Table 23.2:** Criminal courts

	Jurisdiction	**Role and function**
Magistrates' court	Criminal jurisdiction and limited civil jurisdiction. Power to hear summary cases and some 'either way' cases.	Deals with warrants, bail applications, trials, verdicts and sentencing.
Crown Court	Jurisdiction to hear appeals and try 'either way' and indictable offences.	Decides on appeals from the Magistrates' Court, tries cases with not guilty pleas and sentences cases with guilty pleas.
Court of Appeal	Jurisdiction to hear appeals from Crown Court – prosecution only.	May review the facts, the law or the sentence.
Supreme Court	Jurisdiction to hear appeals from the Court of Appeal – prosecution or defence.	Reviews points of law of general public importance.

Magistrates' Court

The Magistrates' courts are tasked with operating efficiently and effectively and are managed by the Ministry of Justice. Almost all criminal cases begin in the Magistrates' Court and over 90 per cent of cases are completed there. Magistrates or Justices of the Peace generally sit in groups of three, although some pre-trial issues can be dealt with by a single magistrate. The magistrates deal with applications for bail and requests by the police for arrest or search warrants. They try summary offences and some 'either way' offences, where they will decide on the verdict and pass a sentence. In ordinary appeals to the Crown Court a magistrate will sit with a judge to hear the appeal. In certain cases the magistrates can make a compensation order for the victim of a crime to allow the victim to avoid taking a civil action for damages. The magistrates are advised on practice and procedure by a legally qualified clerk of the court although the clerk does not participate in the decision making process. District judges can also try cases in a Magistrates' Court but they sit alone.

Civil and criminal jurisdiction

The main role of the Magistrates Court is to deal with minor criminal offences. However they have civil jurisdiction for issues such as recovery of debt, licensing for pubs and clubs and also for betting shops and casinos. Specialist magistrates can deal with family proceedings. These are cases often relating to child protection, family breakdown and adoption.

Pre-trial procedure

When a crime has been committed, reported and recorded, the next stage is an investigation by the police, when a suspect may be arrested, detained and questioned. The case papers are then passed on to the CPS who decide if there is enough evidence for a prosecution.

Plea

After the charges have been read out in court and the accused has confirmed their identity, the accused will be asked to enter a plea. If the plea is guilty, the magistrates will consider an appropriate sentence. If the plea is not guilty, a date will be set for trial and legal professionals will prepare for the prosecution and defence.

Key terms

Mitigating factors – arguments put forward by the defence to persuade the magistrate or judge to pass a lenient (lighter) sentence, for example, the defendant cooperated with police or showed remorse.

Aggravating factors – arguments put forward to persuade the magistrate or judge that a harsh sentence is needed, for example, the defendant committed the offence while on bail.

Key terms

Indictable only case – very serious cases such as murder, manslaughter, rape and armed robbery. They must be tried in a Crown Court.

Reporting restrictions – any details about the case cannot be published by the media. Reporting restrictions may be put in place to protect the accused person.

Key term

Treason – a crime punishable by a life sentence for plotting against the sovereign (queen or king) and the country.

Summary trials

The magistrates listen to the evidence and decide on the facts whether the accused is guilty or not guilty. If a guilty verdict is reached, sentencing takes place and the magistrates consider the defendant's previous record of criminal convictions. They then consult the sentencing guidelines to help to decide a fair sentence. They also consider **mitigating** and **aggravating factors** which may influence their decision. The magistrates can also ask for a report to be prepared by the probation services before making a final decision.

'Either way' cases

When a case falls between being a minor crime and a very serious crime, it is called an 'either way' case. A decision has to be made as to whether the case is tried by the magistrates or by a judge and jury in the Crown Court. The options open to the magistrates depend on how the accused pleads and also on the accused's wishes. The accused may prefer their case to be dealt with in the Magistrates' Court because it will be dealt with more quickly. Alternatively, the accused may feel that they are less likely to be found guilty if the case is decided by a jury of 12 ordinary people.

To make the decision there will be a 'plea before venue hearing'. This is where the accused is asked if they wish to plead guilty.

If the accused does plead guilty, the magistrates hear the case and the accused's previous convictions. However, they still have the power to send the case to a Crown Court for sentencing if they think their powers of punishment are insufficient.

A 'mode of trial hearing' takes place if the accused pleads not guilty or refuses to indicate a plea. The prosecution and defence make statements about where they consider the trial should be held. The magistrates then decide whether or not they will hear the case. If the magistrates agree to proceed, the accused can still request a trial by jury in the Crown Court. If the case is sent to the Crown Court, committal proceedings take place.

Committal

Indictable only cases are automatically sent to the Crown Court. 'Either way' offences may be committed for Crown Court trial with or without a review of the evidence to see if there is a case to answer. **Reporting restrictions** apply at this stage unless the defendant permits publicity.

Youth court

The magistrates deal with young offenders under the age of 18 in a youth court which has a less formal setting, and the panel of three magistrates must include one man and one woman. Hearings are in private and there are reporting restrictions. In 2015 the maximum fine for a child under 14 was £250 and for a young person under 18 it was £1000. The magistrates can also make use of supervision orders, compensation orders, youth rehabilitation orders and detention and training orders.

Crown Court

There are 92 locations in England and Wales where the Crown Court sits. The offences it deals with fall into four categories according to seriousness, as outlined below.

- ▶ Class 1 offences are the most serious and include murder and **treason**. Such cases are usually tried by a High Court judge or an approved circuit judge.
- ▶ Class 2 offences include manslaughter and rape – again these are tried by High Court judges or approved circuit judges.
- ▶ Class 3 offences include all other indictable offences and here it is more common for circuit judges to preside.
- ▶ Class 4 offences include robbery, grievous bodily harm and all 'either way' offences. They are dealt with by circuit judges and recorders.

Trials in the Crown Court are heard by a judge and jury. The jury decides the verdict based on the facts of the case and the judge gives advice on the law and passes sentence.

Jurisdiction

The Crown Court hears trials on indictment and appeals from those convicted in the Magistrates' Court. The locations where the Crown Court may sit are grouped into six circuits and each centre falls into one of three tiers:

▶ first tier – centres which have jurisdiction to deal with all types of Crown Court business and provide a venue for High Court judges to also deal with civil issues

▶ second tier – centres which deal with the full range of the Crown Court's criminal work

▶ third tier – centres which are not usually visited by High Court judges and they deal with less serious criminal cases.

Court of Appeal – criminal division

An appeal can be made by the accused with the permission of the Crown Court trial judge, to the Court of Appeal on grounds involving the facts, the law or the length of sentence. The Criminal Cases Review Commission may bring cases to the Court of Appeal's attention where there may have been a **miscarriage of justice**. The Court of Appeal can also consider sentencing decisions referred by the **Attorney-General**, on grounds that the original sentence was too lenient.

Permission to appeal

Permission to appeal from a Court of Appeal decision must be granted by either the Court of Appeal or the Supreme Court.

Supreme Court

Jurisdiction for criminal cases

The accused or the prosecution may seek permission to appeal to the Supreme Court on a point of law of general public importance. The Supreme Court was established in 2009 and is the highest court in the English legal system dealing with national, criminal appeals.

> **Theory into practice**
>
> Visit the You be the judge website and have a go at the activity called 'You be the judge'. What do you have to think about when completing the activity? What did you find challenging?

Permission to appeal

This applies to appeals and is required to keep the number of appeals for one case down to a minimum. It is also aimed at saving time and costs and being more efficient with decisions.

> **Key terms**
>
> **Miscarriage of justice** – arguments are presented stating that the decision made in court was wrong and that an innocent person has been found guilty.
>
> **Attorney-General** – provides legal advice and support to the government.

PAUSE POINT   Find reported examples of different criminal offences and note the sentences given.

Hint   Look at different types of offences to see how sentences vary.

Extend   Discuss this question: Does the punishment always fit the crime?

The role and jurisdiction of civil first instance and appeal courts

Civil cases are disputes between individuals or organisations; the civil courts determine liability. Many claims relate to workplace injuries, road traffic accidents, medical negligence, contract and consumer cases.

Types of civil issues

The civil justice system deals with a wide range of areas including contract, tort, land law, family law, insolvency and any other matters assigned to the courts by legislation. Generally the civil courts aim to resolve disputes between individuals or organisations.

Case allocation

Civil cases can be allocated to the County Court or the High Court depending on the complexity of the case and the financial limits – cases involving less than £25,000 (£50,000 for personal injury **litigation**) tend to begin in the County Court.

Liability and potential consequences

Civil court action is the last resort to settle a dispute. Prior to taking court action there may have been lengthy negotiations and an out of court settlement may avoid a trial. Court action follows the adversarial process where two opposing sides present their version of events and cross examine witnesses. The judge decides who is liable and decides on a remedy to put right the wrong committed, often by compensation or a court order.

The role and function of courts (civil)

The civil courts are explored in Table 23.3 and in the text that follows.

▶ **Table 23.3:** Civil courts

	Jurisdiction	Role and function
County Court	Civil jurisdiction for first instance trials only.	Deals with small claims and fast track cases up to a value of £25,000, and up to £50,000 for personal injury.
High Court	Civil jurisdiction for first instance and appeal cases. Limited criminal jurisdiction as an **appellate court**.	Hears appeals from the County Court and tries mainly multi-track cases with high value and complex issues.
Court of Appeal	Civil jurisdiction for appeals.	Hears appeals from the three divisions of the High Court on points of law or procedure.
Supreme Court	Civil jurisdiction for appeals.	Hears appeals from the Court of Appeal, and in limited cases from the High Court, on a point of law which is of public interest.
Court of Justice of the European Union (ECJ)	Jurisdiction to deal with breaches of EU law.	Any court can refer a question of European law to the ECJ for clarification.

Key term

Litigation – to argue a case in court.

Key term

Appellate court – a court higher up in the hierarchy of courts which deals with questions about the first instance trial. The questions may relate to the facts, the law or the sentence and the appellate court is asked to reconsider the decisions of the first instance court.

County Court

County Courts deal only with civil issues and they are presided over by a circuit judge or district judge. The judge will read relevant documents before the trial and will play an active role in case management to encourage cooperation and avoid delays. In a civil trial it is the judge who applies the law, decides on the facts and delivers a judgment on liability and an appropriate remedy.

Starting a claim

The claim form identifies the claimant and defendant. It states that the defendant must respond to the claim and must state whether the claim will be opposed. If this response is not made, the claimant could have a default judgment filed in their favour without giving notice to the defendant. The claim form includes details about the complaint and the remedy requested. A statement of the evidence supporting the claim must also be submitted along with the court fee, which is a percentage of the value claimed, for example for a claim of up to £300 the fees would be £35 and for a claim of over £200,000 the fees would be £10,000. If the defendant files a defence, the court will send an allocation questionnaire to both parties.

Allocation to track

Civil cases are allocated to a track which allows for effective case management. The tracks are outlined below.

- Small claims – valued at up to £10,000. For example, a tenant renting a property has paid £8000 for a new boiler for the house. Prior to the purchase, the landlord promised to reimburse the tenant but then refuses to pay even though their responsibility for repairs and replacements is well documented in the tenancy agreement. The tenant can pursue this case as a small claim.

- Fast track – claims between £10,000 and £25,000. For example this could be a claim of £15,000 for compensation from an employer for a workplace injury resulting in pain, suffering, time off work and medical expenses.

- Multi-track – complex claims valued at over £25,000. For example this may be a divorce settlement where the claimant is demanding half of a property valued at £2 million.

Consequences of legal action

It is pointless suing a person or organisation if they have no money. In many cases insurance companies foot the bill for civil actions, so insurance is crucial for both individuals and businesses.

Taking a case to court can be costly in terms of time and money. It can also be extremely stressful with no guaranteed outcome. Court fees, legal representation and costs in an unsuccessful case can easily mount up and separate legal action can follow on from a case where the losing party disputes the costs of the other side. Pre-action **protocols** can be ignored leading to delays, even though these were put in place to encourage:

- more interaction between the parties
- an earlier and fuller disclosure of all of the details of the case
- improved pre-action investigation
- settlement being reached before court proceedings are commenced.

Finally once a judgment is given it can be difficult to enforce, leaving the winning party significantly out of pocket.

▶ Which courts are based at the Royal Courts of Justice in the Strand, London?

> **Tip**
>
> Fees change fast and you should always check the latest recommended fees.

> **Key term**
>
> **Protocols** – rules of behaviour. In this case taking place before a case comes to court to ensure an effective and speedy resolution. For example, before taking a case to a civil court, pre-action protocol is a 'letter before the action', ie making contact with the defendant by letter or email, explaining your complaint and what you are claiming for.

High Court

The senior courts of England and Wales consist of the Crown Court, the High Court and the Court of Appeal. Trials at the High Court take place in London or at one of the 26 High Court centres in England and Wales. Cases are normally heard by one High Court judge, but cases in the Divisional Court of the Queen's Bench are so important that two or three judges may sit in judgment together. Aspects of the High Court are outlined below.

▶ Allocation – high value and complex cases are allocated to the High Court.

▶ Divisions of the High Court – the High Court is split into three divisions which each act as a separate court.

The division with the greatest workload is the Queen's Bench division, which deals with contract and tort cases, often cases concerning debt and personal injury claims.

The Commercial Court is part of this division and hears cases relating to banking and insurance. There is also an Admiralty Court to settle disputes about shipping.

The Chancery division deals with cases involving finance and property including tax, company law and bankruptcy. The Patents Court and the Companies Court form part of the Chancery division. The Family division hears cases about marriage and divorce, family matters involving children and adoption and inheritance cases. High Court judges also hear appeals from County Court judgments.

▶ Civil Procedure Rules – these came into force in 1999 to simplify and update the previous rules. They apply to the County Court and the High Court. The rules relate to case management, court allocation and tracking, documentation and procedures. The rules are accompanied by practice directions which are guidelines relating to applying the rules.

Court of Appeal – civil division

This court hears appeals from the three divisions of the High Court, multi-track cases and specialist cases. The appeal must be on a point of law or practice. An appeal is heard by three or five senior judges.

Permission to appeal

Permission to appeal is needed for almost all appeals and can be obtained from the court of first instance or the appellate court.

Supreme Court – jurisdiction for civil cases

The Supreme Court is the final appeal court for all UK civil cases. It hears appeals from the Court of Appeal and, in limited circumstances, from the High Court. The judges of the Supreme Court are known as 'Justices of the Supreme Court' and depending on the complexity and importance of the case, five, seven or nine Justices will hear the appeal.

Permission to appeal

An appeal from the High Court which misses out the Court of Appeal (sometimes called a leapfrog appeal) must have a certificate granted by the trial judge stating that the case involves an important point of law of public interest. The Supreme Court must also grant permission for the appeal. Cases from the Court of Appeal must have permission to appeal from either the Court of Appeal or the Supreme Court.

> **Research**
>
> Statistics are an excellent way to support your study. Research online to find out about the number and types of cases coming to court. Are you surprised by the variety of cases? Is there anything you expected to see more of – or less?

The Court of Justice of the European Union

This court sits in Luxembourg and judges and the Advocate-General are responsible for decisions which override national laws. The Court of Justice has two functions – a judicial role and a supervisory role. It is important to note that this court is not an appeal court as such. It does not replace the decisions of a lower court with its own decisions. However this court will help national courts to reach their own decisions by clarifying European law and how it should be applied in member states. Aspects of the court are outlined below.

▸ The main court – clarifies any questions put to it from national courts about EU law. Originally it was the only court but after the introduction of the general court, the main court became the superior court with jurisdiction to hear appeals.

▸ Judicial and supervisory role – the main court hears appeals from the general court and deals with disputes against member states and disputes against the institutions of the EU. Disputes against member states involve allegations that a state is acting in breach of European Law. These cases are brought to court by the European Commission or by other member states. Cases against European institutions are used to review European Laws, and to ensure procedures are being followed and powers are not being misused. National courts can ask this court to clarify a point of European Law.

▸ The general court – this court was introduced to reduce the workload of the Court of Justice. It deals with appeals from the Civil Service Tribunal, and with actions for judicial review.

▸ Civil service tribunal – disputes between the EU and its civil servants are heard here.

Application and evaluation of roles and jurisdictions to case decisions, both civil and criminal

The English legal system provides a forum for problem solving and decision making. It provides a systematic approach to dealing with criminal and civil issues both at first instance and on appeal. It operates under strict procedural rules. Though the system has existed for hundreds of years, it continues to develop and adapt to changes in society. It constantly seeks to improve efficiency, keep costs down and balance the workload of the different courts.

Case study

SummerScales for Justice

SummerScales for Justice is a local law firm who deal with all types of legal issues. Their clients are both business organisations and private individuals.

One of the senior partners, Mrs Summerscales, has visited your college. She has offered to take on one learner for a two week summer placement and provide a £1000 scholarship grant. You are extremely excited as you have always wanted to study law and hope to become a lawyer one day. The problem is, many are interested and there is only one placement. In response to the high level of interest Mrs Summerscales has set a series of tasks to ensure she chooses an appropriate candidate who has some knowledge and understanding of law and the legal system. You are going to do your very best to get the placement.

Check your knowledge

1 Research the law and apply it to the following scenarios. You will also need to explain the relevant first instance and appeal court procedure for each using appropriate professional and legal terminology.

   a A manufacturing business has approached the law firm – an employee has been injured at work and he is claiming that the employers were negligent as there was no safety guard on his machine. His sleeve was trapped in the machine and his right arm was crushed. He is claiming in excess of £100,000. The employer admits that they have never paid much attention to health and safety law.

   b A young lady has asked for advice as she has been called as a witness after seeing a fight. A young man punched another who fell to the ground, hit his head on some steps and died.

   c A large, local retailer wants advice. The owner ordered £12,000 worth of Christmas decorations to be delivered in November from a firm in South Wales. She paid for the goods when she placed the order in October. The firm stated that they could not deliver the goods until February. She was furious and demanded her money back, plus compensation. Despite several warnings the firm in Wales are still refusing to refund her.

   d A young man has asked the law firm to represent him in court. He has been accused of stealing from his employer and using the firm's credit card for personal use, running up a bill of £250,000.

2 Find a real case relating to each area of law involved in the scenarios.

3 Produce a short document on the benefits and drawbacks of taking legal action for each scenario.

 **PAUSE POINT**   Choose one type of court and research the types of cases that will be decided there.

Hint   When researching law and case law, make sure your source is telling you about UK law only.

Extend   When researching cases: note the name and year, summarise the facts, state the decision and the reason for it. Try to identify the legal points relating to the case.

Alternative dispute resolution (ADR)

Currently the main use of alternative dispute resolution (ADR) is for family, consumer, commercial, construction and employment cases but it should be recommended for all civil disputes. Parties in dispute are advised that they should attempt to resolve disputes without resorting to the courts. The following methods are examples.

Tribunals

Tribunals exist alongside the court system to deal with cases involving social rights and state welfare. Thousands of cases are decided by tribunals each year. Tribunals are divided into two tiers – the first tier hears cases initially and the upper tier hears any appeals. An example of a tribunal is an employment tribunal which hears cases including those about unfair dismissal, discrimination and equal pay. The tribunal is chaired by a panel of two lay members and a qualified chair person.

Arbitration

In arbitration, both parties allow a third party to make a decision on their behalf. The dispute could be settled by one arbitrator or there could be a panel which includes up to three people. A formal hearing usually takes place in which evidence can be presented by witnesses and experts. Alternatively, the parties might decide to make submissions (ie present their cases) in writing. Whatever the arbitrator decides has to be accepted by both the parties because it is legally binding. The decision can also be enforced by the courts.

Mediation

Mediation is where an independent third party helps the disputing parties find neutral ground to settle the dispute. The mediation may be 'evaluative', where the mediator gives an assessment of the legal strength of the case, or 'facilitative', helping the parties to find a solution. Mediation is often used in cases involving family disputes and break down.

Conciliation

Conciliation is like mediation because an independent person is used to assist making a settlement. However, they play a more active role and make suggestions to the parties. You may have heard of an organisation called 'ACAS' who will intervene in industrial disputes to try to avoid, or bring to an end, strike action.

Negotiation

Negotiation is direct discussion between two disputing parties to find a solution. This is often the parties themselves, but once solicitors are involved they will continue trying to negotiate a settlement even when the case is with the court.

▶ Can you think of a situation where negotiation would be useful?

Comparison with each other and with civil courts

The civil justice procedure has been criticised for the cost, duration, complexity, accessibility and use of an adversarial process. Going to court may require legal representation which can be expensive and the lengthier the case the more expensive it will be. Civil cases often face delays despite case management rules. Legal terminology, rules and procedures all add to the complexity involved in civil action. Decisions in cases can be publicised leading to a loss of reputation. Not everyone can afford to take a legal issue to court and some people are therefore denied access to justice. The fact that cases have a winner and a loser and use an adversarial process drives the parties in dispute further apart whereas ADR tries to bring them closer together. Some of the strengths and weaknesses of ADR are outlined in Table 23.4.

Key term

Precedent – a legal decision that has been made and which should be followed in the future in similar cases.

▶ **Table 23.4:** The advantages and disadvantages of using ADR

Advantages of ADR	Disadvantages of ADR
Quicker and cheaper as many ADR procedures do not need legal representation. ADR also attracts less publicity.	There can be a lack of legal expertise.
ADR is less formal than courts and less complicated, leading to a less stressful experience.	There is a lack of certainty as each case is settled on its own merits and **precedent** does not apply.
ADR schemes are carried out by people with specialist knowledge related to that area of law.	Decisions without the backing of court can be difficult to enforce.
ADR aims to provide a solution which keeps both parties satisfied.	

PAUSE POINT

Produce a poster detailing the different types of ADR that can be used by disputing parties.

Hint

Look online for information about ACAS, ABTA and other trade organisations which have schemes for settling disputes.

Extend

Can you identify any advantages and disadvantages of ADR or taking court action?

Issues

Some of the issues surrounding ADR are outlined below.

▶ Cost – generally for cases heard in court the parties are represented by solicitors and barristers and legal fees can mount up. This is not always the case for ADR as the parties can represent themselves. Court fees for mediation are less than issuing a claim for trial. For an amount claimed of £15,000 to £50,000, four hours of mediation costs £425 plus VAT for each side.

▶ Time – there are fewer delays with ADR. The case is dealt with sooner as it takes less time to arrange some forms of ADR than it does to arrange a court hearing.

▶ Privacy – proceedings are held in private and the parties can agree to keep the details and outcome confidential, whereas most courts are open to the public.

▶ Appeals – depending on the type of ADR used, the decision may not be binding on the other party which could then lead to litigation. Decisions made by ADR do not set precedents for later disputes.

▶ Formality – ADR offers more flexibility than the courts. The procedures are less formal and do not use an adversarial system so the effects on the parties following ADR are likely to be less negative.

▶ Representation – as mentioned above the parties may not need legal representation but there can be an imbalance of power depending on the parties involved.

▶ Accessibility – the aim of ADR was to provide a wider access to justice. Services for dispute resolution are provided by trade associations, voluntary and private operators, and HM Courts and Tribunals Service.

▶ Appropriateness – ADR is not appropriate for all cases, for example if a party feels threatened or needs an urgent solution such as an injunction, then going to court may be the best option. In some cases, if the amount being claimed is very small, the best option may be to do nothing. Parties to a dispute should carry out research and obtain legal advice about whether ADR is appropriate for their case.

B   Investigate the role of the legal profession and lay people in contributing to case outcomes

Different types of judges and their roles

If you visit a court room, you will notice that before the judge enters the room, the usher will say 'all rise' – this is a mark of respect for the judge who holds a very important and responsible office. The role of the **judiciary** is to interpret and apply the law in a fair and objective way. Judges deliver judgments when deciding cases and appeals and give justification for their decisions. They tend to specialise in one area of law and need to have a vast amount of knowledge in order to prepare for a case and then apply legal rules and precedents. Senior judges have a vital role in ensuring that the state does not exceed its powers. The roles of judges are outlined in Table 23.5.

Key term

Judiciary – a system of courts and judges. In the UK there are different levels of judges from part-time judges to senior judges in the Supreme Court.

▶ **Table 23.5:** Judges, roles and courts

Judge	Role	Court
Justices of the Supreme Court	Decide important points of law and act as final appeal court for criminal and civil cases	Supreme Court
Lord Chief Justice	Head of the Court of Appeal, Criminal Division	Court of Appeal
Master of the Rolls	Head of the Court of Appeal, Civil Division	Court of Appeal
Lord Justice of Appeal	Decides on appeals for criminal and civil cases	Court of Appeal
High Court judges	Decide on first instance and appeal cases – criminal and civil	High Court and Crown Court
Circuit judges	Preside over criminal and civil cases	County Court and Crown Court
District judges	Preside over criminal and civil cases	Crown Court and Magistrates' Court
Recorders	Preside over criminal and civil cases	County Court and Crown Court

The judicial hierarchy

You are now fully aware that there are different types of courts dealing with different cases and that the courts are arranged in a hierarchy, with the Supreme Court at the top. Likewise the judges fit into this hierarchy with senior judges at the top.

Appointment, selection, skills, training and roles

Judges are appointed by the Judicial Appointments Commission (JAC). Candidates must be selected on the basis of merit and good character and have five to seven years or more experience post qualification. The candidate must also have a suitable qualification as a legal executive or lawyer. Special selection panels are formed for higher appointments. Court of Appeal judges are formally appointed by the Queen on the advice of the Prime Minister, after the Commission has made recommendations. The Lord Chief Justice is responsible for the arrangement of training for judges. Traditionally judges have worn gowns and horse hair wigs and this continues to be the case for criminal trials but judges hearing civil cases are no longer asked to wear wigs.

Why do you think judges traditionally wear this 'uniform'?

Research

Look at the prospectus for training as a judge at the judiciary website. What skills and qualifications do you need?

Ceasing to be a judge

Judges usually retire at 70 years of age though some continue on a part-time basis. The Constitutional Reform Act 2005 made provision for the dismissal of judges who had breached the judicial code of conduct. The Lord Chancellor and the Lord Chief Justice have joint responsibility for judicial discipline. In 2006, the Office for Judicial Complaints was set up to provide advice and assistance in relation to judicial discipline. Judges can be suspended if they:

- are facing criminal charges
- have been convicted
- are serving a sentence or
- are subject to disciplinary procedures.

Any judge who has been dismissed will have their name and reason for removal made public. Judges may also resign; if they are prevented by reason of permanent infirmity from resigning, the Lord Chancellor may remove a judge from office.

Evaluation of the roles, use, their place in the court system

Critics argue that the judiciary do not reflect society in terms of background, gender or ethnicity. Most judges are privately educated and come from upper or middle class families – women and ethnic minorities are under-represented. The judicial diversity statistics demonstrate this point but also show that steady improvements are being made. The issue of the independence, impartiality and accountability of the judiciary continues to be a topic of debate and an important aspect of the constitution.

Different types of lawyers and their roles

Other legal systems may just have lawyers but in the English legal system there are two types – solicitors and barristers. The division is historical and dates back to the 12th century.

Solicitors and barristers

Solicitors often work in 'high street' private practices and provide legal advice and assistance to clients on many aspects of the law, including personal injury claims, writing wills and family issues. They may appear in court and often represent a client in the Magistrates' Court and County Court. Some solicitors are qualified to conduct hearings in the higher courts. Some specialist firms concentrate on commercial aspects of the law and advise business clients.

Barristers are self-employed legal experts who mainly act as **advocates** for clients by representing them in court and presenting their case to the judge and/or jury. They have the rights of audience in all courts in England and Wales. Barristers draft legal documents and provide independent expert opinions to clients. Some work for the CPS and may appear in criminal courts from the Magistrates' Court up to the Appeal Courts.

The functions of solicitors and barristers are outlined in Table 23.6.

Work

▶ **Table 23.6:** The roles of solicitors and barristers

Solicitors	Barristers
• Most of their work is office based – preparing documents, legally binding contracts and case papers, often using sophisticated software which tracks the progress of a client's case and the costs being incurred. Most people need a solicitor when they are buying a house. This process is called conveyancing. Other solicitors deal with family issues, such as divorce and custody of children. • In a small firm a solicitor may deal with a wide range of legal issues such as minor criminal cases, consumer issues, setting up business agreements for clients and wills. In a very large firm there will be many more specialist roles, for example there may be a whole department dealing with costs and cost litigation. • Many solicitors form partnerships and since 2001 can form a Limited Liability Partnership (LLP). The largest city law firms in London are referred to as the 'Magic Circle' and many law students wish to gain employment with them. Solicitors can represent clients in court. This has traditionally been in the lower courts and it has to be remembered that the court with the greatest workload is the Magistrates' Court. Solicitors can qualify to represent clients in higher courts so many law firms are making **advocacy training** compulsory.	• Under the Bar rules, barristers cannot form partnerships and must be self-employed. However, often they share offices known as chambers, and employ a clerk who allocates their workload and negotiates their fees. Barristers are referred to as specialists, since they concentrate mainly on one area of law, giving expert advice and drafting opinions and solutions to legal problems. They can represent clients in any court and traditionally their main role has been advocacy. • Some cases are passed on to a barrister from a solicitor but it is possible for members of the public to approach a barrister directly. Barristers work under what is known as the 'cab rank principle' – this means that if they have no other commitments they cannot refuse to take a case in their area of specialism. It is a rule aimed at ensuring that every person can access legal representation. • Not all barristers practise at the Bar. Some work for law centres or government agencies, and some large national and international business organisations employ barristers for their specialist legal knowledge. • Barristers tend to be based in large cities, particularly in London, but will travel to courts all around England and Wales to represent clients.

> **Key terms**
>
> **Advocate –** a person who represents a client in court.
>
> **Advocacy training** – advocacy is about representing clients in court. Lawyers need to be trained to present logical and persuasive argument to the judge and/or jury. They must develop the skills needed to successfully question and cross examine witnesses, to apply appropriate laws and sum up their client's case.

Roles

The roles of solicitors and barristers share similarities. They each provide legal advice and representation relating to a range of cases varying according to legal area and complexity. In the past, the solicitor was thought of as a general practitioner dealing with a wide range of cases, whereas the barrister was the specialist. This is no longer the case. A solicitor may specialise and work for a very large law firm in addition to qualifying for rights of audience in the higher courts. A barrister's level of specialism very much depends on experience so the distinction between solicitors and barristers is no longer clear cut. Lawyers need to have rigorous and in-depth training and qualifications. A wide range of legal skills is required for entry into the profession.

Skills

Figure 23.1 shows some of the skills required to become an effective solicitor or barrister

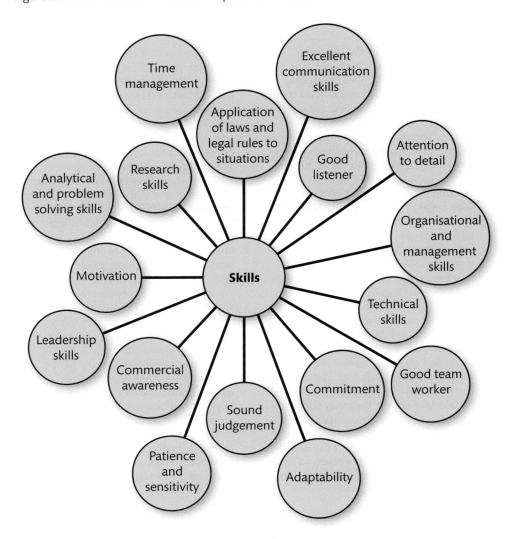

▶ **Figure 23.1:** The skills needed by a barrister or solicitor

---

Discussion

Look at the skills listed in Figure 23.1. In pairs think about what you have learned about the role and work of solicitors and barristers and discuss why you think these skills are crucial to the role. Can you think of any examples where each skill would be useful?

Differences

As shown in Figure 23.1, barristers and solicitors need many of the same skills. However, there are a number of differences between the roles. In the UK, there are a significantly higher number of solicitors than there are barristers and, as you can see below, each role takes a different route to become qualified.

Likewise, there are differences related to regulation:

▶ solicitors are regulated by the Law Society and the Solicitors Regulation Authority
▶ barristers are regulated by the Bar Council and the Bar Standards Board.

The Legal Services Board was set up in 2009 to oversee the way in which the professional bodies regulate standards for the legal profession.

Their employment status also differs:

▶ barristers are self-employed
▶ solicitors are either partners or employees of a law firm.

However, since 2007, Legal Disciplinary Practices (LDPs) have been permitted, enabling firms to employ non-lawyer solicitors, and non-lawyer managers.

The difference in the actual work undertaken has become less easy to distinguish with exclusive rights to conveyancing and advocacy in the higher courts being removed. Many arguments both in favour and against fusion of the professions have been expressed, related to expense, efficiency, talent, specialism, advocacy and independence.

Training and qualifications

Solicitors and barristers go through different training programmes to become fully qualified. The process to become a solicitor is shown in Figure 23.2, and the process for a barrister is shown in Figure 23.3.

> **Key terms**
>
> **Law degrees** – normally studied full time over three years, although there are accelerated and part-time courses. A law degree includes the core areas of study necessary for progression into the legal profession. Degrees are graded as first class honours, upper second class (2:1), lower second class (2:2) and third class.
>
> **LLB Hons** – this is a law degree and stands for Bachelor of Law with Honours.

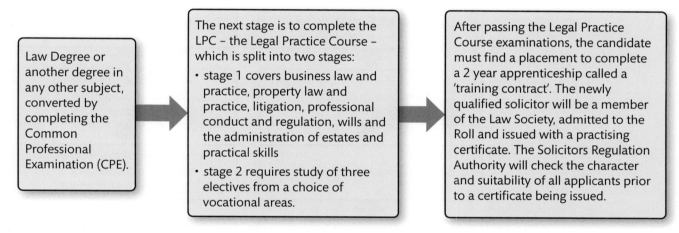

▶ **Figure 23.2:** The route to becoming a solicitor

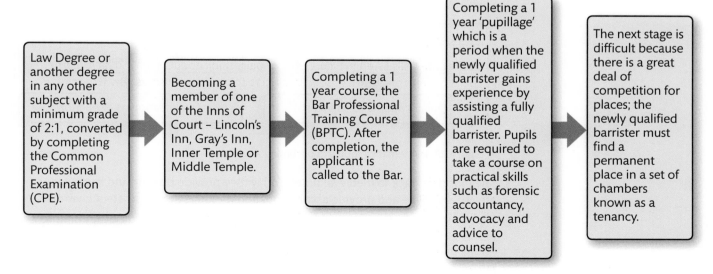

▶ **Figure 23.3:** The route to becoming a barrister

The Law Society is an independent professional body whose aim is to promote the highest professional standards.

Following the Courts and Legal Services Act 1990 and the Access to Justice Act 1999, solicitors can qualify to represent clients in higher courts and since 2008 solicitors can also wear wigs in court. Solicitors may apply through the JAC for judicial appointments and may apply for the status of Queen's Counsel. The Qualified Lawyers Transfer Scheme (QLTS) is available for lawyers who have qualified abroad but who wish to practise in England and Wales.

There are two alternative routes to being a solicitor through being a member or fellow of the Chartered Institute of Legal Executives (CILEX). These routes allow for studying at the same time as working. The stages are shown in Figure 23.4.

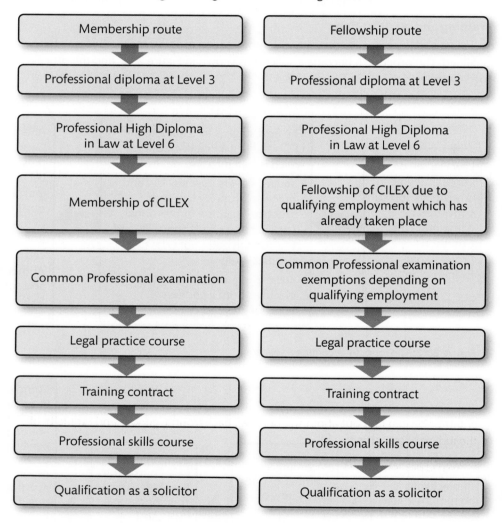

> **Figure 23.4:** Alternative routes to becoming a solicitor

The Inns date back to medieval times. Today they provide training and law libraries, govern discipline and provide accommodation for judges' and barristers' chambers.

Experienced barristers are eligible to apply through the JAC for judicial appointments and after 10 years of experience may apply to become a QC – this is a Queen's Counsel or 'silk'. Being a QC means a barrister has higher status and may command higher fees. Often a QC will be assisted by a 'junior' – a barrister who will complete much of the preparatory work in big cases.

Research

The changing nature of law and legal rules means that solicitors and barristers have to undertake continuing professional development, even when well established. Look online to find out what types of courses these are.

Paralegals

Paralegals are involved in legal work but are not qualified as solicitors or legal executives. They may work for solicitors in local government or for a charitable organisation. Activities range from dealing with clients to preparing legal documents.

Evaluation of the roles, use, their place in the court system and in ADR

The legal profession in England and Wales is highly regarded worldwide and English law is often the law of choice in international trade. Arguments have been put forward both for and against fusion (having one type of lawyer instead of two) of the legal profession but solicitors' and barristers' roles have been brought closer together by recent developments relating to conveyancing and advocacy. Others argue that improvements should be made to the access, cost, breadth and depth of legal education and training so that the legal profession can respond to trends and developments affecting the legal services market.

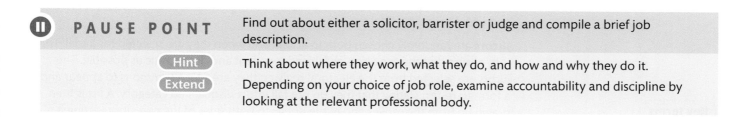

PAUSE POINT   Find out about either a solicitor, barrister or judge and compile a brief job description.

| Hint | Think about where they work, what they do, and how and why they do it. |

| Extend | Depending on your choice of job role, examine accountability and discipline by looking at the relevant professional body. |

Research

Statistics are an excellent way to support study aimed at the merit and distinction criteria. You can find out about the number, background, gender and ethnicity of the judiciary by visiting:

*   www.judiciary.gov.uk
*   www.open.justice.gov.uk
*   www.supremecourt.uk

Participation of lay people and their roles

Lay people have an important role to play in the legal system. They participate in decision making as members of a jury, as magistrates or as lay members of a tribunal panel.

Key term

Lay people – ordinary members of the public who are not legally qualified.

Juries

A jury consists of a number of lay people (12 for a criminal case) who observe the full extent of a case in court. They then consider the evidence and the facts in order to reach a verdict. It has long been decided that a jury can deliver a verdict based on their conscience, even if the law demands a guilty verdict. The judge cannot interfere with the verdict. The jury retire to reach their verdict and are not allowed to communicate with anyone other than the judge or court officials until after the verdict has been delivered. Ideally the verdict should be unanimous but after a period of more than two hours the judge may accept a majority verdict of ten to two.

▶ **Figure 23.5:** Do you know anyone who has served on a jury? What was their experience like?

Selection

Jury service is a public duty and is compulsory. Failure to attend is contempt of court and could result in a fine.

Jurors are randomly chosen both to attend and when they are selected for a trial. This is to ensure that the process is as fair, independent and democratic as possible. The jurors are selected from the electoral register; they are sent a summons to appear and a form to return stating that they do not fall into a disqualified category. A list is then drawn up from the replies and made public to both sides of the case. Jury vetting is a process where potential jurors are checked to ensure that they do not hold 'extremist views'. This is carried out by the police, Special Branch and by checking security records. Counsel for the prosecution or defence may object to a selected juror, but must have a good reason, and the final decision will be that of the judge. If a juror knows anyone else involved in the trial at all, they must say so and will then be asked to stand down. Juries are seen to underpin the right of an individual to have a fair trial. The jury is **impartial** and assesses the merits of the case only on the evidence they hear.

Eligibility

The Criminal Justice Act 2003 made the following points about eligibility.

You are eligible to be a juror if:

▶ you are between 18 and 70 years of age, and
▶ you are registered on the electoral role, and
▶ you have been resident in the UK, Channel Islands or the Isle of Man for at least five consecutive years since you were 13, and
▶ you are not mentally ill, and
▶ you are not disqualified from jury service.

There are grounds for being excused or disqualified relating to age, residency, mental health, criminal record, language barriers, medical or other reasons.

Key terms

Juror – a member of a jury.

Impartial – treating people and situations equally.

Role in criminal and civil cases

Juries are only used in a few cases – in criminal trials in the Crown Court where a defendant pleads not guilty, and very rarely in civil cases related to libel and slander, malicious prosecution, false imprisonment and fraud. In either case, the judge would sum up the evidence and guide the jury to make a decision in line with the evidence that has been presented.

Magistrates

Magistrates or Justices of the Peace (JPs) are volunteers who take on their role in the Magistrates' Court as a public duty. The aim is for the magistrates to represent society in terms of age, occupation, gender and ethnicity.

They are unpaid but can claim expenses. Their role is to deal with summary offences, some 'either way' offences that can be tried and a limited number of civil issues. The magistrates, sitting in a bench of three, make decisions on arrest warrants, on bail, on the verdict and pass sentence.

Selection

To apply to become a magistrate you have to be of good character and in good health. You need to be committed and have spare time to devote to your duties. You must live within 15 miles of the area where you will be working. Magistrates have to sit for a minimum of 13 and a maximum of 70 days per year. Magistrates need to be aged between 18 and 65 but do not need any formal or legal qualifications.

Appointment

There are 47 advisory committees split according to geographical area, with members appointed by the Ministry of Justice, which make recommendations for appointments. Magistrates are appointed by the Lord Chief Justice and are normally expected to serve for at least five years. Members of the police, armed forces and traffic wardens, in addition to anyone working in an occupation where there could be a conflict of interest, cannot be appointed. People with certain criminal convictions and **undischarged bankrupts** cannot be appointed. Magistrates usually retire at the age of 70 but can be removed from office at an earlier age on grounds of misbehaviour or being incapable of carrying out their role.

Training and role

When the magistrates sit in a bench of three, the person in the centre is the chair person who is usually the one with the most experience. The other two magistrates are referred to as wingers but they all have equal decision making powers. Initial training takes place before a magistrate sits in court and each magistrate has a mentor. Magistrates are given core and consolidation training which includes observations and visits to prisons. Training is essential on a continuous basis to keep magistrates up to date with new legislation and procedures. Magistrates can also choose specialist training, for example related to the youth or family court sittings.

> **Key term**
>
> **Undischarged bankrupt** – a person may be declared bankrupt if they have more debts than assets. They will be restricted for a certain period of time in terms of what they can and cannot do financially. During this time, they are referred to as an undischarged bankrupt.

> **Key term**
>
> **Moot** – a role play of an actual case where learners can put forward arguments acting for the prosecution or defence or, in a civil case, for the claimant or defendant.

 **PAUSE POINT**

As a group, transform your classroom into the layout of a court room, either Magistrates' or Crown depending on numbers.

Hint Use a court room plan from the internet or base this task on a previous visit to court to observe cases.

Extend Ask each group member to take on a role and explain it to the whole group or use a script for a **moot** to perform a case.

Evaluation of the roles, use, their place in the court system and in ADR

The advantages and drawbacks of juries versus magistrates are explored in Tables 23.7 and 23.8.

▶ **Table 23.7:** The advantages and disadvantages of juries

Juries	
Advantages	**Disadvantages**
More realistic and just decisions can result from public participation.	Lack of legal knowledge and sometimes intelligence, education and common sense.
Jury decisions cannot be disputed, and add certainty to the law.	Can be biased in relation to certain groups or occupations.
Act as a check and balance against oppressive or politically motivated prosecutions.	Do not always give a true reflection of society.
The tradition of trial by jury attracts public support for fair and objective decisions.	Can be used as a delay in 'either way' cases.
Secrecy in the jury room leaves the jury free from pressure and outside influences.	Juries do not have to give a reason for their decision and this can make it difficult to appeal.
Juries chosen at random should lead to a cross section of society and a fairer decision.	Jury service is not optional and jurors could be resentful.
Having 12 people deciding rather than one should mean there is less chance for errors.	Cost and time involved in jury trials.
Having public participation makes the legal system more open as justice is seen to be done.	Jurors can be vulnerable targets for threats and intimidation.
Juries can make decisions according to conscience.	Jury service can result in stress and distress for jurors.

▶ **Table 23.8:** The advantages and disadvantages of magistrates

Magistrates	
Advantages	**Disadvantages**
Less expensive than using professional judges.	Inconsistent decisions and regional differences.
Local, and therefore aware of issues in the local community.	District judges are legally qualified, quicker and more efficient.
Balanced view as they sit in a bench of three.	Biased in favour of prosecution and police evidence.
Public participation leads to just and realistic decisions.	Not a true representation of society – mainly middle class and middle-aged.
Trained for the role and advised by a legally qualified clerk.	Limited jurisdiction can lead to more referrals to Crown Court.

Assessment practice 23.1

SummerScales for Justice is a local law firm which deals with all types of legal issues. One of the senior partners, Mrs Summerscales, has visited your school/college as a guest speaker. She has asked you to help prepare materials to be delivered at the local Chamber of Commerce meeting. The materials are aimed at helping business people understand the legal system, courts, (ADR) and the people involved in contributing to case outcomes.

You need to prepare a detailed presentation with supplementary notes based on one civil and one criminal case of your choice. This may be based on actual case reports or taken from the local or national press.

You must explain, compare and contrast the legal procedure used to deal with your cases, including any potential appeal routes. Point out the main similarities and differences in criminal and civil court hierarchies and evaluate the methods of solving disputes using civil and criminal courts and ADR.

In a report, explain and compare and contrast the different roles of the legal profession and lay people in coming to a decision for your two cases, including the use of appeal routes. Finally evaluate how effective lay people are in coming to decisions in court cases and participating in ADR. Evaluate how dispute solving in the courts compares with methods of (ADR).

Carry out careful research and plan the order and content of your presentation and report. Make good use of your unit specification, class notes, tasks and time. Make your presentation and report as professional as possible, using legal terminology and referring to case law and statute where appropriate. Practise your presentation and use prompts if necessary. Submit all of your work with a bibliography showing your research resources and reference any quotes.

Plan

- I understand the task and what I am being asked to do.
- I know how confident I am about completing the task and areas where I need clarification.
- I know how to access the resources I shall need for that task.

Do

- I have spent time planning my approach to the task.
- I am confident that I know what I am doing and that I know what it is I should be achieving.
- I can identify when I have gone wrong and adjust my thinking/approach to get myself back on course.

Review

- I can explain what the task was and how I approached it.
- I can explain what skills I employed and which new ones I have developed.
- I can explain what I have learned and why it is important.

Explore sources of law relevant for providing legal advice

Judicial precedent

Judicial precedent is a system based on case law, where judgments in important cases can influence later decisions in similar cases. The system is sometimes referred to as '**stare decisis**'. Precedents are judgments made by judges – not just about verdicts, decisions and sentencing – but wider judgments on how the law is applied in a particular case and what the reason for the decision is in that case.

How it works

The system of judicial precedent works because, from Mediaeval times, we have had a system of law reporting. The decisions in important cases were originally documented in Year Books. Later, people made a living from writing up reports of cases and selling them to lawyers, but the detail and accuracy was often unreliable and inconsistent. In 1865 the Incorporated Council of Law Reporting was set up and controlled by the courts leading to much better information sources.

> **Key term**
>
> **Stare decisis** – a Latin term for judicial precedent. The literal translation is 'let the decision stand'.

Key term

Law Reports – system used to document the judgments of important cases which have an impact on the law and the English legal system. Common reports are:

- WLR (weekly law reports)
- QB (Queen's Bench division)
- Ch (Chancery division)
- AC (Appeal courts).

These reports state the judgments in a case. Lawyers may refer to a particular past case which may influence a decision in a current case and the judge will decide whether or not to follow the precedent. At the front of most legal text books you will find a table of cases which lists all of the cases referred to in that book. You will notice that the case name is often followed by a set of numbers and abbreviations, for example:

R v. Ahluwalia (1992) 4 All ER 889; (1993) 96 Cr App R 133

This means that the Ahluwalia case was heard in 1992 and reported in the All England **Law Reports** in volume 4 for 1992 at page 889. The case was appealed in 1993 and reported in the Criminal appeal reports for that year on page 133.

The hierarchy of courts is important to the system of judicial precedent and controls which decisions should be followed by which courts, as outlined in Table 23.9.

▶ **Table 23.9:** Powers of the courts

Court	Decision made
The Supreme Court	• This court's decisions will be followed by all lower courts in similar cases. • The court itself is not bound by its own previous decisions though generally these are followed unless a change in the law is needed.
The Court of Appeal	The criminal and civil divisions are bound by the Supreme Court. In relation to following their own previous decisions the criminal division has more flexibility as the decision could lead to a person's loss of liberty. The civil division can only depart from its previous decisions if: • a previous decision was made in error or • there are two previous decisions which are conflicting or • there has been a later conflicting decision from the Supreme Court or • a decision was previously made on an assumption of the law without sufficient argument or consideration.
The High Court	• These courts must follow Supreme Court and Court of Appeal decisions. • The Family division and Chancery division deal with civil appeals and must follow its own previous decisions. • The Queen's Bench division has more flexibility as it deals with judicial review and criminal appeals. • The ordinary High Court is not bound by its own previous decisions but can set precedents for the lower courts.
The Crown Court	The Crown Court has to follow the decisions of all higher courts but does not set precedents.
The County Court and the Magistrates' Court	• The decisions of the High Court, Court of Appeal and Supreme Court must be followed. • Cases here do not set precedents.

The system of judicial precedent provides guidelines which can be used by judges deciding present cases, which means like cases should be decided in a like manner. The system relies on the hierarchy of courts which allows for appeals. The flexibility of precedent also means the application of the law can be amended and brought up to date. Important judgments are reported in detail allowing the precedents to filter down through the English legal system.

Binding

If a current case is similar to a previously decided case in a higher court, the **ratio decidendi** of the previous case must be followed as a precedent.

Persuasive

If a persuasive precedent is suggested in court, the judge has discretion (can choose) whether or not it should be followed. Persuasive precedents may come from:

▶ courts which are lower in the hierarchy
▶ **obiter dicta** statements made in a previous case
▶ decisions from cases heard in other commonwealth countries
▶ decisions of superior judges in previous cases who did not agree with the majority judgment – known as dissenting judgments.

Distinguishing

The judge or judges decide whether a precedent is binding, persuasive or appropriate. If the judge considers that the case which has been put forward as a precedent is not similar enough to the present case, then it need not be followed. The judge has distinguished the case on the facts to be too dissimilar.

Overruling

The decision of a lower court in one case can be overruled by a higher court in a different case, on the basis that the rule of law stated in the original case was not appropriate because it was misunderstood. In effect, this changes the precedent which will affect the present and future cases but not the decision in the earlier case.

Reversing

This is when a case is appealed to a higher court and the decision made in the lower court is reversed, changing the outcome for that particular case.

Advantages and disadvantages of judicial precedent

▶ **Table 23.10:** The advantages and disadvantages of judicial precedent

Advantages	Disadvantages
Certainty – by looking at precedents used, lawyers can have some indication as to how a case will be decided.	There are so many previously decided cases that it can be difficult to find the most appropriate precedent.
Flexibility – allows the application of the law to be adapted to modern cases and changes in society.	The *ratio decidendi* can be difficult to extract when several judges have given judgment.
Time saving – the judge has a set of guidelines and uses the decisions made by superior judges.	Although like cases should be treated alike, different judges can use different reasons for distinguishing a case on the facts – this brings in some uncertainty.
Precise – the use of similar cases can mean that the application can be precise as use of the precedent over the years builds up on variations of the facts.	The system is too rigid and a poor precedent may take several years to be amended in a higher court which can overrule it.

Evaluation and application

Because judges are able to use the system of judicial precedent, you could ask whether they apply or make laws. The traditional role of judges is to declare and apply the law objectively and to operate within a system which recognises the 'separation of powers'. This means that Parliament, government and the judiciary all have separate and distinct roles.

▶ Parliament is the supreme law maker.
▶ The government is democratically elected and initiates a programme of **legislative reform**.
▶ The judiciary apply and enforce the law independently and act as a check and balance on the state.

> **Key terms**
>
> **Ratio decidendi** – a Latin term for 'the reason for the decision'. This is the important part of the judgment which forms the precedent that other judges should follow.
>
> **Obiter dicta** – remarks made in the judgment but which do not give the reason for the decision. They are remarks said 'by the way' and can be persuasive for judges in future cases but are not binding.

> **Key term**
>
> **Legislative reform** – changes that are made to the law by making amendments, new laws and removing outdated laws.

However, the distinction between making law and applying it is not so clear cut. Judges have discretion through the system of judicial precedent and by formulating new and original precedents. Applying the law in this way has allowed the judiciary to adapt to social change and continually make advancements in areas such as contract and tort. Some critics argue that judges should have more flexibility in order to protect individual rights whereas others argue that the judiciary overstep their constitutional role.

PAUSE POINT   Think about the reasons for decisions made in legal cases and list several examples.

Hint   Decision making can be very complex. Read a law report containing judgments. Identify reasons for the decisions made.

Extend   Examine the format of the law report to identify those involved in reaching the decision.

> **Key terms**

Acts of Parliament – primary laws created by Parliament. They can also be referred to as statutes, statute law or legislation.

Legislation – the same word is used for singular and plural so if you are referring to several acts of Parliament do not put a letter 's' on legislation.

How acts of Parliament are created and applied to cases

Acts of Parliament are those laws that are created by Parliament itself. They are also known as statutes, statute law or **legislation**.

The legislative process

Parliament consists of the House of Commons, the House of Lords and the Monarch and is responsible for law making. This could involve:

▸ repealing (removing) old and outdated laws

▸ making new laws

▸ consolidating other acts of Parliament

▸ bringing together the laws on one topic.

Ideas for changes in the law may come from:

▸ the Law Commission

▸ pressure groups

▸ political party manifestos

▸ government or private bodies or even private individuals

▸ MPs.

Legislation may also be needed to respond to an emergency situation.

Once a policy objective has been identified and accepted by the government, a 'Green Paper' will be drafted. This is a consultation document aimed at getting feedback from potential interested or affected people or groups. The green paper is followed by a 'White Paper' which contains more specific plans for changing the law.

A proposal for a change in the law is called a 'bill' and there are three types:

▸ public bills, which affect the general public and the whole country

▸ private bills, which may be proposed by a local authority, a public corporation or a large company and will only affect a particular group or area

▸ private members' bills, which are proposed by an individual MP, although these are rare due to a lack of parliamentary time.

The next stages may begin in either the House of Commons or the House of Lords and are shown in Figures 23.6 and 23.7.

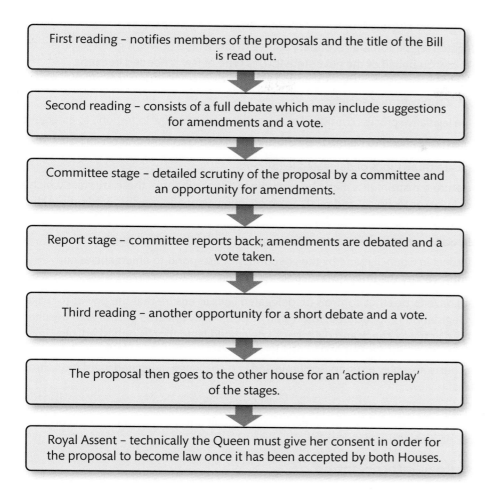

First reading – notifies members of the proposals and the title of the Bill is read out.

Second reading – consists of a full debate which may include suggestions for amendments and a vote.

Committee stage – detailed scrutiny of the proposal by a committee and an opportunity for amendments.

Report stage – committee reports back; amendments are debated and a vote taken.

Third reading – another opportunity for a short debate and a vote.

The proposal then goes to the other house for an 'action replay' of the stages.

Royal Assent – technically the Queen must give her consent in order for the proposal to become law once it has been accepted by both Houses.

▶ **Figure 23.6:** An explanation of what happens when a bill goes through Parliament

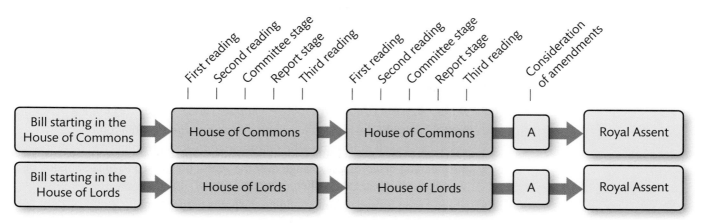

▶ **Figure 23.7:** The legislative process, starting in either the House of Commons or the House of Lords

Research

Look at the Parliament website to examine the types of laws currently being considered. What challenges do you think might be made to any of the laws being considered?

Delegated legislation

Delegated legislation is a secondary source of law where power is given to others to make law on behalf of the government. This type of law is needed because:

▸ the government does not have enough time to debate every detailed rule required for a sophisticated society

▸ the legislative process consists of many stages and is too slow to respond to emergencies

▸ often rules need to be made by those with expert technical or local knowledge.

There are three types of delegated legislation:

▸ statutory instruments made by government departments – these are rules which are detailed or technical and relate to an enabling act made previously to set out the general framework of the law

▸ byelaws made by local authorities or public and nationalised bodies

▸ Orders in Council made by the government to respond to emergencies and approved by the Privy Council and the Queen.

There have to be strict controls on delegated laws to ensure that the power to make new legislation is not abused. Interested or potentially affected parties are consulted and this acts as a check and balance. All delegated legislation is published allowing for concerns to be raised and Parliament has a supervisory role over delegated legislation. The courts also play a supervisory role and can challenge delegated legislation through judicial review.

Critics argue that there is too much delegated legislation with a lack of democratic involvement. They state that supervision is difficult and so there is a lack of control and also a danger of sub-delegation.

Statutory interpretation

The supremacy of Parliament means that Parliament can make any law they wish provided it does not conflict with the law of the EU. Once an act of Parliament has been approved, it comes into force on its commencement date. After that date it must be applied to relevant cases coming to court. The role of the judge or judges is then to interpret and apply the law – often this is not a straight forward task. Acts of Parliament are written by parliamentary counsel who are qualified barristers and expert draftsmen. However, the English language can be ambiguous and unclear, and errors can also confuse the issue. For example:

▸ words can have a double meaning – a jumper can be an athlete jumping or a woollen garment

▸ words can be left out because the draftsmen think they are implied

▸ the meaning of words can change over the years ('bully' used to mean 'superb' or 'wonderful' but has a very different meaning now)

▸ a broad term is used without defining the limits of the term

▸ printing or drafting errors make the meaning difficult to understand

▸ a new situation has arisen which was not foreseen when the legislation was drafted.

Judges have to overcome these problems and decide what the intentions of Parliament actually were.

Rules and aids to interpretation

Judges can use a variety of sources of information to help them to understand, interpret and apply statute law. These are outlined in Table 23.11.

▶ **Table 23.11:** Sources of information used by judges

Intrinsic aids	Extrinsic aids	Presumptions
• Intrinsic aids are anything actually written in the act itself – for example, the title, the preamble or introduction, the sections, sub-sections, marginal notes and schedules. • Since the beginning of 1999 acts are accompanied by explanatory notes and these can also be used.	• Dictionaries and text books, other statutes on the same subject, reports from the Law Commission or other agencies and, in limited circumstances, reports from Hansard which is the official daily report of all the debates in Parliament. • The Interpretation Act 1978 defines a number of commonly used terms.	• Any new law will not fundamentally alter the common law and existing rights will not be interfered with. • Any criminal law will require a guilty act and a guilty mind. • Any new law will not have a retrospective effect. • Any new law will not intend to deprive a person of their liberty. • Any new law will not apply to the Crown or conflict with international law. • Words must be read in context. • The courts must read legislation in a way compatible with human rights.

The following rules are also well established and illustrated by case law examples.

▶ The Literal Rule – the main English approach where judges interpret words with their literal meaning. This approach can be seen to respect parliamentary sovereignty but could lead to an unjust or silly interpretation of the law as illustrated in London and North Eastern Railway Co. v Berriman (1946).

▶ The Golden Rule – this rule recommends moving away from a literal approach if it would lead to an absurd result and substituting a common sense meaning as illustrated in Re Sigsworth (1934). The rule has been criticised for being too wide as there is no common explanation of what would be an absurd result.

▶ The Mischief Rule – this rule dates back to 'Heydon's Case' in 1584 and the guidance is to consider the:

  • problems with the previous law

  • problem being addressed

  • remedy Parliament wanted to provide.

This rule promotes flexibility and aims to avoid injustice as illustrated in Royal College of Nursing v DHSS (1981).

▶ The Purposive Approach – this has been influenced by the European approach to statutory interpretation where judges take a more liberal approach and look to fill in the gaps in the law left by imperfections in drafting.

The Rules of Language are also an aid to interpretation.

▶ Ejusdem generis – specific words followed by general words. The general words refer to things of the same type, for example, cats, dogs, hamsters and other animals, means other domesticated animals and not wild animals

▶ Expressio unius est exclusio alterius – express mention of one thing implies that is all the act applies to – Labrador dogs would not include any other breed.

▶ Noscitur a sociis – words must not be read in isolation and must take their meaning from their context.

Evaluation and application

The rules relating to statutory interpretation, like those relating to precedent, suggest choice and discretion whether the final objective is to:

▶ see the law in the context of 'the bigger picture'

▶ make a decision about interpretation that sits comfortably with the rest of the law as a whole

▶ see the law in context, conducting an analysis of the ordinary meaning and result

▶ look for a just result based on common sense.

Research

Investigate these cases so that you fully understand all of the rules. Try and explain each rule to a classmate using the supporting cases as examples, to fully check your understanding.

Reflect

If you could make a law, what would it be? Write a paragraph to explain your law.

How can you be sure what you have written will be interpreted correctly? Think of the challenges MPs have, to ensure an act of Parliament covers all eventualities.

Other writers point to an interpretation that best suits their political views and views of policy. Other writers have called for reform in drafting legislation, calling for:

▶ a wider use of intrinsic and extrinsic aids
▶ acts to include a statement of purpose
▶ an emphasis on clarity, simplicity and certainty.

PAUSE POINT   Look at an act of Parliament. Note the format, content and commencement date. Does it impose criminal or civil liability?

     Hint   Consider the terminology used and potential problems with interpreting the act.

     Extend   Is the legislative process robust enough to produce laws which give certainty to lawyers providing legal advice? Discuss.

Types of European legislation and their influence on domestic law

Originally six member states of Europe signed the Treaty of Paris in 1951 with the aim of bringing some stability to Europe and preventing future wars. The Treaty of Rome strengthened the aim of unity and recognised that the people of Europe should be brought closer together. The UK became a member state in 1973. This group of member states was referred to as the European Communities but has since been renamed as the European Union (EU). The EU is currently made up of 27 member states. Over the years the aims of the EU have developed to include:

▶ economic and monetary union
▶ a single market
▶ a single currency
▶ common citizenship
▶ common defence and foreign policy.

Consequently many areas of law in England and Wales are affected by European law which is 'supreme' and takes precedence over domestic laws. Some examples are:

▶ competition law
▶ human rights
▶ consumer and employment law
▶ environmental protection
▶ agriculture and fisheries.

Research

In 2016, there was a lot written in the media about Brexit. Research this and decide whether you think the right decision was made.

▶ The flag of the European Union

Types of European legislation

Laws made in Europe are known as:

▶ Treaties – these are international agreements which govern all of the member states of the EU. The treaties create rights and duties and automatically become part of each member state's legal system – this is known as being 'directly applicable'. Treaties are a primary source of EU law.

▶ Regulations – these are a secondary source of EU law and apply directly to member states. They come into force as soon as they are created and must be published in the 'official journal' of the EU.

▶ Directives – set out general guidelines so that member states can bring their own laws into line with the directive within a specified time limit. Directives are not generally directly applicable.

▶ Decisions – these are aimed at particular states, individuals or companies and are only binding to those addressed.

Law making in the EU and impact on domestic law

The main legislative procedure was introduced by the Maastricht Treaty in 1992 and gives equal law making powers to the European Parliament and the Council of the EU on a wide range of areas. The procedure is known as the 'ordinary legislative procedure' (see Table 23.12).

> **Key terms**
>
> **Simple majority vote** – more votes for than against.
>
> **Qualified majority vote** – allows each member state a specified number of votes depending on the size of the state.

▶ **Table 23.12:** EU legislative procedure

Stages	Action	✓	✗
The commission proposes a regulation, directive or decision based on its own views or those of other EU institutions or organisations			
First reading in European Parliament	They may adopt the proposal by a **simple majority vote** or amend it.		
First reading in the Council	They may accept Parliament's position or amend it – vote is by **qualified majority**.	If accepted the proposal is adopted.	
Second reading in European Parliament	They can approve or reject the Council's opinion.	If approved the proposal becomes law. Most proposals are accepted at this stage.	If rejected the whole procedure is ended.
Second reading in the Council	They can approve all of the European Parliament amendments or not.	If approved the proposal becomes law.	If not all amendments are agreed, the proposal moves to the next stage.
Conciliation committee comprising of equal numbers of MEPs and Council representatives	They try to reach a compromise and agree on all amendments.	If they agree, proposal proceeds to next stage.	If they do not agree the whole procedure is ended.
Third reading in European Parliament	They examine the compromised amendments.	If they agree, proposal proceeds to next stage.	If they do not agree the whole procedure is ended.
Third reading in the Council	They examine the compromised amendments.	If they agree, the final draft is signed by the Presidents and Secretaries General of both institutions and published in the 'Official Journal'.	If they do not agree the whole procedure is ended.

Evaluation of influence and impact, and application

Becoming a member of the EU had a major effect on English law and the legal system. Prior to this, Parliament was the supreme law maker, acts of Parliament could not be challenged and, if in conflict with delegated law or case law decisions, statute law took precedence. The situation changed because, if the domestic law of member states conflicts with European law, then European law takes precedence. Judges can now challenge national law if it conflicts with European law and all courts in member states come under the supervisory role of the European Court of Justice when interpreting and applying EU law. Membership of the EU comes with an increased level of rights and duties giving rise to another important source of law in terms of European legislation and case law.

PAUSE POINT   Identify the EU member states and find them on a map. Choose one and find similarities and differences to where you live.

> **Hint**   Think about terrain, culture, main occupations, currency, traditional products and, of course the weather.

> **Extend**   Discuss the advantages and disadvantages of being a member state.

Assessment practice 23.2   `C.P4` `C.P6` `C.M3` `C.D3`

The Chamber of Commerce has asked Mrs Summerscales about what type of information legal professionals rely on when giving legal advice. Mrs Summerscales has asked you to prepare a presentation and report.

Your presentation needs to explain the sources of law supported by relevant examples and case law illustrations. Consider legislation, the legislative process and the impact of both domestic and EU law. You must also explain statutory interpretation and precedent.

Prepare a formal report to evaluate the sources of law and their reliability when giving legal advice. Demonstrate how the legislative process would apply in given scenarios. Explain the rules of precedent and statutory interpretation through accurate application in given scenarios. Analyse the impact of European law has had in domestic law in given situations.

Carry out careful research. Plan the order and content of your presentation and report. Make good use of your unit specification, class notes, tasks and time. Your presentation and report must be of a professional standard, making use of legal terminology and referring to case law and statute where appropriate. Practise your presentation and use prompts if necessary. Check on the format for the report, proof read your work and submit a bibliography showing your research resources and referencing any quotes.

Plan
- I know how I shall approach this task. I know any areas I may struggle with.
- I know where I need any clarification.
- I know what resources I need to complete this task. I know how can I get access to them.

Do
- I have spent time planning out my approach to the task.
- I know how to make connections between what I am reading/researching and the task and identify the important information.
- I know what strategies I am employing and whether or not they are working.

Review
- I can draw links between this learning and prior learning.
- I can explain what I have learned and why it is important.
- I can identify how this experience relates to future experiences in the workplace.

Further reading and resources

Elliott, C. and Quinn, F. (2014) *English Legal System*, London: Pearson.

Huxley-Binns, R. and Martin, J. (2014) *Unlocking the English Legal System*, London: Routledge.

Websites

www.open.justice.gov.uk/courts/criminal-cases/
Information on criminal cases and how they are tried.
www.justice.gov.uk/about/hmcts
Information on HM Courts and Tribunals Service.
www.magistrates-association.org.uk/
More information on the work of magistrates in England and Wales.

THINK ▶FUTURE

Her Honour Judge Hilary Manley

Circuit Judge

After sixth form I studied for a Law Degree (LLB HONS), became a member of Gray's Inn and completed the Bar Vocational Course. I completed a pupilage in Manchester. I practised at the bar for 18 years working from a set of Chambers in Manchester before being appointed as a recorder in 2012. In August 2014 I applied through JAC and was appointed as a circuit judge.

I work at the Crown Court in Manchester, Crown Square. My jurisdiction is 100 per cent criminal and I deal with the full spectrum of cases. I have been approved to deal with sex cases but do not have a 'ticket' (meaning approval) to deal with murder or terrorism cases.

The pre-trial preparation is very important and includes lots of reading – skeleton arguments, case summaries, researching precedent and criminal procedure rules. At this stage I may have to deal with bail applications and make orders, for example for further evidence to be presented. At the trial stage I am responsible for the law, I oversee the trial and make rulings on the law. I have to make sure the questioning is fair and sum up the case for the jury. Post-trial I am responsible for sentencing – this can be the most difficult part of the job. I take into account probation and victim impact reports, aggravating and mitigating factors, and sentencing guidelines. Sometimes I have to make orders relating to the proceeds of crime and I have to deal with people who are in breach of court orders.

The role of a judge is quite solitary, in control of your own court room. However, I do work with between 12 and 15 other judges. We work as a team to share the workload. We often share views and opinions too.

It is really important for a judge to have patience and be a good listener but it is crucial to be able to read a large quantity of information and distil it down to the key issues to be decided. Being organised and having management skills are essential for effective case management and it is important to be able to communicate with people from all walks of life. Up to a point, you need to be able to put yourself in their shoes. In court, it is vital to have authority and to be able to project that authority to keep order.

I really love my role because every day is different and really interesting – the work is never predictable.

Focusing your skills

Planning ahead

Planning is very important when preparing for assignments or exams. Planning for your future learning and career is also crucial. If you were planning for a case soon to start at the Crown Court, what would you consider? Think about the implications of:

- the nature of the case
- the legal arguments
- how long the trial will last
- whether there are any young or vulnerable witnesses
- whether or not the defendant has legal representation.

Take it further

A contingency plan or plan B can be useful in order to respond to changes in the circumstances. For example, what would you do if:

- a defendant used a mobile phone in court
- a defendant failed to turn up for the trial
- a witness is a six-year-old child
- the trial will take at least six weeks
- a defendant has had an argument with their legal team?

Getting ready for assessment

Mary is working towards a BTEC National Extended Diploma in Business and is hoping to progress to study Law at university so she is particularly enjoying this unit. She was given an assignment for this unit and had to produce a presentation with supplementary notes covering:

▸ the jurisdiction of the courts and their alternatives in contributing to case outcomes

▸ the role of the legal profession and lay people contributing to case outcomes.

How I got started

First I carefully read my assignment brief and highlighted the areas it was covering on the unit specification – the content and criteria. I then collected my class notes, handouts and case research relevant to the task. I decided that my choice of cases for this assignment was very important so I carried out some research on local and national cases in the courts and tribunals.

Once I had selected a criminal and civil case, I looked at the assessment criteria and made a list of subheadings to use for my notes and presentation.

What I learned from the experience

▸ I thought it was really interesting to find out about different cases and how they are dealt with and, because I would like to study Law, it was really interesting to find out about the role of solicitors, barristers and judges. It was also interesting to learn that ordinary people can be involved in decision making.

▸ I felt really nervous when presenting. It was a good idea to practise beforehand but when questioned I struggled to find some of the information in my notes – maybe different coloured prompt cards would have been a good idea.

How I brought it all together

I started by making a detailed set of notes and from these I picked out the major points to use in my presentation. I constantly checked my assignment brief and specification to make sure I hadn't missed anything out. Even though the cases I had chosen were being dealt with at first instance, I had to explain appeal routes, possible reasons for appeal and the people who would be involved.

I had to make sure that I included some analysis and evaluation because my aim was to achieve the highest possible grade. I decided to type up my notes so that I could easily refer to them when presenting. For my presentation, I had to make sure my design, font, colours and images looked professional. I proof read everything and made sure that I had used legal terminology accurately. Then I practised my presentation several times. My final task was to put together my references for all the materials I had used and create a bibliography.

Think about it

▸ Have you made a plan so that even if you are working on more than one assignment at a time you will meet your submission date?

▸ Do you have access to all of the relevant class notes? Do you need to check a VLE or access any books from the library?

▸ Ask someone to watch a practice presentation before you deliver it, to comment on your communication skills, for example, body language, eye contact, tone and clarity.

Glossary

5Cs: company, collaborators, customers, competitors, climate.

Accused: person accused of committing an offence.

Active listening: when a person gives physical signals that they are listening to the other person such as nodding their head.

Acts of Parliament: primary laws created by Parliament. They can also be referred to as statutes, statute law or legislation.

Advocacy training: advocacy is about representing clients in court. Lawyers need to be trained to present logical and persuasive argument to the judge and/or jury. They must develop the skills needed to successfully question and cross examine witnesses, to apply appropriate laws and sum up their client's case.

Advocate: a person who represents a client in court.

Aggravating factors: these are arguments put forward to persuade the magistrate or judge that a harsh sentence is needed, for example the defendant committed the offence while on bail.

AIDA: Attention of the customer, Interest to learn more about the product, Desire for the product, Action to purchase when the opportunity arises.

Altruistic: selfless, concern for others.

Ambience: the atmosphere at the event.

Ambiguous: words or phrases which could have more than one meaning or which could be interpreted differently.

Appeal court: reconsiders a decision made in a previous trial.

Appellate court: a court higher up in the hierarchy of courts which deals with questions about the first instance trial. The questions may relate to the facts, the law or the sentence and the appellate court is asked to reconsider the decisions of the first instance court.

Appraisal: an assessment of performance.

Asset: any item of value owned by an individual or firm.

Attendee: a person who is going to attend an event.

Attorney-General: provides legal advice and support to the government.

Attrition: the rate at which employees leave a business.

Austerity: the difficult economic conditions resulting from the government putting measures in place to reduce public spending.

Baby boomers: a generation of the population born between 1946 and 1964.

Bankrupt: when an organisation or individual legally states its inability to repay debts.

Benchmark: a standard to compare things against.

'Blue sky' thinking: approaching subjects with no restrictions on perspectives.

BOGOF: buy one, get one free.

Brand: the identification eg logo of a product or service which is instantly recognisable without explanation (such as the Kellogg's cornflake cockerel).

Branding: producing a unique name or image for a business or product.

Brand personality: human characteristics to which a customer can relate, especially if similar to their own.

Bureaucracy: detailed procedures which have to be followed (sometimes known as 'red tape').

Business-to-business: B2B refers to when one business sells to another business – for example, a stationery business selling to a firm of accountants.

Business-to-consumer: B2C refers to when one business sells to an individual – for example, a stationery business selling wedding stationery to a bride and groom.

Capital employed: the total amount of capital tied up in a business at a point in time. It is calculated as owners' or shareholders' capital + retained profit – drawings.

Capital items: assets bought from capital expenditure such as machinery and vehicles that will stay in the business for more than a year.

Carbon footprint: the amount of carbon dioxide and other gases emitted through fuel consumption.

Case law: cases which have been dealt with by the courts. The facts and decision may have been reported so that they can be referred to again in other similar cases.

Cash flow: the money that goes into and out of a business.

Cash flow forecast: a document that shows the predicted flow of cash into and out of a business over a given period of time, normally 12 months.

Caveat: conditions or limitations.

Claimant: the person or organisation complaining that they have suffered loss or damage.

Client retention: ensuring that customers stay with the business and do not take their custom elsewhere.

Closed questions: questioning technique used to obtain a direct answer. For example, a supermarket might ask 'How often do you buy milk?' and the respondents would have to choose between several options, eg never, once a week, 1 to 3 times a week, 3 to 5 times a week, every day.

Closing balance: amount of cash available in a business at the end of a set time period, for example a month.

Closing inventory: the value of inventory at the end of a financial year.

Commission: A commission is a fee paid to a salesperson in exchange for services in facilitating or completing a sales transaction. Commission could be a flat fee or a percentage of the revenue, gross margin or profit generated by the sale. It could also be charged by brokers to assist in the sale of security, properties, etc.

Communication channel: the method which is used to communicate.

Constitutional law: this branch of law controls the government and how it operates.

Compensation: a sum of money which may be paid to someone (a claimant) who has successfully brought a case against someone else (a defendant).

Consumer: someone who purchases and uses a product or service.

Contingency plan: a back-up plan in case something goes wrong.

Correlation: a connection or mutual relationship between two or more things.

Cost of goods sold: the actual value of inventory used to generate sales.

Credibility: when something or someone can be believed in and trusted.

Credit period: the length of time given to customers to pay for goods or services received.

Credit rating: a score given to individuals on how likely they are to repay debts based upon their previous actions.

Culture: behaviours, habits and values of groups or individuals. It can also refer to 'the way we do things around here': the values and expectations of people in a business that are not written down.

Current account: an account with a bank or building society designed for frequent use, eg regular deposits and withdrawals.

Current assets: items owned by a business that change in value on a regular basis such as stock.

Customer-centric: putting the customer at the centre of operations.

Customer retention: customers who remain loyal to specific brands and businesses.

Debt: money owed.

Defendant: the person alleged to have caused the loss or damage.

Delegated law: Parliament gives some person or body the authority to make laws on their behalf.

Delegation: to give a task to someone else, usually a member of a team, and trust them to do it on your behalf.

Demographic: the statistical data of the population such as age, income, education, gender, race etc.

Demographic trends: the characteristics of a country's population.

Depreciation: an accounting technique used to spread the cost of an asset over its useful life.

Disposable income: the amount of residual money available for non-essentials after paying bills and creditors such as credit cards and store cards.

Dividend: a sum of money paid regularly (usually once a year) by a company to its shareholders. The money usually comes out of profits.

Economies of scale: a term relating to the cost benefit in return for output such as the income return after deducting the cost of a marketing campaign aimed at a mass market.

Economy: the state of a country, such as its wealth, production and consumption of goods and services.

Egotistic: self-important, striving for favourable impressions, conceited.

Elasticity: responsive to price changes.

Empathy: being able to understand the feelings of others, share in another's feelings; demonstrate an understanding.

Environmental factors: those factors outside of the business over which you mostly have no control.

Ethical trends: trends determined by moral principles.

Expected life: how long an asset is expected to be used within a business.

Expenditure: the amount of money you need to cover all your expenses/outgoings, eg your mortgage and bills.

Fatal and non-fatal offences: fatal offences cause death such as murder or manslaughter, whereas non-fatal offences cause harm and injury but not death.

Feasible: likely or probable that something will succeed.

Financial transactions: actions by a business that involve money either going into or out of a business – for example, making a sale or paying a bill.

First instance court: will hear trials. The trial process is adversarial which means the two opposing sides present their cases and cross examine each other's witnesses.

Fiscal: relates to government revenue, for example from taxes.

Fixed assets: items of value owned by a business that are likely to stay in the business for more than one year – for example, machinery. Also known as non-current assets.

Fixed-term contract: an employment contract between employee and employer with a defined end date.

Formal: business-like, factual, technical and professional, providing a record. It can refer to writing, such as formal written feedback.

Fraud: when an individual acquires company money for personal gain, through illegal actions.

Freedom of entry: a business has the freedom of choice to enter or leave the market due to an unlimited number of buyers and sellers.

FTSE: the Financial Times Stock Exchange.

Furnishing enhancements: props that are used to make displayed items more attractive and eye catching. They may also be for sale but not always.

Genre: styles or types.

Gross profit: sales revenue minus cost of goods sold (the cost of the actual materials used to produce the quantity of goods sold).

Happy hour: reduced price items at a predetermined time of the day or week.

Hazard: the HSE define a hazard as anything that may cause harm, such as chemicals, electricity, working from ladders, an open drawer etc.

Headhunter: an organisation that finds and approaches individuals already employed by a business to ask them if they wish to work for another business.

Historic cost: the cost of an asset when it was first purchased.

HM Revenue and Customs (HMRC): HM is an abbreviation for Her (or His) Majesty's, and the HMRC is a British government department responsible for the collection of all types of taxes.

Illiquid: not easily converted into cash.

Impartial: treating people and situations equally.

Indictable only case: very serious cases such as murder, manslaughter, rape and armed robbery. They must be tried in a Crown Court.

Inflation: a general increase in prices and fall in the purchasing value of money.

Informal: less business-like, friendlier and could also mean *ad hoc*. Informal can refer to information given verbally.

Insolvent: when a firm is unable to meet short term cash payments.

Insurance: an agreement with a third party to provide compensation against financial loss in line with the conditions laid down in the policy agreement.

Intangible: items that do not have a physical presence and cannot be touched.

Integrity: being trustworthy and honest.

Interest rate: the proportion of an amount that is charged as interest to the borrower.

Interfirm: between different firms, for example, comparing the performance of two different house builders.

Internal sources of finance: money available to fund expenditure from within the business.

Interpersonal: the ability to build and maintain positive relationships.

Intrafirm: within the firm, for example, comparing this year's results with last year's, or the performance of the York Branch with the Leicester branch of a retail store.

Investment: speculative commitment to a business venture in the hope that it generates a financial reward in the future.

Invoice: a document that is sent by the supplier to the person purchasing goods with terms of reference for payment, eg within 30 days. Sometimes invoices can be sent after an event but, for smaller businesses, are often required to be paid in advance or on delivery.

ISA: individual savings account (a good way to save money without having to pay tax on it).

Jargon: specialist words used by a profession or group of people which not everyone will understand.

Judiciary: a system of courts and judges. In the UK there are different levels of judges from part-time judges to senior judges in the Supreme Court.

Jurisdiction: to have the power to hear legal cases.

Juror: a member of a jury.

LLB Hons: this is a law degree and stands for Bachelor of Law with honours.

Lateral: approaching subjects from alternative perspectives.

Law degrees: normally studied full time over three years, although there are accelerated and part- time courses. A law degree includes the core areas of study necessary for progression into the legal profession. Degrees are graded as first class honours, upper second class (2:1), lower second class (2:2) and third class.

Law of contract: the part of civil law protecting people and businesses who have made agreements, for example about buying and selling goods and services.

Law reports: system used to document the judgements of important cases which have an impact on the law and the English Legal system. Common reports are: WLR – weekly law reports, QB – Queen's Bench division, Ch – Chancery division, AC – Appeal courts.

Lay people: ordinary members of the public who are not legally qualified.

Legislative reform: changes that are made to the law by making amendments, new laws and removing outdated laws.

Legislation: the same word is used for singular and plural so if you are referring to several acts of Parliament do not put a letter 's' on legislation.

Liability: an obligation of a company, or amounts owed to lenders and suppliers.

Liable: in terms of the law, this means someone is legally responsible for their actions.

Litigation: to argue a case in court.

Liquidate: terminate/close down a business.

Liquidity: measures a firm's ability to meet short-term cash payments.

Logistics: the operation and management of getting supplies from one point to another.

Loss: shortfall suffered when total revenue from sales is lower than the total cost of the business.

Loss leader: a product or service offered at a knock down price, possibly even at a loss to the business. This is done to attract additional sales and increase profits and market share.

Market forces: factors created by the economy for the demand and availability of products and services which influence costs.

Marketing mix: factors that a company can control and which will persuade or influence customers to buy its products or services.

Market intelligence: gathering data from different sources which is analysed and evaluated to identify trends.

Market research: systematic gathering, recording and analysis of data about issues relating to marketing products and services.

Market share: the percentage of a given market that a business holds.

Memo: short for memorandum, meaning a brief note about something that needs to be documented, but for internal customer use only.

Micro-merchandising: getting the right products, sizes and colours at the right prices to meet local customer demands.

Millennials: a generation of the population born between 1982 and 2000.

Miscarriage of justice: arguments are presented stating that the decision made by the court was wrong and that an innocent person has been found guilty.

Mitigating factors: these are arguments put forward by the defence to persuade the magistrate or judge to pass a lenient (lighter) sentence, for example, the defendant cooperated with the police or showed remorse.

Moot: a role play of an actual case where learners can put forward arguments acting for the prosecution or defence or, in a civil case, for the claimant or defendant.

Multi-collaborative: collaborating with multiple partners.

Multi-tasking: when more than one task is being performed at the same time.

Net profit: gross profit minus other expenses, for example, rent and advertising.

Networking: the process of connecting groups of people together, for example business professionals.

Non-biased: the questions in the survey are not prejudiced towards or against a group of people, especially in a way that might be considered to be unfair.

Non-tangible: not able to be touched.

Obiter dicta: remarks made in the judgement but which do not give the reason for the decision. They are remarks said 'by the way' and can be persuasive for judges in future cases but are not binding.

Objective: a judgement which is not influenced by personal opinions or points of view, neither biased nor prejudiced and can be validated.

Observee: the event organiser, the person being watched.

Observer: the person that watches the event organiser.

Ofcom: Office of Communications, a regulatory body supervising the communications industry.

Ombudsman: a not-for-profit service, founded in 2002 to provide independent dispute resolution.

Opening balance: amount of cash available in a business at the start of a set of time period, for example a month.

Opening inventory: the value of inventory in a business at the start of the financial year.

Open questions: questioning technique used to obtain a more detailed answer where the respondent can give their opinions and thoughts behind their answer.

Opportunity cost: the cost to a business of making one decision over another, choosing an alternative compared to the next best. For example, the cost of a missed opportunity if you spend your money on one venue which means you cannot spend it at another.

Opulence: an impression of wealth and luxury and possibly glamour.

Output decisions: an economist term relating to maximising profit.

Outside catering: when the business or organisation providing the venue does not also provide the catering.

Outsource: buying services or products from outside suppliers, often overseas, to cut costs.

Overdraft: the ability to withdraw money that you do not have from a current account.

Partnership: comprising two or more people who set up in business together and share all profits and losses.

Passive-aggressive: stubborn and/or sulky (digging your heels and refusing to do something which is your responsibility).

Person specification: the list of requirements that a person needs to have in order to meet the expectations of the job.

PESTLE: political, economic, social, technological, legal, environmental.

Porter's Five Forces: supplier power; threat of new entrants; threat of substitutes; buyer power; rivalry.

Precedent: a legal decision that has been made and which should be followed in the future in similar cases.

Premiums: regular payments made by an individual or company to an insurance provider in return for protection.

Price taker: this is when a company has to accept the prevailing price of a product in the wider market.

Primary research: new research which aims to answer specific issues or questions. It can involve interviews, questionnaires or surveys of individuals or small groups.

Probationary period: a defined 'trial' period where employee and employer can work out if the employee is a good fit for the role and the business.

Profit: the percentage of margin mark-up over the unit cost. Can also be defined as surplus achieved when the total revenue (income) from sales is higher than the total costs of a business.

Protocols: rules of behaviour. In this case taking place before a case comes to court to ensure an effective and speedy resolution. For example, before taking a case to a civil court, pre-action protocol is a 'letter before the action' ie making contact with the defendant by letter or email explaining your complaint and what you are claiming for.

Prototype: an initial version or mock-up of a concept for further development.

Psychology: the scientific study of the human mind and its functions, especially those affecting behaviour in a given context (for example, when buying something).

Psychometric tests: a series of tests that measure personality, skills or behaviour types of prospective employees and are used to compare applicants as part of recruitment and selection.

Public domain: if information is in the public domain it can be accessed by anyone and there are no copyright or legal restrictions on it.

Public liability insurance: insurance cover required to hold an event; cover is usually needed for up to £5 million.

Qualified majority vote: allows each member state a specified number of votes depending on the size of the state.

Qualitative: data providing context and information about how or details about why (customer comments).

Quantitative: numbers, responding to the what, where and why questions.

Quartile: a division of statistical data divided into four equal parts or defined areas. The first part or area is the first quartile, the second is the second quartile, the third is the third quartile and the forth is the forth quartile.

RRP: recommended retail price.

Rapport: a good relationship between people, with good communication and an understanding of the way each other is working.

Ratio decidendi: a Latin term for 'the reason for the decision'. This is the important part of the judgment which forms the precedent that other judges should follow.

Raw materials: any material from which a product is made.

Regulator: external body acting as supervisor to ensure businesses comply with relevant legislation.

Reliability: making sure the method of data gathering leads to consistent results when the input is consistent.

Reporting restrictions: this means any details about the case cannot be published by the media. Reporting restrictions may be put in place to protect the accused person.

Residual value: the value of an asset when it is disposed of by a business, for example, resale value.

Respondent: someone who is giving feedback, i.e. the person answering the questions, or a person who replies to a questionnaire or survey to supply information.

Response rate: the number of people that have responded to a questionnaire either on paper or online. The more people that reply, generally, the more accurate the results are likely to be.

Retail: the sale of goods, usually on a small scale, directly to the public for consumption rather than resale.

Revenue: the income received by a business for selling its products and services.

Risk: the likelihood (chance, high or low) that harm will be done as a result of an identified hazard, together with an indication of how serious the harm could be.

Sales revenue: quantity sold multiplied by the selling price.

Saving: placing money in a secure place so that it grows in value and can be used in the future.

Serendipity: a pleasant discovery that occurs unexpectedly or by accident.

Shareholder: someone who has invested in a company in return for equity, i.e. a share of the business.

Shareholder value: the benefits received by shareholders relative to the number of shares they hold in a business.

Simple majority vote: more votes for than against.

SMART: an acronym used when talking about objectives to ensure that the objective set is specific, measurable, achievable, relevant and time constrained.

Social enterprise: an enterprise that has a social or environmental mission and seeks to have a positive impact on communities or people by investing the majority of the profits made into the cause that they want to help or improve.

Soft copy: a version of a document, such as a pdf, that can be emailed or uploaded to a website.

Staff turnover: this calculation takes the number of employees that left in a given amount of time (usually a year) as a percentage of all employees. For example, ten employees leaving in one year from 100 employees would be 10/100 =10% turnover. The average UK staff turnover is 15%.

Stakeholder: anyone with an interest in the activities of a business, whether directly or indirectly involved, anyone who is affected by a business, including stakeholders such as members of staff and external stakeholders such as customers.

Stakeholder feedback: surveying stakeholders for ideas, compliments, suggestions and complaints.

Strapline: a caption or heading often providing a brief and snappy overview of a product, service or news story.

Stare decisis: a Latin term for judicial precedent. The literal translation is 'let the decision stand'.

Statement of comprehensive income: shows the trading positon of the business which is used to calculate gross profit. It then takes into account all other expenses to calculate the profit or loss for the year.

Statement of financial position: a snapshot of a business's net worth at a particular moment in time, normally the end of the financial year.

Statement of financial situation: a financial document that shows the net worth of business by balancing its assets against its liabilities. It is often called a balance sheet.

Statute law or legislation: another name for an act of Parliament, a written law which affects everyone.

Stereotyping: assumptions about someone or something which may be held by many people and which may be simplified without full thought being given to them.

Slogan: a short, punchy phrase which conveys a memorable message, often used by companies to market their products or services. For example, 'Red Bull gives you wings'.

Solvent: the ability to meet day to day expenditure and repay debts.

Subjective: based on personal opinions and interpretations. Analyses are not possible to validate.

Supply chain: the stages that goods pass through between the producer that makes them and the retailer that sells them.

SWOT: strengths, weaknesses, opportunities and threats.

Tangible: items that have a physical presence and can be touched.

Tort law: part of the civil law dealing with civil wrongs such as negligence or nuisance.

Trade payables: money the business owes from supplies purchased but not yet paid for.

Trade receivables: money owed to a business from sales made but not yet paid for.

Treason: a crime punishable by a life sentence for plotting against the sovereign (queen or king) and the country.

Undischarged bankrupt: a person may be declared bankrupt if they have more debts than assets. They will be restricted for a certain period of time in terms of what they can and cannot do financially. During this time they are referred to as an undischarged bankrupt.

Unit cost: all expenses incurred to manufacture a product or deliver a service including transport, raw materials, labour, premises etc divided by the number of items manufactured.

Unique selling point (USP): an original or individual concept, service or product that is exclusive to your business.

Validity: the process of ensuring data are valid by using original sources or tracing sources back to their original point.

Venn diagram: a logical relationship diagram representing overlaps between categories.

Verbatim: repeating the message exactly as it was originally given.

Viral (advertising/marketing): unsolicited and infectious marketing tactics using social media to attract interest.

Visual merchandising: displaying products and services in a way designed to attract customers' attention.

Visual standards: retailers that have more than one outlet will want to ensure that each site has a visual consistency. The displays are likely to be identical in each of the outlets and they will have a consistent theme and be of the same quality.

Whistle-blowing: informing on someone who is doing something wrong or illegal.

Wholesale: the sale of goods on a larger scale at a lower price, usually sold direct to the retailer to sell on at a profit.

Index